The Smiling Phoenix

THE SMILING PHOENIX

Southern Humor from 1865 to 1914

WADE HALL

University of Florida Press
Gainesville, 1965

A University of Florida Press Book

*Zinc engravings for headpieces were prepared
from linoleum blocks designed and cut by*
MRS. FRANZEE DOLBEARE

FOR
THE FACULTY AND STUDENTS
OF
KENTUCKY SOUTHERN COLLEGE

"They Whom a Dream Hath Possessed"

Contents

Foreword

HUMOR HAS ALWAYS BEEN a tangible quality in American literature although it has varied considerably in time and place. From Captain John Smith's tall tales to the modern fables of James Thurber it has proved a constant element in our writing, sometimes a mere condiment to make the dull or trivial palatable, sometimes a shaping and determining factor. In the hands of Benjamin Franklin it became proverbial wit or incisive satire; with Oliver Wendell Holmes or Henry Thoreau it often took the form of puns or verbal jugglery; with Poe it turned savage; and with Mark Twain it frequently served as a structural device which at the same time permitted significant character differentiation. Twentieth-century writers such as William Saroyan, Tennessee Williams, William Faulkner, and John O'Hara prove that humor definitely remains in the chief literary bloodstream of the country.

The Puritan congregation, too often represented as drowsing in their pews while the sands of the hour glass slipped away and the numbered points of the minister's sermon approached two digits, had more of an awareness of humor than early chroniclers were willing to admit. Nathaniel Ward, a Puritan preacher, could jest about women's fashions while he derided religious tolerance, and

The Smiling Phoenix

Samuel Sewall, a Puritan judge, could mock himself as well as describe his society when he confided to his diary an account of his courtship of an elderly widow. The very ponderousness of the Mathers, devoted as they were to life's seriousness, sometimes became comic, as even Whittier later pointed out. William Byrd, a Virginia contemporary of Jonathan Edwards, wrote humorously both as journalist and as historian. And in the Revolutionary period John Trumbull could be cleverly satiric whether his subject was education or politics.

Readers often think of Southern literature, particularly of ante-bellum Southern literature, as romantic and sentimental, suffused with the odor of magnolias and the thick sounds of dialect. But by 1835 Judge Longstreet had produced *Georgia Scenes,* that classic of the frontier with its revelation of primitive sports and gambling, and William Gilmore Simms had begun his many-volumed series of novels about Carolina life. Both writers revealed a rich vein of comedy, and certainly Simms' Porgy is one of the best of the minor creations of the American portrait gallery. It is true that in the hands of many later Southern writers the ante-bellum plantation became more often the scene of pathos and tragedy than of comedy, so that it remained for occasional local colorists to display the pawky charm as well as the exuberance of rural life. If one tires of the sentimentalism of Thomas Nelson Page and John Pendleton Kennedy and even John Esten Cooke, one can turn to the sly antics of Brer Rabbit as Uncle Remus told of his adventures or to the Creole subtleties of George W. Cable. The point is that humor was present, even in the most saccharine period of Southern writing, and it is perhaps this very humor that makes some of this writing still readable.

Treatises on humor exist for those who wish to define all its functions and special roles. The humor of satire is not the humor of burlesque although the two have an affinity; exaggeration for the purpose of ridicule differs from exaggeration intended simply for entertainment. Humor is sometimes utilized to bring about reform, sometimes resorted to by the political opposition who dare not express their principles in action. Humor can take the form of parody or pasquinade or forthright denunciation—the bludgeon substituting for the scalpel. But beyond the scope of the comic strips literary humor usually has some role, some *raison d'être.*

Southern humor after the Civil War seems to have been affected by two primary factors. First of all, the publishing world and most of the audience were in the North. No Southern periodicals of distinction existed, and publishing houses were small and had limited resources. Consequently, Southern humorists sought a market north of the Mason and Dixon line and consciously tailored their wares to an audience of newspaper and magazine readers. Practical necessity thus required the humorist to work in a limited sphere. Secondly, the events of the 1860's were familiar and recent enough to be rather refractory material for humorous treatment. Southern writers had little desire to reopen old wounds and even less desire to alienate Northern readers. Their resentment sometimes appears indirectly, much as Uncle Remus taunts the white race by means of the most inoffensive of four-legged creatures, but a minority view could be expressed neither vehemently nor boldly. Thus much of the writing with comic overtones was produced solely for entertainment or it dealt with some of the uncontroversial aspects of the times. Neither quality was likely to ensure long vitality.

Periodical humor in general tends to be ephemeral. It is necessarily topical and usually trivial; political cartoons only a few years old lose an astonishing amount of their vigor. It is also unfortunate that much of the post-bellum Southern humor suffers as a result of certain technical aspects. The "phunny phellows" of an earlier period who depended on dialect and deliberate mis-spelling no longer seem very funny. So-called eye humor (even if used by a Josh Billings or an Artemus Ward) strikes us today as naïve. In similar fashion we tend to reject the humor of polysyllabic rhetoric. The jargon of the Pentagon or of Madison Avenue may be funny enough to certain readers, but its original intention was not comic. Modern humorists can still exaggerate, mock, ridicule, parody, or underplay (Art Buchwald in his newspaper columns does most of these things), but they no longer can rely on purely typographical devices. The humor must be in the man, not in the typesetting machine.

But if for various reasons little of the humor so painstakingly assembled and discussed by Professor Wade Hall seems durable or significant in itself, his study is valuable on other accounts. He establishes, for example, that after five grim years and decades of bitter memories, the South could and did laugh. He points out that certain stock figures are funny regardless of conditions and politics—the complaining recruit, the stupid countryman, the migrant, the rustic philosopher, the enterprising manipulator out to make a fast buck. He demon-strates that there was an astonishing amount of humor published and that some of it appeared in very unlikely places—books printed in small towns, local newspapers, agricultural journals. He contends that some of the humorists actually helped to bring about a reconciliation between North and South by stressing their common humanity. And by extensive quotation he proves that some of the humor was, and still is, very funny.

A people is known by its songs, its stories, and its humor. A popular ditty or a joke can spread like wildfire through the country, passing from one phase of society, from one geographical region, to another. Mark Twain thought that the French, the British, and the American forms of humor were different and as an experienced platform performer he had plenty of evidence for his conten-tion. But regardless of distinctions humor can reveal the soul of a people in time of grief and in time of opulence alike. One laughs when one is afraid to cry, bravely, even hopelessly. In the South for half a century people laughed, and in their humor they found a catharsis.

John T. Flanagan

University of Illinois

xi

Author's Acknowledgments

I should like to thank the publishers indicated for permission to quote from the following books:

Colonel Carter and Other Tales of the South by F. Hopkinson Smith, copyright, 1908, by Houghton Mifflin Company.

Dr. George H. Bagby: A Study of Virginian Literature, 1850-1880 by Joseph Leonard King, Jr., copyright, 1927, by Columbia University Press.

Editorials, Sketches and Stories by Quincy Sharpe Mills, copyright, 1930, by G. P. Putnam's Sons and Coward-McCann Company.

James Lane Allen and the Genteel Tradition by Grant C. Knight, copyright, 1935, by the University of North Carolina Press.

Mark Twain and Southwestern Humor by Kenneth S. Lynn, copyright, 1959, by Atlantic-Little, Brown and Company.

Miss Minerva and William Green Hill by Frances Boyd Calhoun, copyright, 1909, by Reilly & Lee Company.

Native American Humor by James R. Aswell, copyright, 1947, by Harper and Brothers.

Rebel Private Front and Rear by William Andrew Fletcher, copyright, 1954, by the University of Texas Press.

Roads of Destiny by William Sydney Porter (O. Henry), copyright, 1918, by Doubleday & Company, Inc.

Sixty Years of American Humor by Joseph L. French, copyright, 1924, by Little, Brown and Company.

Southern Pioneers in Social Interpretation by Howard W. Odum, copyright, 1925, by the University of North Carolina Press.

The American Mind by Bliss Perry, copyright, 1912, by Houghton Mifflin Company.

A review of a book by John T. Moore appearing in the August 13, 1910 issue of the Louisville *Courier-Journal*, copyright by the Courier-Journal Company.

The Life and Letters of Joel Chandler Harris by Julia Collier Harris, copyright, 1918, by Houghton Mifflin Company.

The Local Colorists by Claude M. Simpson, copyright, 1960, by Harper and Brothers.

The Mind of the South by Wilbur J. Cash, copyright, 1941, by A. A. Knopf, Inc.

War Years with Jeb Stuart by William W. Blackford, copyright, 1945, by Charles Scribner's Sons.

Preface

ONE OF THE BEST INDICES to a people's mind is their humor—unwritten folk humor and recorded literary humor—for humor is probably the most nearly honest form of literature. More often than any other it shows with a minimum of pretense how people really feel. A study of humor, therefore, reflects not only a portion of a society's literature but its entire culture.

The period of this study, 1865-1914, was one of great change in the South. A feudal society had been uprooted by the Civil War and a new, more democratic one was being planted by Reconstruction. The South was trying to catch up with the second half of the nineteenth century. It was slowly and sometimes painfully adjusting to life in a civilization that was increasingly dominated by the Industrial Revolution. The attitudes, the emotions, the conflicts of a large segment of the people undergoing these changes are clearly reflected, I believe, in the humor they wrote and read. The attraction of ante-bellum plantation life and the pull of "New South" progressivism, for example, are illustrated in the humor of the day. Joel Chandler Harris could write glowing accounts of the faithful, contented slave and also be a promoter of Henry Grady's "New South" policies.

The Smiling Phoenix

Many other insights into the mind of the South after the Civil War are provided by humor. The desire of the South to vindicate its past is seen in the many stories about ante-bellum days; they constitute a more elaborate defense of slavery than all the prewar polemical tracts. The idea that the Negro was perhaps worthy of freedom but not of full civil rights is also made clear in the humor. The attraction of the Negro personality, however, made him the most popular humorous disguise; and Old Si, Brother Dickey, Uncle Remus, and Old Wash became familiar names.

Virtually all aspects of Southern life are reflected in the humor: politics, religion, education, economics, commerce and industry, and folklore. Various ethnic groups in odd corners were exploited in numerous local-color sketches, most of them published in Northern magazines designed for Northern readers who were eager to learn of the exotic groups south of the Mason-Dixon line.

This study is divided into thirteen chapters. A reading of the study will, I think, show the divisions and order to be logical. Several problems faced me in classifying the humor, especially that dealing with the Negro and the poor white. Since the Negro character touches virtually every area of Southern life, for example, I found it impossible to include all the humor treating him under one heading. He appears in many guises: as a body servant in the Civil War, as an upstart pawn of the carpetbagger and the scalawag during Reconstruction, as a faithful slave in the ante-bellum South, as a dusky philosopher and teller of animal tales, as a conniving picaro, as a political mouthpiece, and as the butt of "coon" jokes. Moreover, the poor white has almost as many facets to his character.

In this study I have tried to give a complete picture of Southern humor written between 1865 and 1914, specifically between the Civil War and World War I. Except for cursory treatment in surveys of American humor and except for studies of a few major writers like Joel Chandler Harris and George Washington Cable, this period of Southern humor has been much neglected. For this reason and because of my own interest in Southern history I chose this time of the South's greatest turmoil and change. Complete research is obviously impossible for so broad a topic; however, I feel that I have surveyed enough material to make the findings of this study valid. I have had at my disposal perhaps the best collection of American humor in existence, the Franklin J. Meine Collection of American Humor and Folklore, now in the University of Illinois Library. I checked all the books, pamphlets, and periodicals for Southern humor in this collection written between the Civil War and World War I. I also used University of Illinois Library resources for works not in the Meine Collection. Other research included a check of the files of my hometown newspaper, the Union Springs (Alabama) *Herald*, for 1867 to 1914. The specimens of humor I collected from this source gave me a clearer idea of the immense popularity of grass roots humor during the period.

Since tastes in and definitions of humor are so unstable, I have made no attempt in this study to define humor. As the reader will probably observe from reading some of the selections I have included, what the public of 1865 considered humorous the public of 1965 may consider merely quaint or ludicrous. I have, therefore, used as a practical, working rule the assumption that what the writers and readers between 1865 and 1914 thought humorous was indeed humorous—at least to them during their time.

Getting a book into print is, of course, never the exclusive work of one person; many people are involved in the several stages from inception to publication. First, I should like to thank Dr. John T. Flanagan, my adviser in the doctoral program at the University of Illinois, who first suggested such a study and then helped me to see it through to completion. Among the many others to whom I am indebted are Dr. Robert W. Oram of the University of Illinois Library, Dr. Alton Morris of the Department of English at the University of Florida, Dr. and Mrs. Lewis F. Haines of the University of Florida Press, Mrs. Franzee Dolbeare of the Kentucky Southern College art faculty, Mrs. Lois Stroud of the Kentucky Southern Library, and Harold Blythe, Jerry Rodgers, Anita Waller, and Mikell Daley, also of Kentucky Southern College. Perhaps most of all I am indebted to Mr. Paul Chalker, who edited the book at the University of Florida Press. I should also like to thank the Humanities Monograph Committee of the University of Florida for permission to reprint the Civil War material from *Reflections of the Civil War in Southern Humor* (Gainesville, 1962).

When I came to this topic I had no idea of what I should find but only a vague assumption that post-Civil-War Southern humor must have been in some way affected by the war. Approaching my material inductively, I let it speak for itself. My findings justify the conclusion that following the Civil War Southern humor underwent extensive modifications. This book is a report on what I found.

The postwar South that is the subject of this book was not unlike that mythical bird, the phoenix, which arises reborn from its own ashes. But the South arose smiling from the ashes of humiliation and defeat—though sometimes smiling through tears. The Southerner's sense of humor helped him to fight a war he believed honorable and to accept the bitter defeat which ended it. Without the escape valve of humor, many a "Rebel" would have succumbed to despair. The Southerner could smile wistfully as he looked back on a proud past and hopefully as he looked forward to an uncertain future. He smiled because he read humorists like Bill Arp, who once wrote somewhat serio-comically that the South was "conquered but not convinced."

WADE H. HALL

Kentucky Southern College

xv

1. Introduction

FRANKLIN J. MEINE has pointed out in the Introduction to *Tall Tales of the Southwest* that Mark Twain and Artemus Ward were the climax, not the start, of American humor. Mark Twain, especially, was saturated in Southern frontier humor, and his first significant story, "The Jumping Frog of Calaveras County," was typical of the tall tales he had heard in Missouri all his life. He had many humorists to draw on for his inspiration and instruction, since in the 1830's, 1840's, and 1850's frontier lawyers, editors, doctors, and politicians frequently doubled as recorders of humor. The humor they wrote was distinct. Meine commented: "This early humor of the South had no counterpart in the humor of any other section of the United States. It was distinctly and peculiarly Southern; and it was provincial, wholly local."

The frontiersmen had a rich field for exploitation. Contrasts in the life of such states as Tennessee, Georgia, Alabama, Mississippi, Arkansas, and Missouri provided them with a multitude of local oddities and eccentric types to record.

The Smiling Phoenix

The humorists who began to write in the 1830's had many things in common. Kenneth Lynn described a typical writer of the period. "The ideal Southwestern humorist was a professional man—a lawyer or a newspaperman, usually, although sometimes a doctor or an actor. He was actively interested in politics, either as a party propagandist or as a candidate for office. He was well educated, relatively speaking, and well traveled. . . ."[1]* James R. Aswell also reported them: "The authors were tramp printers, soldiers, reporters, preachers, doctors, editors, lawyers, politicians, merchants, swindlers, steamboat captains, actors, schoolmasters. They rubbed elbows with the vigorous life of their times and reported it with shrewdly humorous insight."[2]

Prewar

Almost all these men were conservative in politics. Most of them were Whigs. Few supporters of Andrew Jackson were found among them. Lynn pointed out, in fact, that Jackson became the epitome of all they abhorred. The typical Southwestern humorist, he maintained, developed his literary hero as the "Self-controlled Gentleman," who was first seen in the sketches of A. B. Longstreet. The humorist made the reader constantly aware of the gulf between the morally irreproachable Gentleman and the tainted low-life the author described. Lynn concluded that the ultimate purpose of the humor was "to convert the entire community to the temperate values of Whiggery." Although this is probably an overstatement, certainly the typical Southwestern humorist was socially superior to the characters and scenes he depicted, and was politically conscious.

The most popular medium for the humor of the Old Southwest was the newspaper. The New Orleans *Picayune,* the St. Louis *Reveille,* the Louisville *Courier,* the Montgomery *Mail,* and the *Spirit of the Times* founded in New York by William T. Porter, owed much of their popularity to the humorous sketches they published regularly. These sketches were frequently collected and in book form became even more popular. Three representative collections are William T. Porter's *Big Bear of Arkansas* (1845)—the title story was by Thomas Bangs Thorpe—and *Quarter Race in Kentucky* (1846) and T. A. Burke's *Polly Peablossom's Wedding* (1851). Such names as A. B. Longstreet, Joseph G. Baldwin, Johnson J. Hooper, George Washington Harris, Thomas Bangs Thorpe, Henry Taliaferro Lewis, and Madison Tensas became household words among readers of Southern newspapers. William T. Porter's *Spirit of the Times* became the most popular humorous journal of the day.

The Southwestern humorists wrote about subjects that were in direct contrast to the non-Southern themes used by the genteel romancers, who usually tried to emulate Dr. Johnson and Sir Walter Scott. After discussing this European-oriented literature, the critic William M. Baskervill continued: "To this state of affairs a remarkable exception was found in Georgia. Here were the beginnings of a popular literature." Citing Longstreet's *Georgia Scenes* and

* Textual source notes appear at the end of each chapter.

William T. Thompson's *Major Jones's Courtship*, he wrote: "They are, it is true, 'rough and tumble,' but in them we find genuine humor, broad but irresistible."[3]

The "broad but irresistible" part of the humor accounted largely for its great popularity. This coarseness was also its most prominent trait. Many people who in their youth had delighted to read these sketches had reservations later in life about their "vulgar" content. William Dean Howells' censure in 1898 of the humorists of the Old Southwest showed dramatically how the taste in humor had changed since the 1830's. "There was . . . a school of Southern humorists before the war whose drolling my boyhood knew with delight, though when I came far later in life to read 'Georgia Scenes,' 'Flush Times in Alabama,' 'Major Jones's Courtship,' and the 'Sut Levengood [*sic*] Stories,' it was with a very tempered joy in the gouging, biting, and horse-play which form the body of their humour. In fact, they are atrocious, and valuable only to the moralist as expressive of the sort of savage spirit which slavery could breed in people of our kindly and decent strain."[4]

Some doggerel verse published in 1850 in the Galveston *Weekly Journal,* although intended as a burlesque, is a but little exaggerated example of the often bloody humor:

> *They fit and fit,*
> *And gouged and bit,*
> *And struggled in the mud*
> *Until the ground*
> *For miles around*
> *Was kivered with their blood*
> *And a pile of noses, ears, and eyes,*
> *Large and massive reached the skies.*[5]

Henry Clay Lukens summed up the coarse humor this way: "Stepping across the threshold of the nineteenth century, we find our ambitious young literature disposed to be noisy, at times coarse in its frolic, strident, uncouth, and lacking the gentle, harmonious elements of true humor. . . . Fun was boisterous, theatrical, and repellent."[6] W. P. Trent concluded that Sut Lovingood, Simon Suggs, Major Jones, and Ned Brace were all important creations "provided one is not squeamish or puritanical."[7] Certainly the squeamish could find little delight in a humor of boisterous and crude situations, of discomfiture, of rough pranks—a painful humor. C. Alphonso Smith decided that it was this element of pain that distinguished the Southwestern humor.[8]

Exaggeration was another trait of the humor. The tall tale and the lie, in fact, were developed into art forms. The art of lying, for example, has seldom reached such heights as in Joseph Baldwin's character, Ovid Bolus.

Though many of the frontier sketches were exaggerations, they promoted the development of realism in American literature. They emphasized colloquial speech, local mores, and native character types. The humorists were observers of the human comedy during the South's flush times and usually thought of

3

themselves as recording reality rather than writing imaginative literature.[9] Many of their characters read like caricatures today—and obviously they were prone to exaggerate certain features—but their real-life models were living during a rough era, a frontier period when temperance was not a way of life. Constance Rourke, however, maintained in *American Humor* that most of these frontier sketches were "rough fantasies" and had "little or nothing to do with a genuine reality" (p. 64). As could be expected, Vernon L. Parrington attacked the Scottesque stories and novels by ante-bellum Southern writers and commented approvingly on the "few realistic sketches . . . that preserve the authentic ways of backwoods life in their rude vernacular."[10]

Interest in the prewar humorous sketches has steadily increased, while concern for the romantic school of John Pendleton Kennedy has decreased. In his biography, *Dr. George William Bagby*, Joseph King alluded to the reason for these trends. "The romancers of the Old South wrote extravagantly of the cavaliers, the chivalry, the noble lords and beautiful ladies of the past, but the humorists described lovingly the Jack-legged lawyer, the gambling, lying renegade, the simple but shrewd backwoodsman, and the unadorned, bashful country lass of the present. The humorists were the realists, and with all their exaggeration, probably drew a truer picture of life than the romanticists" (p. 62).

Romancers like Kennedy, William Gilmore Simms, and others were not without humor; but their humor was almost always genteel and highly refined. Kennedy's *Swallow Barn* (1832), usually called a novel, is actually a series of sketches—"Court Day," "Opossum Hunt," and "Country Gathering" are examples—in which humor plays a significant role. The book's Frank Meriwether has often been compared with Joseph Addison's Sir Roger de Coverley for his humor.

The humor of the 1830's was by no means the first written in the South. Some critics trace the first Southern humor back to John Smith's exaggerated accounts of his exploits in the New World. Others claim William Byrd of Virginia as the first significant Southern humorist. Although Byrd was an aristocrat and a refined writer generally, he left some sketches that foreshadow the humor of the Old Southwest. Charles W. Kent wrote of the kinship between Byrd and the later frontier school: "The humor of William Byrd, spontaneous, persistent, and original, based upon first-hand observation and not despising the homely even when it was streaked with coarseness, though never depicting coarseness for its own sake, is the exact prototype of the humor of the school to which belonged Longstreet, Baldwin, Hooper, Thompson, Crockett, and others, who unconsciously emulated one or the other of his qualities."[11] This thread of influence may be discovered running throughout Southern humor—from William Byrd to William Faulkner.

The poor white was the most common subject of the sketches of Old Southwestern humor. In studies designed for masculine reading—they were not suitable for polite reading or for the ladies—the shiftless poor white outside the plantocracy came alive. According to Shields McIlwaine, until 1861 the only acceptable version of the poor white was comic. In his study, *The Southern Poor-White,*

McIlwaine divided the early poor white of humor into three types: the hero or Davy Crockett type, the rogue or Simon Suggs type, and the cracker or Ned Brace type (p. 62). The first extensive treatment of the poor white in Southern humor is William Byrd's *History of the Dividing Line,* written in 1728 and published first in 1841. In this account of a surveying trip into western Virginia and North Carolina, Byrd satirized the poor whites of Lubberland whose laziness led them to celebrate the Sabbath all week long. Byrd's depiction of the poor white set the stereotype which has influenced Southern writers since his time. Until shortly before the Civil War the Negro seldom appeared in Southern humor. When he was used by Simms or Poe, he was usually a house or body servant and was always in the background. Longstreet included a few anecdotes with the Negro as the butt, but by the time of Madison Tensas' *The Swamp Doctor's Adventures in the South-West* (1858) the Negro was becoming a not uncommon target of ferocious humor. The only extensive use of the Negro in humor, however, was in the minstrelsy initiated in the 1820's and 1830's by Edwin Forrest and Jim Crow Rice.

Subjects for humorous sketches included peculiar local customs and superstitions, hunting stories, gambling escapades, religion, fights, gander-pullings, horse swaps, militia musters, camp meetings, play parties and frolics, courtings and weddings, marksmanship contests, oddities in character, lawsuits, and political campaigns. Most of these subjects became genre sketches and continued in popularity—especially in oral humor—after the Civil War.

Many of the humorists wrote anonymously and remained anonymous; however, a dozen or so became well known. Baldwin, Bagby, Harris, Hooper, Longstreet—these men especially made their mark in American literature with their humorous sketches.

Joseph G. Baldwin's *Flush Times of Alabama and Mississippi* (1853) deals with the rough and ready civilization of a pioneer area—its eccentric characters, curious customs, and ludicrous scenes. These sketches of primitive manners describe the sharpers, boasters, liars, spread-eagle orators, saddlebag lawyers, jokers, and rascals of the Old Southwest. Baldwin knew what he was writing about because as a lawyer in Alabama he had lived among such characters and conditions. W. P. Trent wrote of *Flush Times:* "If the fighting, swearing, drinking, gambling, hail-fellow-well-met Southwest had produced no other literary monument than this, it would not have broken the Ten Commandments in vain."[12]

Although George W. Bagby made his reputation largely after the Civil War, he created his humorous masterpiece, Mozis Addums, in the 1850's. His "Letters of Mozis Addums to Billy Ivvens" were published in the *Southern Literary Messenger* in 1858. Mozis was the last rustic character creation of the prewar humorists. In Mozis' dialect Bagby was one of the first writers to exploit the humor of illiterate phonetic spelling. The "Letters" deal with the rural Virginian's trip to Washington to patent a perpetual motion machine and his adventures en route and in the city.

The Smiling Phoenix

Jeannette Tandy considered Davy Crockett the first full-fledged Southern humorist. James Fenimore Cooper's Natty Bumppo antedated him in literature, but Davy was the first frontiersman about whom a comic tradition arose. To Kenneth Lynn, Crockett was "a frontiersman who superlatively combined a sense of humor with a mastery of the vernacular. . . . Davy Crockett, in the decade between 1821 and 1831, was a master of frontier humor; in these years he was able to give vent to the feelings generated by a hard and lonely life, and yet by humorously exaggerating them to explode their savagery in laughter; through ingenious expressions he relieved an inner pressure."[13] Parrington called the Crockett autobiography "a striking bit of realism, done after the manner of the Longstreet school," which "reveals the backwoods Anglo-Irishman as an uncivilized animal, responding to simple stimuli. . . ."[14]

One of the first Tennesseeans to write humorous sketches of Appalachian Mountain life was George Washington Harris. He was a typical frontier humorist except that, unlike Longstreet and his kind, he offered no apologies for writing about crude characters and situations. Harris' humor is broad, unrefined, and unabashedly vulgar. His masterful creation was Sut Lovingood, whose adventures burlesque such typical country gatherings as dances, funerals, weddings, and camp meetings. He calls himself a "nat'ral-born durn'd fool" whose mission is to raise "pertickler hell." He is a merciless prankster who delights in pulling crude and often cruel jokes on weak and innocent people. The first of the Sut Lovingood sketches appeared in 1854 in the *Spirit of the Times;* and they continued to come out until 1867, when they were collected as *Sut Lovingood's Yarns.* Many present-day critics believe that in these yarns Southern humor reached its highest level before Mark Twain.

The popularity of Harris was in part responsible for the continuing strain of vulgarity in Southern humor. Postwar critics, however, were generally very censorious of the humor of Harris and his school. In 1907 J. Thompson Brown, Jr., writing on Harris, took to task all American humor for its coarseness: "It is bubbling and irrepressible, and not infrequently lacking in dignity. Worse, perhaps, than aught else, three hundred years has not been a sufficient revolutionary cycle to induce an American to place courteous sympathy before his fun. In brief, American humor is boyish, crude, and boisterous, striking heedlessly, regardless of feelings, propriety, and often even of decency. . . . Within bounds these characteristics might be tolerated, but how easy it is for the truant schoolboy to transgress the limits of noisy though innocent fun-making and become an untiring nuisance."[15]

The motto of Johnson J. Hooper's Simon Suggs was a way of life for many in the frontier South: "It is good to be shifty in a new country." In such a fluid and unsettled society the picaresque rogue thrived. Suggs is typical of the rascal who connives to get ahead; he is a blackleg whose existence is possible only during "flush times." Hooper's *The Adventures of Simon Suggs* (1845), cast in the form of a campaign biography, is perhaps the best picture of pre-Civil-War Alabama cracker life in literature. Although Hooper was a practicing lawyer, he also edited at different times the *Chambers County Times*, the *Alabama Journal*, and the Montgomery *Mail*, in which many of these sketches first appeared. The humor of Suggs' rascally adventures is central; however, political and social satire were important secondary motives for Hooper's creation.

The cornerstone of realistic Southern humor is A. B. Longstreet's *Georgia Scenes* (1835), composed of sketches he had printed earlier in his Augusta *States Rights Sentinel*. His sketches influenced most later Southern humorists including William T. Thompson, Thorpe, Hooper, Baldwin, and Joel Chandler Harris. His accounts of life among the Georgia crackers became a pattern for later humorists and included such "scenes" as a horse trade, a fight, a dancing party, a "gouging" rehearsal, and a militia company drill. In each sketch he attempted to portray life as he saw it around him; that is, he wanted his humor to be documentary as well as entertaining. This objective frequently led him into scenes that were considered coarse and vulgar by the genteel reader. "The Gander Pulling," for example, tells of a popular backwoods sport in which the crackers suspended a greased goose by its legs above the road and passed under on horseback attempting each time to snatch the bird's head off. Longstreet's best known character, Ned Brace, epitomizes his humor. This practical joker is not really vulgar, although occasionally his humor approaches the broad and coarse. The prominent postwar editor Henry Watterson called *Georgia Scenes* "the simplest transcription of the humorous phases of the life and character of the period embraced by them, done in charcoal, without effort and without pretense, and are worthy of preservation because of their fidelity to nature and the truthfulness of detail which marks them."[16] Although the humor has grown somewhat stale, the sociological value of Longstreet's sketches has increased.

Such writers as Longstreet, Baldwin, and Hooper best exemplify the "humorists of the Old Southwest." For several reasons this group is of great significance to the student of Southern literature. Their sketches are, first of all, distinct contributions to American literature. They constitute one of the first concerted attempts by Southern writers to produce literature for its own sake. Moreover, unlike most other Southern literary productions, they were widely read in the South. They were forerunners of the post-Civil-War realistic writers and influenced many of them. Had they done no more than prepare the way for Mark Twain, their work would not have been in vain. But perhaps a revival of interest in them is evidenced by recently published paperback editions of *Flush Times* and *Georgia Scenes*.

War

With tempers at the boiling point it was natural that Civil War humor should be sectional and intensely bitter. Few humorists could then remain objective and level-headed. Even the great humorist-conciliator of the postwar period, Joel Chandler Harris, was ready, as a fledgling writer, to join in the propaganda battle. His unfinished play, *Butler the Beast*, opened with General Ben

Butler saying to an aide: "Well, William, have you sought the city on some pretense or other, to hang a man?"[17] But it was the humor of such partisans as Bill Arp and Petroleum V. Nasby that lightened the burdens of soldiers in the field and of politicians in Richmond and Washington.

Beginning with the election of Lincoln and not abating until Appomattox, the propaganda humorists were busily at work. George Washington Harris' *Sut Lovingood Travels with Old Abe Lincoln* was an early entry in the field. Published in the Nashville *Union and American* between February 28 and March 5, 1861, this series of sketches told how the young Tennessee mountaineer helped get Lincoln safely from Springfield to the White House. As an advance scout, Sut uncovered a plot in Baltimore to murder the President, and hurried to Harrisburg, Pennsylvania, to warn him. Replying to Sut's warning, Lincoln admitted that he had done "the things I hadn't oughter, and left undone the things I had oughter." He then begged the Tennesseean for advice. Sut came to the frightened President's aid by disguising him so that "he looked like he'd been on a big drunk for three weeks." According to Sut's account, only his intervention saved the President and got him to Washington to be sworn in. By implication Sut showed that Lincoln was one of his kind: worthless and idiotic. The sketch revealed the dominant Southern attitude toward the President-elect: he was a man of cowardice, intemperate, boorish, and ugly. Describing Old Abe, Sut wrote that he looked like "a yeller ladder with half the rungs knocked out." He concluded his sketches by comparing Lincoln with a dead frog that had been stretched out of shape. In Washington, Sut gave Lincoln one more bit of advice on how he could get through his term as President: "Jis take the persishion that you haint sponsibil while onder a skeer an hit will kiver your hole administrashun." During the war the spokesmen for the slavocracy ceased being the Well-Bred Gentlemen of earlier humor and became red-necked louts like Bill Arp, Mozis Addums, and Sut Lovingood. They were all radical secessionists.

The work of Charles H. Smith ("Bill Arp") was to the South what Artemus Ward's was to the North. Written in letter form by a supposedly almost illiterate Georgia cracker, the first Bill Arp sketches were published in the Rome, Georgia, paper *Southern Confederacy*. Bill's first letter to "Mr. Abe Linkhorn" appeared in April, 1861, soon after the taking of Fort Sumter. It shows the fierce Southern indignation and pride at the beginning of the war and ridicules Lincoln's demand that the rebels lay down their arms and disperse within twenty days. Bill tells the President sarcastically that it cannot be done in less than thirty days. In his second letter to Lincoln, published in January, 1862, the Southerner laments that "we hav not been able to disperse as yet." After the news of the Emancipation Proclamation reached the South, he published a third letter to the President in December, 1862, in which he reported that the South was still buying and selling Negroes. He added, however, that he knows they soon will all be free and will "rush frantikally forth into the arms of their deliverers, and with perfumed and sented gratitude embrace your exsellency, and

Madam Harriet Beechers toe." Later in the same month Bill wrote his last letter to Lincoln. He told the President that it was possible "that you are usin too much Proklamation" because over eighteen months before he had ordered "the boys to retire and be peasable" but they had paid him no mind. Now that he had "proklimated the niggers free," Bill was afraid that this proclamation would also be disregarded. On a more serious note the Georgia cracker reported that the South was sacrificing willingly in order to whip the North: Southerners "swear by the ghost of Calhoun they will eat roots and drink branch water the balance of the time before they will kernowly to your abolition dyenasty." In the role as adviser to the President, Bill suggested a better route to Richmond than the one the Yankees had been using. Until then, he wrote, the Union army had "been tryin to cum . . . through a mity Longstreet, over two powerful Hills, and across a tremendious Stonewall." He suggested they try going around by the "Rocky Mountings."[18]

Bill Arp, So Called: A Side Show of the Southern Side of the War, published in 1866, contained the four letters to Lincoln and other wartime sketches. Realizing their fiercely partisan nature, Smith explained apologetically: "At the time they were written they were appreciated, because the minds of the people needed relaxation from the momentous and absorbing interests of the war" (p. 5). In the same edition he wrote: "For the sentiments that pervade these letters, I have no apologies to make. At the time they appeared in the press of the South, these sentiments were the silent echoes of our people's thoughts. . . . Of course they contain exaggerations, and prophecies which were never fulfilled; but both sections were playing 'brag' as well as 'battle,' and though we could not compete with our opponents in the former, yet some of us did try to hold our own. At both games we were whipped by overwhelming forces, and we have given it up" (pp. 6-7).

The sketches show that Bill Arp was not only critical of the Yankee invaders; he also castigated Southerners for nonsupport or mismanagement of the war. Georgia's Governor Joseph Brown was a favorite target. One time Bill wrote: "Durn old Brown. He is as big a fool on a proclamation as old Abe Lincoln" (p. 43). Indicting Brown's alleged autocracy, he said: "Joe Brown orders me to jail; I appeal to a special jury and Joe Brown is the jury. I carry it to the Supreme Court, and Joe Brown is the court. . . . Brown's got us, and I reckon it's the best plan to humor the joke. . . . 'Three cheers for Joe Brown,' that's the way to say it" (pp. 50-51). Accusing Brown of Presidential ambitions, "Sometimes I think you are trying to climb too fast, Joe. You see your ideas get so much elevation that your head gets dizzy and your brain begins to swim, and you naturally overlook some things and commit indiscretions which are distressing" (p. 62). He once accused Brown of having the same motto as Louis XIV: "L'état? C'est moi."

Draft dodgers and shirkers also came in for criticism from Smith's acid pen. "It seems utterly impossible to get extortioners in the ranks. Governor Brown thought he would put some of 'em to the useful art of bullet-stopping, so he called for a draft. Enough of the patriotic responded, and there was no draft. But it give 'em a powerful scare, and developed more rheumatics and chronics than was thought possible to exist in a limestone country" (p. 33). The flower of Southern manhood, he feared, was being killed: "We will have a race of people after a while that ain't worth a curse. The good ones are getting killed up, but these *skulkers* and *shirkers* and *dodgers* don't die" (pp. 48-49). Sarcastically, he wrote another time: "Such is the rapid progress of human events in these fighting times, that a man who was only forty last year, can be forty-six this year." If he were a doctor, "I would cure 'em or kill 'em, and then our poor, bleeding country would have sound men or none; and that's the way to stop dodging around" (pp. 78-79).

That the South was never unanimously behind the Confederacy was made clear throughout Smith's Bill Arp sketches. Forgetting that war calls for curtailment of many rights of citizenship, Bill and others excoriated Confederate politicians for the secret legislative session—"perhaps a little the closest communion ever established in a well-watered country"—and the suspension of habeas corpus—"perhaps, when suspended, the most savagerous beast that ever got after tories and traders." In "A Message to All Folks" he summarized major grievances against the Confederate government: "F-E-L-L-E-R CITIZENS: The war, and the Yankees, and old Lincoln and his threats of subjugation, extermination, amalgamation, desolation, and Mr. Toombs' foul domination, is a big thing, terrible and horrible. But old Habeas *hung up*, and secret sessions, and the currency bill, and conscription are far bigger, and awful in the extreme. Our soldiers ought to let the Yankees alone, and come home and fight these savage beasts, and you, my fellow-citizens, ought to arm yourselves with sticks, and rocks, and thrashpoles, and hot water, and pikes, and make a violent assault upon these 'most monstrous paradoxes'" (p. 55). Even the generals tasted his venom: "Since the discovery of America by Pocahontas, the *habeas corpus* has never been suspended over anybody, except three hundred thousand soldiers in the Confederate army. For nearly three years, General Lee and Johnston have had it suspended over all the fighting boys in their commands" (pp. 58-59).

The main object of Smith's war satire was, naturally, the Northerners and especially their conduct of the war. Bill Arp's epithets for the Yankee soldier included "foul invader," "miscegenator," "blue-bellied Yankees," and "blue devil." Northern versions of what their armies were doing were usually exaggerated, he maintained, and in several sketches he attempted to set the record straight. About the Yankee raid—or "battle"—in Rome, Georgia, "I think it highly proper you should git the strait of it from one who seen it with his eyes, and heard it with his years, and a piece of it fell on his big toe" (p. 35). Although fighting against overwhelming odds, the Southern defenders were heroic. "For three days and nights our valiant troops had beat back the foul invader, and saved our pullets from their devouring jaws" (p. 85). But eventually the city had to be evacuated and left to the Yankees. Only a few renegade Negroes remained behind to welcome the enemy. "It is a source of regret, however, that some of our households of the African scent have fallen back into the arms of the foul invaders. I suppose they may now be called miscegenators, and by this time are increasing the stock of *Odour d'Afrique* in Northern society, which popular perfume crowds out of the market all those extracts which made X. Bazin, Jules Haule and Lubin famous. Good-bye, sweet otto of roses; farewell, ye balm of a thousand flowers—your days are numbered" (p. 91). The conduct of the Yankee soldiers in Rome, he reported, was despicable. The "heartless, pitiless invaders" even used tombstones like rocks in building fortifications.

When the war tide was obviously going against the South, Bill Arp could still see some hope for success. Of the mounted Rebel soldier, for instance, "The truth is, that the Confederate cavalry can fight 'em, and dog 'em, and dodge 'em, and bushwhack 'em, and bedevil 'em, for a thousand years. . . . " The Rebel cavalry, he maintained, was invincible (p. 116).

In several sketches Smith was realistic about the chances for a Southern victory. Usually, though, in speculating on a Northern victory he became defiant. Near the end of the war he wrote of Lincoln: "After he has whipped us, then he has got to subjugate us." This, the rabid Rebel asserted, could not be done. All the hullabaloo about Lincoln's freeing of the slave was nonsense, he continued; and, foreshadowing the tone of his immediate postwar pieces, "What does it all amount to?—I want to buy a nigger, and I had just as lief buy a chunk of a free nigger as any other sort. I don't care a bobee about his being free, if I can subjugate him; and if he gets above his color, I will put thirty-nine whelks right under his shirt, and make him wish that old Lincoln stood in his shoes" (p. 115). With these words Smith set the stage for the conflict of Reconstruction.

Southern humor written during the war was by no means restricted to prose. Comic songs and poems were also popular. One of the most popular rebel songs was "Eating Goober Peas," which contained such verses as:

> *Just before the battle the Gen'ral hears a row.*
> *He says, "The Yanks are coming, I hear their rifles now."*
> *He turns around in wonder, and what do you think he sees?*
> *The Georgia Militia, eating goober peas!*

A couplet expressed a longing for the end of the war in these words: "I wish this war was over, when free from rags and fleas, / We'd kiss our wives and sweethearts, and gobble goober peas!"[19]

One of the most widely reprinted poetic satires in the wartime South was the "Confederate Mother Goose," written in the Richmond office of the *Southern Literary Messenger* by Dr. George W. Bagby (then its editor), Innes Randolph, William M. Burwell, Will Washington, and others of the group that became known as the Richmond Wits. Seizing upon well-known weaknesses or shortcomings of Union generals, the wits came up with such gems as the following:

> *Little Be-Pope, he lost his hope,*
> *Jackson, the Rebel, to find him;*

But he found him at last, and he ran very fast,
  With his bully invaders behind him!

Little McClellan sat eating a mellon,
  The Chickahominy by.
He stuck in a spade; and a long time delayed,
  Then cried: "What a great general am I!"

Hey! diddle Sutler, the dastard Ben Butler,
  Fought women, morn, evening and noon;
And old Satan laughed, as hot brimstone he quaffed,
  When the Beast ran away with the Spoon!

Trickery, dickery, slickery Ben [Butler]—
  Eluding and dodging the fighting men—
Was never afraid of a matron or maid,
  But cent for no cotton, or silver, he paid!

Henceforth, when a fellow [McClellan] is kicked out of doors,
  He need never resent the disgrace,
But exclaim: "My dear, I'm eternally yours,
  For assisting in changing my base."

Joe Hooker had a nice tin sword;
  Jack bent it up one day.
When Halleck heard, at Washington,
  He wrote: "Come home and stay."

John Pope came down to Dixie town, and thought it very wise
  To sit down in a 'skeeter swamp and start at telling lies.
But when he found his lies were out, with all his might and main,
  He changed his base to another place, and began to—lie again![20]

Most Southern war humor naturally showed up the foibles of the North. President Lincoln was probably the most popular target of Southern wit, with the cautious General McClellan a close second. A parody of Hamlet's is "McClellan's Soliloquy," by "a Daughter of Georgia." The poem pillories the wavering general who, Lincoln complained, had "the slows." It opens:

> *Advance, or not advance; that is the question!*
> *Whether 'tis better in the mind to suffer*
> *The jeers and howlings of outrageous Congressmen,*
> *Or to take arms against a host of rebels,*
> *And, by opposing, beat them? . . .*

Southern optimism and pride dominate the close: "These Southerners make cowards of us all."[21] After the war only the pride remained.

Transition

Southern postwar humor differed from the prewar humor in many ways. The change did not suddenly take place in April, 1865; it had been in the making for some time, although it had been brought on at least in part by the Civil War. This period of transition covered roughly the years 1860-70; however, the major transition humorist, Richard Malcolm Johnston, continued writing long after 1870.

The overall trend toward a more refined, a more gentle and sentimentalized humor may be seen even in the most prominent of the earlier humorists, A. B. Longstreet. After the war the author of *Georgia Scenes* wrote principally religious essays and articles in vindication of the South.

Writing in 1882, Henry Watterson noted the change: "In the famous speech of Mr. J. Proctor Knott, in 'Texas Siftings,' and in the paragraphs of the late Mr. Hatcher, a marked change . . . is seen; whilst in the more elaborate stories of the author of 'Dukesborough Tales,' and in the delicious fables of 'Uncle Remus,' we discover not merely marked progress in literary handicraft, but a total absence of the merely local tone which abounds in the writing of Longstreet, Harris, Thompson, and Hooper."[22] By 1890 Henry Clay Lukens could characterize the humor of Johnston and other popular humorists as "broader, more brusque, unrestrained, merrier, but always within the corral of honest, inoffensive phrasing. . . ."[23]

In 1870, the year of his death, William Gilmore Simms published in *Harper's New Monthly Magazine* a sketch which shows many indebtednesses to the old frontier humor while observing generally the decorum of the more humane, less coarse humor.[24] "How Sharp Snaffles Got His Capital and His Wife" is a sketch in the manner of Joseph Baldwin's Ovid Bolus. Among hunters in North Carolina, Simms began, Saturday night on a hunting trip was always dedicated to "The Lying Camp." On such occasions lying was made a fine art. "The hunter who actually inclines to exaggeration is, at such a period, privileged to deal in all the extravagancies of invention; nay, he is *required* to do so! To be literal, or confine himself to the bald and naked truth, is not only discreditable, but a *finable* offense!"

One Saturday night Sam Snaffles won the prize for the best yarn by relating how he accumulated enough capital to win his sweetheart's hand. Sam's method of lying is to begin by artfully mixing fact with fiction until he gets his listener to suspend his disbelief. He gradually increases the amount of fiction until at the end anything he says sounds plausible. Sam explains his method to several liars who complain that he has been getting too close to the truth. "And how's a man to lie decently onless you lets him hev a bit of truth to go upon? The truth's nothing but a peg in the wall that I hangs the lie upon. A'ter a while I promise that you shan't see the peg." Sam's big lie concerns how he captured 3,150 geese by stretching a net across a lake where the birds alighted. He also kills a bear while goose hunting and adds the revenue from that source to his capital. This is the way Sam disposed of the bear: "Sold the hide and tallow for a fine market-price; sold the meat, got ten cents a pound for it fresh—'twas most beautiful meat; biled down the bones for the marrow; melted down the grease; sold fourteen pounds of it to the barbers and apothecaries; got a dollar a pound for that; sold the hide for twenty dollars; and got the cash for everything." With such careful attention to detail, not even the most incredulous could disbelieve his story.

With the money from the geese and the bear, Sam has enough capital to satisfy his sweetheart's father; and the two are married. Now, thirteen years later, his wife, Merry Ann, has had thirty-six children. He concludes his yarn with an explanation of how this is possible. "You see, Merry Ann keeps on. But you've only got to do the ciphering for yourself. Here, now, Jedge, look at it. Count for yourself. First we had *three* gal children, you see. Vey well! Put down three. Then we had *six* boys, one every year for four years; and then, the fifth year, Merry Ann throwed deuce. Now put down the six boys a'ter the three gals, and ef that don't make thirty-six thar's no snakes in all Flurriday!" In this late sketch Simms showed a combination of two influences: the subject matter associated with the humor of the Old Southwest and the inoffensive tone and phrasing of postwar humor. He also revealed a knowledge of old folk tales.

Although a contemporary of Simon Suggs, William T. Thompson's Major Jones could almost be a postwar creation because of his innocence and lack of coarseness. John Donald Wade, the biographer of A. B. Longstreet, pointed out Thompson's link to the past and to the future: "After the Civil War Johnston, Joel Chandler Harris, and many other persons of less note, all of them conscious of their indebtedness to Longstreet, kept alive what he had inaugurated. Between Harris and Longstreet there was almost actual contact. It was Thompson who in 1871 secured Harris's services for the Savannah *News.* . . . Could Colonel Thompson fail to tell the young man many anecdotes, lingering in his mind, of Middle Georgia and old Judge Longstreet?" (p. 167).

Major Jones, Thompson's outstanding character creation, is a typical small farmer. He wrote to Colonel Thompson from his home in Pineville, Georgia, a series of letters published as *Major Jones's Courtship* (1843), giving a naïve account of his courtship of Miss Mary Stallins. The courtship is accompanied by many ludicrous episodes before he finally captures the maiden for his bride. The wholesome humor of the Major Jones letters contrasts with most of the frontier humor of the prewar South and previews the dominant postwar humor. Like the later Bill Arp, Thompson wrote of domestic matters: his courtship, marriage, children, relatives, and coon hunts. There is no sting in his humor. Napier Wilt's description of the Major sums up his character: "In Major Jones there is nothing of the rascal and little of the adventurer. He is neither dishonest nor self-seeking; his only vice is tobacco chewing.

14

Jones is a simple, good-natured country lad who refuses to take a serious view of life."[25] A better antithesis of Simon Suggs or Sut Lovingood could not be found than Major Jones, who is shy in the presence of women, goes to church every Sunday, and is a member of a temperance society. In the second series of his letters, published as *Major Jones's Sketches of Travel* (1848), he turns into a first-class homespun philosopher and makes thoughtful comments on what he sees during his trip from Pineville to Quebec.

The writer who best illustrates the changing humor of the Civil War period is Richard Malcolm Johnston ("Philemon Perch"). Contrasting Johnston with A. B. Longstreet, Samuel A. Link in 1900 wrote: "Mr. Longstreet began what another 'native Georgian' took up with . . . a gentler and more loving touch, and put forth with a higher refinement of art—of course reference is made to Richard Malcolm Johnston."[26]

In almost all of his novels and stories Johnston showed a kinship with the earlier humorists of the Old Southwest, but the influence is most evident in his earlier sketches. "The Goosepond School," which describes a small rural Georgia school before the Civil War, was published in 1857 in Porter's *Spirit of the Times*. In it and in most of his early Longstreet-like sketches there is much evidence of social disintegration, but by the mid-1880's his fiction had softened into sweetly sentimental recollections of a quaint and colorful past. Kenneth Lynn in *Mark Twain* described Johnston's transition role: "Appearing between the collapse of the Whig tradition and the advent of Mark Twain, Johnston's early work reveals the death pangs of an old hero and the struggles of a new one to be born" (p. 128). The Self-Controlled Gentleman of prewar humor, Lynn asserts, was becoming the Child-Hero in Johnston's sketches. In "The Goosepond School," for example, students overthrow their despot-teacher; and in "The Expensive Treat of Colonel Moses Grice" the twin sons of a young cracker farmer play an important role.

"The Expensive Treat of Colonel Moses Grice" is one of the sketches from Johnston's first book, *Georgia Sketches* (1864), which reflects his indebtedness to Longstreet's *Georgia Scenes*. Colonel Grice is a militia colonel, a stock character in the humor of the Old Southwest; but he also exhibits the paternalism of the planter that appears in the later sketches by Thomas Nelson Page and Joel Chandler Harris. On a visit to Augusta the colonel persuades a circus troupe to stage a show in Dukesborough. Back home he exults in his role of town benefactor, explaining to the excited people what they can expect to see in the circus. When circus day arrives, the colonel is in his glory. Seeing a young cracker farmer at the show, he decides to play a joke on him and hires a member of the troupe to dress up like a drunk who attempts to ride a bucking horse. The farmer, Bill Williams, rushes into the ring to save his life; whereupon the "drunk" sheds his disguise and the audience gets a good laugh at Bill's expense. But the tables are turned on Colonel Grice when Bill gets the clown to invite the colonel into the ring for a drink of whiskey. All the sketch's horseplay, however, is in good fun.

The Smiling Phoenix

At the end the colonel and Bill make up and have a drink together at a local tavern. Bill's language is always decent and frequently tender. Replying to the colonel's question about the trouble of raising his twins, Romerlus and Remerlus, he says: "I shall raise 'em to give and take. . . . Fact, I wa'n't a-espectin' but one, yit, when Reme come, I thought jes as much o' him as I did o' Rom. No, kurnel, it wouldn't be my desires to be a married man and have nary ar—to leave what little prop'ty I got to. And now, sence I got two instid o' one, and them o' the same size, I feel like I'd be sort o' awk'ard 'ithout both of 'em. You see, kurnel, they balances agin one another in my pockets. No, kurnel, better two than nary one; and in that way you can larn 'em better to give and take" (p. 318).

In this sketch is seen the postwar tendency to combine humor and pathos into a kind of crying humor. In 1891, reviewing a volume of poems by James Whitcomb Riley, Johnston himself made explicit his preference for this mixture: "It is simply wonderful, [Riley's] blending of the sportive and earnest, humor and pathos. One cannot but believe that in the making of these verses his eyes were moist with tears, whether from merriment or compassion, equally tender and sweet."[27]

Like Longstreet and the other humorists of the Old Southwest, Johnston gave his sketches a local tone by writing about picturesque people speaking their dialect. But as a forerunner of the local colorists his humor was more restrained and gentle. Even his own writings show the trend toward refinement. This change is made evident by comparing the first edition of *Dukesborough Tales* (1871) with later editions or by contrasting *Georgia Sketches* (1864) with his novel, *Old Mark Langston* (1883).

Johnston's genre sketch about a fight, "The Various Languages of Billy Moon," published August, 1881, in *Harper's New Monthly Magazine*, lacked the blood and gouging of the Longstreet type fight.[28] Johnston recalled that fights were common in the 1840's, but he claimed that they were less the result of hostility than trials of strength, agility, and endurance. In fact, after a fight "both combatants, though with blackened eyes and bruised faces, panting and hobbling, would repair to the grocery, take a social grog, and, with mutual compliments, have a cordial understanding to repeat the fight at some convenient time after." In this sketch the old-time nose-busting, ear-chewing clash had become clean and picturesque. The rest of Southern humor was undergoing a similar transition. The Civil War had evidently provided enough blood and dirt to last for some time.

Status

After the Civil War the humorist became much more popular but continued to be a second-rate literary man. This was the judgment not only of the critics but of the humorists themselves. Writers like Sidney Lanier were openly apologetic for their humorous works. Most literary people believed that the "literary" man would not content himself with being merely a humorist. Mark

Twain even grew despondent because he was received chiefly as a "phunny phellow." Relatively few writers and critics agreed with Opie Read, who thought that the humorist was just as much a professional man as the doctor or clergyman.

Although George W. Bagby's literary reputation today rests solely upon his humorous works, his biographer, Joseph King, lamented in 1927 that he had spent so much time writing dialect pieces. Churchill Chamberlayne, writing in the *Library of Southern Literature* (I, 144), agreed. "In the circle of his friends . . . it was understood that his efforts of a light kind, irresistibly amusing as many of them are, were but the diversions of a mind that was thoroughly at home in the higher regions of thought. . . . "

Discerning critics of the time, however, were aware of the part played by the humorists in the development of a realistic American literature. In 1917 Maurice G. Fulton defended his extensive treatment of them in *Southern Life in Southern Literature:* "I have devoted much attention to the humorous writers of the South because of my belief that, although much of this work was rough and crude, it was nevertheless very influential not only in the development of American humor but also in that of realistic fiction" (p. vi).

Although humor was still considered subliterary by many people, its popularity was almost universal. As never before, newspapers and magazines were filled with humor. Many a writer got this start in literature by writing publishable humor. As a result of humorous contributions to the New Orleans *Picayune* under the pen name "Drop Shot," for example, George Washington Cable was made a permanent staff member.

The birth of new literary periodicals in the South following the war offered a ready market for the humorist. Although most of them were short-lived, many a humorist received encouragement from seeing his sketches in their pages. The new literary monthlies and weeklies included: *The Land We Love* of Charlotte, North Carolina; *The Eclectic* of Richmond; *Scott's Monthly* and *The Ladies Home* of Atlanta; *The Home Monthly* of Nashville; *The Crescent Monthly* and *The South Western Magazine* of New Orleans; *The Southern Review, Southern Society*, and *Southern Home Journal* of Baltimore; and *The Nineteenth Century* of Charleston.[29] Richard Malcolm Johnston contributed to Baltimore's *Southern Magazine*. Atlanta's *The Sunny South*, edited for a time by Joel Chandler Harris, printed work by Will Allen Dromgoole and lent encouragement to many other struggling local colorists. *The Southern Bivouac*, published at Louisville, was noted for the war humor it printed. Another magazine published in Louisville, *Fetter's Southern Magazine*, brought out works by Opie Read, James Lane Allen, F. Hopkinson Smith, Frank L. Stanton, Maurice Thompson, and John Fox, Jr. The South also had more and better patronized humor periodicals than ever before: the New Orleans *Mascot, Texas Siftings, The Arkansaw Traveler, The Arkansaw Thomas Cat*, and *The Rolling Stone. Texas Siftings* and *The Arkansaw Traveler* had an international following. Even magazines that were not primarily humorous frequently had a regular humor section. Baltimore's *Southern Magazine,* for example, had "The Green Table," and Charleston's *Nineteenth Century* had "Alla Podrida."

A much larger market for the Southern humorist and local colorist existed in the Northern magazine, which from the 1870's through the 1890's was filled with humorous sketches by Southern writers. Northern magazines like *Harper's Weekly, Scribner's Monthly, Harper's New Monthly Magazine,* the *Galaxy,* and *Lippincott's* were especially accessible to Southern writers.

In 1898 C. Alphonso Smith quoted a former Yankee officer in the Civil War on the popularity of Southern writers in the North: "In 1888, in the December number of the *Forum,* Judge Albion W. Tourgee, no partial critic of the South, declared that the Northern magazines had become so monopolized by Southern writers that a foreigner, reading the magazine literature of this country, would be forced to the conclusion that the literary center of the United States is to be sought not in Massachusetts or New York, but in the South. What a literary revolution since 1870 does not that remark indicate!"[30] Frank Luther Mott summed up the Southern writer's vogue in the North in these words: "Lee and Johnston and Early had been defeated in the conflict of '61-'65, but Cable, Craddock, Page, and their cohorts won a complete victory a decade later when they established themselves in the northern magazines."[31]

Southern humorists were featured in every anthology of national humor. Such names as George Washington Cable, Joel Chandler Harris, Charles H. Smith, and Dr. George W. Bagby were familiar to humor readers North and South—and even in England.

Walter Blair's summary of the popularity of nineteenth-century American humor in general applies specifically to Southern humor. "Thus the humor of the stage and the humor of politics brought popularity to the American jester of the nineteenth century, and the numerous publications—newspapers, magazines, comic journals, books, almanacs—and lectures as well helped carry the native humor to a growing number of people."[32] Consequently, the Southern humorist was able as never before to support himself with his pen. Before the war the humorists had been men who were primarily lawyers, politicians, or teachers; after the war it was possible for a humorist to devote his full time to humor. A man like Joel Chandler Harris could make a good living at it.

Trends

The prevailing tone of postwar Southern humor is summed up well in *Ten Wise Men* by William Lightfoot Visscher's comment on the speeches of Governor Bob Taylor of Tennessee. "In his lectures Governor Taylor rambles about amid charming philosophies of life, told in reminiscent anecdote and pointed phraseology. His stories always point a moral and he is ever eloquent in humor and pathos, wisdom and sentiment" (p. 153). In this description are stated or implied most of the traits of postwar humor: optimism, reminiscent detail, moralism, philosophy, pathos, wisdom, sentiment, repose, decency.

Vestiges of the coarse prewar humor lingered, but the dominant trend was toward a mild, refined humor. What the editor of an 1894 humor anthology wrote in the Preface illustrates the current taste in humor: "We have . . . endeavored to guard against the introduction of anything coarse and unrefined, and . . . we trust nothing will be found in these pages to offend the purest and most cultivated of tastes."[33] In an editorial announcement in January, 1889, the editors of *Texas Siftings* set forth their criteria for a humor paper, and incidentally defined the dominant vogue. "We desire to have it distinctly understood that *Texas Siftings* is a paper for the family, and nothing of a vulgar or indelicate character, either in the way of pictures or letter-press, will ever be admitted into its columns. Our aim is to produce an illustrated humor paper that will be acceptable to and welcomed in the most refined American and English homes, and the commendatory letters we are receiving from heads of families on both sides of the Atlantic are most flattering and encouraging." Writing in the *Arkansaw Traveler* of April 25, 1885—itself billed as "A Paper for the Household"—Opie Read commented on this trend. "Mark Twain's last book [*Huckleberry Finn?*] is condemned, American critics say, because it is vulgar and coarse. The days of vulgar humor are over in this country. There was a time when a semi-obscene joke would find admirers, but the reading public is becoming more refined. Exaggerated humor will also pass away. The humorist of the future must be chaste and truthful." Another time Read characterized humor as "the cream that rises to the surface of the milk of human kindness." Indeed, this was a far cry from earlier masculine humor. In the *Arkansaw Traveler* of December 17, 1882, Henry Clay Lukens was quoted as saying that clean humor had a noble objective. "Mirth is natural; it is pure; it is strictly honest. There can be no true ripple of laughter at another's expense. The practical joker is vulgar and mean-souled. His jest is hollow, and only echoes the pain and sorrow of his victim. . . . The mission of mirth is righteous and eternal."

A comparison of the humor of Joel Chandler Harris with that of George Washington Harris will show how much humor had changed. Of the later Harris, Henry Grady said, "He has developed a spirit of humor, gentle, tender, and sportive."[34] His humor, in other words, was the exact antithesis of George Washington Harris'. The new taste led to a deprecation of the humorists of the Old Southwest by critics, anthologizers, and readers in general. In 1901 James L. Ford omitted from his essay, "A Century of American Humor," any mention of the Old Southwestern humorists. Only pre-Civil-War humorists of the rank of James Russell Lowell and Oliver Wendell Holmes were discussed.

Bliss Perry characterized the popular humor of the time as the kind that evoked a smile rather than a laugh. In *The American Mind* he wrote: "The more permanent American humor has commonly been written by persons who were almost unconscious, not indeed of the fact that they were creating humorous characters, but unconscious of the effort to provoke a laugh. The smile lasts longer than the laugh. . . . One smiles over the stories . . . of Thomas Nelson Page. The trouble, possibly, with the enduring qualities of the brilliant humorous stories of 'O. Henry' was that they tempt the reader to laugh too much and to smile too little" (p. 202). This was the way Perry saw humor in the early twentieth century: "Despite the universality of the objects of contemporary American humor, despite, too, its prevalent method of caricature, it remains true that its character is, on the whole, clean, easy-going, and kindly. The old satire of hatred has lost its force" (p. 204). In another place he wrote: "We are less censorious than our ancestors were" (p. 206).

Perhaps the best humorist to exemplify the shifting trends in post-Civil-War Southern humor was Charles H. Smith. As a Yankee-hating cracker he had written venomous Bill Arp sketches during the war and Reconstruction; then gradually he made Bill Arp a good-humored, hard-working Southern farmer concerned mainly with his own domestic affairs. Much of the bad grammar, awkward spellings, and passion of the earlier Bill Arp letters gave way to the philosophical farmer figure smoking at twilight. For the new Bill Arp, "It's a great comfort for me to set in my piazzer these pleasant evenings and look over the farm, and smoke the pipe of peace, and ruminate." The satire of the earlier letters has been replaced by a genial, homely philosophy, wistfully comic, dealing with family and farm life.[35]

Religious sentiment colored much of the later humor of Bill Arp and of most Southern humorists. In *Fogy Days* Dave Sloan's idea of fun was very unlike the humor of a Sut Lovingood or a Ned Brace. "I have thought that the man who loves his God and his fellow man, cannot be adverse to fun, harmless fun. Tying a tin can to a dog's tail is wanton fun; to fight dogs and chickens, is cruel fun; to profane the Sabbath with unrighteous merriment, is sacrilegious fun; but to surprise suffering humanity with acts of kindness, and with timely aid, is heavenly fun" (p. 240).

Repose became characteristic of much of the humor. The element of repose is so pronounced in such books as Eliza Calvert Hall's *The Land of Long Ago* (1909) that it almost lulls the reader to sleep. Bill Arp's farm and home sketches are also sleepy, as is the retrospective work of Thomas Nelson Page. Much of Joel Chandler Harris' humor has the same trait, and it may be characterized as he described the peaceful life at Shady Dale in *Gabriel Tolliver*. "Before, during, and after the war, Shady Dale presented always the same aspect of serene repose" (p. 33).

Didacticism was another common trait. Humor was not only supposed to entertain; it must teach a lesson. Joel Chandler Harris' comment on *Huckleberry Finn* applied as well to his own work, and to most postwar Southern humor: "It is history, it is romance, it is life. Here we behold a human character stripped of all tiresome details; we see people growing and living; we laugh at their humor, share their griefs, and, in the midst of it all, behold we are taught the lesson of honesty, justice, and mercy."[36] This didactic motivation was evident in the sketches appearing in *Texas Siftings*, the *Arkansaw Traveler*, and other humor sheets which condemned such "evils" as bicycles, tobacco, and liquor. And the reform sheet par excellence was, of course, W. C. Brann's *Iconoclast*, published in Waco, Texas. Fred L. Pattee attributed the didacticism of postwar humor to the great moral awakening brought on by the Civil War.[37] Whatever the cause, the humor of Harris, George Washington Cable, and others certainly had a philosophical depth and purpose unknown in previous Southern humor.

During the postwar period the Negro became the dominant character in Southern humor. In poems and sketches by Irwin Russell, Joel Chandler Harris, and Thomas Nelson Page, a type hitherto sketched chiefly in caricature began to assume humanity—even though humanity with grotesque traits. Throughout the period the caricature of the Negro was gradually becoming character, and by 1914 it was possible, though still not typical, to treat the Negro without the impediment of the slapstick and buffoon tradition. It was true, however, that this character was usually a white man's Negro; or as Claude Simpson has recently described Page's old-time darkies, "the jolly illiterates who are conceived as the white man wishes them to be."[38] Page's Negro longed for the days of slavery and disapproved of most of what had happened since 1861. He was especially critical of meddling Yankees and of upstart members of his own race. In the subliterary "coon" humor of the period, both the old-time darky and the "new" Negro were objects of ridicule. The Negro was laughed at both for remaining an Uncle Tom and for pretending to the white man's status. Writers of the stature of Joel Chandler Harris, however, usually did not stoop to this level.

In addition to the backward-looking freedman, the fine-mannered but impoverished planter was a creation of the postwar period. He held to antiquated notions about society, and generally had a hard time adjusting to the new social and economic order. But the unreconstructed Southerner, male or female, was almost always lovable in his weaknesses and poverty.

These vestiges of the old regime were parts of the attempt by Southern humorists to reconstruct the ante-bellum South with all the unpleasantness removed. In the work of Page this objective reached its greatest fruition. In his fiction the readers saw pictured an admirable and charming South, one in which master and slave were closely bound by ties of love and paternalism. Most of the sketches dealing with ante-bellum life purported to set the record straight by giving a "correct" view of slavery times. Mary Ross Banks' *Bright Days in the Old Plantation Time* (1882) was only one of the many books written with this mission as their motivating force.

The past, or remnants of the past, by no means monopolized postwar

Southern humor. There was also renewed interest in the low life of the present. Although there was some attempt by reconciliation humorists to exclude prewar and postwar Ransy Sniffles from fiction, in the works of Will Harben, Mary Noailles Murfree ("Charles Egbert Craddock"), Mrs. Ruth McEnery Stuart, and others, the Southern poor white had national attention focused upon him. The postwar poor white in humor, however, was usually more respectable and less coarse than his prewar father and grandfather.

In many odd corners of the South a rich variety of fresh types waited to be exploited by humorists. Crackers, creoles, mountaineers, moonshiners—all were potentially humorous to the reading public which had had little or no live contact with them. Their strange way of speaking, their superstitions, their religion, their feuds, their recreations—all were so different from the usual that they were likely to be amusing. Around the turn of the century the cowboy was added to the list.

In the humor dealing with the poor white a sense of place was likely to be important. The Middle Georgia setting of Harry Stillwell Edwards' stories was indispensable to their full impact. Likewise John Fox's Kentucky mountains, Samuel Minturn Peck's Alabama hills, and George Washington Cable's New Orleans were important elements in these authors' works. Most of these writers who portrayed life in the South's odd corners were members of the so-called local-color school which dominated American humor from the 1870's to the 1890's. The vitality of the national movement owed much to the talent of Southern writers like Cable and Craddock.

Southern low life as a subject produced a new realism, another trait of postwar humor which at first seems to be inconsistent with refined humor. In the Preface to *Southern Lights and Shadows*, a collection of Southern sketches, William Dean Howells explained the apparent inconsistency: "To be sure, this development of post-war realism was on the lines of those early humorists who antedated the romantic fictionists, and who were often in their humor so rank, so wild, so savage, so cruel, but the modern realism has refined both upon their matter and their manner." This comment recalls Howell's own definition of realism as a depiction of the decent average. To many Southerners this was also the definition of realistic humor.

Much of the popularity of humor in the postwar South was probably attributable to its attempts at realism—to depict things as they were. This had been a strong motivation for the humorist of the Old Southwest, and with some refinement it remained so for the postwar humorist. The realistic vogue was part of the reaction against the sweet sentiment offered by the ladies' books and the popular romances. In the anthology of 1894 Howells noted the postwar reaction to Sir Walter Scott, and added: "The most noticeable characteristic of the extraordinary literary development of the South since the Civil War is that it is almost entirely in the direction of realism. . . . Evidently [Southern writers] believed that there was a poetry under the rude outside of their mountaineers, their slattern country wives, their shy rustic men and maids, their grotesque humorists, their wild religionists, even their black freed men, which was worth more than the poetastery of the romantic fiction of their fathers." A surfeit of extreme romantic fiction helped to explain the new popular humor with its insistence on genuineness and reality, its attempt to show things as they were, its studies from life, not books. As editor of the *Southern Literary Messenger*, Dr. George W. Bagby in 1860 wrote: "We desire especially to obtain home-made, purely Southern articles—tales, stories, sketches, poems, that smack of the soil."[39] Many postwar Southerners attempted to write such pieces.

Not since the days of Washington Irving had there been such emphasis placed upon an exploitation of folklore in humor. B A. Botkin has written that "folklore and local color were the soil from which sprang the broad humor, the racy idiom, the anecdotal verve, and the gorgeous yarn-spinning of . . . Charles Henry Smith ('Bill Arp'), Joel Chandler Harris, Mark Twain. . . ."[40] To this list of Southern humorists who owed a debt to folklore could be added George Washington Cable, Anne Virginia Culbertson, Mary Noailles Murfree, and most of the other humorists who dealt with the life about them.

The vogue of looking at life through the eyes of a child became popular after the Civil War. The transitionist Richard Malcolm Johnston had retreated to childhood scenes and characters when the controversies and conflicts of the war and Reconstruction filled the present. In *Mark Twain and Southwestern Humor* Kenneth Lynn has pointed out that Joel Chandler Harris believed that in the Gilded Age one could discover enchantment in America only by becoming a child again. He noted that Uncle Remus once remarked, "Folks aint half as smart when they grow up as they is when they're little children" (pp. 184 ff). The flowering of this approach to humor was, of course, *Huckleberry Finn*; but humorists farther south also made frequent use of the device.

For the first time in Southern literature women wrote as equals with men. Grace King, Ruth McEnery Stuart, George Madden Martin, Kate Chopin, and Mary Noailles Murfree were almost as well known as Page, Harris, and Edwards. In some states women almost monopolized the writing field. In his life of John T. Moore, Claude Green, for example, noted that from 1870 to 1900 most literature in Tennessee was written by women (p. 26).

Before the Civil War there were few humorists among Southern women writers; in fact, most people believed that women could write only of morbid, melancholy, and sentimental subjects. In an 1886 anthology, *The Wit of Women*, Katharine Abbott ("Kate Sanborn") attempted to disprove this belief and to prove "that women are not deficient in either wit or humor." She cited Rufus Griswold's *Female Poets of America* and commented sarcastically: "The general air of gloom—hopeless gloom—was depressing. Such mawkish sentimentality and despair; such inane and mortifying confessions; such longings for a lover to come; such sighings over a lover departed; such cravings for 'only'—'only' a *grave* in some dark, dank solitude. As Mrs. Dodge puts it,

'Pegasus generally feels inclined to pace toward a graveyard the moment he feels a side-saddle on his back'" (p. 14). Miss Abbott's collection of female humor includes Katherine MacDowell ("Sherwood Bonner") of Mississippi and Mary Noailles Murfree of Tennessee. A later collection of women's humor, *Laughing Their Way* (Bruere and Beard), included a chapter on local colorists of the South and discussed Grace King, Ruth McEnery Stuart, Mrs. George Madden Martin, and Corra Harris. Each of these women had made a name for herself in humor after 1865 and before 1914.

The influence of the woman on post-Civil-War Southern humor was great. Not only did she write much of the humor, but she formed a large segment of the reading audience and her tastes could not be ignored. *Texas Siftings* was only one of the periodicals that had a "Ladies Department"; on June 19, 1886, it offered these bits of information: "Mrs. Cleveland will be giving the President some points on Home Rule before long. . . . It is not etiquette for a Queen of Spain to nurse her own child, and Maria Christina has always been deprived of this pleasure."

Since so much of post-Civil-War Southern humor was retrospectively oriented, it naturally tended to pathos. Pathos was implicit in much prewar writing (Longstreet's sketches, for example), but it was not until after the war that it became an almost indispensable ingredient. Joseph King said of George W. Bagby that the Virginian anticipated this quality in two prewar sketches. "'Good Eatings' and 'My Uncle Flatback's Plantation' have the quaint humor and dreamy pathos, the reminiscent sentimentality that inevitably crept into nearly all of the writing about the plantation that followed the war. It was as if the author had a premonition that the old order was doomed, and that already it was a thing of the past, to be written about with retrospective warmth" (p. 177). After the war Bagby, Page, and a host of other humorists knew that the past was irrevocably doomed. All they could do was call up the sweet memories of the past and surround them with an aura of glorification. The intertwining of humor and pathos that characterized most postwar Southern writing is described by Churchill G. Chamberlayne in an essay on Bagby: "Although Dr. Bagby's reputation rests to so large an extent upon his humorous writings, it may be held that he was at his best when he was at his most serious. As a matter of fact a vein of seriousness runs through all his work; for even those of his writings that are justly celebrated for their rare fun contain single lines or long passages full of an indefinable pathos that stirs the heart to its depths. . . . On the other hand, again, in his most serious compositions his irrepressible humor will not infrequently show itself, thus lighting up what otherwise might be thought a shade too sombre. This rare faculty of so combining the serious with the light that neither the one nor the other is unduly prominent, and neither is lost in the other, is one of the most distinguishing characteristics of Dr. Bagby's genius."[41]

The humorist who could make the reader cry as well as laugh was in much demand. Writing in the *Arkansaw Traveler* of April 25, 1885, H. S.

Keller said of crying humor: "When a man makes you laugh to button-bursting propensity, and advertises a weep and a tear in the next column, you can begin to make up your mind to the fact that he is not a humorist. He is something more—he is a genius." The appeal of crying humor seemed to be almost universal. In an obituary on A. W. Kelly ("Parmenas Mix"), Opie Read commented casually, "His blending of humor and pathos was wonderful— a tear of joy, a tear of sadness."

In his unpublished study of post-Civil-War humor magazines, William Linneman noted the excessive sentiment that crept into the periodicals: "A large vein of sentimentality ran through the humorous newspapers, and a little even crept into the illustrated slicks. This sentiment was especially noticeable in the short stories. . . . The regional humorists, who were the editors of these comic newspapers, liked to point out the serious qualities of their publications and praised each other for their tenderness. They compared themselves to Charles Lamb and Tom Hood. . . . The juxtaposition of these two seemingly contrary temperaments is well shown by the name of one of these papers: *The Through Mail Magazine of Humor and Pathos,* published at Bloomington, Illinois, ca. 1885" (p. 280).

Many humorists considered pathos and humor so closely allied as to be inseparable. A drawing of "Humor and Pathos" opposite the title page of William L. Visscher's *Ten Wise Men* (1909) shows the two interlocked within a single circle. In "A Retrospect of American Humor," published in 1901, W. P. Trent concluded that humor "is constantly tending to run into pathos." Looking at the popular mixture of humor and pathos in 1912, Bliss Perry wrote, "Most philosophers who have meditated upon the nature of the comic point out that it is closely allied with the tragic." He then added, "It is only the humorist who sees things truly because he sees both the greatness and the littleness of mortals; but even he may not know whether to laugh or to cry at what he sees."[42]

Women writers and women readers influenced the increased emphasis on pathos in humor. In a biography of James Lane Allen, Grant Knight has written that the Kentuckian's pathos was "so much to the liking of the feminine taste that it aroused only an occasional protest, such as that of *The Chicago Times.* . . . Mr. Allen's chief lack as a story-teller seems to be in the element of humor. Not altogether that which makes people laugh, but rather showing in the prevailing tendency to stir the fountains of tears rather than appeal to any other human feeling" (p. 88).

In her edition of the *Memoirs of Judge Richard H. Clark,* Lollie Belle Wylie reviewed a recently published sketch and revealed the attraction of crying humor to her. "If anyone would like to laugh, and then cry in quick transition, let him read 'Puss T.'s Defense.' . . . Indeed, if he has any humor and pathos in his soul he will do so, whether he likes to or not—in fact, he will both laugh and cry at the same time, and cannot help himself . . ." (p. 236).

One of the worst offenders in the matter of crying humor was the woman with a man's name, Will Allen Dromgoole. What Andrew Lang said of Bret Harte also applies to Miss Dromgoole: "His mixture of the serious, the earnest, the pathetic, makes his humour not unlike the melancholy mirth of Thackeray and Sterne."[43]

Other humorists who emulated Dickens in blending humor and pathos included Sherwood Bonner, Opie Read, and Joel Chandler Harris. In *Ten Wise Men* William L. Visscher said of one of Opie Read's Negro dialect poems ("W'en de Col' Win' Blows"): "Here is one of his little darky sketches in rhyme that illustrates how faithfully he portrays nature, even in its homeliest moods, and it also shows how humor and pathos commingle in his work, proving once more that the two are of a 'Siamese twindom,' in that one cannot live apart from the other . . ." (p. 134).

The trend to pathos and sentiment is apparent even in Joel Chandler Harris. The most obvious indication is a comparison of the two versions of "A Story of the War." In the first version of the story, published in the Atlanta *Constitution* in 1877 and called "Uncle Remus as a Rebel," Harris has the old Negro kill a Yankee soldier who is threatening the life of his master. In the later version which appeared in *Uncle Remus: His Songs and His Sayings* (1880) the Yankee is only wounded by Uncle Remus and recovers to marry his intended victim's daughter.

Religious sentiment was another common element of postwar Southern humor. William J. Burtscher even prefaced his *Yellow Creek Humor* with "A Prayer," which ends "Make me an optimist. Help me to practice what thy ministers preach. Help me to preach what thy saints practice. Help me to go about doing good. In His name; Amen." A common tendency of the period was for stories and sketches to end on a note of religious sentiment. Humorous accounts of the Civil War were also sprinkled liberally with religious passages.

One of the happier results of the Civil War was the quickening of the nationalistic impulse in the South. This feeling was promoted by and reflected in Southern humor. Although continuing primarily to deal with Southern types, it was considerably less provincial than the humor written before the war.[44] Nationalism was also increased in the South by the Spanish-American War and World War I. Sectionalism was likewise decreased by other times of distress: recessions, yellow fever epidemics, the assassinations of President Lincoln and President McKinley.

Humor was the most important branch of Southern literature between 1865 and 1914, and the humorist was the most significant Southern writer of the period. During these trying years of transition he did much service for his section. He lightened the burdens of Reconstruction and he led his fellow Southerners to see the necessity for reconciliation with the North. His humor of the Civil War made the Southern reader proud of the Lost Cause. And the progressive philosophy of Joel Chandler Harris, Henry Watterson, Henry Grady, and others helped the South to make the transition from an agrarian to an agrarian-industrial economy. Humor helped prepare the South for the twentieth century, while at the same time it promoted a historical awareness.

Writing in 1901, W. P. Trent summed up the contribution of American humorists to American life: "Living or dead, they have been the benefactors of their people. It may suggest a coarse taste, it may even be uncritical, as superfine criticism now goes, to maintain that their work is an integral and not the least valuable part of American literature; but, however this may be, it seems safe to prophesy that whenever America ceases to produce good humorists, and men and women ready to smile and laugh with them, the country will cease to be the great nation that now engages our love and pride."[45] What Trent said about American humorists in general is even more applicable to those of the South writing between 1865 and 1914. As "benefactors of their people" they helped Southerners to smile wistfully as they looked back on a ruined society, and hopefully as they looked forward to a brighter future.

Notes

(Short titles are used in the citations. See the Bibliography for complete information.)

1. *Mark Twain,* 52, 65.
2. *Native American Humor,* xi-xii.
3. "Southern Literature," 96.
4. "American Letter," 231.
5. In Boatright, *Folk Laughter,* 1-2.
6. "American Literary Comedians," 786.
7. "American Humor," 60.
8. Alderman & Harris, *Library of Southern Literature,* VI, 2490. Hereafter cited as *Library of Southern Literature.*
9. See Simpson, *Local Colorists,* 3.
10. *Main Currents,* II, 158.
11. *Library of Southern Literature,* XI, 5037.   12. "American Humor," 62.
13. *Mark Twain,* 35.
14. *Main Currents,* II, 170-71.
15. *Library of Southern Literature,* V, 2100-2101.
16. *Oddities in Southern Life,* 2.
17. Julia Harris, *J. C. Harris,* 46.
18. See Tandy, *Crackerbox Philosophers,* Chap. V, for a good estimate of Smith's early works.
19. In Bodkin, *Southern Folklore,* 716.
20. In DeLeon, *Belles, Beaux and Brains,* 268-70.
21. In F. Moore, *Anecdotes, Poetry and Incidents,* 358.

22. *Oddities in Southern Life,* viii.
23. "American Literary Comedians," 795.
24. In Hibbard, *Stories of the South,* 32-90.
25. *Some American Humorists,* 56-57.
26. "Southern Humorists," 497.
27. *Lippincott's Magazine,* XLVIII, 511.
28. In *Humorous Masterpieces from American Literature,* I, 236-52.
29. See J. King, *Bagby,* 138.
30. "Possibilities of the South," 303.
31. *American Magazines, 1865-1885,* 48.
32. "Popularity of 19th Century American Humorists," 190.
33. Shoemaker, *Choice Humor,* iii.
34. Quoted in Wiggins, *Harris,* 121.
35. See Blair, *Horse Sense,* 172 ff.
36. Quoted in Pattee, *American Literature Since 1870,* 308.
37. *Ibid.,* 43.
38. *Local Colorists,* 14.
39. Quoted in J. King, *Bagby,* 81.
40. *Southern Folklore,* 419.
41. *Library of Southern Literature,* I, 145.
42. *American Mind,* 167-68.
43. Lang, *Lost Leaders* (London, 1889), 72.
44. See Henneman, "National Element."
45. "American Humor," 64.

2. The Civil War

THE CIVIL WAR was not a laughing matter. It was the bloodiest and bitterest war the world had hitherto known. It was the culmination of ill will between the North and the South, which had been in the making for decades. It created hatred which took years to dissipate. It killed off the nation's ablest men. It was an American tragedy which could have been avoided. But it was one of the most justifiable wars ever fought, for it showed that the destiny of both North and South must inevitably be one. The business of the war, therefore, was grim and serious because its outcome was to determine the future of "the last best hope of man."

Although a tragedy, this "irrepressible conflict" was not without its lighter side. Comic relief helped lighten the darkness of the tragedy for the people at home and for the men at the front. Of all those affected by the war, the Southern soldier was probably without peer in finding humor in it. "The Confederate soldier was distinguished for his cheerfulness, and I cannot look back on the scenes around the Confed campfires without amazement at the temper of the men who carried the muskets. I wonder how hilarity and sport could animate bivouacs in an atmosphere of discomfort and danger.

"Around a campfire, feasting on an ounce of raw pork and cornbread made of unhusked meal, jokes of striking humor and sallies of keen wit always lightened the gloomy hours; on the march every passing person caught shots of ridicule which would almost make a mule laugh; and a line of soldiers on the march, halted for a tardy commissary train, gave occasion for merry-making and fun as sparkling as rippling water dancing in the sunlight."[1] Thus the Southern soldier laughed as he fought and died, and his laughter was recorded in chronicle, fiction, and folklore.

The later popularity of humorous accounts and anecdotes of the war is perhaps astounding in this more sober mid-twentieth-century. It must be remembered, however, that this was a country—split though it was—which made heroes of its humorists, a nation whose slain President had been its most prominent humorist. The times were serious, but the ultimate aim of much of the humor was also serious. A joke, some sage once remarked, is the most solemn thing in the world. Hence the increased popularity of humor among post-Civil-War Americans was no indictment of their lack of seriousness; it was rather a testimony to their concern for it.

The most popular means of disseminating humor in the postwar South was the newspaper. For many years newspapers were filled with war humor. The following anecdote published on December 7, 1867, in the Union Springs, Alabama, *Times,* is typical: "We have read many amusing specimens of soldier wit during the late war; but as good as we have seen was the reply of a Virginia cavalryman to a North Carolina infantryman. It was on the march toward Adairsville, in November, 1863, a cold, bright morning, while the troops were lying along the road waiting for obstacles to be removed in front. A fellow came jogging down the line on an old flea-bitten frame of a horse, and as he passed a chap greeted him with—'I say, mister, you are mighty like a brother of mine the hogs eat up.' The cavalryman did not relax a muscle, but looking the 'tar heel' straight in the face, replied: 'Well, my friend, 'tis a monstrous pity they hadn't finished the family while they *war a eatin',*' and moved on amidst shouts of laughter."

The Sunny South, published in Atlanta, carried a regular column called "The Gray and the Blue" which contained minutiae of the war, including many humorous selections. Southern magazines which featured the humor of the camp included *Scott's Monthly Magazine* of Atlanta (1865-69) and the *Southern Bivouac* of Louisville (1882-87). The quality of such popular stuff was not always high, but it filled empty columns and the readers liked it.

Postwar collections of campaign humor became best sellers. Usually the anthologies contained material representing both the blue and the gray. Occasionally some bitterness and bias were evident in the selections, but most of them were good-natured and contributed to a better understanding between conqueror and conquered. Through the catharsis of laughter much ill will was purged away. Indeed, the Civil War as a subject for humor has continued popular in the twentieth century. A recent anthology edited by Katharine M. Jones, *New Confederate Short Stories,* contains stories of humor by such writers as Caroline Gordon, O. Henry, James Street, and Frances Gray Patton.

Many of the ablest writers in the South dealt with the humor of the war. In fact, for some of them the war provided the inspiration for their best work. In a 1907 essay on Thomas Nelson Page, Charles W. Kent concluded that this Southerner's "best short stories are those that record in true Hanover negro dialect war time in Old Virginia."[2] Other humorists from Maryland to Texas spent much ink in relating or creating the humors of the late war.

In addition to their obvious motive of entertainment, the humorists contributed to a fuller understanding and an objective interpretation of the war. Some of them even made significant contributions to the development of realism in American literature. Rebecca Washington Smith placed them in the vanguard of realistic treatments of the war. "The first and the most consistently realistic attitude toward the war in the literature before 1870 is to be found in the fiction created by the popular humorists. . . . Charles H. Smith's Bill Arp, the spokesman of commonsense in the Confederacy, is not unlike Artemus Ward in his blunt, kindly views. Arp, Mrs. Arp, the children, Tip, Potash, and all the 'runagees' and slackers of middle Georgia mingle together in a scene that is not romantic. The humorists deliberately set out to tell the truth."[3] Although Charles H. Smith's realistic comments on the war appeared chiefly before April, 1865, he continued his bitter denunciation of Black Republicans and turncoat Rebels through his rustic mouthpiece Bill Arp into the 1870's.

The war furnished an inexhaustible supply of incidents for humorists to use in their imagery. In the Atlanta *Constitution,* Sam W. Small, for example, had his Negro creation, Old Si, describe a grasshopper plague on his two-acre homestead in this manner: "An' yer nebber seed sech forrigin' an' instrueshun ob truck in de feel's sence de days when de Linkum army cum 'long hyar!"[4] So the fact and folklore of the war were assimilated into the stock of humorous metaphor. From Joel Chandler Harris to William Faulkner, Southern writers have drawn freely from this reservoir.

The Soldiers

The most popular subject of the Civil War humor written after the war was logically the soldier. His war experiences were exploited in poetry, in fiction, in memoirs, and in anecdotes. The humor dealt with soldiers of all ranks from privates to generals. Even soldiers from European countries, in the South as observers, were the subject of funny sketches. Not even the Yankee soldier was excepted.

Most of the humor concerning the Yankee soldier was satirical. Using satire, the Southern humorist gave vent to feelings of hurt and wrong that he felt the South had suffered at the hands of the Northern soldiers. There was no more vulnerable target for the South's satire than General Ben Butler, known popularly below the Potomac as "Beast" Butler, the Union general who gained fame—or infamy—as military commander of New Orleans after its fall. *The American Cyclops,* a poem by J. Fairfax McLaughlin, impaled Butler with the poniards of heroic couplets. A passage from the poem (pp. 17-18), published in 1868, will illustrate the "Beast's" popularity in Dixie.

> *Oh! hapless hour, when from the stormy North,*
> *This modern Cyclops marched repellent forth,*
> *To slake his thirst for blood and plundered wealth,*
> *Not as the soldier, but by fraud and stealth;*
> *To waft the gales of death with horror rife*
> *On helpless age, and wage with women strife:*
> *To leave Baltimore and New Orleans*
> *The drunkard's name, or worse, the gibbet's scenes;*
> *To license lust with all a lecher's rage,*
> *And stab the virtue of a Christian age:*
> *This single crime will fix a beastly name,*
> *Fresh in immortal infamy and shame.*

For many years the name Butler, along with Grant and Sherman conjured up repulsion in the Southern mind and rebellion in the Southern heart. The Southern humorist capitalized on their public images and caricatured them even more.

An anonymous poem parodying the contemporary English poet-laureate Tennyson's "Come Not When I Am Dead" was probably written, the paragrapher for the Union Springs *Times* noted (September 4, 1867), by a soldier who had been present at the siege of Vicksburg.

> *Come not when I'm asleep,*
> > *To rain huge fragments on my lowly head,*
> *To cause with fear my tingling veins to creep,*
> > *Or add me to the patriotic dead!*
> *There let the Minnies fall and Parrots fly—*
> > *But thou—pass by!*

Whether written during or shortly after the war, the humor of the parody is of the nervous kind found in the works of authors "who were there" and can see danger in a retrospect of mixed humor and fear.

Fictional humor by post-Civil-War Southern writers dealing with soldier life includes sketches by Will Harben, Charles H. Smith, Sidney Lanier, George Washington Cable, and Joel Chandler Harris.

Will Harben's *Northern Georgia Sketches* contains one story set during the War Between the States. Like many postwar humorous stories, "The Courage of Ericson" shows how the opposing sides of the war could be reconciled. It is the story of the estrangement of a Rebel boy and his Union-sympathizing girl, and their subsequent reconciliation as a result of his being wounded in a battle near the girl's house. When the boy first shows up at the girl's house, she affects to depise him because of the uniform he has on; but when she sees that he is wounded and hears that the Yanks are out looking for escaped Rebels, she tries to save him by getting him to dress in her dead brother's Federal uniform. He patriotically refuses, but faints in time for the girl and her father to dress him in the Yankee uniform before the search party arrives.

The girl tells the Yankee captain who comes in that the boy's mind has been affected by his wound and that he is irrational. Should he come to, she tells the Union officer, he might even say he's a Reb. "Once he declared to us that he was actu'ly President Jeff Davis. Thar's no tellin' what idea may strike 'im next." Sure enough, when he regains consciousness and sees the hated uniform of the enemy on him, he shouts belligerently: "Why, who's done this heer? . . . I ain't no Yankee soldier. I'm a rebel dyed in the wool." He is unable to convince the search party, however, and when they leave he mutters: "I didn't 'low you'd play sech a dog-mean trick on me, Sally. . . . I'd ruther a thousand times 'a' been shot like a soldier than to hide in Yankee clothes." While he is convalescing at his girl's house, his partisan fervor is gradually lessened; and when the news of Lee's surrender comes he can say: "I'm awfully glad it's all over. . . . I'm satisfied. I was shot by a Yankee ball an' nussed back to life by a Union gal, so I reckon my account is even." Like the stronger union of states forged by the fiery war, so two young people are ultimately reunited by the pressures of opposing sympathies. They are brought together by a Georgia local colorist.

Sidney Lanier was a child of his time in using excessive sentiment. To relieve the heavy sentimentality of his war novel, *Tiger-Lilies,* Lanier occasionally employed grotesque humor. According to Aubrey Harrison Starke in *Sidney Lanier* (p. 106), the novel reveals a mixture of "the serious and the comic, the sublime and the grotesque, the pathetic and the ludicrous." Much of the material for the novel came from Lanier's own war experiences. One such experience, described by Starke, concerns his unfortunate hesitation to "borrow" a clean new shirt off the corpse of a Union private. "He hesitated for a moment, but quickly deciding that he could not take the shirt, moved on. Within a few minutes he had repented his squeamishness, reminding himself of his sore need of a whole garment, and urging upon himself the strong probability that the Federal would not, under the circumstances, begrudge the transfer. By the time he had returned, however, he found to his chagrin that a less tender conscienced mate had dexterously captured the shirt" (p. 50). This reluctance to take clothing off a Union corpse became almost a genre sketch in literature dealing with the war; later Sarge Wier and Sam Watkins also recorded such incidents.

Lanier's kinship with the earlier backwoods humor is made explicit in *Tiger-Lilies,* not only in the grotesqueness but in its treatment of pain. Again Starke has the description. "Lanier's sense of humor was seldom subtle; he liked puns, and minor physical discomfiture amused him tremendously; the most amusing part of the description of the ball in Chapter XII is ridiculous to the point of utter improbability. Rübetsahl as King Arthur and Cranston as Lancelot fight a duel which almost ends in the death of Cranston but the spectators think it only a part of the masquerade" (p. 96). Throughout the novel Lanier demonstrated that his humor retained vestiges of the older coarseness of the school of George Washington Harris and Johnson J. Hooper. A veteran of the war, he surely had material for realistic sketches that would have shocked the sensibilities of his readers; but he bowed to convention.

Although remembered primarily for his local-color sketches of the Louisiana Creoles, George Washington Cable also treated the Civil War soldier in his fiction. The novels *Dr. Sevier* and *The Cavalier* both contain war humor. *The Cavalier,* at least partly autobiographical, is the record of the war experiences of a nineteen-year-old "cavalier," Richard Smith of New Orleans. As a member of a scout unit his work was extremely dangerous; however, the tension was relieved by many touches of humor, much of it played on him. Because of his youth he was often the butt of harmless practical jokes pulled on him by the older, more experienced soldiers. Cable, writing in the first person, exploited the humor in the cavalier's innocence and immaturity. His reactions to trying or unusual situations, for example, are often amusing. One day he single-handedly captured a Yankee soldier. "'I surrender,' [the Yankee] said, with amiable ease. I stepped back a pace and he drew out and straightened up—the tallest man I had ever seen. I laughed, he smiled, laughed; my eyes filled with tears, I blazed with rage, and in plain sight and hearing of those ladies [refugees the boy is escorting to safety] he said, 'That's all right, my son, get as scared as you like; only, you don't need to cry about it.'

"'Hold your tongue!' I barked my wrath like a frightened puppy, drawing back a stride and laying my eye closer along the pistol. 'If you call me your son again I'll send you to your fathers'" (pp. 39-40). Having the cavalier tell his own story in his own words makes the "education" of the young recruit in the ways of war even more touching and humorous.

The creator of Uncle Remus also dealt often with the Civil War soldier in his fiction. Like most of his works, Joel Chandler Harris' war stories were written to show both North and South that the adversaries were people who were kind and honorable and had fought for what they thought was right. Although himself a Georgian, in all of his war fiction Harris presented a very sympathetic picture of the North. The heroine of the novel *A Little Union Scout* is, in fact, a Federal spy. Most of the stories in *Tales of the Home Folks* ignore the grimmer aspects of the war on both sides.

In *The Shadow Between His Shoulder-Blades,* Harris used as a narrator his humorous Georgia cracker, Billy Sanders. Most of the humor in the novel derives from the manner in which Billy Sanders tells his adventures. Sitting on the tavern veranda in Shady Dale and surrounded by curious auditors, Billy tells—in cracker dialect—of the part he played as a soldier in the conflict. He had acted as a nineteenth-century Sancho to a local aristocrat, Wimberly Driscoll, who had returned home wounded but before long was "sufferin' from the corns on the foot he left in Virginia." Thirsting for battle glory, the two decide to set out in search of General Forrest's outfit. As they are leaving, Driscoll's Negro mammy puts up a big howl, and Sanders comments for the benefit of his Yankee listeners, "Ef one of you Northern fellers could 'a' heern 'er, you'd 'a' got a bran' new idee in regards to the oppressed colored people" (p. 12). Most of the novel is concerned with the entertaining but dangerous adventures of the aristocrat and the cracker during the war. As a reconciliationist, Harris never allows Billy Sanders to express anything reprehensible against the Yankees; on the contrary, Billy's harshest criticism concerns a Southern opportunist.

Well into the twentieth century the favorite pastime of Civil War survivors, it seems, was the writing of war memoirs, many of them with a humorous slant. These memoirs provide intimate glimpses of soldier life by men who were soldiers. As the war receded into the past, their recollections became extremely conciliatory, with little or no criticism of the North. They were written by privates and generals and by men representing all the ranks in between. Most of them purport to tell what actually happened, although many professional writers used their war experiences as a springboard for works of the imagination. Joel Chandler Harris, for example, combined fact and fiction in *On the Plantation*. George Washington Cable served briefly in the Confederate cavalry and probably used his experiences as the basis for his story of the raw young recruit in *The Cavalier*. Neither Harris nor Cable was ever a violently partisan Rebel, and in the reflective aftermath of the war each saw the absurdity of the conflict.

There was probably not an officer on either side who did not at least plan to write his memoirs of the important part he played in the war. Or if he happened to die before accomplishing this mission, usually an obliging kinsman would immortalize his deeds on paper. Frank A. Montgomery performed this service in *Reminiscences of a Mississippian in Peace and War* for his relative, Major W. E. Montgomery, whose command was called the "featherbeds . . . because they always scattered at night and slept in their own or other people's houses" (p. 116). These memoirs include many amusing incidents, such as how the major once escaped from his Union guards. After he was captured, the major was taken to a house surrounded by cane. Pretending that something was wrong with him, he asked his guard to walk around the yard with him. While they were promenading, the guard asked him about the game in that part of the country, and the major replied that there were plenty of bear. Just then a noise was made in the cane by a cow or a mule, and the Rebel, seeing his chance, shouted, "There's one now," and taking his captor off guard he made his escape into the cane. Surely many an unreconstructed Southerner delighted to read of such ingenious escapes perpetrated on the unsuspecting Yanks.

Most memoirs were written with a twofold purpose: to entertain and to inform. In the Preface to his *War Years with Jeb Stuart,* Lieutenant Colonel W. W. Blackford, C.S.A., wrote that he hoped his sketches would be useful to the historian and entertaining to the general reader. He achieved his entertainment motif with touches of humor scattered throughout the book. He recalled that once when he was captured by his own men at night they wouldn't believe that he had on a Confederate uniform until he allowed them to feel the lace on his sleeve.

Humorous incidents such as the following after the surrender at Harpers Ferry relieve the pathos and gruesomeness of his history: "The men of the surrendered garrison, not having been exposed to the weather, were not all sunburned, and this paleness to us at the time looked peculiar in soldiers, contrasting so strongly with our berry-brown complexions. As we marched along the street one of our troopers sang out to one of the men on the sidewalk, 'I say, Yank, what sort of soap do you fellows use? It has washed all the color out of your faces,' at which our side cheered. To this the man retorted, 'Damn me, if you don't look like you had never used soap of any sort.' Shouts of laughter greeted the reply from our men as well as the Yanks, and our man called back as he rode on, 'Bully for you, Yank; you got me that time'" (p. 146). If Blackford is to be believed, all was not animosity between Rebs and Yanks. Although they fought each other when commanded to, humor was a common ground on which both sides could meet without guns and sabers.

But relations between the blues and grays could be bitter. A passage of grim humor shows how harmless fun could turn into tragedy. "Rather a curious incident happened one day between the infantry lines, which at that place were about three hundred yards apart. About midway there was a farm house and around it wandered a solitary turkey which a Yankee skirmisher shot and then ran forward to secure amid cheers from his side; as he stooped to pick up the turkey one of our men shot him dead and ran forward to get the prize amid cheers from our side. Just as he stooped to pull the turkey from under the Yankee, a shot from their side killed him and wild cheers from their side arose; and there they all three lay one on top of the other, neither side wanting turkey any more" (pp. 243-44). Blackford offers an explanation for the tragic incident. "Men in the infantry have such a hard time of it and see so little fun that when a chance offers they are just like children." But the toys of soldiers are guns loaded with ammunition.

A simple event, according to Blackford, could be the occasion for the greatest merriment. He remembered, for instance, the time when a cat broke the tension of waiting for a Yankee attack. "Just then a young Lieutenant sitting at the end of the table . . . got so nervous that he slipped under the table; this started a titter among the others, which an instant later burst into an irrepressible roar of laughter from a most unexpected event. As I have said, the common above the fly was a resort for cats from the town at night, and these cats, hearing the fearful noise above them, and seeing the long stream of fire shooting towards them from the heavens, became completely demoralized and went scampering by as fast as they could run, back to the deserted houses where they made their homes. One huge tomcat, however, came tearing down the hill with eyes flaming, claws out, and hair on end, directly towards my fly. He was going so fast that he could not avoid the pit in which the fly stood, but came dashing, spitting and sputtering with one bound flop on the table, and with another clear out at the front and away" (pp. 273-74). The entire group was convulsed with laughter. The appearance of the cat relieved everyone—including the young lieutenant under the table. Not only did such incidents do much to sustain the soldier; after the war had been lost, the defeated South could read of them and in the resultant laughter could gain strength for the future.

Blackford gave many glimpses of the unheroic side of military life, from the stealing of corn for the horses to the slaughtering of men in battle. Though his record is often frank, it contains little or no malice toward the former enemy. He prefers to write about how he and his men were forced to meet the demands of the war in foraging food. Like almost every Confederate unit, they were frequently hungry; hearing a cow bell one day, he sent out a detail to capture a small heifer. Unwilling to wait for the meat to be cooked, they ate it raw; and Blackford remembered "I was surprised to find how good it was. Indeed I could discover no difference between this and rare beef steak, it was so warm and nice" (p. 286).

George Cary Eggleston, the brother of the author of *The Hoosier Schoolmaster,* feeling a bond of sympathy to his Virginia forebears, served as an officer in the Southern army. In 1874 he published at the request of William Dean Howells "my reminiscences of life as a Southern soldier," *A Rebel's Recollections.* When Howells first approached him to write his memoirs, he says in the Preface to the fourth edition, he hesitated because "at that time war passions had only just begun to cool"; but deciding that he could do something to bring about better feeling between the North and the South, he relented.

Eggleston's personal record of the war contains many humorous sidelights, from comments on Southern female patriotism to inflation in the Confederacy. The intensity of feeling by Southern women is illustrated by a conversation he says he overheard between two ladies. The first lady said: "I'm sure I do not hate our enemies. I earnestly hope their souls may go to heaven, but I would like to blow all their mortal bodies away, as fast as they come upon our soil." The second lady replied quickly: "Why, you shock me, my dear; I don't see why you want the Yankees to go to heaven! I hope to get there myself some day, and I'm sure I shouldn't want to go if I thought I should find any of them there" (p. 61). The Hoosier Rebel again tells of several ladies living near where a battle was about to commence. They rushed from their house to ask General Nathan Forrest what they could do to help. Eggleston recorded that the impatient General told them, "I really don't see that you can do much, except to stand on stumps, wave your bonnets, and shout 'Hurrah, boys!'" (p. 66).

Inflation was always a problem in the Confederacy; but when the South seemed certain to lose the war, it became chronic. Eggleston condensed the problem into anecdotal form by relating the conversation between a Union and a Confederate picket. The Federal asks if times are hard with coffee $40 a pound, but the Rebel answers truthfully: "Well, perhaps it is a trifle uppish, but then you never saw money so plentiful as it is with us. We hardly know what to do with it, and don't mind paying high prices for things we want" (p. 81).

F. E. Daniel in his *Recollections of a Rebel Surgeon* also has something to say about Confederate inflation. "I remember one day I bought a wagon-load of home-tanned leather from a countryman, and without unloading it from the wagon, sold it to the town storekeeper at $1200 profit; and made $2000 on a barrel of peach brandy after drinking off of it a week" (p. 146). The spokesman, "the Old Doctor," reminisces to Daniel about many other things too. Most of his memories are humorous, some are sad and pathetic, but all are based on fact. He says that the incidents related in his memoirs have little to do with the professional duties of the army surgeon, "but are for the most part recollections of fun, frolic, fishing or flirting, as the case may be, 'endurin' of the war,' in the doctor's 'sappy' days" (pp. 7-8). Although disapproving of slavery and secession, the Old Doctor had cast his lot with his native Mississippi when she left the Union.

Early in his recollections the Doctor articulated the way he and most of the South wanted to look back at the war—through rose-colored glasses. Once when talking about the blot of slavery, he stopped and explained to his imaginary auditor: "But look here, Dan'els, I don't like to talk about unpleasant things; it's against my principles, and it's against the principles of my Retroscope" (pp. 12-13). His Retroscope, he told his biographer, was like a telescope in that it brought the past closer; but it was unusual in its way of bringing out "conspicuously and in bold relief, all the pleasant things, all the funny things, all the amusing or ridiculous memories, and of suppressing or effacing the painful, disagreeable ones, or rounding off the rough edges, at least." He then summed up his Retroscopic creed. "It's a fact. When we look back at the war, with all its horrors and sufferings, it is remarkable that my memory brings to light mainly the funny side, or the pleasant side, of those days of privations and sacrifice and suffering" (p. 13). Throughout the book when he was on the verge of describing the war realistically, he remembered his Retroscope and changed his tone.

The Smiling Phoenix

The first sketch, which he entitled "Sunshine Soldiering," deals with his first days in the army, when, he says, "We just ate, and flirted, and drilled, and *played* soldier." When his company was shipped from Jackson to Corinth, he took with him a valise containing broadcloth shirts, patent leather shoes, linen shirts, and fancy socks and ties; but all this fancy stuff was left behind when an order came down that all clothing would be carried on the back. He remembered that "instead of fine clothes we were reduced to a coarse gray flannel shirt, blue cotton pants and a belt." Thus began the dispelling of his romantic notions about war. Life as a whole in the army remained pleasant, though, until his company started on a forced march. "On our first march I found my knapsack too heavy, and I went through it to lighten it. I took out my extra drawers, my extra undershirts, my extra socks (we wore a flannel topshirt all the while; didn't *need* change), I couldn't throw any of them away; my towel and soap, couldn't spare them; my smoking-tobacco— couldn't find a blessed thing that I could throw away, except two sheets of letter-paper and two envelopes, on which I had expected to write to my sweetheart; fact!" Nevertheless, his Retroscope had little trouble showing the light side of army life.

The humor of "The Doctor Gets Dinner" is as close as the Old Doctor ever came to the painful humor of before the war. This sketch concerns the time the company cook got sick and the men had to take turns cooking. Knowing very little about cooking—but keeping ignorance a secret—the narrator, "a little pale-faced, beardless, dandified medical student," decided to cook all the rations he received from the commissary at one time. George, one of his messmates, told him to cook about a peck of rice; so he filled the four-gallon camp-kettle half full, finished filling it with water, and set it on a hot fire. "Presently it began to boil, and, oh, horrors! to slop over." George suggested that he put the excess in the eating vessels; so he filled the coffee-pot, and all the tin cups, plates, and pans—but the rice kept expanding. Looking around for something more to hold the huge surplus, they saw their friend Bright's big horse-leather boots. George suggested they put rice in them, assuring the doctor that it would cool before Bright could awaken and put his feet into them. They both agreed that this would be a good joke and filled Bright's boots with steaming rice. Unfortunately for their joke, at that moment the captain called to Bright that a lady was there to see him. "Bright sat up, rubbing his eyes; and as quick as he could, seized one boot, and socked his foot into the scalding rice; when, gee-whiz! what a howl went up, of mingled pain, wrath and surprise! He made the atmosphere thick with a most florid rhetoric; and with his scalded foot still smoking, and redolent of rice, lit out after me and George with a six-shooter in each hand." Although the physical pain is central here and provides most of the humor, the sketch does not suggest the sadistic Sut Lovingood school. The humor derives rather from the unexpected happening.

Like most war memoirs, Daniel's recollections offer dramatic interpretations of soldier life not found in more somber history. The destruction of food when retreating is an example. The Doctor lamented the necessity of destroying food when there were thousands of men hungry; however, he managed to salvage some of it by handing it out to passing infantrymen. He recalled the serio-comic scene. "Well, sirs, it was the funniest sight you ever saw (however, as you didn't see it we'll say the funniest sight imaginable), to see about six miles of bayonets, each one bearing aloft a side of bacon, or a ham, or a bolt of jeans! The hot sun made the grease run out of the meat in streams, and it trickled down on the feller's faces, and necks, and backs, and then the red dust would settle on it, and it was a funny combination; they looked like a bedraggled *Mardi Gras*" (p. 92). Such descriptions have to be taken from real life. They are too ludicrous for fiction.

Mixed in with his humorous recollections were many pathetic scenes. He remembered, for example, a dead boy who still clutched an ambrotype in his cold hands. "We took it tenderly from his grasp; it was the picture of a plain, faded, wrinkled old woman of the commoner sort, the poorer country people. It was his *mother*. Ah, to his childish eyes she was not old, nor wrinkled, nor ugly, nor faded, nor common. To him she was beautiful; she was young; she was the apotheosis of all that was lovely and lovable" (p. 95). Daniel did not apologize for this tearful picture. To him and to most of his contemporaries as well, pathos and humor were but the two sides of the same coin.

Horrors that offer no such cathartic cleansing by tears frequently intruded; but remembering his "principles," he dispelled them. One day he explained to his biographer why he was in bad humor. "I've been lookin' thro' the wrong end of my Retroscope, contrary to my principles, and before I was aware of it, there had come trooping before my mental vision a whole lot of unpleasant recollections, and it has depressed me somewhat, and I haven't gotten entirely over it, altho' I have taken a bath and disinfected myself" (p. 97). Disinfecting himself with a mixture of James Whitcomb Riley and Mark Twain, he vowed to think only of pleasant things. However, the night-mares of the past continued to rise up occasionally in his memory.

He used an emphasis on trivial incidents as an effective way of keeping down bad memories. For instance, he recalled a mock-serious report he submitted one time to the medical director of the hospital where he was a staff doctor. When the director indicated that medical officers should show more zeal in their work by submitting more detailed reports than the usual four lines saying perfunctorily that everything was satisfactory, the young doctor decided to have a little fun with the language. He wrote a report of twenty-four pages, which said no more than the earlier four-line reports. He prefaced his verbiage with:

The English language is happily so constructed that a great many words of diverse origin and derivation can be so brought to bear as to convey one and the same idea; and consequently, one best versed in the resources of the language will naturally be most facile in its use. Thus, I said, to give an illustration: Instead of saying as Dr. Brown did yesterday, that the bread was a little scorched, it might be expressed thus:

In consequence of inattention, ignorance, incompetence, temporary absence or preoccupation of the colored divinity who presides over the culinary establishment of Ward 3, vulgarly called the "cook," a part of the nutriment, the subsistence, the "grub," a very essential part, which was that day being prepared and intended for the alimentation and sustenance of the unfortunate beings who, by accident, exposure or fate were at that time sick or wounded, and lying prone on a roughly extemporized bunk in a building near by, by courtesy called a hospital, sick, wounded or else convalescent, and dependent on others, ourselves, to-wit, and deprived, doubtless much to their sorrow and regret, of the privilege of being at the front in the trenches or on the lines of battle, battling for their country; to-wit, the bread, being too long exposed to the oxidizing influence of the oven, has been somewhat scorched, burnt, or otherwise injured, being thereby rendered unwholesome and unfit for the purposes for which it was intended; to-wit, the nourishment of the said sick, wounded or convalescent soldiers (pp. 120-21).

Writing in this manner, the Doctor was able to string out his report for twenty-four pages "and didn't say anything except that the bread was burnt in cooking."

Daniel held no grudges against the Yankees. In fact, in one of the few scenes in which he treated the enemy directly, his life was saved by a Union soldier. He had held up his handkerchief to indicate surrender, but evidently the Yanks didn't know what that meant, he said, because they kept shooting at him. He added parenthetically that "it was a clean handkerchief, or I would not have much blamed them for not recognizing it." Anyway, he saw that his only chance was to roll over and play dead. This he did; whereupon a Yank came up, took him prisoner, and saved his life (pp. 134-41).

The small amount of satire in the book is mild and is directed toward soldiers who tried to stay away from the front lines by pleading sickness. One shirker, he remembered, described his illness this way: "Well, Doc . . . I mostly don't know 'zackly what ails me. I've got a misery in my chest, a soreness in my jints, a-a-kinder stiffness in my back, and a hurtin' all-l-l over!" (p. 152). The Old Doctor recalled that he once told the "chief . . . medicine-giver of ward three" to go back to his regiment "and tell your colonel to make you head chief, medical or otherwise, bullet-arrester; you'll be good to stop a bullet from some less important person" (p. 157).

An anecdote of a dandy whom several ladies begged to sing for them incidentally exposed one of the most common ailments of the soldier: "'Oh, Miss Sue,—I cawn't sing, you know; only a little for my own amusement,' said this swell, with an air that, as Sut Lovingood would say, made my big toe itch; I felt like kicking him." Finally he was persuaded and began in his little falsetto, "W-h-y—am *I* so w-e-a-k and *w-e-a-r-y*—" At this point one of the graybacks shouted from a distance: "Hits 'cause you've got the di-ur-*ree*, you Sunday galoot!" (p. 162).

The admiration of Southern belles made the hardships of war seem more bearable. In a poem obviously parodying Longfellow, Daniel celebrated a roommate's alleged love affair. Entitled "The Clever Quartermaster; or the Fate of the Flirt," it began:

> *Miss Maggie:*
> *Let me tell you a good story*
> *On my room-mate, Captain Riddle;*
> *Captain Riddle, Quartermaster*
> *Of the Post of Chattanooga;*
> *Riddle, with the auburn tresses*
> *All combed back so slick and shiney;*
> *Riddle, with the whiskers auburn* (pp. 180-81).

The Old Doctor also remembered fondly his own flirtations. One of them was with a Miss Vannie Vogle of Chattanooga, "the daintiest little darling of them all," who, when he first met her, would not say anything or even open her mouth. Deciding to take advantage of all opportunities, he tried to kiss her; but she broke away and ran to a porch where she "spat out a mouthful of brown juice." Looking at him reproachfully while wiping her mouth with the back of her hand, she said: "You fool—didn't you see I had snuff in my mouth?" (p. 171). Fortunately, not all of his affairs were with the snuff-dipping girls.

Though in his recollections he concentrated on the humorous side of the war, Daniel was never unaware of its tragedy and deeper significance. Summing up his war experiences, he wrote, "But, upon the whole, I am glad I lived in wartimes. I trust to God that I may not live to see another war—but I am glad to have been through that one, and to have seen and experienced what I did" (p. 259). Like most thinking survivors of the struggle, he understood the salutary effect on the nation; also like most, he preferred to think of its pleasant and amusing side.

In 1881 Alexander E. Sweet and J. Armory Knox established in Austin the humor magazine *Texas Siftings*. After four years they carried it to New York where it lasted until 1897. In 1882 the two men published a selection of pieces from the magazine, and in 1883 they issued the original *On a Mexican Mustang through Texas*. Like so many other books of the time which exploited the habits and foibles of particular states, this one professes to be a recounting of the authors' experiences on a trip through their native state. It touches on the Civil War soldier in several places. A reporter who accompanies the authors part of the way is a Confederate veteran. One time, he says, some Yankees mistook a herd of cows for Rebel soldiers. "They trained two of the guns on the cattle while we were scattering. The cows, not having any more sense than we had, waited to be shelled. They staid there until the gunners

41

got the range. We saw afterwards that the carnage was dreadful: tenderloin steaks and soup-bones were found scattered over the country for miles. We rejoiced that none of us were hurt: we did not wish to add to the bitterness of the fratricidal struggle" (pp. 497-98).

The reporter's war adventures are usually slapstick and, unlike Daniel's memoirs, have very little significance outside farce. Another representative adventure has to do with a pig-stealing scheme which misfires. Going through Louisiana by forced marches, since "the first troops that went out from Texas were in very much of a hurry, because they feared that the war would be over before they could reach the tented field," they passed a farmer who was driving his pigs under the house for safekeeping. After camping for the night, the reporter and a buddy decided to go back and steal some fresh pork. With the reporter standing by ready with a club, the ill-fated friend went under the house to drive the pigs out. Hearing a noise near the exit, the reporter lammed a pig on the back of his head. The pig turned out to be his friend who was crawling out to tell him that the farmer had moved his pigs again. The reporter had hit his comrade-at-pig-stealing so hard that he had to carry him back to camp. The reporter commented on that episode: "From that hour I instinctively felt that the cause of the Confederacy was hopeless" (pp. 590-93).

A much more significant memoir of the war is Sergeant A. M. Wier's *Old Times in Georgia.* Wier's account of life in the ranks is much more realistic—sometimes grotesque—than most humorous memoirs. Although crudely written, Sarge's reminiscences smack of real life. For instance, he describes realistically the trouble he and three buddies had trying to divest a dead and stiff Union soldier of a new overcoat. Their difficulty was compounded because the corpse's arms were stretched out straight on either side. In Sarge's words: "They raised him on his feet and one of 'em got on one side and another on the other side and were trying to bend the stiff arms, when the fellow that was holding him up gave a quick jerk which turned the dead body and brought the stiff arms around with it and the open palm slapped Ned in the face, and it smacked as natural as if the yankee had er been alive and done it. Ned didn't stop to ask questions." In fact, the poor soldier didn't stop running until he got to camp; and no one could convince him he hadn't been hit by a ghost. From then on "he wouldn't have nothing to do with getting overcoats that way, and so he froze to death pretty soon after that, one night on picket" (p. 4). Sarge's unaffected account of this incident tells more about the underclothed Confederate soldier than reams of official reports in Richmond.

Wier relates many realistic hospital stories of wartime. His telling about a young Texan who bled to death after a leg amputation reminds one of his listeners about his own painful experience in a military hospital. As the war wore on, the listener says, the draft age was raised and raised until it finally put him in the eligible category. He decided without hestitation that he had to develop a disqualifying ailment. "So the first thing you know my back was in such er bad fix that I couldn't move a chair from one side er the fireplace to the other, and it was soon norated all over the settlement that Brown's a plum invalid, and some 'lowed it was spinal affection, and some 'lowed it was liftin' too much when I was young, and some 'lowed one thing and some 'lowed ernother, but me and the old 'oman and the gals knowed what it was" (pp. 9-10). Brown was safe until a conscript officer caught him carrying a big hickory log. Though he continued complaining about his back, he was taken in for a physical examination. Because of his alleged disorder he was sent to a hospital for a painful turpentine burn cure. This treatment consisted of setting cups of burning turpentine on his bare back and then cutting the resultant blisters. After undergoing such an ordeal, Brown's condemnation of the medical profession is understandable. He concludes, "I've hated hospitals and doctors from that day to this, and I always expect to."

Although Sarge Wier is proud of war heroes like Lee, Jackson, and Longstreet, he constantly comments on the cruelty of war. He concludes that "war's er bad, bad thing" (p. 37).

With the passage of time Charles H. Smith's bitter picture of the war mellowed and turned sentimental. Eventually he came to see that not all Yankee soldiers had been villains, but he still preferred the South. In *Bill Arp: From the Uncivil War to Date, 1861-1903,* his daughter wrote: "The Confederacy was a passion with my father. He loved to honor the old South and her veterans" (p. 13).

In his old age Smith wrote sentimentally of the war experiences of the original Bill Arp. After remarking that Arp had once stolen the General's apple brandy, he added a goodly portion of pathos. "He was a good soldier in war. He was the wit and wag of the camp fires, and made many a homesick youth laugh away his melancholy. He was a good citizen in peace. When told that his son was killed he looked no surprise, but simply said: 'Major, did he die all right?' When assured that he did, Bill wiped away a falling tear and said, 'I only wanted to tell his mother'" (p. 63). Smith had almost spent himself on war topics while the war was still being fought. When the clamor of Reconstruction died down, he restricted most of his writing to domestic subjects of the present.

In 1882 Carlton McCarthy, who had been a private in the Army of Northern Virginia, published his *Detailed Minutiae of Soldier Life,* a eulogistic account of the Confederate soldier fighting against overpowering odds. Humor and pathos mix in this book of memoirs, whose dominant mood is melancholy.

Like F. E. Daniel, McCarthy related how many a soldier's romantic notions about war were soon dispelled. Describing the typical soldier's outfit, which included an elaborately furnished knapsack and a haversack, he wrote: "It is amusing to think of the follies of the early part of the war, as illustrated by the outfits of the volunteers. They were so heavily clad, and so burdened with all manner of things, that a march was torture, and the wagon trains were so immense in proportion to the number of troops, that it would have been impossible to guard them in an enemy country. Subordinate officers thought themselves entitled to transportation for trunks, mattresses, and folding bedsteads, and the privates were as ridiculous in their demands" (pp. 19-20). Once the reality of war hit them, they reduced their baggage drastically, until "reduced to the minimum, the private soldier consisted of one man, one hat, one jacket, one shirt, one pair of pants, one pair of drawers, one pair of shoes, and one pair of socks" (p. 26).

Other romantic preconceptions of war also quickly melted away. One was that soldiers should be as uncomfortable as possible and "glory in getting wet, being cold, hungry, and tired. So they refused shelter in houses or barns, and 'like true soldiers' paddled about in the mud and rain, thinking thereby to serve their country better" (p. 30). Another quickly discarded notion was that one Confederate could whip a dozen Yankees. The former private admitted that this was "literally true sometimes, but, generally speaking, two to one made hard work for the boys" (p. 32). Perhaps the most quickly rejected preconception of war was the belief that one should get wounded as soon as possible. "Many became despondent and groaned as they thought that perchance after all they were doomed to go home safe and sound, and hear, for all time, the praises of the fellow who had lost his arm by a cannon shot, or had his face ripped by a sabre, or his head smashed with a fragment of shell" (p. 33). Men soon found out that getting wounded was the next thing to getting killed, and that often a simple "hero's" wound could prove fatal.

McCarthy's treatment of common soldier life is excellent. There is, for example, the almost perfect vignette of a straggler from the march. "An accomplished straggler could assume more misery, look more horribly emaciated, tell more dismal stories of distress, eat more and march further (to the rear), than any ten ordinary men" (p. 54). Other glimpses of military low life include foraging raids on farmers' hog pens, cornfields, and cow pastures. Many of these raids terminated in hilarious failure. One rabbit hunt, without benefit of guns, however, ended in success—at least for one officer, who "worn out with the long, weary march, sick, hungry, and dejected, leaned his back against a tree and groaned to think of his inability to join in the chase of an old hare, which, he knew, from the wild yells in the wood, his men were pursuing. But the uproar approached him—nearer, nearer, and nearer, until he saw the hare bounding towards him with a regiment at her heels. She spied an opening made by the folds of the officer's cloak and jumped in, and he embraced his first meal for forty-eight hours" (p. 70).

Some of McCarthy's humor seems related to the familiar coarse fun of prewar days. The following brief sketch is evidence: "An artilleryman, camped for a day where no water was to be found easily, awakened during the night by thirst, went stumbling about in search of water; and to his great delight found a large bucketful. He drank his fill, and in the morning found that what he drank had washed a bullock's head, and was crimson with its blood" (pp. 70-71). He also tells of several stragglers who came into camp one night and found a large pot of soup which they drank, though it tasted peculiar. The next morning they checked to see what had given it the odd taste and found that it had been "strongly impregnated with the peculiar flavor of defunct cockroaches." The author also remembers having eaten a muskrat that was "skinned, cleaned, buried a day or two, disinterred, cooked, and eaten with great relish" (p. 71).

Chapter VII, "Fun and Fury on the Field," concerns the cheering, laughter, fun, and pathos of fighting. McCarthy describes a battle where he was an on-the-spot witness: "As we approach, a ludicrous scene presents itself. A strong-armed artilleryman is energetically thrashing a dejected looking individual with a hickory bush, and urging him to the front. He has managed to keep out of many a fight, but now he *must* go in. The captain has detailed a man to *whip* him in, and the man is doing it. With every blow the poor fellow yells and begs to be spared, but his determined guardian will not cease. They press on, the one screaming and the other lashing, till they reach the battery in position and firing on the retiring enemy."

McCarthy proved that even the heat of battle could be an occasion for humor. He told of a big brawny fellow who at Gettysburg, when the artillery fire was at its height, burst out singing, "Backward, roll backward, O Time in thy flight: / Make me a child again, just for this *fight!*" A fellow near him interrupted with "Yes; and a *gal* child at that."

The ex-Rebel could even find humor in defeat. During a retreat, he said, a Southern artilleryman was approached by a Yankee cavalryman who shouted for him to surrender. The Reb didn't stop. The Yank became indignant and shouted, "Halt, d——n you; halt!" Still the Reb continued to walk. "Halt," repeated the cavalryman furiously, "halt, you d——n s—— of a ——; halt!" McCarthy continued, "Then the artilleryman halted, and remarking that he didn't allow any man to speak to *him* that way, seized a huge stick, turned on the cavalryman, knocked him out of his saddle, and proceeded on his journey to the rear." It was well that the Southern soldier could see humor in defeat, for it was his humor that buttressed him in the dark days of the war and its aftermath.

Another amusing account of low life in the Confederate army is William Andrew Fletcher's *Rebel Private Front and Rear*. Born in Louisiana, Fletcher moved with his family to Texas, where he enlisted in the Confederate army when the war started. His delightful sense of humor is evident throughout the record of his war experiences. The style of *Rebel Private* is unpolished but lively.

Fletcher remembers that he had a hard time staying healthy enough to fight in the war. On arrival at Richmond he found that he had a case of measles. Then he developed the itch, which actually turned out to be body lice. After that he came down with the mumps. When he recovered from that, he slipped from a persimmon tree and had to return to the hospital. Finally he had an attack of jaundice. When he at last recovered from all these maladies, he was ready for service.

At least he thought he was ready for service, until another health specter haunted him in camp. This time it was diarrhea. In the following words he records his meeting with this malady and the cure he found for it: "I, with a number of others, had quite an amusing experience—with a happy ending—and it was this: We were sufferers from camp diarrhea, as it was called, and up to that time we had found no cure. So, entering the battle, I had quite a great fear that something disgraceful might happen and it was somewhat uppermost in my mind; but to my surprise the excitement, or something else, had effected a cure. I inquired of some of the others and they reported a cure" (p. 16).

The most that can be said for the Rebel private's humor connected with food is that it is mildly nauseating. For example, until he discovered a cat's claw in his portion, sausage had been a favorite dish with the men. His description of cattle to be slaughtered and the meat taken from them is, to say the least, unpalatable. "In every brute there was depicted the wanting condition of the owner. The once pride of the family was slowly but surely starving to death and the end was near, for there were numbers that one would think when they lay down that they never would rise again until skinned and carted away to their last resting place—the soldier's stomach. The most of this meat, when cooked, would turn to jelly and one would think of sweetening. It was not necessary to have a peg to hang it on— throw it against a tree and it would stick. Need not necessarily be a nearby tree, as there was little danger of its being stolen, as each fellow had enough of the kind. After being thrown against the tree it had the appearance of some hideous picture of a sea monster trying to climb down, as the tendons would stick where they came in contact with the tree and would slowly stretch from the weight of body whether the entire piece would go to strings, or not. We never made a test, but I have often pulled meat off—if such it could be called—when the meat was from two to four inches below where it first stuck. If the reader of this undertakes to make test to prove the correctness of this statement, I would ask him to go for his material where he can get fair samples under like conditions. Here was where it was reported that some men ate the unborn calf if it was spotted. This word 'spotted' was to denote one that had the hair on" (pp. 71-72). Typical of the memoirs written by foot soldiers, *Rebel Private* relates in serio-comic exaggeration the deprivations of the war.

Fletcher's humor is sometimes almost Freudian. One can only speculate as to what he had in mind when he reported the following scene on a visit to a Yankee infirmary. "I was somewhat amused, however, with one fine-looking, intelligent young fellow, who, from appearances and conversation, had lived on the bright side of life; he was on his feet and slowly moving about; he said, 'Reb, look what you fellows have done for me. I would rather that bullet had gone through my head, and I guess my girl will hunt another fellow when she hears of it' " (p. 38).

Another time his humor seems to border on the sadistic. One time he and a friend see a mass of moving people—Yankee soldiers and Negro civilians mixed in—and decide to have a little fun by firing on the mounted enemy, "not carying a straw whether we hit a negro or not." He recalls the scene with macabre humor. "We turned loose with our carbines, three charges each— terror reigned, and there was as if by magic, a dismounting, jumping from carts and wagons; and I guess there were a number of mothers who forgot their babies, and grandmas and grandpas who forgot, for the time, that there was such a thing as rheumatism" (p. 90).

In addition to being at least semi-sadistic—he liked to tease cowards in battle—Fletcher must have been a tough and brave soldier. Remembering an operation on a serious wound in his hip, he writes: "Without further question they commenced to cut and from the way the knife pulled the muscle, I took it to be very dull, and was expressing my views in very forcible terms when one of them remarked: 'If you don't hush up we will leave you.' My reply was, 'It don't hurt as badly when I am cursing' " (p. 43). He recalls, however, a medicine he once tried to no avail. "While in the line, I thought of my gin and opened a bottle, and the most of the boys did the same. I was not used to drink, but wanted to test gin as a fear tonic; so I partook of the remedy freely, but the bullets would make about the same impression at each visitation, and when we were marched off, the most of one bottle was gone and the bullets sounded the same old way" (pp. 141-42).

Foraging was as much a necessity in Fletcher's outfit as in McCarthy's. Corn patches, beehives, and hen houses were especially attractive objects of foraging expeditions. Chicken stealing was reduced by hungry soldiers to a science. Some directions devised by an old Negro are guaranteed by Fletcher to work "where chickens roost low."

When you get under their roost, let the chickens get through with their low croaking, and stop operations—if they do hear something and start it again, wait till all is quiet and commence again. Put your hand on the roost (back up is best), move it along the roost until you touch a foot; the chicken will raise up, slip your hand under and when he puts his foot down on your hand, you will know about the size of the chicken and direction of its head. If you don't want the chicken, or its head is toward you, turn your hand and draw from under its foot and the chicken will put its foot back on the roost. If you want the fowl, change so your hand will be on the other side of the roost. This will put its head from you. Repeat operation and when one foot is on your hand, slowly slip your hand to touch the other foot and it will raise and put that foot on your hand. When both feet are on your hand, raise a little, then when the chicken's body is clear of the roost, lower gently, at the same time swing across breast and raise left arm at the shoulder. When chicken's body is under, give quick up motion with chicken and downward clamp with your arm. As you are doing this, grab the neck with left hand, and with the other hand clamp its head, give a twist and pull and neck is broken. Hold for a moment— this hard squeezing and lack of freedom to flutter will quiet the nerve instantly. Holding by head, lower the chicken until ground is touched and turn loose. If on the floor, hold to the head till it touches the floor. This can be repeated as often as wished, and the darker the night the better, as the owner cannot peep through a crack and see you, and as he hears nothing he would at once leave, and if light is seen, one has time to creep away (pp. 57-58).

This method worked for Fletcher and many others during the war, but he had his reservations about its practicality in the electric age. "I guess one would be less at ease now, for the electric snap light would be on his mind."

On the way home to Texas after the surrender, Fletcher stopped for lodging at a house infested with rats. In the concluding pages of his memoirs he describes how he helped rid the house of the vermin by putting a sack over a rat hole and running the rats into it. The work was interrupted only briefly when a rat ran up a girl's dress. Once back home in Beaumont, he applied for work at the sawmill where he had worked for $35 a month plus room and board before the war. He was offered $16 doing the same work, but declined, saying, "Four years lost and wages cut." There was only one resort left him. "So I went home and gathered up father's old carpenter tools and went on a job at a dollar and a half a day, about one hundred feet from the place where I left off work" (p. 158).

One of the most delightful memoirs of the war is Sam R. Watkins' *"Co. Aytch,"* written in 1881-82 and published first in the Columbia, Tennessee, *Herald*. At a time when most popular writers were romanticizing the war, Watkins wrote with a surprising realism. Some of his Rebel soldiers drink, gamble, and swear; some are cowards. Since he wrote from memory, some of his facts are inaccurate. Another limitation is his coolness toward Yankees, which sometimes breaks through when he recounts war atrocities. But all in all the book is vigorous and readable. One of the book's dominating features is its humor. Writing in the Introduction to the 1952 reprint, Bell Irvin Wiley says: "Soldiering also had its brighter side, and it is in presenting this aspect that Watkins is at his best. His humor is so irrepressible that it frequently breaks through the most serious passages to blend mirth with tragedy." The critic concludes his commentary with this judgment, "No memoir by a Rebel participant is richer in intimate detail of common soldier life than this engaging story told by Private Sam R. Watkins of the First Tennessee."*

---

* Wiley's *The Life of Johnny Reb* (Indianapolis, 1943) is an excellent study of the common soldier of the Confederacy. Wiley has also edited Lt. William N. Wood, *Reminiscences of Big I,* a Virginian's memoirs of his experiences as a Confederate officer. The recollections are not primarily humorous but contain amusing incidents, such as "The Cat Wouldn't Cook Done" in which Wood relates that a cat was still too tough to eat after two days' boiling.

Watkins himself limited his scope by explaining that he was not writing a history, but merely the observations of a private in the rear ranks of the army. History tells of the great men and events of war, "But in the following pages I propose to tell of the fellows who did the shooting and killing, the fortifying and ditching, the sweeping of the streets, the drilling, the standing guard, picket and videt, and who drew (or were to draw) eleven dollars per month and rations, and also drew the ramrod and tore the cartridge" (p. 47).

The satiric tone of much of the book appears early when Watkins, in discussing the events that led to the war, spoke of the leaders of the two sides. Of President Lincoln and Vice-President Hannibal Hamlin, "The other side selected as captain a son of Nancy Hanks, of Bowling Green, and a son of old Bob Lincoln, the rail-splitter, and whose name was Abe. Well, after he was elected captain, they elected as first lieutenant an individual of doubtful blood by the name of Hannibal Hamlin, being a descendant of the generation of Ham, the bad son of old Noah, who meant to curse him blue, but overdid the thing, and cursed him black" (p. 46).

Satire also colors the author's handling of officers and even noncommissioned officers. Once, he says, after a battle he noticed that the military hierarchy from corporals to captains had torn all the fine lace off their uniforms. When he asked several why they had done this, their reply was, "Humph, you think that I was going to be a target for the Yankees to shoot at?" Watkins comments caustically, "You see, this was our first battle, and the officers had not found out that minnie as well as cannon balls were blind; that they had no eyes and could not see. They thought that the balls would hunt for them and not hurt the privates. I always shot at privates. It was they that did the shooting and killing, and if I could kill or wound a private, why, my chances were so much the better. I always looked upon officers as harmless personages" (p. 55).

Scenes of stark realism and grotesqueness that are the antithesis of typical postwar treatments are frequently inserted. He remembers the time in Virginia he was with a group which went to relieve a guard unit. "If I remember correctly, there were just eleven of them. Some were sitting down and some were lying down; but each and every one was as cold and as hard frozen as the icicles that hung from their hands and faces and clothing—dead! They had died at their post on duty. Two of them, a little advance of the others, were standing with their guns in their hands, as cold and as hard frozen as a monument of marble—standing sentinel with loaded guns in their frozen hands!" (p. 62). His description of the Chickamauga battlefield the day after the battle could not be made any more gory. "Men were lying where they fell, shot in every conceivable part of the body. Some with their entrails torn out and still hanging to them and piled up on the ground beside them, and they still alive. Some with their underjaw torn off, and hanging by a fragment of skin to their cheeks, with their tongues lolling from their mouth, and they trying to talk. Some with both eyes shot out, and with one eye hanging down on their cheek. In fact, you might walk over the battlefield and find men shot from the crown of the head to the tip end of the toe" (pp. 118-19). There is probably no scene in prewar humor with realism this vivid. Other passages are just as bloody. For instance, Watkins tells of a cannon ball that tore a buddy's head off, "spattering his brains all over my face and bosom," and of visiting an Atlanta hospital and seeing in the rear of the building "a pile of arms and legs, rotting and decomposing." But even in the midst of describing a battle, he pauses to insert an anecdote. He remembers, for example, a funny incident during the battle of Shiloh. "As we advanced, on the edge of the battlefield, we saw a big fat colonel of the 23rd Tennessee regiment badly wounded, whose name, if I remember correctly, was Matt. Martin. He said to us, 'Give 'em goss, boys. That's right, my brave First Tennessee. Give 'em Hail Columbia!' We halted but a moment, and said I, 'Colonel, where are you wounded?' He answered in a deep bass voice, 'My son, I am wounded in the arm, in the leg, in the head, in the body, and in another place which I have a delicacy in mentioning'" (p. 65).

Desertion was a perennial problem in the Confederate army. Watkins recalled with horror the punishments meted out to deserters and men who had gone AWOL. Deserters were often shot, and AWOLers were usually whipped unmercifully and branded in full view of their comrades. "And when some miserable wretch was to be whipped and branded for being absent ten days without leave, we had to see him kneel down and have his head shaved smooth and slick as a peeled onion, and then stripped to the naked skin. Then a strapping fellow with a big rawhide would make the blood flow and spurt at every lick, the wretch begging and howling like a hound, and then he was branded with the letter *D* on both hips, when he was marched through the army to the music of the 'Rogue's March'" (p. 71).

No memoir of common soldier life was ever complete without mention of the lice that infected virtually every man. "Every soldier had a brigade of lice on him, and I have seen fellows so busily engaged in cracking them that it reminded me of an old woman knitting." At first, Watkins says, the men were embarrassed when they discovered they had lice and would go off by themselves into the woods to delouse; but when they found out that almost everybody was crawling with the little vermin, they lost their self-consciousness. "Pharaoh's people, when they were resisting old Moses, never enjoyed the curse of lice more than we did." Entertainments built around lice became popular, with louse races common everywhere. Watkins recalls the champion louse racer in his outfit. "There was one fellow who was winning all the money; his lice would run quicker and crawl faster than anybody's lice. We could not understand it. If some fellow happened to catch a fierce-looking louse, he would call on Dornin for a race. Dornin would come and always win the stake. The lice were placed in plates—

this was the race course—and the first that crawled off was the winner. At last we found out Dornin's trick; he always heated his plate" (p. 76).*

Although occasionally harsh on the Yankees, he is usually objective when he mentions the enemy. Before the Battle of Perryville he stood picket duty on one side of the street in the town, with a Yankee picket within talking distance on the other side. They got quite chummy that night "and made a raid upon a citizen's pantry, where we captured a bucket of honey, a pitcher of sweet milk, and three or four biscuit" (p. 81). The next day they were trying to kill each other. Another time, like Sidney Lanier and Sarge Wier, he tried to rob a dead Yankee. "In passing over the battlefield [at Murfreesboro], I came across a dead Yankee colonel. He had on the finest clothes I ever saw, a red sash and fine sword. I particularly noticed his boots. I needed them, and had made up my mind to wear them out for him. But I could not bear the thought of wearing dead men's shoes. I took hold of the foot and raised it up and made one trial at the boot to get it off. I happened to look up, and the colonel had his eyes wide open, and seemed to be looking at me. He was stone dead, but I dropped that foot quick" (p. 95). After relating that grotesque experience, he adds, "It was my first and last attempt to rob a dead Yankee." Other men, however, were not so squeamish.

The only time the author mentioned specifically killing anyone he showed regret. He recalls painfully that his victim "was the prettiest youth I ever saw. When I fired, the Yankees broke and run, and I went up to the boy I had killed, and the blood was gushing out of his mouth. I was sorry" (p. 195).

Almost everyone in the army, he writes, had a nickname—from generals down to privates. Had the war lasted ten years, "we would have forgotten our proper names" (p. 89). Common nicknames included Sneak, Apple Jack, Devil Horse, Old Snake, Greasy, Buzzard, Hog, and Brutus.

Practical jokes, always popular among the common people of the South, flourished during the war. Larking or snipe hunting was a favorite. Watkins described the way it was done in the army. "The way to go 'a larking' is this: Get an empty meal bag and about a dozen men and go to some dark forest or open field on some cold, dark, frosty or rainy night, about five miles from camp. Get someone who does not understand the game to hold the bag in as stooping and cramped a position as is possible, to keep perfectly still and quiet, and when he has got in the right fix, the others to go off to drive in the larks. As soon as they get out of sight, they break in a run and go back to camp, and go to sleep, leaving the poor fellow all the time

---

* In *Rebel Private* (pp. 17–18) William A. Fletcher also touched on the ubiquitous louse. This was the procedure, he recalled, for delousing an affected pair of pants or a shirt: "Our plan was, when they got so thick that they were hardly bearable, to make a fire of a small amount of straw or leaves and hold the garment over the blaze and from the heat they would drop off, be burned, or be ready for the next fellow. If one was well stocked with big fat fellows, it would remind him of popping corn. The uneducated may think I have said too much for truth of this subject; but if he or she will ask some old 'battle-scarred soldier' he will give you a few lines more."

holding the bag" (pp. 106-7). Watkins was party to a larking expedition one time, but later regretted having taken part when the sleepy-eyed and exhausted young greenhorn brought his bag back to him the next morning.

When foraging didn't supplement their food stores sufficiently, soldiers often had to resort to other devices. Sometimes they even had to go rat hunting. Watkins recalled a time when he and several other hungry men caught a large rat in an old outhouse. "We skinned him, washed and salted him, buttered and peppered him, and fried him. He actually looked nice. The delicate aroma of the frying rat came to our hungry nostrils. We were keen to eat a piece of rat; our teeth were on edge; yea, even our mouth watered for a piece of rat. Well, after a while, he was said to be done. I got a piece of cold corn dodger, laid my piece of rat on it, ate a little piece of bread, and raised the piece of rat to my mouth, when I happened to think of how that rat's tail did slip. I had lost my appetite for dead rat. I did not eat any rat. It was my first and last effort to eat dead rat" (pp. 108-9).

Usually a soldier had to do his own laundry, but occasionally he could find a colored woman near camp to do it for him. Watkins found such a washerwoman in Aunt Daphne, whose husband Uncle Zack—when awake—would entertain him with his talk about his religion. One time Uncle Zack told him about the night the devil visited him and took him to hell. Once in hell the devil "jes stretch a wire across hell, and hang me up jes same like a side of bacon, through the tongue." As the Negro continued, his memory became more vivid.

"Well, dar I hang like de bacon, and de grease kept droppin' down and would blaze up all 'round me. I jes stay dar and burn; and after while de debil come 'round wid his gun, and say, 'Zack, I gwine to shoot you,' and jes as he raise de gun, I jes jerk loose from dat wire, and I jes fly to hebin."

"Fly! did you have wings?"

"O, yes, sir, I had wings."

"Well, after you got to heaven, what did you do then?"

"Well, I jes went to eatin' grass like all de balance of de lams."

"What! were they eating grass?"

"O, yes, sir."

"Well, what color were the lambs, Uncle Zack?"

"Well, sir, some of dem was white, and some black, and some spotted."

"Were there no old rams or ewes among them?"

"No, sir; dey was all lams."

"Well, Uncle Zack, what sort of a looking lamb were you?"

"Well, sir, I was sort of specklish and brown like."

Old Zack begins to get sleepy.

"Did you have horns, Uncle Zack?"

"Well, some of dem had little horns dat look like dey was jes sorter sproutin' like."

Zack begins to nod and doze a little.

"Well, how often did they shear the lambs, Uncle Zack?"

"Well, w-e-1-l, w—e—l—l," and Uncle Zack was fast asleep and dreaming no doubt of the beautiful pastures glimmering above the clouds of heaven (pp. 140-41).

Such interludes must have provided Watkins with comic relief from the worries of warfare.

Watkins came out of the army only one notch above the rank he went in. Ironically, the only promotion he ever got was for breaking ranks and picking up a deserted flag. He comments mock-seriously: "And had I only known that picking up flags entitled me to promotion and that every flag picked up would raise me one notch higher, I would have quit fighting and gone to picking up flags, and by that means I would have soon been President of the Confederate States of America" (p. 180). Thousands of readers have been glad that he stuck to being a private; otherwise there would be no "*Co. Aytch*." Without Watkins' book and other humorous memoirs of the war, our present-day knowledge of the period would be sadly incomplete.

The reunited nation delighted to read anecdotes of Civil War soldiers—great and lowly. Many of the stories were apocryphal, but truth (or lack of it) did not bother a people busy making Stonewall Jackson, Jeb Stuart, and the common soldier into legends. Rare was the book written about the war which failed to include a section variously called "Humors of the Camp," "Comic Aspects of Battle," or "The Light Side of the War."

The novelist and former Confederate captain John Esten Cooke mentioned the necessity for humor in King's and Derby's *Camp-Fire Sketches*, a collection of Civil War pieces. "The humorous side of the drama may be less inspiring and exciting, but it is more amusing and characteristic. . . . The main object is to show how men in positions of grave responsibility, enough to crush out all tendency to fun, yet showed a marked tendency to enjoy the 'sunny side' of things, and laugh when ruin itself stared them in the face" (p. 554).

While Cooke was occupied with writing down the humor of Stuart and Jackson, another chronicler of Civil War humor, Lieutenant Colonel W. W. Blackford, had an amusing story to tell about Cooke. In the section of *War Years with Jeb Stuart* entitled "Captain Cooke Dodges a Shell," he records a comic incident at the Battle of Mechanicsville.

While we were all sitting on our horses in a conspicuous part of the field, a battery noticed us by a round. One of the shots passed screaming a few inches over our heads. We were not so well accustomed to artillery then as we became afterwards, and most of us involuntarily ducked our heads. Capt. John Esten Cooke, while so doing, bowed a little too low, lost his balance, and fell sprawling on the ground. We were all a good deal shocked, for we did not doubt for a moment that his head had been carried off. Stuart leaned down from his saddle and in a most sympathizing voice said, "Hallo, Cooke! Are you hit?" But Cooke jumped up looking very sheepish as he dusted himself and said, "Oh, no, General; I only dodged a little too far." The reaction of feeling from

53

the uneasiness we had felt for him, and his ludicrous appearance as he scrambled back into his saddle, still covered with dust, was perfectly irresistible, and we laughed until we could scarcely keep our seats in our saddles. For months after, almost every time Cooke appeared at the breakfast table, the General would call to him, "Hello, Cooke! Are you hit?" or "No, General; I only dodged too far." He [Stuart] loved a joke, and would ring the changes on one until a better one turned up.

A Confederate general as admired as Stonewall Jackson was bound to figure in many humorous stories. One anecdote in which Jackson was involved shows the adulation the Southerner accorded his military leaders. A Virginia planter had given almost all he had to the Confederacy; he had kept for his own use only one ten-acre lot of corn. One day he was exasperated to see a troop of cavalry riding through his corn, and he angrily threatened to report them to President Davis. But when he discovered that their leader was Stonewall Jackson, he changed his tone completely and babbled excitedly, "God bless you, General Jackson! I am so glad to see you! Go back and ride all over my field, damn you, ride all over my field! Get down, and come into my house. I am so glad to see you. Ride all over my field, all over it—all over it! Bless your soul, I'm so glad to see you."[5] Jackson's men admired him extravagantly too. Because he said he liked the taste of whiskey too much, he was a teetotaler; but this prohibition did not extend to his men, who drank frequent toasts to him. These two subjects are combined in the following anecdote told about Jackson by George Cary Eggleston in *A Rebel's Recollections.* "On one occasion, a soldier who had imbibed enthusiasm with his whiskey, feeling the inadequacy of the devotion shown by drinking to an absent chief, marched, canteen in hand, to Jackson's tent, and gaining admission, proposed as a sentiment, 'Here's to you, general! May I live to see you stand on the highest pinnacle of Mount Ararat, and hear you give the command, "By the right of nations front into empires,—worlds, right face!"'" (pp. 155-56).

The Yankees contributed to making Jackson into a legend. It was widely believed among Union soldiers, for example, that Stonewall never slept. The Yanks had good reason to place his powers above those of the average man, for time and again his maneuvers startled both sides. One of Cooke's anecdotes about Jackson (in *Camp-Fire Sketches*) contains as much truth as humor. He wrote that when Jackson was told that General McClellan was close by with a large army, he asked if the Yanks had many beef cattle with them. When he was told yes, he said with a dry smile, "Well, I can whip any army that comes well supplied with beef cattle!" (p. 563). Jackson's insistence on strict discipline also contributed to the building of his legend. Sam Watkins said of him: "He did his duty himself and was ever at his post, and he expected and demanded of everybody to do the same thing. He would have a man shot at the drop of a hat, and drop it himself" (p. 60).

Although many of the heaviest burdens of the war fell on Robert E. Lee, even he was not without humor. Biographies of Lee almost always include incidents which show his humor. One anecdote concerns the time at Petersburg when he visited one of his major generals and in the course of the talk asked about the condition of his subordinate's lines. The man told him they were in good shape, but when they visited the lines, they found no work had been done. Noticing the spirited horse the major general was riding, Lee suggested a remedy for both the lines and the horse. "I would suggest to you that *these rough paths along these trenches would be very admirable ground over which to tame him*."[6] Cooke recorded an incident during the Chancellorsville campaign when a young officer rode up in haste to report to Lee that the Yanks had attacked. Lee is supposed to have said, smiling, "Well, I heard firing, and I was beginning to think it was time some of you lazy fellows were coming to tell me what it was all about" (pp. 563-64).

Cooke also vouched for the spirit of General Fitzhugh Lee. "He was full of humor, as brave as steel, without any 'official dignity' whatever in his manner, but at all times the hearty soldier, loving his jest dearly and never in low spirits, whatever the outlook might be." Cooke also reported that Lee once told him that his great ambition was "to have a company of Negro minstrels this winter—all mulattoes" (pp. 567-69). Thus was humor helping to romanticize and legendize Southern war heroes.

Other popular war figures in humor were Colonel W. H. F. Lee; General Richard Ewell, whose humor was generally profane; and the daring raider Captain John Morgan. But the Southern patriot with by far the greatest reputation for humor was General Jeb Stuart. Cooke called him "the gayest probably of all the Southern generals" and noted that his staff consisted chiefly of young men who loved fun. The General's banjo player accompanied him everywhere. Cooke reported a meeting between Stuart and a former West Point classmate while the former was on a reconnaissance mission in 1861. Stuart said to his former friend, "I didn't know you were on our side," to which his companion responded by pointing to his command, a Federal battery just coming into sight. They both had a good laugh over the confusion and went back to their respective sides (p. 555). From then until the end of the war, Stuart's humor figured in stories told from the Potomac to the Rio Grande.

Blackford idolized his commander and recorded many instances of Stuart's love of humor. Sometimes Stuart was but a laughing observer. "Once during the night I had an adventure with a dog which amused General Stuart and my comrades of the staff no little, though it was not at all amusing to me. Passing a country house, General Stuart told me to go in and find out if the man had seen or heard anything of the enemy. He waited at the gate of the yard while I dismounted and went in. The house stood fifty yards from the road, and halfway to it a large bulldog dashed out and made a furious attack upon me. We were now very near the camps of the enemy and it would not do to use firearms, so I received the dog on the point of my sabre, inflicting a wound in the shoulder which, though arresting his first attack, placed him upon his guard and only infuriated him the more. He circled round and round just out of reach of my thrusts, uttering savage growls which showed plainly enough what he would do if he could get hold of me with his teeth. Stuart roared with laughter and called out continually, 'Give it to him, Blackford,' for he had an instinctive love of fighting and enjoyed seeing the battle, and but for the order about firearms I would have made quick work of it with my pistol" (p. 174). As much of the humor in this sketch comes from the *way* Blackford relates it as from the incident itself, though comic it surely must have been when Stuart witnessed it. According to Blackford, when Stuart was almost captured by the enemy at Verdiersville, he lost his hat and haversack to them, much to the amusement of his troops. But the General retaliated in kind a few days later when he captured General Pope's coat and hat at Catlett's Station. Later when Pope's headquarters was captured, a full-dress uniform belonging to the Federal general was brought to Stuart, who sent it to a friend in Richmond. There the uniform was displayed in a book store with a card which read: "Headquarters in the Saddle" and "The Rear Taking Care of Itself" (pp. 97-98).

Stuart's recklessness was the subject of many humorous stories. Eggleston wrote of one of his daring performances, "after capturing a large number of horses and mules on one of his raids, he seized a telegraph station and sent a dispatch to General Meigs, then Quartermaster-General of the United States army, complaining that he could not afford to come after animals of so poor a quality, and urging that officer to provide better ones for capture in the future . . . " (pp. 126-27). In spurring his men on, Stuart made frequent use of his humor. Blackford told of an incident in which Stuart, passing by some men who told him they had been on picket duty for thirty-six hours without food, gave the men a little "pep" talk which made them forget their hunger. "Oh nonsense! You don't look starved. There's a cornfield over there; jump the fence and get a good breakfast. You don't want to go back to camp, I know; it's stupid there, and all the fun is out here. I never go to camp if I can help it. Besides, I've kept your company on duty all this time as a compliment" (pp. 134-35). Although this incident was related as a humorous story, the General meant his words to be taken seriously. The compliment he paid the men was a genuine one.

Cooke recorded the time Stuart made common horse sense sound humorous. Once when an officer reported to him that his command must fall back because a rain had dampened their powder and made their guns useless, Stuart told him, "No . . . hold your ground. If the rain wets your powder it will wet your enemy's too." About General Stuart, Cooke wrote: "He made a frolic of war, in fact, and nothing ever seemed to cast him down or made him in the least doubtful of the result. He was always laughing, paying compliments to ladies, or roaring out his camp songs when he was not fighting hard, or working hour after hour at his desk."[7] At the head of his marching column Stuart would amuse some of his men—and terrify some—by singing such songs as: "If you get there before I do, Oh, tell 'em I'm a-coming too!" Stuart could agree with Joel Chandler Harris who once said that humor was a good thing to die by.

Foreign soldiers sent to the South by their governments as observers were occasionally the source of much amusement because of their Old World attitudes and their strange accents. A Prussian assigned to Jeb Stuart's staff, Major Heros Von Borcke entertained his Southern comrades with his antics. In *War Years with Jeb Stuart* Blackford devoted more space to Von Borcke's theatrics than to many critical battles (pp. 156-60). He related one of the Prussian's entertainments held in a private home before Stuart and his staff. A sheet was stretched across the hall against which the shadows of the actors were cast. When the scene opens, Von Borcke is sitting on a couch dressed in a large nightshirt stuffed with pillows. He begins to groan and a nurse appears and sends for a doctor. A ridiculously dressed medic comes in and gives the patient a deep draught from a bottle, "and then, on the sly, the doctor takes one too, to the great delight of the audience." Between groans of agony the patient manages to tell the doctor the things he has just eaten at a dinner party. To relieve him, the doctor reaches down his throat (or appears to) and "pulls in succession, and holds up for inspection, a pair of deer's horns, some beef's horns, cabbages, stalks and all, quantities of oyster shells, etc., etc., and finally a pair of boots." At each delivery an assistant takes out a pillow from Von Borcke's nightshirt, and the patient utters excruciating cries of relief—until finally he is considered cured. He then jumps up, embraces the doctor, and the two begin "swigging at the bottle of physic . . . until they become tipsy, and the performance closes in an uproarious dance of doctor and patient. . . ." Blackford concluded his account with this critique: "The wit and humor displayed in this performance I have rarely seen equalled and its effect on the audience was convulsive. All the negroes on the place were allowed to come in to see it and their intense appreciation of the scene, and their rich, broad peals of laughter added no little to its attractions."

Another hilarious performance recorded by Blackford had Von Borcke playing the part of a blushing maiden. The sketch showed an Irishman courting his sweetheart. This is Blackford's description of Paddy's beloved: "Von Borcke was transformed into a blushing maiden weighing two hundred and fifty pounds and six feet two and a half inches tall; a riding skirt of one of the girls, supplemented by numerous dainty underskirts and extended by enormous hoops according to the fashion then in vogue, hung in graceful folds to conceal the huge cavalry boots the huge damsel wore. Her naturally ample bosom palpitated under skillfully arranged pillows, and was gorgeously decorated with . . . jewelry and ribbons, while 'a love of a bonnet,' long braids of hair, and quantities of powder and rouge completed her toilet, and in her hand she flirted coquettishly a fan of huge dimensions." Von Borcke's suitor was a colonel dressed as an Irishman, complete with red nose. As the two promenaded around the room arm in arm they made comic love conversation. Their disguises were so good that no one suspected their identity. Only when they began to waltz and the maiden's hoop skirts flew up "that twinkling amid the white drapery beneath, the well-known boots of Von Borcke betrayed the first suspicion of who the lady was." And then "as suddenly as they had come they vanished, waltzing out through the open door and followed by convulsive roars of laughter from the delighted audience."

The Prussians seem to have sent over a battalion of observers, for another amusing Prussian attached to the Southern army was a Captain Scheibert, a man with artistic as well as military talents and the subject of several comic sketches by Blackford. One episode deals with the time the fat little foreigner agreed to aid Mrs. W. H. F. Lee, visiting her husband near an encampment, in touching up an oil sketch of "a small-size female head" which she had just finished. When they had finished working on the portrait, they placed it on a chair to dry. Later during an animated conversation the Prussian accidentally—and unknown to himself or anyone else—sat down in the chair that held the wet picture.

When the time came for him to go Mrs. Lee thanked him cordially, and told him she would keep the picture as a souvenir of their pleasant acquaintance, and turned to get the picture for him to take a last critical survey of it. Where was the picture? "Bless my soul!" said the Captain, "I laid it down on one of the chairs, but I don't see it now." Then they looked and looked. "Oh!" said Scheibert, "the wind must have blown it under the piano!" "Here it is," said Mrs. Lee, screaming with laughter, as she peeled the unfortunate picture from the broad seat of Scheibert's white trousers, leaving the lovely face, somewhat blurred, transferred thereto most conspicuously.

Scheibert backed out from under the piano and without taking leave, or stopping to get his hat, cane and gloves in the hall, bolted across the fields for our camp. We saw him coming, waving his arms wildly and roaring like a bull with laughter. He threw himself on the grass, still convulsed, rolling over and over, and every time he turned that side up there was a bright picture of a lovely face on the seat of his trousers. It was a long time before he could find breath to tell us about it, and then you may rest assured we enjoyed the joke (pp. 207-8).

Blackford's light touch and deft style have preserved well the original humor of the episode.

Of the other amusing incidents in which Scheibert is a central character, one of the best is Blackford's account of his poor horsemanship, "a never-ending source of amusement to us." The fat Prussian's sloppy habit of tying his belongings to his saddle with strings and straps often caused him to lose items. Once sent by Stuart with an order for reinforcements, he "in his headlong impulsive way dashed off with it at full speed, but to Stuart's horror took by mistake a road which led directly towards the enemy." The General quickly ordered a courier to try to catch him before he reached the Yankees; but Scheibert, seeing a horseman following him, mistook him for an enemy and spurred his horse on faster, with a bundle coming loose at nearly every jump of his horse. Fortunately the courier intercepted him just short of the enemy lines. Blackford ends: "To retrace their steps and find the scattered property was no easy task but poor Captain Scheibert at last appeared, sadly crestfallen and greatly to the relief of Stuart's mind" (pp. 208-9).

Humorous stories by the thousands—some true, some half true, and some lies—were chronicled about lesser known men. Daniel's *Rebel Surgeon,* for example, tells of an engineer who demonstrated to a group of gullible officers that a toad could swallow coals of fire without harm. Catching a large toad, he then sent his colored boyservant for some live coals and prepared for the exhibition. "He went cautiously towards the toad, and with thumb and finger thumped a live coal right plump in the frog's path—right before his face. Well, sirs, that old toad stopped, straightened up, turned his head on one side and took a square look at the coal. It must have been just what he was looking for, as he seemed pleased to meet it. His eyes shone with a new light, and he made a grab at the coal and swallowed it with apparent relish. Fact. His eyes sparkled still more, and beyond doubt he registered the mental reflection that that certainly *was* the much talked of 'hot stuff.' " Since skeptics in the group insisted the toad would die, the engineer had him put in a wooden box and shut up over night. The Old Doctor concludes his story with a comic snapper. "As I live, boys, next morning that toad was not only alive, but gave unmistakable evidence of being hungry! He recognized the major and winked at him; and when a candle-bug . . . was thrown in the box, the frog snapped him up like a trout would a minnow; fact" (pp. 113-17).

The humor of the Southern foot soldier—at least it was humorous in retrospect—became legendary. Daniel remembered a fat young fellow of about twenty-two, who, pretending concern over an older man in the company, approached him after a double-timing exercise and, gasping for breath, suggested, "Sergeant—I wouldn't—make—the—men double-quick up the hill; it tires Mr. Russell so bad!" Mr. Russell, about fifty, was seated on a log gently fanning himself (pp. 22-24).

The company wit was always the most popular man in the outfit. Writers of war memoirs seldom had trouble remembering him. In "*Co. Aytch*" Sam Watkins painted the character sketch of his company's favorite. "A big strapping fellow by the name of Tennessee Thompson, always carried bigger burdens than any other five men in the army. For example, he carried two quilts, three blankets, one gum oil cloth, one overcoat, one axe, one hatchet, one camp-kettle, one oven and lid, one coffee pot, besides his knapsack, haversack, canteen, gun, cartridge-box, and three days' rations. He was a rare bird, anyhow. Tennessee usually had his hair cut short on one side and left long on the other, so that he could give his head a bow and a toss and throw the long hairs over on the other side, and it would naturally part itself without a comb. Tennessee was the wit and good nature of the company; always in a good humor, and ever ready to do any duty when called upon. In fact, I would sometimes get out of heart and low spirited, and would hunt up Tennessee to have a little fun. His bye-word was 'Bully for Bragg; he's hell on retreat, and will whip the Yankees yet'" (p. 97).

Even the preacher could play the humorist. Daniel told of an Episcopal minister, who was also captain of their company, whose custom it was to hold frequent prayer meetings for his men. He suddenly, however, stopped these meetings with the explanation that "he had been fighting the devil all his life, and now that he had the Yankees to fight in addition, doubling on him as it were, he couldn't do justice to both" (pp. 46-47).

In "*Co. Aytch*" Watkins also pokes gentle fun at his company chaplain, a very learned divine from Nashville who began his first service with a prayer which sounded to Watkins like: "Oh, Thou immaculate, invisible, eternal and holy Being, the exudations of whose effulgence illuminate this terrestrial sphere, we approach Thy presence, being covered all over with wounds and bruises and putrifying sores, from the crowns of our heads to the soles of our feet. And Thou, O Lord, art our dernier resort." The prayer continues in this tone of polysyllabic profundity *ad infinitum* and leads Watkins to comment, "In fact, he was so 'high larnt' that I don't think anyone understood him but the generals." The minister finally began to preach a roaring war sermon, damning the Yankees, saying they should be fought in this world and their ghosts chased into the next. And then, in Watkins' words, "About this time we heard the awfullest racket, produced by some wild animal tearing through the woods towards us, and the cry, 'Look out! look out! hooie! hooie! look out!' and there came running right through our midst a wild bull, mad with terror and fright, running right over and knocking down the divine, and scattering Bibles and hymn books in every direction. The services were brought to a close without the doxology." During the attack at Chickamauga the same chaplain was riding along inciting the men on. With shells screaming through the air, he was saying: "Remember, boys, that he who is killed will sup tonight in Paradise." Then a loud soldier shouted to him, "Well, parson, you come along and take supper with us." Suddenly a bomb burst near the preacher and he put spurs to his horse and was next seen advancing to the rear, with almost every soldier yelling, "The parson isn't hungry, and never eats supper." But all this taunting was good-natured; chaplains were generally held in high esteem among the men (pp. 113-14).

In *A Rebel's Recollections* Eggleston sketched some odd characters he knew in the Southern army—characters like Jack Hawkins, one of "our assortment of queer people," who was inoffensive and timid but who sang "bold robber songs in the metallic voice peculiar to vocalists of the circus." He recalled old Denton, who would describe sumptuous imaginary feasts on an empty stomach. "'You ought to have dined with me today,' he would say. 'I had a deviled leg of turkey, and some beautiful broiled oysters with spanish olives. I never eat broiled oysters without olives. You try it sometime, and you'll never regret it. Then I had a stuffed wild goose's liver. Did you ever eat one? Well, you don't know what a real tidbit is, then. Not stuffed in the ordinary way, but stuffed scientifically and cooked in a way you never saw it done before'" (pp. 186-87). Eggleston also remembered "the most ingenious malingerer I ever heard of" who "was never off the sick-list for a single day." He was completely inured to "the gibes of the men, the sneers of the surgeons, and the denunciations of the officers." After being dismissed from one hospital, he would start toward his unit "and continue in that direction till he came to another infirmary, when he would have a relapse at once, and gain admission there." The doctors used all manner of remedies to get rid of him. "They burned his back with hot coppers; gave him the most nauseous mixture; put him on the lowest possible diet; treated him to cold shower-baths four or five times daily . . . but all to no purpose." Only the end of the war relieved them of him (p. 191).

The camp storyteller, "big, strong jolly" Bill Hicks, remained a pleasant and poignant memory for F. E. Daniel. Once, the Old Doctor recalls, Bill told of a dogfight, realistically "imitating the big dog how *he* 'went,' and the little dog how *he* 'went.'" After he had told several times how the big dog would jump at the little dog and go "gh-r-r-rh" and how the little dog would catch the big dog by the leg and go "br-e-w-r-r-rer," Tump Dixon, a bully from an adjoining camp, came up and insisted he tell the story again. When Bill refused, the bully pulled out a six-shooter and leveled it at his head and said: "How-did-that-big-dog-go?"—and Bill showed him. Then he said: "How-did-that-little-dog-go?"—and Bill showed him again. The performance was repeated until the boys were yelling with laughter and Bill got mad. "Tump left presently, and any time after that, if one wanted to get a fight on his hands he had only to ask Bill 'how the big dog went?'" (pp. 30-33).

Other sketches of Bill include the time several men found him sleeping soundly under a tree, tied up his jaws, crossed his hands on his breast, and had begun his burial service when the "corpse" was awakened by a call to report to the captain's tent. But Bill did not allow his "undertakers" to go unpunished. Another time when the author and Bill fell out of ranks to pick blackberries, they heard strange voices and in trying to hide, Bill plumped down into a bumblebees' nest. Daniel's recollection of the scene is semi-sadistic. "He ran again—you bet he did! and such a sight I never saw—Bill running like a scared deer, and fighting those bumblebees off with both hands, and every now and then, as one would get in his work, to hear Bill yell was just too funny for anything in this world, unless it be a Wild-west show" (p. 37). This sketch shows that, even with the postwar trend toward a less painful, less sadistic humor, discomfiture was still the source of much mirth. Immediately following these incidents, however, Daniel returned to the more typical humor of his time. The lines drip with sentiment and pathos. "Alas, poor Bill! He was a fine young man, an Apollo in form, and a model of strong physical manhood. Had he lived he would surely have had a career of usefulness. But like thousands of others of the flower of the youth of the South he was needlessly sacrificed to what the South believed to be principle . . ." (pp. 43-44). The war had made a difference in humor.

The author of *Detailed Minutiae of Soldier Life* sketched in caricature the military types he found in his company. These types include the "General" of the mess, who knows all about forthcoming campaigns—with details; "the Bore" or "the Old Auger," who begins to tell a story and takes hours to get to the point; "the Singing Man," who sings the men to sleep with "Virginia, Virginia, the Land of the Free" and "Dixie"; "the Recruit," with "his nice new clothes, new hat, new knife for all the fellows to borrow, nice comb for general use, nice little glass to shave by, good smoking tobacco, money in his pocket to lend out . . ."; "the Scribe," who could write a two-hour pass and sign the captain's name better than the captain himself; "the Mischievous Man," who would volunteer to shave a man with a big beard and moustache with his own razor, but would walk off after shaving half his face; "the Forager," who could tell "if there was buttermilk anywhere inside of ten miles" and who would get the spareribs if anybody in the country was killing a hog; "the Commissary Man," who never had any sugar left over, or any salt or soda or coffee; "the Honest Man," "who would not eat stolen pig," but would "take a little of the gravy." In addition, McCarthy lists "the Bully," "the Argument Man," "the Lazy Man," and "the Worthless Man" (pp. 194-204). Most of these types were exploited in postwar Southern humor.

The Negroes

Negroes contributed more to the war than merely keeping their white masters' clothes clean and entertaining them with anthropomorphic stories of their religion. The Aunt Daphnes and the Uncle Zacks did their part, but it was a small one. A far more important role was played by the valet who accompanied his owner to the war and remained with him until the war ended—or one of them was killed. Many are the stories of Negroes who fought heroically to protect their masters. Armistead Churchill Gordon's "Envion" is about just such a faithful slave who fought by the side of his master until the master was killed. Envion then buried him on the battlefield and went home to tell his mistress the sad news. His conduct in the war is his consolation in old age. He soliloquizes: "I ain't nothin' but a poor good-for-nothin' nigger; but it does me some good ter remember dat I fit in de battle 'long side o' de braves' man dat was in dat wah; an' dat when I come back I tuk keer o' young Miss Agnes."[8] This selection by Gordon sets the pattern for most postwar pictures of the Negro in the war: faithful, comic, and scornful of the invaders. The Negro who escaped into the Federal armies and freedom is seldom treated.

In *His Defense and Other Stories* by Harry Stillwell Edwards, "Captain Isam" tells how a Negro bodyguard decides to help in the actual fighting and gets the regimental colonel's permission to organize the other valets into a fighting unit. What happens is a farce. Justifying his petition to the colonel, Isam says, "You see, Mas' Alec, hyah ez thirty-two niggers waitin' on folks in dis hyah camp, holdin' hosses, cleanin' brasses, an' cookin'; an' hit don' look right for dese lazy rascals ter be er-settin' roun' while fightin's goin' on, an' dey bosses out yonner somewhar, reskin' dey lives ter keep 'em fum bein' stole an' runned off by dem Yankees." After permission is granted, Isam keeps his dusky troops drilling for hours each day in preparation for their first battle. He also decides he'd better get the rules of warfare straight before his initiation and asks a white officer, "Boss, when we gets dere an' goes ter fightin', ez hit 'g'inst de rules ter tek res' an' shoot? Some er dese niggers can't hit er mount'in ercross er hog-pen 'lessen dey teks res'. Ef dey can't tek res', 'spec' er heap er Gen'l Bragg's powdah an' shot be wasted right dere dis mornin'." As zero hour approaches, Isam begins lining his men up for the charge and giving them orders. "Berry Bowles ez de bigges' an' de fus' man in de line, an' he mus' lead de way an' y'-all des foller right erlong en es tracks. Berry, you mek fer dat pine ovah yonner on de ridge, an' I'm comin' 'long berhin' de las' man; an' de fus' nigger what bre'k ranks ez got me ter run ovah 'fo' he leave. I done gi' y'-all fair warnin'; an' ef anybody git dis sword stuck frough 'im, ain' my funer'l march!" As they are about to leave, a cannon blows up a short distance away and the Negroes scatter. They begin praying and soon a mighty revival is in progress, complete with spirituals. The platoon advances only at the command of a white officer with a pistol in his hand. Their conduct under fire, however, was not very exemplary. Isam later explains that as they were advancing a cannon ball landed nearby and the Negroes fled in terror. "Dey runned ober me, an' 'fo' I knowed what my name was, de groun' was full er guns an' tracks. I got on top er stump an' hollered loud ez I could holler, an' 'fo' Gord, de onliest nigger en sight was Berry, what done fell over er log, an' was des layin' dere prayin' fer somebody ter tell es Mas' George ter sen' de doctor quick. I knowed dere warn' no use er my stan'in' up dere fer fo' thousan' Yankees ter be shootin' at, an' I got down an' went 'long back, sorter singin' ter merse'f ter let folks know I warn' anxious ter leave." When he gets back to safe ground where the other Negroes are, he begins rationalizing their behavior and the need for him to stay behind the lines. "An' den hit come ter me dat ev'y nigger dere was worf er thousan' dollahs, an' some er dey marsters was po' white men, an' couldn' 'ford ter lose er nigger. So I said I reck'n Gen's Bragg an' Mas' Alec done look atter dat little bunch er Yankees out en front, an' I better stay back dere an' keep dem niggers an' waggins fum bein' runned off." Thus bravely standing guard duty behind the lines Isam figures he saved the Confederacy $32,000 worth of Negroes and a wagon train at Chickamauga.*

Uncle Remus, however, is better able to adapt to the demands of war than Isam. His is a much more serious contribution too. Although he remains behind to protect his white women, he briefly enters the war to save the life of his beloved master. Joel Chandler Harris records this Civil War adventure in "A Story of the War" (in *Uncle Remus*). In the sketch the old Negro tells Miss Theodosia Huntingdon, his employer's sister down from Vermont, of his war experiences. When the war first started, he says, "hit didn't strike me dat dey wuz enny war gwine on, en ef I hadn't sorter miss de nabers, en seed fokes gwine outer de way fer ter ax de news, I'd a 'lowed ter myse'f dat de war wuz 'way off 'mong some yuther country." Soon, however, the war came closer; and when all the white men were gone from the place, his "ole Miss" sent for him and said, "Remus, I ain't got nobody fer ter look arter de place but you." Pledging that his mistress could "des 'pen' on de ole nigger," he says he took over the plantation "en you better b'leeve I bossed dem han's." Sounding like his white master, he says he worked the slaves hard, but adds: "But dey wuz tuk keer un. Dey had plenty er cloze en plenty er grub, en dey wuz de fattes' niggers in de settlement."

He then proudly explains how he defended the plantation when the Yankees came. After hiding the cattle, horses, grain, and hogs, he says, "I put on my Sunday cloze en groun' my axe. Two whole days I groun' dat axe. De grinestone wuz in sight er de gate en close ter de big 'ouse, en dar I tuck my stan'." When the Yanks came they ransacked the place, but Uncle Remus took up a protective vigil near Ole Miss and Miss Sally. After the Federals left he took his gun to go see about the stock, but on the way he spied a Yankee sniper firing from a tree. As Remus watched, he suddenly saw his master riding down the road toward the sniper. He recalls his quick action: "I know'd dat man wuz gwineter shoot Mars Jeems ef he could, en dat wuz mo'n I could stan'. Manys en manys de time dat I nuss dat boy, en hilt 'im in dese arms, en toted 'im on dis back, en w'en I see dat Yankee lay dat gun 'cross a lim' en take aim at Mars Jeems I up wid my ole rifle, en shet my eyes en let de man have all she had." As Remus finishes this part of his story, his Northern listener asks indignantly, "Do you mean to say that you shot the Union soldier, when you knew he was fighting for your freedom?" But Uncle Remus is ready for her question. "Co'se, I know all about dat, en it sorter made cole chills run up my back; but w'en I see dat man take aim, en Mars Jeems gwine home ter Ole Miss en Miss Sally, I des disremembered all 'bout freedom en lammed aloose." The wounded soldier

---

* A different version of the Negro's conduct under fire is found in Thomas Wentworth Higginson, *Army Life in a Black Regiment*. Higginson's view of the Negro is admittedly biased, but he had occasion to observe the Negro as colonel in command of the first colored regiment mustered during the war, the First South Carolina Volunteers.

was cared for, the old Negro adds, by Miss Sally; and pointing to Miss Theodosia's brother, says "en now dar he is." Like almost all of Harris' work dealing with the war, this story shows how the war eventually united the nation more strongly than ever. The symbol of this union is the marriage of a Northern man and a Southern woman.

Like Uncle Remus, the slaves left behind on the plantation are usually accorded the responsibility—at least in fictional humor—of "protecting" or "looking after" the women. In addition, they break bad news of a loved one's death to the mistress (Sherwood Bonner, "Gran'mammy" in *Suwannee River Tales*, 1876), they take her to see a wounded son or husband (Jeannette Walworth, *Uncle Scipio*, 1896), and they constantly worry about the safety of their masters fighting far away from home. Jeannette Walworth's picture in *Southern Silhouettes* of a doting mammy was duplicated many times in humorous sketches: "What a despot she was! What a gentle, tart, coaxable, domineering old paradox, whom we children loved and feared extravagantly and unreasonably" (p. 133). When her master's son left for the war, she gave him a black quart bottle filled with her special preparation and said, "H'it's balsam apple and whisky. It's mighty good for cuts en bruises, en ef my chillun git hurt, Mammy won' be nigh 'em to ten' 'em lak she wants t' be, but you jes' rub dat balsam apple inter de place right quick en h'it mebbe be de savin' ub yo' libes, son. If you git out'n it, write to Mammy for some mo'" (p. 138). Thus Mammy figures that, in a sense, she can accompany her young master to the battlefield.

One of the infrequent treatments of the unfaithful Negro, however, is found in this same sketch. Mammy's husband deserts to Vicksburg, where he believes he will get "a guv'ment mule en ten acres er groun' by goin' arter it." Mammy is depressed by her husband's absence, and when her son leaves too, she cannot stand her lonesome cabin any longer and reluctantly follows them. Unable to stay away from her white people, however, she returns after the war to help them "reconstruct" their lives.

On the other hand, John T. Moore's stories of Negroes and the war are solidly and consistently in the faithful darky tradition. Paralleling the sentiments of Edwards' Isam are those of Moore's Dick in *Ole Mistis*, who, hearing the noise of a battle being fought near his master's plantation, asks indignantly, "Whut dese Yankees wanter cum down heah an' take our niggers 'way frum us fur ennyway? Whut we done to dem? All we ax 'em ter do is ter let us erlone." In this war sketch, "Dick," Moore becomes polemical, writing in such defensive passages as the following: "Where Dick got the sentiments he expressed I cannot say; but I do know that Dick was no exception to his race. Darkey like, he was for his home and his white people first, though the freedom of all his race lay on the other side." Seldom was a Southerner so explicit in his defense of "the peculiar institution" of the South. "Some day there is going to be a great monument put up in the South by the southern people. And on its top is going to be a negro—not the mythical slave with chains on him and terror in his face, which fool artists, who never saw a negro slave, and fool poets, who never heard one laugh, are wont to depict—but the jolly, contented, rollicking rascal that we knew and loved; the member of our household and sharer of our joys and sorrows. On its top, I say, there is going to be that kind of negro, as he was, and he is going to be represented in the act of picking cotton, with a laugh, while he refuses with scorn a gun with which to fight his master for his own freedom. When that is done, it will be the crowning monument of the age." Into these words Moore condensed a popular Southern—and national—attitude toward the slave in the postwar period. Using this attitude as a hypothesis, Southern humorists filled their writings with contented slaves.

The most devoted war Negroes of the lot are, naturally, those delineated by the arch-apologist for the South, Thomas Nelson Page. His Uncle Balla, in *Two Little Confederates,* is the epitome of the faithful slave during the war. When his mistress tells him that he is free to leave, he answers her with a puzzled question. "Hi, Mistis . . . whar is I got to go? I wuz born on dis place an' I 'spec' to die here, an' be buried right *yonder*"; and he points toward the graveyard and continues with a pledge: "Y'all sticks by us, and we'll stick by you" (pp. 49-50). Uncle Balla knew that the future was to be a trying time for both white and black Southerners and that in union there was strength.

The unenthusiastic reaction to freedom was often depicted comically. Opie Read's "An Ivory Smile" in *Odd Folks,* is said to be based on fact. A Kentucky planter before the war decides to make his favorite slave, Amos, a present of his freedom for Christmas. The owner recalls the scene in which he first said:

"Amos, I am going to give you something which many of the world's greatest men have died for, and for which any great man would shed his blood. Amos, I give you freedom."

He did not bound into the air, as I had expected; he wiped his mouth with the back of his hand, and quietly said: "I 'lowed you gwine gimme dat 'possum dog."

"What! You old rascal," I exclaimed, "would you rather have a dog than your freedom?"

He looked up and thus replied: "Er ole man kin hab comfort wid er 'possum dog, sah, but when freedom comes ter er ole man it makes him feel foolish."

Unlike most fictional Negroes, however, Amos made the most of his freedom; and during the war he saved his former owner's life and told him that at last he had forgiven him "fur not makin' me er present o' dat 'possum dog." To most postwar humorists the "good" Negro refused to exercise his new freedom during the war. Even if he left to seek "a guv'ment mule en ten acres er groun'," he returned before long with an empty stomach and a begging mouth.

The Poor Whites

Although Union sentiment was strong among poor whites in East Tennessee, Southwest Virginia, Northwest North Carolina, North Alabama and Mississippi, and Western Georgia, the poor white generally aligned himself with the slaveowner to present a united front when the war came.[9] Historians have posited many explanations for the phenomenon of the poor white fighting "the rich man's war": he was harangued by secessionist orators like William L. Yancey, he didn't like the thought of equality and competition with the Negro, and he did like excitement. Once in the army he was usually a good fighter—he had been shooting rabbits and squirrels since he was big enough to hold a gun in his hands—but he couldn't abide the strict military discipline, and desertion was very common. More likely than not, he had a good reason for deserting: his family was starving; consequently the deserter is most often presented sympathetically in postwar humor. In Joel Chandler Harris' *On the Plantation* a man who deserted to return to his starving family defines a deserter as one of "these here fellers what jines inter the army an' then comes home arter awhile without lief or license" (p. 138). Harris also treated the deserter in "At Teague Poteet's," in which he pictured Georgia crackers dodging Confederate conscript officers and usually outwitting them.

An Alabama cracker deserter is the subject of Samuel Minturn Peck's "Far from the Front," one of the *Alabama Sketches*. The Alabama local colorist notes the waning of enthusiasm for the war among the poor whites living in the hills of Western Alabama. In Biblical style Peck wrote of the hard times the poor women were having. "And it came to pass that many of the wives of the poor non-slaveowning whites who dwelt in the hills sometimes asked themselves if they were not paying too dearly for the possibility of some day owning a negro, and other benefits promised by secession." This sketch is about a man who deserts to his starving wife and children about the time the war ends. Because Lee surrendered before the man's absence was found out, no one ever knew of his desertion except his wife.

Another story by Peck, "Pap's Mules," tells how a cracker family's mules were saved from Yankee soldiers by the heroism of two small children. The poor Cline family was living life about the same as always, when the Widow Barbour, who delighted in terrifying people with her gossip of imminent Yankee raids, came by to warn them and to chastise them for going about life as usual. "The day o' wrath's at han', Susan Cline . . . an' you pore critters are washin' clo'es, churnin' milk, an' bilin' soap!" Having just come from the nearby village of Oakville, she describes for the Clines the ludicrous preparations being made there for defending the town. The villagers are not deluded into thinking they can successfully keep back the enemy, but to surrender the town without even a token struggle would be unthinkable—and dishonorable. The Clines don't appear to be upset by the widow's bad tidings; but that night their small boy saves their mules by taking them into the swamp in case the Yankees should come by.

Meanwhile Oakville is preparing for her heroic but futile defense. The mayor's patriotism reaches its high-water mark. "The old mayor was . . . proud. What was a war governor beside a raid mayor! To repulse the enemy had been beyond his expectation; and when it was discovered at daylight that they were fifteen hundred strong, while the Home Guard were but fifty, his honor remarked to a friend that no braver defense was recorded in the pages of history."

After the raid is over and the Yankees leave, the Widow Barbour conducts a survey of the damage done, hoping to find a lot; but she is especially disappointed to find little touched at the Clines'. "'The fence is all thar and the beegums is standin'. Nothin's tore down,' she sighed, regretfully. 'Howsomever, I don't hear no hens cacklin',' and her eyes brightened. 'But thar's the old black sow sunnin' herself agin the fence fat as ever,' she added sorrowfully." To her dismay she even finds the mules safe. She could glean no bad news at the Clines' to spread around the community. In fact, while she's there, John Cline returns from Oakville with startling information. "Word's come that Lee's surrendered, and the war's done." Many another suffering poor white considered that good news.

An incident in Sidney Lanier's *Tiger-Lilies* shows the widespread discontent with the war among poor whites. A Tennessee deserter's family is more concerned about what the neighbors will say than about the service he could have rendered the Confederacy had he stayed with the army. His brother gives him a tongue-lashing. "Hit don't make much diff'ence to me now, whether we whips the Yanks or they whips us. What good'll it do ef we do conquer 'em? Everybody'll be a-shoutin' an' a-hurrahin' an' they'll leave *us* out of the frolic, for we is kin to a deserter! An' the women'll be a-smilin' on them that has lived to git home, one minute, an' the next they'll be a-weepin' for them that's left dead in Virginny an' Pennsylvany an' Tennessy—but *you* won't git home, an' *you* won't be left dead nowhere; they cain't neither smile at you nor cry for you; what'll they do ef anybody speaks yer name? Gore Smallin, they'll lift their heads high an' we'll hang our'n low. They'll scorn ye an' we'll blush for ye" (p. 155). If this reaction is typical, family shame for deserters was common all over the South; but contrary to Lanier, desertion doesn't seem to have been much of a family stigma among poor whites.

In *Christmas Eve on Lonesome* by John Fox, Jr., "The Army of the Callahan" is a humorous sketch in which the author relates how the proprietor of a crossroads store in Western Virginia got protection against Union raiders from Kentucky. When the storekeeper heard that raiders were coming to destroy the property of Confederate sympathizers in the settlement, he pulled a hoax designed to save his property. The hoax was in the form of a forged order from Jefferson Davis to a gullible and vain old man in the community, commanding him to muster a home guard to protect the property of the Confederate citizens. The plan almost backfired on the merchant when the commander of the guard appointed him commissary general with the duty of supplying his army of free-loaders with rations. The property of the Rebels was not harmed when the raiders came through; but not because the home guard defended it, for the men broke ranks and fled in fear when the enemy first appeared.

Although Thomas Nelson Page concentrated in *Two Little Confederates* on the effect of the war on the slavocracy, he touched on the poor whites at the periphery of plantation life. Describing the poor whites who lived in the community known as Holetown, he wrote: "They were inoffensive people, and their worst vices were intemperance and evasion of the tax-laws" (p. 31). At the outbreak of the war most of the eligible men in Holetown enlisted in the Confederate service, but many of them soon tired of army discipline and returned to care for their poverty-stricken families. Consequently Holetown was frequently searched for deserters. The two little Confederates have many amusing adventures hunting the runaway men in the community, and they once capture a member of the conscript guard. The poor-white women warn their menfolk by blowing on a horn; they called it "jes' blowin' fur Millindy to come to dinner," but there must have been many Millindys because horns sounded all through the settlement when soldiers were near.

Many poor-white men took the war casually. When they fought, they fought like the devil, but when they got tired of it they went home. Sometimes they returned to fight again. In *Two Little Confederates* Page recorded the defiant words of a returned soldier to his commander. "Cun'l . . . I ain't no deserter. I ain't feared of bein' shot. Ef I was, I wouldn' 'a' come here now. I'm gwine wid you, an' I'm gwine back to my company; an' I'm gwine fight, ef Yankees gits in my way; but ef I gits tired, I's comin' home; an' tain't no use to tell you I ain't, 'cause I *is*,—an' ef anybody flings up to me that I's a-runnin' away, I'm gwine to kill 'em!" (p. 114). Knowing the man will make good his pledge and threat, the colonel agrees to his terms.

Not all poor whites took the war so lightly. In "The Bushwhackers" Mary Noailles Murfree told the story of a young mountaineer in Unionist East Tennessee who proudly fought in the Confederate army. To his mother's complaint that he was too young to enlist, he threatened, "I'll jes' set an' spin like a sure-enough gal ef ye won't let me go an' jine the army like a boy." One day a Rebel company camped nearby and he joined it. Saying goodby to his girl, he proudly announced, "An' I ain't no hand ter dodge bullets, nuther." In his company he was nicknamed Baby Bunting because of his youth, and he became popular with all the men, who often made him the butt of their good-humored pranks. The only cruelty in the sketch was the beating of Baby Bunting by one of his own cowardly comrades, which caused the boy to lose an arm. The Yanks were always mentioned favorably.

While her son was fighting for the Confederacy, the mother at home lamented his decision to join the Rebel side. She told a neighbor, "Ye know I war fur the Union, an' so war his dad. . . . My old man had been ailin' ennyhows, but this hyar talk o' bustin' up the Union—why, it jes' fairly harried him inter his grave. An' I 'lowed ez Hil'ry would be fur the Union, too, like everybody in the mountings ez hed good sense. But when a critter-company o' Confeds rid up the mounting one day Hil'ry he talk with some of 'em, an' he was war stubborn ever after. An' so he jined the critter-company."

After his arm was amputated, Hilary returned home where he found everyone frightened by bushwhackers, who were threatening the area. The boy's mother lent a note of unconscious humor to the tense situation. "It air powerful selfish, I know, ter hope the bushwhackers'll forage on somebody else's poultry an' sech, but somehows my own chickens seem nigher kin ter me than other folkses' be. I ain't never seen no sech ten-toed chickens ez mine nowhar." The men of the neighborhood, however, banded together and fought off the bushwhackers when they attacked. Like so much postwar fiction, the story ends on a note of religious sentiment. Men who had been through the hell of war supposedly had had a foretaste of the real hell and wanted to avoid going there.

In 1871 Dr. George W. Bagby, under the pseudonym Mozis Addums, published a poor white's "Histry uv the Waw" in the *Southern Magazine*.[10] Although the work is a masterpiece of irony, Mozis maintained in the "In-troducktory" that his only objective was to write for money. His history would be a departure from the usual. "Far frum imitating the exampul of the Waw Department at Washintun, and tellin uv the truth recklissly and regardliss of konsekenses, I shall not hesitate, whenever it suit my puppus, to tell the most infunnul lies that ever issued frum mortul man. . . . I make out my kase in my oan mind befo startin, and then wuk the facts up to it." His history, he continued, would be partial to the South, "becaws I don't know ennything about the other side (altho' I've red thar ofishul repotes, and thar still mo reliabul newspapers) and don't want to know nuthin 'bout it." The book would also be "the only trewly vallibul historrikul Wuk which has apeard since the Book uv Jobe—which he was a good histoarianer, be-caws he confined himself to a narrytiv uv his oan suffrins, with a okashunal excurshun discriptiv uv wild asses, waw-hosses, and the hevinly boddies." By offending as many people as he could, he thought his history would gain notoriety and thus a large sale. "The world is full of corns, made to be trod on, espeshly by histoarians uv thar own times; and I be durn ef I dont inten to tred on as menny uv 'em as I possibly kin. But Confedrit corns, I shell tred litely on um." Mozis' history of the war, therefore, is written exclusively from a Southern viewpoint.

The Folks at Home

The Southern noncombatants during the Civil War frequently suffered as much as the soldiers. The women, the children, and the aged left behind were often without protection and adequate supplies. What food they had was subject to be commandeered by foraging soldiers of both sides. To keep family valuables safe they had to be buried, and livestock had to be hidden in swamps; sometimes even these precautions were not effective. After enemy troops passed through with their flaming torches, many families did not even have a house to sleep in. In spite of deprivation and separation from loved ones, however, postwar humorists could still find humorous subject matter in the folks that stayed behind.

If memoirs of prison life were usually grim, a few were amusing. During the war Jane Tandy Cross was imprisoned for her Southern sentiments. Out of her prison experiences she wrote a series of amusing and pathetic letters dealing with prison life which she published as *Six Months Under a Cloud*. The Virginian Sara Agnes Pryor recorded her Civil War experiences in *Reminiscences of Peace and War* (1904), her most popular book. An indication of the book's humor is Ellen Glasgow's mention of it in a letter to a friend: "Last night I sat up spellbound until I finished it, beginning with laughter and ending in real tears. . . . The tragedy of it I can understand, for it is not difficult to be tragic—but the delicious, piquant, never-failing humor— the humor that brightens tears, this, I confess, has taken me completely captive."[11] Women writers and women readers did much to promote the vogue of such crying humor in the postwar South.

One of the most popular Southern writers, Thomas Nelson Page, wrote many stories set during the war; but none has been more frequently read and enjoyed than *Two Little Confederates*. This book is an entertaining account of boys' life on a Virginia plantation during the war. The patriotic fervor of the little Rebels, Frank and Willy, leads them to organize drills, using wooden guns made for them by Uncle Balla, the faithful old Negro driver. A dozen or so little black boys fill in the ranks. Their exciting war adventures include catching a Rebel soldier raiding their hen house, and being caught by Yankee soldiers. One of their not unusual pastimes was observing battles fought near their home. One day, while they were watching a battle and were a little too close to the front, bullets got to flying near them and the colored boys with them.

"What's them things 'zip-zippin' 'round my ears?" asked one of the negro boys.
"Bullets," said Frank, proud of his knowledge.
"Will they hurt me if they hit me?"
"Of course they will. They'll kill you."
"I'm gwine home," said the boy, and off he started with a trot (p. 133).

Harris' *On the Plantation: A Story of a Georgia Boy's Adventures During the War* is based at least partly on the author's war experiences as a printer's devil on the Joseph Addison Turner plantation in Middle Georgia. Most of the humor in the novel comes from the "Georgia boy," Joe Maxwell, who was full of pranks and tricks and had a reputation for humor. The main business of the book is to show plantation life—often austere, dangerous, and tragic but also exciting, humorous, and rewarding—along the route of Sherman's march to the sea.

Samuel M. Peck's local stories of the Civil War have a gentle humor and an absence of sectional bitterness characteristic of Southern humor written after Reconstruction. Two of the stories in his *Alabama Sketches* are set on the home front—"The Maid of Jasmindale" and "Under the White Rose-Tree." The first is the love story of a returning Confederate soldier who visits an Alabama friend and falls in love with his sister. The young couple's romance goes smoothly until the Alabama belle overhears her lover and her brother laughing and talking about Katie, and assuming this to be her lover's Kentucky girl, she shuns him and becomes incommunicado when he's around. When the Kentuckian discovers the cause of her strange behavior, he puts their romance back on course by laughingly explaining: "Why—Katie is the name of a cannon in our battery. The boys used to name the guns for their sweethearts. I named my gun Katie because I was ashamed to confess I had no sweetheart." He seals their reconciliation by chiding: "And you were jealous of a gun!"

The plot of "Under the White Rose-Tree" is concerned with how a middle-aged bachelor is made to realize his love for a next-door spinster by the exigencies of war. Miss Melinda entrusts Professor Winston with her grandmother's gold thimble to bury just before the Yankees raid the town. After elaborate preparations he finally decides on putting the thimble and his prize watch in a tobacco box and burying it under his rose tree. The Yankee raiders come and one is billeted on the professor's front porch. The first night after the professor buries the treasure he has a nightmare: he dreams that his watch is talking to him and reminding him that it hasn't been wound. The watch is in danger of running down—something that hasn't happened in thirty-five years! Awaking from his bad dream, the professor steals from the house, digs up the box, winds the watch, and replaces it in its cache. While he is doing this he is being watched by the good-for-nothing son of his colored cook, who quickly goes to the hiding place to steal the treasure. Another person, however, has also been watching the nocturnal prowling, the Yankee sentinel bedded on the front porch; and he intercepts the Negro boy and returns the box to the professor before he leaves the next day. This little serio-comic episode makes the professor and his neighbor aware of their affection for each other. The sketch contains no hint of bitterness against the Union troops. The hero of the story, in fact, is the Yankee soldier who saves the professor's watch and his ladyfriend's thimble.

As unlikely as it may seem, humor played a significant part in the bloody epic that was the American Civil War. It was humor which helped to keep the South fighting against insurmountable odds for four years. In the face of hunger, inadequate clothing and supplies, and superior numbers, the Southern soldier was sustained by his sense of humor. W. W. Blackford testified to the importance of laughter to the Rebel soldier: "War develops an infinite amount of wit and humor among soldiers. In every company there were aspirants for the honor of being the 'funny man' of the command, whose study it was to get off good jokes; and between the companies of a regiment there was rivalry as to whose man should produce the best and make a regimental reputation. Every conceivable subject on the line of march was made to contribute to this harmless amusement and the officers encouraged it, submitting good-humoredly to being sometimes the victims themselves. The clatter of tongues and merry laughter along a dusty road would make one think they belonged to the weaker sex, bless their dear talkative hearts" (p. 146).

Post-Civil-War humor about the war was many-faced and many-toned. Certain general characteristics, however, emerge from the potpourri. Throughout the era 1865-1914 the Civil War was second only to the Negro as subject for Southern humor. Newspaper and magazine columns were filled with the humor of the war. Novels, sketches, memoirs, and short stories frequently used war themes. Unlike that written during the war, this later humor was likely to be more conciliatory than condemnatory and defiant. It was a humor that pointed with pride to the gallantry of the South's fight for independence, but it also admitted the postwar need to convert the swords into plowshares. Although not generally as realistic as the earlier humor of the Longstreet school or that written during the war, it was the most consistently realistic of the postwar period. Realism bordering on naturalism is especially prominent in the memoirs of men like Sam Watkins and Carlton McCarthy, who had served in the ranks. Pathos and religious sentiment were other elements of war writing, often juxtaposed with vestiges of the coarse humor of before the war.

In the humor the slave was usually pictured as the Faithful Darky, who accompanied his master to war or stayed at home to tend the plantation and protect "Ol' Mistis" from the Yankees and unruly free Negroes. He would have no truck with the invaders who were trying to take him away from his rightful owners. Some slaves, like Harry S. Edwards' Isam, intervened in the war itself but failed ludicrously to become good soldiers. Others, like Harris' Uncle Remus, supported the Cause on the home front.

Although the poor white living in the mountainous areas of the South was likely to be Union in sentiment, the majority of the poor whites supported the Confederacy. They fought valiantly under slaveowners to protect a regime in which they had very little vested interest. In humor they were typically depicted as good and brave soldiers, but not very responsible or reliable ones. The poor-white deserter, in fact, became a familiar type in the newspapers and magazines.

73

The Smiling Phoenix

The War for Southern Independence was the American Iliad—full of tragedy, heroism, pathos, sacrifice, hatred, and humor. Some postwar Southern humorists pointed up a defiant pride. Thomas Nelson Page, for example, in *The Burial of the Guns* had a Confederate sergeant write a note which reads: "We aint surrendered; just disbanded, and we pledges ourselves to teach our children to love the South and General Lee; and to come when we're called anywheres an' anytime, so help us God" (p. 80). But a much more realistic and representative attitude was taken by Sam Watkins. Relating a cock fight in Atlanta in which the rooster named Southern Confederacy (Fed for short) was killed, he allegorized: "He was a dead rooster; yea, a dead cock in the pit. Tom went and picked up his rooster, and said, 'Poor Fed, I loved you; you used to crow every morning at daylight to wake me up. I have carried you a long time, but, alas! poor Fed, your days are numbered, and those who fight will sometimes be slain. Now, friends, conscripts, countrymen, if you have any tears to shed, prepare to shed them now. I will not bury Fed. The evil that roosters do lives after them, but the good is often interred with their bones. So let it be with Confed. Confed left no will, but I will pick him, and fry him, and dip my biscuit in his gravy. Poor Fed, Confed, Confederacy, I place one hand on my heart and one on my head, regretting that I have not another to place on my stomach, and whisper, softly whisper, in the most doleful accents, Good-bye, farewell, a long farewell'" (pp. 188-89). Most writers acknowledged that, like the namesake rooster, the Confederacy was dead beyond resurrection. The task for the living generation was, as General Lee urged, to make the South a better section within the Union. The humorists set about their work.

Notes

1. W. Stewart, *Spirit of the South*, 107.
2. *Library of Southern Literature*, IX, 3851.
3. "The Civil War," 11.
4. *Old Si's Sayings*, 115.
5. Botkin, *Southern Folklore*, 12.
6. *Ibid.*, 242-44.
7. King & Derby, *Camp-Fire Sketches*, 560-62.
8. *Library of Southern Literature*, V, 1906.
9. Dowdey, *Experiment in Rebellion*, 379-80.
10. VIII (Jan., 1871), 70-72. It ran through the year.
11. *Library of Southern Literature*, X, 4276.

3. Reconstruction

SURELY IF THE WAR WAS TRAGIC, its aftermath in the South was more so. To extreme deprivation were added misrule and persecution. In Virginia hill dialect Mozis Addums, telling his "History uv the Waw," described Reconstruction: "It is a consoundid hard thing to git knocked down and stompt on, and then git up and pull out a very small pockit-puss and pay the man whar knockt you down everry cent you've got in the world; but it is the fate uv nations, and sich is life."[1] Just as during the war, humor came to the rescue, dispelling somewhat the gloom of those dark days. Writers whose humorous works touched on Reconstruction included Charles H. Smith, George W. Bagby, Joel Chandler Harris, Sidney Lanier, Jeannette Walworth, and Sam W. Small. Sherwood Bonner's *Like Unto Like* (1878) and George Washington Cable's *John March, Southerner* (1894) are but two of the many novels dealing with Reconstruction. In *Like Unto Like* Miss Bonner, for example, portrayed the types of a Southern town on the eve of the election of 1876.

75

The Smiling Phoenix

Through his cracker mouthpiece Bill Arp, Charles H. Smith commented with humorous cynicism, but with an underlying seriousness, on the attempt of the North to reconstruct its conquered province. His letter to "Mr. Artemus Ward, Showman," dated September 1, 1865, and reprinted in *Bill Arp, So Called,* was one of the first Southern reactions in humor to the loss of the war. The Louisville *Courier-Journal* said of it, "It was the first chirp of any bird after the surrender, and gave relief and hope to thousands of drooping hearts."[2] He wrote Artemus Ward that he'd been wanting to say something to someone "to soften down my feelin's" and to keep from exploding. In the letter he called the imprisonment of Southern leaders "a blamed outrage" and was generally very critical of the conduct of the victors. Although a good Confederate during the war, now he says he's a good Union man. But this doesn't mean that Bill Arp is ashamed of his part in the war or that he will grovel in the ruins at his master's feet—not at all! His pride is screamingly evident. "I've dun tuk the oath, and I'm gwine to keep it, but as for my being subjergated and humilyated, and amalgamated and enervated, as Mr. Chase says, it ain't so—nary time. I ain't ashamed of nuthin, neather— ain't repentin—ain't axin for no one hoss, short-winded pardin. . . . I tell you, my friend, we are the poorest peepul on the face of the yearth—but we are poor and proud. We made a bully fite, selah, and the whole Amerikan nation ought to feel proud of it." The letter seems as challenging and defiant as it is conciliatory, but such a mixed tone reflected the feelings of most Southerners in the fall of 1865. If, coming from a recently defeated enemy, its tone is sharp, it should be remembered that the South was just beginning to feel a military occupation harsher than any the nation would ever impose on a foreign enemy. In view of this, it is perhaps remarkable that the letter contains only honest indignation and little bitterness. Throughout the period, Smith's use of the Bill Arp personality allowed him to express his opinions freely about the course of Reconstruction, and this he did.

Virginia, as well as Georgia, had its humorist writing words of cheer in the midst of ruin. "Dr. George W. Bagby made Virginia smile at his humor," wrote Douglas S. Freeman in the Richmond *News Leader* (October 10, 1923), "when smiles were as rare as gold in the land of Confederate money." J. L. King quotes Freeman's tribute to Bagby's contribution to postwar Virginia: "One can imagine how Virginians who were rigid in the struggle for a living would relax as they saw Dr. Bagby coax humor from their diet, their courtships, their large families and their diversions. From relaxation came laughter and new hope. Little as it is realized, Dr. Bagby is to be included in any intelligent list of the half dozen men who did most for Virginia in the years immediately following the war" (p. 166). This is, indeed, high praise. It is not merely the overenthusiasm of a minor writer's biographer; for had not Smith's Bill Arp and Bagby's Mozis Addums continued to write their amusing observations in dialect, many a Southerner would have had no cause to laugh.

Although an acceptance of defeat was implicit in most postwar humor, there were a few unreconstructed Rebels who refused to lay down the sword. In humor their sentiments break out in such a poem as "I'm a Good Old Rebel," by Major Innes Randolph. The hatred for the Yankees and what they stood for was so intense it seems pathetic and funny today. The opening lines of the poem, which became a popular song, state clearly the position of the writer.

> *Oh, I'm a good old Rebel,*
> *Now that's just what I am;*
> *For this "fair land of freedom"*
> *I do not care a damn.*

Beginning with this omnibus assertion, the author becomes specific and lists what he most hates.

> *I hates the Constitution,*
> *This great Republic too;*
> *I hates the Freedman's Bureau.*

Then he rises to his climax.

> *But the lyin' thievin' Yankees,*
> *I hates 'em wuss and wuss.*[3]

A much more realistic and less emotional reaction to Reconstruction is found in Joel Chandler Harris' *Gabriel Tolliver.* Dedicated to James Whitcomb Riley, the novel is critical only of unreasonable radicals and not of Reconstruction generally. The main plot concerns the murder of an unscrupulous Union League organizer, and the radicals' accusation of the young Gabriel Tolliver as a party to the crime. The most active character, however, is the humorous Georgia cracker, Billy Sanders, whose mirth permeates the entire book. Home from the war, Billy helps straighten things out in Shady Dale, the scene of the novel. This includes helping Gabriel escape from his Federal captors and proving his innocence. But Billy's service to the community went beyond being a mere "straighten-outer" of things. Although never an avid Rebel, his time in the army afforded him a rich background to draw on for humor. "He had mingled with public men, and, as he himself contended, had been 'closeted' with one of the greatest men the country ever produced—the reference being to Mr. Lincoln. Mr. Sanders had to tell over and over again the story of how he and Frank Bethune didn't kidnap the President; and he brought home hundreds of rich and racy anecdotes that he had picked up in the camp. In those awful days when there was little ready money to be had, and business was at a standstill, and the courts demoralised, and the whole social fabric threatening to fall to pieces, it was Mr. Billy Sanders who went around scattering cheerfulness and good-humour as carelessly as the children scatter the flowers they have gathered in the fields" (p. 112). Kind references to Lincoln inserted throughout their work by Harris and other humorists helped the South to swallow the bitter pill of Reconstruction. Harris seldom gave more than cursory treatment to unreconstructed Rebels. One of the few in *Gabriel Tolliver* is the title character's grandmother, whose sentiments are, "Show me a piece of blue cloth, and I'll tear it to pieces" (p. 312). Sometimes radical Reconstruction caused more intersectional ill will than the war had.

The Conquered Province

Many humorists pictured radical misrule in the South in realistic, if often exaggerated, sketches. Most of them were extremely bitter about the wholesale disfranchisement of white Southern voters, and vented their feelings in excoriating attacks on radical rule. Although Northern humorists had patriotically stood for the Union during the war, many had their eyes opened to the intolerable political conditions in the South. On December 21, 1870, the Union Springs *Times* printed the following excerpt from a lecture on Reconstruction delivered in Boston by "the distinguished Ohio Radical" Petroleum V. Nasby: "I saw cadetships sold for dollars. I met judges of courts in the Southern States who, ten years ago, were hostlers in livery stables in the North, and whose knowledge of criminal law was gained from standing in the prisoner's dock."

Criticism of corrupt home-grown politicians was often direct attack. In his *Reports* Joseph Gault lashed them. "As to statesmen who is [*sic*] pushing themselves into the lawmaking powers of the State in 1865, after Lee's surrender, and raised their salary from $5 per day to $9—I say march them in another band of Pope's priests and kings, adulterers and fornicators, beggars and swindlers for taking $9 per day and making poor soldiers pay $2 per year for laying on the tented fields of battle four years and returned without one dollar in their pocket, and their wives and children destitute" (p. 55). Without the help of scalawags in the Southern governments, Reconstruction would certainly have been shorter and less severe.

The following paragraphs gleaned at random from the pages of the Union Springs weekly show the reaction of Southerners to Reconstruction politics.

A negro in Virginia is gradually turning white. During the seven days fight around Richmond, he observed a small white spot on his arm. This has increased until one-third of his body is white, and the skin is as soft as an infant's. The Louisville *Courier* thinks he ought to hurry and register before it is too late (July 17, 1867).

We learn that one negro shot another on Tuesday upon the plantation of Mr. A. Mabson, a few miles from town. The wound is serious. For the Sentinel's information, we would say that it is not known, whether this was an "attempted assassination of a Union man by bitter rebels" or not. We are inclined to the belief that it was only an attempt of one negro to kill another—nothing more (October 2, 1867).

Perhaps the fretful tone of the paragraphs can be better understood when read in the light of the paper's official policy, stated in a subscription advertisement in the October 2, 1867, issue. "Politically it will constantly struggle, without fear or favor, for the uncompromised rights of the south and will aim in the future to be what it has been in the past, THE WHITE MAN'S ORGAN, opposed in toto to mongrelism come in what shape it may." Newspapers in larger towns and cities of the South were not usually so partisan. There was much in Southern life, however, to be partisan about.

With most qualified former Confederates ineligible to hold office, political positions were often filled by illiterate white trash. Many such white Southerners who worked with the Yankee victors were called "scalawags" by ex-Confederates. According to W. C. Elam, writing in 1871, "Scalawags are verminous, shabby, scabby, scrubby, scurvy cattle." The scalawag, the Southerner continued, "renounces all his previous professions and practices, slinks from his own color and kindred, and foregathers with dirty freedmen, to gain whose favor and votes he maligns all respectable citizens and incites the colored rabble to all sorts of absurd pretensions, or worse, to deeds of violence and blood." Elam concluded his character study by indicting the scalawag as the cause as well as the consequence of the war.[4]

James J. McDonald in his *Life in Old Virginia* offers a comic account of a court presided over by an illiterate justice of the peace. The case involved an assault on a constable in which the defendant threw a bucket of slop water on the constable's head from a second-story window. The trial was a farce because the justice knew nothing at all about law. When the plaintiff and defendant presented themselves at the justice's house, his wife told them he was "out in the low ground a' grubbin' an' burnin' bresh." She called him with two long blasts from "a conch shell horn." When, during the trial held under a big pine tree, the scalawag justice was asked about a certain law, he admitted, "I don't know much about the book laws. I never went to school but two days in my life. It *rained like all scissors* both days, and the teacher didn't come nary day of the two, so I quit wastin' time and went to work, and I've been at work ever since. I'll think this thing over, an' let ye know." The man had become a justice because he had taken no part in the war and had held no office before the war, and was thus eligible under the Reconstruction Acts. The attorney for the plaintiff was a recent law-school graduate. The defendant had no attorney, but was represented by friends, one of whom scored a victory when the young lawyer quoted Blackstone to make a point. The friend of the defendant objected to quoting Blackstone on the laws of Virginia because "everybody in the county knows that *Blackstone is no lawyer,* but only the keeper of a summer resort on Blackstone's Island, up the Potomac River, on the Maryland side." The gullible magistrate agreed. About that time six of his honor's young shoats broke loose from the pig pen, and the defendant's friends asked if they might help catch them. This done "after numerous upsets, and tumbles over one another, and amusing slips of 'tail holds'," the grateful justice granted their request for a postponement until *"some more convenient date,"* which never came (pp. 183-88).

Opie Read presented a somewhat more favorable picture of Reconstruction government in *The Carpetbagger,* a novel he collaborated on with Frank Pixley. The book concerns the carpetbagger governor of Mississippi, Melville Crance, a former Chicago auctioneer who had come South after the war to seek his fortune. Rather than perpetuate carpetbag and scalawag misrule, he rebels against several of his cronies and graciously relinquishes the governor's chair to a duly elected Democrat, who is both a native Mississippian and a Confederate war hero. The fictional governor even falls in love with a proud Southern widow, and after his regeneration, he wins her hand.

A not so attractive portrait of the carpetbagger is Hotchkiss in Harris' *Gabriel Tolliver.* Hotchkiss is a black villain unrelieved by any shade of brown; he is the Radical Carpetbagger incarnate. Using a scathing language unusual for him, Harris wrote: "He belonged to the Peace Society, and yet nothing would have pleased him better than an uprising of the blacks, followed by the shedding of innocent blood. . . . He held the Southern people responsible for American slavery, and would have refused to listen to any statement of facts calculated to upset his belief. He was narrow-minded, bigoted, and intensely in earnest" (pp. 290-91). In the novel the mild-mannered Harris suggested that the North and the South would never learn to understand and appreciate each other until such extremists on both sides were silenced. Harris did his share in fiction by having Hotchkiss shot by a secret assassin.

For the many radical Mohammeds coming South offering salvation to the freedman, Allah was the Republican party. These men of destiny tried to instill in the Negro a love of and awe for the political party that had freed them. Many of these young radicals were well educated and harangued the former slaves with an oratorical style and language incomprehensible, but impressive, to the illiterate Negro. Myrta Lockett Avary in *Dixie After the War* gave an account of a young carpetbagger addressing a group of Richmond Negroes in 1867.

Dear Friends: I rejoice to find myself in this noble company of patriots. I see before me men and women who are bulwarks of the nation; ready to give their money, to work, to die, if need be, for freedom. Freedom, my friends, is another name for the great Republican Party. ("Hise yo' mouf tellin' dat truf!" "Dat's so!" "Halleluia!" "Glory be tuh Gawd!") The Republican Party gave you freedom and will preserve it inviolate! (Applause; whispers: "What dat he spoken 'bout?" "Sho use big words!" "Dat man got sense. He know what he talkin' 'bout ef we don't!") That party was unknown in this grand old State until a few months ago. It has been rotten-egged!—("Now ain't dat a shame!") although its speakers have only advocated the teachings of the Holy Bible. ("Glory Halleluia!" "Glory to de Lamb!" "Jesus, my Marster!") The Republican Party is your friend that has led you out of the Wilderness into the Promised Land!

The glories and halleluias reached a climax, and two shouting sisters were carried out. "Disshere gitten' too much lak er 'ligious meetin' tuh suit me," a sinner observed (p. 230). Although not consciously funny, Republican agents used many such ludicrous appeals in trying to bind the freedman to the radical party.

The freedman looked to the Republican party for the promised salvation— and he was exploited. He was given the vote, only to have it controlled by his liberators. He was given political office, only to have it manipulated by his white mentors. But the Southern humorists knew where the blame lay, and in their writings the Negro is commonly shown to be an innocent pawn in the hands of unscrupulous carpetbaggers and scalawags. In *Gabriel Tolliver*, for example, Harris has the ex-Confederate Major Tomlin Perdue lecture Gabriel. "The trouble is that some of the hot-headed youngsters want to hold the poor niggers responsible . . . and the niggers are no more to blame than the chicken in a new-laid egg. Don't forget that, Tolliver. I wouldn't give my old Minervy Ann for a hundred and seventy-five thousand of these white thieves and rascals; and Jerry Tomlin, fool as he is, is more of a gentleman than any of the men who have misled him" (p. 261).

Nevertheless, the easily impressed and tractable Negro was corrupted, and his corruption was recorded. A historian used humor to illustrate the misrule of Reconstruction legislatures. "A North Carolina negro legislator was found on one occasion chuckling as he counted some money. 'What are you laughing at, Uncle?' he was asked. 'Well, boss, I'se been sold 'leben times in my life and dis is de fust time I eber got de money.' "[5]

Negroes who held high governmental positions were frequently the object of the Southern humorist's satire. Opie Read, for example, printed a satirical poem, "The Negro Judge," in the *Arkansaw Traveler* of May 5, 1883. The following is a quatrain from the poem:

> *I sets all day on my bench in de shade,*
> *Widout any thought ob de hoe an' de spade,*
> *An' de plow an' de mule, an' de maul an' de wedge,*
> *For de folks hab made out ob me a jedge.*

On December 17, 1882, Read satirized the colored justice of the peace.

Col. Jasit and Capt. Fomas were arraigned before a colored justice of the peace, having been arrested on a charge of committing a robbery. The prisoners pleaded guilty, and the justice with great solemnity asked:
"Col. Jasit, yer acknowledges de crime?"
"Yes, your honor."
"How much ob de money did yersef git?"
"Five hundred dollars."
"Capt. Fomas, yersef is guilty, is yer?"
"Yes, sir."
"How much ob de money did yersef git?"
"Only ten dollars, your honor."

81

The Smiling Phoenix

"Ah, dis flings a new light on de subjeck. Col. Jasit, have a cheer and sot down, sah. Capt. Fomas, stan' war yer is. De law is mighty plain in such matters. Colonel, yer got five hundred dollars, an' is entitled ter de respeck ob dis court. Captain, yersef is a petty thief an' is 'titled ter no respeck. Colonel, yersef is honorably discharged. Captain, I sends yer ter jail, sah. I wants yer all ter un'erstan' dat when yer monkeys wid dis nigger yer monkeys wid a man."

Sweet and Knox, the authors of *On a Mexican Mustang*, commented humorously on the civil rights granted the Negro in Texas.

As far as depriving the negro of his vote is concerned, white Democrats have no such desire. On the contrary, they sometimes encourage the colored voter to vote as often, and in as many different places, as is possible on election-day.

In conclusion, I will state that there is in Texas a disposition, on the part of some of the most influential Democrats, to do everything in their power to improve the colored race; and the fact that in the larger cities, and particularly in Houston, many of the negroes are nearly white, should certainly convince the most skeptical that there is no prejudice against the race (p. 637).

When this picaresque book was published (1883), however, Southern whites had regained most of their former political power—sometimes by using "radical" tactics.

In *Uncle Scipio* Jeannette Walworth exposed the abuse of the jury system during Reconstruction. In selecting jurymen for a trial a lawyer asked a Negro prospective juror if he had ever served on a jury, to which he replied, "Oncet," adding, "It were when ol' Dave Rooney kilt his wife. The jedge he try mek we bring in a verdic' uv manslaughter in de fus' degree, but we wur'n big 'nough fools to call killin' a woman manslaughter, so we all twelve 'gree unanimous on 'accidental deaf,' an' got de ol' man off. Some folks is rank ongrateful in this worl'. You think ol' Dave ever gin any one of us so much as a sweet tater for gittin' him off? No, sir, not the wroppin' uv a finger" (p. 258).

A poem included by McDonald in *Life in Old Virginia*, "Lookin' Fo' de Candeedate," expresses the enthusiasm and naïveté of most freedman voters.

> *Jes' befo' de 'lection*
> *He cum soon an' late,*
> *Now I'se gittin' lonesome*
> *Waitin' at de gate.*
> *Mistuh! can yo' tell me*
> *Whar is dat Can-dee-date?*
>
> *Hope de Lawd will spar' him,*
> *His talk was powerful great.*
> *I 'spect he'll do a heap*
> *Now fo' dis ol' state.*
> *Mistuh! please do tell me*
> *Whar is dat Can-dee-date?*

This gullible voter awaiting the fruition of campaign pledges can be taken as symbolic of all the postwar Negroes who were promised everything and delivered nothing.

Probably the most critical commentator on radical Reconstruction policy among the humorists was Charles H. Smith. His first caustic denunciations of Reconstruction plans came in *Bill Arp, So Called* (pp. 140-48), published in 1866. Commenting on immediate postwar conditions in the South, he wrote: "Well, if the war is over, what's the use of fillin up our towns and cities with soldiers any longer? . . . The fact is, General Sherman and his caterpillars made such a clean sweep of everything, I don't see much to reconstruct." Nevertheless, he made a counterproposal for reconstructing the South. "There wasn't nothin to do but jes to go off and let us alone. We've got plenty of statesmen—plenty of men for governor." As a qualified man for governor he named Joseph Brown, who, he says, is "standin at the door with his hat off."

Of the policies in effect, he singled out "that oath about gittin letters" which extended even to women. Coming to the defense of Southern womanhood, he warned, "They can't vote, nor they can't preach, nor hold office, nor play soldier, nor muster, nor wear breeches, nor ride straddle, nor cuss, nor chaw tobacco, nor do nothing hardly but talk and write letters. . . . Better leave the women alone."

It was ridiculous, he advised, to try to reconstruct Southern whites when the Federal government hadn't even succeeded in reconstructing the Negro—even with the aid of the Freedman's Bureau. He wagered, "I'll bet a possum that some of 'em steals my wood this winter or freezes to death. Freedman's buro? freedman's humbug I say."

Bill Arp made it plain that he was no slavery agitator. In fact, he wrote, "Nobody wants any more slavery. If the abolitionists had let us alone we would have fixed it up right a long time ago, and we can fix it up now." He added an argument used since ante-bellum days: "Our people have got a heap more feelin for the poor nigger than any abolitionist." He backed up this assertion by boasting that although Rome (Georgia) was a poor town, he would bet that more money could be raised there among the white people to build a Negro church than the $37 it took "the Boston Christians" three weeks to raise.

Although occasionally making overtures to the North, the dominant tone of the book is defiant. In such language as the following, Smith made it clear that he would not be humbled by Yankee threats: "Who's sorry? Who's repenting? Who ain't proud of our people? Who loves our enemies? Nobody but a durned sneak. I say let 'em hang and be hanged to 'em, before I beg 'em for grace." Implicit, however, in his proud protests is a plea for mercy.

Harking back to the war, he attacked Southern "tories," who for selfish reasons had pledged loyalty to the Union. He proposed a barter. "We want to trade 'em off. By hoky, we'll give two of 'em for one copperhead, and ax nothin to boot."

Complaining about Northern journalists who were really agitators, he attacked "newspaper scribblers who slip down to the edge of Dixey every twenty-four hours, and peep over at us on tip-toe," and then run back home shouting: "He ain't dead. . . . Don't withdraw the soljers, but send down more troops immegeately." Singling out one popular Northern periodical, he wrote: "And here's your 'Harper's Weekly' a-headin all sich—a-gassin lies and slanders in every issue. . . . Wish old Stonewall had cotched these Harpers at their ferry. . . . We'd a-made baptists of them sertin. . . ."

Taking all things into consideration, however, he decided "there's a heap of things to be thankful for." He listed specifically: "I'm thankful the war is over— that's the big thing. Then I'm thankful I ain't a black republican pup. I'm thankful that Thad Stevens and Sumner and Phillips . . . ain't no kin to *me*. I'm thankful for the high privilege of hatin all such. I'm thankful I live in Dixey, in the State of Georgia, and our Governor's name ain't Brownlow. Poor Tennessee!" Scalawag governor of Tennessee, William G. Brownlow was disdained by most Southerners. Bill's commentary on the restrictive laws in Tennessee regarding former Confederates came in a verse couplet: "Sweet Land of Liberty, of thee / I could not sing in Tennessee."

Bill Arp's belief in Southern solidarity led him to attack the Chattanooga *Gazette* for its "exaltations of Northern bravery and Southern treason." But he extended the hand of reconciliation—with, however, a requirement. "When you make an effort to convince Mr. Harper's Weekly and the Black Republicans that our people, from General Lee and Mr. Davis down to the high privates, are just as good and brave and honorable as they are, I'll harmonize with you." Then he decided that perhaps the paper should do some harmonizing within its own state because, he observed, Rome was being overrun by refugees deserting Tennessee.

In "Bill Arp Addresses His Constituents" he expressed his thanks for having been elected to the Georgia Senate. Then on a less serious note he said that the Senate had been busy trying to figure out "whether our poor innocent children, born durin the war, were all illegal and had to be born over agin or not. This last pint are much unsettled, but our women are advised to be calm and sereen." Then on the more explosive subject of the radical Republicans, he wrote that he didn't encourage cussing in anyone, but, "If there is in all history a good excuse and a proper subject, it is upon them heartless, soulless, bowelless, gizzardless, fratrisidal, suisidal, parasidal, sistercidal, abominabul, contemptibul, disgustabul individuals." He ended his avalanche of abusive words by concluding that the Civil War was "the hardes war to wind up that history records." Touching on the subject of suffrage, he stated that he didn't understand the logic of not allowing Negroes to vote in Connecticut, where there are so few, and of insisting that they vote in Georgia, where there are so many. He added, though, that perhaps he didn't know all the facts; but one thing he did know was that "as sure as I am two foot high a nigger is a nigger I don't care where you smell him." He concluded his letter to the electorate on a note of hope. "My fellow-people, let me in conclusion congratulate you on having a governor once more, as is a governor. Oh there is life in the old land yet, and by and by we'll transport them black Republicans into the African desert, and put 'em teaching Hottentots the right of suffrage."

A letter which is largely a defense of the Southern right to secede is "Bill Arp to His Old Friend." The friend is John Happy, then living in Nashville, "where you can study Paradise Lost without a Book." He admitted that the South wasn't much then, "but we did have sovereign States before the war." He appealed to the past to show the right of secession. "From the time of Hamilton and Jefferson down to 1861, the right of a State to dissolve her own partnership has been argued by powerful minded men, and there has been more for it than agin it. . . . Massachusetts and Connecticut were for it at one time, and bellered round and pawed dirt amazin to git out. . . ." Therefore, he couldn't understand why the South wasn't allowed to leave the Union. "I wouldn't have a nigger or a dog to stay round me that didn't want to." He said he'd been told that the North wanted the South to stay in to help fight "furrin" wars, but he doubted if Dixie would respond now. "Dodds says before he'd pull a trigger for Thad Stevens, he'd have his soul transmigrated to a bench-leg'd fice, and bark at his daddy's mules 2,000 years."

Reviewing the history of Amerian slavery, Smith put blame principally on the North for bringing over the Negroes. Then, he continued, when the Yankees found that the Northern climate didn't suit the slaves "they begun to slide 'em down South." In a more conciliatory vein he wrote of the postwar scions of the slave traders, "If they had held out the hand of fellowship, we would have made friends and buried the hatchet." Instead they yelled treason. With his dander again up, Bill Arp fumed. "Now, the idea of several millions of American freemen being guilty of treason at once! . . . Treason the dickens! . . . Where's Dan'l Webster? Where's the history of the American Revolution?" He then answered his implied question. "No, it ain't treason or reason—but it's devillish, infernal, inhuman hate"; and this hate is indicated, he maintained, by their keeping Jefferson Davis in prison. He posited a comparison. "If Mr. Davis's honor and integrity and patriotism and true courage were weighed in a balance against Sumner's and Stevens's and all his enemies, wouldn't he outweigh them all?" For all his defiant bombast, his concluding statement—as well as the collective tone for the entire letter—was one of pathos. Smith appealed to the reader's sympathy by writing that "if there ever was an afflicted people that needed friends, it's us." In the postscript, again assuming the pose of a hardened, proud Rebel, he asked his friend in Tennessee, "Is Brownlow dead yet? I'm writing his obituary, and thought I would like for the sad event to come off as soon as possible."

Bill Arp continued to be at odds with the Reconstruction plans of the North in *Bill Arp's Peace Papers*, published in 1873 and containing pieces written during and after the war. In one selection, dated March 8, 1867, he mentioned that he had intended to remain in obscurity, but because of the many requests for "my views about the momentus state of our sufferin kountry," he had decided to take up his pen again.

The Smiling Phoenix

The "Dedikashun" to the volume made plain his continued Southern bias: "To the unarm'd, unleg'd, uney'd, unpenshun'd, unwept, unhonor'd and unsung soljiers of the Confedrit States." In the "Prefase" he summed up his disagreements with the way things had been going since Appomattox. "The fakt is, it aint the war that our peepul is mad about no how. It is this confounded, everlastin, abominabal peace—this tail to the comet—this rubbin the skab off before the sore gets well." Since, to many Southerners, Ulysses S. Grant, President from 1869 to 1877, symbolized radical Republicanism, Bill even took a jab at this sacred cow of the enemy. "I'll bet Grant a thousan dollars agin the best bull terryer dog he's got, that if he lives 25 years, he'll be set down in history as a reglar aksidental bust. I'll bet there was ten thousan soljiers in the Yankee army who would have made a better fite, and a hundred thousan who would hav made a better president." Because of the one-sided opinions expressed in the book, Bill concluded his prefatory section with a kind of apologia, a slight indication that he was beginning to mellow. "Spontanyous combustions are sed to be always exskusable, and if the sentiments which bubble up in this volume dont soot sum foaks, they will be gratyfide to see what a fool a man can make of himself without tryin."

In "Bill Arp Before the Rekonstruktion Committee—(Supprest Testimony.)" he used a structural device which allows him to express freely his sarcasm and defiance. When one of the men on the "Destruktion Committee" asked him if he lived in "the State of Georgy," Bill answers, "I'm in a state of oncertainty about that. . . . We don't know whether Georgy is a State or not. I would like for you to state yourself, if you know. The state of the kountry requires that this matter be settled, and I will proseed to state—" But he is interrupted and asked his age, to which he replies smart-alecky, "That depends on sirkumstances. . . . I don't know whether to count the last five years or not. Durin the war you foaks sed that a State couldn't seseed, but that while she were in state of rebellyun she were ded. Now you say we got out and we shant git back agin in 1870. A man's age has got sumthin to do with his rights, and if we are not to vote, I don't think we ort to kount the time. That's about as near as I cum to my age, sur." The interrogation finally gets under way, but Bill continues his surly retorts to the committee. As an example, he tells one of the investigators that the South will obey their laws as long as it has to, but warns that "you'll ketch it in the long run." When another member of the committee asks what the South would do with General Sherman if the United States should go to war against England or France, he answers, "Sorry you mentioned him. We'll hav to hire him, I rekon, as a camp fiddler, and make him sing 'Hail Columbia' by fire-light, as a warnin to the boys how mean it is to burn sittys and make war on defenceless wimmin and childern." In answer to a question about his present opinion of the Negroes, he says that the only difference between their prewar and their postwar status is that they now are more evenly distributed. He boasts to the committee, "Sum of us don't own as many as we used to, but evrybody has got a nigger or two now, and they'll all vote em or turn em off.

86

A nigger that wouldn't vote as I told him, shouldn't black my boots." Time and time again genuine pathos breaks through this exterior bravado. Throughout his Reconstruction letters, in fact, runs the plaintive cry, "How much more are we to endure?" A hard shell covered a sentimental core, as his later works were to reveal.

But when Smith wrote the selections in this volume, he was not yet ready for the bucolic philosopher role. He was still too close in time to the emotions of the war to forgive his former enemies completely. "I'm not rekonsiled. I thought I was, but I ain't. I've been tryin to make peace, and make friends sinse the confounded old war was over, but it won't do" (p. 201). Bill Arp's internal struggle was evidently representative of the conflicts that remained with the South until the last Confederate veteran died.

Like most thinking Southerners, he was aware that slavery had to go sometime. His bone of contention was with the way it went—the cataclysmic overturn of a long-established social and economic system overnight. He whined in retrospect. "Them good old nigger days was jest blotted out like fallin into a celler. If we could have slid into it quietly and slantendikular, if slavery could have sorter tapered out and freedom sorter tapered in, everybody could have got used to it" (p. 202). Had Bill thought about this a little more, he would have realized that the blame for the sudden emancipation of the slaves lay mainly on Southern extremists who had goaded their states to secession. The great majority of the people in the free states had no wish to abolish slavery in the slave states; like Lincoln, they merely wanted to preserve the Union. It was only the exigencies of the war to save the Union that forced Lincoln finally to issue the Emancipation Proclamation.

Before completing the volume, Smith got in a last thrust at the "lying" Northern newspapers. A friend of his, Bill wrote, said that sometimes a paper succeeds by lying—the New York *Herald,* the *Tribune,* and John W. Forney's paper he gave as examples—but that it has to be well backed. "The *Herald* has got so now it can quit party and set back in a cheer and tell the truth in its old age; like an old spekulator who has made a fortune by cheatin and lyin and then puts his money in stocks and retires. He [the friend] says that political papers lie from 90 per cent down to 10, and that Forney is the only editor who ever went full up to a 100 and kept it there" (pp. 207-8). Bill Arp was well qualified to attack newspapers with a definite political slant; he himself had been writing in like manner since 1861. But like the *Herald,* he would soon "quit party and set back in a cheer," and view things more objectively.

The civil rights bills passed by the radically controlled Congress were almost unanimously attacked by Southern humorists, who saw in them little actual concern for the Negro but rather a method of perpetuating the radical political regime. Years before Joel Chandler Harris took upon himself the role of conciliator, he wrote somewhat critically of Northern intentions. In W. T. Thompson's Savannah *Morning News,* he wrote in 1871, "There will have to be another amendment to the civil rights bill. A negro boy in Covington [Georgia] was attacked by a sow lately and narrowly escaped with his life. We will hear next that the sheep have banded together to mangle the down-trodden race."[6] This piece, however, was more an effort to write for an audience than an expression of the writer's feelings. Harris had been a boy during the war, and his largely pleasant war experiences did not leave the bitter memories felt by Bill Arp and others who had matured on the battlefield.

Even the placid Sidney Lanier attacked radical Reconstruction in a dialect poem he entitled "Civil Rights."[7] He had been living for some time since the war in Prattville, Alabama, where he was principal of an academy; but the danger from unruly free Negroes there caused him to leave. Knowing, therefore, the Negro as intimately as he did, he was very much opposed to the so-called civil rights bills, which many Southerners feared would incite Negro atrocities. The immediate provocation for the poem was Charles Sumner's Supplementary Civil Rights Bill, passed by Congress in 1875 and the last piece of Reconstruction legislation. To many horrified ex-Confederates the bill seemed to confer social equality on the former slaves. Written in twenty-eight couplets of iambic heptameter, Lanier's poem expresses Southern reaction to the bill in the dialect of the Georgia cracker.

> *I jes was startin' out to like 'em some agin;*
> *And that was not an easy thing, right after what had bin!*

The speaker was an old man who had lost his son and everything else he had to the Yankees, and still they did not let up.

> *And when I stands aside and waits, and hopes that things will mend,*
> *Here comes this Civil Rights and says, this fuss shan't have no end!*
> *Hit seems as ef, jest when the water's roughest, here of late,*
> *Them Yanks had throwed us overboard from off the Ship of State.*

Using a rustic dialect, Lanier was thus able to express political views that might have been censored had they appeared in standard English.

The presence of Negro soldiers in the occupation army in the South added insult to defeat. F. E. Daniel, "the Rebel Surgeon," recorded at least two brushes with colored troops. One incident concerns a white illiterate piney woods preacher in Mississippi, whom Daniel says he heard preach shortly after the war. Taking for his text, "My brethren, all things happen for the best," the preacher describes the trials and hardships of his life, but adds that "God knows best, and we must bow to His will." Relating his postwar experiences to his text, he continues: "Now, I come home from the army after the break-up, and my little house was burnt; all the fences burnt; my two mules stolen and nothin' on this green yerth left me 'cept a blue sow—and *by the grace of the Lord she pigged in the spring*—givin' me a show for my meat in the fall, and the mule I rid all endurin' of the war where I was chapling to Captain Carr's comp'ny. But I took heart. I got the nabers to jine in, and we put up a little log house. I borrid a plow, and with that one pore so' back mule, I broke up a little patch for cawn. The cawn was up and in the tassel, and needed one more plowin' to lay it by. Hit was promisin'; and with my growin' shoats I thought to stave off starvation for a while longer, and I was puttin' my trust in Providence, when what should happen but some of them nigger sogers from the garrison over thar (pointing with his thumb over his shoulder in the direction of Jackson), jes' stole my mule, and killed and carried off the *l-a-s-t* one of my shoats, not even sparin's the old blue sow." With his congregation expecting him to say that all this misfortune happened for the best, he pauses—then he damns the occupation: "Now, brethern and sistern: That *may* have all been for the best—but I'll be everlastin'ly durned my old buttons if I can see it!" (pp. 283-84).

Southerners could launch epithets at their conquerors, but they had no power to back them up. According to Daniel, shortly after the war a Jackson, Mississippi, newspaper editor shot at and narrowly missed some Negro troops he caught in his apple orchard. He was handled rather roughly by the military authorities and taken to jail. Indignant townspeople gathered, but were powerless to do anything but disapprove verbally. One ex-Rebel was saying that the editor should have killed the bunch of them, when the commander of the Negro garrison came up to him and threatened, "You damned old rebel scoundrel—you say it is right to shoot a union soldier for taking a few green apples?" The withered ex-major hastily backed down, according to Daniel's recollection. "'Was they green? Was they *green?*' quickly exclaimed the old major, who was terribly frightened and began to tremble and apologize. 'Oh, no; not if they was *green.* I wouldn't shoot a soldier for taking a few *green* apples. No, I thought they was *ripe.* No, not if they wasn't ripe. No; I wouldn't if they was green—.' And he backed out of the crowd still mumbling his disclaimer amidst shouts of laughter" (pp. 279-80).

To condemn the occupation forces and radical Reconstruction generally, the Southerner had to be less direct and slightly more subtle; it was best for him to disguise either himself or his message. A popular device used by humorists to articulate criticism was the Negro mouthpiece, who indicted the outsiders for what they were doing to his white people, to his race, and to his Southland. Old Si, the popular creation of Sam W. Small of the Atlanta *Constitution* (his pieces were collected in *Old Si's Sayings* in 1886), was just such a darky, speaking the sentiments of his white ventriloquist. Old Si is the perfect "White Folks' Negro." His attitude toward the radicals and the Republican party is extremely critical. His people, he asserted, could expect no favors from the radicals. "Dey gibs de nigger nuffin but de pick'd bone, an' don't gib him dat ef dere's a bonedus fackry any whars handy!" (p. 43). Explaining why the Republican party in the South was beginning to decline and why Negroes wouldn't save it, "When de 'publican train hab got no pervisions on 'board an' de dimmycrats has planty of bacon ter eat, an' is allus greasin' de 'publican track wid de meat-skins, de niggers takes mighty little stock in dat train—dat's so!" (p. 48). Smart Negroes, Si suggested, should be able to see that eventually Southern Democrats would derail the Republican train.

The Smiling Phoenix

When the promises of the radicals failed to materialize, many Negroes began to take stock and found that they had been hornswoggled. Old Si listed his complaints against the Republican party. "I charge de 'publicans wid fawty akers ob land an' a good mule dat I nebber got; den wid 'bout twenty dollars dat 'scaped troo de Freedmen's bank; den, wid loss' time foolin' 'round an' shoe ledder tromped out in persessions an' seech; an' . . . ef de 'publican party wuz ter shake hit's pockits wrong side out'ards an' den sell all de niggers back inter slavery de money wouldn't git a cl'ar reseet fur dere fust yeah's stealin'!" (p. 53). Again he accuses the Republicans of extorting money from him through the Freedman's Bank. "De Lawd made de nigger, but dis heah freedman bizness wuz what turned de nigger inter de cussed fool dat he is ter go 'round 'sportin' dem as cheet him outer his home an' his money. I tell yer, I lef' de tail ob my coat wid my pockit-book in it in dat Freedman Bank trap— an' sence dat I'me preachin' dis same sarmon!" (p. 70).

One of the best and most picturesque statements of the differences between the Republican and the Democratic plans for the postwar South is Old Si's contention that the Republicans are for reconstruction and the Democrats for reform. To illustrate the difference he speaks metaphorically, "Well, de reconstrucshun hit am like bustin' up de hoss power to a co'n mill an' tryin' fur to put hit togedder in anudder way from de man whar made it! . . . An' de reform, dat means dat yer takes de ricketty ole hoss power ter pieces, fixes all de parts inter de same shapes dat dey wuz at de fust, tightens up de braces and de sockits and den puts dat whole hoss power up jess 'zactly de same, but a heap more substantial dan hit wuz when yer fust got it from de factry!" (p. 62).

As Old Si continued to write his sketches, it became more evident that he was a Democrat. He saw in that party the best hope for the Southerner—black and white. His belief in it led him to attack Independents. "Er In'erpenden' candydate in dis heah town is like er blin' hoss tryin' ter fine his way inter a strange co'n-field—de good-eye hosses don't stop roun' wid him, dey goes on ter de gap in de fence—an' when hit comes ter polyticks de nigger kno's whar dat gap is, you kin jes bet yer las' nickel!" (p. 72). No contemporary of Old Si would have failed to substitute "Democratic party" for "gap."

Old Si was perfectly aware of the venal nature of the freedman and continually lectured him on it. Satirizing political barbecues, he wrote, "Dere's mo' seduckshun ter de averidge nigger in er pone er lite bred dan in forty flatforms, an' when de licker circulates de only freedum dat de nuely enfrancheesed wants is er clar track ter de votin' poles . . ." (p. 76).

In a sketch on carpetbaggers he decides that "hits time fur dem ter git skase!" When someone asks him if they aren't the freedman's guardian, he replies sarcastically, "I takes time ter notice dat dey gyards de nigger mighty close ter see dat he don't git nuffin widout dey gittin' de bigges' sheer, ef dey can!" Again speaking metaphorically, he characterizes the carpetbaggers. "Yer see, dey's er kind ob perliterkil bed bugs, dem fellers is, and de nigger's gittin' pow'ful tired ob habbin' dem 'round in his bed—an' he's gwine ter put sum dimmycrat turpytime on de bed slats dis fall!" (p. 61). All his readers who had ever been troubled with bedbugs—and this probably included most of them—knew what turpentine would do to the pests.

"Waving the bloody shirt"—keeping the Northern electorate reminded of the war and its challenge to the Union—was a favorite pastime among Northern politicians for many years after the war ended. Old Si had his own definition of the term. When he is told that it "is taken as a sign of the lies told up north about outrages and murders upon negroes down here by the rebels," he says he hasn't seen any "outrage niggers" in Georgia and adds, "Old Si done bin 'round heah 'nuff fur ter kno' dat when dey takes a bloody shu't . . . offen a nigger down heah dey's gwine ter leab dat nigger in de cold wid a nakid back an' a mighty hankerin arter somebody else's gyarment" (p. 48).

Times had changed since the Negro was the legal ward of the white man— or so Old Si found out one day much to his chagrin. With his new civil rights he had to shift for himself as the white man's equal. Small dramatized the predicament of the irresponsible Negro by having Si ask the son of his former master for fifty cents to go to the circus. The white man informs him that it will now cost him a dollar because with his civil-rights equality he is as good as the white man. When the cost of freedom strikes so close to home, Old Si gets riled up and truly condemns civil rights. "I tole dem niggers dey was spilin' de horn when dey wanted dem sibil rights, an' hyar's de truf of it, p'int blank . . . 'twixt us I say dam de sibil rights, 'speshilly when de circus is 'round" (p. 97).

By 1876 the Southern white man had won back much of his former power in politics. The Negro voter was being gradually disfranchised. After a primary election in which the colored voters were excluded, Old Si tells of seeing a Negro racing for the train with a carpetbag in his hand. The traveler explains why he's leaving Atlanta for his home town. "Lissen to me, boy! We's done been free nigs onter 'lebben years, hain't we? Dere's been lots ob leckshions round har since den, hain't dere? Now, when it has come to pass in dis yer city ob Atlanta dat one ob de fust gen'lemen ob de town run for aldyman, and don't eben say, 'Hyar, Ben, is a little sumfin to keep your upper lip stiff,' its time fur an ole niggah like me to go off to his ole home and die" (pp. 40-41). Thus white supremacy came back to the South.

But the winning back of his old pre-eminent position was not accomplished overnight by the white man. It was near the end of the century before all Southern states had adopted white primary laws. Sometimes the white man gained political supremacy honestly at the ballot box as more and more whites were given back the vote, but often the ex-Confederates had to resort to the same tactice used by the radicals. In *Dixie After the War* Myrta Avary related the following anecdote as typical at many polling places. A father was before the ballot box, talking of a letter he had just received from his son in Europe, when someone came up and used the son's name and voted. But the old man was equal to the occasion. "Why, my dear boy, so glad you got back in time to cast your vote!"—and the two strangers walked off with affectionate arms around each other (p. 292).

"Charley Knight's Strategy," from Jeannette Walworth's *Southern Silhouettes*, shows another way one small Southern town ridded itself of its carpetbaggers. In this sketch a white man successfully runs his former slave for tax collector and then acts as clerk for the illiterate Negro. By controlling tax collections, the white clerk was able to break the backbone of the corrupt carpetbag rule in the county.

Yet another method used by the responsible whites to regain political power was controlling the Negro vote. In Samuel Minturn Peck's *Alabama Sketches*, for example, "The Political Split in Oakville" shows how a young lawyer wins office by a clever coup which delivers to himself the Negro vote. The occasion is the biennial election of a mayor in a small Western Alabama town. The incumbent, Colonel Jackson, is considered a sure winner over his lawyer opponent, Charles Lawton, because he controls the Negro vote and the whiskey ring. He also has the support of the Negro political boss, Lucullus Williams. A victory for Lawton looks very unlikely because he realizes that in order to win he must get a sizable minority of the black vote, and this looks impossible. However, he discovers that Williams has a rival, a Negro carpenter, Jim Lawrence, who offers his aid free. "I ain't much of a speechifyer, Marse Charlie," Jim told him, "but I'm a powerful han' at still-huntin', and I'll jes' cirkilate roun' 'mong de colored folks an' git yer all de votes I kin, for I jes' bodaciously 'spises dat biggerty nigger, Lucullus Williams, wursuren pisen."

Jim, though, has little success with his canvassing because Lucullus is buying votes with whiskey. Lawton's political future, indeed, looks dark. He even asks Jim if his stand for repealing the hog law won't get him Negro votes, but Jim tells him that "dey don't care nothin' 'bout no hog law. Dey jes' laughs an' say hit's easier to pick up de white folks' hogs in a pen than gwine roun' loose."

All seems lost until Lawton's fiancée suggests a big supper for the Negroes the night before the election after all the saloons are closed. She suspects that they will all be hungry after drinking Jackson's whiskey for several days with little food. So a feast is planned in the courthouse, and "the things negroes like best" are on the menu: sardines, gingercake, tinned salmon, watermelon, "two-fors" (two-for-five-cent cigars), bread, pickles, and cheese. Jim thinks the idea is brilliant. "You ax me will dey go down to de court-house to a good supper! Bless God, Marse Charlie, dem hongry niggers'll follow me down dar like a drove o' razor-back hogs." Jim believes that he and Dick Newton, a friend of Lawton, can capture most of the votes this way: "Yes, Marse Charlie, jes' leave dis nigger business to Marse Newton and me. We gwine trap dem niggers like patridges." Quietly, transportation is arranged; and on the night before the election not a Negro voter misses the supper. After all get inside and sufficient food for the night is taken in, the door is locked. Peck shows the triumph of the strategy with this description of election morning: "The battle was indeed won, for next morning Dick Newton unlocked the door of the banquet-hall, and Jim and his aides marched three hundred negroes across the street to the polls in blocks of six, each with a Lawton ticket in his hand."

Within a few years there were not three hundred Negro voters in a dozen such Alabama towns, for the Negro had been effectively disfranchised. The period when the Negro wielded significant political power in Southern towns is recorded best in such humorous sketches as "The Political Split in Oakville"—stories written by men who had lived through this turbulent era of Southern history.

The slave was often bewildered by freedom, for he had no clear notion of what it meant. Listening to his Republican saviors, he was likely to think that it was a panacea, a heaven on earth. One contemporary humorist-critic characterized the new freedman in these words: "Thousands of negroes lounged about the country enjoying their newly-found freedom and living without work by pilfering the poverty-burdened people. Their chief occupations were voting and conducting religious revivals, and their highest ambition was to live in town."[8] John T. Moore's Negro mouthpiece also painted in "His First Ku-Klux" (*Uncle Wash*) a picture of the reaction to freedom. "After the niggers wuz sot free . . . they wuz lak sheep widout a leader, an' didn't kno jes whut to do. Menny uv 'em tho't somebody wuz gwinter tak keer uv us—like es not Marse Lincoln—jes lak ole Marster useter do—an' so dey loafed aroun' till dey mighty nigh starve, waitin' fur de forty acres uv lan' an' de mule dat had been promised 'em fur votin' wid de 'Publicans." Many Negroes fully expected that the magical freedom would cause their skin to change from black to white. Miss Avary recorded the actual question of a newly freed slave: "Ole Miss, now I'se free, is I gwi tu'n white lak white folks?" (p. 193).

Freedom brought with it, however, many responsibilities and burdens the slave had not known. After the first glow of freedom died, the Negro's personality was likely to undergo a change. The title character in Harris' *Gabriel Tolliver* detected such a change, ". . . the negroes were no longer cheerful. Their child-like gaiety had vanished. In place of their loud laughter, their boisterous play, and their songs welling forth and filling the twilight places with sweet melodies, there was silence" (p. 114).

In this changed condition the writers saw many possibilities for humor. In *The Southerner* Walter Hines Page, writing under the name of Nicholas Worth, recorded his impressions of the newly freed Negro. Old Aunt Maris, a cook, reacted in this way to the news that she was free: "Dey say dat de niggers'll be free. I ain't gwine ter have none o' deir freedom, I ain't. May de good Lord carry me erway in er chariut o' fire" (p. 7). The Negro, Page asserted, often released freedom tensions in religious enthusiasm. Their shouting and rolling on the church floor was a socially acceptable way of again becoming the irresponsible and carefree people they once were.

But not all were fearful of their new freedom. Some luxuriated in it. James J. McDonald painted in *Life in Old Virginia* a serio-comic portrait of Aunt Dorcas. For several years after she was freed she would walk down the middle of the road, stop suddenly, raise her eyes and hands heavenward, and cry out in exuberant thanksgiving, "Th-a-ank Je-e-sus I'se free-e! Ya-a-s my Je-eus I'se free-e!" Then she would continue on her route, collecting the white folks' laundry (p. 172).

The list of humorous subjects connected with the Reconstruction Negro is almost endless. His adulation of the slain Emancipator, for example, was exploited in many jibes. Joel Chandler Harris wrote the following squib: "The colored people of Macon celebrated the birthday of Lincoln again on Wednesday. This is the third time since last October."⁹

The official reconstruction program by Congress, although ostensibly designed for his benefit, often puzzled even the Negro. He was probably more confused about the Freedman's Bureau than about any other part of the program. William Ludwell Sheppard remembers his mammy's impression of the bureau this way: "You know this Freedman's Bureau? . . . Well, they tells me—Lawd knows what they calls it bureau for!—they tells me that ef a colored pusson goes down thar and gives in what he wuz worth—women either, mind you—that the guv'mint would pay um."¹⁰

Overwhelmingly illiterate when freed, the Negro had many benefactors—mostly Northern—who tried to educate him. Hundreds of Yankee schoolteachers converged on the South, burning with the mission to educate the former slaves. The Alabama humorist Francis Bartow Lloyd joined with many Southern writers in satirizing this new kind of Yankee invasion. "The 'Nigger' School Marm" in *Sketches of Country Life* shows the fruitless efforts of one such missionary. One day the teacher was asking her colored scholars such catechism questions as "Who made you?" Everything seemed to be going along fine. Most of the answers were intelligent and doctrinally sound. She paused in her questioning to send one boy to the spring for water, and then resumed, repeating her earlier question "Who made you?" This time, however, she received a rather startling answer. "Adam." When asked for an explanation, the little heretic answered, "Dat nigger what God made has done gone to de spring to fetch some watah."

While the schoolmarms were busy trying to make the Negro the white man's equal educationally and while the radical Congress was busy trying to make him equal politically, Charles H. Smith was busy making Bill Arp attack all these "fool ideas." "Bill Arp on Nigger Equality," one of the *Peace Papers,* is his treatise on the subject. He begins by defining President Grant's concept of equality. "I don't want to speak disrespekful of Mr. Grant nor myself, but I'm obleeged to think that either him or me is a fool. He beleeves in nigger equality and I don't—that is to say, he beleeves a nigger is as good as a Southern man, though not quite as good as a Yank." Using the Southern stereotype of the Negro as a beast of burden, he shows—at least to a white supremacist's satisfaction—why there can be no equality of the races. "The nigger wasent made to keep a post offis nor set on a jewry. He wasent made for intelektual persoots. He was made to dig, and ditch, and grub, and hoe, and plow a mule, and tote things about for white foaks, and nothin else don't soot him, and that don't soot him as well as doin nothin." Most of Smith's readers probably failed to see the incongruity of the almost illiterate cracker's thesis that Negroes were unintellectual *per se*. Bill Arp firmly believed that the white man was by nature civilized and the Negro by nature savage. In the following colorful imagery he shows this innate difference between the two races: "A blak Alabama nigger is jest the same as his great gran daddy was in Afriky two thousan years ago. He's got sivilized and behaves sorter decent, but it's bekaus he lived with white foaks, and is obleeged to. If you turn him loos on an island by himself, he'll relaps into a vagabon in ten years. He'll quit wearin close and go to beatin tin pans and eat lizzards before you git out of site." Such were the sentiments of one of the most influential and respected humorists in the postwar South. Nearing the end of his tract, in order to show that he is not callous, Smith states the stock Southern argument. "But I ain't agin the nigger. I like him. . . . I don't want them radikals to be foolin him about his own natur, and puttin fool ideas in his head." He concludes with one of the best examples of distorted logic in Southern humor. Attempting to prove his thesis that Negroes are naturally inferior, he cites "evidence" which he considers conclusive. "My daddy ownd 'em for fifty years, and they barely larned to make a hoe handle."

The Freedman

Some of the most amusing incidents in postwar Southern humor relate to the Negro and the Ku Klux Klan. Although the Klan was organized and existed for the very serious mission of keeping the Negro in his place and of reinstating white supremacy, the methods and paraphernalia of the secret society were comic as well as frightening. A Klan costume might consist of a long white robe, a high cardboard hat decorated with stars and pictures of animals, a white mask with holes for eyes, and a long tongue of red flannel. Often the Ku Kluxer's horse was draped in a long flowing sheet. The ghostly rider frequently carried a cow's skull—sometimes even a human being's—and a rubber tube which he placed under his robe to allow for huge consumptions of water.[11]

When a Negro met such an apparition, his fertile imagination was set in motion and his later recollections of the visitation were almost always exaggerated. Myrta Avary gave an example of this. "A Ku Klux captain tells me that one night as he rose up out of a graveyard, one of his negroes passed with a purloined gobbler in possession; he touched the negro on the shoulder. The negro dropped the turkey and flew like mad, and the turkey flew, too. Next morning, the darkey related the experience to his master (omitting the fowl). 'How tall was that hant, George?' 'Des high ez a tree, Marster! an' de han' it toch my shoulder wid burnt me lak fire. I got mutton-suet on de place.' 'I was about three feet taller than my natural self that night,' says Captain Lea. George wore a plaster on his arm and for some time complained that it was 'pa'lised'" (p. 277).

By way of newspapers and posters the Klan broadcast its cryptic proclamations. In *Gabriel Tolliver* Harris wrote that one morning Shady Dale was plastered with placards printed in red ink and with the image of a grinning skull and crossbones (p. 263). The placards were written as a proclamation, dated Den No. Ten, Second Moon, Year 21,000 of the Dynasty, and read:

To all Lovers of Peace and Good Order—Greeting: Whereas, it has come to the knowledge of the Grand Cyclops that evil-minded white men, and deluded freedmen, are engaged in stirring up strife; and whereas it is known that corruption is conspiring with ignorance—

Therefore, this is to warn all and singular the persons who have made or are now making incendiary propositions and threats, and all who are banded together in secret political associations to forthwith cease their activity. And let this warning be regarded as an order, the violation of which will be followed by vengeance swift and sure. The White Riders are abroad.

Thrice endorsed by the Venerable, the Grand Cyclops, in behalf of the all-powerful Klan. (. (. (. K. K. K. .) .) .)

No less ludicrous is a real proclamation actually circulated in Montgomery, Alabama, in April, 1868.[12]

> K. K. K.
> Clan of Vega.
> HDQR'S K. K. K. HOSPITALLERS.
> Vega Clan, New Moon,
> 3rd Month, Anno K.K.K. 1.

ORDER NO. K. K.

Clansmen—Meet at the Trysting Spot when Orion Kisses the Zenith. The doom of treason is Death. *Dies Irae.* The wolf is on his walk—the serpent coils to strike. Action! Action!! Action!!! By midnight and the Tomb; by Sword and Torch and the Sacred Oath at Forrester's Altar, I bid you come! The Clansmen of Glen Iran and Alpine will greet you at the new-made grave.

Remember the Ides of April.

By command of the Grand D.I.H.

> Cheg. V.

Placards with garbled text such as the following were often left pinned on doors and trees by the Klan:[13]

> The Raven Croaked
> and we are come to Look on the Moon.
> The Lion Tracks the Jackal
> the Bear the Wolf
> Our Shrouds are Bloody (But the Midnight is Black)

One who was favored with a visit from the Klan seldom saw any humor in the situation or in the hooded figures, but white men were usually amused by accounts of how the hosts had acted and reacted. Especially terrifying was the consumption by one figure of gallons of water, with some accompanying remark like, "It was hot in hell today and I am thirsty." This was enough to make the Negro do or refrain from doing just about anything. In *Sequel of Appomattox* Walter Fleming described a typical visitation. "In the middle of the night a sleeping negro might wake to find his house surrounded by a ghostly company, or to see several terrifying figures standing by his bedside. They were, they said, the ghosts of men he had formerly known. They had scratched through from Hell to warn the negroes of the consequences of their misconduct. Hell was a dry and thirsty land; and they asked for water. Bucket after bucket of water disappeared into a sack of leather, or rubber, concealed within the flowing robe" (p. 254).

The appearance and conduct of the mysterious night visitors often convinced the superstitious that such men were supernatural. The black imagination would again embellish the details. Myrta Avary recorded the recollection of a Negro who told of his ghostly guests begging for water, saying, "Dey ain' had nay drap sence de Yankees killed 'em at Gettysburg. An' den, suh, when he han' 'em er gode-full, dee say: 'Kin you let me have de bucket? I'se jes come f'om hell an' I'se scotchin' in my insides.' An' den, mun, dat ar hant des drink down dat whole bucket at a gulp, and I hyern it sizzlin' down his gullet des same ez you done flung it on de coals! I ain' gwi fool longer nothin' lat dat! Some folks say it's white folks tryin' tuh skeer we-all, but, suh, I b'lieve it's hants—er Old Satan one!" (p. 276). Sometimes the supernatural-appearing figure would intercept a black on the road and insist that the frightened man shake hands with him. Afraid to refuse, the trembling Negro would hold out his hand only to have a skeleton's hand thrust into it.

After one such visit from the Klan, the intimidated person was likely to change his politics. Sarge Wier told in *Old Times in Georgia* how "a mighty big talking nigger," visited by a Ku Kluxer shortly before an election, was led to change his voting sentiments. The ghostly visitor asked for water and drank gourd after gourd as it was handed out to him. Finally in desperation the Negro pleaded with his wife, "In de name of de Lord, old 'oman . . . hand the bucket erlong out here with the gourds, and let the gentleman get his water and be er going." When the man "drank" the bucket of water and asked for more, the Negro, his wife, and his children rushed out of the house and across the field, screaming in terror (pp. 32-34). A Klan visit not quite so terrible but just as effective is recorded by Joel Chandler Harris in *The Chronicles of Aunt Minervy Ann.* Soon after the war Minervy Ann's good-for-nothing husband became a political leader in the county, joined the radical Union League, and got elected to the state legislature. The Klan's call was made to suggest that he be a little more humble in his speech and actions (pp. 1-33).

Frequently the Klan would converge on a political meeting, reducing the group to chaos. Young Gabriel Tolliver witnesses such a scene. He watches as thirteen mounted Knights of the White Camellia break up a rally in a church. This is what he saw and heard.

97

The Smiling Phoenix

Three times this ghostly procession marched around the church. Finally they paused, each horseman at a window, save the leader, who being taller than the rest, had stationed himself at the door.

He was the first to break the silence. "Brothers, is all well with you?" his voice was strong and sonorous.

"All is not well," replied twelve voices in chorus.

"What do you see?" the impressive voice of the leader asked.

"Trouble, misery, blood!" came the answering chorus.

"Blood?" cried the leader.

"Yes, blood!" was the reply.

"Then all is well!"

"So mote it be! All is well!" answered twelve voices in chorus.

Again the ghostly horsemen rode round and round the church, and then quickly disappeared into the darkness. At first the Negroes were too paralyzed with fear to move; then they panicked to the door, yelling (pp. 251-52). Harris, like almost all postwar Southern writers, was sympathetic to the Klan and its objectives—as long as Klansmen kept from physically injuring or lynching Negroes. Harris felt that such methods were necessary to show the upstart freedmen that the white man was not asleep.

A similar visit of the Klan is the subject of John T. Moore's "His First Ku-Klux" in *Uncle Wash*. And another political meeting in a church is broken up by the ubiquitous Klan in "The Ku-Klux-Klan and the Negro 'Convention,'" by "Amicus," in the *Sunny South* for June 27, 1886.

Whenever the Klan was attacked by Yankees, Southern humorists sprang to its defense. Sidney Lanier's dialect poem, "Them Ku Klux," ridicules Northern reports of Klan atrocities. The poem's narrator is an old man who has spent "nigh upon twenty year" sitting on his "front pyazer" observing the human comedy. One day he was sitting in his usual place when a neighbor, Jeems Munro, ran across the field, exclaiming about the doings of the Ku Klux Klan, which he had read about in a Pennsylvania paper. Part of the Yankee report read like this:

> . . . *the Ku Klux went*
> *That night that was so rainy,*
> *And they tuck up a poor old colored man,*
> *And carved him, and jinted him; made him stan'*
> *On his head and eat up hisself. . . .*

The cracker narrator inserts an explanation about Jeems, a Yankee who had bought some land from him "When things was crinky-cranky, / Jest after the war," adding "And spite of his Yankeeness, he has bin / A fust-rate honest neighbor." Jeems, however, has one major fault: he will not believe "That all o' them Ku Klux lies he's hearn' / Is fools' and rascals' labor." Therefore, the Southerner asks the credulous Yankee for proof.

Did you ever see, or feel, or hear,
Or taste, or smell, or think you was near,
A Ku Kluxin' assassin?[14]

This poem reduced the Yankee misconceptions of the Klan to acrid laughter.

Although immediately after the war the Klan had been helpful to the South in ameliorating radical Reconstruction, as time went on the hooded order became a refuge for rascals who were bent on sadistic fun; and in 1869 General Nathan Forrest, the Grand Wizard, ordered it disbanded. The Ku Klux Klan continued to exist, but much of its social respectability was taken away. The early Klan and other secret white societies, however, had been instrumental in replacing Southern society in the old historic grooves from which the war and Reconstruction had jarred it.

The New System

The freeing of the slaves brought chaos to the South's labor system. It upset a labor market that had been an integral part of Southern life since early colonial times—a market which both whites and blacks were adjusted to from birth. The change even affected the poor whites, who now had to compete with black labor on the open market, although they refused to do domestic labor and other "nigger work." A number of freedmen decided to exercise their new freedom by leaving their former masters. They were sure that their revised status would miraculously supply all their needs—or that the "guvmint" would. When they found out that they had to look out for themselves, they often returned to their old masters or resorted to petty thievery.

Although many former slaves chose to remain with their old masters, scarcity of labor remained a problem on many plantations. In "Mas' Craffud's Freedom" Harry Stillwell Edwards showed how one planter solved his problem.[15] The humorous story centers around Major Crawford Worthington, the feudal lord of Woodhaven, who during the war had commanded an elite cavalry outfit, the gentlemen of Worthington's Guards. After the war he persuaded a gullible Yankee general to detach two German soldiers to his plantation, ostensibly to keep peace among the Negroes, but actually as an incentive to make lazy, unruly laborers work. With their blue uniforms the two German-Americans, "Captain" Sneifleheimer and "Captain" Sprintz, awed the free workers into passive obedience. An example of how they kept them in line is Captain Sneifleheimer's threat when he comes upon some Negroes loafing in the fields. "Vadt for you tek Mejjer Verdington's money und sleep mid de day? Gainse sur la vork quvick, und be een a hurry mid eet, or I'll pblow oud your prains mid de gun! Hoof!" This warning has enough force to make everybody suddenly very industrious. The guttural words of the German really find their mark in one old man, who later reprimands one of the leaders of the mutiny. "You fool wid dat Yankee, nigger, an' you git er bullet in your skin! Keep away fom dem sort er folks, an' don't you put faith in nobody what talks down dey throats. When you hyah er man rumble 'way down yonder in es throat, hit's des de same as thunder down behind er cloud. Fus' news you git, lightning'll be er-reachin' out fer you." Even after the soldiers are discharged from the army they stay on at Woodhaven, wearing their same old blue uniforms. The ex-Confederate's plantation thrives and by 1869 he is a wealthy man—thanks to the Union army.

Once the magic of freedom had turned into disillusionment and their stomachs had begun growling, the former slaves sometimes tried to find work. Often in their searchings for that elusive freedom which the war had brought them, they were carried far from their ancestral plantations and from the paternalism that slavery had bred. *Eneas Africanus* by Harry Stillwell Edwards is the story of a faithful old Negro who is separated from his owner in 1864 and spends eight years searching for his old home. In this allegory of Reconstruction, Eneas is the archetypal freedman seeking the security and status of his former master. Just before his death he returns from "out o' de wilderness," bringing a silver cup, symbol of amicable race relations between white and black, to his beloved "Marse George," who passes it on in trust to his recently married daughter.

Forced to compete on the open labor market, many Negroes found they were ill equipped to earn their living. McDonald used an anecdote in *Life in Old Virginia* to illustrate how the extreme prewar division of labor among slaves worked to the freedman's disadvantage. When two freed women apply to a white lady for work, she asks them what they can do—cook? wash? clean house? To each question she receives a negative answer. Finally one of the Negroes discloses their work experience. "Sukey, heah, she keep flies off Marster, an' I hunt fo' ol' Missus specks" (p. 245).

Many planters, though, were not as fortunate as Edwards' Major Worthington. Left with no Negro labor, they had to do the work themselves. McDonald also described the serio-comic predicament of an old gentleman who couldn't get labor to lay by his corn; against the advice of his wife he decides to do it for himself. He hitches up his mules and sets to work. As the sun gets higher the day gets hotter, and the old man begins to shed piece after piece of clothing, scattering them all over the field. His wife sends her one remaining servant, the cook, down to the field with water; and she is horrified by what she sees. "I tells you Missus . . . I'se feered ol' Marster don' loss his mind. He don' flung away mos' ev'ry stitch uv his clothes, an' he was rarrin' an' pitchin' 'bout de lazy, sorry niggers, de Yankees, an' 'mancipation. It's de truff ef evah I tol' it Missus, dat de words ol' Marster was a sayin' was jes' mos' laik ol' time 'tracted meetin' preachin' as evah I heerd in all ma bo'n days" (pp. 175-76). The sight of men whose hands had never known the plow working in the fields must indeed have been ludicrous as well as pathetic.

The white lady was also affected in her house work by emancipation. She frequently had to do menial jobs for which earlier there had been half a dozen servants. Myrta Avary, a contemporary historian, used an anecdote to show how pathetic was the woman unused to domestic work. An Atlanta woman, one day shortly after the war, was struggling with her washing, when a group of

Union soldiers, among them a kindhearted Irishman, came into her yard to get some water. Seeing her delicate hands and arms streaked with blood, the Irishman was touched.

"Faith an' be jabbers!" said Pat, "an' what is that you're thryin' to do?" "Go away and let me alone." "Faith, an' if ye don't lave off cleanin' thim garmints, they'll be that doirty—" "Go 'way!" "Sure, me choild, an' if ye'll jis' step to the other soide of the tub without puttin' me to the inconvaniance—" He was about to pick her up in his mighty hands. She moved and dropped down, swallowing a sob.

"Sure, an' it's as good a washerwoman as ivver wore breeches I am," said Pat. "An' that's what I've larned in the army." In short order, he had all the clothes hanging snow-white on the line; before he left, he cut enough wood for her ironing. "I'm your Bridget ivery wash-day that comes 'roun'," he said as he swung himself off. He was as good as his word. This brother-man did her wash every week. "Sure, an' it's a shame it is," he would say, "the Government fadin' the lazy nagurs an' God an' the divvil can't make 'em wur-r-k" (pp. 118-19).

Unfortunately there were not many chivalrous Pats in the occupation army.

One not very happy consequence of the destruction of slavery was the sharecropping system. *On a Mexican Mustang* by Sweet and Knox gave a good definition and evaluation of the system. "In theory, farming on shares is a good thing for the colored agriculturalist. A white man furnishes land, teams, and implements; the negro furnishes the labor; the crops, when harvested, to be divided equally between landlord and tenant. In practice, and in the division of the shares, it does not work so satisfactorily for the tenant. The landlord gets the first share; the storekeeper, who furnished coffee, bacon, and clothing for the tenant, while he was making the crop, gets the other share; and the tenant, for his share, gets cussed because he did not make more cotton and corn. The negro farmer has been heard to hint, that, if he could afford to keep a bookkeeper, his share might be more satisfactory to himself" (pp. 632-33).

The illiterate freedman was an easy prey for unscrupulous white planters. In a half-humorous, half-serious anecdote McDonald shows how the poor Negro was exploited. One reports to his former owner on his sharecropping experience. "I wucked Mustuh C——'s co'n crap on half shar's, an' kaze uv de drouf dar war'nt mo' dan half a crap rais', an' Mistuh C—— he say to me dat dar's no use 'sputin' 'bout it, kaze de half crap dat wuz raise mus' sholy go fo' de lan' an' de mules. I don quit 'sputin' wid him, an' I don quit wuckin' on sich shar's as dat" (pp. 176-77). This situation became a stock anecdote, and it appears often in the writings dealing with the Negro.

The merchant who staked the colored sharecropper during the working season was often just as unscrupulous as the dishonest planter. Jeannette Walworth wrote in *Uncle Scipio* of an incident in which a Negro's former master tries to help him out by going over his account with the merchant who holds a mortgage on his cotton crop. The major intends to find out why Eben has nothing coming to him from the four bales of cotton he has made; he has the merchant's clerk read out the list of items Eben had bought on account. "One gallon of whiskey, six plugs of tobacco, one jar strawberry preserves, one ditto quince—" The major interrupts the reading to ask what Eben wanted with the jar of strawberry preserves and one ditto quince. Eben scratches his head pensively and then says apologetically, "I eet de strawberries, marse, but I don't recall no ditto. No, sir (waxing more positive), all I axes is justus. I owns up t' de strawberries, but you must scratch out dat odder. I don't know nuthin' 'bout de jar er ditto. I think thar's a mistake somewhar', I does indeed. I don' recall buyin' no ditto." The clerk resumes the list of items that Eben has bought or has had foisted off on him by the merchant: one quart of whiskey, one peck of meal, one peck of dried apples, six pounds of pork, one gallon of molasses, one photograph album—and again the major interrupts to chide Eben for buying such an impractical item. Eben explains, "That were a mistake, too, marse. I done tuk de stopper out'n dat bottle of whuskey too soon. A nigger feels mouty rich arter one drink, marse, en I jus' look roun' fur somethin' t' tek home to Mandy, en de clerk, he say dat book would look tiptop on de chimbley, en I 'lowed he knowed, but Mandy, she sorter differ wid 'im. She tuk dat book en she sent it swingin' thro' de a'r." With this, the major dismisses the clerk and lectures first the merchant and then the Negro. "As long as you've got the right to set up your shops like mushrooms in every man's field, if you want to, and ply these poor idiots with your vile whiskey, just that long their year's labor will go to enrich you and impoverish them. Eben, you've swapped masters, that's all. You used to be called my slave, now you belong to Mr. Tim Barnes [the merchant], and he makes you jump a little harder than I ever did" (pp. 139-41). This exploitation of the Negro by white farmer and merchant did not stop with the end of Reconstruction; it continued on into the middle of the twentieth century.

The Southerner—black and white—was mainly concerned with staying alive during the lean years of Reconstruction. He was usually too busy earning a living to care much about the political aspects. The following paragraph illustrating this primary concern is taken from the Union Springs *Times* of June 5, 1867. "A go-ahead planter in a neighboring county was approached by a troubled neighbor, perhaps more of a politician than planter, who was discussing the state of the country, especially the bill converting the Southern States into military districts. The go-ahead planter heard him through, and asked if the bill prohibited the making of corn; being answered in the negative, he responded: 'If it don't, then d--n Congress and the bill. Let 'em rip. I am going to make corn.'" This situation, with many variations, appeared often in postwar humor.

Mozis Addums (George W. Bagby) wrote an essay on "Bein Po'." In it he says, "Thar is pepul in Virginyer so ded po' . . . they can't do nuthin, and they never even tries. Thar is pepul so po' they'll let you treet every time, 'thout even sayin 'look here, now,' like they was goin to treet in thar turn. . . . Thar's hundreds so durn po' they orter be kill'd."[16] For postwar Virginia, Mozis wasn't exaggerating very much either; there was too much truth in the essay.

The South was a long time recovering economically from the disaster of the war. Many factors contributed to the slowness of recovery: widespread property destruction in the war, the corruption of Reconstruction legislatures, the Reconstruction laws, the apathy of Southerners—the list is endless. One of the factors usually put near the top of the list of those contributing to the recovery is industrialization. In 1877 Sidney Lanier, however, wrote an amusing children's poem, "Hard Times in Elfland," in which he seemed to blame industrialization for many of the South's ills.[17] A poor poet's small child asks, "Papa, is hard times ev'ywhere?" and the poet tells of the poverty that has reached even Santa Claus, who "had no belly—not a sign." Santa Claus lost all he had as a result of investments in a celestial Grand Trunk Railway, which was designed to carry dead souls to heaven and unborn babies to earth—and Santa Claus on his annual tour. The railroad, however, was never built because lawyers' fees and the like consumed all the capital. Santa was even forced to sell his reindeer at a bankrupt sale; now he has to make his rounds through the sleet and snow by foot, and he has developed a cough. But bravely poor old Santa continues to distribute the toys he makes in his own home since his toy factory was wiped out. This light poem can be read merely for its entertainment value; or it can be taken as an allegory of the postwar South. Since Lanier was not very enthusiastic about the South's attempts to industrialize, an allegorical interpretation is not far-fetched: Elfland is the South; Santa Claus is the Southern planter taken in and ruined by the industrialist and stock broker; and the lesson that the gullible Santa learns is the one the Southerner must learn. Lanier believed that industrialization had been the South's undoing. Whether read as allegory or as society verse or both, the poem is truly one of his most delightful and successful efforts.

Several of Lanier's humorous dialect poems also have an underlying economic seriousness. His dialect poems, called by Aubrey Starke "a sort of poetical counterpart of A. B. Longstreet's realistic *Georgia Scenes*" (p. 148), show that he saw the South's problem as one of inducing the poor whites to farm the land intelligently. "Thar's More in the Man Than Thar Is in the Land" is a poetic essay in economics.[18] It shows how Jones, a poor cracker farmer of Jones County, Georgia, ruins himself by not staying on his land. Jones is so poor—"his mules was nuthin' but skin and bones / And his hogs was flat as his corn-bread pones" —he decides to pull up stakes and move to Texas, where he'd heard that "Cotton would sprout / By the time you could plant it in the land." He sells his property to a man named Brown, and leaves. Brown moves to the farm, works hard, and prospers. One day the destitute Jones returns on foot from Texas "to see if he couldn't git sum / Employment." The successful Brown takes him in, feeds him, and tells him the moral of his experience, "whether men's land was rich or poor / Thar was more in the *man* than thar was in the *land*." Thus Lanier suggested to his generation of Southerners that they make the best of what they have. The green fields over yonder usually turn out to be mirages.

In his *Yellow Creek Humor* (p. 66) William J. Burtscher expresses much the same sentiment.

103

The Smiling Phoenix

There was a young farmer whose name was Brown,
He packed up his trunk and he moved into town;
There came a panic that gave him alarm;
So he packed his trunk and came back to the farm.

In two humorous dialect poems Lanier advocated diversified crops as one solution to the South's farm problems. In "Jones's Private Argument"[19] the selfish cracker farmer spreads the word that farmers should plant only corn "and swear for true / To quit raisin' cotton!" When all the other farmers plant corn, Jones gleefully exclaims that "cotton will fetch 'bout a dollar a pound / Tharfore, I'll plant *all* cotton!" Implicit in the poem is Lanier's suggestion that farmers plant some of both; thus they wouldn't be dependent upon price fluctuation in one crop.

Again, in "Nine from Eight,"[20] Lanier argued for diversification of crops by showing what usually happens when only one crop is planted. Ellick Garry had borrowed money on his unmade cotton crop; and when the time came to pay up, he hadn't made enough to come out even. Coming back from the cotton gin, he stopped and began figuring in the sand, working "A 'rethmetic sum that wouldn't gee." Talking to himself, he says, "My crap-leen calls for nine hundred and more. / My counts of sales is eight hundred and four." He tries to subtract nine from eight to see how much he is in the clear, but finds that it can't be done. Like Farmer Jones, he had put all his crops into one category: cotton. When King Cotton suffered, Farmer Garry suffered even more. In these poems Lanier showed how, as a humorist, he related himself closely to the life and problems of his time. Perhaps in these dialect poems he contributed more to the welfare of his native South than in any of his works of "pure" literature. (Dave Sloan published in *Fogy Days* (pp. 148-55) an address to a Georgia farm group in which he too urged diversified farming.)

The problems created by the war were not solved by Reconstruction. Indeed they were often added to and intensified. Politicians, as always, were more interested in getting into power and perpetuating their position than in the welfare of those left destitute by the war. Of the postwar writers, the Southern humorists were among the few who wrote the truth without regard to the consequences. Much of their humor was sociological, but this was a period when survival was many a man's first concern. Much of the humor was realistic, but there was little about Reconstruction that could be romanticized. Their humor helped the South over the darkest era in her history, and it gave inspiration to succeeding generations.

Notes

1. *Southern Magazine,* VIII (Jan. 1871), 71.

2. Quoted in Tandy, *Crackerbox Philosophers,* 115.

3. Botkin, *Southern Folklore,* 717.

4. "On Scalawags."

5. Fleming, *Sequel of Appomattox,* 225-26.   6. Julia Harris, *J. C. Harris,* 96.

7. *Poems and Poem Outlines,* I, 40-42.

8. Srygley, *Seventy Years in Dixie,* 364.

9. Julia Harris, *J. C. Harris,* 96.

10. In Howells & Alden, *Southern Lights,* 145.

11. Fleming, *Sequel of Appomattox,* 253.

12. *Ibid.,* 257-58.

13. Avary, *Dixie After the War,* 269.

14. *Poems and Poem Outlines,* I, 191-94.

15. In Palmer, *Dixie Land,* 37-56.

16. Quoted in J. King, *Bagby,* 129.

17. *Poems of Sidney Lanier,* 159-67; first published in *The Christmas Magazine* (Baltimore, 1877).

18. *Poems of Sidney Lanier,* 180-82; first published in the *Georgia Daily,* 1869.

19. *Poems of Sidney Lanier,* 183-84.

20. *Ibid.,* 177-79.

4. Reconciliation

CIVIL WAR IS SAID to engender the bitterest kind of hatred. Having just completed such a war in which brother fought brother, it was not easy for Northerners and Southerners to shake hands and forget. But out of the stillness at Appomattox came many attempts at reconciliation; none were more earnest and more fruitful than those of the humorists. In their efforts influential humorists like Opie Read even took it upon themselves to lecture Confederate heroes. Twenty years after the Civil War, Read wrote in the *Arkansaw Traveler* (August 29, 1885): "Mr. Jefferson Davis says 'The United States are.' Why not say 'Mississippi are.' Mississippi is composed of counties. Then why not say 'The county are.' The county is composed of townships or districts. Progressive grammar, Mr. Davis, teaches us to say 'The United States is.' How would this sound, 'The United States are a great country.'"

Not much progress was made before 1876, but the succeeding decade saw a reunion that in many ways was stronger than the prewar federation. Paralleling and contributing to this change in North-South relations was a renaissance in Southern literature. By the early 1870's most of the old literary voices in the South—Simms, Longstreet, Kennedy, Thompson, Baldwin—were dead or silent. From the literary darkness of the early 1870's, however, emerged a new spirit and a new school of Southern literature which included Lanier, Cable, Irwin Russell, Richard Malcolm Johnston, Joel Chandler Harris, and Thomas Nelson Page. All the writers in this new school wrote some humor; some of them (Johnston and Harris, for example) were professional humorists. Like earlier Southern writers, they were Southern and sectional, but unlike the earlier, they were not provincial, for they had no "peculiar institution" to defend. Sectional bias in literature largely gave way to a literature of reconciliation. Southern humorists were among the first to realize that the South had nothing to gain by remaining recalcitrant and unapproachable. The future, they knew, lay with a united country.

Most Southern writers agreed with George Cary Eggleston, the Hoosier Confederate, who, in a speech strangely titled "Southern Literature" and delivered at a banquet of the New York Southern Society in 1887, said: "I am firmly convinced that there is no Southern literature, that there never was a Southern literature, that there never will be a Southern literature, and that there never ought to be a Southern literature. Some very great and noble work in literature has been produced by men of Southern lineage and birth and residence."[1] Literature, he postulated, is never provincial. Good Southern literature, therefore, is good American literature. Rooted in the South, it is but the flowering of one branch of the national literature, which has many branches.

Although many of the battle wounds were still bleeding, the war had not become a forbidden topic in the humor of reconciliation. At intersectional meetings, for example, speakers frequently used humorous anecdotes dealing with the war. In 1887 at a meeting of the Democratic party the toast was offered: "The Union of the States, Indivisible Forever." Zebulon Vance, former Confederate officer and later wartime governor of North Carolina, answered it. "In selecting me to respond, Mr. President, I hope the committee were not influenced by the supposition that I might be peculiarly qualified to speak thereon because of having tried both sides of that question."[2] When former enemies could laugh about their earlier disagreements, reunion—real reunion—was possible.

Although when he wrote it he was one of the most unreconciled of Southerners, Bill Arp, in the "Dedikashun" of his *Peace Papers,* lists his conditions for a "shore enuf lasting and unpretended peace . . . when the peepul of these United States, so called, shake hands and make frends over the green graves of their heroes . . . when the patriotism and honor of our brave boys is rekognized by their northern brethren, so called." At that time not remotely conciliatory, but rather defiant, Bill did recognize the eventual necessity of more than physical reunion. After a while his requirements were actually met, and both Lincoln and Lee became national heroes.

The stated or implicit aim of much of the humor was thus to reunite the

North and the South. If the power of the pen could be wielded to break the Union (though perhaps not openly anti-union, the writings of Mrs. Stowe and the Abolitionists contributed ultimately to disunion), postwar writers North and South believed it could again be employed to cement the nation. Thus, much of the humor was calculated with this objective in mind. As evidence, Shields McIlwaine, the author of *The Southern Poor-White*, stated that in the postwar South the poor white was deprecated as subject matter because "to depict new Ham Rachels and Ransy Sniffles would have been poor strategy in allaying the prejudices of the two sections" (p. 107). The Southern humorist as a rule tried, by subordinating or eliminating coarse characters and situations, to make his section appear as attractive as possible to the outsider.

The humor of the period reflects all the reconciliation devices that reunited the country, from appeals to nationalism and the concept of the "New South" to the efforts of the North and the effect of time. Throughout their works, humorists tried to show that underneath an exterior of pride and prejudice all Americans were the same and that during national crises sectional feelings would disappear. Later writers even showed this impulse at work during the war. George Washington Cable in *The Cavalier* (1901), for instance, had a Southern girl sing the "Star Spangled Banner" for a dying Yankee captain.

The aim of responsible Southerners from politicians to journalists was to reunite the country. Any occasion was appropriate for promoting reunion. On New York Day at the Tennessee Centennial celebration in 1897, the Tennessee governor and humorist Bob Taylor remarked that "whatever the difference between the North and the South may be in climate, in wealth, in conditions and environments, we are all one people, with common hopes and a common destiny, and may God bless our people of every section."[3]

Taylor is a good example of the Southerner who could see good in the North as well as in the South. In *Bob Taylor's Magazine* (February, 1906), using his characteristic spread-eagle oratory in the essay "Yankee Doodle and Dixie," he praised both sections of the country.

When the angels of the Lord had laid out and completed the second paradise on earth—which I think the Cherubim and Seraphim named Dixie —when they had rested under the shade of its trees, and bathed in its crystal waters and breathed the perfume of its flowers, they spread their wings on its mellow air and mounted upward towards the skies. They hung a rainbow on the clouds, and pursuing its gorgeous archway northward over hill and vale and mountain, and across the Potomac and Ohio, they alighted to tie its nether end to earth, and behold! there lay stretched out before them another empire of transcendent beauty, and lo! they made a third paradise, and called it the Land of Yankee Doodle; the rainbow still rests with one end on Dixie and the other on Yankee Doodle, its radiant arch overshadowing a race of the bravest men and the most beautiful women that the sun in heaven ever shone upon. . . .

It is true that the Northerner still says "You hadn't ought to do it," and the Southerner says "I've gone and done it," but the sectional line which separates them, and which was once a bloody chasm is now only the great dividing line between cold bread and hot biscuits.

Men like Henry Watterson, editor of the Louisville *Courier-Journal*, who believed that the future lay with a "New South," worked untiringly for understanding and a real reconciliation. Watterson noted in the Preface to his collection of Southern humor, *Oddities in Southern Life and Character*, that his objective was to promote "a better understanding among classes of people hitherto kept asunder by misconceptions and prejudices the most whimsical." The book, published in 1882, showed that indeed much of the South was an "odd corner" of the nation, but that this "differentness" did not make it less a valuable part of the whole.

LaSalle Corbell Pickett, noted most for her humorous works, also wrote histories of the war. Of her best-known history, the one about her famous husband, *Pickett and His Men*, the Atlanta *Constitution* wrote, "She makes no timid apologies in deference to changed conditions; but at the same time she writes in such sweet temper that her work throughout breathes the violet aroma of complete reconciliation."[4] Mrs. Pickett's work was typical of other Southern women, and some men, whose almost forgotten works exhale "the violet aroma" of reconciliation. The works of Thomas Nelson Page and Joel Chandler Harris offer occasional examples.

Another woman, the local colorist Mary Noailles Murfree, was careful to exclude sectionalism from her Southern studies. In a letter to her publisher accompanying the manuscript of *Where the Battle Was Fought*, she wrote, "The scene is laid in the South, in 1871, but no sectional feeling is manifested nor indication of any political bias."[5] An economic motivation, of course, was partly behind this mood because the larger part of the book and magazine market was still in the North. At the end of *The Southerner* Walter Hines Page ("Nicholas Worth") showed even more plainly that his purpose had not been to antagonize his Northern readers. "If any reader of what I have written shall find anywhere a single word of bitterness, I pray him to rub it out." But reconciliation was the order of the day.

George Cary Eggleston was another writer of humor who aimed at reconciling the two former enemies. Of the first success of *A Rebel's Recollections* in the North and South he wrote in the edition of 1905, "I was satisfied that my work had really ministered somewhat to that reconciliation between North and South which I had really hoped to help forward." First published serially in William Dean Howells' *Atlantic Monthly*, the memoirs of his Confederate service had met with a cordial response in New England. Early in his recollections Eggleston assured the reader that "it is no part of my purpose to write a defense of the Southern view of any question" (p. 2). For him all such defenses had been vitiated by Appomattox.

Although apologetic for the South, Thomas Nelson Page in such stories as

"Marse Chan" and "Meh Lady" helped to erase the bitter sectional hatred. In the laughter and tears of his stories much ill will was purged away. The novel *Two Little Confederates* contains passages showing kindness and compassion on both sides. The two little Confederates, for example, one day come upon a dying Union soldier pleading for a drink of water. They bring him some and later help carry his body to their house and bury it in the garden. After the war the dead soldier's mother comes south looking for his grave; and finding that a Southern family had respected him and had given him a decent burial, out of gratitude she sent them clothing and two new guns for the two little ex-Confederates. In the same novel Page shows the Yankee soldiers to be generally courteous. When an officer has to search a house for Rebel officers, he apologizes to the lady. "I hope, madam, that you ladies will not be alarmed. . . . You need be under no apprehension, I assure you. . . . I am sorry to be forced to do violence to my feelings, but I must search the house" (pp. 101-2). With such evidences of kindness on both sides, the North and South could not remain irrevocably separated.

Of all the Southern humorists Joel Chandler Harris was probably the one who did most to reconcile the earlier belligerents. "We had enough war in 1865," he once said. Ray Stannard Baker characterized the tone of his works in these words: "Indeed, there is not one unkindly or fault-finding or cynical line in all the volumes of Uncle Remus's writings. Though brought up in the South in war time, and though he saw much of the terrible ravages of the victorious Union army, there is nowhere in his work so much as a touch of sectional hatred. Many of his stories deal with the troublesome days of civil discord, and yet all tend to heal and soothe the bitterness between North and South."[6] Harris was able to do so much because he was one of the most widely admired American writers. The historian Lucian L. Knight described his fellow Georgian's popularity: "With his cabin songs of the old regime he has literally put a girdle of music around the globe, and even in the library of the New England scholar, he has made the southern cotton patch as classic as the Roman arena."[7] No sectional writer could have won such universal acclaim.

Explicit examples of reconciliation talk are not hard to find in Harris' works. The title character in *Gabriel Tolliver* is frequently a mouthpiece for the author's views of reunion. At a political barbecue Gabriel makes a speech, using as his theme a statement made to him by a judge. "Why should a parcel of politicians turn us against a Government under which we are compelled to live?" (p. 44). This stoic philosophy helped many a Southerner agree to shake hands with his former enemy. In the editorial announcement that ushered in *Uncle Remus's Magazine,* in 1907, Harris stated explicitly the plan which had been behind his Uncle Remus stories and most of his other work. He wrote that the magazine would be Southern by reason of its environment, but that all its motives and policies would be "broader than any section and higher than any partisanship." Though pleased with that provincialism which provides a variety of types, he pledged that "those who will be in charge of the magazine will have nothing to do with the provinciality so prevalent in the North, East, South, and West which stands for ignorance and blind prejudice, that represents narrow views and an unhappy congestion of ideas."[8] Throughout his literary life Harris tried to erase misunderstanding and prejudice between the sections wherever he found it.

When humor dealing with the war or Reconstruction lapsed into bitterness, the writer would usually make amends by ending his criticism with a plea for national unity. After a bitter attack on the Beast Butler, J. Fairfax McLaughlin, the author of *The American Cyclops*, ends with a call for reconciliation (p. 27).

> *Haply my country's freedom still remains,*
> *And with the night have passed oppression's chains.*
> *Oh, may the storms which settle o'er our land*
> *Be gently lifted by th' all-saving Hand;*
> *The dove return; fraternal discord cease,*
> *And millions join the Jubilee of Peace!*

Out of the dissipating sectional hatred came a demand for national oneness. A major aim of the Southern humorist was being reached.

Many writers appealed to a common heritage and common prewar heroes in reconciling the nation. Anecdotes of American figures which both North and South could honor became popular. Washington, Jefferson, Jackson, Patrick Henry, Davy Crockett, Sam Houston—all these and more furnished subjects for humor which helped to remind all sections of the nation of their common past. Some writers went as far back as Sir Walter Raleigh and Captain John Smith for their subjects.[9]

John Esten Cooke, Thomas Nelson Page, and others sought subjects for their humor in colonial days. The celebration of the centennial of the Revolution in 1876 intensified Americans' awareness of their common history. By 1900 Benjamin Wells could say of the South, "She is learning to turn her eyes more and more from secession and reconstruction to the romance of her colonial history, and of the Revolution."[10] During the same year Thomas Nelson Page, earlier a Southerner of Southerners, wrote a story, not about the South at all, but about "Santa Claus' Partner" in New York. Two years earlier the Tennessee local colorist Will Allen Dromgoole had focused on a national hero of prewar days in "Old Hickory's Ball" and in other stories about Andrew Jackson.

The Fourth of July was still a day for celebrating all over the nation. Wier in *Old Times in Georgia* showed how this holiday helped point up a common heritage. In the sketch "An Old Time Fourth in Flat Ground" an old-timer, after hearing a procession of speakers make excuses for the mother country, gets up and criticizes them for hurrahing too much for England and not showing enough American patriotism. He tells the startled crowd, "Me and my folks come to hear old England cussed, and if nobody else won't cuss her I'll be dadrab my buttons if I don't do it. . . . I say d--n old England and hurrah for George Washington and the brave men what followed him and stuck to him through thick and thin." In addition to the Revolution, other American wars were subjects of reconciliation humor: the War of 1812, the Mexican War, the War for Texas' Independence, and various Indian battles. The Virginia humorist Dr. George W. Bagby epitomizes the Southerner who passed from sectional loyalty to national loyalty because of his awareness of an all-American past. The spirit of reconciliation is the motivation for an address he delivered at Trenton, New Jersey, in 1882, "Yorktown and Appomattox," in which he drew a parallel between two climactic events of America's two greatest wars.

Lincoln was rapidly being made into a national hero. During the war Southern humorists had excoriated him as a meddling "nigger-lover," but after his assassination they began to find much good in the man who had freed their slaves. They concluded that at his death he was the best friend the South had. In 1906 Myrta Lockett Avary could paint a very sympathetic picture of the wartime President without fear of criticism from fellow Southerners. The historian included in *Dixie After the War* an anecdote about Lincoln which showed him to be forgiving and kind toward the South. "His last joke—the story-tellers say it was his last—was about 'Dixie.' General Lee's surrender had been announced; Washington was ablaze with excitement. Delirious multitudes surged to the White House, calling the President out for a speech. It was a moment for easy betrayal into words that might widen the breach between sections. He said in his quaint way that he had no speech ready, and concluded humorously: 'I have always thought "Dixie" one of the best tunes I ever heard. I insisted yesterday that we had fairly captured it. I presented the question to the Attorney-General and he gave his opinion that it is our lawful prize. I ask the band to give us a good turn upon it'" (p. 43). In that little speech he demanded from the defeated South a song—nothing more. Such generosity, even if the anecdote is apocryphal, would have made recovery from the war easier in the South.

Harris' spokesman in *Gabriel Tolliver,* the humorous countryman Billy Sanders, tells Alexander Stephens, the one-time Vice-President of the Confederacy, of his attempt to kidnap Lincoln and what he really thought of the President. "Well, sir, I thought, an' still think that he was the best all-'round man I ever laid eyes on." Stephens replies, "He certainly was a great man. . . . I knew him before the war. We were in Congress together" (p. 120).

A concept related to history and historical figures, nationalism as a unifying force was frequently exploited by the humorists. This force impressed upon the people North and South the fact that they were actually one with a common history, a common language, a common culture, and common ideals. They were all Americans. The Kentuckian Eliza Caroline Obenchain (she wrote as Eliza Calvert Hall) produced local-color sketches that showed the basic national unity of the American people even when they differed on the outside. An advertisement for *Aunt Jane of Kentucky* reads: "The humor of the book is softened and refined by being linked with pathos and romance, and the character drawing is done with so firm a hand that we seem for the moment to live on the highways, around the hearthstones, and in the gardens of that country neighborhood, smiling over its joys, weeping over its sorrows, and realizing afresh our common humanity, our kinship with the children of the Kentucky soil."[11] Like Mrs. Obenchain's books, all reconciliation humor was likely to be so "softened" and "refined" by pathos that it called forth as many tears as smiles. There were few good belly laughs in the humor of reconciliation.

The poet-humorist of the Atlanta *Constitution*, Frank L. Stanton, wrote many poems that stressed nationalism. "The Warship Dixie" in *Comes One with a Song*, for example, is a poem of reconciliation which expresses joy over a United States cruiser named "Dixie" and manned by ex-Confederates. Its significance Stanton compresses into one couplet. "She means we're all united—the war hurts healed away, / An' 'Way Down South in Dixie' is national today."

Southerners even went so far as to recognize the arch-abolitionist poet John Greenleaf Whittier as a national bard. Though John Trotwood Moore was the author of many partisan Confederate poems, he also wrote a poem to the memory of the dead Quaker poet in which he characterized Whittier as having "The heart that throbbed for others, / The mind that thought no wrong."[12] Reconciliation was almost complete when a Southerner could write these words about a radical abolitionist.

In many of his stories the North-Carolina-born O. Henry suggested a nationalism in which North, West, and South were each to play an important part. In such stories as "The Duplicity of Hargraves" and "The Rose of Dixie" he staged a contrast between the North and the South. Although he gently satirized foibles of both sections, he was also fair to both. The theme of these stories is not sectionalism but reciprocity. To O. Henry art was not sectional, and he often protested the labeling of his stories as local-color sketches. He once said that "so long as a story is true to human nature all you need to do to fit any town is to change the local color."[13] He proved this statement in "A Municipal Report." The truth of the human heart, he maintained, can be told as well in a story set in New York as in Alabama. The Southern humorist became in O. Henry more cosmopolitan than Southern. His stories are clearly in the tradition of reconciliation humor, for he could see from both Northern and Southern vantage points. Having lived all over the country from North Carolina to Texas and New York and having no vested interest in any one place, he had the perspective necessary to view both sections without prejudice. Katharine Jones' *New Confederate Short Stories* (1954), which includes several written before 1914, contains stories which emphasize the nationalistic impulse. In the Preface Miss Jones wrote: "In all these stories, the War, the Union, and the Confederacy are viewed, explicitly or implicitly, as a national heritage. In 'Two Renegades,' by O. Henry, the Confederacy joins forces with the Union in the face of a South American firing squad. . . . There are Yankees and Rebels in these stories, but first of all they are Americans."

The most articulate humorist using appeals to nationalism was of course Joel Chandler Harris. Beginning early in his writing career, he stressed the basic similarity of American types. In an editorial he called "Georgia Crackers: Types and Shadows," published in the Atlanta *Constitution* of September 28, 1879, he pointed out parallels between William T. Thompson's Major Jones and James Russell Lowell's Hosea Biglow, the typical Cracker and the typical Yankee. Major Jones "is not only typically Georgian, but typically national. . . . Major Jones is Brother Jonathan thinly disguised in a suit of Georgia linsey-woolsey. We might compare the Major with Sam Slick; but we prefer to stand him up alongside Hosea Biglow, a serious literary study of the typical Yankee. Examine them critically, and the parallel is complete. Bring Hosea Biglow to Georgia, turn him loose in a pine thicket, show him a bunch of dogwood blossoms, make him acquainted with the joree and the jay, give him a suit of jeans (which he would probably bring in his carpetsack), and then you have your Major Joseph Jones, who is 'yours till deth.' Take the Major to New England, let him tamper with the climate and learn how to save tobacco instead of giving it away, and there is your Hosea Biglow. Being typical, they are national; being national, they are well-nigh identical." Harris had concluded that the local character is at the same time national because the American national character is a composite made up of many local types.

A few days later "The Puritan and the Cracker" appeared in the *Constitution* and he continued to stress that both Major Jones and Hosea Biglow were equally national types. "Major Jones and Hosea Biglow are characters that will live because they are locally perfect and typically national. Each represents a section, and each is as identically American as the other. . . . One is the hero of an episode purely pastoral in its surroundings, and the other is a provincial politician of the most intense pattern. . . . The contrast between the pastoral instincts of Major Jones and the political pretensions of Hosea Biglow, while it does not disturb their resemblance to each other, is, nevertheless, perplexing in another direction. The popular idea in the North is that every Southern man is engaged in political discussion, while every Yankee is shrewdly attending to his private affairs. And yet here is Mr. Hosea Biglow, the typical Yankee, discoursing of politics continually; while Major Joseph Jones, the typical Southern cracker, is engaged in imparting confidentially to his friend, the country editor, the installments of the only pastoral love story in American literature." In other words, Harris underlined his assertion that the two stereotypes of local characters are interchangeable by pointing out the paradoxical fact that in at least one way Major Jones is more Yankee than Southern and that Hosea Biglow is in one way more Southern than Yankee. Continuing this vein of criticism in 1881, Harris stated that "if the South is ever to make any permanent or important contribution to the literature of the world, we must get over our self-consciousness" and accept literary criticism unflinchingly. The Southern writer, he was sure, must be willing to accept the sometimes harsh verdict of objective critics and readers everywhere—even outside the South. Only then could he merit a place in American and world literature.[14]

Southern humor after the war, therefore, remained largely provincial but lost most of its sectional tone. It was caught up in, reflected, and helped form the spirit of nationalism that worked to rejoin the divided country. Another Harris comment on sectionalism in literature reflects the opinion of most Southern humorists of the period: "What does it matter whether I am a Northerner or a Southerner if I am true to truth, and true to the larger truth, my own self? My idea is that truth is more important than sectionalism, and that literature that can be labeled Northern, Southern, Western, or Eastern is not worth labeling at all."[15] With such judgments the literary standards of Southern humor—and of literature in general—were being raised.

A war is always followed by the ringing of many wedding bells celebrating the union of erstwhile enemies. This was especially true after the Civil War because the enemies had so much in common. Postwar humor showed the symbolic reunion of the nation in the marriage of a couple, usually consisting of a Northern officer and a Southern belle.* The stock situation had the couple meet during the war under critical circumstances—usually the belle's family was starving—and as a result of the officer's befriending the poor girl's family, a romance began to develop. When the war ended, he returned to make official his declaration of love, and they got married and lived happily ever after, each praising the other's section of the country. Rebecca Washington Smith found that "The most popular and dramatic motive in Civil War literature was that of the Union soldier-lover and the Southern girl" (p. 41).

By 1884 even Bill Arp could see some good in the intermarrying of Northerner and Southerner. He put in his *Scrap Book:* "There is a power of difference in human stock. The pure breed of Yankees never was a favorite with me. When it is judiciously crossed it does very well and I have known some mighty good grades to come from a mixture of the Yank with the old Southern blooded stock" (p. 287). In the same volume Smith commented approvingly on the fondness of Southern men for Yankee schoolmarms. "They go for 'em quick, and it's a pretty fair bargain, for there is money on the one side and rebel blood and independence on the other, and that's a good compromise" (p. 275).

One of the stories in Louise Looney's *Tennessee Sketches* fills out the formula. In "Gray Farm Folk" a young lady persuades a Union officer to remand an order to burn their plantation home. After the war the young ex-officer, realizing his love for the Southern girl since he first met her, searches her out, finds her in Washington, and takes her to the altar.

In many of Thomas Nelson Page's stories the reconciliatory marriage occurs. The title character in "Meh Lady," after much mental anguish, acknowledges her love for a Federal captain and marries him, knowing that just a few months before he had been an enemy of her country. Page was not to be taken in completely by the literary vogue, however. True-blue Virginian that he was, he could not see a Virginia belle marrying a Yankee soldier with no Old Dominion

---

* Southern writers were not alone in the exploitation of the intersectional marriage theme. John W. DeForest, *The Bloody Chasm* (1881), and Maurice Thompson, *A Tallahassee Girl* (1881), and *His Second Campaign* (1883), use the marriage of a Southern girl and a Northern suitor to effect a symbolic reconciliation.

115

connections. William Dean Howells' comment on how Page resolved the dilemma is itself amusing. "I am rather glad that he keeps so entirely to the Virginian atmosphere [in his stories] that even when a Virginian girl must give herself to a Union soldier, it is to a Union soldier of Virginian lineage, and of her own blood at no great cousinly remove."[16] Howells' reading of Page was correct because the Virginian usually makes it plain that the Yankee bridegroom is a nephew or grandson or cousin of some prominent Southerner.

The fictional marriages in Joel Chandler Harris are perhaps the best examples of this method of reconciliation. "Aunt Fountain's Prisoner," to illustrate, is the story of a wounded Federal soldier who is nursed back to health in a Southern home and eventually marries the only daughter of the household.[17] Reading an advertisement in the paper for Tomlinson butter, the narrator of the story is astonished to see that the aristocratic old Tomlinson place has been turned into a dairy farm. Soon afterwards while in the neighborhood he visits Aunt Fountain, once a slave owned by the Tomlinsons, to find out what has happened to the family. The woman goes back to the war to explain the change. She tells of how she rescued an injured Yankee soldier, Fess Trunion, from a gully, where he had been left by Sherman's advancing army. The soldier, she says, was in a pitiful condition: he had a fever, pneumonia, and a broken leg; but she carried him to the Tomlinson place nearby, where he recovered. The narrator then visits the plantation, where he meets an industrious Fess Trunion. "He told me laughingly of some of his troubles with his hot-headed neighbors in the early days after the war, but nothing of this sort seemed to be as important as his difficulties with Bermuda grass." The Yankee-Southerner had combined his know-how with a temperate Southern climate and had made a success. The narrator notes admiringly, "There were comforts and conveniences on the Tomlinson Place not dreamed of in the old days." Harris appends the moral of one Yankee's success in the South. "I do not know what industrial theories Trunion has impressed on his neighborhood by this time, but he gave me a practical illustration of the fact that one may be a Yankee and a Southerner too, simply by being a large-hearted whole-souled American." Harris, like many another humorist, saw an ideal combination in the progressive, scientific, and practical Yankee and the gracious, cultured, tradition-regarding Southerner.

Sometimes, as in Page, the Yankee officer is kin to the Southerners he befriends. In *Gabriel Tolliver* Harris explored, in addition to relationship, the conflict between hatred of the enemy and attraction to his good looks. Two girls are talking. "And, oh, Nan! you know the Yankee captain who is in command of the Yankee soldiers here? Well, his name is Falconer, and mother says he is our cousin. And would you believe it, she wanted to ask him to tea. I cried when she told me; I never was so angry in my life. Why, I wouldn't stay in the same house nor eat at the same table with one who is an enemy of my country." "Nor I either," said Nan with emphasis. "But he's very handsome" (p. 131). The motto *omnia amor vincit* was proved to be just as effective in the post-Civil-War South as it had been in Chaucer's day.

A later novel by Harris, *A Little Union Scout,* explores further the anguish of the love of a man and woman on opposite sides of the war. This time it is the woman who is the Unionist. The story concerns a notorious Union spy who is revealed as a woman when she is captured by the narrator of the story. The captor falls in love with the spy, in spite of her nefarious work, and gradually wins the indignant and rebellious girl. When the Southerner himself is captured by Union soldiers, she helps him escape. Harris used their parting to illustrate the absurdity of sectional loyalties. The Unionist says to the Rebel: "Do you care enough for me to desert your comrades and fling your principles to the four winds? Do I care enough for you to leave my people and give my sympathies to your side?" He answers her searching question. "I do care enough for you to leave everything for your sake." When their passions have cooled somewhat, however, they decide against deserting either side. The little spy admits, "I am not myself today. Duty has been poisoned for me, and I shall be wretched until this war is over." But as the Southerner leaves to rejoin his command, he exclaims passionately, "If you'll say the word . . . I'll go with you." Just as passionately, she responds, "I can't! I can't! . . . Do you say it, and I'll go with you." Neither willing to make the other a deserter, they part, planning to meet a year later in a nearby tavern. After the year passes, they meet and marry. Thus the power of love triumphs over extreme partisanship in two people; and Harris seems to suggest that it can triumph on a larger scale—a national scale— as well. The North and the South had, as it were, to fall in love and be wedded before complete reconciliation could be accomplished. Individual marriages helped, but a national marriage of sections was necessary.

Certain events contributed greatly toward better understanding between, and a closer union of, the North and South. Many of these events are reflected in humor: the election of 1876, the Memphis yellow fever epidemic, the Spanish-American War, and World War I. Most of these events were critical to the future of the nation, and they showed that in times of crisis the nation closed ranks.

One of the first events that contributed materially to reunion was the election settlement of 1876. Samuel J. Tilden, the nominee of the Democrats, received a majority of the electoral votes and was apparently the winner over Rutherford B. Hayes, the candidate of the Republicans; but in four states—including three in the South—the election results were disputed. The dispute was settled by negotiation, with Hayes getting all the contested electoral votes. Rumor held that the Republicans had agreed to withdraw all troops from the South and appoint a Southerner to the cabinet if the three Southern states would certify the Republican electors. In effect, the North was admitting that the South was best qualified to solve its own problems. Some Southerners, however, were anything but happy over the gentleman's agreement. Sam W. Small's Old Si expressed his reservations about Hayes' victory, but he said there would be no war over the controversy because Southern whites had gotten their fill of fighting several years before. As he put it in *Old Si's Sayings:* "Dey fit, an' dey mought fite agin, fer

117

ter sabe fo' millium ob niggers; but when it comes ter fite'n fer jess one ole white man, an' dat man a Norfern feller, dey's gwine ter ax ter be 'scused fum de skirmidge . . ." (p. 113). After the election of Hayes, Old Si laments that he can't distinguish between a " 'publican" and a "dimmycrat" any more. Addressing members of his race, " . . . niggers, sense Hays got in de cheer an' gotter doin' 'bout, fust wid dis han' an' den wid dat, dese whole polyticks 'pears ter me like one ob dese flying hoss mersheers at de state fa'r whar gits so fas' dat all de hosses is strung tergedder, an' yer can't 'stinguish one frum tudder" (p. 50). He concludes sadly that it's impossible to tell "whedder de 'publican hoss is swallerin' de democrat hoss, er hit's tudder way." He was sure, however, that the Democrats had sold out to the black Republicans. His reaction to Hayes' appointment of a Georgia Negro as consul at Malaga is skeptical. Distrust of the President's intentions is implicit in Old Si's words: ". . . de presydent ain't gwine ter send no nigger counsul [*sic*] whar de grapes grow—grapes is fer white folks, all de time! An' when you reeds in de papers dat he's sent er nigger fer consul er returney ef law ter Malagy, er enny whar' else, you kin jess put hit down dat's some place dat no white man wants, an' whar' de nigger'll find his fees moughty skase an' his feed skaser!" (p. 52).

Opposition to Republicanism was growing; Old Si's criticism of a compromised President was but one manifestation of it. Partly as a result of the election settlement in 1876, the Democrats increased in power and numbers. One rumor circulated by Republican partisans had it that when the Democrats should come into power the Rebels would take over the country. Old Si put the damper on that rumor. "Well, hit's fool talk, dat's what hit is, fur de white folks in Geo'gy is no mo' rebels dan I tell yer. A hoss is got less foolishniss dan a colt and kno's whar de troff is soon as he heahs de co'n rattle inter hit. Dem what was rebels is 'bout ter eat co'n an' is stayin' inside de palin's . . ." (p. 69). Si knew human nature too well to go along with those who thought that Southerners would cause trouble, just when they were about to reach the trough of political spoils for the first time since before the war. No, the Tilden-Hayes election controversy had been the beginning of more political power for the white South. They were not going to risk a promising future for a repetition of Fort Sumter and its consequences.

Another event which helped dissipate sectional hatred was the series of yellow fever epidemics in the 1870's. A poem in cracker dialect by Sam Small, "Bob Sutton at Memphis," shows how the nation was drawn closer by Yankee response to the suffering at Memphis. Blankets, ice, and other supplies were sent down from the North "afore we call'd twice" and helped save many lives. In the piece a near victim of the epidemic relates his change of attitude after his life is saved by a Yankee blanket.

> *Well, brother, I've been mighty solid*
>   *Agin' Yankees, yer know, sence the wah—*
> *An' agin' reconstrucktin' was stolid,*
>   *Not kearin fer Kongriss ner law;*

> But, John, I got onder that kiver,
>   That God-blessed gift o' the Yanks,
> An' it saved me frum fordin' "the river,"
>   An' I'm prayin' em oceans o' thanks!

Through the yellow fever survivor, Small stated his belief that crises would always bring the country closer together.

> I tell yer, old boy, thar's er streak in us
>   Old Rebels an' Yanks thet is warm—
> It's brotherly love thet'll speak in us
>   An' fetch us tergether in storm;
> We may snarl about "niggers an' francheese,"
>   But whenever thar's sufferin' afoot—
> The two trees'll unite in the branches
>   The same as they do at the root!

The last two lines deserve a rereading because they paint a vivid love-picture of the reconciled North and South. In times of distress the "branches" as well as the "roots" of the national tree would be united.

The South had always been proud of her military tradition, and when the United States was again threatened with war in 1898, former Confederates—officers, men, and civilians—answered the call to arms. The South was again as ready to defend the Union as she had been before 1861. Preluding this avenue of reunion, on May 31, 1884, the *Arkansaw Traveler* printed an anecdote of the Civil War in which Confederate and Federal units in Southern Missouri fought a common enemy—rattlesnakes. The sketch ends: "They agreed to camp together, and during the social night, when 'reb' and 'yank' sat around the same fire, the great bloody war was forgotten. Each man—true human nature—told lies of the number and size of the snakes he had killed. This was the first evidence of coming peace. It proved to men who never before had seen each other that there existed a great enemy of mankind against which they should all be united." And in *Comes One with a Song* by Frank L. Stanton, "A Southern Volunteer" recites his Civil War experiences fighting for the South, but ends each stanza with "But if this here Union goes to war, / Make one more gun for me!" He had the opportunity after the American ship "Maine" was blown up in Havana harbor.

In *Old Plantation Days* Martha Gielow told how the Spanish-American War fanned national patriotism in a small Alabama town. The sketch "Mammy Joe Tells of the Sinking of the Merrimac" shows how war news of the bravery of her "Marse Rich" caused an old Negro woman to react. She spreads the word that her former master's son sank a ship and then walked the water to safety. She adds religiously, "I jes looks fer Marse Rich ter be translated, an' 'spects de nex' thing we hyar, de charrot will have tuk him up inter hebben." The entire town is excited by a native son's heroism and flags are flown all over. At first, only Confederate flags are in evidence, but this partiality is soon remedied. "When the evening train came in from Selma, however, the Stars and Stripes, which had been telegraphed for, were unfurled by the side of the mementoes of the Lost Cause. The flag of the nation took on a new meaning, and for the first time since the war, the 'Stars and Stripes' floated peacefully over many proud mansions and devastated Southern homes." Thus reconciliation comes to the last stronghold of Confederate sentiment, the small Southern town.

"Uncle Aaron's Greeting: A Monologue" from *Plantation Songs* by Martha Young ("Eli Sheppard") shows the amusing reaction of an old darky to news that a son of the South is fighting in the Yankee army. When he hears that the son of his former master is back from fighting in Santiago, Uncle Aaron goes up to the Great House to welcome him. On the way he reminisces about "our war" and compares it with the present one. "Our war wa'n't played to dis tune!" He continues:

> *Marcy! in our war my master*
> *And four hundred 'listed one night!*
> *Ev'y one had his several hosses,*
> *Nigger cook, nigger boy, nigger man;*
> *Besides from dis ve'y plantation*
> *Mos' a whole endurin' brass ban'.*

He speculates skeptically on what the new war is about.

> *Well, times is obleeged to change,*
> *And de ole ways is mos' wo' out:*
> *Young folks, and new ways, and new wars—*
> *Wonder what dis new war is about:*
> *Never heard of no Spaniards in my time,*
> *De Lord must have made 'em sence.*
> *In Cuba? Freein' mo' niggers?*
> *Dar's enough on dis side of de fence.*
> *A passel of skittish free darkeys*
> *As won't let ole folks teach 'em sense.*

Like all "uncle" and "auntie" personalities in humor, Uncle Aaron speaks the mind and sentiments of his white creator. Nearing the Great House, he sees to his amazement a Yankee flag flying over the house. He whispers a warning to his grandchildren accompanying him.

> *Marcy me! what'd dat on de tower?*
> *Yankee-flag, des sho as I'm born!*
> *Heah, chil'en, slip down and hide*
> *Right heah is dis ruslin' high corn—*
> *Dem Yankees sure found dat Marse Tom*
> *Was des come home for a spell,*
> *And dey done come and took dat boy*
> *Ter deir Dry 'Tugas Prison, or hell!*

120

They hide in the corn and peep out to see Marse Tom sitting on the porch. Uncle Aaron is overjoyed at seeing the white man but is shocked by the blue uniform he is wearing. Over the initial shock of seeing the white man in a Yankee uniform, Uncle Aaron gets more details on Southern participation in the war.

> *You say you follered Joe Wheeler*
> *   To de rifle-pits down at Caney?*
> *Dat's right. Us follered dat Wheeler*
> *   From Tupelo to Kintuck—like you say.*
> *And you say Wheeler rallied 'em on*
> *   And won de whole glorious day!*

But he can hardly believe that the great Confederate General Wheeler is now fighting for the "enemy" flag.

> *But you say he rallied his men*
> *   Round dat flag, and led men from New York?*
> *I sholy believe my senses*
> *   Gwine ac' like a mustang—and balk*
> *And us all des one country now,*
> *   Same as had no Great War at all?*

He is still a little puzzled at what he has seen and heard.

> *All I know is: With things gwine like you say*
> *   Den us nigh to de golden sho',*
> *Whar dey eats des butter and honey,*
> *   And whar Yankees ain't Yankees no mo'.*

This humorous poem by an obscure Southern writer is an excellent exhibit showing how the Spanish-American War made comrades of former enemies, at home as well as on the battlefield.

No Southerner was ashamed of the Stars and Bars or the Confederacy; however, times had changed since the Civil War, and the only new wars the South would fight would be under the Stars and Stripes. Frank A. Montgomery's *Reminiscences of a Mississippian in Peace and War*, published in 1901, showed pride in the part Mississippi played in the Civil War; but the author ended the book on a note of reconciliation. "The star of Mississippi which once seemed to have been quenched in the blood of her sons, and made the paradise of slaves, once more shines with renewed luster amid the bright galaxy of her sisters, and with them henceforth 'one and inseparable' will shine on forever!" By 1901 reconciliation was almost a reality.

World War I made the reunion of the nation complete. The dedication of Lucian Lamar Knight's *Memorials of Dixie-Land*, published just after the war, shows how united the North and South were by then: "To the Sentiment of Brotherhood Which a Great World War Has Intensified and Strengthened in the Heart of a New America." But pride in the Confederacy was not dead. "But in keeping with the broadest spirit of nationality, I desire, in a subordinate way, to inscribe these pages to two Confederate soldiers, each of whom went to his grave a devoted champion of the Union." The humor of the period but reflected the trend toward unity—a unity accelerated by certain climactic events.

Before the Civil War, W. T. Thompson's Major Jones in his *Travels* toured the North—more than 4,000 miles and 14 states—and in his observations he said that such travel would do a Southerner much good. The Southerner would learn a lot about his Northern brethren. "He will find all sorts of peeple thar—sum that is examples of patriotism, intelligence, and enterprise, and sum that ain't no manner of account on the face of the yearth, only to kick up a eternal rumpus and keep the world in a everlastin stew about ther new-fangled fooleries. . . . Thar's a good deal of ignorance and prejudice at the North, to be shore, specially about matters what don't consarn ther own interests; but it is to be hoped that whar ther is so much patriotism and intelligence, they will sum day larn to mind ther own bisness, and leave other peeple's consarns to be regulated by ther own consciences and ther own judgments" (p. 206). This passage could just as easily have been taken from the observations of a later Bill Arp, had Bill made such a trip. The tone and the recommendation are in the immediate postwar tradition. It was Major Jones' last bit of advice which the North finally decided to take after Reconstruction had failed. When the North concluded to let the South solve its own race problems (largely after 1876), a true reconciliation of the two sections became possible. The North gave up trying to reconstruct the South according to a Yankee blueprint; and the literature of reconciliation, which increased after 1876, usually pictured the South as best able to handle her own peculiar problems.

Long before Northern politicians realized the futility of radical Reconstruction and stopped waving the bloody shirt, Northern humorists were promoting reunion. Bill Arp, for example, praised Josh Billings at his death because "in all his great and curious utterances he had never written a line that showed prejudice or malignity to our people or our section."[18] Another Yankee humorist, George Peck, dedicated his humorous war memoirs "To the Boys in Blue and the Boys in Gray, who got real spunky at each other some years ago," but "who have decided to be neighbors and friends again, ready to protect and defend each other against the world. . . ." Thus Northern humorists were among the first and most influential of their section to make reconciliation overtures to the South.

While the war was still going on, many Yankee soldiers did their best to make a good impression on the South. In *On the Plantation* Joel Chandler Harris painted a not unpleasant picture of Union troops, and this one a group usually mentioned only in scorn, foragers from Sherman's army. "Joe Maxwell saw a good deal of these foragers, and he found them all, with one exception, to be good-humored." The exception was not even a real Yankee, but a German. The kindness and jocularity of Sherman's men on the march to the sea are illustrated by what they call out to Joe, a small boy who is sitting on a fence watching the passing columns. They direct good-humored jests at him, such as "He's a bush-whacker, boys. If he bats his eyes, I'm a-goin' to dodge!" (p. 229). Had Northern politicians but retained *their* sense of humor when planning the Reconstruction program, reconciliation could have taken place long before it did.

After the war many Union soldiers in the occupation forces were sympathetic to the South and opposed the Congressional Reconstruction program just as much as Southerners did. Such a friend of the South was the young captain in charge of the detachment of Federal troops stationed at Shady Dale in Harris' *Gabriel Tolliver*. The young officer tells Billy Sanders that he is a Democrat from a family of Democrats. He assures the Georgian that he does not believe in Negro suffrage and detests the radical Reconstruction being forced upon the South. But, he explains to the genial countryman, as a soldier he unfortunately has to obey orders regardless of how obnoxious they may be to him personally. He is aware of Southern hatred for the occupation forces, and he is forgiving. Harris describes the officer's reaction to Southern contempt: "He had observed all this, and he was wounded by it; and yet he had no resentment. Being a Southerner himself, he knew that the feelings which prompted such actions were perfectly natural, the fitting accompaniment of the humiliation which the radical element compelled the whites to endure" (pp. 319-23). The sympathetic Union officer is, of course, fictional; but Harris had much real evidence on which to base the character.

In addition to the compassionate occupation soldier, there were Democratic politicians in the North who generally opposed the Republican plan of reconstruction. In a letter to "Mr. Tammany Hall" in February, 1866, *Bill Arp, So Called* paid tribute to all such Southern sympathizers in the North, while jibing at the radicals. "We are whipt at last, Old Tammany. We rebs are conquered, subdued, and subjugated, not by bayonets or bullets, but by your friendly overtures, your manly speeches." Such gracious gestures, Bill continues, have made the South as docile as it had been hostile; and adds, "Thank the Lord that there are good men north of Dixey." Then he makes a recommendation and a promise. "Don't be alarmed, don't receed, don't take back nothin; be calm and sereen, and we of the rebellious South will wipe out the last spark of hatred to such as you." The Georgian admits harsh criticism of the North, but he maintains that it was provoked. "We've said some hard things, Mr. Hall; we've tried to scorch and blister and excoriate but you see we were goaded, gored by bulls—Trumbulls and Republican bulls." Though the body of the letter is at least half-way conciliatory, Bill Arp cannot resist a postscript of defiance. "I'm gittin to be highly loyal, Mr. Hall; I know I am; for a feller tried to sell me a little nigger to-day, *and I wouldn't buy him.* I heard of a bill that's comin up to bind out the niggers for 99 years, and I'm agin it. Darnd if I'll vote for more than 50. You can tell Thad. Stevens of these hopeful signs" (pp. 174-81). Such an ironic juxtaposition of sentiments was common to the Northern and Southern humorists who were still close enough to the war to smell the cannon fumes. Forgiveness and vengeance were thus continually battling for pre-eminence in their minds.

In *What Happened to Me,* her often humorous autobiography, Mrs. Pickett related how the friendly gestures of Northern men of importance, like Lincoln and Grant, gradually won her over. At Lincoln's death she recorded the reaction of her husband, General George Edward Pickett. "My God! My God! The South has lost her best friend and protector in this, her direst hour of need" (p. 174). The kindnesses shown her and her family by her husband's prewar friends now in the Union army did much to reconcile her. She occasionally gave way to outbursts of bitterness, but these didn't last very long. Once, for example, she became angry when a Yankee general was accorded some military honor and General Pickett was not; and she told her young son that he must hate all Yankees. Soon thereafter, however, another Northern general was kind to them and brought some candy for the baby. Making an exception to her earlier command, she told her son, "You must never be a politician and—you may love this one Yankee a tiny bit, and may suck a piece of his beautiful candy" (p. 198). From then on she continued to add names to the list of Yankees for her son not to hate. After her husband was pardoned by the Federal government, the family returned home from exile in Canada and often entertained Yankee visitors. Once they were invited to visit President Grant at the White House and were pleased that he never referred to Southerners as "Rebels" but as "you fellows on the other side."

An economic fact that helped in the reconciliation was the patronage by the North of Southern writers. Surveying Southern fiction after the war, Bliss Perry wrote: "The public for these stories . . . was still largely in the North and West, and it was the magazines and publishing-houses of New York and Boston that gave the Southern authors their chief stimulus and support. It was one of the happy proofs of the solidarity of the new nation."[19] This circumstance had also contributed to the nation's solidarity because a writer, like anyone else, will not slap the hand that feeds him—even if that hand reaches out from a sleeve of Union blue.

Travel helped the Northerner understand the South and some of the thousands of Yankee tourists swarming over the South after the war became aware of and sympathetic to the South's problems. Of the many Northern writers who came south, the local colorist Constance Fenimore Woolson—sometimes claimed as a Southern writer—is one of the most significant. A grandniece of James Fenimore Cooper, Miss Woolson was born and educated in the North, but during the 1870's she and her mother lived for six years in Florida and the Carolinas. She learned to appreciate and to understand the South's indigenous problems, and in her Southern sketches she advised the North that the South must be left alone to solve these problems. The title story in *Rodman the Keeper* shows her comprehension of, and sympathy for, Southern pride. The Yankee Rodman tells a proud and haughty Southern girl, "Nothing can change you . . . I know it, I have known it all along; you are part of your country, part of the time, part of the bitter hour through which she is passing. Nothing can change you; if it could, you would not be what you are, and I should not—But you can not change." Such feeling and understanding were necessary from the North before the South would be reconciled.

A more explicit statement of self-determination is found in "King David," another sketch from the same volume. This is the story of a New England school-master's failure to rescue "the Children of Ham" soon after the war. David King —his dusky charges soon corrupt it into "King David"—has come south with glorious visions of educating the downtrodden race; but he has trouble com-municating with those he would uplift. The Negroes want a Southern Negro minister to teach them and no one—white or black—from the North. A spokesman tells him the heart of the difficulty when they are celebrating the Northerner's going away. "Our service to you, sah, all de same . . . but you hab nebber quite unnerstan us, sah, nebber quite; an' you can nebber do much fo' us, sah, on 'count ob dat fack—ef you'll scuse my saying so. But it is de trouf. We give you our t'anks and our congratturrurlations, an' we hopes you'll go j'yful back to your own people, an' be a shining light to 'em for ebbermore." The North was beginning to realize that the freedman as well as the ex-Rebel could best be handled by letting them handle themselves.

Another example of how travel helped the Yankee become more sympathetic toward the South is the narrator's wife in Harris' example-rich *Gabriel Tolliver*. Returning to her native New York from a visit to her husband's home town in Georgia, she chides him. "Cephas, you ought to be ashamed of yourself for not going to see those people. . . . Why they are the salt of the earth. I never ex-pected to be treated as they treated me. If it wasn't for your business, I would beg to go back there and live" (p. 5). Her short sojourn in the South had meant a complete change in her views and feelings. Her experience was typical of that of many Northerners whose changed attitudes contributed to the adoption of a hands-off policy toward the South's domestic problems. This allowance of the North made the South more amenable to reconciliation.

When the South admitted that slavery wasn't good—at least wasn't good eco-nomically—she was in a better mood to be reconciled with the North that had taken it away from her. Soon after the war Southern humorists began admitting that slavery was morally and economically bad and stating that its abolition had been a good thing. Even those who had earlier been radical proslavery humor-ists, like Bill Arp, were known to acknowledge—when Yankees weren't within earshot—that slavery had been the blight of the South and could not have lasted.

In George Washington Cable's *Dr. Sevier* (1885) the central character is a Unionist who is convinced all along that the South is wrong. This admission of Southern wrong, however, was not unanimous among Southern writers. At the other extreme was Thomas Nelson Page, who revered the mythical Old South so much he could not forget that the war and the freeing of the slaves were responsible for the destruction of that beautiful society. A society—even one built upon slavery—in which gracious living was a way of life could not, he maintained, have been bad. Joel Chandler Harris was a moderate between these two extremes. Rebecca Washington Smith has plotted the attitudes of these three popular writers this way: "The commonsense and humor of Harris stand midway between Page's reverence for the Old South and the disillusioned view of the war in the writings of George W. Cable before 1899" (p. 39). Harris even went so far as to state that the war had been good for the country. "I am keenly alive to the happier results of the war, and I hope I appreciate at their full value the emancipation of both whites and blacks from the deadly effects of negro slavery, and the wonderful development of our material resources that the war has rendered possible."[20] Yet in his Uncle Remus sketches Harris portrayed the slave, despite the "deadly effects," as quite content and happy with his lot. He took this position because he wanted no vestige of prewar controversy to stand in the way of postwar reconciliation. The slave pictured as persecuted and abused by his owner would have been an obstacle to reunion. Mrs. Smith has written about him: "Through all his works about wartime . . . a few ideas run consistently. There is no real racial antagonism between white man and black, if each keeps his place; the South was wrong in the issues for which the war was fought, but not disgraced; commonsense bids both parties to forget hatreds and help each other." (p. 38).

The memoirs written by many ex-Confederate officers suggest that to them in retrospect slavery seemed wrong. W. W. Blackford, though he had fought valiantly for the South, stated in his *War Years with Jeb Stuart*, written before 1905, that he was glad the Confederacy had failed. When a Confederate lieutenant colonel could accept this view, points of contention between North and South tended to disappear.

When the Southerner became convinced of the moral wrong of slavery, he often tried to allay his feelings of guilt by not thinking about slavery at all. One of Bill Arp's sons asks him, in *Farm and Fireside*, to tell a story about runaway slaves, and Bill explains the practice. "I had almost forgotten that there ever was a runaway nigger. . . . It is seldom that we old folks talk about [slavery] to our children. We tell them frequently of our frolics with the little darkies, and how good old Aunt Peggy was to us, and how we used to hunt with Big Ben and Virgil and Uncle Sam, and we repeat some of the ghost stories they used to tell us and all that, but the idea of slavery hardly ever comes in" (p. 313). Much of the unpleasantness of the prewar period—that originated by the abolitionist as well as by the slaveowner—had to be forgotten by both sides before they could shake hands and face the future together.

Although by the end of the century most Southerners were convinced that slavery had been wrong, they were not willing to accept all the blame for the institution. They knew their history too well for that. As late as 1902 Bill Arp could get his Rebel dander up when a Yankee blamed the South for the miserable condition of the Negro, and in *Bill Arp* his defense forced him into an extreme position. "If slavery was a sin at all, which I deny, it was not our sin . . ." (p. 319). After the turn of the century, however, such an exchange of hot words was a rarity. By then both sides had agreed to accept a share of the responsibility for slavery, and the South had almost stopped defending it.

The Civil War was salutary in many ways. For example, it showed that the destiny of the states was to be one and that in this more perfect union there would be no legal slavery. Nevertheless, in the South many humorists began to conclude that the Confederacy and the war were absurdities, that from the standpoint of the South both had been mistakes. After a farcical career in the Confederate army, Mark Twain had separated himself from it, and he later satirized in "The Private History of a Campaign That Failed" the pseudo-chivalry that he saw in the pretensions of the Confederacy.

The dreams of glory in battle that led many a young Southern boy to enlist soon turned into a gory nightmare for him. Even the humorous accounts of the war stressed the useless carnage. His experiences made one participant see that "The war was a mistake and a failure. All wars are mistakes and failures."[21] Recalling the slaughter, the author of "*Co. Aytch*" often lamented that "my heart grows sick." He referred to the conflict frequently as that "unholy and uncalled for war." The restrictive discipline of the military didn't correspond to the recruit's preconceived notions of army life, either. Bill Arp made this clear. "I began to realize what war was, and that civil law was silent, dead or sleeping, and that nobody had any rights save the generals and their officers."[22] Men who had been at the front were thus among the first to see the tragic absurdity of the military settlement of sectional differences.

The idea of a Southern Confederacy was the subject of some good-natured and some derisive humor. Joseph Gault in his *Reports*, for example, wrote that the men were "humbuged into the field." Gault even attacked the theory of secession as absurd. He said that in 1832 South Carolina had been thwarted in her nullification plans; then in 1850 "when they awoke up from a nap of 18 years and rubbed their eyes and yawned and stretched their limbs, they said if they could not nullify the laws of the United States, by G-d they had the right to secede, and did secede" (p. 5).

O. Henry's short story "Two Renegades," in *Roads of Destiny*, reduces the idea of the Confederacy to one big joke. At a meeting of Confederate veterans in Atlanta, the narrator is astounded to see Barnard O'Keefe, a "Northerner born and bred." The explanation is simple, he is told: O'Keefe owes his life to the Confederate government, which four months earlier had saved his neck in Panama. As the Yankee unfolds the plot it becomes more and more absurd. Down in Panama, he says, while the canal talk was going on, he met a Doc Millikin, "an old medical outrage," a Mississippian and "the red-hottest Southerner that ever smelled mint. He made Stonewall Jackson and Robert E. Lee look like Abolitionists." The Rebel's home was near Yazoo City, "but he stayed away from the States on account of an uncontrollable liking he had for the absence of a Yankee government." O'Keefe participated in a Colombian revolution and was captured and sentenced to be shot. He appealed to the American consul for aid, but got none; finally he got permission for Doc to visit him in jail. When the Southerner arrived, O'Keefe implored him, "Doc, can't you suspend hostilities on the slavery question long enough to do something for me?" The doctor chided him because the Union government wouldn't come to his aid, "Since your country has gone back on you, you have come to the old doctor whose cotton you burned and whose mules you stole and whose niggers you freed to help you." Forgetting past injustices, the doctor agreed to help and told him that there was one government that could rescue him "and that's the Confederate States of America, the grandest nation that ever existed." O'Keefe said he had trouble seeing how a government that had been dissolved forty years could help him; but when the doctor insisted he take an oath of allegiance to the Confederate government, he went along. "I, Barnard O'Keefe, Yank, being of sound body but a Republican mind, do hereby swear to transfer my fealty, respect, and allegiance to the Confederate States of America, and the government thereof in consideration of said government, through its official acts and powers, obtaining my freedom and release from confinement and sentence of death brought about by the exuberance of my Irish proclivities and my general pizenness as a Yank." The time for his execution drew near, and still no release. Four days before his doomsday he told the doctor that he'd "sleep better if you had a government that was alive and on the map," and that he couldn't help feeling that his "chances of being pulled out of this scrape was decidedly weakened when General Lee surrendered." Two days before he was to be shot, however, he was mysteriously released. In joyful amazement he went to the doctor's house and there the Rebel explained how the Confederate government had saved his life. The Southerner had secretly negotiated his release with $12,000 in bribes—in Confederate money from Yazoo City. This bit of kindness had reconciled the Yank and the Reb. O'Keefe shouted "Hurrah for Jeff Davis!" and Doc Millikin responded in kind: "The next tune I learn on my flute is going to be 'Yankee Doodle.' I reckon there's some Yanks that are not so pizen." Though O. Henry was poking fun at the Confederacy, the story does illustrate the necessary state of affairs before the North and South could be reconciled. Each had to recognize in the other the good as well as the bad.

The absurdity of the war is nowhere made plainer than in Joel Chandler Harris' *Home Folks*. The theme of brothers, a Union captain and a Confederate private, fighting each other is the principal one in "The Comedy of War." He also shows the absurdity of a war in which one minute a Union picket and a Confederate picket are swapping tobacco for coffee and tea, and the next minute are killing each other. The story focuses on fighting near the two brothers' home. Their father Squire Fambrough and their sister Julia still live at home, though the two armies are close by. To the old man and his daughter there seems to be no real animosity among the soldiers. "By far the most boisterously ferocious appendages of the two armies were the two brass bands. They were continually challenging each other, beginning early in the morning and ending late in the afternoon; one firing off 'Dixie,' and the other 'Yankee Doodle.' It was 'Yankee Doodle, howdy do?' and 'Doodle-doodle, Dixie, too,' like two chanticleers challenging each other afar off."

Julia tries to read, but the noise interrupts her. She reacts fretfully: "There's the shooting again! How can I read books and sit quietly here while the soldiers are preparing to fight?" Her father becomes irritated too, and wishes they would start fighting—and annihilate each other. "Half of my niggers is gone . . . one side has got my hosses, and t'other side has stole my cattle. The Yankees has grabbed my grist mill, an' the Confeds has laid holt of my corn crib. One army is squattin' in my tater patch, and t'other one is roostin' in my cow pastur'. Do you reckon I was born to set down here an' put up wi' that kind of business?" Harris thus allowed the squire, at least, to show no partiality; he hates both sides for what they are doing to his place. When his daughter suggests they leave the farm until the war is over, he refuses "to be a-refuggin' an' a-skeedaddlin' across the country like a skeer'd rabbit." He boasts, "I hain't afeared of nary two armies they can find room for on these hills! Hain't I got one son on one side an' another son on t'other side? Much good they are doin', too. If they'd a-felt like me they'd a-fit both sides."

Two enemy parties meet at the old man's place, and among the men are his two sons. Not recognizing his sons yet, but knowing what enemies should be doing to each other in war, he tells both groups, "I don't like to be harborin' nary side. It's agin' my principles. I don't like this colloguin' an' palaverin' betwixt folks that ought to be by good rights a-knockin' one another on the head." Still unaware that they are nearby, he explains to a Union officer why his two sons chose the sides they did. "One of my sons is in the Union army, I hear tell, an' the other is in the Confederate army when he ain't in the hospital. These boys, you see, found their old daddy a-straddle of the fence, an' one clomb down one leg on the Union side, an' t'other one clomb down t'other leg on the Confederate side."

Always an objective critic of the war, Harris spoke through the squire and showed a perfect balance of sentiment. To reconcile both sides, Harris knew that he had to picture each partly right and partly wrong, perhaps with a little more right on the Union side, since it was the victor. But he had to do this without making the South appear the villain. He achieved his objective admirably in such a story as this. Like the squire, Harris was not a little confused by the many mix-ups and incongruities of the war. Soon after the squire is reunited with his sons, news arrives that Lee has surrendered. The old man thinks that finally all the confusion will be cleared up; but when he is told that the Confederate colonel commanding the local units is a Connecticut man and the Union colonel is from Virginia, he stutters perplexedly: "Lord 'a' mercy! . . . I'm a-goin' off som'ers an' ontangle the tangle we've got into." This, to Harris, was the major problem facing the nation after the war. This problem could be solved, the writer reasoned, by the South's admitting that the war had been a mistake and the North's taking some responsibility for starting it.

Some years after the March to the Sea, the Georgia journalist-humorist Henry W. Grady, wrote for *A Message from Atlanta's Immortals*: "I want to say to General Sherman, who is considered an able man in our parts, though some people think he is a kind of careless man about fire, that from the ashes he left us in 1864 we have raised a brave and beautiful city; that somehow or other we have caught the sunshine in the bricks and mortar of our homes, and have builded therein not one ignoble prejudice or memory." In these words Grady proudly asserted the reality of a "New South."

After Reconstruction officially ended in 1876, talk increased about a New South among Southern businessmen, journalists, writers, and others. The New South was not to be at all a "reconstructed" South in the radical Republican sense, but a South which would catch up industrially and economically with the second half of the nineteenth century—a progressive, forward-looking South. The Old South had been feudal; the New South must be industrial. And this New South must be promoted and reflected in literature. The pen must be used as much in support of this new concept as it had been to defend slavery. It was. Near the end of the century William Dean Howells could write: "One of the most interesting facts of our literary growth since the Civil War is the rise of a school of writers who express with striking fidelity certain moods and phases of the New South."[23] The humorists and local colorists had recognized the urgency of the call, and had answered it almost to a man.

The businessman and the promoter became new Southern heroes. Henry Watterson reflected this trend when he dedicated his *Oddities in Southern Life and Character* "To My Friend, Walter N. Haldeman, A Representative of the Business Progress, No Less than of the Newspaper Development of the South. . . ." *Bob Taylor's Magazine* was but one of the Southern periodicals devoted to propagandizing the New South. Industrial developments were given full coverage in the magazine. In one issue the editor proclaimed, "One river locked and dammed is far more important to Southern progress than ten thousand joint discussions between professional 'spellbinders'" (II, 485). The masthead of Atlanta's *Sunny South*, founded about 1875, stated its editorial objectives: "Devoted to Literature, Romance, Science, Education, and Southern Progress."

Even such admirers of the old regime as George Cary Eggleston, after picturing the leisurely life of the old Virginia in *A Rebel's Recollections*, hastened to add that though life then had been wonderful, still progress must be made. And the retrospective Martha Young dedicated *Plantation Songs for My Lady's Banjo* "To my father who was one of the noblest types of the Old South, and who bore forceful part with the heroic upbuilders of the New." Rebecca Washington Smith wrote of Thomas C. DeLeon, a Southern journalist and romancer who had been on Jefferson Davis' staff in his youth: "He was a colleague of Grady and Watterson in the New South movement, and carefully devised his rather trite romances to argue for reconciliation" (p. 54).

A business and commercial society was inevitable if the South was to progress. The conservatism of the past with its prejudice against commercialism had to go. Though some old-timers held out, many of the younger generation threw a binding tradition to the winds. A few, like Walter Marion Raymond, author of *Rebels of the New South*, even became socialists.

Pride in the progress of the New South was reflected in the writings of the humorists. "The Sunny South," from Dave Sloan's *Fogy Days*, showed this pride and mixed with it a new defiance of the North that was bred of progress. He jibed at the Yankees by accusing them of unloading the slave on the South when they discovered that he was not profitable in the North. Then he confronted them with an industrial threat.

> *Now we grow, even more than they,*
> *And in progression shall compete;*
> *We'll make our cotton into cloth,*
> *Thus their own plans will defeat.*

Sloan's verses certainly make execrable poetry. Their inclusion here is on sociological grounds rather than esthetic, for they do show how the enthusiasm for the New South permeated the writings of almost all Southerners—even tenth-rate humorists. Yet Sloan concluded his book by extending the hand of friendship even to the industrial North. He admitted, "I have made a few cuts at our brethren across the north line—not in anger nor in hate, but in truth, as I understand it." But malice must be put behind, and he welcomed them south to "come in peace, and bring their machines, their brains and their money with them." The success of the economic motivation for reunion had, indeed, been great when he could end with kind words for the Republicans. "If I was born with hair on my head and a democratic seed inside, and you were born with or without hair on yours and a republican seed inside, why let them both sprout and grow." Whenever it became a matter of tolerating Republicans or hampering economic growth, even the most avid Confederate could find it in his heart to stomach the party of Lincoln and Grant.

Although the South courted the North for capital with which to industrialize, many new factories were financed by local subscription. The desire for factories became evangelistic in some communities. In the early 1880's, in fact, a cotton mill was born at a revival service in Salisbury, North Carolina, when an evangelist preached to his congregation on the text: "NEXT TO THE GRACE OF GOD, WHAT SALISBURY NEEDS IS A COTTON MILL!" Salisbury responded to the invitation.[24]

Such influential newspapers as the Atlanta *Constitution* edited by Henry W. Grady and the Louisville *Courier-Journal* edited by Henry Watterson, assisted by hundreds of smaller daily and weekly papers, pushed for more and more factories. Grady preached the gospel of progress, not that of the mint-julep reaction. His inspiration was Horatio Alger, not Sir Walter Scott. He was one of the most prominent and influential of the New South promoters. Using humor frequently to make a point, he wrote and spoke all over the nation, trying to get the South to go modern. Grady's early efforts in journalism were the "King Hans" letters, full of the racy humor that came to be characteristic of most of his work, which he wrote as a casual correspondent for the Atlanta *Constitution*. Later as its editor he published such writers as Charles H. Smith, Sarge Wier, and Betsey Hamilton. The *Life of Henry W. Grady Including His Writings and Speeches* was edited by Joel Chandler Harris, and carried praise of him from Harris, James Whitcomb Riley, Henry Watterson, and other humorists. It is of course well known how the speech "The New South" which he delivered in New York on December 22, 1889, became a rallying cry for the promoters of a modern, progressive South.

Grady's best known humorous story is "The Pickens County Funeral," and he turns this burial in the mountains of Northern Georgia into a description of the economic situation of the South. In his biography, James W. Lee summarized it.

He said the grave was dug through solid marble, but the marble head-stone was from Vermont. That it was in a pine wilderness, but the pine coffin came from Cincinnati. That an iron mountain overshadowed it, but the coffin nails and screws came from Pittsburgh. That hard woods and metals abounded, but the corpse was hauled on a wagon from South Bend, Indiana. That a hickory grove was near by, but the pick and shovel handles came from New York. That the cotton shirt on the dead man came from Cincinnati, the coat and breeches from Chicago, and the shoes from Boston. That the folded hands were incased in white gloves which came from New York, and around the poor neck that had worn all its living days the bondage of lost opportunity was twisted a cheap cravat from Phil-adelphia. That the country, so rich in underdeveloped resources, furnished nothing for the funeral but the poor man's body and the grave in which it awaited the judgment trump. And that the poor fellow lowered to his rest on coffin bands from Lowell carried nothing into the next world as a reminder of his home in this, save the halted blood in his veins, the chilled marrow in his bones, and the echo of the dull clods that fell on his coffin lid (pp. 59-60).

This macabre mixture of humor, pathos, grotesqueness, and truth served like an anguished scream for the local exploitation of Southern resources to advance the New South.

Not all voices were unanimous in heralding the millennium of the New South. Some of the praise for it was much qualified, and there were even reser-vations about the value of industrialization. Sidney Lanier was suspicious of the so-called progress it brought with it. Fletcher Douglas Srygley recorded what T. W. Caskey, the subject of *Seventy Years in Dixie*, thought of the new era. "There have been wonderful changes, in material things, in this country dur-ing the last seventy years, and the changes, during the same period, in social customs, political economy, educational methods and religious institutions, have been equally marvelous. The new order of things differs widely from the old, but who will say the former is better than the latter?" (p. 371). Many older Southerners had a tough time adjusting to the new faster way of life. Some could not adjust at all. Jeannette Walworth tells of such an anachronism in a story from *Southern Silhouettes*, "Why a New Doctor Went the Rounds." The old doctor could not keep pace with the new commercial society—his records system, for example, was chaotic—and he had to give up his practice.

With increased industrialization came greater labor problems. John T. Moore stood with the progressives of the New South, but he was not blind to the abuse of labor by factory owners. He exposed child labor in the Southern cotton mill in *The Bishop of Cottontown.* The novel, published in 1906, is a mixture of sentiment, humor, propaganda, romance, and realism.

One commentator on the post-Reconstruction South, Rebecca Washington Smith, has written that Grady's "The New South" could serve as a text for every war story Joel Chandler Harris ever wrote (p. 38). As chief editorial writer for the Atlanta *Constitution,* Harris certainly matched the paper's editor in his enthusiasm for business and industry; but the sensitive and perceptive Harris was much disturbed by the materialism and corruption that accompanied the New South. In *Uncle Remus's Magazine* under the character and rubric of Billy Sanders, Harris frequently attacked business greed and the evils of monopolies.

Remembering the tranquility of the prewar South, perhaps, Dave Sloan penned awkward lines to show his disapproval of the Yankee influence in what was happening.

> *The war has brought its bad results,*
> *And our customs it has changed,*
> *Are learning fast the Yankee plans,*
> *From the right we have been estranged* (pp. 36-37).

New factories meant more jobs, and country people flocked to the towns and cities to work in the cotton mills and garment factories. Humorists from Lanier to Sarge Wier pointed out the dangers of leaving the farm to seek better pickings elsewhere. The author of *Old Times in Georgia* warned crackers against going to town to make their fortunes. In a sketch he called "Moving to Town" he told of seeing a prosperous-looking farmer and his family pass by his place on their way to Atlanta. Two years later, he said, the family returned to the country, all their money gone, their property sold, and their daughters ruined. Sarge was even skeptical of the emphasis placed on formal education in the New South. In "Pluckett Thinks There Is Too Much Schooling" he satirized boys and girls who learn in school to farm and keep house. To contrast the school of practical experience—the one he went to—with the new formal education, he told of coming upon a recent agriculture school graduate stranded in the road with a broken wagon axle. The educated farmer did not know what to do, but Sarge immediately chopped down a pine sapling, made a new axle for the wagon, and showed the college kid up.

Just how new was this New South that the humorists and almost everyone else were promoting? Some observers seemed to think that the change from the ante-bellum era was not very great. As soon as 1907 Thomas C. DeLeon wrote in *Belles, Beaux and Brains of the 60's* that Henry Grady's term was merely a rallying cry and not a statement of fact. "Grady knew that there was not—and could be no 'New South.' He knew that it was the same old South, bracing her every sinew and girding up her loins for a fresh struggle with the conditions of day-after-tomorrow, out of the methods of day-before-yesterday. He knew, thinker that he was, that the habits and traditions of three centuries could no more be whistled down the wind by a word than they could be uprooted by the sword, and what he knew then exists today" (p. 446). Although DeLeon's conclusion was not quite accurate, a later critic agreed with his major hypothesis. In the Preface to *The Mind of the South* Wilbur Cash admitted that the South had been affected by industry and commerce. "Nevertheless, the extent of the change and of the break between the Old South that was and the South of our time has been vastly exaggerated. The South, one might say, is a tree with many age rings, with its limbs and trunk bent and twisted by all the winds of the years, but with its tap root in the Old South." Cash, of course, was dealing with the *mind* of the South. Outwardly the change had been great. By 1914 the conquest of the South by the North was more complete and fundamental than it had been in 1865. By World War I the South openly imitated the North in industry, culture, and most other areas. The New South that humor had done so much to further had become nationally oriented.

Time has always been the best healer of wounds. Distance in time makes wrongs and bitterness seem less poignant. So it was with the North and South after the Civil War. As early as 1887 the editors of a collection of war humor could write: "Federal and Confederate chieftains sit side by side in the Senate chamber, and unite in the councils of our chosen ruler. Peace and joy have spread their silver wings over the desolations and bereavements of the past, and today we are one people, one country, united under one flag."[25]

Men who had fought in the war were often the first to let time bind up their wounds. Sometimes it didn't take long, either. In his comic memoirs *Rebel Private Front and Rear,* William A. Fletcher wrote that just after the end of the war he was accosted by a North Carolina infantryman who asked him if he had any bacon. He answered yes, and was told, "Grease and slide back into the Union." Till then Fletcher had been despondent over losing the war, but as he thought of that humorous bit of advice, he decided it was a very wise suggestion. Back home in Beaumont, Texas, he fraternized with the Union soldiers on duty there and became thoroughly reconstructed. This was the best course, he wrote, because he "had seen service enough to learn not to pine over the bygone or carry hatred for a victorious foe" (p. 146).

Two other Confederate veterans added their testimonials to Fletcher's: Dave Sloan and Sam Watkins. Sloan wrote: "Though a secessionist and a confederate soldier, I rejoice that the Union of the States has been preserved, and pray that this Union may never be severed" (p. 213). The historian of *"Co. Aytch"* also thought the past should remain there and not intrude on the present or the future. "The past is buried in oblivion. The mantle of charity has long ago fallen upon those who think differently from us. We remember no longer wrongs and injustices done us by anyone on earth. We are willing to forget and forgive those who have wronged and falsified us. We look up above and beyond all these petty groveling things and shake hands and forget the past" (pp. 229-30).

Time helped soften the feelings of many a professional humorist against the North. Charles H. Smith and George W. Bagby are two good examples of the softening trend. In his old age Bill Arp could find much about the North to like. In 1880 Dr. Bagby traveled in the North and wrote a series of letters for the Baltimore *Sun,* which show how the once fiery Rebel had at last found some good in the Yankees.

A humorous story by George Madden Martin of Kentucky shows how Confederates in a border state finally learned to see some good in Republicans. "The Confines of Consistency" is set in 1879, when "Republican" was still a dirty word to many Southerners.[26] It concerns the political education of Emily Louise, twelve, who one day is unable to go to school because she is told that a grocery store by which she must pass has become a "Poll," evidently a dreadful place. She has heard that her teacher is a "Republican"; so the next day at school she decides to find out more about Republicans. She asks her friend Hattie what one is, and Hattie answers, "A Republican—why—people who are not Democrats—of course." Hattie also tells her that a child is what his father is. On the way home from school Emily Louise asks William what a Republican is. "It's—well—it's the sort you don't want to have anything to do with." At home she asks Aunt Louise if she is a Democrat, and gets the reply, "What else could you dream I am?" Tom tells Emily Louise that her father is a Republican; and remembering what Hattie told her, she asks Aunt M'randa if that doesn't make her a Republican too. But the cook assures her, "Co'se yer ain't chile; huccome yer think sech er thing? Ain't yer done learned it's sinnahs is lumped wi' 'publicans—po' whites, an' cul'd folks an' sech?"

All this leaves Emily Louise in a dilemma and faced with a decision: Should she desert her Democrat aunts or turn traitor to her Republican father? She finally resolves her problem by asking William, "What is a person when they are not either Democrat or Republican?" William tells her such a person is a Mugwump. The next day in school she writes in Hattie's album. "Dear Hattie: I am a Mugwump and your true friend. Emily Louise MacLauren."

That same day Emily Louise is chosen by her teacher to present flowers to a visiting celebrity—the wife of the Republican President of the United States. She is chosen for this honor because her father is a Republican. At the presentation ceremony the President's wife kisses her on the cheek, and the other children all envy her. At home she tells her aunts of her exciting day; they are proud and she is puzzled. She goes outside and sits on the doorstep because "she needed solitude for the readjustment of her ideas." "With the kiss of Republicanism upon her cheek" she has become a school and home celebrity. She has always thought everyone hated Republicans. With the passage of a little more time, tolerance for Republicans spread more deeply into the South; and a person no longer had to call himself a Mugwump to keep peace in a divided family.

Historians tell us that the South lost the war. It took many years and many federal laws and many federal marshals to convince its people of that fact. Slowly, however, the South has acknowledged that she came out on the short end;* but at the same time she has resolved to win the commemoration of that Lost Cause. And as soon as the ink was dry on Lee's signature at Appomattox, monuments began going up from Maryland to Texas, honoring Lee, Jackson, Longstreet, Stuart, "the Confederate Soldier," "the Spirit of the Confederacy," or simply "Our Heroes." In 1961 the Civil War Centennial began, and the South intensified its celebration of the Lost Cause. Some wag remarked early in the commemoration that the South may have lost the war but she certainly was going to win the Centennial.

Women have been largely responsible for this Confederate cult. In his letter of 1865 Bill Arp presented the problem to Artemus Ward. "You may reconstruct the men, with your laws and things, but how are you going to reconstruct the women?" This question proved prophetic, for the women were the hardest to reconstruct; and even now the United Daughters of the Confederacy is very much alive. In 1908 Frances Boyd Calhoun, author of the humorous classic *Miss Minerva and William Green Hill,* wrote in a biographical sketch for the back pages of the book: "While eligible to join the Daughters of the American Revolution, I never have done so, preferring to give my time and attention to the Daughters of the Confederacy—of which organization I am a most enthusiastic member, being president of the local chapter. I am a Southerner of Southerners."

In 1866 the fiery Bill Arp let it be known in *Bill Arp, So Called* that he was still proud of being a Southerner, regardless of the way the war had turned out. "I've taken up a motto of no North, no South, no East, no West; but let me tell you, my friend, I'll bet on Dixie as long as I've got a dollar. . . . I'm a good Union reb, and my battle cry is Dixie and the Union" (p. 139). He could have added "in that order" because Dixie did indeed retain his first allegiance, and that of many another hard-core Rebel. To this day many a Southerner still gets his keenest emotional thrill in hearing "Dixie," played by the Boston Symphony Orchestra or by a small-town high-school band.

When a Confederate hero was not shown proper respect, a true-blue Southerner would become obstreperously articulate. The reputed refusal of a clerk in the War Department to lower the flag at the death of Jefferson Davis was the occasion of the satirical "Little Purp" by Dave Sloan. Two lines describing the clerk will show the tone of the poem. "The little fice, with noisy mouth, / Like all his breed, he's a barker."

Governor Bob Taylor of Tennessee made it plain that he considered Dixie to be America's answer to the Garden of Eden. In one of his speeches he told of a politician who shouted from the stump, "Fellow-citizens, I know no North, I know no South, I know no East, I know no West," to which a barefooted boy shouted back, "You'd better go an' study jog-er-fey!" The boy, Taylor judged, was right. The governor said he believed in sectional lines and sectional pride

---

* As I write this note (October, 1962), Mississippi is again being reminded, in what historians may come to call the last battle of the Civil War, of the sovereignty of the federal government.

"so long as they are not the demarcations of prejudice." He believed in sectional patriotism; consequently he loved Dixie best, where "oranges and magnolias bloom, except when blighted by a blizzard from the land of Yankee Doodle."[27] In another speech he described the Maxon-Dixon line. "There it is, a great crimson scar of politics across the face of the grandest country God ever made. There it is, and there it will remain, the dividing line between cold bread and hot biscuit."[28] There would always be a difference between the North and the South, even if this difference was only in food.

By 1914 most Southerners respected the Union as well as the Confederacy. A song often sung at Confederate reunions shows how love of the Union and love of the South were juxtaposed in many minds. "We Are Old-Time Confederates" praises Jefferson Davis, Lee, Johnston, Jackson, and other heroes; but the last stanza reads: "Now our country is united, / . . . It's good enough for me."

In his war memoirs Sam Watkins made a statement that expressed the sentiment of most of his contemporaries. "Secession may have been wrong in the abstract, and has been tried and settled by the arbitrament of the sword and bayonet, but I am as firm in my convictions today of the right of secession as I was in 1861." Then he quickly adds: "The question has been long ago settled and is buried forever, never in this age or generation to be resurrected" (p. 49). By 1914 "in this age or generation" could have been omitted. Reconciliation was an accomplished fact.

Notes

1. In Shurter, *Extempore Speaking*, 139-40.
2. Hilton, *Funny Side of Politics*, 219.
3. Taylor, *Echoes*, 64.
4. Advertisement in Pickett, *Yule Log*, 166.
5. Parks, *Craddock*, 79.
6. "J. C. Harris," 601.
7. *Memorials of Dixie-Land*, 496; Atlanta *Constitution*, Mar. 19, 1911.
8. Quoted in Odum, *Southern Pioneers*, 152.
9. Botkin, *Southern Folklore*, 155 ff.; McDonald, *Life in Old Virginia*, 92 ff.
10. "Southern Literature," 505.
11. In Obenchain, *Sally Ann's Experiences*, 29.
12. *Songs and Stories*, 192-93; *Clark Horse Review*, IX (Mar. 20, 1894), 384.
13. Quoted in Fulton, *Southern Life*, 515.
14. Quotations are from R. Wiggins, *J. C. Harris*, 181-83, 195.
15. Quoted in Fulton, *Southern Life*, 512.
16. "American Letter," 258.
17. In *Stories of the South*, 131-74.
18. *Farm and Fireside*, 254.
19. *American Spirit*, 246.
20. *Stories of the South*, 140.
21. Srygley, *Seventy Years in Dixie*, 353.
22. Quoted in Fleming, *Sequel of Appomattox*, 38.
23. "American Letter," 231.
24. Kendrick & Arnett, *South Looks at Its Past*, 125.
25. King & Derby, *Camp-Fire Sketches*, 7.
26. In Bruere & Beard, *Laughing Their Way*, 41-45.
27. *Life Pictures*, 272-73; Botkin, *Southern Folklore*, 278.
28. Quoted in Visscher, *Ten Wise Men*, 146.

5. The Image

THE NOSTALGIA THAT ENVELOPED most of the South after the Civil War accounts for much of that large body of postwar Southern humor dealing with ante-bellum life.* A civilization, a way of life which many of the humorists had known as children, had been annihilated. If the plantation system was virtually uprooted by the freeing of the slaves, the whites and Negroes outside the slavocracy were also affected. The four years of the war had in fact shaken the foundations of a society that the South had been building for over two hundred years.

The postwar South was indeed different from the prewar South, and to escape its harsh reality many writers and readers looked to the past. The humor-

* In their *Humor of America*, pp. 398-99, Max J. Herzberg and Leon Mones incidentally provided an excellent defense for this chapter in the following passage: ". . . a great deal of humor is aroused by gentle playing in our memories among the scenes of our childhood. The songs of days that are gone, photographs, enmities, rivalries, triumphs of those days, all seem to be surrounded with an aura of nostalgic magic that does not sink into the light of common day when we grow up, and that strikes us in our later life as wistfully serio-comic."

ists were prominent among those writers who chose the ante-bellum South for their setting and subjects. And of subjects there were a plenty: the comic, illiterate darky; the well-intentioned, but naïve aristocrat; the blustering frontiersman. Bathed in a nostalgic humor, these characters became stereotypes.

The Plantation

In addition to entertainment, the humorists had a serious purpose in their interpretations of ante-bellum life. Most of their work was defensive, emphasizing the good times of the past. "What we really have in the literature of the Reconstruction era," Wilbur Cash has written in *The Mind of the South*, "is, in its dominant aspect, a propaganda. Its novels, its sketches and stories, are essentially so many pamphlets, its poems so many handbills, concerned mainly, as is common knowledge, with the Old South, and addressed primarily to the purpose of glorifying that Old South . . ." (p. 142). Cash's judgment on literature in general is even more applicable to humor, for there were few Southern humorists, from Joel Chandler Harris to Martha Gielow, who did not propagandize for the Old South by purging it of its unpleasantness. Robert L. Taylor of Tennessee in April, 1909, reiterated the original aim of the *Taylor-Trotwood Magazine*, which he edited jointly with John Trotwood Moore. "It is one of the purposes of this magazine to aid in keeping ever fresh and green the history and traditions of the Old South. . . ."

Although most of the humor dealing with the Old South was propaganda, some of this propaganda had high literary value. Even Cash applauded Joel Chandler Harris. "Plainly having in it the will to render the Old South as an idyl, Uncle Remus nevertheless succeeds in being an authentic creation, in catching almost without exaggeration and without false feeling a fact and a mood which actually existed" (p. 143).

Whether this world of the Old South, reflected in the idealistic humor of later writers, actually existed is debatable. Certainly there was much good feeling between slaves and their masters and mistresses; nevertheless, as a rule, the past was seen through rose-colored glasses. The pain and the suffering of the period were typically excised from humor. Stephen Leacock's explanation of Harris' popularity emphasizes the idealism of his humor. "In Uncle Remus it is not the mere animal stories that please as incident: that is nothing: it is the strange vision into a pictured world, a 'nice' place where we too would fain fit in."[1] Leacock added that the true humorist is an optimist and "must present the vision of a better world, if only of a lost one." A society that had ceased to exist, like the Old South, could be made to conform to anyone's ideas of a better world.

Many a humorist saw a vision of a better world in the prewar South. Whether this vision can be corroborated by the historian is immaterial to the literary critic, who must address himself to the reality in a writer's mind. What the humorist thought or remembered as having been true had a much stronger hold on his imagination than any fact of history. Writers generally admitted they were selecting the best from the old society for presentation; nevertheless they maintained that their idealistic pictures of ante-bellum life were true to the spirit of the period, if not to the fact. In the Introduction to *Southern Silhouettes,* Jeannette Walworth justified her sketches by writing that the old order was passing into legend and tradition and that she was helping fill the need for one who was part of that order truly to record its day. Her sketches, first run in the New York *Evening Post,* are, she wrote, "not the work of imagination, but are accurate outlines of actual entities, written with the loving desire to do away with some of the misconceptions that have militated against a true appreciation of what is noblest and best in the people of whom they treat." The critic or historian interested in the *Zeitgeist* of the postwar South can learn much from this reconstruction of the ante-bellum period. Most humorists saw no need for photographic realism in treating the Old South; their own workaday world provided realism enough. The past was the province of romance. Thomas Nelson Page late in the century wrote: "In the South . . . the conditions for a literature now exist as perhaps they do not exist in any other country or section. An heroic past is already assuming the proper romantic perspective for a literature."[2] The romanticizing of the Old South had begun, however, long before he declared conditions propitious. It had started before the guns were silenced by Appomattox and continued after *Gone with the Wind.*

The attraction of the romantic past over the sordid present is well illustrated in words written by Grace King, who was old enough to remember the days before the war. Although she accepted Southern defeat and the new era more readily than most of her contemporaries, she remembered the days of her girlhood with the nostalgia typical of humor dealing with the past. Her words are a good defense for the humor discussed in this chapter.

Do you remember, you who can remember as much as fifty years ago, when your ears hardly reached above the dinner table, the stories your elders used to tell over the wine and nuts? . . . What a pleasant world that was to be sure, into which we were born fifty years ago in New Orleans; what a natural, what a simple world! . . . And do you remember how those great Papas of ours went to war? And how God did not act toward them as they would have acted toward Him had they been God and He a Southern Gentleman? . . . And do you remember what followed? . . . The fighting the Papas had done in war was nothing to the fighting they did afterward, for bread and meat; and the bitterness of their defeat was sweetness compared to the bitterness that came afterward. Bayonet in hand was easier than hat in hand. . . . Who of us, who inherit want as surely as our fathers did wealth, has not at one time or another made a pilgrimage to that Gibraltar of memory, the home of our childhood, of our Olympian beginnings? Leaving behind us the sordid little rented house . . . we have threaded the streets to stand on the sidewalk opposite some grim, gaunt, battered, old brick mansion, filled with shops below and a mongrel lot of tenants above, trying to fit our past into or upon it. "Is that the balcony," we ask our-

selves, "from which on gala days we used to look upon a gala world? . . .
Is that the doorway through which our great Past made its entrance and
exit? Is that the courtyard where our slaves worked for us? That the building in which they were born to work for us?" . . . To you who have not
made that pilgrimage I say, do not attempt it; you will never find what
you seek. Thread the way to it only in memory, if you would find it.[3]

For many Reconstruction-weary Southerners, the "Gibraltar of memory" became their only release from gaunt reality.

The most attractive defense of slavery is the postwar humor of the so-called
plantation school. A contemporary of Thomas Nelson Page or Joel Chandler
Harris, who read of the carefree life of the darky and the gracious, cultured
society of the planter, must have wondered why there had to be a war to ruin
such a civilization. Each person, black and white, could claim a link in the plantation chain of being. Everyone was content because everyone "belonged." Not
all Southerners, however, were of the school of Page and Harris: George Washington Cable led the unpopular minority in pointing out the tragedy and bru-
tality of slavery. But the idealized interpretations of the past by Page were far
more popular with the public—North and South—than the more realistic ones of
Cable.

Works of humor frequently contained passages which were undisguised apo-
logias for the ante-bellum plantation system. Sweet and Knox in *Mexican Mustang*, for example, used the following argument: "Abundance of hog, hominy,
hoecakes, and molasses; a liberal license in the matter of break-downs and camp-
meetings,—this, with Sunday frolics, went to make the 'poor, down-trodden African' the happiest of mortals in the 'ole timey days 'fore 'mancipation.' If they
did get whipped when they did what was wrong, do we, in these days of universal freedom, not whip certain of our criminals? If they were for certain crimes
bound with chains, as we used to see the 'man and brother' depicted on the
title page of abolition tracts, do the officers of the best government the world
ever saw not bind with chains those who break the laws?" Sweet maintained that
the life of the slave was superior to the life of the freedman. He recalled the
good life of the slave and then wrote, "I look around, and I see the 'colored gentleman' of to-day indolent and shiftless, filthy and ragged, lying asleep in the
sun. I enter his miserable cabin, and I see his wife as dirty and ragged as he is.
I find his children sick, and on the way to an early grave for lack of intelligent
care and medical aid." The polemist quickly assured the reader that he was no
defender of slavery; it is gone, and he is glad; but, he added, ". . . when I look
at the present and the past without prejudice, I can see that the colored man of
to-day, with his freedom and all the rights of citizenship, stands more in need of
sympathy than ever did the slave of ante-bellum days." To back up his assertion, the humorist quoted from an interview with a former slave. Replying
to the question whether he wanted the old times back, the Negro had said,
"Oh, no, young massa! I knows it's better fur de young folks dat dey am free;
but as fur me, I'd rather, if de good Lord willed it, be gittin' my vittuls in ole

massa's kitchen dan be skirmishin' roun' for grub like we has to do now" (pp. 75-78). The old man had had a hard time since freedom came.

The popularity then of literature with a plantation theme is almost unbelievable today. It soon became a dominant subject in Southern humor. Francis Pendleton Gaines, the historian of the *Southern Plantation,* described its popularity. "Humorists drew increasingly upon the plantation; authors, especially Cable and Page, gave readings from their own works; lecturers amused audiences with anecdotes of the old regime; cartoonists, minstrel managers, touring companies of jubilee singers, all assisted in making vivid the general conception" (pp. 74-75). The Northern magazines were filled with Southerners' plantation sketches. Gaines pointed out that as late as October, 1901, the *Century Magazine* carried in that one issue Page's "Bred in the Bone," Harris' "Rosalie," and Mrs. Virginia F. Boyle's "The Triumph of Shad." Many Northern writers also used plantation material: Frank R. Stockton, James Whitcomb Riley, Maurice Thompson, Stephen Crane, to name a few. Southern magazines also regularly printed plantation stories and sketches. Beginning in its issue of June 13, 1891, the *Arkansaw Travler,* for example, serialized Mrs. C. C. Scott's novel of the past, *Sis and Bud: Plantation Sketches of the Ante-Bellum South.*

The arch-humorist of the plantation school was Thomas Nelson Page. In his novels and short stories set in the prewar period, romantic shades rise up to laugh and to chatter. He touched with pathos, humor, and love the best of the plantation life "befo' de wah." As a Virginian of aristocratic lineage, Page lamented the passing of the feudal South and looked back longingly to it as an escape from the harsh reality of Reconstruction. H. A. Toulmin, in *Social Historians,* said that Page "is a Virginian, speaking in the manner and way of the Virginia gentleman as he is, courteous, kindly, with a gift of humor and a capacity for story telling that is modest, well-bred, never bitter, a man of large heart and ample views" (p. 5). In *Southern Plantation* Gaines succinctly concluded that Page "wrote the epitaph of a civilization." In stressing the departed glory of the South—from his first published poem, "Uncle Gabe's White Folks," to his death—the corpus of his humor was a final triumphant reply to the abolitionists.

"Unc' Edinburg's Drowndin'," "Meh Lady," "Polly," *Red Rock,* "Marse Chan"—in fact, all his literary work contains an appealing, usually nostalgic humor that makes the reader wish he could have been around when the character originals were flesh and blood. Already in *In Ole Virginia* the title character in "Unc' Edinburg's Drowndin'" fills the sketch with his amusing reflections, such as, "Dees monsus 'ceivin' critters, women is, jes as onreliable as de hind leg of a mule; a man got to watch 'em all de time." The story also shows many attractive characteristics of the old regime: its splendor, the cordiality between the races, the fraternity between master and slave, the slave's sense of belonging, and the joy of living then.

Some of Page's stories leave the reader wondering who was master and who was slave. Drinkwater Torm in "Polly," for example, openly tyrannizes over his master. Drinkwater Torm was so named by his master, because, the Colonel said, "if he were to drink water once he would die." Each time Torm gets drunk the Colonel threatens to sell him. "I'll sell him tomorrow morning; and if I can't sell him I'll give him away." But Torm keeps on drinking and never worries about his future because the threat has been made many times and never carried out. Anyway, the imbibing slave knows that he is indispensable to his master.

Page's principal contribution to Southern humor was his delineation of the happy slave. His Negroes became type characters who begat numerous offspring and held their popularity into the twentieth century. The Page Negro was simple, contented, credulous, philosophical, picturesque, and comic; he had great talent in singing, dancing, storytelling, and reuniting estranged white lovers. He remained unquestioningly loyal to his white folks during and after the war. He was critical of upstart freedmen, and obtained solace from the hard life of freedom by living in the past. "They have passed away in the ruins of the Southern aristocracy, and that is why these characters with their delicate sentimentality, their genuine pathos, and their pervasive humor strike a responsive chord in every heart."[4]

Although Page treated the contented slave intensively, his range of types is extremely limited. He considered chiefly the old family manservant and neglected the younger Negro, Negro life before and after the war, and relationships among Negroes themselves. It remained for other writers in the plantation school to fill in the gaps.

Page was not the pioneer of the plantation school. That honor is usually accorded Irwin Russell, whose "befo'-de-wah" poems inspired most of the later writers in plantation humor. Of Russell's best-known composition, Page wrote, "His cantata 'Christmas Night in the Quarters' is the best delineation of negro life yet written, and is pitched on an artistic key which contains a suggestion of the possibilities possessed by the old life of the negroes as a field for either music or romance."[5] Henry Clay Lukens spoke of the poet's cotton and rice field Negroes. "Irwin Russell's plantation fac-similes of life and frolic at 'De Quarters' were perfect in ensemble, symmetry, and laugh power."[6]

The most famous part of *Christmas Night in the Quarters* is "The Origin of the Banjo." Beginning with an explanation of why "de ha'r is missin'" on the possum's tail, the speaker tells of Noah and the flood and how the banjo came about.

> *Now, Ham, de only nigger whut wuz runnin' on de packet,*
> *Got lonesome in de barber-shop, an' c'u'dn't stan' de racket;*
> *And so, fur to amuse hese'f, he steamed some wood an' bent it,*
> *An' soon he had a banjo made—de fust dat wuz invented.*

Using possum-tail hairs for strings, Ham entertains everybody on board with a hoe-down. The section tells why the Negro loves the banjo and possum.

Now, sence dat time—it's mighty strange—dere's not de slightes' showin'
Ob any ha'r at all upon de 'possum's tail a-growin';
An' curi's, too, dat's nigger's ways: his people nebber los' em,—
Fur whar you finds de nigger—dar's the banjo an' de possum!

Like virtually all the plantation-school humorists, Russell saw the Negro condescendingly as a comic half-human.

Ironically, the plantation myth was so strong and pervasive in the late nineteenth and early twentieth centuries that it captured even the educated Negroes' imagination and obscured the historical reality. For example, two prominent Negro writers, Paul Laurence Dunbar and Charles W. Chesnutt, born in the North but influenced by the Southern image, wrote in the Page-Russell plantation tradition. Though their works exhibit some differences, the casual reader would find their plantation writings indistinguishable from Page's in subject, tone, and approach. Four collections of short stories show Dunbar's debt to Page: *Folks from Dixie* (1898), *The Strength of Gideon* (1900), *In Old Plantation Days* (1903), and *The Heart of Happy Hollow* (1904). In these stories Dunbar tacitly agreed with Page that slavery was the best way of life for most Negroes and that freedom brought the black man misery and want. A principal difference between Dunbar and Page, however, is that the Negro writer focused on life in the slave quarters and treated slave life apart from the master and the Big House. But, like Page, he depicted the comic side of the slave's life as typical and largely ignored its tragedy. Chesnutt, although firmly in the Page and Joel Chandler Harris tradition, was more likely to show the occasional cruelty and oppression of slavery. His humorous folklore tales in *The Conjure Woman* (1899), however, are suggestive of Harris.

Although given the title of "Virginia realist," Dr. George W. Bagby also purged the plantation system of much of its dross in his ante-bellum sketches. In the Introduction to *The Old Virginia Gentleman,* a collection of Bagby's works, Page evaluated his contribution to Southern humor. "Next to Poe, the most original of all Virginia writers was he whose reputation in his lifetime mainly rested on humorous sketches of a mildly satirical and exceedingly original type. . . ." Asserting that Bagby was not a fictionist but a realist, Page claimed that he was "so purely realistic that no one can read, even at random, a page of his genre sketches and not recognize at once the truth of the picture, and—if he be a Virginian—point to its original." Writers who had lived and written during the ante-bellum period—William A. Caruthers, William Gilmore Simms, John Pendleton Kennedy, Philip Pendleton Cooke, and others influenced by Walter Scott—had pictured Virginia life too idealistically for Page; Bagby was the "first to picture Virginia as she was."

Bagby seldom used the nostalgic darky-narrator popular with Page, Joel Chandler Harris, and F. Hopkinson Smith. Although set in the postwar South, Smith's *Colonel Carter of Cartersville* contains many glimpses of the earlier days. The colonel's likable, comic manservant, Nebuchadnezzar called "Chad," relates many humorous incidents of the good old days in Virginia. The story's narrator, for example, tells of a visit to see the colonel and, finding him absent, of being entertained by one of Chad's stories. Chad reminisces of the time his wife-to-be Henny almost got him into serious trouble with the colonel's father. Finding a goose roasting in the kitchen stove, she cut off a leg and ate it. Horrified at what might happen, Chad tried to deny that a goose was intended for dinner, and served everything but that. When confronted with the evidence that one had been picked and prepared for the meal, he reluctantly brought in the maimed goose and placed it on the table with the one leg on the upper side. Immediately a lady guest chose the leg, and a gentleman guest asked for the other. Chad's description of the scene cannot be paraphrased. "Major, you oughter seen ole marsa lookin' for der udder leg ob dat goose! He rolled him ober on de dish, dis way an' dat way, an' den he jabbed dat ole bone-handled caarvin' fork in him an' hel' him up ober de dish an' looked under him an' on top ob him, an' den he says, kinder sad like:—'Chad, whar is de udder leg ob dat goose?' 'It didn't hab none,' says I. 'You mean ter say, Chad, dat de gooses on my plantation on'y got one leg?' 'Some ob 'em has an' some ob 'em ain't. You see, marsa, we got two kinds in de pond, an' we was a little boddered to-day, so Mammy Jane cooked dis one 'cause I cotched it fust.'" The master broke off the dialogue by remarking ominously to Chad, "I'll settle with you after dinner." After dinner, the master, his guests, and a trembling Chad walked down to the duck pond to investigate the strange one-legged fowls; and, in Chad's words, "dar was de gooses sittin' on a log in de middle of dat ole green goose-pond wid one leg stuck down—so—an' de udder tucked under de wing." The relieved Chad pointed out to the master that they had but one leg; whereupon the master, "his face gittin' white an' he a-jerking his handkerchief from his pocket," shouted "Shoo!" at the geese. Chad remembers. "Major, I hope to have my brains kicked out by a lame grasshopper if ebery one ob dem gooses didn't put down de udder foot!" With his cane held up ready to strike, the master angrily exlaimed, "You lyin' nigger, I'll show you." But the frightened Chad managed to cry out, "Stop, Marsa John! 't ain't fair, 't ain't fair." To the master's question Chad slyly replied: "Cause . . . you didn't say 'Shoo!' to de goose what was on de table." This quick thinking saved him, and the next day Marsa John told Chad he could have Henny for his wife (pp. 63-70).

The sketches of John Trotwood Moore show how pathos had become an inseparable twin of humor. The "Old Mistis" is a good example of postwar crying humor. Set in the 1840's in Middle Tennessee, the story deals with the unto-death devotion of Jake, a young slave. His master, Colonel Dinwiddie, whose motto is "The proper study of mankind, sir—with due respect to Alexander Pope—is horsekind," owes gambling debts to a man who wants to pay court to the colonel's daughter. The artificial plot also has another important character, the daughter's true love, who plans to enter one of the colonel's horses, Ole Mistis, in a race with a $50,000 purse. With this money the colonel can pay his debts, throw the villain-suitor out, and allow his daughter to marry her choice. At the race Jake, who is to ride Ole Mistis, is told that if he wins he can have his freedom; but Jake is disappointed in that promise. He says, "I'll win it enyway, ef I can, Marse Jim. Whut I wanter be free fur—whut'd I do erway frum ole Marster an' Ole Mistis?" The race is close, Ole Mistis wins by a nose. But Jake loses his life; just past the finish line he is hurled off and his body lies mangled on the track. He dies in his mistress' arms. Most of the story's humor comes early and centers around the running fight Jake has with his mother, Aunt Fereby, over his love of horses. Pathos triumphs completely in the end.

The humor of another story in the same collection by Moore, "Miss Kitty's Fun'ral," derives chiefly from the comic Old Wash, who narrates the plot. Wash tells of Miss Kitty's love for her cousin and how their love is thwarted by her father. Rebuffed, the cousin goes to a foreign country, participates in a revolution, and is reported killed. Meanwhile the father dies and Kitty is being courted by a sharp lawyer, Captain Estes, whom she doesn't love but will marry, since no one else is eligible. Just before the loveless wedding, luckily, her cousin arrives to claim her love, telling everyone the announcement of his death was an obvious mistake. Throughout the sketch Old Wash's humorous comments, expressions, and descriptions help retain reader interest. Wash's description of lawyer Estes, for example, shows Moore's talent for striking figures of speech. "Ef he wasn't free wind at de rasho ob 16 ter 1, an' de onlimited coinage ob brass, my name ain't Washingtun! Why, he cu'd talk on fo' things at de same time, pocket er fee on bof sides ob er case, an' keep one eye on de bar-room an' de yuther on de church steeple. He cu'd play poker lak er gambler, drink lak er Kansas drought, an' pray lak er country deacon. He cu'd get drunk lak er sinner, an' yit stan' highes' es er saint; make lub wid one eye to Miss Kitty an' yit keep de yuther solemnly sot fur ole Marster lak St. Paul watchin' fur revolushuns!" The absurd plot holds absolutely no interest for the modern reader; it probably held little for the late nineteenth-century reader. What attraction and charm the story has comes entirely from the personality and language of Old Wash.

Still another story from the book, "A Cavalry Drill in Old Tennessee," is, strictly speaking, not a plantation sketch; however, since its central character is of the plantation class, it is included here. The occasion is a mounted cavalry drill and the action concerns the trouble an old Mexican War veteran, Colonel Dick Posey, has with his farmer-soldiers. The colonel's first problem is Jim McHyde, who rides in half-drunk on a steer decorated with cowbells. This, however, is not serious since most of the men had paid a visit to the grocery, which is also the saloon, before reporting for drill. Not knowing very much about drill commands, the colonel has a hard time getting the men to fall in. As this task is almost accomplished, the cannon is fired and the formation is broken. It takes twenty minutes to re-form the ranks. The colonel orders the arrest of McHyde, who had been told to fire the cannon *after* drill. "As the only safe place was the rear end of the bar-room, forty of the company immediately volunteered their services to take the luckless Jim there and keep him till further orders. Two were detailed, and Jim was forced to 'treet' them on arrival." When again the drill is ready to proceed, Colonel Posey admits to his men that the only rule he knows about cavalry drill is "Set straight in yer saddle, turn out yer toes, an' ride at the enemy!" He elaborates extensively on his rule, defining each word in detail and demonstrating what he means by sitting up straight in the saddle. "Second, gentlemen, you must ride at the enemy. Now 'at,' gentlemen, is a very little word, but it is bigger than a bombshell in battle, and means more than everything else; in fact, gentlemen, it's about the chief thing of this important rule, although it appears so small. Ef you'd leave out all the other words in this rule, and jes' git into yer saddles an' say *at* 'em! and then do it, you'd come mighty nigh knowin' all the rules of war. Don't gallop around nor ride about, then stop, but *at,* straight *at,* and do it dam fast, to keep yer courage up!"

After these elaborate preliminaries, they try the drill—unsuccessfully—because most of the men anticipate Colonel Posey's commands. The old man tries to be patient, and tells them that "this milertary business ain't nothin' but common sense rigged up with a sword an' a cocked hat"; but all his efforts are to no avail because someone has left the stableyard open and from it the colts make for their dams on the drill field. Pandemonium is everywhere. Moore concludes the sketch by relating the colonel's bold stroke. "To one less gifted than the Colonel, the day's drill would have ended in confusion and disgrace. Not so with him. Riding to the front, with a look on his face as if he had expected all this and it was a part of his program, he issued a command never before heard in military science—nay, not even in the Mexican war. Rising in his stirrups, he shouted, in his deepest voice: 'Halt, and suckle colts!'" This farce is perhaps the most consistently entertaining of Moore's sketches. It is also the one in which he writes least like his age.

The plantation system had been paradise for the slave, according to the postwar humorists. Master and slave were bound in a brotherhood not equaled since ancient Greece. At Christmas these genial relations reached a climax. W. L. Visscher's "Chrismus in de Ole Time," in *Harp of the South,* describes the good times had in the quarters on Christmas Eve. "Hear the fiddle, bones and banjo; / People there are gay to-night." On Christmas morning the slaves converge on the Big House where they " 'Ketch' the white folks' 'Christmas gift.' " The ever-generous planter's family has gifts for all.

In *Plantation Poems* Eloise Sherman recreated "An Old-Time Christmas" on a plantation. All the accoutrements of the season are there: the fruit cakes, home-cured hams, mistletoe and holly, the yule log, and of course eggnog. The Big House is a scene of elaborate preparations for the Christmas festivities.

147

The Smiling Phoenix

Big House in a flurry,
Kitchen up side down,
White folks givin' orders,
Niggers flyin' roun':
Ev'ybody busy
Es de time draws nigh,
Dat's how we kep' Chris'mus
In de days gone by.

All was sweetness and light at Christmas—and most of the remaining days of the year. The slave was the property of his owner, but he also had property of his own, usually given him by his master at Christmas. Torm in Mrs. Sherman's "Personal Property" is very protective of a hat his master has given him. He says proudly, "De head, hit b'long to Marster, but / De hat, dat b'long to me." Torm is proud of owning a hat—and of being owned by his master.

Several of Jeannette Walworth's *Southern Silhouettes* deal with plantation life before the war. " 'Mely Jane's Wedding" shows how well the slaves were treated by their owners, even to the extent of allowing a Negro bride to use for her own the left-overs from her young mistress' wedding. All the provisions for the two ceremonies are the same; only the casts are different. Humor permeates the entire story, but 'Mely Jane's wedding is a farce. The preacher who performs the ritual uses the occasion to preach a sermon on gluttony. "Sistern and breddern, we is meet togedder to jine dis man and dis woman in de bonds of holy widlock. Leas'ways I is meet to jine 'm' en you is meet prinsupply, I tek it, outer a hankerin' arter de flesh pots uv Egypt." He continues his sermon on frivolous entertainment and lusts of the flesh, and concludes, "We is all meet here t' rej'ice over 'Mely Jane Benson's takin' Pete—Pete—whar yo udder name, nigger?" With the ceremony concluded, even the parson succumbs to the "fleshpots uv Egypt" and partakes freely of the wedding food.

The attempt of a Yankee governess to do her part in enlightening the plantation South is the plot of "Colonel Sutton's Governess." Her reaction to the slave's acceptance of his bondage provides most of the humor. She is shocked, for example, when she is told, "I'se Mandy. Miss says I'se gwine to be yo' nigger." She is also horrified at the evident lack of religious training for the slaves. When she asks Mandy who made her, the girl responded: "Nobody didn't mek me, less'n 'twere Mammy, en she mus' 'a jes' started me, 'cause I war'n but jes' half made w'en she die. I'se twicet as big as I wuz w'en Mammy die." The sketch is dominated at the end by a religious sentiment, however, because the Boston girl converts the little heathen by reading to her from the Bible. Especially in humorous sketches by women the religious-sentimental ending became a stereotype.

The title character in Mrs. Walworths' *Uncle Scipio* spends much of his time reliving the happy days in Mississippi when he was a slave. Scipio can recall very minute details from the past. For proof, read his gossipy, discursive recollection of "de ve'y las' fox hunt our folks hed befo' de racket commence w'ich broke we all up . . . It was prime fun fur de young folks er huntin' uv dem foxes. En w'en Mars Billy Ranson, dat were Miss 'Tildy's onlies' brudder (ol' Mr. Ranson ain't had but two chillun), he come 'long wid his houn's, en Miss 'Tildy on her little w'ite mar', wid a blue ridin' skyirt an' cap, an' de Parker boys, an' de Millers, three of 'em, 'cludin' Jeff, which brought 'long der extry horses, en our boys, wid our hounds a mekin music, I tell you, sir, de ol' meetin' ground down thar', just inside our big gate, look gay fur true" (p. 39). To the former carriage driver all the glory of his long life was in the past. The book's Northern narrator listens to Uncle Scipio's spoken memories because "nothing pleased him better than an opportunity to talk about old plantation days and his wi'te folks." Scipio's recollections of his white folks are a mixture of pride, humor, pathos, and longing. The old Negro utters wistfully: "My w'ite folks was de fus' quality uv de land . . . ev'y thing min's me uv ol' times now. Seems lak I wuz countin' milestones all 'long de way fum de cabin do' t' de gates uv de golden city en yherin' voices a callin' t' me out'n de burryin'-groun' up yonder under de locus' trees. W'en de cott'n's ready to be pick, en de co'n hangs ripe, it's marster's voice I hears" (pp. 18-19). Such plaintive cries must have evoked tears as well as sweet smiles from the sentimental reader, whose vote could probably have been counted on in a referendum to re-enslave the Negro.

A frank contrast of "freedom times" with "old slave times"—the latter winning on every point—is the core of "The Old Slave Regime" in Dave Sloan's *Fogy Days*. The stanzas, like almost all humorous poetry of the period, lack literary merit. The diction is poor, forced rimes abound, and the overall effect is awkward. The poem does, however, illustrate the attitude toward slavery dominant in the postwar South. It is a defense of the system, containing such bold lines as "Southern slavery may have been sin, / But the Bible does not show it." To prove his premise, Sloan proposed a testimony from one who had known both slavery and freedom.

> Let's have old Sambo take the stand,
>   Let old time nigger tell the truth,
> Which times were best, freedom times,
>   Or the old slave times of your youth.

He reminded the imaginary Negro on the stand of the "freedom" and indulgence he enjoyed under slavery.

> Have you forgot your little thefts,
>   Of all the chickens you have stole,
> Of the tater patches you have robbed,
>   Couldn't count them for your soul.

The Smiling Phoenix

The happy slave became the miserable freedman when the jealous Yankee interfered. Sloan stated his case bluntly.

> *There never was a happier race,*
> *If they could have been left alone,*
> *'Twas hatred that stirred up the fuss,*
> *The Yankes were jealous of our bone.*

Such defenses of slavery did not necessarily indicate a white man's desire to return to "old slave times." They rather constituted an offensive defense of a system and a section that the humorists believed had been so much maligned.

Religion, the defense asserted, helped make the slave's life a not unhappy one. Emotional by nature, the slave found release in his religion. To the average plantation Negro, the Christian religion was more than a mere set of abstract principles deduced from a book called the Bible. His religion was real and close. Led by the plantation "exhorter" (who became a full-fledged preacher after the war), he usually interpreted the Bible in an extremely anthropomorphic way. A good example of comic misinterpretation of Scripture and the intruding of the slave's real world on his religious world is Martha Gielow's "Er White Horse Turnt Loose" in *Old Plantation Days*. A sermon was purportedly "Preached in the Bethlehem Chapel, near Greensboro, Ala." The parson's text was from "Reberlations": "Er white horse turnt loose in hebben an' de reins throw'd ober his nake, an' you kin hyar de soun' uv his hoofs echoin' ter Goshum." This meaningless text was minutely explicated and blown up into a full-length sermon. The sermon made about as much sense as the text, but the preacher's congregation responded not to his meaning but to his rhythm. The exhorter always ended his sermon at the climactic moment for a generous collection. His appeal might run like this: "Now, my Bredren, I wants ter tell you one mo' thing, an' dat is dis: Dar is three things what is necessary fer er preacher ter have fer ter preach de gospel. Knowledge in de haid, de sperit in de heart, an' money in de pocket. Now, I is got de knowledge in de haid, an' de sperit in de heart, but, Bredren, I ain't got no money in de pocket. . . . I only calls on you fer ter s'ply me wid one uv dem." The slave in postwar humor was perennially happy. He was happy, according to the humorists, because he knew how to enjoy every duty of life from picking cotton to going to church. We may note, though, that unlike the slave depicted in Southern humor, the Negro of the ante-bellum spirituals is a creature of grief and woe longing for a heavenly home.

The religion of the slaves was one of the main themes of Edmund K. Goldsborough's *Ole Mars an' Ole Miss*, although he treated their secular recreations too. He wrote in the Introduction: "My subjects are all typical Eastern-Shore-of-Maryland darkies, some of whom 'had erligion, 'longed ter de Babtis' church an' wuz monstus pious.' Others danced, sang, played the banjo, fiddled, fished and frolicked in Talbot County 'Befo' de Wah.'" The life he portrayed was a pleasant one for master and slave. The Negroes were allowed their own pastimes, of which churchgoing was chief. Preaching was a social occasion and worship was just one part of the service. A service might consist of a recipe for Aunt Phillis' pancakes which some of the ladies of the church had asked for; an announcement that the deacons would buy watermelon seeds with last Sunday's collection, package them, and raffle them off; an announcement of a "rebate" (debate) to be held shortly on "Ef'n uh man er woman hab salbation in deah hyarts, will dey be feared ter babtiz wha shirks is?" (p. 33). Debates were a popular diversion, and the more absurd and abstruse the topic, the better. One "rebate" at "Zion Babtis' Chuch" was based on "secon' chapta Zacharyhy, 6 vus: 'Ho, ho, cum forth an' flee fum de lan' ub de north, saith de Lawd; fuh I hab spred you uh broad ez de fo' winds ub heabin saith de Lawd.' " The objective was to decide "ef'n Ho, ho wan' uh Chine er Japne, who wuz he?" (p. 75). The slave's misinterpretation of the Bible is seen in the comment of one of the debaters on the sons of Noah. "De Bible tells us plain ez plain kin be, dat Noahy had three sons— *Sham*, Ham an' *Jap*heth. Sham ez befo' mentioned wuz uh white pusson; Ham wuz uh cullud pusson, an' *Jap*heth mus' uh bin uh Japne" (p. 83). Very seldom was anything conclusive decided at one of the debates.

Goldsborough's romantic sketches of ante-bellum plantation life are generally effective. His dialect is usually authentic, and his understanding of the Negro's mind is thorough. His character sketches of plantation types are memorable. Sometimes in one sentence he sketches fully a character. "Little Billy was as black as a tar pot, short of stature, very bow-legged, cunning as a fox, and smart" (p. 91). Goldsborough is solidly in the Page plantation tradition.

Another attractive picture of plantation life before the war is Mary Ross Banks' semi-autobiographical *Bright Days in the Old Plantation Time.* Her objective, she declared in the Introduction, was to present "a correct view of a Southern child's life in the days of slavery." She hoped her book would help remove the false ideas about slaves as beasts of burden; she remembered them only as a "free-from-care and happy race." Her book claimed to be accurate, since Southerners "will readily recognize negro character, dialect, and love for their old owners, as we all knew and experienced it prior to the war."

Most of the sketches are told in the words of Bet, the author's childhood nurse, who always reflects the plantation mind. Like most slaves, she despises "po' white trash." Commenting sarcastically on their lack of roots, "Dey allus min' me er some folks I heerd erbout in Alerbam onct, what lived close ter my miss's brother, de gin'ral. Dem folks moved erbout ser much, twel one ol' rooster what dey had, ev'y time he'd see er kivered wagin comin' down de road, he'd des lay down on hiz back, an' stick hiz foots up in de air, an' wait fur somebody ter come 'long, an' tie hiz legs terguther, reddy ter be flung in the wagin fur de fam'ly ter move" (pp. 69-70). To Bet, quality folks, white or black, stayed on one place.

She has no criticism of the aristocracy; her tales consistently show the amiable relations between slaves and their owners. She tells her little white charge, for example, of the time the white church was used for a Negro funeral. The sermon lasted five hours, she recalls, "an' I des tell you, honey, ef de Lord iz got enny mussy on sinners, he sholy opened the hebenly gate, an' tuck dem niggers inter glory dat night" (p. 73). Another entertainment for the slaves was corn shucking, which Bet calls "de mos' consequenshus time er de whole year, 'cep' Chris'mus an' fofe-er-Jewly." Bet also comments on other slaves, and like the familiar Negro after the war, is usually very critical of their foibles. She predicts, for example, that the marriage of "ol' Kalline" to a "young nigger, what ain' much ol'n dat las' gal uv her'n" won't last beyond Christmas. The device of using a slave or former slave to tell stories to young white children, seen here in Bet's stories to the author when a child, was used throughout postwar humor. It dramatizes better than anything else could dramatize the supposed intimacy between whites and blacks in the days before 1861.

Mrs. Pickett also shows in "Mammy Borry" (*Yule Log*) the typical old-time Negro attitude toward the poor white. As a child, the author recalls, she once got into trouble with the overseer's children and went to Mammy Borry to have it settled. The old nurse chastised her for having anything to do with poor whites. "Come 'long, now, chillun, en 'semble yo'se'fs 'roun' me en lemme ax you how of'n is I told you 'bout 'soshatin' wid po' w'ite folks. Dey don' lak niggers 'kaze dey nebber ownt none, en dey don' lak ladies en gemmans 'kaze dey kyan' nebber be ekals wid 'em. You chillun is jes' lak de birds in de Bible; you kyan' play wid pots en kittles en smutty t'ings, widout gittin smutty lak dey is."

The slave was often pictured as turning routine work into play fests. The Virginian James J. McDonald, after stating in *Life in Old Virginia* (p. 232) that "Tidewater Virginia was virtually the slave's paradise," substantiated his assertion by showing the good times at such work occasions as shuckings.

> *Dis co'n it are good,*
> *An' dat yo' den all know,*
> *It's on dis yere plantation*
> *Dis good co'n did grow.*
> *Shuck co'n,*
> *O, shuck co'n.*

Two of Will Harben's *Northern Georgia Sketches* deal with slaves. Despite their titles, "The Whipping of Uncle Henry" and "The Sale of Uncle Rastus" are both favorable pictures of slave life. The first sketch shows the slave's tyranny over his master and his scorn of the poor white. While his master is away on business in North Carolina, Uncle Henry is to take orders from the overseer; but he refuses. The old Negro explains to his mistress that he can't respect the overseer because "thar ain't no pore white trash in all this valley country as low down as all his lay-out." To discipline his slave with a whipping, the master cuts short his business trip and returns to his plantation. He takes Uncle Henry to the woods to administer the punishment, but first they have prayer. The master prays first and then the slave, who tells the Lord, "I may have brought trouble an' vexation to Marse Jasper, I don't dispute that, but he had no business puttin' me under that low-down, white-trash overseer an' goin' off so far." Uncle Henry swears to the Lord that nobody is going to whip him for disobeying a low-down, poor-white overseer. Seeing his slave's side of the case, the master agrees to let Uncle Henry be his own boss when the master is away. No more trouble was had with Uncle Henry, who turned out three times as much work as any other slave on the place.

"The Sale of Uncle Rastus" also has a happy ending. Because of imminent bankruptcy, an owner is forced to put his slaves up for sale. At the auction the Negroes try not to think of possible family separation, and joke about how much each of them will bring. Uncle Rastus prances around on the auction block and teases the crowd. "Who gwine buy me? . . . I been er li'l sick, but I'm pickin' up now, en kin hol' my own wid any nigger in dis county. Who want me? Speak up quick." Just as the slaves are about to be sold, their owner's estranged brother steps up, bids $20,000, and returns the family intact to his joyful brother. Thus in these two sketches a postwar humorist refutes two slave nightmares: whippings and the cruel separating of families. The defense of an extinct way of life goes on.

If one can believe the humorists, the Negro was never so fortunate as when he was a slave. Bill Arp dispelled in *Farm and Fireside* another bugbear of slavery: he made a joke out of the plantation police force, the patrol or "pat-roller." To the theft-inclined slave, he wrote, it was a fine game. "Many a good story have they told us boys how they fooled the patrol and got away. It was more of a frolic than a fear, and one success made them bold and ready for another. Such was negro life in our young days; and it wasn't so bad, so very bad, after all" (p. 317). Though few people wanted to return to those days, most agreed that it hadn't been too harsh on the Negro.

The slave was a perennial favorite as a subject—usually the butt—for short jokes and anecdotes. Two from Jacob Stroyer's *My Life in the South* will illustrate this method of exploiting the slave's personality. Stroyer told an anecdote of a slave who received many beatings for being lazy. An old Negro woman one day suggested that he let the Lord help him with his work. The indolent slave agreed to this, did half the task assigned to him, and then lay down under a tree. The overseer came by and whipped him again for doing only half his work. A short time later a preacher called on him and pleaded with him to stop serving the devil and begin serving the Lord, who would help him to be a better man. The slave's rebuttal was that if the Lord wouldn't help him out when he gave Him a chance, he couldn't trust the Lord. The skeptical Negro never became a Christian.

Another of Stroyer's anecdotes deals with the slave's propensity to steal.

153

He wrote that during fodder-pulling time the slaves would frequently steal green ears of corn and secretly roast them. One time a slave barely managed to conceal an ear of roasting corn in his shirt bosom when the overseer walked up. Suddenly the corn thief realized that some live coals had stuck to the corn. He jumped up, rushed down to the creek, and jumped in to put the fire out. He explained later to the overseer that he just went down to cool off. In the postwar period such jokes made up the bulk of oral humor. Their only interest today is to the literary historian, to whom they reveal much about the attitude of the period toward the Negro.

The humorists usually associated certain personality traits with the slave. His supposed slyness was one of the subjects most often exploited. F. D. Srygley relays two stories told by T. W. Caskey in *Seventy Years in Dixie* which illustrate this trait. During slavery times, Caskey said, he bought two opossums from a Negro boy, who explained their strange appearance by telling that he had cut off the head of the smaller one because he had "squashed it up monst'us bad w'en I kill 'im." He explained the absence of a tail on one by saying he had cut it off "so de 'possum'd look sorter squar' like." Caskey swallowed the explanation, took the "possums" home, and had them prepared for dinner. After he and his family and a guest had eaten all but one piece, the guest, an expert on physiology, commented that the bones didn't look like opossum bones. He pieced the bones together and concluded that they had just eaten a cat. This news almost caused a riot at the table. Caskey was at first angry, but he soon saw that apologies would not be appropriate. "I wavered no longer, but boldly stuck my fork into the last remaining piece of the misrepresented animal, and quietly finished my dinner" (pp. 114-18).

The other story by Caskey shows how a slave cleverly avoided a whipping. His mistress was a widow who had her punishments administered by the overseer. Whenever one of the house servants needed a whipping, she would send the victim to the overseer with a note which read, "Please whip the bearer and oblige." The carriage driver had already received one whipping that way, and when he was again sent on a similar errand, he gave the note to the wood chopper, telling him, "Ole Missus say how you got ter fotch dis yere note to de boss!" The illiterate and unsuspecting wood chopper, glad to get off from work, took the note to the overseer and amid cries of innocence was given a sound beating (pp. 281-83). However, in spite of occasional whippings and other minor punishments and inconveniences of slavery, the consensus among the postwar Southern humorists was that the golden age of the Negro had been when he was in bondage to the Southern white.

The slaveholding class was not nearly so popular a subject for humor as the slave, but many comic accounts of the aristocracy were written. Virginius Dabney's *The Story of Don Miff* (1886), for example, is a humorous novel treating the slaveowning class in ante-bellum Virginia. Although it deals with slaveowners largely apart from their slaves, the book is a valuable discussion of the old Southern life. Much of it consists of the author's reminiscences of "the follies of his youth"—the follies of a youth of leisure spent in conversation and beer drinking with his friends.

In the autobiographical *Recollections of a Southern Matron* (1867), Caroline Howard Gilman portrayed her parents with humorous touches. She told, for instance, an anecdote illustrating her father's fondness for his old clothes. The visit of a peddler was always a big occasion on the plantation. One day as her mother was looking at a glass pitcher, the Jewish peddler began his sales spiel. "Ver sheap, only two dollars—sheap as dirt. If te lady hash any old closhes, it is petter as money." This gave her mother an idea and she sent for a pair of the colonel's old pantaloons to trade for the pitcher. Looking at the worn trousers, the peddler protested that "te closhesman's give noting for dish," but he agreed to exchange when the lady threw in a waistcoat and coat with the pantaloons. The colonel was furious when he discovered his hunting clothes gone. "I believe, if they could, women would sell their husbands to those rascally peddlers." He continued his ranting as he left for hunting.[7]

The first part of Mrs. Pickett's humorous autobiography, *What Happened to Me,* is a backward look to the planter aristocracy. Her memories of an aristocratic childhood are all nostalgically amusing. Her arrival, she notes, had been unwelcome because her family had made elaborate preparations for a son. They had even planned to name him Thomas La Salle. But she came anyway. "I made my arrival in the middle of the night, the middle of the week, the middle of the month, almost the middle of the year, near the middle of the century, and in the middle of a hail-storm." Her father was away in Philadelphia when she was born, but those present were downcast. Her mammy said, "Lordy, Lordy, Marse Doctor . . . he ain't no boy-chile. It's a po' li'l gal-chile." The doctor said, "A girl? Why! Damn him!" She describes her grieving mother, "My poor, disappointed, heart-broken mother turned her face to the wall." Only the mammy regained her composure enough to comfort the poor, forsaken, unwanted girl-baby. "Come 'long to yo' mammy, honey. She ain't gwine to 'sert you ef you is a gal-chile, po' li'l lamb! You can't he'p yo' calamity no mo' dan we-all kin. Mammy knows hit's terrible. En yo' pa, he gwine cuss eb'y last nigger on de plantation 'bout hit. . . . I suttinly is sorry, but dar ain't nuttin' so bad dat hit couldn't be wusser, en you mouter been twins—gal twins!" To make matters worse, she is not only a gal-chile, but a cross-eyed gal-chile. Mammy tried to explain one of the deformities to the poor, shocked father: "I dunno, Marse Dae, how de po' boy happened to be a gal. I 'clare it wuz none of we-all's doin's, but I reckon de reason she's cross-eyed is her bein' born lak she was in de middle of de week a lookin' bofe ways for Sunday" (pp. 3-5).

When three weeks later her grandmother arrived and offered to take the baby home with her, the offer was eagerly accepted and LaSalle was placed in a "settin'-aig-basket" and taken away. At her grandmother's Mammy Dilsey chastised the carriage driver for bringing her in such a basket. "How you-all know dat some misforchunement ain't gwine to come 'count er projickin' wid her lak dat? De chile mout crow, or she mout cackle, or she mout take her arms for wings en flop 'em, or she mout peck, or eat wu'ms, or walk wid her toes stuck in'ards. She eben mout have fedders." All the house servants at her grandmother's place crowded around to admire her. Uncle Charles' reaction was typical of her reception there. "Is dat Miss Lizzie's chile? Niggers, you-all hyer dat? Take off your hats en bow en cutchy, ebby last one er you, for dis is yo' Miss Lizzie's chile en mistisses' gran'chile, de young missis dat de Lord is done en sont down to earth for us to take a intrus' in, to work for, en to teach manners to, en to send to school." After pledging to "slave" for the little white child, he offered up a prayer to "concentrate our li'l missis to de bressed Lord. . . . Oh, Lord, de Father of de fatherless, dat letteth not a sparrow fall to de groun' widout Dy knowledge en counts de very hairs upon dar heads; disremember dis Dy he'pless chile who has been fotch to us dis day th'oo trials en triberlations in a settin'-aig-basket. I beseech De, oh Lord, to watch over her, clothe her in raiment en vestures en feed her on manna en lead her li'l foots into de straight en narrer paths to de glory of Dy righteousness. Harken up her voice to sing Dy praises en lift up her han's to do Dy wu'k en keep her in Dy holy keepin'. Oh, Lord bress dis our li'l baby for de sake of Dy own en Miss Mary's li'l baby, li'l Marse Jesus, amen." With such a consecration as this, LaSalle couldn't help but lead a charmed life. But Ole-Granny-Aggie was taking no chances and refused to let her be put in a certain cradle because "Marse Jasper's twin done en die in dat cradle, en all de rabbits' foots in de worl' ain't gwine charm away de ha'nts en keep off de ebil eye ef you puts her in dat cradle to sleep." Just in case granny was right, she was put in a trundle bed (pp. 14-17).

After a rather unpropitious beginning, LaSalle grew up loving and being loved by the Negroes who raised her. Slaveowners, she asserts, had little to do with their children until they were almost grown. Like LaSalle, the babies had colored wet nurses and played with colored children when they were growing up. LaSalle was also entertained with stories told by the older slaves. Her favorite was Uncle Bosum, who claimed royal blood and would tell stories of his regal ancestors. Uncle Jack, his father, he said, had been an African king and in the United States had worked at the College of William and Mary. Uncle Bosum delighted the credulous little girl. "Yo Uncle Jack had charge of all de books at de college en dey says ev'y time he'd dus' de books dat Marse Robert Dinsmore give to de college he'd stop en read de abertisement writ on 'em, 'Ubi Libertas Ibi Patria,' en say to hisse'f, 'I wonder why on earf Marse Robert Dinsmore want to separate dat po' couple for, when he was rich en could a bought Libi en Pat bofe hisse'f 'stead a orderin' de yuther man to buy Libi en sayin' he was gwine to buy Pat' " (p. 54).

Throughout her memoirs, Mrs. Pickett tried to picture plantation life as an idyl for both slave and master. Her grandmother's place was called Holiday's Point, she says, because of the many holidays her grandfather had given his slaves. "The community held that if my grandfather had framed the almanac he would have put into it twice as many days as did the Arabs and Romans, that he might have more holidays to bestow upon his slaves" (p. 64). Christmas was a gala occasion on the plantation for master and slave, with Christmas gifts lovingly exchanged across the freedom line. Servants working away from home returned at Christmas to complete the one big happy slaveowner family. Always the defender of the slavocracy, she explains why some servants might be away from home. "Many of my grandmother's servants had been away from the home plantation, being allowed to choose their places of service and to return if they did not find them satisfactory" (p. 75).

The placid plantation life was almost at an end, however, when her father took her to Lynchburg Seminary in 1859. She left her home remembering the loving gifts and farewells of the slaves, and especially Uncle Charles, who brought her "a nest of guinea eggs, a box of sweet gum which he had been collecting for months, a string of chinquapins and some dried haws." A premonition that all this was to be suddenly swept away came with John Brown's raid at Harpers Ferry, which occurred just before she left for college. On the way to Lynchburg she and her father met Colonel Robert E. Lee, who had just captured Brown. Lee and her father talked of the effect hanging Brown would have on the slave. Her father, she recalls, told the future hero of the Confederacy: "I asked my foreman, who is a representative of his race, if he did not think we ought to hang old John Brown. He looked at me earnestly for a while then, shaking his head slowly, said 'I knows, Marse Dae, dat po' Marse John done en bruk de law, killin' all dem mens; but den, Marse Dae, even ef po' Marse John did bre'k de law, don't you think, suh, dat hangin' him would be a *li'l abrupt?*'" (p. 85). Lee laughed and replied, "I think that just about expresses the sentiment not only of the colored people but of many others." Unfortunately hotheads on both sides did not agree. John Brown was hanged, the Republican Lincoln was elected President, Fort Sumter was fired upon, and Mrs. Pickett's plantation idyl was doomed.

Mrs. Pickett's account of ante-bellum plantation life was written from an undisguised aristocratic point of view. Because he was not of the aristocracy, Joel Chandler Harris perhaps understood plantation life more fully and depicted it more completely than Mrs. Pickett or any other humorist. In his writings, the whole plantation appears not with Mrs. Pickett's gentleness nor Page's glamor, but with a completeness of understanding not equaled by either. As a boy and young man Harris had lived on the Joseph Addison Turner plantation in Middle Georgia, where he could view that society intimately but without bias. His pictures of the ante-bellum plantation are typically pleasant and even romantic, yet he does not exclude the darker side of the life. Julia Collier Harris, his daughter and biographer, described his realistic portrayal of plantation society. "He never let the glamorous memory of happy days on the Turner plantation, when his work in the printing-shop was enlivened by runs with the bird-dogs, or by hours of wonderful interest in the negro cabins, blind him to the darker aspects of slavery, such as the sufferings of fugitives, the tragedy of mixed blood, the separation of families or the occasional cruelties of overseers, and in this respect he differed from most of the Southern writers who distinguished themselves in the same field."[8] He also treated the tragic implications of slavery for the free Negro. The title character of his "Free Joe and the Rest of the World," though his name was spoken humorously, was not a happy person. Harris said of him: "He realized the fact that though he was free he was more helpless than any slave. Having no owner, every man was his master" (p. 12). Harris knew of the kindness of the slaveowner—Joseph Addison Turner was the ideal master—but he also knew that the system was inherently evil and no amount of indulgence could change that.

Jeannette Walworth's "Tony's White Angel" from *Southern Silhouettes* is another sketch of the tragic free Negro. "Perhaps if Tony had been given any choice in the matter, he would not have chosen to be born free, at a time when the pains and penalties attaching to that condition so far outweighed its factitious advantages."

A plantation setting became popular for children's books. Harris helped initiate the tradition with his "Little Mr. Thimblefinger" series, which comprised six books, the first of which was published in 1894. He introduced the series with this sentence: "Once upon a time there lived on a plantation in the very middle of Middle Georgia a little girl and a little boy and their negro nurse." The little girl's name was Sweetest Susan, the little boy was called Buster John, and the nurse was Drusilla. Of the last, Harris explained, "She was their playmate—their companion, and a capital one she made." Although these were children's stories, here as well as in his adult writings Harris tried to show that in spite of the tragedy of slavery it did not brutalize the Southerner as abolitionists and radical Republicans suggested.

Another children's classic using the ante-bellum plantation as a setting is Mrs. Louisa Clarke Pyrnelle's *Diddy, Dumps, and Tot* (1882). The structure of the book is similar to the Uncle Remus stories in that an old Negro tells stories to young white children. Thomas Nelson Page wrote that the book was unexcelled by any Southern story in tenderness and humor. Her purpose was the same as that of other writers of the plantation school: to refute the "slanders" of Mrs. Stowe and other abolitionists by showing the pleasant and happy relations between master and slave.

Harry Stillwell Edwards' *Two Runaways* had the same objective as Mrs. Pyrnelle's book. In the Preface to the collection, however, Edwards admitted that he was dealing with "the brighter and better parts of the older negro character, and of some of the people whose lives touch or touched his." The title sketch tells the delightful story of Major Worthington and his slave Isam. The major had noticed that each year Isam went absent without leave for a couple of weeks. One year he decided to watch the slave to see where he went. His discovery of Isam's secret was the beginning of a new life for the major.

On the way to Isam's hideaway the first year they passed the Negro burial ground, but Isam bragged that he was not afraid. "Ain't nuthin' go'n' ter tech ole Isam. All dem in dere is dun boun' en' sot." He explained to his master what he meant. "Well . . . w'en er sperrit gits out'n de flesh, de only way hit can be boun' en' sot es ter plug er tree." He then showed the major a pine tree in which a plug had been driven for each grave in the cemetery. When the major took out his knife and started to pick at a plug, Isam went into hysterics. "Don', Mass' Craffud! don't do it, honey; you mout let de meanes' nigg'r on de place git loose, en' dere ain' no tellin' w'at 'u'd happ'n. You git de chill 'n' fev'r 'n' cat'piller 'n' bad craps, sho' 's yer born." Just to make sure his master believed him, he presented evidence to show the validity of the superstition. "One time, lightnin' busted er tree ov'r dere, en' seben er dem plugs drap out; en' dat summer de typhoid fev'r struck seben nigg'rs, en' de las' one uv 'm died spang dead."

The two runaways arrived at Isam's hideaway without any interference from Negro spirits. They were completely without provisions, not even food for which they had to forage. They were loose and free, master and slave. Their unequal social relations were suspended and they were boys again.

A farcical episode concerns Major Worthington's providential rescue from a deer. When a deer rushed Isam on the way back from a foraging expedition, the major came to his aid and tangled with the animal, while Isam was safely escaping to the top branch of a nearby haw bush. The Negro, however, supported his master orally in his death struggle, shouting: "Stick ter 'im, Mass' Craffud, stick ter 'im! Wo' deer! wo' deer! Stick ter 'im, Mass' Craffud!" The major continued to wrestle with the mad deer, all the time ordering, then begging, Isam to help him. But Isam was safely in the tree, paralyzed with fear, and he chided his master for his anger and begged the Lord to forgive him for it. "You mustn't let de sun go down on yo' wraf! O Lord . . . don' you mine nuth'n' he es er-sayin' now, cos he ain' 'spons'bl'. Lord, ef de bes' aingil you got wuz down dere in his fix, en' er fool deer wuz er-straddlin' 'im, dey ain' no tell'n' w'at 'u'd happ'n, er w'at sorter lang-widge he'd let loos'. Wo' deer! wo' deer! Stick ter 'im Mass' Craffud, stick ter 'im. Steddy, deer! Steddy, Mass' Craffud!" The major continued to plead with the frightened Negro to come down and help him get loose from his death grip with the deer, but Isam logically replied: "Good Gawd, Mass' Craffud . . . dere ain' nuthin' I woodn' do fur you but hit's better fur one ter die 'n two. Hit's a long sight better." Finally the slave told his master flatly that there was nothing that could get him to come down out of the tree because the Lord had saved him by putting him there, and there he expected to stay. As the major's hold on the deer seemed to weaken and the slave thought his master doomed, Isam began praying anew for him, and implored the Lord: "He's b'en er bad man. He cuss 'n' sware, 'n' play keerds, 'n' bet on horse-races, 'n' drink whisky. . . . En' he steal—good*ness*, he tek ter steal'n' like er duck ter water. Roast'n' yers, watermilluns, chick'n—nuthin' too bad fur 'im. . . . Tek him by de slack er es briches en' shek 'm ov'r de flames, but don' let 'im drap. . . ."

While Isam's impassioned last rites were going on, the major was devising a stratagem to get Isam out of the tree. Then he called to Isam that he recognized in the beast's eyes the face of the dead Negro whose plug he had been picking on at the graveyard. The desperate major warned the slave that "he and I will never give you another hour of peace as long as you live." This revelation worked a miracle, and suddenly Isam was more frightened of the loose spirit than the live deer. He jumped from the tree, leaped on the deer, and saved his master's life. The major did not hold his slave's temporary cowardice against him, and every year until the start of the war the two runaways left society for the swamps and lived "loos' en free" in a strange brotherhood binding master and slave.

When George Washington Cable started writing about early nineteenth-century Creoles he found an almost virgin theme. He was fascinated by these people of mixed blood, and in *Old Creole Days* (1879) and *The Grandissimes* (1880) he explored in local-color sketches the effects of miscegenation. In the 1880's he was considered the peer of Henry James, William Dean Howells, and Mark Twain. Richard Chase has written of him, "George Washington Cable is remembered, if at all, as a local colorist who wrote quaint, pathetic, and humorous tales about Creole life in Louisiana, and who sometimes gave his characters a dialect speech too irksome to read."[9] Speaking more highly of Cable, Edmund Wilson in *Patriotic Gore* (pp. 584-85), his incisive study of Civil War literature, stated that every student of American literature should read five of Cable's books—*Old Creole Days, The Grandissimes, Strange True Stories of Louisiana, The Silent South,* and *The Negro Question.*

Old Creole Days followed the popular mode of blending humor and pathos. A delicate humor is evident in one of the best-known stories of the volume, "Madame Délicieuse." This tells of a short little doctor, his fifteen-year alienation from his Creole father, and their reconciliation through the offices of the doctor's fiancée. General Villivicencio thinks his son is a coward and has disowned him because he refused to become a soldier. He hears from Madame Délicieuse, however, that his son actually is a world-renowned scientist; and he decides that perhaps he has been too harsh. The reconciliation is thwarted, though, when the general is attacked by an opposing political faction. He goes to his son, expecting him to challenge the accuser to a duel. At first the scientist refuses, but then gives in and goes out looking for the culprit. Happily the duel never comes off; the fiancée reveals that she wrote the accusation herself just to show the general his son's loyalty and bravery. The old man is pleased and reunites the family, now brightened by the adorable Délicieuse. Most of the story's humor is of character, most vividly seen in the characterization of the old Creole general with his old-fashioned ideals of honor.

Cable's pictures of Creole life were considered libelous by most Creoles and many non-Creoles. The historian Alcée Fortier declared that "his descriptions of Creole life and his types of the Creole gentlemen and lady are utterly incorrect."[10] Perhaps Fortier's criticism was prompted by such a passage as the following from *The Grandissimes*. It displays the laughable Creole egotism of the artist M. Raoul Innerarity. One day he appears at a drug store where various items are often left for sale. Behind him is a little Negro boy lugging a large rectangular package. Raoul goes up to the proprietor and announces, "I 'ave somet'ing beauteeful to place into yo' window." Tearing off the wrappings from the package, he reveals a painting which he tells the drug-store man is called "Louisiana rif-using to hanter de h-Union." The druggist peers at the painting and remarks that the subject must be allegorical. Raoul protests, "Allegoricon? No, sir! Allegoricon never saw that pigshoe. If you insist to know who make dat pigshoe—de hartis' stan' bif-ore you!" After making this startling announcement, the proud artist continues, "'Tis de work of me, Raoul Innerarity, cousin to de distingwish Honoré Grandissime. I swear to you, sir, on stack of Bible' as 'igh as yo' head!" The druggist asks the "distinguished" artist if he wants the picture put into the window for sale. The haughty Creole answers equivocally. "'Sieur Frowenfel'! I think it is a foolishness to be too proud, eh? I want you to say, 'My frien', 'Sieur Innerarity, never care to sell anything; 'tis for egshibbyshun'. *Mais*—when somebody look at it, so . . . you say, '*Foudre tonnere!* what de dev'!—I take dat ris-pon-sibble-ty—you can have her for two hun'red fifty dollah!' Better not be too proud, eh, 'Sieur Frowenfel'?" (pp. 145-49).

Cable's "lies" were answered in books, in newspapers, in magazines, and in such anonymous pamphlets as the *Critical Dialogue Between Aboo and Caboo on a New Book; or A Grandissime Ascension.* This dialogue, edited by "E. Junius," is itself a small masterpiece of satirical wit. It purports to be the publication of a manuscript, found on the shores of Lake Pont-chartrain, which records the conversation between the returned shade of the illustrious LaCreole family (Aboo) and a living member of that family (Caboo). The conversation was ostensibly taken down by an eavesdropping reporter who then lost his manuscript on the beach. The Editor's Preface gives the *raison d'être* of the pamphlet. "The subject of this 'Critical Dialogue,' is the last work of the Dignissime George William Cable,—'The Grandissimes,'—which work is but a sequel of the 'Old Creole Days.' They were both given as *novels* and they have been taken for HISTORY. The most historical and honorable creole families are therein pasquinaded." The Preface continues with a direct attack on Cable. "There was in Louisiana, long ago, a Choctaw Chief on whom had been inflicted the disgraceful name of *Mingolabee*, le Chef-Menteur, the Great-Liar. . . . Have we not, just now, in the very heart of

161

the good and beautiful City of New Orleans, a Magnissime Mingolabee-Romanticist?—We have."

In the dialogue Cable's "misrepresentations" are exposed and condemned. Lamenting the untrue picture given of Creoles in *The Grandissimes,* Aboo tells his latter-day kinsman: "By chance, somewhere, the other day, fell, unhappily, into my hands a book *grandly* entitled 'The Grandissimes,' but whose fit title should have been 'The Fictions of Ridicule'; which book is neither historical nor romantic, in any true sense of what we term history or romance. It has been, evidently, most submissively, written for the prejudiced and inimical North, *against* the olden customs, habits, manners and idiosyncrasies of the Southern Creole population of Louisiana, therein so slanderously misrepresented. . . ." Identifying his target in a pun, Aboo attacks Cable directly and personally. "The Grandissime Imaginer of this non-historical, non-romantic, half-comical, half-dramatic, or rather melo-dramatic—and wondrously artistic,—elucubration, is, we have been told, a native of Louisiana; he is, besides, a pert, waggish, flippant, somewhat bold upstart, brazen-faced witling, who supplies the Northern literary market with that sort of adulterated, but gratifying, stuff: How disloyal, how basely unfilial, how despi-*cable!*" Thus runs the dialogue, and after he has been properly impaled on a wall of criticism, a chorus of bullfrogs sings the praises of "le Chef-Menteur."

Cable perhaps isolated certain peculiarities of the Creoles, but objective critics have not been blind to his merits as a humorist. Stephen Leacock, for instance, said that in him "the South produced a humorist in the highest sense of the word, and one whose works reached two continents. . . . His was the humor of that high type that does not excite the loud laughter, exploding over single strokes of comicality and single incongruities of words, but that is interwoven as a golden thread in the texture of depicted life."[11]

Kate Chopin's *Bayou Folk* contains comic glimpses of aristocratic Creoles (in "Madame Célestin's Divorce," for example), but concentrates on the lower class of Creoles and Cajuns. Grace King used humor in her stories (*Balcony Stories, Monsieur Motte,* and others) which attempted to set the record straight on the misrepresented New Orleans Creoles. Molly Moore Davis also exploited the personality of the Creole in humorous sketches. The world of the Creole was strangely different from the rest of the South. In language and culture it was actually outside the mainstream of Southern life. To the Northern reader, however, it was not stranger than the world of the Tennessee mountaineer, not stranger than the South itself, so recently enemy territory. Sketches of the ante-bellum Creole aristocrat merely showed another odd corner of the Southern past.

To the depressed postwar South all its glory seemed past. Ante-bellum society appeared to be the only possible source of pride. To be sure, the slavocracy had not been perfect. It had had its imperfections and abuses. But a defensive, bleeding South make it look almost as white as Robert E. Lee's soul looked to a Daughter of the Confederacy. Debunking of the plantation school would not gain momentum until the time of O. Henry, who in many of his stories would poke gentle fun at the then solid tradition of baronial splendor in the Old South—the legend of Corinthian columns, marble halls, and troops of faithful slaves ready to die for ol' marster. When O. Henry came along, however, the tradition was beginning to outlive its usefulness. In its time it had helped the South hold up her head when there was nothing in the present, or in prospect for the future, to justify any pride.

Elsewhere

Ante-bellum life outside the plantation ran a poor second to the slavocracy as subject matter for postwar humor. Although some pictures of poor whites were sketched by prewar humorists with aristocratic backgrounds, the postwar depiction of the ante-bellum poor white was largely the work of the man with a humble background himself. These later sketches were often Crockett-like and were written by men to whom the period meant pioneering, hard work, and good times. They never gained the popularity of the idyllic plantation stories of Page, Bagby, or the later Harris. They retained too much of the crude humor of the Old Southwest to please the more refined taste of Gilded Age Americans. Indeed, many of the Southern humorists who pictured the pleasant life before the war as an aid in reconciling the nation avoided treating the low life because it was often crude and repellent and could have done little to make the Northerner think more kindly of the period.

The first part of Frank A. Montgomery's *Reminiscences of a Mississippian* is filled with his account of life in Mississippi during her "flush times": the shooting matches, the camp meetings, and other frontier activities. One anecdote deals with the ubiquitous Methodist circuit rider. Once, as Montgomery told it, a circuit rider was stopped by a bandit who demanded his money. The preacher had no money, and the outlaw told him to dismount and prepare to die. The parson received permission to pray once more before his death. "He kneeled down by the side of a log, and, with closed eyes, prayed fervently for his own reception into heaven, for the salvation of the world, and, above all, for the pardon and salvation of the sinful man who was about to imbrue his hands in his blood." When finally the preacher finished his prayer and opened his eyes, the robber was gone (p. 25). In this and in similar anecdotes the lawlessness of the frontier South was made dramatically plain.

Since thousands of settlers poured into the new "western" states—Indiana, Illinois, and other states of today's Midwest—from Virginia, the Carolinas, and especially Kentucky and Tennessee, the early humor of Southern Illinois and Indiana is very similar to that of the Old Southwest. An example from Southern Illinois is Mrs. T. E. Perley's *From Timber to Town: Down in Egypt.* Her description of a camp meeting shows a kinship with the humor of farther South. "A satturdy nite a lot o' fokes frum the river an' furdes' frunteer settlemunts pored in ontell all the tents an' camps wus cram full an' a site hed ter sleep in ther waggins an' when preechin' begun ever' bench wus occerpide an' a long row o' chers cleen roun' the pulpit" (p. 155).

Unlike the humor of the plantation school, accounts of frontier life were likely to touch on the Indian. Bill Arp, for example, wrote a realistic and sentimental account of the removal of the Cherokees to the West in 1835. He told of the Indians broken hearted over being forced to leave their ancestral homes, of the forced march to the Mississippi River, and of the startling death rate. "We started with 14,000 and 4,000 of 'em died before we got to Tuscumbia. They died on the side of the road; they died of broken hearts; they died of starvation, for they wouldn't eat a thing; they just died all along the way." Disillusioned by the treatment of the Indian, the Georgian concluded, "I'd rather risk an Injun for a true friend than a white man."[12]

F. D. Srygley's record of the life of the frontier preacher T. W. Caskey, *Seventy Years in Dixie,* purports to tell of actual frontier events. Though many of the sketches deal with religion, they show a kinship in their frankness with the prewar school of Longstreet humorists. A realistic fight, for example, is narrated by an old deacon who described early life in Arkansas (and North Carolina). "When we fust settled in Arkansaw we jes had to fight almost day an' night to keep up the morals uv the country. I didn't care a cent fur religion in them days, but always did stand squar' for good morals. . . . My father wuz always a law-abidin' citizen, but he'd fight ever' time when a man tried to run over the morality uv the country. He fit Uncle Sam Dangrum in North Car'liny, before any uv us ever seen this country, an' bit off his nose—bit the thing clean off up to his head an' swallered it! Uncle Sam Dangrum wuz a tryin' to run over the morals uv the country, an' my father jest couldn't stan' that, an' so they fit, an' off come Uncle Sammy's nose. We all called him Uncle Sam, an' so did everybody else, but he won't no nat'ral kin to us. Well, that wuz about the biggest bite any uv my folks ever took, an' it come mighty nigh a bein' more'n we all could chaw! You see, it wuz ag'in the law to bite off a man's nose in them days, an' so we all had to light out fur Arkansaw" (pp. 237-39).

Most of the sketches and anecdotes, however, are more refined. The following anecdote, for example, makes good-humored use of comic exaggeration. An old mountaineer is telling the author of the time his gun hung fire when he aimed at a chicken a short distance away. "She sputtered, an' spootered, and sizzled till the chicken got tired waitin' and went over in the field to hunt June bugs. I had both eyes shet, fur the sparks wuz jest a b'ilin' out'n the tech hole, an' I dasn't take 'er down from my shoulder, 'cause I knowed she'd go off *some* time that day, an' when she *did* go, I knowed she'd git whatever wuz before 'er. So thar I wuz, as blind as a owl, an' a dodgin' the sparks worse'n a blind mule in a yaller jackets nes', an' 'bout that time a old sheep trotted out before the gun, jest as she went off, an' got the whole load right behind the shoulder, an' keeled over deader'n a shad" (p. 59).

Srygley constantly used such comic incidents to enliven and illustrate his narrative of the old times. In the chapter "Old-Time Dentists and Dentistry" he relates the story of the Negro preacher who one day used as his text, "And there shall be weeping and gnashing of teeth." Asked by an old brother in the amen corner what folks without teeth were going to do, the parson promptly explained. "Dis tex', brer Joe, am not to be implied to dem whar aint got no teef ter mash. Dey dat got teef ter mash, mus' mash, as de tex' say, an' dey whar aint got no teef ter mash, mus' gum it!" (p. 107). The Negro's religion was always a popular topic in humor.

Since the subject of the book was a preacher, obviously most of the humorous sketches have religious themes. They reveal much about the status of the frontier church and its position on controversial issues, such as drinking. The frontier church's stand on whiskey was much more lenient than the later church's. To illustrate, Srygley recorded the conversation of two prominent church members who had been to town to lay in supplies for the annual revival. "How much 'sperits' did you git?" "Ten gallons." "Jest sech stinginess as that will sp'ile the meetin' an' kill the church. I got twenty gallons, myself, an' you are jest as able to support the gospil as I am, if you wuzn't so dog stingy" (p. 176).

Another religious sketch, reminiscent of earlier humor, is entitled "For Snake Bites and Thy Stomach's Sake." It discusses the problem resulting from the conversion of a saloon keeper. The problem concerns the proper way to dispose of the new Christian's stock of whiskey. After much prayer and careful thought, the members decide to buy up the whiskey and then pour it out. But as soon as the revival closes, the temperance fever dies down; and on the day appointed for the disposition of the liquor no one is eager to pour any out. Several members suggest its value as a substitute for camphor, in making bitters, and in treating snake bites. Convincing themselves of its medicinal value, the members decide to divide up the whiskey. Then someone raises the question as to which whiskey was best for which purpose and someone else suggests tasting it. The tasting becomes so popular that "in less than an hour that little band of loving brothers was a howling mob of drunken backsliders. They whooped, they yelled, they embraced each other with maudlin affection and sang sketches of revival hymns."

Funerals were a social occasion in frontier society. Frequently friends and relatives would not see each other from one funeral to another. Businessmen in all fields looked upon the gatherings as an excellent opportunity to push their business. Srygley described the commercial and social aspects. "Jockeys went to funerals to sell or swap horses; candidates, to electioneer; road overseers, to 'warn hands'; schoolteachers, to circulate their 'articles' and make up schools; sheriffs, to serve warrants, subpoena witnesses and summon jurors; creditors, to collect debts; and farmers in general, to 'lease' land, buy mules, sell bee-trees and ask hands to log-rollings, house-raisings and corn-shuckings." And, Srygley continued, if a person had no practical reason for attending, he would go "because everybody else would be there—men, women, boys, girls, babies and dogs." It was sometimes a wonder that the corpse was not forgotten in the hubbub. Visiting preachers were always recognized and given a special place to sit. Usually they were asked to lead in prayer or direct the singing. Sometimes their commercialism was more blatant than the lay-men's. Srygley tells of an old preacher who had walked a long way to get to a funeral. Asked to open the meeting by leading the singing, the old man rose with the hymnal in hand and looked out over the vast audience. "Breether-ing, as bein' as I'm here, I'll open the meetin' fur brother Buncomb, an' then he'll preach the funeral sarmint accordin' to a previous a-p'intment. But while I'm before you, I want to say as how my main business over here is a huntin' of some seed peas, an' if any body here has got any to spar', I'd like to know it after meetin'" (pp. 197-200).

Most frontier churches believed in the "call" to preach; that is, a man became a preacher because the Lord had somehow informed him of this mission. Sometimes the Lord's voice had been clearly audible. A favorite place for hearing it was in the field behind a plow on a hot summer day. Srygley recorded the case of a man who was known to be waiting and praying for the call to preach. Several community skeptics decided to play a trick on the unsuspecting man and thus expose the "calling" theory as a fraud. On a hot day in June one of the doubters concealed himself in a tree near the field where the would-be preacher was plowing. When the farmer got within earshot, the skeptic called him by name and told him in a solemn, sepulchral voice to go and preach the gospel. Without checking the source of the voice, the plowman raised shouts of thanksgiving, left the field, and at the next meeting of the church was ordained a minister. For a long time area skeptics used the story to show that both a preacher and a church could be deceived as to a call to the ministry (pp. 231-32).

One more humorous religious sketch will show the extent to which religion permeated the frontiersman's life. Even the doubter went to church, though probably because he had nowhere else to go. At an experience meeting, Srygley reported, an old sinner and backslider reviewed the history of his miraculous escapes from damnation: he was first saved by the death of his beloved little daughter; later he backslid and the death of his second child called him to repentance; again he backslid and a third child was taken by God to put his feet back on the heavenly road; then his wife was taken for the same purpose. Now, he rejoiced, he was all alone—but saved. A skeptic arose to comment on the lurid testimony. "Well, I must say, the Lord has managed this case very badly. He has killed one good woman and three innocent little children trying to save this old back-slider, and the chances are that the devil will get the old humbug yet. The next time he gets drunk and goes to pieces generally, there will be no wife or beloved little children to kill, and how will God ever get him straight any more? If I had been managing this case, when I had to kill that first child to get the old fraud straight, I would have broken his neck with a stroke of lightning, and sent him on to glory just as soon as I got him on the right track" (pp. 236-37). The subjects and tone of these religious sketches suggest that Srygley and Caskey were aware of the hypocrisy of much of the frontier—and latter-day—religion and used this means as a way of exposing the abuses.

A semi-historical account of the flush times of West Tennessee (in the 1820's and 1830's), with many amusing sketches of pioneer and backwoods life, is *Old Times in West Tennessee* by "A Descendant of One of the First Settlers." Like Srygley's, this book shows the continuation of the realistic tradition of the humor of the Old Southwest. Though softened somewhat by the intervening years, the humor is essentially of the old tradition with its coarse and painful incidents, its panther and bear hunts realistically related, its practical jokes, its accounts of camp meetings, of circuit lawyers, of the motley array of humanity that inhabited the frontier.

There are few humorous sketches more realistic than the author's account of an ax wound. After a mustering drill, the village bully Ab Gaines is challenged to a fight by a blacksmith; but because the bully is too drunk to fight, it is postponed. Returning home from a drinking fest a few days before the proposed bout, Ab passes a squatter's house and sees a man beating a woman in the front yard. Ab rushes to the poor woman's rescue. When he reaches the yard the man has the woman by the hair of her head and is slinging her around. Ab jerks him loose from the woman, knocks him flat on his back, and begins pounding him in the face. The woman, freed from her attacker, turns upon the well-intentioned Ab. "Seizing an ax that lay near, she sent it into his back up to the eye, leaving it sticking in him, with the remark: 'Now, let my husband alone.' Ab rolled off the squatter, crying out, 'Murder! murder!' "

The husband gets to his feet, pulls the ax from Ab's back, and leaves on his horse for the doctor. When the doctor arrives and examines the wound, he finds that the ax has gone in close to the liver, breaking ribs and cutting off a part of the liver, which he took out. The wound is so deep and the bleeding so bad the doctor pronounces it fatal. He speaks frankly to the mortally wounded man: "There is no hope for you, Ab . . . the bleeding is internal and can't be stanched. If you have any worldly affairs about which you want to leave instructions, it will be well that you go about it." Ab replies that he has no instructions about worldly affairs, but adds: "Only one request will I make. You say there is no hope; then my last request is, that you will send up to the store and get me a gallon of whisky." The whiskey is brought to the dying man; he drinks to satiation; and the next day the doctor finds him alive with an empty jug by his side. Although he recovers from the "fatal" wound, he is never quite the same again. He even has to apologize to the blacksmith for not being able to meet him in their planned fight (pp. 132-37).

The anonymous author devoted a section of his book to memories of Davy

167

Crockett and his folksy way with the backwoods voter. Crockett's plain style in speechmaking contrasted sharply with the spread-eagle style popular with most politicians of the day. The author inserted a copy of one of Crockett's speeches made during the canvass of 1829 "as a specimen of the amusing interest the representative of thirteen counties in West Tennessee afforded to the newspaper men of those days" (p. 175).

A comic sketch reminiscent of Sidney Lanier's "The Power of Prayer" is the account of the first steamboat that came up the Big Hatchie River. Everyone turned out to see the boat from the river banks. "Every available twig, limb, sapling or stake, from the river bank for many yards back was put in requisition to hitch and fasten the horses to." To get a better view, many people climbed trees. When the puff of the boat was heard as it approached, the press of the crowd became intense. The boat came into sight, and the delighted spectators hailed its appearance with shouts and yells. Where the crowd was thickest, the captain made her fast. The people pressed in even closer to gawk and to hear the speech of welcome. Unfortunately it never came off. "Just then the engineer raised his valves and let off steam, and the scene that ensued beggars all description. Men, women and children broke as for dear life, some shrieking and screaming amid the deafening noise of the blowing-off steam, which had reached its culminating point in the boilers. The frightened horses had broken loose, where they could, and were tearing helter skelter through the woods and up the road, and those that could not break loose were rearing, pitching and dancing around the trees and places that held them. Everything looked as though the devil had broken out of his harness. Many were so badly frightened that they did not stop running or look back until they were out of breath, and the frightened horses never stopped until they got home" (p. 259).

Such writers as this "Descendant of One of the First Settlers" not only entertained their reader with humorous sketches of frontier life, they also provided him with an insight into the frontier mind and living conditions. Sometimes such humorists recorded history more accurately than the historians.

The Southern aristocrat naturally looked to the past as his finest hour. To many a non-aristocrat the "fogy days" before the war were also the best days. In retrospect the past was a haven from harsh reality that one could dream about and conjure up as in memory. In the Preface to his *Fogy Days* Dave Sloan expressed the hope that his book would provide for the young "amusing portraitures of the days of 'yore'" and for the old, "pleasing reminiscences." His book, composed of poetry and prose, was designed, he continued, "to illustrate some of the scenes and customs of the days of fogyism." A prefatory poem, "The Innovations of the 19th Century," sets the mood and approach for the memoirs. In it, and wherever he compared the fogy days with the present, the past came out best.

SOUTHERN HUMOR/*Image*

To-day every man's for himself,
  Hindmost left to the devil's care,
The tickling game's the winning card,
Man must tickle to get his share.

In the Introduction, also in verse, he was even more explicit in stating his attitude and objective.

Old-time happenings will set afloat,
Made up of story and anecdote.
Contrast to-day with fogy times,
Show them up in bungling rhymes.

The memoirs recorded what appeared to him in his old age as an idyllic boyhood and young manhood spent fishing, hunting deer and fox, playing practical jokes, and attending country frolics. A gentle nostalgia hovers over most of the poems and sketches. For example, in verses he called "South Carolina Home" he reminisced plaintively.

Ah! Those were rosy, daisy days,
  But now have gone, gone glimmering,
Love to think of those happy days,
Whilst our life away is simmering.

In a sketch picturing "An Olden Time Fox Chase" he compared past amusements with those of the present and preferred the earlier ones. The present, he asserted, has nothing to match the excitement of a prewar fox hunt. Commenting on the present's degenerate custom of dressing dogs in silks, he also showed his attitude toward the Negro. "I thought it bad enough to try to 'histe' the nigger over the heads of the white folks, but now it comes to 'histing' the dogs over both—what next? I like the dog and I like the nigger, but I like them in their places." Sloan's sketches of backwoods life and character are often graphic. Describing the "rude and illiterate" mountain people, he recalled a "buxom mountain lassie" who one day "was seen coming from a mountain gorge, with her rifle, sleeves rolled up and bloody arms, and, upon being questioned, indifferently replied that she had 'jist kilt a bar beyant the Terrapin!'" The mountaineer's isolation from the outside world was almost complete. According to Sloan, a mountaineer's daughter, when told of a proposed railroad to cut across the mountains, reacted in these words: "Uncle Jim says ef he war to see one of them relerodes acomin', he'd leave the world and take a saplin'; Dad says ef he seed the dern thing he'd drap rite down on the yearth." Their comic reaction to the first train was not unlike the reaction of other backwoodsmen to the first steamboat.

Good times were an important part of frontier life. In "A Rabun County, Georgia, Frolic" Sloan told of a dance he attended when he was a young man. He remembered that he had been pushed into a dance "contest" with the belle of the valley. As they danced he tried elaborate steps which he

169

was sure would throw the backwoods girl into confusion, but she not only kept up but bettered him. "I made a pass and she coquetted, I cornered and she chassed, I shuffled and she sidewized, I pigeon-toed and she wire-toed, I double-shuffled and she gave the toe-whiz, I gave a jim-crow lick and she kill-krankled, I struck a break-down and she hit the hurricane, I went into a jig and she jiggareed, and for every lead I'd make she'd call me and go one better. . . ." Remembering such pleasant experiences of life before the war, he could hardly be blamed for preferring those times to the bleakness of his old age.

The Alabama philosopher-humorist Rufus Sanders, who was Francis Bartow Lloyd's Sage of Rocky Creek in *Sketches of Country Life,* was so captivated by the past of his youth that he tried to go back in time to observe "Christmas in the Good Old Way." The present generation, he wrote, "live too infernal fast and git old too blame soon." He decided, therefore, to go back to the slower and more youthful past by returning to the village of his childhood, where the present had not made serious inroads. He took this geographical journey into the past in order to celebrate Christmas in the old-time way. In Panther Creek he went to a candy pulling and a "weddin' match," he attended a scrub horse race, and he danced in the front yard Christmas night. Once again back in the mundane present, he thanked the Lord "for Xmas as it use to be, and Xmas as I found it last week down in the old Panther creek settlement." Most humorists had to revisit the past in memory; Rufus Sanders found a way to visit it in fact.

Everything seemed to be bigger and better all over in the olden times. The authors of *On a Mexican Mustang* told of meeting a pioneer who had come to Texas from Mississippi in '46, and who had in the meantime mastered the art of piscatorial prevarication. For Sweet and Knox the old-timer recalled that before the war he caught a mudcat weighing ten pounds. He put him on a string with some smaller fish and went down creek. When he returned, he saw a moccasin lying coiled around the string of fish. The string broke and the big cat began flopping around, mad. Then, in the old-timer's words, "That old cat, sir, jest wriggled up to the moccason as he lay coiled around the bunch of fish. He took two coils of the snake in his mouth, and shuck her like a dog shakes a rat. Fur about half a minute it rained small catfish and goggle-eyed perch all around whar I stood. The snake's back was broke in two places, and he was chawed up considerable." The old man concluded his fish story by saying that he was so pleased with the performance of the fish that he "histed him back into the crick; and he is thar now, for all I know." Somehow the bear, the deer, the fish seemed larger and stronger when viewed from the vantage point of forty or more years later.

But the present did keep intruding on the past, even in the remote sections of the South. In William L. Visscher's "The Kentuckian's Lament" (*Harp of the South*) a man revisits the scenes of his boyhood, and unlike Rufus Sanders, can see only changes.

That little crick has gone plum' dry, the mill
  is all to' down,
An' blamed ef they ain't tuck the spot to build
  er onry town,
An' whar the big-road uster run thar's growin'
  weeds an' grass,
An' thar's a cut, clean thro' the hill, fur railroad
  kyars to pass.

Disillusioned by his inability to return to the past of forty years before, the narrator returns to his second home "Kase I don't like the changes that the times has gone an' done."

Sarge Wier's scenes from the fogy days in *Old Times in Georgia* contrast sharply with the dull, degenerate present. Applying the contrast to the church, he says that people used to walk to the Lord's house gladly, but now they won't. "They have to offer premiums to get folks to go to church." Camp meetings, Christmas times, corn shuckings for the Negroes, wedding pranks, even the singing of hymns—all have changed for the worse since the war. At present, he maintains, the old-time wedding pranks would make the newly married couple mad; but before the war they had been taken as a matter of course, as one of the hazards of getting married. He recalls that in a common prank the cord slats of the nuptial bed were cut so that when one person turned over both would hit the floor. Sheep and cow bells were tied about the bed, and "if a fellow wiggled some of the bells would tap." Another harassment for the couple was having the women put the bride to bed and the men put the groom to bed with her. The only way to escape this embarrassing custom was for the groom to promise to buy peach brandy for the men. Couples won't stand for this good-natured joking today, he concludes, but in the fogy days it was as natural as getting married. "Pranks of this kind were common them times, and the girls and boys and the old and young enjoyed and aided in the sport, and nobody ever thought of getting mad, but it made a couple lay uncomfortably still all night" (p. 116).

The life of Major Tom Noodle seems much more adventurous and humorous than it probably was, as W. T. Carden recorded it in Major Tom's name, in *A Tennessee Ignoramus*. In this comic autobiography Noodle showed plainly that the most memorable years of his life were already remote. Most of his writings are trifles, but they reveal a quick wit and a striking mode of expression reminiscent of Mark Twain. After announcing that he was born in three states—"poverty, ignorance, and Tennessee"—he went on to describe the last region. "Tennessee is bound on the north by feuds, blue grass and liquor; northeast by mountains and pride; east, by tar, turpentine and poor people; south, by peaches, watermelons and peanuts, negroes, cotton and sand; and west, by water, chills, frogs and mules. Its principal crops are cotton, corn, wheat, babies, and trouble. It also raises fine horses and women and other beasts of burden. It produces more brave men, fools, politicians

171

and office seekers than any other State in the Union" (p. 21). And he gave much more of the same.

Beginning at the beginning with a burlesque of genealogy, Major Noodle then announced that family trees were nonsense because they all led to the same root—Adam and Eve. Nevertheless, the author had investigated his origins and "found that I was part Scotch, part Irish, and part fool" (p. 23). The rogues' gallery of his relatives included several very queer specimens; for instance, "Aunt Puss was single. The center of her nose looked like an ace of diamonds; her eyes like a deuce of spades; her mouth like a queen of hearts; and her ears like a tray of clubs" (p. 33). And then "Grandad Pennymint was as honest as a dollar and as close as the bark on a hard-shell hickorynut tree" (p. 48).

Life in the Tennessee Cumberlands of his youth had not been so bad. Noodle described such rural pleasures as hunting, good food, dances, log-rollings, and debates. But, he added, "Time and conditions in the main changed fast and innovations crept in" (p. 38). Only in memory can these pleasures be relived.

The general postwar distaste for painful humor is evident in Noodle's memoirs. Although dealing with the same period and people as the Sut Lovingood sketches of George Washington Harris, he would have nothing to do with sadistic humor. "There is a divinity which shapes our ends—but a chestnut shingle shaped mine. I am quite tenderhearted. I can feel the pain when I see any living thing suffer. I can hardly take the life of any being. I hate to kill a chicken. It actually grieves me to kill a weed. I never put anything here and I have no right to take anything away" (pp. 54-55).

The major had grown up, however, in a coarse age, and he had been very much a part of it. Perhaps he meant the confession to apply to him only at the time he began his autobiography; a few pages further on he evidently forgot what he had written about killing and gave a realistic description of how he once prepared an opossum for the table. "Mam told me to dress my opossum. I asked which suit to put on it—one of mine or one of Hezzy's. She described the process, which seemed to me to be more of undressing than dressing. I took the animal from under the kettle, put a stick across its neck and pulled its hind legs until I heard its neck pop and its eyes and tongue ran out. That did not kill it, however. I slammed its brains out against a rock, but that did not kill it. I, then, cut off its head with a dull axe. I do not know whether that killed it nor not. I secured a pan of boiling water and put some ashes in it and wallowed the opossum therein. I did not get much of the fur off. I put it in the pan again and kept it there but it refused to slip. I pulled it off in bunches, but I could not get all the hairs. I next sandpapered the brute. That did little good. I took an old razor and shaved and scraped it. I singed it and finally skinned it. Opposums are somewhat hard to clean. I had trouble with that one—but it was extra good when cooked with sweet potatoes" (p. 88). This sketch can perhaps confirm the trend toward painless humor because nowhere does Noodle indicate pleasure in the killing and skinning. And in the last two sentences of his description he does use two popular devices of the postwar literary comedians: the comic understatement and the unexpected snapper.

No portrayal of the early backwoods South failed to mention religion. A sketch by Major Noodle poked gentle satire at the Reverend Gabriel Straddle-bags, "an old Methodist preacher of the chicken-eating variety." The time was remembered when the itinerant minister had stopped by the author's grandad's, and upon being asked for the latest news had replied that he knew no news worth telling " 'cept this cold snap wuz a leetle severe on my livestock. I lost 3 cows, 5 yearlings, a calf, thirteen shoats, three kids, a grandson, and 11 lambs" (p. 80). Such a straight listing with one incongruous item was a popular trick.

Name-humor was another device of the period exploited by Noodle. He would locate his home for us. "Our community was known by the name Scacegrease. It was ten miles from Smigginsville, ten miles from Tummy-holy, ten miles from Needmore, ten miles from Sandblister, and some said ten miles from Tophet Station" (p. 84).

The book is actually an omnibus of humor. It contains such additional items as a grotesque comic account of bathing and dressing a corpse and sitting up at the wake, misadventures while fishing, and comic essays on his nose and on his bachelorhood. In this book the author showed how the postwar humorist, especially the non-professional, was influenced by the new taste, yet was also drawn by the more realistic fun of the Old Southwest. The popular humorists—Joel Chandler Harris, Thomas Nelson Page, Sam Small—as a rule guarded against the attraction of the older tradition. The one- or two-book writers had no large following to alienate with frank descriptions of how to kill an opossum.

The humor of the Old Southwest, however, remained a potent influence into the period. Most of the later humorists had learned their trade at the feet of Longstreet, Baldwin, G. W. Harris, and W. T. Thompson; it was hard to forget the way their mentors had written. A backwoods sketch in Charles H. Smith's *Farm and Fireside*, "The Georgia Cracker and the Gander Pulling," showed his debt in subject and treatment to the A. B. Longstreet who wrote "Gander Pulling." There is little difference, Smith began, between the Georgia cracker and the Alabama or Tennessee cracker. "The Georgia cracker was a merry-hearted, unconcerned, independent creature, and all he asked was to be let alone by the laws and the outside world." One of the principal amusements of the crackers was gander pulling, and the author told how he witnessed a pulling in 1847 that lasted two hours, one in which the original Bill Arp came out the victor. It took place on a Saturday morning at the Blue Gizzard court ground. Smith first set the stage for the contest. The properties included a tree with a fork about ten feet from the ground. "A long slender, springy pole was resting in the fork with the large end pressed to the ground and fastened with stobs crossed on either side and driven firmly in the clay. This incline raised the long end of the pole quite high in the air, and to that end was looped a plow line, and to the lower end of the line another loop was slipped over the crimson feet of a venerable gander and left him swinging, head downward, just high enough for a horseman to reach it easily as he rode underneath. The doomed bird gave an occasional squawk, and, with wings half open and neck half bent, looked with inquisitive alarm upon the proceedings. The feathers had been stripped from its neck and a thick coat of grease put on instead."

With the stage set and the victim ready, the heroes came on the set. Each of the twenty participants paid one dollar into a pot to go to the winner. The men lined up on plow nags at the end of a path leading to the dangling gander. At eleven o'clock the mid-nineteenth-century cracker version of the medieval tournament was ready to commence. Eight "whippers," four on either side of the path, were stationed "to see to it that no man's nag moved towards the gander with less alacrity than a gallop." The old squire supervising the tournament pleaded mock-seriously for humane treatment of the gander. "Thar he are hangin' without a friend. Tote fair boys, tote fair; and put him out of his misery as quick as you ken, in reason."

The fun began. The horse of the first knight stopped suddenly in front of the gander, throwing its owner onto the ground—much to the delight of the crowd. The shame-faced cracker explained, "We'uns hain't got no geese at our house . . . and my animal never seed one afore as I knows on." Other men took their turns, but the gander's greased neck made it hard to grasp and hold while racing forward on a horse. Meanwhile the gander was suffering from the many attempts. "The poor bird swang to and fro and flapped his wings and squawked loud and long at the terrible squeeze and the more terrible elongation of his oesophagus." Rube Underwood's turn came, but when he got close to the bird "the gander's head collided square in Rube's face and some swore got in his mouth" and "effen he had jest shet it he would have had the prize." Soon a short recess was called to regrease the gander.

The second half of the sport began, and Bill Arp finally won the prize. The first time he tried he had a miscarriage because he grabbed the gander's head instead of its neck. "Bill got the right grip this time and in a trice had given the neck a double and something had to break as the pole and the line swiftly followed his motion. For a moment it seemed uncertain what would break or what had broken for the strained tendons popped like a whip as Bill's nag went on at full speed. For a little while the quivering, headless body swung backwards and forwards and was then at rest. . . . The crowd gathered round to see the gander's head that he held high in his hand—the warm blood trickling from the arteries." Bill Arp was the hero of the day and was twenty dollars richer to boot.

His memories of the gander pulling caused Smith to comment, "I could have seen more of them, but I did not care to, just for the same reason

174

that a kindhearted man does not wish to see but one hanging." The softened and refined sensibility of the later time led Smith to make this judgment, but it was not strong enough to keep him from describing what he had seen. To many a humorist a description of a coarse or brutal scene from the past in no way violated the taste of the day. These rough sketches from the Old South only served to point up how much more refined society had become since then.

The lower class Creoles and Cajuns of Louisiana were treated extensively in humor by such writers as George Washington Cable and Kate Chopin. "Posson Jone'" from Cable's *Old Creole Days* is set in early New Orleans and owes much to the old frontier humor tradition. Claude Simpson has placed the title character: "The parson, despite his calling, is one of those 'half horse, half alligator' men who abound in American frontier humor, and he exhibits his physical strength at the circus, just as he betrays his knowledge of cards and liquor."[13] Cable's sketch contrasts two very different types of old Louisiana: Jules St.-Ange, a dissipated wastrel, an "elegant little heathen," and Parson Jones from one of the Louisiana "provinces," whose "bones were those of an ox." They are perfect foils: a city dandy and a backwoodsman, a dilettante in religion and a fanatic who sometimes backslides. Most of the comedy comes from the incongruity of their friendship and the ludicrous picture of a drunk parson. The men visit gambling parlors and saloons and then, when the parson is thoroughly drunk, attend a buffalo and tiger fight in Congo Square. Here the apostate minister takes a baby tiger in his arms and harangues the crowd. "The tiger and the buffler *shell* lay down together! You dah to say they shayn't and I'll comb you with this varmint from head to foot! The tiger and the buffler *shell* lay down together. They *shell!*" Though showing kinship with the rougher humor, the sketch ends with the religious-sentimental peroration of Cable's age. "In all Parson Jones's after-life, amid the many painful reminiscences of his visit to the City of the Plain, the sweet knowledge was withheld from him that by the light of the Christian virtue that shone from him even in his great fall, Jules St.-Ange arose, and went to his father, an honest man."

Cable and Kate Chopin created a new world for the reading public, the world of the Cajuns. In *Bonaventure* Cable described their picturesque life, and in *Bayou Folk* Mrs. Chopin helped fill in the picture. "Boulot and Boulotte," from *Bayou Folk*, for example, is a comic sketch of twins whose family decided it was time they put their naked little feet into shoes. The two Cajun children go to town to buy shoes but return home carrying their new possessions. Boulotte explains: "You 'spec' Boulot an' me got money fur was'e—us? . . . You think we go buy shoes fur ruin it in de dus'? *Comment!*" In this volume and later in *A Night in Acadie* (1897) Kate Chopin showed the mingled humor and pathos of these peculiar Southerners.

The realistic fight of the old Southwest is spoofed in *Echoes* by Governor Bob Taylor of Tennessee. A new preacher accidentally insulted a mountain bully in his first sermon and was challenged by him to a fight. The parson agreed, but before they tangled he kneeled and, like Frank Montgomery's Methodist preacher, won his fight with a prayer. "O Lord, thou knowest when I killed Bill Cummins, and John Born, and Jerry Smith, and Levi Battles, that I did it in self defense. Thou knowest, O Lord, that when I cut the heart out of young Sliger, and strewed the ground with the brains of Paddy Miles, that it was forced upon me, and that I did it in great agony of soul. And now, O Lord, I am about to be forced to put in his coffin, this poor, miserable wretch, who has attacked me here to-day. O Lord, have mercy upon this soul, and take care of his helpless widow and orphans when he is gone!" When the bloodthirsty parson finished his prayer and opened his eyes, all he saw of his opponent was a cloud of dust in the distance. The bully had met his match in bluffing, if not in fighting (p. 176). In these stories the tough was becoming less the hero than the shrewd coward.

Another genre picture in the Old Southwest was the horse swap. In the *Memoirs of Judge Richard H. Clark,* as edited by Lollie Belle Wylie, the narrator gets a good deal, and in Dave Sloan's *Fogy Days* an innocent is taken in. On a trip from Savannah to Albany in Georgia, the young lawyer Richard Clark was approached near Vienna by two men. One of the men was drunk and insisted on swapping horses with Clark. The stranger had a fine bay horse and Clark's mare was small and suitable only for the saddle. Clark offered five dollars to boot, and to his surprise the drunk accepted. Soon the swap was made and each rode off on his new horse. The lawyer was extremely pleased with his good swap, until he found out that his new horse had been stolen. Afraid of being left stranded with his saddlebags, he threw honesty to the winds and hurried out of the county before his stolen horse could be recognized. The Judge concluded: "This was the first, last and only horse-swap I ever made. I now wish some other swaps had been forced upon me, since it seems it is the only way by which I can make a profit" (p. 204).

Dave Sloan's first experience in horse trading was not quite so rewarding. Traveling in Georgia on his "splendid young sorrel mare named Frances," he met a cracker, "a small, stoop-shouldered freckle-faced, red-haired man, about forty years of age, wearing a wool hat, blue jeans coat, coperas breeches and home-tanned shoes without socks." This man was riding "a sluggish looking old sway-back, clay-bank mare, with flax mane and tail." The two horses were so different outwardly that Sloan was astounded when the cracker proposed, "That's a right snug critter you've got there, how'd you like to swap her?" The cracker was not surprised at Sloan's astonishment; his own horse, he said, had deceived experienced horse experts. Some of the most famous horses in the world, he declared, are the most unsightly looking. His critter had royal blood coursing through her veins. He called Sloan's attention to "her pointed ears, wide nostrils, the full swelling veins, the symetry [*sic*] of her limbs; said she was with foal by the celebrated horse Steel (a horse that I had seen, and the most famous horse of that day) and that the colt would bring five hundred dollars when it was six months old."

Young Sloan was still skeptical and objected to the old mare's color. The shrewd swapper immediately responded to the challenge by replying that "her color was one of the best evidences of her value, and asked me if I had not, myself, observed that all circus horses were selected for intelligence, and that the white and spotted, and especially the claybanks [were selected] for ring purposes. . . ." Noting that his victim was weakening, the wool hat asserted that normally he would never think of parting with her but that now he was on his way to the "MAS-SE-SIP" and couldn't take her all the way. Only this circumstance forced him to offer such a good trade. The gullible Sloan's opinion of the old mare and the cracker had undergone a complete change. "This same old, ungainly animal, had become the great object of my desires. I observed closely, and in great admiration, the pointed ears, the wide nostrils, the swelling veins, and magnified the royal blood coursing through the intelligent animal's veins." The more closely he examined the animal, the more desirable she became. He had to have her. The wool hat insisted that he should get a large sum to boot, but "bein' as it wus me, and it wus as it wus, he'd take a hundred dollars." Sloan had only ten dollars, and after much deliberation the sharper agreed to accept that.

When the proud boy arrived home a few days later, he displayed the magnificent beast to his father. "I expatiated to my astonished parent on the pointed ears, the wide nostrils, the symmetrical limbs, the royal blood, the foal, the intelligent color—caught my breath and was about to take a new start—when my father exclaimed 'fiddle sticks.'" His father was so mad about the swap that he gave the old mare away. The boy Sloan, however, still believed that time would vindicate him. "Yes, I felt as confident of a glorious victory over my parent, as I afterward did in Charleston on the great evening of secession, when I blew my old hunting horn down the streets, that it would be but a breakfast spell to wipe out the yankees." But in both he had been mistaken. He thought the birth of a prize colt would clear his reputation as a horse trader, but the colt turned out to be but "a little, weazelly, mud-colored, sway-backed, crooked-shanked, long-eared m-u-l-e." And, oh yes, the South lost the war.

Molly Moore Davis' "A Snipe-Hunt: A Story of Jim-Ned Creek" describes how a greenhorn from the East—"the States"—is initiated into frontier life by being taken on a snipe hunt.[14] The Easterner was very pleased when he was invited to go on the hunt because he felt that at last he was being accepted by the other men. On the appointed night the men took their victim deep in the woods, where they gave him a big sack with a barrel hoop to keep it open and a lighted tallow candle. One of the men instructed him. "Now, Bud, . . . you jest scrooch down behind this here sack an' hold the candle. You kin lay the rifle back of you, in case a wild-cat or a cougar prowls up. An' you whistle jest as hard an' as continual as you can, whilse the balance of us beats aroun' an' drives in the snipe. They'll run fer the candle ever' time. An' the minit that sack is full of snipe, all you've got to do is to pull out the prop, an' they're yourn." As soon as the greenhorn got into position, the other men left ostensibly to "drive in the snipe," but actually to go home. Early the next morning the exhausted and embarrassed victim dragged himself into the settlement, but instead of being angry he was eager to pull the same joke on "that biggetty drummer from Waco." Sam Watkins' wartime snipe hunt was no different, even when it was called larking.

The politics of the fogy days was always a popular topic. In the writings of such a bucolic humorist as Rufus Sanders (F. B. Lloyd, *Sketches of Country Life*) politics played an unusually large role. According to Sanders, almost everybody around Rocky Creek was interested in politics. There was, for example, Uncle Billy Hornady, "the outdoinest campaigner that ever cast a ballot or whipped a fight in forty mile of Rocky Creek." He was always in the very middle of every campaign "with about a pint of corn juice under his shirt and a smile on his face as broad as a barn door." "Goshermighty durn" was Uncle Billy's favorite exclamation, and he used it liberally in his political speeches. One speech helped Andrew Jackson get the presidential votes in Rocky Creek over Henry Clay. "Fellow citizens. Where was Henry Clay durin the battle of New Orleans? Goshermighty durn! He was at home warmin the seat of his pants in a soft cushion chair, and playin poker at a dollar an ante, goshermighty durn! But where was Andy Jackson durin the Battle of New Orleans? Goshermighty durn! Up to his neck in blood and fire and thunder, goshermighty durn!"

Rufus himself became something of a politician. In his satirical "Rufus Sanders' Maiden Speech" he told of his own electioneering in the 1850's for justice of the peace. He was a Democrat and his opponent was a Whig, but they both supported free whiskey for everybody. He demonstrated that he was a master politician on the occasion of his first speech. Addressing the electorate as "Fellow citizens and citizenesses, Whigs and Democrats, one and all," he told them that he was running for office for their good in general "and for my good in particular." He listed his personal qualifications designed to please everybody. "I am a Democrat, but my good old grandfather was a Whig among the Whigs. I am a hard-shell Baptist, but mother is a shoutin Methodist and all her folks are straight-lace Presbyterians." Someone shouted approvingly, "He'll do; he covers all the ground." His concluding statements gathered in the few remaining holdout votes. "So, fellow-citizens, while I am a Democrat, all wool and a yard wide and somethin like three feet thick, I am not a one-sided Democrat. I am for the stock and no dog law and free whisky, and if my platform don't suit you I can change it at your earliest convenience." With an appeal like this, he couldn't have lost the election.

A fitting conclusion to this discussion of the image of the prewar South in postwar humor is a tale out of *Northern Georgia Sketches* by Will Harben. "A Humble Abolitionist" depicts the awkward relations between the poor white and the slave. The Gill family nervously awaited the arrival of their first and only slave, Big Joe, who had been given to Mr. Gill in lieu of money owed him by a bankrupt planter. Both Mr. and Mrs. Gill were against slaveholding, but they saw no other way to get their money back. Still Mrs. Gill was apprehensive about Big Joe. "We are purty-lookin' folks to own a high-priced, stuck-up quality nigger," she told her husband. They prepared for the arrival of the slave as if he were a guest. Mrs. Gill provided a feather bed and store-bought sheets for him, luxuries even their neighbors didn't enjoy. A gossipy neighbor warned her. "Big Joe feels his dignity tuck down a good many pegs by bein' put off on you-uns, that never owned a slave to yore name. The other darkies has been a-teasin' of 'im all day, an' he's sick an' tired of it." As the time drew near, the poor woman grew more nervous. She even put a carpet on the floor of Big Joe's room so he "won't have to tech his bare feet to the floor while he's puttin' on his clothes." Other neighbors came over to taunt them about owning a slave. One asked, "Are you goin' to make 'im say Marse Gill, an' Mis' Lucretia?" Another reminded them, "Folks like you-uns, an' we-uns fer that matter, don't know no more about managin' slaves raised by high-falutin' white folks than doodle-bugs does."

The next day Big Joe arrived. The Gills were awkwardly solicitous, but the slave sullenly refused to talk or to eat the special breakfast Mrs. Gill had prepared for him. His new owner told him sympathetically, "I know how you feel; most o' yore sort has a way o' thinkin' yorese'ves a sight better'n pore white folks. . . ." Mr. Gill tried unsuccessfully to penetrate the insolent reserve of the Negro. Finally that night he got through to the slave, who explained that he was heartbroken because his sweetheart had been set free and now would have nothing to do with him because he was still a slave. Suddenly Gill saw a solution to all their problems: set Big Joe free and make everybody happy. This he did. The next day Big Joe left and Mrs. Gill exclaimed with relief, "I wouldn't pass another day like yistiddy fer all the slaves in Georgia."

Before 1861 the poor whites and the aristocrat had little in common. The war, however, caused them to unite against a common enemy, the North. Afterwards they formed another united front against radical Reconstruction and civil rights for the Negro, a front that has survived to the present.

Notes

1. *Greatest Pages,* 174.
2. "Literature in the South," 756.
3. Quoted in Bruere & Beard, *Laughing Their Way,* 31-32.
4. Rollins, "Negro in the Southern Short Story," 51.
5. "Literature in the South," 748.
6. "American Literary Comedians," 796.
7. In Wauchope, *Writers of South Caro-*lina, 168.
8. Quoted in Odum, *Southern Pioneers,* 147.
9. "Cable and His Grandissimes," 373.
10. *Louisiana Studies,* 117.
11. *Greatest Pages,* 157-58.
12. In Manly, *Southern Literature,* 327-29.
13. *Local Colorists,* 257.
14. In Howells, *Southern Lights,* 200-218.

6. Survival

THE ANTE-BELLUM South was not all in the past. Vestiges survived into the postwar period and beyond. Two types especially from the slavocracy lived on: the aristocrat and the slave. Frequently they were treated together as ludicrous but lovable anachronisms. Though objects of laughter, they were seldom objects of ridicule. They were merely men and women who had survived their day.

On no group of people did the freeing of the slaves have a greater impact than on the aristocracy. Men used to having from one to many slaves to do their bidding suddenly had these servants taken away. The result was bewilderment and often an inability to adjust to the new conditions. Only a few faithful old freedmen remained to oversee the decline and fall of their former masters and mistresses. Myrta Avary in *Dixie After the War* tells of a lady who was astounded when her former slaves no longer obeyed her. When reminded that the Negroes were free, that they did not belong to her any more, she asked with puzzlement, "If they don't belong to me, whose are they?" (p. 152). The idea that Negroes were property was as old as America, and even an emancipation proclamation could not uproot this belief overnight.

The Aristocrat

The Southern humorist was generally careful not to poke low fun at the fortunes of the fallen aristocrat. The former gentry, including high Confederate officers and their wives, often had to stoop to selling pies, flowers, and molasses on the streets to Yankee soldiers as well as to former slaves. Such activities of the fallen aristocracy seldom, however, appeared in humor. The aristocrat in literature was often pictured as indigent, but he still had too much pride to peddle or to beg. One of the few examples of satirical humor directed at him was published in Opie Read's *Arkansaw Traveler* for June 27, 1885. The sketch was entitled "Aristocrats."

"Your people used to belong to the aristocracy of this state, did they not?" was asked of an Arkansaw man.
"Yes, sir, the leading people of the land."
"Always resented insults, didn't they?"
"Yes, my father fought three duels."
"Brave and honorable, wasn't he?"
"Yes, the very soul of honor."
"I suppose you intend to follow his example?"
"Of course I do."
"I am glad to know it; but say, don't you remember that you bought five dollars worth of goods at my store some time ago?"
"That so? Well, we always trade with our friends."
"Yes, but you haven't paid me yet."
"Haven't?"
"No, you haven't."
"Well, whose fault is it?"
"Yours, of course, for I have sent my collector around several times."
"No, sir, it's your fault."
"I don't see how you make that."
"Why it's as plain as daylight. You shouldn't have let me take the goods, but speaking about aristocracy, let me tell you what's a fact, there's nothing like blood. Well, so long. Send your collector around occasionally. I'll always treat him with politeness."

If the war changed the economic condition of the aristocrat, it had trouble changing his character. He usually retained to the end his aristocratic temperament, though occasionally somewhat readjusted, and even passed some of it on to his children. In the Introduction to his picturesque and humorous sketches of life in old Virginia, A. G. Bradley wrote, "The Civil War, with its far-reaching consequences, succeeded in utterly dislocating the rural economy of the South, but it could not change the personalities, the habits, the traditions, and methods of thought of the men who had grown up under the system it destroyed." Time, however, did what the war could not do immediately.

Many portraits of fallen aristocrats mixed the humorous and the pathetic. The pathos is augmented when faithful servants who refused to leave them reflect their white folks' hour of need. In "Mammy's Story" (*Black Mammy*) by William L. Visscher, an old servant describes the desolation of her master.

> *Yes, suh, he's livin' here alone,*
> *Asceptin' color like my own;*
> *Ole Mis' is gone to glory,*
> *An' all de yuthers dey's away.*

Aunt Mandy and Uncle Billy in Martha Gielow's *Old Plantation Days,* loyal to their "Marse Willie" killed during the Civil War, also remain with their mistress, who has lost her mind.

Most humorists treated the fallen aristocrat at least cursorily. James Lane Allen's "Two Gentlemen of Kentucky" (in *Flute and Violin*) describes the attempt of a "befo' de wah" Southerner and his Negro servant to adapt to a new life. George W. Bagby's "Old Virginia Gentleman" is an essay which Thomas Nelson Page described as "a beautiful and pathetic portrait of the last of the Cavaliers." Popular too were novels like Mary Noailles Murfree's *Where the Battle Was Fought* and F. Hopkinson Smith's *Colonel Carter of Cartersville.* The old-time Southerner was also often eulogized in poetry.

A short story by Thomas Nelson Page, "My Cousin Fanny" (*Burial of the Guns*) shows a characteristic trait of the fallen aristocrat: his (or her) pride. An old maid, "proud as Lucifer," refuses to leave her ancestral plantation ruined by the war, and lives there with a faithful old Negro couple. She has, of course, many amusing eccentricities. She is afraid of cows, horses, sheep, bugs, anything that crawls. Her attitude toward Yankees remains unreconstructed. She visits a relative in New York, and on the train she meets a chivalrous gentleman she refuses to believe is a Yankee. She relates the incident to her cousin. "He told me his name, but I have forgotten it, of course. But he was such a gentleman, and to think of his being a Yankee! I told him I hated all Yankees, and he just laughed, and did not mind my stick, nor old umbrella, nor bundles a bit. You'd have thought my old cap was a Parisian bonnet. I will not believe he was a Yankee." The sketch is inundated by pathos. Cousin Fanny is finally forced to sell her home and board out. She dies one Christmas night after returning from an errand of mercy to a sick friend.

Pride is also the theme of one of the *Tennessee Sketches* by Louise Looney. "Aftermath of the Old Regime" records Mrs. Pennington's refusal to adjust to the new age. Although she has lost all in the war, she will not let that fact change her attitude toward life. She refuses to allow her daughter Hattie to go to a party because the girl doesn't have suitable clothes to wear. "If we cannot appear as we once did, we can stay away—there is an exclusiveness even in poverty." Mrs. Pennington is a semi-invalid and likes to be waited on by a particular servant because "she remembers what I was in my time." The mother will not allow her daughter to marry a certain suitor because she considers him below Hattie in breeding. The Southern aristocrat's innate hostility to the commercial class is evident in her defense of her position. "As I recall him he is bluff, off-hand; there is something intensely commercial about him. He laughs loud, too, my daughter. I remember he once occasioned me a severe headache by his violent laughter in the parlor; my nerves were positively unequal to his continued cachinnation. . . . The Waylands [his family] are not much blood—in trade every one of them." After Mrs. Pennington's death, Hattie's mammy finally persuades her to marry the scion of the commercial family. On her death bed the mammy vows that she will not die until the two are married. As she dies, the wedding takes place. The New South, Mrs. Looney's sketch implies, must be made up of the best from both traditions.

Two stories in Samuel Minturn Peck's *Alabama Sketches* treat the poverty-stricken aristocracy. "The Old Piano" tells the story of the reunion of a very poor lady and a former Confederate officer. The officer had written the lady a love note while he was a guest in her home during the war, but the note had dropped down into the keys of the piano on which he had placed it for her to find. She did not know of his love for her until she managed to save enough money to have the piano tuned and found the fifteen-year-old note. "The Dragon Candlestick" has a dreamlike ending which makes for ludicrous reading today. An indigent widow and her daughter have only a set of candlesticks left to them by a cousin. A mysterious letter accompanying the candlesticks directs that the candles be lighted only "when fortune jeers." Deciding that fortune has jeered enough, the mother and daughter light the candles and find a box of fifty large diamonds hidden in the candlesticks. Their lawyer tells them that they have enough wealth now "to pay off the mortgage on your home, redeem your plantation that has been sold for debt, and still leave a handsome sum for a safe investment." Unfortunately such windfalls were seldom a part of reality.

Jeannette Walworth drew several serio-comic pictures of the unfortunate aristocracy in *Uncle Scipio*. The dashing ante-bellum debutante often became a stoic after the war in the struggle to survive. But if she stooped to enter the crude commercial world, there was always a guardian Negro around to criticize her for soiling her lily-white hands. Uncle Scipio, for example, disapproved of his former mistress who kept up the house "by sellin' her poultry en her butter en truck." His slain master and her husband, the old Negro commented, would surely be hurt if he knew about it.

Several sketches of aristocratic women appear in Mrs. Walworth's *Southern*

183

Silhouettes. "Unreconstructed" is a character study of a "high-bred, high-principled, fastidious lady of the old school." She was left unchanged by the war, but there has been a change. In place of slaves working the plantation, she now rents the land to the Negroes. This is the difference: "She is the 'Widder Somers' to them, and they are her tenants. They are not 'her people,' and she is not their 'ol' Miss.'" Two stories, "Poor Miss Mollie" and "Ol' Miss," show women with glorious pasts but bleak presents. "Miss Flo's Harvest" tells how a poor aristocratic lady supported herself after the war by making clothes for the Negroes. Protracted-meeting time in the summer was when Miss Flo reaped her main harvest. These revivals were always climaxed by a ceremonious baptizing in the creek; and since all the Negroes wanted to be well dressed for that occasion, they came to Miss Flo. Before the war her father had owned many blacks; now his surviving daughter was a seamstress to these former slaves. This year a servant of her former lover comes to borrow Miss Flo's dead father's coat. He explains that he has to be especially well dressed this time because he is to be a "toter" at the baptizing. " 'Stracted meetin' and big baptizings were prolific of hysteria. The sisters were much given to shouting themselves into a state of collapse, and the interest of good order demanded that there should always be some four or five muscular 'toters' detailed to bear the squirming, kicking, moaning mass of humanity into the receiving room prepared for the sufferers."

Miss Flo lends him the coat, remembering that once she and the Negro's employer had planned to get married. The war came. Her fiancé returned with a wooden leg and their affair gradually tapered off. But now the Negro finds in the lining of her father's coat a love letter that her lover had written her four years ago and that she has not seen. Suddenly the affair is on again.

Another of Mrs. Walworth's *Southern Silhouettes* is "The Colonel." This is a sharp contrast between life before and after the war. The colonel had been a potentate; now he is just another farmer. The old times were the best times to him. He tells the younger planters of one of the differences. "What does December mean to you boys? It means a lot of sulky freedmen sitting around in their cabins cussing you and the store-keepers and the commission merchants for their penniless condition, while they keep their heels warm with your fence-rails. It used to mean hog-killing time, and by the time eighty or a hundred fat hogs were hanging up in my smoke-house frozen stiff, the whole quarter lot was reveling in crackling bread, and back-bones, and chitlings."

The colonel's attitude toward Negroes has little changed since he lost his slaves: he is still the indulgent father watching over prone-to-err children. He finds it difficult to break himself of certain plantation observances, such as having his horse saddled and brought around each morning at exactly the same hour and hitched to the horse-rack under the cottonwood tree outside the front gate. This ritual appears absurd after the war, but the colonel insists that his morning rounds do affect the work done now by freedmen. Another custom he continues is riding with a cowhide whip in his hands. The author comments: "The Colonel will have to be more thoroughly reconstructed than he is yet, before he can bring himself to ride around the place bare-handed." Mrs. Walworth sums up the aristocrat's philosophy in these words: "He looks backward without shame and forward without trepidation."

The Confederate general in Grace King's "A Drama of Three," from *Balcony Stories,* cannot adjust to his new status. Though left destitute by the war, he insists on living as if nothing has changed. His attitude toward the Negro remains the same. When Pompey is late with his mail, he complains to his wife. "I tell you, Honorine, Pompey must be discharged. He is worthless. He is trifling. Discharge him! Do not have him about! Chase him out of the yard! Chase him as soon as he makes his appearance!" His wife has to remind him that they do not own Pompey or even hire him to bring the mail, that he does it out of kindness to oblige them. Around the first of each month the general anxiously awaits the delivery of a letter from an anonymous donor containing the $30 he uses to pay the rent. When the letter doesn't arrive on time, he accuses Pompey of tampering with his mail. Sometimes he even accuses the parvenu Journel, his landlord and grandson of his father's overseer, of the theft. But the money always arrives and the rent is paid. In both *Balcony Stories* and *Tales of a Time and Place* (1888) Grace King treated the passing of the feudal aristocracy and the coming of commercialism. Tragedy and pathetic humor mix in the struggle of people whose social system has collapsed.

In *Where the Battle Was Fought* Miss Murfree described to perfection the stereotyped fallen aristocrat. She reproduced Southern sentimentality and irrational conservatism in a mildly satirical tone that presaged O. Henry. General Vayne, the gentleman of the Old South, "stormily counselled mildness, calmness, conservation, above all, consistency." She derided his politics. "'I am, and have always been, strictly tolerant,' continued General Vayne,—'conservative in my views. Conservatism, sir,' declared the tolerant man, with an extreme look in his eye, 'is the moral centripetal force that curbs the flighty world'" (p. 6). The general was courageous, highhearted, impractical, and opinionated; and Miss Murfree exposed his vices and his virtues. Though poor, the old man maintained his pride and his bearing. "He bore himself with a noble dignity which might well have befitted Julius Caesar, but which consorted absurdly enough with the uncouthness of the bare ruin where he lived; with his hunted condition, never out of sound of the hue and cry of his debts; with the well-worn seams of his coat—a suggestive contrast to his perfect and immaculate linen, that in making the most of its virtues he only offered another annotation upon the history of his struggle between gentility and poverty" (p. 3). Although unreconstructed, the general no longer bothered to bait, or even to argue with, the enemy. His was one way the fallen aristocrat reconciled himself to the new conditions. "'Ah well,' said General Vayne, waving the war, the Federal army, and the nation generally into a diminishing distance with his expressive left hand, 'I have—a—dismissed them—from consideration. Let them go! Let them go! Nowadays I am no wrangler. I leave all questions of public policy as a bone of contention for the Political Dogs to gnaw!'" (p. 6).

Caricature was a favorite method of the humorists in picturing the aristocrat. In *Sketches* A. G. Bradley appended to a physical description of "The Doctor: An Old Virginia Fox Hunter" this passage: "I may add, moreover, that he was unquestionably non-progressive, that he was decidedly not modern, while to the end of his days he was so reactionary that the sound of a railway irritated him; and, finally, that he was, beyond a doubt, eminently picturesque." Then Bradley exaggerated his portrait even more. "He hated Yankees; he hated your new-fangled houses; he hated railroads; he hated towns; he hated breech-loading guns: sights and sounds and things that he was not familiar with at five-and-twenty, he would have nothing of when he was between sixty and seventy." He hated the new but he dearly loved the old fox hunt. In another Bradley sketch, "An Old Virginia Foxhunter," the Doctor's servant tells about such an old-time hunt—"the most magnificent lie," declares the narrator, "I ever heard recited in cold blood and in detail, and by a member of the church too. Uncle Ephraim's exaggerated account includes such passages as this one: "Yes, suh, fo' Gawd I's tellin' you de solemn troof. Dem ar dawgs run dat ar ole fox fur two days an' two nights clar through. . . . It wur de day befo' Christmas, dey struck dat ar fox's trail, and when de Jedge quit off hunt'n at sundown he done tell me ter foller dem hounds and see whar they's gwine ter. Well, suh, I follerd 'em all dat night. I follerd 'em all Christmas Day and all dat night too, and when I caught up wid 'em jes as sho' as yo' born, suh, it wur over in Hanover County about'n hour after sun-up, and fo' de Lawd de fox was walkin', and de hounds was walkin', dey was all walkin', widin a few yards of one nur'r."

The domestic tyranny of Negro servants is brought out humorously in this sketch and in "Mar'se Dab after the War." In the latter sketch Uncle Reuben criticized Dabney Carter Digges for marrying beneath him and not bearing himself as an aristocrat should. Digges had fought as a Confederate officer, but after the war he decided that he had to adjust to the new times. He found that his severest critic was Uncle Reuben. "Mar'se Dab . . . is a mighty good man, but he ain't like his pa. I bin raised with quality folks, and knows what they is. Thar ain't no fambly in the State as held thorselves higher or more 'sclusive than our folks done uster. But Mar'se Dab! Lor'! he don't seem to have no respect for hisself or fambly." The freedman complains that the white man is acting too much like ordinary white folks "that ain't had no raisin' wuth speakin' 'bout. . . . Now, sah, I bin *raised*, I has! I bin *raised!* I ain't growed up like a sassafras bush in a ole turn'd-out anyhow!" But he didn't have the ear of Mar'se Dab as he had had Dab's father's. "I ain't suited to these times nohow. A heap a hurrain' an' fuss was made 'bout dis yer friddom an' that; but I b'lieve I'd as lief things had stayed as they wur." Certainly under the old system he had more influence with his white master.

Of F. Hopkinson Smith's most significant book, *Colonel Carter of Cartersville*, the critic F. L. Pattee observed that it was "one of the most sympathetic studies of Southern life ever written; its sly humor, its negro dialect, its power of characterization, its tender sentiment, its lovable, whimsical central figure, and its glimpses of an old South that forever disappeared, [made] it one of the few books of the period concerning which one [might] even now prophesy with confidence."[1] If today the book is almost forgotten, its title character is one of the most lovable and humorous survivals of the Old South in literature. The indigent colonel and his servant, the faithful Chad, are the epitome of the postwar master and his colored servant. Although the colonel moves to New York, he is a true unreconstructed Confederate. His card reads "Colonel George Fairfax Carter, of Carter Hall, Cartersville, Virginia." The author notes that he omits "United States of America" because it would "add nothing to his identity or his dignity" (p. 11). The old man is completely impractical, never worries about money, and is naïve about business and people. His philosophy is an extremely optimistic one: one should never mix the cares of the world with good food. "Salt yo' food, suh, with humor. . . . Season it with wit and sprinkle it all over with the charm of good fellowship, but never poison it with the cares of yo' life. It is an insult to yo' digestion, besides bein', suh, a mark of bad breedin'" (p. 28).

The colonel may not worry, but Chad, acting as his guardian, does. Like Bradley's Uncle Reuben, Chad feels that it is his responsibility to look after his white boss. The Negro tells the narrator: "You know, Major, same as me, dat de colonel ain't nuffin but a chile, an' 'bout his bills he's *wuss*. But I'm yer, an' I'm 'sponsible. 'Chad,' he says, 'go out an' git six mo' bottles of dat old madery'; an' 'Chad, don't forgit de sweet ile'; an' 'Chad, is we got claret enough to last ober Sunday?' an' not a cent in de house. I ain't slep' none for two nights, worritin' ober dis business,—an' I'm mos' crazy" (p. 53). Indeed, the poor colonel gives Chad cause to worry. When, for example, the servant tells him the grocer has been by, he never suspects that it was a dunning call, but assumes that it was a friendly visit. "You don't say so, Chad, and I was out: most unfortunate occurrence! When he calls again show him in at once. It will give me great pleasure to see him. . . . He has shown me every courtesy since I have been here, and I am ashamed to say that I have not once entered his doors. His calling twice in one evening touches me deeply. I did not expect to find yo' tradespeople so polite" (pp. 62-63).

Colonel Carter is always hospitable—even though he might have to borrow supplies from his guests with which to entertain them. One of his guests observes privately that he was "hospitable to the verge of beggary." The old Southerner was enthusiastic and visionary, tender-hearted and happy as a boy, proud of his ancestry, his state, and himself, and an unswerving believer in states' rights, slavery, and the Confederacy. The colonel was beyond reconstruction.

One of Colonel Carter's most amusing visionary schemes is his proposal to connect Cartersville with the sea by way of the Cartersville and Warrentown Air Line Railroad. When asked whether there will be any advantage to the railroad in building the twelve additional miles, he replies indignantly, "Any advantage? Major, I am surprised at you! A place settled mo' than one hundred years ago, belongin' to one of the vehy fust fam'lies of Virginia, not to be of any advantage to a new enterprise like this! Why, suh, it will give an air of respectability to the whole *thing* that nothing else could ever do. Leave out Carter Hall, suh, and you pa'alyze the whole scheme" (p. 30). To Colonel Carter a business deal must have something to give it respectability. Again he shows his ineptitude in business when he demands that a foreclosure clause be taken out of the prospectus for the railroad. "This fo'-closure business has ruined half the gentlemen in our county, suh. But for that foolishness two thirds of our fust fam'lies would still be livin' in their homes" (p. 35). His plan for a railroad is absurd, but his friends are so taken in by his sincerity they do not have the heart to tell him. One of his confidants laments privately: "I couldn't raise a dollar in a lunatic asylum full of millionaires on a scheme like the colonel's, and yet I keep on lying to the dear old fellow day after day, hoping that something will turn up by which I can help him out" (p. 43).

Colonel Carter's railroad plans never reach fruition, but the discovery of coal on his property in Virginia makes him a wealthy man. Thus Chad no longer has to worry about keeping the old man out of the poorhouse. He can now indulge his quaint, eccentric, and lovable weaknesses to satiation. Akin to the Southern gentlemen of Page in "Marse Chan," "Meh Lady," and "Polly," Colonel Carter of Cartersville is one of postwar humor's most appealing characters.

The devotion of a former slave to her master is the theme of another story by Smith, "A Kentucky Cinderella" (in *The Other Fellow,* 1899). She tells the narrator of her love for her dead master and concludes: "An' I love him yet, an' ife he was a-livin' to-day I'd work for him an' take care of him if I went hungry myse'f."

O. Henry dealt with the theme in several short stories. Usually he satirized the aristocratic tradition. In "The Rose of Dixie," "The Emancipation of Billy," and "A Municipal Report" the North Carolinian poked gentle fun at the stereotype. The first story concerns a Southern colonel who undertakes to edit a magazine exclusively in the interest of the sons and daughters of Dixie. The second story deals with the freeing of the son of an aristocrat from the weight of the past. Set in Nashville, "A Municipal Report" shows in caricature the devotion of a former slave to his mistress—even to the

188

extent of murdering her violent drunkard husband. But the key to O. Henry's attitude toward the past comes in an aside paragraph. "I desire to interpolate here that I am a Southerner. But I am not one by profession or trade. I eschew the string tie, the slouch hat, the Prince Albert, the number of bales of cotton destroyed by Sherman, and plug chewing. When the orchestra plays Dixie I do not cheer. I slide a little lower on the leathercornered seat and, well, order another Wurzburger and wish that Longstreet had—but what's the use?"[2]

O. Henry's extreme attitude was certainly not typical of Southern humorists even of his time. Eventually, however, it took this recognition of the absurdity of the aristocrat's conservatism before the South could free itself from an encumbering past. But as late as William Faulkner's Gail Hightower in *Light in August* the tramping hoof beats of the past continued to divide and oppress—and inspire—the Southern mind. Not all the philosophy and influence of the uncompromising fallen aristocrat were interred with his bones.

The Darky

The most popular type character in postwar Southern humor was the old freedman, who no less than his erstwhile master longed for the secure days of slavery. Humorists generally pictured the fawning old Negro mumbling at the back doorstep of the Big House where he waited for his former owner to rescue him from some distressing predicament, or sitting on his own doorstep dozing in the sun and dreaming of the days that had been. His attitude toward his present status is summed up in a statement and a question. "Marse Lincoln gun me freedom. Whar' my Chris'mus?"[3] Sam Small's Old Si contrasted slavery and its security with freedom and its want. Before the war, he says in *Old Si's Sayings,* his Marse Aleck used to give him a gold dollar on the first day of every month. Now, "Well, ebber sence freedom I'se been pine'en jess ter feel er gole dollar—jess ter know dat er nigger's han' wouldn't git burned ef hit touched one, but ebery time I see one hit wus in er bank winder wid a big glass twixt me an' hit" (p. 161).

Frequently the freed Negro acted as self-appointed guardian of his former owner. The two were in literature an almost inseparable pair. In *Uncle Scipio* Jeannette Walworth has the Northern narrator comment on the loyalty of Scipio and his helpmeet to their former owners. "I marveled at the strength of the tie that still bound this aged couple to the 'white folks,' from whom time and circumstances had freed them bodily, but towards whom their memories seemed to revert with reverential affection" (p. 20). Scipio is an archetype of the obsequious Negro—the fawning menial who would never advance beyond the threshold with his head covered.

F. D. Srygley in *Seventy Years in Dixie* noted the family loyalty as well as other common traits. "They feel great pride in the old family name and reputation, and delight to tell how 'I fotch up dese yer chilluns to be 'spectable an' hones'.' They have contempt for 'all dese yer smart Ellick nig-gers w'at growed up sence freedom come out,' and they never tire of drawing contrasts between 'de laz'ness o' dese yer young bucks' and 'de way dem fiel' han's use ter hump deyselves fer me an' de ole boss 'fo' de war.'" This affection, the writer continued, was reciprocated by the whites. "Devotion to those old mammies and daddies is one of the marked traits of Southern character" (p. 50).

In his nostalgia for the slavery days of his youth, one freedman pines in poetry "fur a sight ob Tennessee" in John T. Moore's *Ole Mistis* (pp. 352-54). Now an exile in the North, he would gladly become a slave again to go back home.

> *Yes, marster, dat's er fac' you say,*
> *De ole man he am free—*
> *But I'd be er slave ergin*
> *Fur jes' er bref ob Tennessee!*

The faithful darky thus became a stock character in Southern (and na-tional) humor. No book of humor ignored him, and few books of fiction failed to include him. Northern writers from Ben King, the "Michigan Bard," to Charles W. Chesnutt, the Ohio Negro writer, exploited his character. No Southern humorist failed at least to attempt to delineate him.

Politicians seldom made speeches without a liberal sprinkling of darky jokes. Governor Bob Taylor of Tennessee, for example, made frequent use of them in his speeches and writings. Commenting on the accusation made by his political enemies that he granted pardons indiscriminately, the governor recalled a case and allowed his public to decide what they would have done. His old mammy had come begging him to pardon her jailed husband. "I'se toted you in my arms when you wuzzen no bigger dan a minnit." The governor asked what her husband was in for. "Jis fur one po' little ole ham, Marse Bob. We wuz outen meat, an' Jim he jes went down to Mr. Smif's smokehouse, he did, an' tuck one po' little ole ham, an' dey tuck him up fur dat an' put 'im down dar in the pen, an' he ain' no good fur nuffin nowhar. We needs him at home, Marse Bob, an' I wish—" The governor interrupted to ask why Jim was needed at home if he was so useless. "W'y, laws bress yo' life, Marse Bob, we'se out er meat ergin!" Marse Bob pardoned Jim.[4]

An anecdote printed on June 6, 1885, in the *Arkansaw Traveler* is a com-mentary on an old Negro's reaction to freedom and his inclination to petty theft.

"How are times down in the country, uncle?" asked a white man of an old negro.
"Porely, sah, porely."
"What is the cause?"
"It's de comin' o' dese Yankees, sah."
"How did they cause hard times?"

"By t'arin' down all de ole smokehouses, sah."

"Why did that make any difference?"

"Whut? Why did dat make any difference? Confoun' 'em, sah, da tore down de log houses an' built brick ones in dar place. Da needn't be so purticular. Nobody wan't gwine ter steal nuthin.'"

Criticism of the North was often put into the mouth of the Negro. A historian illustrated the prevalence of miscegenation with the following anecdote. "In Florida a northern tourist remarked to a negro woman, 'They say Southerners do not believe in intermingling of the races. But look at all these half-white coons!' 'Well, Marster,' she answered, 'don't you give Southern folks too much credit fuh dat. Rich Yankees in de winter-time; crap uh white nigger babies in de fall. Fus' war we all had down here, mighty big crap uh yaller babies come up. Arter de war 'bout Cuba, 'nother big crap come 'long. Nigger gal ain' nuvver gwi have a black chile ef she kin git a white one!'"⁵ Much of the humor in which the Negro figures was obviously propaganda in defense of the "Southern Way of Life."

The pioneer in treating the unreconstructed free Negro in dialect was Irwin Russell. He is usually given the honor of having started the national literary movement which included Joel Chandler Harris, Thomas Nelson Page, George Washington Cable, James Lane Allen, Paul Lawrence Dunbar and a host of others North and South. Certainly he was one of the first to give the Negro a prominent place in poems and sketches. Page testified that "It was the light of his genius shining through his dialect poems—first of dialect poems and still first—that led my feet in the direction I have since tried to follow."⁶ Russell's poems breathed with the spirit of the Negro as he lived in literature: his quaint humor, his shrewd philosophy, his childlike innocence, his emotional religious nature, his belief in superstition, and his folklore. In addition, Russell showed the Negro's love of dancing and music, his slyness in a trade and his injured innocence when detected in a fraud, his child-like conceit, his love for his old master, and his common horse sense and homely proverbs. A. A. Kern, writing in the *Library of Southern Literature* (X, 4606), paid Russell this tribute: "It is his distinction to have discovered not only a new literary form—the negro-dialect poem—but also a new literary field—that of negro life—which has since been the most widely cultivated of all the fields in Southern literature." Though the quantity of Russell's work was slight, he wrote several poems which became models for later Southern humorists. His "Christmas-Night in the Quarters," discussed in Chapter 5, was one of the most widely known and anthologized poems of the period. Some of his poems are bagatelles, like "Nebuchadnezzar," about an old Negro plowing and talking to his mule. Other poems are a defense of the old way of life. In "Mahsr John" (*Poems*), a one-time slave pictures his master's wealth before the war and then contrasts it with the present.

The Smiling Phoenix

Well, times is changed. De war it come an' sot de niggers free,
An' now ol' Mahsr John ain't hardly wuf as much as me;
He had to pay his debts, an' so his lan' is mos'ly gone—
An' I declar' I's sorry fur my pore ol' Mahsr John.

Despite the short span of his life (Russell died in 1879, only twenty-six) he became a historian of the Negro and pointed the course of Southern literature.

Clifford and Sidney Lanier share with Russell the honor of being pioneers in the discovery of the literary value of the Negro. Actually a prose sketch by Sidney Lanier in Negro dialect, written in 1865, predates Russell's work; but Lanier was always apologetic about his dialect poems, and Russell was not. The Lanier brothers in collaboration wrote three poems which were experiments in portraying Negro character and dialect. "The Power of Prayer: Or, the First Steamboat Up the Alabama," sold to *Scribner's Monthly* in 1874, is written in iambic meter and triplets (*Poems and Poem Outlines*). The poem's narrator, a blind aged Negro, hears his first steamboat and thinks he is having a supernatural visitation. After his daughter Dinah has placed him "Whar de ribber-roads does meet," he is left alone and he suddenly hears "Somebody holl'in' 'Hoo, Jim, hoo?'" He thinks at first it must be his dead wife.

> *My Sarah died las' y'ar;*
> *Is dat black angel done come back to call ole Jim*
> *f'om hyar?*

Then he decides it can't be Sarah because of its noise. "Fus' bellerin' like a pawin' bull, den squealin' like a sow." He concludes it must be the devil.

> *De Debble's comin' round dat bend, he's comin',*
> *shuh enuff,*
> *A-splashin' up de water wid his tail and wid his*
> *hoof!*

Sure that the devil has come for someone, the narrator prays the Lord to spare Dinah and to take him instead: "Lord, ef you's clarin' de underbrush, don't cut her down, cut me!" Eventually the sounds of the steamboat die away, and he tells his daughter joyfully of the power of prayer.

> *When folks starts prayin', answer-angels drops*
> *down th'u de a'r.*
> *Yes, Dinah, whar 'ould you be now, jes' 'cepting*
> *fur dat pra'r?*

The superstitious imagination of the literary Negro made for delightful reading to an audience eager to learn more about the recently freed slave.

In "The Power of Affection; or, Voting in Alabama" a faithful Negro explains why he's voting for his ol' Marster.[7] His former owner, he says, has never turned his back on him and has even given him work "when work was mon'sous slim." This was more than the radicals had done.

When de creek was up an' drowned de corn, an' riz
  to dis here door,
Who gin' me 'lasses an' meal an' sich? Congress?
  no more'n dat limb.

He has worked for and believed in equality, but in vain.

I'se voted ev'ry 'lection yit for Ekal rights; I'se tore
My insides out a holl'rin fur em; I'se yit ole nigger Sim.

His wife Mehaly can read, and "She says de Rads jis loves us nigs, like gar fish loves de brim." The old Negro confesses that he too has strayed, but now he sees the light and is back on the right path—the path that leads to his former master's back door. He castigates the radicals.

Dey's rid our votes to offis till our backs is skinned
  an' sore;
  Dey's fooled young *mules wid* collar straw, *dey* caint
  fool uncle Sim;
Don' tel me nuffi'n 'bout votin', Boss, I'se fur ole
  Marster shore:
  He *nuvver went back on dis black chile: I aint*
  gwine back on him.

Thus the Lanier brothers joined other humorists in showing how postwar politics drove many a Negro back to his old master.

Another early Southern humorist who used the old-fashioned Negro extensively in her work was Sherwood Bonner of Mississippi. Before 1876 she had published her "Gran'mammy" stories, probably the first Negro dialect stories widely read in the North. Longfellow predicted that she would be the American writer of the future. She delineated to near perfection the darky type in *Dialect Tales*, especially in such tales as "Aunt Anniky's Teeth," "Dr. Jex's Predicament," and "In Aunt Mely's Cabin." The first two stories are farces. The third is a pathos-dominated story of a white man who flees the law by seeking refuge in an old Negro woman's cabin.

"Aunt Anniky's Teeth" is a comic sketch of "a funny, illiterate old darkey, vain, affable, and neat as a pink"—the perfect picture of the white folks' fawning slave. Aunt Anniky was an excellent nurse, and for nursing the author's mother back to health she was rewarded with a set of false teeth. This was her reason for wanting store-bought teeth: "I has gummed it fur a good many ye'rs . . . but not wishin' ter be ongrateful ter my obligations, I owns ter havin' five nateral teef. But dey is po' sogers; dey shirks battle. One ob dem's got a little somethin' in it as lively as a speared worm, an' I tell you when anything teches it, hot or cold, it jest makes me *dance!* An' annuder is in my top jaw, an' ain't got no match fur it in de bottom one; an' one is broke off nearly to de root; an' de las' two is so yaller dat I'se ashamed ter show 'em in company, an' so I lif's my turkey-tail ter my mouf

193

every time I laughs or speaks." After Anniky gets the teeth installed, she is a hilarious sight. "She had selected them herself, and the little ridiculous milk-white things were more fitted for the mouth of a Titania than for the great cavern in which Aunt Anniky's tongue moved and had its being. The gums above them were black, and when she spread her wide mouth in a laugh, it always reminded me of a piano-lid opening suddenly and showing all the black and white ivories at a glance. . . . It was observed, to her credit, that she put on no airs of pride, but was as sociable as ever, and made nothing of taking out her teeth and handing them around for inspection among her curious and admiring visitors."

But, alas! she lost her teeth—and in a most unusual way. It happened when she was nursing Uncle Ned, whose wealth, "apart from a little corn crop, consisted in a lot of fine young pigs, that ran in and out of the house at all times." One night she gave her patient up as dying, and after deciding that she could do nothing more to help him, she went to sleep. During the night the patient, in a delirium, shouted for some cracked ice, but his nurse did not awaken. He began reaching wildly for something to assuage his fever, and finally made contact with the glass which contained Aunt Anniky's teeth. In his words: "I pulled it to me, an' I run my han' in an' grabbed de ice, as I s'posed, an' flung it in my mouf, an' crunched, an' crunched—" He soon discovered his mistake, but too late for Aunt Anniky's teeth. She was furious; and to compound her anger, he even refused to give her the young pig he had promised if he should recover. He pleaded that he was angry too. "I don't pay nobody nothin' who's played me a trick like dat." At a hearing before the author's father, Aunt Anniky maintained that it was Uncle Ned's anger that had broken his fever and saved his life, and since she had been responsible for the anger, she deserved her pig. The white judge decided that perhaps the best way to solve the problem would be for the two to get married, and after much discussion they agreed with him.

In "Dr. Jex's Predicament" Uncle Brimmer's white folks move from Mississippi to Kentucky. He decides to follow them and to do so walks the entire distance. Though the family has only a three-room house, they put him up in the loft of the separate kitchen; and he soon becomes the mainstay of the family. One time Uncle Brimmer gets sick, and the pompous, fat, effeminate, and white Dr. Trattles Jex is sent for. The doctor starts to climb a ladder leading to the window of the old man's loft-room, but before Dr. Jex can get to the top, Uncle Brimmer sticks his head out to tell him there's not enough room inside for both of them. Dr. Jex is a ludicrous sight on the ladder, examining the Negro through the window and dodging the red underwear flying in the breeze. As luck would have it, a loose bull rushes into the yard, sees the fluttering red of Uncle Brimmer's underwear, and charges the ladder, knocking it away from the window. This leaves the fat little doctor clinging frantically to Uncle Brimmer's neck and dangling his feet wildly, while below the bull awaits his opportunity. Soon, however, the owner arrives and takes the bull away. But Dr. Jex's pride is shattered beyond repair.

Thomas Nelson Page's ideal Negroes are crushed by the responsibilities and hardships of freedom. They long for the good old days. Several appear in the collection *In Ole Virginia*. "Marse Chan," Page's most beloved story, tells of the devotion of Sam to his master during the war and to his memory following the war. The slavery days were "de bes' Sam ever see! Dey wuz, in fac'! Niggers didn' hed nothin' 'tall to do—jes' had to 'ten' to de feedin' an' cleanin' de horses, an' doin' what de marster tell 'em to do, an' when dey wuz sick, dey had things sont 'em out de house, an' de same doctor come to see 'em whar 'ten' to de white folks when dey wuz po'ly. Dyar warn' no trouble nor nothin'." The concluding passages of the story cover Marse Chan's death in battle and his funeral at home. The casket scene with the dead man's fiancée shows the complete triumph of pathos. Sam recalls, "I couldn't see, I wuz cryin' so myse'f, an' ev'ybody wuz cryin'. But dey went in arfter a while in de parlor, an' shet de do'; an' I heahd 'em say, Miss Anne she tuk de coffin in her arms an' kissed it, an' kissed Marse Chan, an' call 'im by his name, an' he darlin', an' ole missis lef' her cryin' in dyar tell some one on 'em went in, an' found her done faint on de flo'." The appeal of such once popular stories was, of course, not in the plot or characters (except for the Negroes), but in the manner of their telling—a pathetic story unfolded in comic Negro dialect.

Page's "Meh Lady" also illustrates the humor of method. Ole Billy, the teller of the story, is typical of the loyal, sympathetic, humorous house servants that Page idealized. Billy's quaint similes add many humorous touches to the story. For example, Meh Lady as a little girl looked "white 'mong dem urr chil'ns as a clump o' blackberry blossoms 'mong de blackberries." During the war he "protected" the white folks left on the place. But afterwards none of the family was left to give Meh Lady away to her Northern suitor. "Who gives this woman to this man?" the minister asked at the wedding. "I don't know huccome 'twuz, but I think 'bout Marse Jeems an' Mistis when he ax me dat, an' Marse Phil, whar all dead, an' all de scufflin' we done been th'oo, an' how de chile ain't got no body to teck her part now 'sep jes' me; an' now when he wait an' look at me dat way, an' ax me dat, I 'bleeged to speak up; I jes' step for'ard an' say, 'Ole Billy.'"

In "Unc' Edinburg's Drowndin': A Plantation Echo" Page showed the wistful longing for earlier times of still another Negro. This one's contrast of the present with the past introduces the story. "Dese heah free-issue niggers don't know what Christmas is. Hawg meat an' pop crackers don' meck Christmas. Hit tecks ole times to meck a sho'-'nough, tyahin'-down Christmas. Gord! I'se seen 'em! But de wuss Christmas I ever seen tunned out de best in de een . . . an' dat wuz de Christmas me an' Marse George an' Reveller all got drownded down at Braxton's Creek. You's hearn 'bout dat?" Encouraged, Uncle Edinburg launches into his oft-repeated story filled

195

with his memories of the pleasant times of slavery. He was proud of his master. "He sutney set a heap o' sto' by me; an' I ain' nuver see nobody yit wuz good to me as Marse George." Commenting parenthetically on a political campaign in which his master was elected to office, he says, "'Lections wuz 'lections dem days; dee warn' no baitgode 'lections, wid e'vy sort o' wurrms squirmin' up 'ginst one nurr, wid piece o' paper d' ain' know what on, drappin' in a chink; didn' nuttin but gent'mens vote den, an dee took dee dram, an' vote out loud, like gent'mens." In retrospect, Edinburg could see only the plesant times he had when a slave.

Several stories in Page's *Bred in the Bone,* including the title story, deal with darkies. One of the most amusing, though mildly grotesque, is "Old Jabe's Marital Experiments." Before the war the fact that Old Jabe belonged to one of the best families in the area helped him in getting his many wives. After the war he continued to rely on his former owner for food, work, and wives. The white man asked him why he kept on coming back, and Jabe in return demanded, "Ef I don' come to you, who is I got to go to?" Jabe's idea of emancipation, Page commented, was somewhat one-sided. One day he visited his former mistress, preparatory to courting her cook. When the white lady expressed shock at the reason for his visit and asked about his wife Amanda, he exclaimed, "'Mandy! Lord! 'm, 'Mandy was two back. She's de one runned away wid Tom Halleck, an' lef' me. I don' know how *she* is. I never went ahter her. I wuz re-ally glad to git shet o' her. She was too expensive. Dat ooman want two frocks a year. When dese women begin to dress up so much, a man got to look out. Dee ain't always dressin' fer *you!*" He told the astonished white woman that one of the two wives he'd had since Amanda had died. He had spent money for two doctor's calls and decided that was enough. When his former mistress asked him why he didn't send for the doctor until his wife got well, he explained: "Well, m'm, I gin her two chances. I think dat was 'nough. I wuz right fond o' Sairey; but I declar' I'd ruther lost Sairey than to *broke.*" His last wife, he told the now horrified lady, had been dead two days; and he was now in the market for a new one.

"Mam' Lyddy's Recognition," also from *Bred in the Bone,* shows Page's attitude toward the "uppity" freedman. In this story an old mammy has her head temporarily turned by bad advisors who tell her she must demand "rec'nition" from the white people she works for. Things are in a mess until she realizes her error and again becomes the fawning servant she was obviously born to be—the one Page approved. Throughout his writing career Page continued to portray the Negro as a comic figure somewhere between horses and humans.

Appropriately enough, the volume of poems Page collaborated on with A. C. Gordon was entitled *Befo' de War.* In almost all these poems, dedicated "To the Memory of Irwin Russell Who Awoke the First Echo," the Negro is pictured as lamenting the departed days "befo' de war." Some of the poems are trifles, some are so filled with pathos there is little room for humor, but most of them make nostalgia humorous. One Negro, for example, in "De Ole 'Oman an' Me" cried that his wife had made life miserable for him since the war. She had put on airs, stopped cooking "possum-fat an' ash-Cake-pone," and was now insisting that he learn his ABC's. He summed up.

> 'Tis "Mister Brown" an' "Mistis Brown,"
>   Ontwel it seems ter me
> We's done gone changed our nat'rel selves
>   F'om what we used to be.

In "The Lament of Orpheus" another Negro contrasted the Virginia reel, which the First Families of Virginia used to dance, with what they danced now.

> I know de white folks knows a heap,
>   An I'se jes' an ole nigger
> Wid brains 'bout big enough ter keep
>   F'om gittin' hurt—no bigger;
> But, somehow, it do look ter me
>   Like things had got alarmin',
> Ter see an ole-time F.F.V.
>   A-dancin' dis new Garmin.

The darky did not hesitate to criticize his white folks when he felt they had changed for the worse.

But the Negro's harshest criticism was reserved for his own race, sometimes his own children. In "Virginia Creepers" the black speaker told how his ole mistis used to call his children Virginia creepers because they were so slow and lazy. Now, that freedom had come, they were absolutely worthless.

> I'm gittin' w'ared out wid dis here thing
>   O' t'ilin' fur all o' you;
> Sometimes I wishes de ole slave ways
>   Was back fur a week or two.
> "How come?" Jes 'dis: ter make you work!
>   De niggers never did lay
> Out on a bench in de sunshine den.
>   An' sun deyselves all day.
> "Ferginyer Creepers" was bad, at fus';
> "Ferginyer Sleepers" is p'int'ly wus'!

"Ichabod" is another lament over the passing of the old times. After deciding that "All o' de glory's done departed," the Negro commentator said there was much concern for books among Negroes now, "an' too little grubbin' / 'Mongst de corn."

197

The Smiling Phoenix

Gordon's poem, "Ebo," shows an old freedman's reaction to his educated son. Ebo was sent to school when he was fourteen, and there they taught him such nonsense as that the world was round like a ball. Ebo's father knew the world was flat, and he proved it by pointing to the water bucket placed on the shelf at night. At sunrise, he said,

> "Dat 'ar water's
> In dar still;
> Ef de y'arth turned over
> It 'ud spill!"

The worried old man concluded that if Ebo kept on learning, "Nex' thing, he'll be provin' I'se a fool!"

By the end of the century the Page and Gordon Negro had become, North and South, the popular public image of the black man. Their concept of the Negro as inferior by nature to the white man was an obstacle to his gaining citizenship rights. After all, their Negro himself acknowledged his inferiority and indicated clearly that he did not want his civil rights. He was but the white man's burden.

The Georgian Harry Stillwell Edwards carried the setting for his sketches of Isam and Major Worthington from the prewar into the postwar period. Stories in the later collection, *His Defense,* continue the hilarious adventures of the "two runaways." Unlike Page and Gordon, Edwards attempted no real defense of slavery or the "Southern Way of Life." Nevertheless Isam is a genuine "befo' de wah" Negro who of course remains with his master after freedom. "Isam and the Major" is a comedy of errors about the major's niece's coming to live with him. The major and Isam make elaborate plans for the arrival of a six-year-old girl. Since they've never seen the girl, they're not sure what to provision the house with. Isam, however, offers helpful suggestions in the cosmetics line. He suggests buying one of "dem dere t'ings what womanfolks jab powder in deir face wid." They buy the powder puff, ten pounds of powder, a gallon of cologne, and tops for the child to spin. When the six-year-old arrives, she is sixteen.

"The Hard Trigger" is a comic account of an affair of honor in which the major participates. On the dueling grounds Isam thinks he is hit by a stray bullet, and begins screaming "Oh, Lordy! I'm killed, I'm killed, I'm killed!" The attending physician examines the old man and discovers that the bullet had been stopped by an old watch the major had given him. Although Isam can not tell time—he always checks the sun in addition to looking at his watch—the major makes him a present of a new one next day.

At first glance, "The Woodhaven Goat" looks like a humorous sketch in the familiar tradition, but a closer examination of the story shows that the humor arises not from the pain the characters are caused but from the comic predicament they find themselves in. The fun begins when a goat in the orchard outside the back yard, trying to reach the luxuriant leaves of a cherry tree, overturns a bee hive. Isam sees the mishap and calls out to Mas' Craffud, "Dere's gwine ter be trouble hyah, sho'ly. Ef dere's anyt'ing 'twix' you an' de back do' up dere, better move hit." A mule is the first victim of the bees. In great pain the beast begins running around in a circle and gets its feet tangled in the plow and the lines. Edwards gives the scene a touch of Sut Lovingood. "Presently he made a rush for the gate, and finding it closed, started on a wild career around the yard, gathering bees as he gathered momentum. Woodhaven for the time being had been converted into a two-ring circus. The goat, with his horns laid on his back, had the orchard, and the mule the back yard. As the mule came round, the excitement increased, for the plow was swinging out on the chain-traces, knocking over benches and tubs, skinning the shade-trees, and thundering against the weather-boards of the buildings."

The major is cut off from the porch, but he finally finds under the kitchen a place of safety from the swinging plow. Poor Isam is attacked by the bees *and* the goat before he has a chance to find refuge. "Isam got his enemy by the horns and tried in vain to hold him; but there were no rests or breathing-spells—the bees attended to that. The man and the goat rolled over, half rose and fell, and mingled their voices like warriors of old engaged in deadly combat." Watching from under the kitchen, the major, remembering another episode in which he alone had fought a deer because Isam had refused to aid him, shouts with glee. "Better for one to die than two; it's a long sight better." Continuing his parody, "Don't cuss, Isam, don't cuss! If ever a man had a call to pray, you've got it now. Stick to him, Isam, stick to him! Whoa, goat! Whoa, goat! Whee!" The major exhausts himself from too much laughing. Isam finally manages to flee the goat. He is later found down the well. "Maddened with pain, covered with bees, and fleeing from the face of the awful goat, he had leaped upon the well-curb, grasped the chain, and rattled down into the cool waters. He was triumphantly hauled up again; but he refused to leave his place of refuge until assured that the war was entirely over. A little vinegar and soda soon restored him to his usual size."

The poems of the Alabama humorist Howard Weeden are solidly in the tradition of the postwar Negro with an ante-bellum soul. In *Shadows on the Wall* (1898), *Bandanna Ballads* (1899), *Songs of the Old South* (1901), and *Old Voices* (1904) Miss Weeden wrote of the old-time quality Negro. In addition to amusing poems, the volumes also contain portraits or caricatures by the author, who was an artist with brush as well as pen. F. P. Gamble described her full treatment of the Negro. "Her themes are of his work, his pleasures, his taste for good 'vittles,' his love for old Marse, his faithfulness, and his hope of crossing Jordan into happiness." This description is almost a summary of all postwar humor dealing with the type. "In all of her work three strains of negro character are discovered: humor, a kind of reminiscent pathos, and religious emotion. For, despite the vulgarity of the false black-face minstrel, the negro is truly humorous, though much of his humor is unconscious."[8]

The poems in *Bandanna Ballads* are typical of all Miss Weeden's work. In his Introduction to the collection, Joel Chandler Harris wrote that the poems "flutter across the page as shy and as delicate as the yellow falling leaves of the mimosa blown past a dear old lady's window years and years ago." In this one statement Harris revealed much about the delicate, nostalgic taste in humor of his contemporaries. Like Page's sentimental darkies, Miss Weeden's Negroes look to the past for all the brightness in their lives. In "Old Times," for example, one admits,

> *I ought to think 'bout Canaan, but*
> *It's Ole Times crowds my mind,*
> *An' maybe when I gits to Heaben*
> *It's Ole Times dat I'll find!*

Another former slave is dying.

> *I changed my name, when I got free,*
> *To "Mister" like the res',*
> *But now dat I am going Home*
> *I likes de ol' name bes'.*

In the same poem, which Miss Weeden calls "The Old Boatman," the black speaks lovingly of his ol' Marster, who used to call him Rome.

> *He's passed Heaven's River now, an' soon*
> *He'll call across its foam:*
> *"You, Rome, you damn ol' nigger, loose*
> *Your boat, an' come on Home!"*

As this poem illustrates, Miss Weeden's works contain a large amount of religious sentiment. Other humorists also treated the Negro's religion, but they usually exploited his comic exegeses of Biblical passages and other less serious aspects of his faith.

A Negro woman protests being typed as a "befo-de-wah" darky in "Aunt Judy and the Painter." A painter asked Aunt Judy to dress in a plain blue dress and a red turban for her portrait.

> *I can't allow my picture took*
> *De way you wants to draw—*
> *A-leavin' off my Freedom-look*
> *For fashions 'fore de war.*

She was emphatic in her refusal to wear those marks of the slave; in fact, she said, "Dat's 'zactly why de war was fought— / To end dem same bandannas!"

In "The Banjo of the Past" Miss Weeden returned to the popular belief that the Negro had more fun while he was a slave. Here one of them explained why banjos were not played much any more.

Dem banjos b'longed to by-gone days
When times an' chunes was rare,
When we was gay as children—'case,
We didn't have a care.

But when we got our freedom, we
Found projeckin' was done;
Our livin' was to make—you see,
An' dat lef' out de fun.

We learned to vote an' read an' spell,
We learned de taste ob tears—
An' when you gets dat 'sponsible,
De banjo disappears!

This poem implies a parallel between the Negroes before they were free and Adam and Eve before they ate the forbidden fruit of knowledge. In other words, to Miss Weeden and others like her, while the Negro was a slave he was in a state of carefree innocence. When he tasted of the fruit of freedom, burdens were placed on his shoulders.

Some of her poems are bagatelles which exploit specific facets of the comic Negro character. In *Songs of the Old South*, "Mullen," for instance, deals with the Negro's trust in home remedies over store-bought medicines. Of course doctors are all right,

But if you is sick an' wants to be cured,
Jis' git you a good mullen stalk!

De mullen don't need fer to feel of your pulse,
Nor to ask about how do you do:
De tea when you've swallowed hit knows where to go
'Dout askin' no questions of you.

Miss Weeden's main theme, however, was the longing of the freed slave for the old days when ol' Marster did the worrying—and ol' Mistis did the doctoring.

F. Hopkinson Smith's Chad spent much time reminiscing about the glorious days at Carter Hall before the war. "Dem was high times. We ain't neber seed no time like dat since de wah. Git up in de mawnin' an' look out ober de lawn an' yer come fo'teen or fifteen couples ob de fustest quality folks, all on horseback ridin' in de gate. Den such scufflin' round! Old marsa an' missis out on de po'ch, an' de little pickaninnies runnin' from de quarters, an' all hands helpin' 'em off de horses, an' dey all smokin' hot wid de gallop up de lane" (p. 54). Such idyllic glimpses of the past showed the postwar reader that the slave not only had fun in the quarters but also enjoyed vicariously the amusements of the gentry.

Other Negro characters who lived in the afterglow of slavery were drawn by Sam Small. Their memories of slavery became more and more idealized as that period receded into the past. The poems and sketches in *Old Si's Sayings* fit neatly into the darky pattern. In "Uncle Ben's Christmas,"

> *Dere isn't no Christmas for me,*
> *De times is too hard, an' gits harder*
> *De longer we niggers is free.*

His plantation days, the speaker continues, were "jubilee days in Georgy" because "de niggers, same as de white fokes, / Lib'd on de fat ob de land." He recalls the generosity of his master on Christmas morning when he would distribute presents to all the slaves and fete them with eggnog. But times have since changed.

> *But dem days is gone far away, sah,*
> *And we ain't got no marster any mo';*
> *De nigger looks out for hisself, sah,*
> *And can't keep de wolf from de do'.*

The freedman's continued loyalty to his white folks is the theme of "Old Ben and the Bailiff." Called before a judge for assaulting a bailiff who had come to evict his former owner's daughter ("Old Marse's onlies' chile") for not paying her rent, he wins his case. When he had assaulted the officer, "I wuz back on de ole plantation / An a-actin' on dat line!"

Small's prose sketches are frequently political. In "Experiences in Emancipation" the free Old Si meets his former master on the street and reminds him that Christmas is near. The white man says he can't be as liberal as before the war, but offers Si instead a copy of the Declaration of Independence, the Constitution including the Fifteenth Amendment, a civil rights bill, and a check on the Freedman's Bank. After Si refuses each of these gifts, the white offers him a copy of "one of those elegant emancipation proclamations." But Si wants something more than words on a paper. "I wants somefin' comfotin' an' 'stantial, somefin' like feed an' kiverin, 'kase dis ole nigger, like all de rest, is left out in de cold—put too much 'pendence 'pon dat manserfashun prockymashun what put de nigger in the wrong pew—too high up in de church—an' he had to come out!" The Negro was still essentially a chattel in the humorists' paternalistic system.

According to Old Si, the Georgia darky loved his home. The Negro gave his opinion of a senator's proposal to create a Negro state in the Northwest. Southern Negroes would migrate there only on one condition. "Well, ef he wuz ter cum down hyar wid er box-kyar full ob alfydabits dat de hole face ob de territory wuz ripe wid watermillion patches an' all de cross fences wuz kep' warm wid de blackberry bushes, an' dat all de shanties wuz next doah ter de spring, an' dat de gubment garanteed ter keep up everybody's wood-pile, an' dere wuz sandy roads full ob fat dedhed hogs, an' rashens ob army obercoats wuz issher'ed ebery few days, I 'low dat some ob dese darkies mought take excurshun tickets up dar durin' de summer!" Love for the Southland, Old Si believed, was a trait all Negroes had retained.

The past became dearer as it got more remote. Every year, Old Si observed, "de good ole times seems fur ter git furder away fum de country." The philosopher blamed the predicament on emancipation. He put it metaphorically. "Well, sah, 'fore de wah de white folks and dere niggers went 'long on de same train, on de same road, bound for de stashun whar de fiel's ob plenty jess spread out on bofe sides de track an' free fur all. . . . But now when dey put in dat 'manserpashun switch hit allers seems fer ter open when de nigger train comes 'long an' de white fokes takes de right fork an' de nigger takes de lef'. . . . De white fokes goes on up de grade an' des berry well on de ole camp-groun's, but de nigger train it strikes inter de woods an' de passingers is mighty lucky ef dey don't git dump'd inter de swamp ob despare."

Although most of Old Si's sketches had political implications, he also took time to chastise members of his own race for their indiscretions. He even told of the precautions he planned to take against grave-robbers. "I'se gwine ter put on my will dat I'se ter be berried in de dark ob de moon, wid cotton ties aroun' de coffin, an' den hab de hed an' foot-boards sot up nacherally, jess half er mile ter de lef' ob de remains—dat's me!"

Old Si gave voice over and over to the changes that had taken place since the war. One of them he could explain in his *Humorous Sketches;* namely, the reason white folks didn't have as much time to work as they had had. "Kase 'fore de wah de white fokes nebber riz tell de roosters crowed. Now, wid so menny loose niggers in de land roosters is pow'ful skase, an' when er white man ress' onder de 'lusion dat day don't break tell somethin' hollers he's lierbul ter loose de ten o'clock trane ebery day in de yeah!" (p. 52). For thousands of readers of the Atlanta *Constitution* Old Si was the archetype of the "good" Negro. He was a white folks' Negro. He looked upon himself and life as his white overlords wanted him to.

John T. Moore's comic Old Wash has the humor, imagination, weird fancy, and affectionate loyalty of the other darky types, but he also has a shrewder, more selfish side. A critic writing in 1910 for the Louisville *Courier-Journal* said that Wash "looks out always for his own advantage. He schemes to stand well with the widows. He dwells upon the delights of good liquor and tobacco. His stories show how he turns everything to his own profit. His observations upon life are full of worldly wisdom, even satire. . . . He has all the anecdotal and traditional weaknesses and predilections of his race. He is a good raconteur and tells some thirty odd stories with great point and no little humor and rough wit. He deals with widows, mules, goats, preachers, ghosts, Ku Klux. . . . The author knows his Tennessee, and the dialect is true to his life as well as the accessories and scenery of the region in which Uncle Wash places and elaborates his funny jokes."[9]

The Wash stories reveal Moore's tangible debt to the humor of the Old Southwest. "The Wolf Hunt on Big Bigby" in *Songs and Stories* continues the tradition of the tall tale. Reminiscent of Thorpe's "Big Bear of Arkansas," it tells of a particularly good crop year. So well did things grow that a farmer refused to plant pumpkin seeds on his land because he found families living in the pumpkins that had grown the year before. Squatters had moved in and made homes for themselves by hollowing out the pumpkins, building chimneys, and putting in windows and doors.

In "The Spelling Match at Big Sandy" Wash tries spelling—he was tutored by a Boston lady for six months after the war—and when he is told by the schoolmaster that he has made an error, he gets mad and starts an argument. During the ruckus some hot candy is overturned and drops through cracks in the floor onto some hogs under the house. In squealing pain, the hogs break through the floor, the Negroes begin scattering, and Wash jumps through a window. Only after he has stopped running does he realize that he has been injured during the excitement. Claud B. Green, Moore's biographer, offered one explanation for the coarse element in the stories. "Wash was created," he wrote, "not to amuse a young white boy with priceless tales of Brer Rabbit and Brer Fox [like Uncle Remus] but to entertain an adult white man who liked his humor strong and earthy" (p. 84). Many of Moore's stories were, in fact, published in Nashville men's magazines like *The Horse Review* and the *Taylor-Trotwood Magazine*. As a local colorist, however, he also wrote for a larger audience and used the popular combination of humor and pathos.

One of Moore's best stories, "Tom's Last 'Furage,'" contains what was once thought the correct proportion of humor and pathos. In court for stealing a pig, the Negro pleads his case before his former owner, now a judge. Tom defends his theft by recalling his war record of foraging for his young master when that was the only way to get food. Now, he says, the white man is ready to sentence him for doing in peacetime what he had been encouraged to do in wartime. Tom doesn't understand the difference. He doesn't know that the "foraging" of the war has become "stealing" now. Disregarding the present illegality of what he has done, the old Negro makes an impassioned speech in his defense, reciting his war experiences when he commandeered eggs, chickens, and hams from Chattanooga to Atlanta. Tom's recital brings laughter, then tears, to the men in the court, and his case is dismissed. Of Moore's handling of this story, Green commented, "This progression from laughter to tears, from the humorous to the serious, was standard in the formula for short-story writing to which Moore subscribed, but in this particular instance he handled it well. The sentiment does not overflow into sentimentality and the humor has an indigenous quality about it which rings true" (p. 84).

Most of the Uncle Wash stories, however, contain less sentiment and often tend to be pure farce. "How Old Wash Mixed the Lambs," for instance, is a boisterous account of a baby-switching by Wash, who has drunk too much apple brandy at a Negro frolic. His slyness is the theme of "How Old Wash Sold the Filly" in *Ole Mistis*. Wash leaves his wife with the horse and wagon, and comes into the narrator's office. The Negro explains that he has read in horse journals every year for the past few years that owners of harness horses should not sell yet, for each year the price was going to go up the following year. Wash needs to sell his own horse, but he has followed this printed advice. One year, after reading the prediction, "I tuck de filly back home, stopped de chillum frum skule, sold de 'possum dog, lied erbout my taxes, shet off the missionery fund fer de church, closed down on de preacher, an' spent de money in forty-cent oats an' fifty-cent cohn to stuff hit erway in dat filly fur de cummin' ob de angel!" But each year in fact the price has gone down—from $300 the year Wash first thought about selling to the present $50. Nothing ever goes right for poor Wash. "Why, boss, ef I'd buy er carload ob ice in Augus' an' ship it to Hades dey'd cum er big freeze down dar befo' it got dar, an' dey wouldn't be no demand fur it de naixt day." Suddenly there is a loud crash outside, and Wash rushes away. He returns to announce that he has just sold his filly to the L. & N. Railroad for five hundred dollars—plus five cents for his wife's broken jaw. "I tell yo', boss, dey ain't nuffin lak crossin' our fillies on a locomotive to improve de breed in dis state."

Perhaps Moore's most amusing farce is "Bre'r Washington's Arraignment," also in *Ole Mistis*. Here the darky turns his pride in having been a slave to his own advantage. He tells of the time they had him up "befo' de jedge at Nashville fur makin', without license, er leetle ob dat licker dat makes kings ob us all." The liquor he had made, he quickly assures his auditors, was not run-of-the-mill stuff. "I don't mean dis heah stuff dese po' white trash makes up in de mountings so strong an' vile dat when yo' oncork a bottle ob it on dis yearth it make de debbil sneeze in de reguns below." Continuing the preface to the account of his arraignment, he explains lyrically how his "sho' nuff whisky—whisky dat sho' nuff white folks drink" is made. "Yo' must make it in October . . . er 'bout de time de fall poet begins ter write his poem on de golden rod, when de leabs begin ter turn purple an' golden, an' de air am crisp an' sparklin', an' de spring water am full ob fallin' nuts an' de 'romer ob de sweet night dews." He finally returns to his story, boasting that he had no notion of staying long in jail for making good whiskey—"now ef I made mean whisky dat ud bin ernudder thing, an' I'd bin willin' to plead gilty an' say far'well." His prejudice against poor whites shows in his recollection of his imprisonment. The law played a mean trick on him, he says, "fur dey sot me down in de same pen wid er lot ob po' white trash frum de mountings dat had bin cotch in de act ob makin' wild-cat whisky! Gord, suh, hit made me mad, fur I wan't used ter 'soshatin' wid dat kind o' white folks!"

At the trial the shrewd old man gives gustatory proof of his skill. He uncorks a jug of fourteen-year-old whiskey he's had his wife dig up and bring in. "I handed dat decanter to de fus' juryman—he jes' smelt it an' fell ober in er dead faint, callin' out, sorter dream lak, 'Not gilty, not gilty!' "

205

The other jurymen are equally impressed. But Wash is not finished with the court. He feels that he's been wronged and he wants redress. "An' now, gemmen ob de jury, sense dis Newnighted States govment dun see fit to 'raign me, I wanter 'raign hit. . . . Men lak him [Wash's master] an' yore fathers, gemmen, tuck my ancesturs out ob de jungles ob barbarity an' led us inter de blessed temple ob religun an' light. Dey made slaves ob us ter do it, gemmen, but I thang Gord I wuz erlowed ter be er slave in dis wurl fur de sake ob bein' etunnally free in de naixt." Then, to the delight and approval of the court, he indicts the United States government for ruining his life by setting him free. "But in my ole aige, heah cums dis Newnighted States guvermen' an' sots me free. An' O, Marsters, dey sot me free indeed— free frum de friends I lubbed, free frum de cumperney ob gemmen, free frum de good things ob de wurl, an', wuss ob all, free frum de sight but not de appertite ob dat licker dat makes kings ob us all! 'Stid ob drivin' er cheeriut an fo' down de pike ob de valley ob plenty, I mus' plow er leetle tow-haided muel on de flinty hillsides ob poverty. 'Stid ob 'soshatin' wid learned men who sot in de counsils ob dis country an' de cotes ob de kings, I mus' be cussed an' mocked by de hill-billy an' de po' white, or forced to 'soshate wid low-lived an' low-mannered niggers an' fiel'-han's. An' 'stid ob drinkin' de 'lixir ob life frum de decanter ob de gourds, in my ole aige, I'm forced ter drink de branch water ob poverty frum de gourd dat grows in de barn-yard ob toil." Reaching a fever-pitch, Wash asks, "Gemmen, kin yo' do it? Marsters, will yo' sen' de ole man up?" Naturally, they can't. Wash's adroit mixture of religious sentiment, pathos, and humor, his apotheosis of the past, and his appealing presentation win his acquittal by the jury. The judge gives him fifty dollars toward the taxes on his future runs.

This farce presents another perfect stereotype of the literary darky. Everything that Wash says confirms the traditional Southern white position on the Negro. The only defect in the picture is that one suspects that the old scoundrel is well aware of what he is doing and is merely adapting to the exigencies of the situation and of his audience.

Paul Laurence Dunbar, the Ohio poet-humorist, portrayed the Negro extensively in his poetry. Though a Negro himself, he adopted the typical Southern white opinion of his race. A passage from one of his *Poems of Cabin and Field* reveals his kinship with Page and his school. After surveying his old plantation home, a former slave asks:

> *Whah's de da'kies, dem dat used to be a-dancin'*
> *Ev'ry night befo' de ol' cabin do'?*
> *Whah's de chillun, dem dat used to be a-prancin'*
> *Er a-rollin' in de san' er on de flo'?*

The old man decides to stay on and oversee the deserted plantation because "it hol's in me a lover till de las'."

So I'll stay an' watch de deah ol' place an' tend it
Ez I used to in de happy days gone by.
Twell de othah Mastah thinks it's time to end it,
An' calls me to my qua'ters in de sky (p. 29).

The popular humorists had not only brainwashed whites to believe the legend of the past; their writings seemed to convince even the Negroes.

Colonel Romulus Field's body servant Peter in James Lane Allen's "Two Gentlemen from Kentucky" is another stereotype of the faithful old Negro. Allen's interpretation of Peter is frankly idealistic and somewhat sentimental, but the lovable old character is one of the strangest looking figures in American humor. Among other oddities, his coat is embroidered with Bible texts. In addition to being the colonel's servant, Peter is a preacher. Once when he offers his services to a colored congregation he is not "called" because he has a broken leg, because he wears his boss' clothing which is too big for him, and because he preaches in the old-fashioned way. Peter's account of how he happened to marry his wife is one of the most amusing episodes in the story. At a revival in which he is the preacher, his future wife is converted after much "wras'lin' wid 'erse'f." The fateful incident occurs at the baptizing which closes the meeting. The big social and religious event is held in a creek where the current is swift. He baptizes each convert in turn, and then he comes to Phillis. "En me en 'er j'ined han's en waded out in the creek, mighty slow, caze Phillis didn't have no shot roun' de bottom uv 'er dress, en it kep' bobbin' on top de watter til I pushed it down. But by-en-by we got 'way out in de creek, en bof uv us wuz tremblin'. En I says to 'er ve'y kin'ly, 'When I put you un'er de watter, Phillis, you mus' try en hole yo'se'f stiff, so I can lif' you up easy.' But I hadn't mo' 'n got 'er laid back over de watter ready to souze 'er un'er when 'er feet flew up off de bottom uv de creek, en when I retched out to fetch 'er up, I stepped in a hole; en' 'fo' I knowed it, we wuz flounderin' roun' in de watter, en de hymn dey was singin' on de bank sounded mighty confused-like. En Phillis she swallowed some water, en all't oncet she jes grap me right roun' de neck, en say mighty quick, says she, 'I gwine marry whoever gits me out'n dis yere watter!'" The two victims of the total immersion are eventually married. The sketch ends, however, with a pathetic account of the colonel's death, and afterwards, of Peter's.[10]

Martha Young's Negroes are creatures of her nostalgia. Most of the poems in her *Plantation Songs* are set before the war when her subjects are actually enjoying the good life, but in "Hog-Killin' Times in Dixie Land" she describes the joy in the slave's heart during the slaughtering season and contrasts it with his later glumness. The colored speaker laments that these times are over—"Lost with the things of long ago"—but "We fit ourselves to new time,—though / The olden days we ne'er forget."

Uncle Stephen Demby in Edmund K. Goldsborough's *Ole Mars an' Ole Miss* is another who reminisces about "dem days" when everything was better.

To Uncle Stephen they had been times to brag about—and brag he does! Of his master's plantation he says, "All de niggahs on dat plantation slep' wid sheets on deah beds. Mars Nickey didn't hab, an' he wouldn' hab no common niggahs." The times were slower and the land was flowing with milk and honey. "Why, hunny, ebin de peaches an' watahmillions wuz bigger dem deys, kase dey didn't grow up so fars; dey tuck deah time; an' ez fuh oysters an' fish, why dem deys you cud walk out in dat cobe not fudder dan yo' nees, an' git all de oysters you wan', an' set rite at dat stake an' pull in de fish tell you go 'stracted, an' de wile ducks quackin' all 'roun' you" (pp. 115-18). It is no wonder that the Negro wanted to return to those days of indolent plenty.

A popular pastime for many years after the war was the mock-serious threatening of ignorant Negroes with re-enslavement. To perpetuate their own power, radical Republicans would sometimes start rumors before elections that a vote for a Democrat was a vote for the return of slavery. Many freedmen believed the threat. One of Goldsborough's Negroes was convinced that the election of the Democrat Grover Cleveland meant that Uncle Billy would again be sold into slavery. Some white jokesters decided to exploit his fear, and put up notices announcing that on a certain day all former slaves in the state would be sold at auction. On the appointed day Uncle Billy appeared on the block, and the mock bidding started, with his resigned pronouncement ringing in the ears of the laughing onlookers: "I's glad ter be uh slabe, ef'n uh gemman buy me" (p. 59) Thus the backward-looking freedman was put to the ultimate test and chose slavery.

LaSalle Corbell Pickett's nostalgic *Yule Log* is a book of memories describing "how hit use' ter be in de ole, ole times 'fo' de war." Something of Mrs. Pickett's approach is revealed in her attitude toward ante-bellum life. "The reminiscence of the far-away life lingers with us like the fragrance of the snowy magnolias" (p. 9). Speaking the language of Mammy Borry, she described the earlier happy lot of the ox-cart driver and contrasted it with the poverty of the present. "My ole man is gittin' too ole ter be a gee-in' en a haw-in' lak he is, but 'pear lak hit's moughty hard fer 'im ter gib up breckin' in de oxens. He allers wuz so proud er his ox-teams, en proud er his ox-kyarts, too, fer he us' ter stan' ter hit dat a ox-kyart wuz de kingdomes', soshubles', roomies' chariotable ebber rid in, en he nebber wuz ez happy ez when he wuz a gee-hawin' a load er de nayberhood gals ter a ball er ter a camp-meetin', en hit mos' bruck his heart ter come down ter one steer en a single kyart; but dat's freedom. We won' nebber see de ole times no mo'" (pp. 37-38).

The plaintive cry of the freedman for the good old times is heard just as clearly in Martha Gielow's *Old Plantation Days*. This Alabama writer used the popular device of having an old Negro, man or woman, tell reminiscent stories to a white child. Those times were undoubtedly the best, but Mammy Joe found some solace in her religion. "When I sets hyar an' looks out upon de changes, hit seem all wrong—an' sometimes hit seem lak de Marster done fergit us all—an' mos' pertic'lar dem what is ole an' no 'count—what ain' got nobody 'sponsible fer 'um dese days. But den, dat's des de debble er temptin' uv me. I knows dat He do keer" (p. ix). Conjuring up poignant memories of the past, she looked toward the Big House and recalled for her little white listener how it was. "Lawd, chile, I can' hardly stan' it, an' when I sets hyar lookin' ober dar, I thinks erbout de times befo' de war when de quarters looked lak er city, an' when de plantation was lak er hive uv bees, wid de han's at wuck. I can see ole Mistis right now, walkin' erlong lak er queen, froo de quarters whar we all fairly worshipped her" (pp. 22-23).

Poor Mammy Joe had lived under white supremacy so long that she never questioned its validity. She accepted the inferiority of her race, and in order to think respectfully of herself, she had to disavow her color. She told the white child, "I don' lak ter call myse'f er nigger, kase, pertic'lar speakin', dar ain' but one sho' nuff nigger, an' dat's de *debble*. We black folks ain' 'zackly niggurs, you know, honey, we is des black-skinned white folks" (p. 28).

According to Mrs. Gielow too, the freedman still sought out his white folks for advice on topics ranging from money to matrimony. In "Uncle Tom's Matrimonial Difficulties" a black went to the son of his former owner for help with his love life. He wanted to divorce Aunt Becky because "she ain' es young es she wuz, an' she boss me so." He also had his eye on a younger girl. However, before any divorce action could be taken, Uncle Tom's prospective bride ran away with someone else, Aunt Becky locked him out of his house, and he was left with the problem of getting reconciled with his present wife. Again he went to the white man and promised: "Ef you will jes' he'p me out onct mo', I gwine fotch you de bigges' water-million I kin raise in my patch nex' year, an' de fus' possum what go up de 'simmon tree dis fall." In postwar humor the Negro always knew his problems could be solved magically by his white folks.

Although the freed slave often left his former master, he usually realized after much searching for a better life elsewhere that that better life was still with the white people he had known all his life. In an essay in the *Century Magazine* (March, 1892) Richard Malcolm Johnston used an anecdote to illustrate the return of one man to his former owner. The white man asked why he was returning. "Well now, Marse Jack, I gwine up en tell you jes how 'tis. I wuck fer dah man all las' year, en I wuck hard, en I make him a good crop. Well, now de troof is, I did git f'om him a few, but, min' you, jes only a few, merlasses en tobarker, en one hat, en a pa'r o' shoes, en one little thing en 'nother. Well, den, Chris'mus come en he say, 'Jim, I gwine make out our 'count.' En den he tuck he piece o' paper, en he pen, en he ink-vial, en he 'gin a-settin' down, en when he thoo wid dat job, he 'gin a-addin' up, en a-put'n' down, en a-kyar'n'; en he kyar'd, en he kep' on a-kyar'n', ontwel, bless your soul and body! Marse Jacky, when he got thoo, he done kyar's off all what was a-comin' to me! En so I makes up my min', I does, to leff dar, en pewoose myself back to you, whar I knows dey not gwine be no sich kyar'n' as dem." The faithful freedman of humor could always trust his old master. He couldn't trust the radical politicians, the carpetbaggers or the scalawags, members of his own race, or other white planters; but he knew his former owner would be straight with him.

In *Yellow Creek Humor* William J. Burtscher sketched many servile Negroes. He described Uncle Deb as "an old-fashioned ante-bellum darky, who brought with him into the twentieth century no education, no money, no property—nothing but the politeness and the manners which he absorbed from the ladies and the gentlemen whose slave he was" (p. 22). In this statement Burtscher unknowingly made the most serious indictment possible of a system he was evidently trying to defend. The politeness and manners which the slave absorbed from his owners were a poor substitute for all the things he was denied. In several sketches Burtscher even reveled in the ignorant Negro, who to him was comic. Burtscher saw humor, for example, in the fact that an old Negro couldn't count to one hundred or did not know how old he was. The first stanza from a dialect poem, "Living Like a White Man," makes Burtscher's haughty attitude more explicit.

> De sun keep on a-shinin',
>   An' de wint'r wood am cut;
> De hick'ry nuts bin gether'd,
>   An' dun piled up in de hut.
> De panic hit am ovah,
>   An' dis am what I 'low—
> I'm mighty nigh a-livin'
>   Like a white man now.

It was probably words like these that spurred the Negro on in his determination to break segregation barriers. He wanted to live like civilized human beings—"like a white man."

The death of a devoted old servant was the occasion of much tear-shedding by white people. In "The Passing of Mammy" (*Plantation Songs*) Martha Young gave a sentimental and yet humorous account of such a deathbed scene. A white woman rushes to the bedside of her dying mammy, who tells her that though the colored preacher has said white folks can't get beyond the door of heaven, she will ask for a special dispensation.

> And I'll ax de Good Lord: Please, Sah! Massa!
> Des give my li'l' Missy a seat,
> And some nice li'l' gol'en slippers,—
> Fit yo' neat li'l' feet;
> And a gol'en crown fer you, Lady!
> Ef I ax him he'll fix you up right—
> Dough you is—Mammy's li'l' Lady—
> Dough you is—only—des white.

210

Of course, neither Miss Young nor her readers did more than smile at the quaint notion that heaven was reserved for colored people only. It was common knowledge among them that in heaven all people were white.

The old-fashioned Negro was extremely suspicious and critical of the new Negro, the educated Negro. Speaking his white creator's mind, the typical darky took the enlightened Negro to task for trying to act like white people. In Irwin Russell's "Dat Peter" the speaker ridicules a Negro for wearing store-bought clothes and a five-dollar hat and for oiling his hair and concludes sarcastically: "I guess he thinks he's white." He decides the best thing for such an "uppity" Negro to do would be to rent a little patch of land and "settle down to crapping" or else "De debbil's gwine to set him back afore his game is done."[11]

The Negro does much to enliven the pages of James McDonald's *Life in Old Virginia*. One of the frequent subjects of humor was the Negro's weakness for petty thefts. McDonald recorded the persuasive defense of one who was caught stealing a turkey shortly after the war. "Jedge, it happen'd dis yere way. I was tukken down wid a misery in ma side, an' I wa'nt able to go to cuttin' no co'd wood laik I'd bin a doin', an' jus as I wuz a gwine to de sto' to ax Mistuh B---- to lemme hav' a few poun's o' bacon 'twill I gets rid o' de misery in ma side, an' den as I cums pas' Mistah C----'s cuppen fence dar sot dis yere young tukkey right dar, suh, and I sez to mase'f, ef de Lawd spars me I shore gwine cut Mistuh C---- a co'd an' a ha'f uv good wood fo' dis yere tukkey. Dat's jes' wat I say, I aint tellin' yo' no lie, suh. I suttinly will wo'k out dat tukkey, shore's I live. W'en I tuk dat tukkey I didn't hav' grease enuff in ma cabin to grease a spider. I don et it all up 'fore I seed dat tukkey. Dat's how cum I taik dat tukkey. I clar 'fore de Lawd dis is de fust time I evah was *kotched* takin' tukkey in ma life" (pp. 194-95). The shrewd presentation worked on the judge's sympathy—as it was calculated to do—and the trial never came up. More important than the surface humor of the sketch is its revelation that Negroes—especially the humble Uncle Tom type—were usually let off light for minor crimes. As sub-human-beings they were not supposed to have the highly developed sense of right and wrong of the white man.

A stock situation in Southern humor has been the digressive, involved direction. McDonald had a Virginia freedman give the following directions to a stranger for getting to a certain Captain Pat Clay's house: "Keep de straight road 'twell yo' comes to a 'new cut' road. Do'an yo' turn in dar, kase dat aint de road yo' takes. W'en yo' gits right smaht ways fum dat place whar yo' sees de new cut road, yo' keeps de straight road pas' Captain Jim Lanes 'wintah cuppen' (cowpen); it's right in de pines whar he shelter his cattle in de wintah time. Den yo' turn dar an' keep de straight road 'twell yo' gits to a pole gate made outen pine saplin's. Do'an yo' go in dar, kase dat whar Captain Tom Jinkins live. Den yo' keep de straight road 'twell yo' comes to a big sycamore, right smaht skirt o' pines, some on 'em right smaht

211

size an' yuther ones jes' young saplin's, kase dar whar de saw mill war las' year, an' dey cut all de bes' timber outen dar 'fore dey move de mill. Dey suttinly mus' use a heap o' timber in town, kase dat mill wuz a sawin' mos' night an' day, an' dey sont ev'ry blessed stick o' dat timber to town, an' dey axed fo' mor'." He concludes that digression, but still he goes on. "W'en yo' gits outen dat clearin' whar de saw mill war, yo' comes in sight o' Captain Ned Daingerfield's house, right down on the crick sho'. Den de nex' house yo' sees straight down de crick sho', yo' knows it's Captain Pat Clays. I 'spect he's de gentleman yo' is lookin fo'" (pp. 214-15). The Negro's leisurely life before the war had supposedly made him a great teller of long, rambling stories filled with reams of irrelevant information. This sketch is a good illus·tration of that supposition.

The Negro of humor acknowledged his decline in status since slavery, but he had not declined enough to lose his disdain for white trash. His attitude is perhaps best summed up in this jingle:

> *You can't make a livin'*
> *On sandy lan';*
> *I'd ruther be a nigger*
> *Than a po' white man.*[12]

Almost without exception, the darkies cannot abide the poor white. Part of this dislike is attributable to a fear of competition on the labor market. Mrs. Jeannette Walworth's Uncle Scipio, for example, makes fun of "po' w'ite trash" from the North who after the war tried to usurp the Negro's rightful place in the cotton field. "Mister w'ite man, he come 'long en hire some lan' frum de man'ger fur so many poun's er lint t' de acre. Mister wi'te man, he start in might brickitty. He gwine show mister nigger w'at was w'at. Nigger got t' stan' aside w'en mister w'ite man mek up he min' to work. . . . But w'en de sun git hot, en de grass growin' so fas' you kin hear it; yes, sir, I sez hear it; den whar mister w'ite man! Kyurl up in de shade watchin' mister nigger git'm out'n de grass. Dar' whar' he be" (p. 46.) The poor white's low manners and general coarseness naturally repulsed the genteel freedman who had known gracious living on his owner's plantation.

The Uncle Remus of Joel Chandler Harris is the best depiction of the literary Negro. Uncle Remus is not the Faithful Black, the Martyred Uncle Tom, or the Black Sambo of earlier literature. True, he had a bit of each of these stereotypes in his character; but more accurately than any one, he reflects the idealized image of the ante-bellum regime. Uncle Remus' place in the tradition is emphasized by Hyder Rollins. "Remus is an idealized, aristocratic old darky, whose dominant traits are pride in Miss Sally and her boy and contempt for poor white trash and freed niggers."[13] Uncle Remus is *the* postwar survival of the prewar darky. He is also one of the most memorable characters in American literature. In the Introduction to *Uncle Remus,* the first volume of the stories, Harris knowingly presented the mythological nature of his creation. "If the reader not familiar with plantation life will imagine that the myth-stories of Uncle Remus are told night after night to a little boy by an old Negro who appears venerable enough to have lived during the period which he describes—who has nothing but pleasant memories of the discipline of slavery—and who has all the prejudices of caste and pride of family that were the natural results of the system . . . he will find little difficulty in appreciating and sympathizing with the air of affectionate superiority which Uncle Remus assumes as he proceeds to unfold the mysteries of plantation lore to a little child. . . ."

Harris did not attempt to create, as many of his contemporaries were doing, a lovable old darky who would convince his readers that the "peculiar institution" of the South had been right. Instead, he drew a character who is true to the spirit of good feeling that exists between whites and blacks regardless of time and condition. His delineation of Uncle Remus did much to reunite the torn nation because it showed convincingly that slavery had not meant an irrevocable separation in enmity of the races.

Harris distinguished his animal stories told by Uncle Remus and others from his Negro character sketches. He stated that he was "presenting a phase of Negro character wholly distinct from that which I have endeavored to preserve in the legends. . . . Only in this shape, and with all the local allusions, would it be possible to adequately represent the shrewd observations, the curious retorts, the homely thrusts, the quaint comments, and the humorous philosophy of the race of which Uncle Remus is the type."

The first Uncle Remus volume contains examples of genre sketches common to all humor of the time. "Uncle Remus's Church Experience," for example, is a comic satire on the bickering, pettiness, and fights in Negro churches. In "Uncle Remus and the Savannah Darky" and "Turnip Salad as a Text" he lectures his own race. "Uncle Remus with the Toothache" is a comic bagatelle with no serious implications for anyone. "The Phonograph" shows the old Negro's naïveté and wonder at new gadgets. In "As to Education" he expresses his skepticism of education for the colored man. Any one of these sketches could have been written by Sam Small or Opie Read—but with much less artistry and impact.

In addition to revealing Negro folklore, Uncle Remus' animal tales are also a commentary on the friendly relations between the freedman and his white folks. In other words, to many readers the setting for the tales was more significant than what happened to Brer Rabbit. In his recent book on Mark Twain, Kenneth Lynn has written: "To Twain, the most meaningful part of the Uncle Remus stories was the part that Harris had contributed—the 'frame', which dramatized the relationship between Uncle Remus and the little boy . . ." (p. 242). Thomas Nelson Page also noted the significance of the frame and of the storyteller's personality. "Reading 'Uncle Remus,' we are not studying animal myths nor learning phonetic arrangements; we are translated bodily to the old man's fireside in his cabin, listening with 'Miss Sally's Little Boy' to Uncle Remus himself as he tells us stories the merit of which as stories springs directly from the fact that Uncle Remus knows them, is relating them, and is vivifying them with his own quaintness and humor and impressing us in every phase with his delightful and lovable personality. . . . The stories caught the ear of the South, and touched a chord which opened wide the doors of memory. With 'Uncle Remus' and 'Miss Sally's Little Boy,' whoever came across them lived over again his own childhood, laughed over the stories, told with inimitable fidelity and art, which he used to hear at the fireside 'in the dear remembered days' and wept a little also over the memories that they recalled."[14]

Uncle Remus, the product of the plantation system, has the outlook of the aristocrat. He gives advice to upstart young Negroes who mistake freedom for license. The Uncle Remus writings of Harris, therefore, were written with a serious intention: to educate the freedman and to reconcile the North and the South by showing the past and present amicable relations between the races. Harris made his intention clear in the Introduction to *Uncle Remus*. "I am advised by my publishers that this book is to be included in their catalogue of humorous publications, and this friendly warning gives me an opportunity to say that however humorous it may be in effect, its intention is perfectly serious. . . ." Uncle Remus was just as much a propagandist for the South as John C. Calhoun had been before the war; but unlike Calhoun's his propaganda had for its objective reunion, not disunion. Like another Harris storyteller, Aunt Minervy Ann, Uncle Remus refuses to be taken in by carpetbaggers and equality talk. Nor will he stoop to Old Si's pastime of castigating the Yankee for setting him free. He was a middle-of-the-roader at a time when this was almost an untenable position.

In Harris' novels the postwar darky is always prominent. Refusing to join the Union League, Uncle Plato in *Gabriel Tolliver* explains to the organizers. "I wuz des ez free twenty year ago ez you all will ever be. My marster has been good ter me fum de work [sic] go. I ain't stayin' wid 'im bekaze he got money. Ef him an' Miss Sa'ah di'n'a have a dollar in de worl', an no way ter git it, I'd work my arms off fer 'm. An' ef I 'fused ter do it my wife 'd quit me, an' my chillun wouldn't look at me. But I'll tell you what I'll do: when my marster tu'ns his back on me I'll tu'n my back on him" (p. 179). Thus another picture of the Loyal Freedman.

Harris took the darky of transient humor and made him into a permanent contribution to world humor and literature. He achieved superbly his ultimate objective, which is perhaps best expressed in the dedication to the Frost edition of the Remus stories. "I seem to see before me the smiling faces of thousands of children—some young and fresh and some wearing the friendly marks of age, but all children at heart—and not an unfriendly face among them. And while I am trying hard to speak the right word, I seem to hear a voice lifted above the rest, saying: 'You have made some of us happy.' And so I feel my heart fluttering and my lips trembling and I have to bow silently, and turn away and hurry into the obscurity that fits me best."[15] In a much later edition of *Uncle Remus* Marc Connelly summed up its author's contribution to humor. "Artemus Ward, Josh Billings, Petroleum V. Nasby and other contemporary symbols of dialect humor almost always wrote with labored humor about ephemeral subjects. Harris, like Hans Christian Anderson and Aesop, wrote of the permanent."

Although Harris' work is conventional in form, it is not typical of most humor of that kind. By the turn of the century the faithful old Negro and his companion, the fallen aristocrat, had become stock figures of caricature. It looked then as if Southern writing would forever create only fawning uncles, aunties, mammies, and proud but poor aristocrats. Again, however, O. Henry came to the rescue, and in "The Guardian of the Accolade" (*Roads of Destiny*) reduced the tradition to a big joke. According to this iconoclastic author, Uncle Bushrod has given sixty years of faithful service to the Weymouth family "as chattel, servitor, and friend." At the time of the story he works at the Weymouth Bank, where "he was something between porter and generalissimo-in-charge." The scion of the Weymouth family, Mr. Robert, is, to Uncle Bushrod's dismay, a profligate and a heavy drinker.

One night returning to the bank—he has his own key—to pick up some records for the Sons and Daughters of the Burning Bush society, Uncle Bushrod is surprised to hear another key in the lock. Unnoticed, he watches Mr. Robert come in with a satchel, go to the vault, and return with the satchel bulging. The "guardian of the accolade" is convinced that Mr. Robert is planning to embezzle the bank's money and thus drag the Weymouth name in the mud. To prevent this he follows the white man to the train station and remonstrates with him. What the astonished bank robber has in his valise will "destroy de name of Weymouth and bow down dem dat own it wid shame and triberlation." When Mr. Robert gets angry, the old Negro reminds him of his authority. "I got a right, suh, to talk to you dis 'er' way. I slaved for you and 'tended to you from a child up. I went th'ough de war as yo' body-servant tell we whipped de Yankees and sent 'em back to de No'th. I was at yo' weddin', and I wasn' fur away when yo' Miss Letty was bawn. And Miss Letty's chillun, dey watches to-day for Uncle Bushrod when he come home ever' evenin'. I been a Weymouth, all 'cept in colour and entitlements." Disgusted, the embezzler thrusts the valise into Uncle Bushrod's hands and boards the departing train. Later when Mr. Robert meets the friend with whom he has planned a fishing trip, he has to explain why the two bottles of bourbon are missing. It was "an infernally presumptuous old nigger belonging in my family that broke up the arrangement." Up to the denouement, the story has all the ingredients of a typical darky sketch: his pride in the family name and his guardianship over it, his tyranny over his white folks, and of course the usual humor, pathos, and religious sentiment. The O. Henry twist at the end is quite a shock to the reader, for only then does he know that it was a sham. The darky becomes a conceited and grotesque fool.

The Smiling Phoenix

Although O. Henry could poke acrid fun at it, he could not completely do away with the literary tradition. In September, 1908, for example, the *Taylor-Trotwood Magazine* published a genre sketch by Sarah Anne Hobson, "Mammy Tap," which affirmed the continuing popularity of darkies in Southern humor. Miss Hobson still described the mammy in these words: "Loyal and true, uncompromising in her standards of the olden times, scorning the freedom that was thrust upon her, she remains in the South one of the last connecting links between the old civilization and the new" (VII, 525). By the end of the century, however, the old-time darky was no longer an attractive subject for humor. O. Henry and other debunkers of the tradition, the continually changing taste in humor, the rise of the Negro politically and economically, and the surfeit of such portrayals—all contributed to the lessening of the vogue. Back in 1882 Opie Read had already lamented in the *Arkansaw Traveler* the decline of the real person. "The old time negro is gradually passing away. His head is as white as his native cotton field, his form is bent and his shambling gait is toward the grave. . . . In the years that come, he will have no representative. His children are ashamed of him. They ridicule his odd dialect, laugh at his traditions and scorn his religious fancies. Years ago he was an oracle. . . . He read but two books, nature and his own mind. He once held high rank among the village boys. They would not think of fishing in a pool condemned by him. His dogs were the best. His stories were the richest" (July 9). By 1914 the Negro was even on his way out of humor. He and his unreconstructed master eventually ceased to be a vital source of popular humor and were relegated to social and political history and to folklore.

Notes

1. *History,* 269.
2. Porter, *Strictly Business,* 148-72.
3. Gaines, *Southern Plantation,* 63.
4. Visscher, *Ten Wise Men,* 151.
5. Avary, *Dixie After the War,* 397.
6. Quoted in Holliday, *Southern Literature,* 369.
7. *Library of Southern Literature,* VII, 3036-38.
8. *Ibid.,* XIII, 5722-23.
9. Quoted in Green, *Moore,* 85.
10. *Library of Southern Literature,* I, 57.
11. Quoted from Fulton, *Southern Life,* 413-14.
12. Kendrick and Arnett, *South Looks at Its Past,* 48.
13. "Negro in the Southern Short Story," 47.
14. "Literature in the South," 748-49.
15. Quoted in Julia Harris, *J. C. Harris,* 589.

7. The Postwar Negro

IN 1890 HENRY CLAY LUKENS noted that "the freedman is one of the liveliest and strongest forces in our varicolored national caricature."[1] This was not always so. Before the Civil War the Negro, if treated at all, was almost always a background character; his personality remained virtually unexploited in written humor. As Hyder Rollins said, "If the negro appears in other ante-bellum short stories [than those of Kennedy and Poe], either he or his creator is of little importance."[2] After the war this was all changed. The school of local colorists in the South was composed of men like Thomas Nelson Page, Harry Stillwell Edwards, and Joel Chandler Harris who made their reputations with short stories or sketches in most of which the Negro plays a leading role.

The popularity of the character was tremendous. Various blacks—from the darky to the new, emancipated Negro—dominated Southern humor from 1865 to 1914. Racial conduct and character were exploited in modes ranging from the "coon" joke through the minstrel to the short story and the novel. Dialect poems, jokes, and short sketches filled the columns of such periodicals as *Texas Siftings*, the *Arkansaw Traveler*, the *Taylor-Trotwood Magazine*, and hundreds of other magazines and newspapers throughout the South. The Negro's speech, his dishonesty, his superstitions, his courtships, his religious fanaticism, his comic singing and dancing—all these alleged vagaries and eccentricities were topics of humor. And the written was minuscule compared to the vast unrecorded folk humor that grew up around the Negro character.

Unfortunately, much of the written humor was manufactured by people who were unsympathetic and used the coon as a literary device only. When the Negro became a popular subject, mercenary writers climbed aboard the bandwagon. Dialect, for example, was frequently used merely as machinery, as in the coon poems of Opie Read and William Lightfoot Visscher, and not as an integral part of the piece. In such humor the Negro's physical and psychological features were usually exaggerated beyond recognition. In much he became the Comic Animal.

Northern humorists, especially the minor ones, also exploited the Negro personality. Timothy Sullivan, for example, in his *Plantation and Up-to-Date Humorous Negro Stories* included coon stories dealing with the Negro's religion, superstitions, and amusements, allegedly collected on a trip through the South "where he has seen the happiest of all races in their natural and simple moods."

One of the commonest stock jokes showed the supposed indifference of the husband to his spouse. The male's infidelity was taken as a matter of course, and his wife had little trouble in forgetting him when he was dead. The *Arkansaw Traveler* of November 28, 1885, showed how long a woman would remain faithful to her husband's memory.

Judge (to a negro who had been summoned as a witness)—"Is this man your husband?"
Woman—"He's my step-husban'."
Judge—"What!"
Woman—"I says dat de gennerman is my step-husban'!"
Judge—"How do you make that?"
Woman—"Wall, sah, yer see dat jes' 'bout de time my fust husban' wuz buried, dis gennerman come er steppin' er long an' I married him."

In spite of these perversions, writers like Harris, Charles Egbert Craddock, Will Allen Dromgoole, Anne Virginia Culbertson, and many others portrayed the freedman in a humor which had more than transitory significance.

Those dealing with the Negro showed a definitely condescending attitude toward him, even the most liberal humorists. Many—Thomas Nelson Page was one—became concerned about the potential political power of the Negro and did all they could to show him as dangerous and irresponsible. In Page's "How Andrew Carried the Precinct" (*Pastime Stories*), a faithful black servant saves an election for a white man opposed by a "dangerous" mulatto. Page advocated elementary education for all Negroes and higher education for a few selected ones; but to him the race was unquestionably inferior. He and others like him admired the leader Booker T. Washington, who never asserted for himself or his race—at least publicly—a claim to equality with the white man. Almost all the humor, therefore, assumed the inferiority of the Negro. A poem by Leo C. Evans entitled "The Color Line" illustrates this attitude. After describing the beauty of a woman—her eyes, hair, teeth, lips—the writer abruptly tears the picture apart.

> She had one imperfection—
> The Color Line's in sight;
> I didn't love dear Becky; 'cause
> Dear Becky wasn't white.[3]

This racist attitude toward the freedman was predominant in both the North and the South. The Negro never seemed to mind being thus ridiculed in humor; or if he did, he didn't have the political and economic power to make his objections heard. And few were articulate enough to fight back in print.

The color line more and more came in for treatment in humor. A change in race relations is reflected by Mrs. Pickett in *What Happened to Me*: the gradual alienation of whites and blacks, the erecting of a wall between the races that cut off communication. Under slavery the races had lived together intimately. They had reputedly understood each other. Now with freedom they were being separated by racial prejudice and conflicting interests. Mrs. Pickett showed this trend incidentally in her young son's prayer when he found out that his white nurse was to be replaced by a colored one. "Our Father who art in Heaven, please send me a white nurse because nobody else can, and because when black hands touch me my soul crawls around inside and I get icicles and creepy things all down my back, and oh, dear Lord, our Father who art in Heaven, I'd rather have no supper than have their black hands cut it up for me, and I'd rather be dirty as the pigs than have them wash me, and I'd rather not go out doors and see the birds and flowers and other children and things play and pick the buttercups that the policemen don't care if we pick because they grow wild, than have their big black-white eyes watching me. So, our Father who art in Heaven, please send me a white nurse quick, for Christ's sake. Amen!" (p. 316). His mother explained to him that before the war all Southern children had had colored nurses, that she had loved her mammy almost like a mother. But her attempt didn't make the boy change his opinion toward black people; unlike his mother, he had not been wet-nursed by a mammy.

The use of dialect has accounted for much of the popularity of American humor since the Civil War. Although Irish, Italian, German, and other dialects have been widely used, in the South the Negro has been by far the most popular. To many readers before 1914 any story written in Negro dialect was funny regardless of theme or intention. Although some humorists used it merely to exploit the vogue, many other recorded Negro speech accurately and artistically.

219

The Smiling Phoenix

To writers like Joel Chandler Harris and Thomas Nelson Page it was a means of revealing the real Negro. Ambrose Gonzales, the author of *The Black Border*, wrote in the Introduction to his stories that he had used Gullah dialect only as a "vehicle for carrying to the reader the thought and life of an isolated group among the varied peoples that make up the complex population of this Republic."

Harris seldom failed to capture perfectly the idiom of the Negro. When in *Gabriel Tolliver* a thief was caught in the chicken house, Harris captured the mind and speech of the colored offender in one pleading sentence. "I wish you'd please, suh, excusen me dis time." William Dean Howells revealed one of the reasons for the almost universal appeal of the dialect: the laughter resulted from the discrepancy between the subject matter and the intellectual level of the speaker. Howells said of "Marse Chan" and "Meh Lady": "These pieces, and others akin to them, are felt out to the last halting syllable, with equal patience and frankness, in a speech which is always below the material; for Mr. Page's wish is to show how great and beautiful things appeared to humble witnesses who could not quite utter them."[4] Unfortunately, though, dialect had the tendency to make all Negroes comic as well as humble. Many readers assumed that because a story or a poem was in dialect it was necessarily a humorous piece. This fact became one of the main obstacles to the serious treatment of the Negro in American literature, for it made the colored man appear grotesque and funny even when he was supposed to be taken straight and serious. Harris, however, used dialect for realism and was critical of those who abused its use. In the Introduction to *Uncle Remus* he labeled as "intolerable misrepresentations" the speech of the minstrel stage.

Negro dialect sketches and poems filled American newspapers, magazines, and books until well into the twentieth century. (Even today a newspaper series, "Hambone's Meditations" by J. P. Alley, is syndicated throughout the South.) Southerners were often accused of exploiting it by turning out sub-literary junk. Thomas Nelson Page in 1891 felt the need for defending its users. "Whilst it has unquestionably been carried to unwarrantable excess, most of the Southern writers have used dialect simply as the vehicle to convey local color, and, marked as is the realistic, it is subordinated in their work to the romantic."[5] Already, however, dialect writing was on the decline. The means had too often become the end.

Folklore

Recently Professor John T. Flanagan has written: "To me one of the most exciting and interesting approaches to literature in the twentieth century is provided by the study of folklore and its impact on writing."[6] Professor Flanagan applied his statement to all of literature; it is especially pertinent to Negro humor. A large part of Southern humor centered around Negro folklore. His superstitions, his quaint (and to him logical) explanations of why certain things are, his belief in the supernatural, his vivid and wild imagination—all these combined to make his folklore tales popular with the whites. The student of Negro humor cannot ignore folklore.

The most conspicuous example of Negro folklore is the animal tale. Animals that talk are not a peculiar contribution of the Negro to humor; they have been around since Chaucer—and Aesop. In German beast epics Brer Fox was known as Reineke Fuchs and in French as Maître Renard. The animal tale is common to most literatures of the world. In American humor the recorder of Negro folklore tales who stands above all others is Joel Chandler Harris. His Uncle Remus stories are not a collection of black-face comicalities or a miscellany of coon wisecracks; they are a serious contribution to American literature. Harris was even afraid that his use of dialect might induce some readers to think of them as being on the level of the minstrel. But their genuineness as folklore is attested to by Harris himself in a letter to the *Folk-Lore Journal* of London. "It is a misfortune, perhaps, from an English point of view, that the stories in that volume are rendered in the American Negro dialect, but it was my desire to preserve the stories as far as I might be able in the form in which I heard them, and to preserve also if possible the quaint humor of the Negro. It is this humor that gives the collection its popularity in the United States, but I think you will find the stories more important than humorous should you take the trouble to examine them. Not one of them is cooked, and not one nor any part of one is an invention of mine. They are all genuine folklore tales."[7] Harris based his tales on African myths and animal stories he had heard from slaves during his boyhood in Putnam County, Georgia; however, it was his genius that preserved the stories and set them in their immortal form. Each tale is carefully contrived.

Harris wrote the Uncle Remus tales to exploit the humor and folklore of the Negro, to reconcile North and South by showing amicable relations between whites and blacks, and to characterize the Negro. Kenneth Lynn has offered yet another reason: in the tales Harris found solace for the materialism of the Gilded Age. Utilitarianism in education, Harris felt, had failed to initiate children into the mystery that is in all life. He thought that children and the former slave were alike in their love of mystery and their attraction to black African lore; therefore when he started writing the tales he used the framework of an old Negro telling them to a small white child. Like Mrs. Stowe's Uncle Tom and Little Eva and Mark Twain's Huck Finn and Nigger Jim (and more recently Faulkner's Lucas Beauchamp and Chick Mallison), Harris' two characters are isolated from the prosaic world of white adults. In Uncle Remus' cabin the old man and the little boy enter another world of beauty, mystery, terror, laughter. To them it is a more believable world than the one outside. In their make-believe world the old Negro and the white child delight in stories of the triumph of the weak—the rabbit—symbolically perhaps the Negro. Lynn concluded that Harris showed that the bears and wolves of the adult materialistic world of business could be outwitted and bettered. Harris' interest in the folklore of the tales was genuine but incidental; his real interest lay in their implications for weak and downtrodden humanity.[8]

As Harris admitted, his Uncle Remus stories were popular mainly for their humor. A recent critic has said that the humor of the tales is "like molasses stirred into hominy grits."[9] Toulmin in his *Social Historians* is probably right in stressing the fact that it was humor that made the tales so appealing and popular. This humor he described as "kindly in its bearing, apt in its application, commingling satire, gentle ridicule, and the legitimate failings of the actors in a pleasing whole. It is American humor; the basic, fundamental qualities are the breath of the spirit of a Mark Twain" (p. 145).

The humor of the tales is based largely upon exaggeration and ridiculous comparisons. Brer Rabbit comments on high prices in these words: "I'm des about ez fat ez de mule mon had, which he hatter tie a knot in his tail fer ter keep 'm fum slippin' thro de collar." The tricks played by the animals on each other afford much humor. Uncle Remus and the little boy are delighted each time Brer Rabbit tricks and outwits Brer Fox or each time Brer Terrypin wins in a contest of strength with Brer Bar. Uncle Remus' mimicking of animal calls and signals is also amusing. The old Negro's knowledge of backwoods life seems exhaustive. Humor also derives from the assumption of the dress and personality traits of humans by the animals. The rabbit, for example, is curious, sly, and weak; the wolf is stupid; the fox is curious; and the terrapin is slow and self-armored.

Several of the sketches deal in a cruel humor reminiscent of the humor of the Old Southwest. "The Awful Fate of Mr. Wolf" (*Uncle Remus*), for example, tells of how Brer Rabbit killed Brer Wolf by pretending to offer a chest as a refuge from the dogs. When Brer Wolf is securely in the chest, Brer Rabbit takes a kettle of boiling water and pours it through holes he has bored ostensibly to give Brer Wolf air. With the hot water streaming in on him, Brer Wolf asks: "W'at dat I feel, Brer Rabbit?" "You feels de fleas a bitin', Brer Wolf." "Dey er bitin' mighty hard, Brer Rabbit." "Tu'n over on de udder side, Brer Wolf." "W'at dat I feel now, Brer Rabbit?" "Still you feels de fleas, Brer Wolf." "Dey er eatin' me up, Brer Rabbit." These were the last words of Brer Wolf "kase de scaldin' water done de bizness." Most of the Uncle Remus stories are not quite so unfeeling as this one; but as a rule they are all more akin to the humor of the Old Southwest in situation and approach than are Harris' more conventional writings.

Uncle Remus includes the representative and best known Negro folklore stories by Harris. To an extent, all the animal stories in the book are allegorical. The only figure approaching a fixed symbol, however, is Brer Rabbit, the weak and helpless but sly and mischievous mask for the Negro. The Bear, the Wolf, the Fox are his adversaries who symbolize threats, sometimes from the white world and sometimes from his own colored world. From the first sketch, "Uncle Remus Initiates the Little Boy," Brer Rabbit remains alive only because he lives by his wits. When Brer Fox tells him he wants to "have some confab,"

Brer Rabbit rightly suspects foul play and retorts, "All right, Brer Fox, but you better holler fum whar you stan'. I'm monstus full er fleas dis mawnin'." An appropriate commentary on the shrewdness of Brer Rabbit is Uncle Remus' closing remark. "En Brer Fox ain't never kotch 'im yit, en w'at's mo', honey, he ain't gwineter." In fact, the rabbit outwits all the stronger animals. According to Uncle Remus: "Fox atter 'im, Buzzard atter 'im, en Cow atter 'im, en dey ain't kotch 'im yit."* Brer Rabbit finally meets his match in Brer Terrypin, a weaker and slyer animal than he, when the terrapin wins a race by stationing members of his family at each post in the race. Another sketch in which Brer Rabbit is not allowed to get away with his rascality deals with his attempt to swindle Brer Buzzard out of his share of a crop they worked on halves. In this sketch the rabbit becomes the white landlord and the buzzard the Negro sharecropper.

Many of the tales are etiological. "The Story of the Deluge and How It Came About" shows how a great apocryphal flood happened. Uncle Remus says that back in the days when "creeturs had lots mo' sense dan dey got now" the animals held an assembly "fer ter sorter straighten out marters en hear de complaints." During the session an elephant accidentally stepped on a crawfish "en dey wa'n't nuff er dat Crawfish lef' fer ter tell dat he'd bin dar." All the crawfishes got mad and raised a ruckus. When another was stamped to death, they could restrain themselves no longer and "dey bo'd inter de groun' en kep' on bo'in twel dey onloost de fountains er de earf; en de waters squirt out, en riz higher en higher twel de hills wuz kivvered, en de creeturs wuz all drownded; en all bekaze dey let on 'mong deyselves dat dey wuz bigger dan de Crawfishes."

Other stories explaining origins or phenomena are "How Mr. Rabbit Lost His Fine Bushy Tail," "Why Mr. Possum Has No Hair on His Tail," and "Why the Negro Is Black." There was probably no more popular subject for Negro folklore than his color. In "Why the Negro Is Black" Uncle Remus explains racial differences to the little white boy. "Way back yander. In dem times we 'uz all un us black; we 'uz all niggers tergedder, an 'cordin' ter all de 'counts w'at I years fokes 'uz gittin 'long 'bout ez well in dem days ez dey is now. But atter w'ile de news come dat dere wuz a pon' er water some'rs in de naberhood, w'ich ef dey'd get inter dey'd be wash off nice en w'ite, en den one un um, he fine de place en make er splunge inter de pon', en come out w'ite ez a town gal. En den, bless grashus! w'en de fokes seed it, dey make a break fer de pon', en dem w'at wuz de soopless, dey got in fus' en dey come out w'ite; den dem w'at wuz nex' soopless, dey got in nex', en dey come out merlatters; en dey wuz sech a crowd un um dat dey might nigh use de water up, w'ich w'en dem yuthers

---

* One of the many versions of the tar-baby story is recorded by Mary Ross Banks in *Bright Days in the Old Plantation Time* (pp. 204-16). This tale is close to Uncle Remus's version through Brer Rabbit's escape in the briar patch, but Mrs. Banks added another episode in which Brer Wolf tries another trick. Sis Wolf sends word to Brer Rabbit that her husband is dead and that before he died he insisted that only Brer Rabbit lay him out. Brer Rabbit goes to see the body, but suspecting a trick, he decides to make sure that Brer Wolf is dead. "Brer Rabbit tuck out hiz backerbox, an' groun' up some rabbit-backer fine like snuff, an' sprinklet it in brer Wolf's nose, an' dat made brer Wolf sneeze, so den brer Rabbit knowed brer Wolf wuz 'playin' possum.'" Again the sly rabbit escapes death.

come 'long, de morest dey could do wuz paddle about wid der foots en dabble in it wid der han's. Dem wuz de niggers, en down ter dis day dey ain't no w'ite 'bout a nigger 'ceppin de pa'ms er der han's en de soles er der foot." The tale has an explanation for other races too. Uncle Remus tells his little auditor that Indians and Chinese have to be counted along with the mulattoes but that they differ from them because "dem w'at git ter de pon' time nuff fer ter git der head in de water, de water hit onkink der ha'r."[*]

Generally, the attitude of Uncle Remus toward the little boy is one of affectionate condescension. He will not be hurried into a story nor will he explain a point or continue a story he's stopped—at least not until another sitting. The white boy's occasional incredulity is ignored or brushed off lightly by the old Negro. Once when Uncle Remus speaks of the reality of witches, the boy says his papa has told him there are no witches. But Uncle Remus has a ready answer: "Mars John ain't live long ez I is. . . . He ain't bin broozin' 'roun' all hours er de night en day." Uncle Remus' faith in his legends could not be shaken by education or reason.

Second only to Harris in exploitation of Negro folk tales in humor was Anne Virginia Culbertson. In her sketches Aunt 'Phrony and Aunt Nancy tell "how" and "why" tales to their white charges. In artistry some of her stories rival even those of Uncle Remus. "How Mr. Terrapin Lost His Beard," for example, is one of the best constructed of the folklore tales (*At the Big House*). After a Negro frolic in the cookhouse, which the white children are allowed to watch and enjoy, Aunt 'Phrony is persuaded to tell what she insists is an Indian story of how the terrapin lost his beard. Before she begins the story proper she explains that she will not be "talkin' 'bout de li'l ol' no-kyount tarr'pins de has dese days" but " 'bout de ol' time Tarr'pin whar wuz a gre't chieft an' a big fighter." In those days Tarr'pin and Mistah Wi'yum Wil' Tukkey were good friends. There was, however, one point of dissension: the terrapin had a beard and wattles; the turkey had none and was jealous. He decided to take them from the terrapin and asked: "I wish, suh, you lemme put 'em on fer a minnit, so's 't I kin see ef I becomes 'em ez good ez w'at you does." His friend lent them to him; but after admiring himself in the water, he decided to keep them, saying: "I b'lieve I becomes 'em mo'n w'at you does, 'kase my neck so long an' thick seem lak I needs 'em ter set hit off mo'n w'at you does wid dat shawt li'l neck er yo'n whar you keeps tuck 'way in yo' shell half de time anyways." But the terrapin maintained that he couldn't part with them. He chased the turkey unsuccessfully. He consulted conjurers for aid, and they told him they'd put little bones in the turkey's legs to slow him down. All this, however, was to no avail. Aunt 'Phrony concludes her tale. "But seem lak de conjers thought Mistah Tarr'pin wuz faster'n w'at he wuz, er dat Mistah Tukkey 'z slower'n w'at *he* wuz, 'kase Tarr'pin ain't nuver ketch up wid him

---

[*] In *What Happened to Me* (pp. 48-52), Mrs. LaSalle Corbell Pickett included a more detailed telling of this same tale. See also James J. McDonald, *Life in Old Virginia* (p. 211), for an old Negro's explanation of why Sunday was set aside as a day of rest.

yit, an' w'ats mo', de tarr'pins is still doin' widout by'uds and wattles an' de gobblers is still wearin' 'em an' swellin' roun' shown' off ter de gals, steppin' ez high ez ef dem li'l bones w'at de conjers putt dar wan't in der laigs. . . ."

Negro folk tales often involved a belief in conjurers. During her tale about the terrapin and the turkey, Aunt 'Phrony stops to explain to a white child what a conjurer is. "Well, now, honey . . . I dunno ez I kin jes' rightly tell you, but deys w'at de Injuns calls 'medicin'-men' an' dey doctors de sick folks an' he'ps de hunters ter git game an' de gals ter git beaux, an' putts spells on folks an' mek 'em do jes' 'bout w'at dey want 'em to."

Other tales told by Aunt 'Phrony include "Mr. Hare Tries to Get a Wife" and "The Woman Who Married an Owl." Both of these stories, she tells the children, are Indian tales. The occasion for the first story is a nutting expedition. When Aunt 'Phrony and the children have found all the walnuts they want, they sit down to rest and see a hare run by near them. This prompts the story of "de time Mistah Hyar' try ter git him a wife." The hare, she begins, had spent his life frolicking around as "a no-kyount bachelder"; but one day he took stock of himself and decided it was time to get married; "so he primp hisse'f up an' slick his hya'r down wid b'argrease an' stick a raid hank'cher in his ves'-pockit an' pick him a button-hole f'um a lady's gyarden, an' den he go co'tin' dis gal an' dat gal an' tu'rr gal." But the poor hare had no success because, Aunt 'Phrony reasons, "he done so many mean tricks an' wuz sech a hyarum-skyarum dat dey wuz all 'feared ter tek up wid 'im."

Finally the hare decided on a foolproof scheme to get a wife: he spread the word "dat a big meetin' bin hilt an' a law passed dat ev'yb'dy gotter git ma'ied." Surely, he thought, this plan would bring him a wife. A day was appointed when all the "creeturs" were to meet and mate. They all dressed in their "Sunday clo'es" in preparation. Aunt 'Phrony describes the meeting. "De gals dey all stan' up in line an' de men go struttin' mighty biggitty up an' down befo' 'em, showin' off an' makin' manners an' sayin', 'Howdy, ladiz, howdy, howdy!' An' de gals dey'd giggle an' twis' an' putt a finger in de cornders er der moufs, an' w'en a man step up ter one uv 'em ter choose her out, she'd fetch 'im a li'l tap an' say, 'Hysh! g'way f'um yer, man! better lemme 'lone!' an' den she'd giggle an' snicker some mo', but I let you know she wuz sho' ter go wid him in de een'." Still the hare had no success. When the selection was over, every man had a wife but him—and no woman was left over for him. But the hare was not discouraged yet. He consoled himself: "Ef I kain't git me a gal, I kin git me a widdy, an' some folks laks dem de bes', anyhows." To put this new plan into effect he broadcast among the gullible "creeturs" that another law had been passed which said that the world was overpopulated and there must be a big battle to kill off some of the people. This plan, he was sure, would result in many widows and he would get a wife. His scheme, however, didn't work because soon after the battle started his deception was found out, and he was given a good beating by the other animals. The story ends: " . . . an stidder gittin' him a wife he got him a hide dat smart f'um haid ter heels." Aunt 'Phrony adds that "w'en my daddy tell dat tale he useter een' her up dis-a-way, 'An mebby Hyar' git de bes' uv 'em, atter all, 'kase w'en you git a hidin', de smart's soon over, but w'en you git a wife, de mis'ry done come ter stay.'"

"The Woman Who Married an Owl" is Aunt 'Phrony's story about an owl that turned itself into a man and was courted by an Indian girl. One of the skeptical children asks how a girl could mistake an owl for a man; and though Aunt 'Phrony, like Uncle Remus, is little bothered by logic or probability in her tales, she reasons: "Well, honey de tale ain' tell dat, but I done study hit out dis-a-way, dat mo'n likely de gal bin turnin' up her nose at some young Injun man, an' outer spite he done gone an' got some witch ter putt a spell on her so's't de Owl 'ud look lak a man an' she 'ud go an' th'ow husse'f away on a ol' no-kyount bu'd."

Another storyteller creation by Miss Culbertson is Aunt Nancy. One of her favorite stories is "Why Moles Have Hands." One day, reminded by a dead mole the children show her, she tells her story about "huccome moleses have han'ses." There was a time, she begins, when "de moleses useter be folks, sho'-'nuff folks, dough dey is all swunk up ter dis size an' der han's is all dat's lef ter tell de tale." The moles used to be high and mighty folks. "W'ats mo', dey wuz so uppish dey thought de yearf wuz too low down fer 'em ter run der eyes over, so dey went 'long wid der haids r'ared an' der eyes all time lookin' up, stidder down." This superior attitude did not please the Lord, who said to Himself, "Who is dese yer folks, anyhows, war gittin' so airish, walkin' up an' down an' back an' fo'th on my yearf an' spurnin' hit so's't dey spread kyarpets 'twix' hit an' der footses, treatin' my yearf, w'at I done mek, lak 'twuz de dirt un'need der footses, an' 'spisin' der feller creeturs an' excusin' 'em er being common, an' keepin' der eyes turnt up all de time, ez ef dey wuz too good ter look at de things I done mek an' putt on my yearf?" He is angry at such behavior and He does something about it. In Aunt Nancy's words: "So de Lawd He pass jedgment on de moleses. Fus' He tuck an' made 'em lose der human shape an' den He swunk 'em up ontwel dey 'z no bigger'n dey is now, dat 'uz ter show 'em how no-kyount dey wuz in His sight. Den bekase dey thought derse'fs too good ter walk 'pun de bare groun' He sont 'em ter live un'need hit, whar dey hatter dig an' scratch der way 'long. Las' uv all He tuck an' tuck 'way der eyes an' made 'em blin', dat's 'kase dey done 'spise ter look at der feller creeturs. But he feel kind er saw'ry fer 'em w'en He git dat fur, an' He ain' wanter punish 'em too haivy, so He lef' 'em dese silk clo'es whar I done tol' you 'bout, an' dese han's whar you kin see fer yo'se'fs is human, an' I reckon bofe dem things putt 'em in min' er w'at dey useter be an' mek 'em 'umble." Aunt Nancy adds a moral to the tale. "An' dat orter l'arn you w'at comes er folks 'spisin' der feller creeturs, an' I want y'all ter 'member dat nex' time I year you call dem Thompson chillen 'trash.'" One of her little Northern charges indicates that he can't see any use for moles; but Aunt Nancy maintains that "de Lawd have some use fer ev'y creetur He done mek." Moles, she reminds him, eat bugs and worms. "Sidesen dat, jes' gimme one'r de claws er dat mole, an' lemme hang hit roun' de neck uv a baby whar cuttin' his toofs, an' I boun' you, ev'y toof in his jaws gwine come bustin' thu his goms without nair' a ache er a pain ter let him know dey's dar. Don't talk ter me 'bout de moleses bein' wufless! I done walk de flo' too much wid cryin' babies not ter know de use er moleses."

These folk tales told by Negro spokesmen and recorded by Harris, Miss Culbertson, and others were a part of a way of life that emancipation and education soon terminated. Older Negroes continued telling the legends after the war, but many of the younger freedmen scoffed at such vestiges of a superstitious and enslaved past. The educated Negro thought he had discovered infinitely better explanations for the "how" and the "why" of things.

The Freedman

After he was freed, the Negro had to begin shifting for himself. If he was now his own master, he was also his own provider. This new status of responsibility was a hardship to many freedman. Even the one who refused to cut the strings that bound him to his old master found that things were not the same. The Emancipation Proclamation and the Thirteenth Amendment had, in effect, meant a new birth for the American Negro. He was on his own, and his experiences provided many themes for humorists.

According to the general view, the freedman was carefree, irresponsible, and improvident. Some lines in *Plantation Songs* by Martha Young show this stereotype:

> *Times is change sence niggers is free,*
> *But he still love to laugh, and dat I see—*
> *Us'll mortgage up de mule, and de calf, and de cow—*
> *And get out of payin' some way how!*
>
> . . . .
>
> *And whatever happen at de end of de year*
> *Nigger happy to-day and to-morrow don't keer!* (p. 68).

The indigent freedman, the humorist said, could always depend on his white folks to get him out of a famine. The younger Negroes, not trained by slavery, would not do so well. In *Mexican Mustang* Sweet and Knox put the following sentiments into the mouth of an old man: ". . . de risin' generation ob de cullud people is a gwine to de debbil as fas' as dey can, yes, sah, for a fac'. . . . De ole timey niggers ain't got much sense, but dey is hones', an' most ob dem works; but de young folks is de no accountest trash! Sakes alive, sah! dey cares for nuffin but polertics and whiskey" (p. 78).

The Negro was consistently treated as an oddity and an object of amusement per se. His alleged weaknesses for lying and stealing—even his religion —were considered appropriate themes for humor. In appearance he was frequently made to look like a baboon. Old Si, for example, tells an anecdote about "a big fat negro, with a pair of lips like sides of middling meat." He was con-

227

sidered fair game for any humorist or would-be humorist—from the paragrapher for the Union Springs *Times* in Alabama to O. Henry in New York, whose weekly, *Rolling Stone,* offered such examples of Negro humor as this:

Please decide a bet for us. My friend says that the sentence, "The negro bought the watermelon of the farmer" is correct, and I say it should be "The negro bought the watermelon from the farmer." Which is correct?

Neither. It should read, "The negro stole the watermelon from the farmer" (p. 233).

The humorist depicted the Negro stealing not only watermelons, but chickens from the chicken house, hams from the smokehouse, roasting ears from the cornfield, and anything else that was not tied or nailed down. He was frequently pictured as trying to get by without working. In the *Arkansaw Traveler* of October 3, 1885, for example, the following squib appeared: "The cotton picking season has opened and the 'smooth' negro from town has gone down into the country to shuffle cards, 'shoot craps' and make his living by the sweat of another man's brow."

The Negro who refused to go on playing the role of Uncle Tom was usually pilloried. If he attempted to get an education, he was ridiculed as an upstart and an asserter of equality with the white man. In "A Gentleman Vagabond" (*Colonel Carter and Other Tales*) F. Hopkinson Smith described sympathetically a former slave who had raised himself from "the pit of slavery" and was now a valet in the North. But a Southerner disliked the Negro's "affectation" and commented sarcastically: "Yes, I know—education and thirty dollars a month. All very fine, but give me the old house-servants of the South—the old Anthonys, and Keziahs, and Rachels. They never went about rigged up like a stick of black sealing-wax in a suit of black co't-plaster. They were easy-goin' and comfortable. Yo' interest was their interest; they bore yo' name, looked after yo' children, and could look after yo' house, too. Now see this nigger of Jack's; he's better dressed than I am, tips round as solemn on his toes as a marsh crane, and yet I'll bet a dollar he's as slick and cold-hearted as a high-water clam. That's what education has done for *him*." As suggested in this passage, much of the Southern dislike of the "new" Negro was motivated by economic jealousy.

Even leaders like Booker T. Washington, President of Tuskegee Institute, contributed to the caricature. Washington, to illustrate the vanity of the Negro and his desire to show off his knowledge, frequently told an anecdote. General Sherman had been told that colored guards would sometimes allow doubtful persons to pass just to exercise their authority to do so; so he decided to check the report. He disguised himself and tried to pass by a colored sentry, who stopped him and asked for the countersign. Sherman gave several incorrect ones—Roxbury, Medford, Charleston—but (Washington would conclude, adding the punch line) the Negro was not to be taken in. "Now seea heah—yo' can go fru th' whole blamed joggrafy, but Massa Sherman he done say that nobody can get pas' me wifout sayin' 'Cambridge'!"[10]

Often the upstart is ridiculed by a member of his own race—usually an old "uncle" or "aunt." In Walter Hines Page's *The Southerner*, in reply to a question about his opinion of a new school for Negroes, Uncle Ephraim says, "Don' set no sto' by it. . . . Dey has dere, 'cordin' to what I hears, de stuck-up young niggers what 'brudder yer dis' and 'brudder yer dat'—preacher niggers what ain't got no ol'-fashion' 'ligion. Dey don' think much on 'em 'bout here" (p. 142.) In addition, Uncle Ephraim represented a majority of his race in his attitude toward the Negro in the professions, especially law and medicine. Once when he was sick, the old man was administered to by a colored physician. When he was well enough to protest, this is what he said: "See here. I don' wan' no nigger a-doctorin o' me. I'se good enough to have white doctors when I'se sick. I'se allers had 'em, same as ol' Marster had afore me" (p. 152). This preference for white doctors and lawyers still persists among many Negroes.

A most amusing story is Sherwood Bonner's "Hieronymus Pop and the Baby." In addition to its farcical humor it also contains an implicit criticism of the new educated Negro.[11] The complete story is worth reciting here. One day 'Onymus Pop, a small Negro boy, is told by his mother to mind the baby while the family goes to a hanging. He is disgruntled. "It was either to tend the baby, or mix the cow's food, or to card wool, or cut wood, or to pick a chicken, or wash up the floor, or to draw water, or to sprinkle the clothes—always something." The little boy never has a minute's peace. His mother even makes him study the alphabet, which is being taught him by his sister Savannah "who went to school, put on airs, and was always clean." When the family leave, he tries to put Tiddlekins to sleep, but in the heat the baby stays awake and frets. Taking stock of the trouble, Hieronymus decides that nothing is wrong with the baby that a cooling-off won't cure. He studies how this can be accomplished, and suddenly thinks of the well where they put milk, butter, and fresh meats to keep them cool. "If I was ter hang Tiddlekins down de well," he reflected, "'t wouldn't be mo' dan three jumps of a flea befo' he's as cool as Christmas." Quickly he puts his idea into execution, stuffing the little baby into the bucket and taking off his suspenders to tie him in. In the coolness of the well, the baby stops crying; and Hieronymus lies down and goes to sleep. He is, however, soon called away to a dog fight, forgetting all about his little brother cooling off in the well.

When the Pop family returns from the hanging, they find the house deserted. Then Savannah remembers pompously, "I witnessed Hieronymus . . . as I wandered from school. He was with a multitude of boys, who cheered, without a sign of disapp*er*ation, two canine beasts, that tore each other in deadly feud." Mother Pop translates for the rest of the family. "Yer don't mean ter say, Sissy, dat 'Onymus Pop is gone ter a dog-fight?" Realizing that the boy has deserted the baby, they all begin a search, "under the bed, in the bed, in the wash-tub and the soup-kettle; behind the wood-pile, and in the pea vines; up the chimney, and in the ash-hopper," but the poor baby is nowhere to be found. They finally call in the hound, and he leads them to the well and the baby. Mr. Pop mutters, "Dar'll be annuder hangin' in town befo' long, and *Hi won't miss dat hangin'*."

229

Tiddlekins is pulled up cautiously. "He looked like a jack-in-the-box. But he was cool, Tiddlekins was, no doubt of that." To revive the child, they decide to give him a whiskey bath, and send down to a white neighbor's for some bourbon. The child becomes warm and lively, and even winks at his father, lying "on his back, placidly sucking a pig's tail." When Hieronymus comes home, Mr. Pop takes down from the mantelpiece "a long thin something" and leads the erring boy by the left ear out to the woodpile. In this and other humorous sketches Miss Bonner showed the dramatic possibilities of the Negro in brief fiction. She was one of the first writers to use the genuine dialect, the first Southern woman to deal with the Negro, and the first writer to treat him separate from the white man. Her humor is typically farcical but restrained. Her satire—the new Negro in Savannah Pop—is usually gentle.

The educated Negro was usually ridiculed as merely pseudo-educated. His talk was filled with malapropisms. *Texas Siftings,* for example, printed the following anecdote (February 2, 1889).

Gilhooly—Sam, if President Harrison were to invite you to accept a position in his Cabinet what would you do?

Sam Johnsing—I should be obleeged, sah, ter notify him dat sarcumstances repugnant to de acquiesce would prevent my exceptin' de inwite. I has a two-dollar job ob whitewashin' on hand, sah.

An anecdote in the *Arkansaw Traveler* (February 10, 1883) also poked fun.

"I hear that your son is becoming quite an educated man," said a gentleman to a negro acquaintance.

"Er edycated man, why I reckon he is. Dat boy ain't afraid ter talk ter nobody. Dat boy, why boss, he can get on de train an' talk to de conductor."

Connected with and growing out of the humorous treatment of the Negro was a concern for the serious problems associated with the freedman. In sketches by Harry Stillwell Edwards ("De Valley an' de Shadder," "Minc"), Jeannette Walworth ("Blind Joe and the New People"), Charles Chesnutt (*The Wife of His Youth, and Other Stories of the Color Line*), and Paul Laurence Dunbar ("The Ordeal at Mt. Hope," "At Shaft II") such themes as lynchings, murders, labor unions, and prejudice appear. And out of the earlier caricatures of the Negro was developed a new type by Sarah Barnwell Elliott ("An Accident") and Thomas Dixon (*The Leopard's Spots, The Clansman*): the dangerous brute-Negro. Throughout the period 1865-1914, however, the comic, carefree, harmless darky remained the most popular type in humor.

Like Miss Bonner's sketches, those by Will Allen Dromgoole follow the trend toward treating the Negro apart from white characters. Before the war he had almost invariably been shown as a background figure in connection with his white owners. Now he was beginning to play major roles—often the only roles—in humorous stories. Two stories in the collection *Cinch* by Miss Dromgoole deal exclusively with Negro life; the one or two whites are negligible.

"George Washington's Bufday" is an account of the confusion in the mind of an ignorant old woman between the name of her son and that of the Father of the Country. Taking butter in to sell, George Washington's mother leaves him at home to mind the baby, after having scolded him for wanting to go fishing instead. Approaching town, she meets a gang working on a bridge. One of them tells her that they are trying to finish the work today "bekase we don' work ter-morror. Hit's George Washin'ton's bufday." She is astounded that the birthday of her son should be a holiday, but she doesn't want to appear unknowledgeable. "Shet yo' mouf. I don' want hear none yo' big talk. I wonder if yer takes me fur a fool, or a what? Letting on I don't know when's George Washin'ton's bufday! Hit ain' ter-morrer, I tell yer. Ter-morrer ain' no mo' his bufday dan it's mine. I reckon I ought ter know when George Washin'ton wuz bawn. I reckin I wuz dar, at de bawning."

With this pronouncement she goes on her way, not understanding why the workman is laughing and calling out after her, "Look out, folkses; look out. Dar goes de ol'est 'oman in de worl'."

In town she tells the merchant that she will return the next day. He tells her that he will be closed in observance of George Washington's birthday. When she shows surprise, he explains, "We all love George Washington, Aunt Jane." She goes to her wagon very puzzled. "Dat chile sholy been and done something and not let on ter we-alls, his pappy and me." Then she remembers something that confuses her even more: George Washington was born in the summer and it is now February. As a last resort to clear up her quandary, she consults Marse Tom, her husband's old master. He would surely tell her the truth; but he only confirms what the others have been saying: the next day is a holiday in celebration of George Washington's birthday.

Still not clear about it all, she nonetheless makes up her mind to celebrate the birthday, too. She returns to the grocery store, buys back a pound of the butter, two pounds of cheese, and a dozen sticks of striped peppermint candy. "Ef ev'ybody else ain' gwine to begrudge de chile de celebrating, I reckin sholy his own mammy ain' gwine do dat. . . . I'se gwine straight home and kill a hin." She plans a feast complete with raisin cake. At home Little Wash doesn't understand his mother's sudden change in attitude toward him, his sudden rise to greatness. Preparations for the dinner go on until Uncle Jake, the father and husband, returns at night. He hears the tale and laughingly explains that the townspeople had been talking about another George Washington. For a minute Aunt Jane looked as if she might become angry; then she laughs, and says "I done kilt a hin . . . and it's got ter be et, naw, sah; George Washin'ton am gwine hab dat bufday. He been mighty handy he'ping 'bout de baby and all, and he kin hab two bufdays dis year well ez not." Thus Miss Dromgoole proved again that the Negro independent of the white man could be a fascinating subject for humor.

"Sweet 'Lasses" has no white characters at all. The story concerns the rivalry between two colored sections of town expressed here in a cakewalk contest.

The Smiling Phoenix

Liza Ann, called "Sweet 'Lasses" by her beau, is to compete with a rival from the other section. Her sweetheart has told her that he wants to walk her home after the contest and help her eat the cake—if she wins it. This she determines to do. She squeezes her feet into a pair of size-two red shoes. It is painful, but she remembers her beau's promise and bears it. At the cakewalk her tiny red slippers create a sensation. But her opponent has pulled a sly trick: she has taken pains to dress up the rest of herself so that her loose shoes won't be noticed when she walks. She walks first and finishes in a storm of applause, one admirer telling her that "dey ain' been no sech walkin' as dat, not sence de war." On the other hand, Sweet 'Lasses' midget shoes prove her ruin, for when she starts to walk, a stitch breaks, then another and another, and she begins to limp; and finally the shoes rip open. She loses the prize; her beau takes the winner home with her cake. Sweet 'Lasses holds her tears until she gets home; then she lets loose, sobbing. "Hit ain' de angul cake . . . I don't keer nothin' 'bout de ole angul cake; I don't keer fur de money flung 'way on de shoes, an' I don't keer 'bout dey-alls laffin' at me,—*but I heerd him call dat yaller gal his Sweet 'Lasses!*" The everyday life of the freedman continued to offer almost unlimited possibilities for humor.

Though published in 1922, Ambrose Gonzales' *The Black Border* includes humorous sketches of Carolina and Georgia coastal Negroes written before 1893. Gonzales wrote in a Gullah dialect, however, which is almost unreadable. Domestic life from weddings to debates is pictured in these sketches. "Waiting till the Bridegrooms Come" is a typical piece from the collection. Minzacter Singleton, middle-aged, is hauled into court by Julia Singleton, who accuses him of throwing her over and marrying "Paul Jenkin' grumma jes' 'cause 'e got fo' cow en' I ent got no cow." As evidence of their marriage she presents a certificate—a "stuhstiffikit" she calls it—but it only states, "I marry Mistuh Singleton to Missis Singleton." Both her brother and her "locus pastuh" (local pastor) refuse to testify in her behalf. Desperately, she sighs, "Please Gawd . . . I gone en try fuh ketch my juntlemun en' I fetch'um yuh, en' *him* lie. Den I gone en' ketch my bredduh en' fetch'um yuh, en' *him* lie. Den I gone en' ketch de stuhstiffikit en' *him* lie; en' fin'lly at las', I ketch de locus pastuh en' fetch'um yuh, en', 'fo' de Lawd, *him* lie. Now, I gwine home en' fetch de six bridegroom' w'at bin to dis wedd'n' w'en I marry dis juntlemun—w'ich my sistuh Amy bin one un de bridegroom'—en' I know berry *well* dem will crucify dat dis is my juntlemun." But "de six bridegrooms" never come to certify her marriage, and she is left without a husband. Joel Chandler Harris and a few other humorists occasionally wrote in Gullah, but because of its difficulty it was never a popular medium.

Two sketches from *His Defense* by Harry Stillwell Edwards deal with humorous incidents. "Charley and the Possum" is an account of how a country Negro wins his case when he is brought into court for allegedly stealing a town Negro's steel trap with an opossum in it. The special jury is composed of country Negroes, and shrewdly appealing to their prejudice, he is found not guilty. Later a juror rationalizes the verdict: a possum is clearly no man's property until actually in his possession; the trap had been stolen not by Charley but by the opossum that happened to be attached to it.

"The Gum Swamp Debate" is ostensibly about a contest of wits on this resolution: "De pen am more pow'ful dan de powder." Actually it is a verbal battle between two types: the old-time Negro preacher and the "school darkey." The schoolman gets the better of every argument the older man puts forth on the power of the pen. He even refutes the argument that Lincoln freed the slaves with a proclamation. "An' dat writin' what Mr. Linkum nail up on de courthouse do'. Was you niggers free fum dat dey? No, sah. We had ter kill six hunderd million uv dem Yankees, an' dey had ter kill all our white folks, fus'; and hit took 'leven years ter do hit. Talk erbout de pen! Hit was de powdah sot you free." The darky was gradually losing out to the more militant, semi-educated man.

The Negro's habit, while plowing, of talking about, and to, his mule was the subject of many humorous poems. Will Allen Dromgoole's "Balaam" is a monologue in which the speaker seems to excoriate his mule, but underneath the barrage of criticism his fondness for the beast is evident. The name of the mule was carefully chosen.

> *'Cause I name him dest accordin'*
> *Ter meh religus lights;*
> *Name him fur de man 'uz sent*
> *Ter cuss de Isullites.*
>
> *Fur dis de stubb'nis' critter,*
> *I reckin, in de lan';*
> *En dat's huccome I name him*
> *Des lack dat Bible man.*

Balaam is the laziest and most stubborn mule in all creation.

> *Ef de worl' uz all a-burnin',*
> *En hit uz jedgmint day,*
> *Dat triflin' mule not lif' a huf*
> *Ter git out Satan's way.*[12]

Though Irwin Russell is best known for his portraits of slaves, he did not neglect the freedman of his day. He touched on most of the traits considered peculiarly Negro: his superstition, his ignorance of the world, his awe of legal terms, his trust in his religion, his childlike attitude toward nature, his habit of talking to animals, and above all, his pervasive humor. "Selling a Dog" deals with one's shrewdness in closing a deal and getting the better end of it. A fast-talking darky tries to sell to a white man a dog who "kin smell a 'coon fur half a mile." The owner insists, "I don' like to sell him, fur he's wuf his weight in gol'," and assures his victim, "If *you* didn't want him, sah, he nebber *should* be sol'." Pot-liquor is too good a watch dog to part with, the super-salesman continues, but "You kin hab him fur a dollar, seein's how it's *you*." Clinching the sale, "Don't you tell nobody, now what wuz de price you paid." And the Negro smugly chuckles to himself.

> *Dar! I's done got rid ob dat ar wretched dog at las'!*
> *Drownin' time wuz comin' fur him mighty precious fas'!*
> *Sol' him fur a dollar—Well! An' goodness knows de pup*
> *Isn't wuf de powder it'd take to blow him up!*[13]

To many, however, a man's best friend was truly his dog. William L. Visscher's "Jube's Old Yaller Dog" in *Harp of the South* shows the intense love of one old man for his dog. Jube is close to eighty, he says, "An' all dat's left fur me to love / Is dat ole yaller dog." He reminisces about pleasant times.

> *We's hunted, many a livelong night,*
> *De 'possum an' de coon,*
> *An' cotch 'em by de silvah light*
> *Of many a Southern moon.*

And he closes with a pledge to his faithful friend.

> *An' long as I is got a bite*
> *Er hominy an' hog,*
> *Ise gwine to 'vide—you jis' is right—*
> *Wid dat ole yaller dog.*

The love of fishing—even to the neglect of bread-and-butter matters—came in for a lot of mild satire. Sweet and Knox had this to say in *Mexican Mustang*. "He is calm and placid in presence of wire-grass in the cotton, unruffled and tranquil when surrounded by cockleburrs, patient and submissive when it rains (so that he cannot work), resigned and serene when the cow gets into the corn; and he will at any time curb a turbulent desire to hoe out ten acres of cotton, suppress a delirious craving to grub up roots, and choke back an impatient longing to destroy a patch of weeds, if the clouds show indications that catfish will bite" (pp. 633-34). Fondness for fish frys was another oft-exploited subject. Much later Roark Bradford in his *Ol' Man Adam an' His Chillun* showed a fish fry in heaven as the genesis of the world.

Ruth McEnery Stuart was a pioneer in writing about the transitional Negro. Her characters are generally more realistic than those of Harris, Page, or Paul Laurence Dunbar. The latter, however, was somewhat influenced by her earlier sketches. She was one of the first writers to show the Negro in his home life independent of his relations with the white man. After reading "Carlotta's Intended" and others of her stories, Kate Chopin wrote this: "Her humor is rich and plentiful, with nothing finical or feminine about it. Few of our women writers have equalled her in this respect. Even Page and Harris among the men have not surpassed her in the portrayal of that child-like exuberance which is so pronounced a feature of negro character, and which has furnished so much that is deliciously humorous and pathetic to our recent literature."[14]

With some twelve volumes of stories to her credit, she was perhaps the most prolific of the humorists treating the freedman.

Of the dozens of sketches she wrote, one of the most popular was "The Gentleman of the Plush Rocker" (*Napoleon Jackson*). It is a story of Rose Ann, a washerwoman, "not none o' yo' fancy laund'esses, but jes a plain grass-bleachin', sun-dryin', clair-starchin', muscle-polishin' washerwoman." It is even more the story of her indolent husband, Mr. Napoleon Jackson, Esquire, who is "the gentleman in starched linen, if you please." Usually found reclining in a chair near Rose Ann's washstand, "he was, as seen at a glance, a man of color, of leisure, of family, and of parts." It does not seem to worry him that his wife supports him and the children. Nor does Rose Ann mind working for her lord; she even likes to do it. Anyway, she explains, "He didn't *work* whilst he was *co'tin'* me an' *stop* arter he got *married*. No, sir. He co'ted me settin' down fannin' or layin' in de clover whilst I flung de hoe. An' I swapped off de hoe fer love an' duty arter I got married, 'ca'se a wash-bench is better'n a potato-hill to raise chillen roun'. No, I know it ain't none n' his fault. He *can't* work, 'ca'se his mammy she *marked* him so. She had been overworked befo' he was born, an' she marked her chile fer *rest*." The story is a panorama of washtub scenes with pickaninnies scampering around, of Negro laughter, talk, play, singing, dancing, working, shirking, of superstitious fear of "sperrits." It closes with a comic mock trial of Napoleon Jackson for vagrancy, in which Rose Ann's eloquent defense of her gentleman of leisure wins his acquittal.

The sketches in *Aunt Amity's Silver Wedding* are representative of Mrs. Stuart's treatments of the Negro. "Petty Larceny," "The Hair of the Dog," and "Thanksgiving on Crawfish Bayou" all portray the Negro humorously. The title story is set on the Louisiana coast and shows the ludicrousness of the attempt to ape the white man's ways. Aunt Amity is a former slave who, hearing of a white couple's celebration of their silver wedding anniversay and the gifts they get, decides to have one of her own. She has been told that anyone—black or white—can have a silver wedding. To get all the details straight, she consults a white lady, who, among other things, asks her if she expects all her guests to bring silver presents. Aunt Amity replies, "Well, mostly dimes an' two-bitses an' maybe fifty-centses; an' it mought be dat a few would drap us a dollar." She hurries to explain that she's planned a big feast for the celebration and that the donors will be repaid. She rationalizes. "You can't have but one silver weddin' in a lifetime, an' I wants to have it rackless, whilst I'm a-havin'!" Her husband is not to share in the silver presents because she's been married to "dat husban'" only "jes about five yeahs." She continues the revelation of her plans to the startled white woman, saying "dat's one o' de p'ints I come to insult you about. Sence Frank is been married five yeahs, I don't see why he can't draw for a wood weddin'." She hopes that he would get "a load o' fire wood or fat pine for kindlin'." The white woman is too amused to tell her that silver weddings are for people who have been married to each other for twenty-five years, and the anniversary plans go on. All the Negroes in the community gather for the occasion, and everything is fine until Aunt Amity's former husband appears uninvited to ask for his share of the silver presents. Her five-year husband beats him up, however, and he leaves. The celebration continues as Frank plays his fiddle and all the guests prepare to dance the "Ferginia reel." Aunt Amity's own silver wedding was a success.

Mrs. Stuart's stories depict the Negro as a humorous character, but seldom as a comic animal. She showed the Negro as still somewhat bewildered and ill adjusted to the ways of the white world; but she never suggested that he was incapable of eventually adapting to it. Meanwhile the transition period was a rich field for humor. In 1916 Hyder Rollins complimented Mrs. Stuart is these words: "Unless, then, one follows after the Clansmen, Mrs. Stuart, by her choice of the typical present-day Southern Negro as the hero of her stories, has opened the only field that still remains for the portrayer of negro character."[15]

Religion

His intensely personal religion was probably the Negro subject most written about. His extreme anthropomorphism and his fondness for camp meetings, protracted revivals, orgiastic baptisms, and love feasts were exploited by almost all Southern humorists. The humor of his conversion and his subsequent backsliding, the human weaknesses of his minister, the literalness of his interpretation of Bible stories—all are reflected in the humor of the day, from cursory glimpses in newspaper fillers to more detailed treatment in short stories and novels. Since most of the humor in religion was unintentional on the Negro's part, the sensitive writer was careful not to make him into an insincere, fun-loving, hedonistic hypocrite.

Outsiders were bound to misunderstand the religious impulse in a race to whom religion was so real, to whom Japheth, Jonah, Joshua, and Jesus were almost as real as the neighbors across the cotton patch or down the alley. Lest her readers think him sacrilegious, Martha Gielow stated explicitly in *Old Plantation Days* that "the negro is the most religious of all people, and . . . their constant use of the Lord's name is neither disrespectful nor irreligious— but comes from their daily familiarity of appealing to Him as a person ever present to hear and see their joys, their woes, and their prayers" (p. 183).

Perhaps in no area is dialect more likely to be confusing and misleading than in the humor depicting his religion. In such a poem as "The Old Man's Lament," included in Sam Small's *Old Si's Humorous Sketches,* the sentiment and religious pathos are genuine and should not be laughed at. A representative passage reads: "But I'se ready fer ter go—I'se lonesome down heah / A-watchin' an' waitin' de comin' o' day!" Such poems were designed to evoke a joyous sympathetic smile and a sentimental tear or two.

The Negro often used religious and secular imagery indiscriminately. In "Christmas Times Is Come" (*Boner's Lyrics*) by the North Carolinian John Henry Boner, the intimate association of the earthly and the spiritual is made dramatically clear. The poem, which includes a narrative in dialect of the birth of Christ, frequently juxtaposes religious and secular imagery.

> *De Chrismus possum am a-bakin' mighty snug,*
> *So han' aroun' de tumbler en de little yaller jug*
> *Wid de co'ncob stopper, en de honey in de bowl,*
> *An' a-glory hallyluyer en a-bless yo' soul.*

Since religion permeated every area of the Negro's existence, the humor of his religion covers the gamut of his life. Religion touched every type—from the hardened sinner to the well-intentioned but ignorant church member. James J. McDonald, in *Life in Old Virginia*, told of an old sinner who applied for membership in Shiloh Church and was ordered first to mend his ways. This he vowed to do and prayed to God for forgiveness and permission to join the church. "De Lawd he say to me, I wish yo' bettah luck dan I has, Stephen, kase I'se be'n tryin' to jine dat chu'ch fo' mo' den fohty years mahse'f!" (pp. 281-82).

On May 29, 1867, the Union Springs *Times* poked gentle satire at the confusion of Scripture and the idea that age was a sure index of knowledge and wisdom, even in religion.

A negro named Ephe, who was a regular attendant at church, was proud of his Bible learning. He was sawing wood one day, while his master's son, a lad of about twelve years, was looking on, and now and then asking questions.

"Which of the Apostles do you like best?" asked Ephe.

"Well, I don't know," drawled the boy.

"I like Sampson," said Ephe, "he was so strong, and piled up dem wicked folks so."

"Why, Ephe," replied the boy, "Sampson wasn't one of the Apostles."

Ephe put down his saw, and looked at the youngster a moment in amazement, and then asked him with an air of triumph:

"Look here, white boy, how old am you?"

"Twelve," replied the boy.

"Well, I'se forty; now, who ought to know the best, I ax you dat."

Visions were a popular pastime among devout church members. A vision of heaven and hell is recorded by Charles Colcock Jones in "The Vision of Daddy Jupiter" (*Negro Myths*). Jesus takes an old man on a tour of hell where he sees Satan. Daddy Jupiter recalls the experience: "Satan, him bin dah wid eh pitchfork, an eh black head wid screech-owl yez, an eh red eye, an eh claw-han, an eh forky tail." The imagery of the vision had most likely been affected by the lurid descriptions of hell and the devil Jupiter had heard expounded from the pulpit.

Many were afraid that the Lord was overburdened by the numerous prayer petitions that daily ascended from earth, and in Visscher's "Sorry for the Lord" from *Harp of the South* a little girl has compassion for the Lord because "de niggah wants so monst'ous much." One, she said, prayed "for Christmas time de whole year roun'" and, in addition,

> *He axed to have de chicken roos'*
> *Down on de lowes' limb,*
> *An' turkeys jes' on top de fence,*
> *In easy reach er him.*

She begs the Lord to chastize such lazy, good-for-nothing Negroes.

The preacher was a big man in the community and figured in most religious humor. Sometimes, however, he had trouble with some of his recalcitrant parishioners—with Uncle Remus, Old Si, and Uncle Ephraim. Uncle Ephraim, from Walter Hines Page's *The Southerner* is skeptical of well-dressed preachers. When one asked him for money to help convert the heathens, a dialogue took place.

> Young man, let de heathens git da'r own money. I ain't got none ter spar.
> But ter give to them is to give ter de Lord.
> Let de Lawd mek His own money, den.
> Yes, brother, but de Lord—He do not—
> He kin mek it, ef He want any. Didn' He mek wine outen water? and, ef He kin do dat, He kin make money outen some'in or ne'r, if He need enny small change. You go 'long 'bout your bus'ness" (p. 357).

In 1913 the preacher was still having his troubles with the church members. On March 14 of that year the Bullock County (Alabama) *Breeze* published the following anecdote.

> The goose had been carved, and everybody had tasted it. It was excellent. The negro minister, who was the guest of honor, could not restrain his enthusiasm.
> "Dat's as fine a goose as I evah see, Bruddah Williams," he said to his host. "Whar did you git such a fine goose?"
> "Well now, pahson," replied the carver of the goose, exhibiting great dignity and reticence, "When you preaches a speshul good sermon, I never axes you whr [*sic*] you got it. I hopes you will show me de same consideration."

At the church service, of course, the preacher was undisputed monarch. For most of his sermon he chastized his congregation for such transgressions of the law of God as drinking, cursing, dancing, and "de sin ob fancy dressin'." In Irwin Russell's "A Sermon for the Sisters" a preacher takes the women in his congregation to task for this last sin. He tells them of the vanity of putting on airs and affecting graces and of dressing up in "stylish coats" and "Philadelphy breeches." As proof of where all these sins can lead, he cites Joseph in the Bible, who was sold into slavery for "struttin' in dat streaked coat ob hisn." Since his sermon is directed mainly at the women, he adds, "He'd had a dozen fancy coats ef he'd 'a' bin a 'ooman!" Joseph, he reminds them, learned his lesson; and he advises the women also to take heed.

Now, sistahs, won't you copy him? Say, won't you take lesson,
An' min' dis sollum wahnin' 'bout de sin ob fancy dressin'?
How much you spen' upon yo'se'f! I wish you might remember
Yo' preacher ain't bin paid a cent sence somwhar in November.[16]

A climax of the service was reached at collection time, when the preacher would by various devices extort from his membership their nickels, dimes, and occasional half dollars. A preacher of Russell's uses the title of the poem as his sermon text (in *Poems*). "Half-way doin's," he reminds his congregation, got Adam and Eve into trouble and still lead people astray. Ending on a high note,

I see dat Brudder Johnson's 'bout to pass aroun' de hat,
An' don't let's hab no half way doin's when it comes to dat!

One of the best character creations of Southern humor is Alexander Sweet's Reverend Whangdoodle Baxter, pastor of the Austin, Texas, Blue Light Tabernacle, whose sermons appeared as a regular feature in *Texas Siftings*. In the sermons the preacher berates his flock for chicken stealing, gambling, and—most of all—not supporting the Lord's work. His sermons, masterpieces of the type, are filled with malapropisms. This excerpt (November 10, 1888) from one of his discourses will show their typical manner and matter. "Before closin' my remarks to dish heah brilliantine assemblage, I wish ter say sumfin about my celery. De outlook for de future am preposterous. I tole yer about how many buttons found dar way inter de hat when hits bein' passed. Only yesterday I read dat a machine had been discovered what makes 2,000 buttons ebery minit. Ef dat ain't a gloomy outlook for dem what serves at de altar I givs up. Some ob de nickels what goes inter de hat has got holes in 'em, and I berlieves dat ef it was possible ter put de hole in de hat widout puttin' in de nickle some ob you would do hit for a fac'. Not all de coins . . . am nickles. Most of 'em am copper cents. Nebber ontil I become de pasture of dish heah brilliantine concatination did I realize de meanin' ob de sayin' ob St. Paul: Alexander de coppersmiff did me much evil." The Reverend Whangdoodle Baxter occasionally commented on such secular matters as the tariff, the Populists, and the free coinage of silver; but he spent most of his energy trying to keep his erring flock in the fold.

The preacher often became explicit in his sermons, calling by name members of his flock who had erred. How to persuade the preacher not to mention his sin of adultery is Bre'r Torm's problem in Harry Stillwell Edwards' "Tom's Strategy" (*Two Runaways*). One Saturday on the way to a rendezvous with a woman not his wife, Tom passes the church and is surprised to hear the Reverend Joshua Sims preaching to an empty house. Tom quickly realizes that he is rehearsing his Sunday sermon and stops to listen. The theme is "Shake off yo' weights," by which he means that his sinning members should rid themselves of their weighty sins. As Tom continues to listen in secret, the Reverend Mr. Sims becomes personal, calling sinners by name and listing their transgressions. "Here's Bre'r Dan! Here's Bre'r Dan! Bre'r Dan got weights, an' 'e ain' shake 'em off. What es dem weight's name? Too much corn en 'is crib fur de size er 'is crop! Too much cott'n en 'is crib fur de size er 'is patch! Too many chickens en de pan fur two hens an' er rooster! Too many shotes erbout Chrismus fur er no-sow man. Shake off yo' weights, Bre'r Dan; shake 'em off!" Tom enjoys the attacks on his fellow church members—until the parson starts on him and then his laughter freezes on his lips. "W'at es Bre'r Torm's weights? He heah ter see dis 'ooman, an' yonder ter see dat 'ooman; fus' one way an' den ernudder, an' er wife down yonner home t'ink 'e gone huntin' ev'y time 'e take 'is gun." Tom knows that he must somehow induce Mr. Sims to revise his sermon. Finally he hits upon the strategy of inviting the old preacher home for a sumptuous dinner of possum and taters. The plan succeeds, and the next day the sermon attacks all those rehearsed—except Bre'r Torm.

Trance meetings were popular. To the outsider these services were usually strange and ludicrous. Under the heading "A New Religion," the Union Springs *Times* on October 3, 1868, published an anecdotal paragraph on them. "The Monroe Advertiser says the negroes around Forsyth, and in other places in Middle Georgia, have discovered or invented what they term a 'New Religion.' They assemble at their place of worship, and, to all appearance, go through the usual ceremonies of divine worship. When this is concluded, the congregation rises to its feet and begins singing one of those wild, weird songs peculiar to the African race. This has a singular effect upon the ignorant minds of Cuffee and Dinah; they shout, go crazy, and fall down in a trance, which lasts sometimes as long as three days. During these trances they have wonderful visions, which they relate with great relish and seeming earnestness." In such meetings the Negro could give full vent to the emotional side of his nature.

Among many congregations the most eagerly awaited occasion was the celebration of the ordinance of foot washing. In *Cinch* Will Allen Dromgoole gives in "A Day in Asia" an account of the celebration by the Hard-Shell Baptists, colored, in the town of Asia. When the great day arrives many of the brethren can not restrain themselves till they get to the meeting, but begin their shouting and singing along the way. For Widow Brown this is to be an especially rewarding day: she plans to have a special guest for dinner, the Reverend Benjamin Franklin George Washington Henderson, who is to officiate at the foot-washing service. The preacher is fat, fifty, and well fed by the members of his several churches. The widow meets him and invites him to her house for some "nice lill' barb' cue shoat," but he has already been invited to eat with Lill' Sis Moore. The widow is indignant. "Sis Moore's mouf ain't no pra'r book . . . en no dicshuner, neider, ef it *do* op'n en shet." Mrs. Brown throws herself on the mercy of the minister. "You tek dinner at my house, Brudder Hen'son. De good book say yer boun' ter kep keer ob de widder en de orf'n, Brudder Hen'son. Hit doan sey noth'n' bout young gals ez runs roun' arter folks ter eat dey peegs up." But the preacher refuses to change his mind.

The foot washing gets under way. Among the eager participants there was Aunt Milly, who claimed to be "mos' two hundred, I reckin. I sho' am,—fur I wuz here fo' de war, chile. Dat I wuz. I'se boun' ter be nigh two hundred." The belle of Asia, Sis Moore, was there in all her glory; the Widow Brown mumbles to herself threateningly during the singing. "Look at dat! Look *et* dat! Dat yaller nigger think she mighty fine, *I reckin,* becase she tuk de cake et de walkin' last night. Nice way ter glorify de Lawd. Ef I gits my han's on dem eyes, I ull bus' her wide op'n *ef* I gits my han's on her, de low-live triflin' hussy,—." During the prayer the widow peeps at the parson, who is "fairly wras'lin' in pra'r"; then to her increased ire, she sees his fingers part and him stealing a look at her hated rival. Sis Moore takes no part in the foot washing, for she has been to school and has learned "when's the proper time to wash yer feet, an' it be *Sadday night.*" Throughout the service the widow's hatred of that "yaller gal" increases, but she manages to keep it under control. After church the preacher, sure enough, leaves with the "hussy"; but there is some consolation for the distraught widow. Crossing a creek near the church, he slips on the log and falls astraddle it. Widow Brown restrains herself no longer and shouts gleefully: "Dar now! Dar now! Ain' you glad God made yer forkid?" She then invites some of the other brethren to dinner, feeling in a manner repaid for her misery by seeing the parson in such a ridiculous position.

In *The Heart of Old Hickory* are two other sketches by Miss Dromgoole which treat the Negro's religion. One story is a mixture of humor and religious pathos; the other is a farce. In "A Wonderful Experience Meeting" the church members at Nebo decide on a testimonial meeting to celebrate Christmas in preference to the more worldy amusements like cakewalks. The testimonies given at the meeting provide a good picture of the ignorant Negro's materialistic concept of heaven. Shaky Jake tells of being "transfloated up inter de heab'ins" while in a "tranch"; but once there he is ashamed to go in with his rags on. "I knowed I ud nuver be able ter keep up wid de style dey uz all containin' ob up dar, when de front do' opened en Marse Jesus Hisse'f walked out on de front peazzy." Marse Jesus assures him that his clothes are all right and calls out to the doorkeeper, "Peter, jes' let Unc' Jake step inside dar a minit." Inside the golden gate Jake drops his hat on the doorstep and shades his eyes from the glory. In Jake's words: "Well, brudderin, He jes' glanced down et dem golden streets en den up et my ole rags, en sez He, 'Unc' Jake, jes' rip up one ob de bricks out'n dat pavemint en go buy yo'se'f some close; den come up dem golden sta'rs ter de ballroom. . . . Spen' it all; en' what's lef' go buy yo'se'f some oyschers wid hit.'" Then Jake awakes from his vision and sees the poverty around him. But he does not despair. "I'll git dar bimeby, en de pavemints ull keep, 'ca'se dey's gol', en de ain't no thief, en no mof, en no rus' fur ter cranker ob 'em. So sez I, bress de Lawd! I kin wait fur de Chris'mus ober yon'er."

According to another member's vision of heaven, Old Jordan, after he gets his golden slippers and his crown and harp, is told by the King, "Hab a seat on de throne, Brudder Jordan, en res' yose'f whil'st yo' room's afixin' fur yer."

While they are waiting, He tells Old Jordan that in heaven whites and blacks exchange skin color—"dey des' swops places." The last experience is that of Mose, to whom heaven is a place where "de wood pile hit lay et de front do', free ter der nigger en de white dest erlack" and where "de nigger wuz called ter de fus' table, same's all de res'." All the visions show the extreme anthropomorphism of the illiterate Negro's religion.

In "Who Broke up de Meet'n'?" Aunt Sylvia reviews the scandal that "broke up de meet'n'" at the "Pisgy meet'n' house, an' tuk Brudder Simmons inter the cote, an' plumb made dey all furgit all about the feet-washin' what dey allus winds up de big meet'n' wid, ever' onct a year." She relates all the incidents, but since each event is a link in the chain leading to the great catastrophe, it is impossible to place responsibility on any one person. At the preacher's trial a lawyer, she says, lists the events in this order. "De rooster crowed! ole mis' jumped ag'in' de cow; de cow kicked Eli; Eli want ter kill de cow; ole mis' want ter jail Eli; Ike fotched him ter meet'n', wid de dog; de widder hugged Ike, de dog bit de widder; de gals laffed; de preacher gin out de wrong chune; de sisters fit de preacher, en de meet'n' bruk up. En now," Aunt Sylvia says the lawyer concluded, "*who* bruk up de meet'n'?" The chain of events is reviewed several times, but no one is able to answer the question.

Summer revival time among Southern Negroes was the social, as well as the religious, event of the year. For weeks plans were made for the meetings, the women hoarding food, fattening the fryers for the preacher and other dignitaries who might take dinner with them, getting ready the pallets for the guests who would come for the meetings; the men getting the crops in shape to be left alone for a week or two and laying in secret stores of moonshine whiskey. For weeks before the meetings started they were advertised by word of mouth, by crudely lettered signs, and by such posters as the following:

NOTICE!   STOP!   NOW READ!

Where are you going the third Sunday in August? I am going to DeRidder, La., to a Tribe meeting at the Starlight Baptist Church. We are going to have ice cold lemonade free for all visitors and plenty of ice water. We will name some of the preachers:

Rev. McHome, from Natchitoches, a son of thunder;
Rev. McCrow, from Leesville, the world's wonder;
Rev. Hy Williams, from Alexandria, a tall black angel;
Rev. Samuel Phanor, from Cane River, a light that sits on a hill can't be hidden;
Rev. Charley Marrow, from DeRidder, master of arts;
Rev. McCall, from Lake Charles, master of ceremonies;
Rev. J. K. Walker, from Cravens, a burning light;
Rev. Ishmon, from Bon Ami, a hero;
Rev. Bennett, from Fullerton, a noble spokesman.[17]

There was seldom a dearth of preachers at the big meetings.

The services were usually very emotional and sincere, but they also contained possibilities that were humorous to the outsider. McDonald in his *Life in Old Virginia* recorded that once during a revival meeting a scoffer asked a preacher,

"How far off yo' reckon de devil is fum yere?"

"How ol' is yo' Bre'r Petah?" asked the preacher.

"Well, suh, I 'spect I'se 'bout fohty foh."

"W'en yo' wuz b'on inter dis worl'" said the preacher, "de devil wuz jes' fohty foh years behin' yo', an' all I'se got ter say is, dat ef he aint cotched up wid yo' hit 'taint yo' own fault" (p. 278). Shouting was common during the meetings. McDonald wrote that a Sister Patsey in a fit of ecstasy shrieked, "Lawd, jes' giv me one mo' feath'a in ma wing o' faith, an' I'se gwine flyin' to you." "Deah Lawd," the preacher added, "ef yo' has one mo' feath'a to spar' please sen' it to Sistah Patsey soon's yo' kin" (p. 279). Once a new preacher had pictured vividly the horrors of hell—the fire and brimstone and the condition of the condemned souls—but without any response from the congregation. Finally he struck a spark by describing eternity in this manner: "Does yo' know w'at etern'ty is? Well, I tell yo'. Ef one uv dem li'l sparrows w'at yo' see roun yo' gyarden bushes wuz to dip his bill in de 'Lantic Ocean an' taik one hop a day an' hop 'cross de country an' put dat drop uv watah into de 'Cific Ocean, an' den he hop back to de 'Lantic Ocean, jes one hop a day, an' ef he keep dat hoppin' up 'twell de 'Lantic Ocean wuz dry as a bone, it wouldn't be break o' day in etern'ty" (pp. 280-81).

The hymns were rousing ones filled with many local allusions and personal petitions addressed to heavenly figures. McDonald reported that songs like the following were popular:

> *I'se got on de back uv de Baptis' mule,*
> *Sinner doan' yo' stan' dar lookin' laik a fule.*
> *De bridle bit am silva, de saddle am gol'.*
> *An' I'm boun' fo' to go to Aberhams fol'!*
>   *An' I'll ride,*
>   *Yas I will*
> *An' I'll ride right on to glory!* (p. 280).

The camp-meeting hymn with its everyday images became a regular feature in the *Arkansaw Traveler*. The following typical stanza appeared on April 28, 1883.

> *Ole sister Mary drapped her pride*
> *An' all at once got sanctified,*
> *An' when she fell down for ter pray,*
> *She tuck up wings an' flew away.*

A poem by Sidney Lanier, "Uncle Jim's Baptist Revival-Hymn" (in *Poems*), uses homely details as symbols showing the church overrun by the cares and concerns of the world. Employing farming imagery, Lanier pictured the Baptists in the grass, while other denominations had done better at keeping the grass (sin) under control. His use of "Mahster" for God shows that the Negro best understood God in terms of his own environment. Most Negroes of the time were Baptists—hence the use by humorists of the Baptist as the representative church.

The use of personal, homey images pervades Martha Young's "Hymns of the Black Belt" in *Plantation Songs*. Many of the songs become quite familiar with Biblical personages, speaking of "Sister Mary and Martha" and stating:

> *I am a-gwine to Bethlehem,*
> *Gwine to meet Marse Canaan and Shem,*
> *Gwine to fit on de shoes of John.*

Heaven was the promise of a better life. There the Negro would live like a white person. "Oh, de white chillen has dere heaven down heah, / But de niggers wait fer dere's up Dar!" Unc' 'Ronymus Dan's idyllic vision of the recently buried Unc' Sol turned a cold meeting into a hot one. It pictured what to the Negro was a paradise.

> *Uncle Sol sat under dat Fritter Tree,*
> *Whar fritters hung thick as leaves do be;*
> *When he hongry he des hatter retch up, I see,*
> *And grab a good handful offer dat tree.*

The chant, an important part of the service in which the congregation joined the minister or song leader in rhythmic singing, was the inspiration for Anne Virginia Culbertson's "Whar Dem Sinful Apples Grow."[18] This literary chant covers Adam in the Garden of Eden, the formation of Eve, and the Fall. The application comes in the last stanza.

> *Oh, sinner, is you in de Gyardin uv Eden?*
> *('Way down yonner)*
> *Is you on dem sinful apples feedin'?*
> *('Way down yonner)*
> *Come out, oh, sinner, befo' youse driven,*
> *De debil gwine git you ef you goes on livin'*
> *'Way down yonner whar dem sinful apples grow!*

In the heat and enthusiasm of the revival many souls were converted—at least for a while. Backsliding was one of the most common sins. Frank L. Stanton's "The Backsliding Brother" in *Songs from Dixie Land* concerns one who has been drinking. The tipsy convert is warned of his backsliding by a screech owl which seems to be telling him: "En Satan gwine ter roas' you at de Judgmint Day!" At least nine-tenths of the converts backslid by the time a new big meeting rolled around to put their erring feet back on the straight and narrow road.

Although the Negro was usually a member of one of the fundamentalist sects, occasionally he joined a high church, such as the Episcopal. Sometimes he joined because he was the rector's yard man or his wife was the bishop's cook. The colored Episcopalian in Samuel Minturn Peck's "The Trouble at St. James" (*Alabama Sketches*), is sexton of the church. Dan's pride in being a high-church Episcopalian is evident throughout the sketch. He tells a stranger to Oakville of the trouble at St. James since the new minister arrived. Mr. Crofton had his first trouble with the choir. "You know, sah, dat choirs is always mighty bumptious. De cullurd people's got a sayin', dat when de Devil comes to church he sits in de choir." After the new minister had finished with the choir, the sexton recalls, he "regerlated de Sunday school, an' de Daughters o' de King, an' de Brothers o' St. Andrew, an' de Woman's Auxillerary." Then he turned on the low-church element and put them in their lowly place.

The real trouble at St. James came during Lent. The vestry voted to put in a water-run motor for the organ, and agreed to pay the water company so much each quarter. The worldly wise Dan asserts parenthetically that this trouble "growed out o' de fact dat de contract warn't drawed up on paper." Higgins at the water company complains that St. James is using much more water than it is paying for—more water than any other church in town. During Lent he asks Dan when the revival is going to stop, and Dan explains that they are *not* holding a revival. Higgins then suggests that they stop whatever they are having because they are using too much water. Baptists and Methodists, he says, can stop their protracted meetings when they want to. But the sexton patiently explains: "De Babtises an' de Methodises kin stop when dey likes, kaze dey begins when dey chooses, but hit ain't so wid de Church. Dis Lenten season is as regerlar as de heavenly bodies. . . . If Mr. Crofton was to stop Lent 'fore Easter hit would be jes' as scannerlous as if de Methodis' preacher was to dance de German."

Shortly thereafter Higgins and Mr. Crofton have an argument, and Higgins swears he will get even. The minister refuses to pay any more, because, Dan reports, he had investigated "an' found out dat de church was payin' as much for de use o' de water-power as de broom-factory, or de city fountain, which run day an' night." Higgins gets angriest when the choir rehearses the "Hallelujah Chorus." Dan's mention of this music suggests an aside, and he says to his amused listener: "Did yer ever chance to know dat chorus, sah? Well, sah, hit's de glorifyin'est chune ever I hyerd. De spranners hallelujahed high up in de trebles, den de basses roared hit down low, an' de 'traltos an' de tenors pitched hit back an' forth in de middle; den dey all sot in an' shouted hit together, an' see-sawed an' zig-zagged up an' down de scales, while de organist played wid his all fours, an' ever' stop pulled out to de very een." All the time, Higgins was outside "watchin' dat water runnin', an' cussin'." Higgins's desire for revenge becomes unbearable, and he strikes through the organist—they shake hands and the organist's hand "swole twice de size o' de other." Of course, he cannot play for the Easter services, but Mr. Crofton assures Dan that the Lord has provided a substitute. "Is—is He gwine sen' a angel to play de organ tomorrow?" Another man has agreed to play, and Dan is amazed at the pastor's good luck. "If Mr. Crofton hadn't been a Christian an' a minister, I would 'a' sholy 'spicioned dat he toted a rabbit's foot, 'kaze ever'thing was a-turnin' out so fine."*

Higgins doesn't know about the substitute organist. On Easter Day he hears the organ and becomes furious; he will turn off the water. But Dan has taken certain precautions. "I jes' drapped some sand an' grabbel in de hydrant so Higgins can't unscrew it." Higgins gets his wrench and waits for the "Hallelujah Chorus." Then he tried to unscrew the plug. Dan pictures him. "Wid ever' shout Higgins got madder an' madder, till in de middle of de chorus he braced his feet an' brought a jerk what busted de wrench, an' he went over back'ards in a turrible fall across de roots of de tree, an' dar he laid wid a broken leg." The incident has a happy ending, however. Higgins is taken into the rectory where for two months he recuperates. "Lo an' behole, nex' time de bishop come, Higgins was confirmed."

Most of the miscellaneous humor dealing with the Negro is worthless from both a literary and a sociological standpoint. Even a trifle like this joke from the Union Springs *Times* of July 3, 1867, illustrates, however, two traits of postwar Negro humor: its immense popularity and its sub-literary nature.

Well, Sambo, what's yer up to now-a-day?
Oh, I is a carb'ner and jiner.
He! I guess yer is. What department do you perform?
What deparment? Why, I does the circular work.
What'd dat?
Why, I turns de grindstone.
G'way.

The joke also suggests an attitude. Frank L. Stanton's "Happy Lan'" in *Songs of the Soil* illustrates the most commonly held concept of the period: the Negro as a happy, carefree child.

> *Three niggers with a banjer—talk 'bout the "Sunny South,"*
> *They sing like watermillions was a-melting in their mouth;*
> *Jest happy as three blackbirds six miles from any trap.*

The darky, the white humorists thought, was bound to have his fun regardless of the consequences. The white man might even envy what he assumed to be an immense capacity for enjoying life. "Happy as a nigger" became a Southern folk saying.

* See Sam Small, "Old Si against the Choir" (*Old Si's Sayings*), for a similar account of a colored choir. Describing how the choir sang "All Hail the Power of Jesus's Name," "de 'oman dat sings de sopranner squealed out on de 'all hail' tell yer'd er thought dar wuz a sto'm in full blas' outside; an' jess den she gib out, an' de tenner tuck up de strane an' work'd on de power like he wuz tryin' to coff up er fish bone!" Then the others come in. "De alto gals an' de base fellers wurkin' dere bellusses fer all dey wuz wuff, an' de mixin' ob de song goin' on tell noboddy on de yearth cood a tole whedder de song begun wid Jesus' name er all hail, er how it wuz 'fore de Lawd, I forgot what dey wuz singin' 'fore dey tackl'd de secon' line!"

The question of whether the white man influenced the black man's speech or vice versa is still being debated. Certainly no objective observer can fail to see that there has been influence on both sides. One of the most amusing books in Southern (and national) literature shows the influence of the Negro's speech, his superstitions, and his general attitude on a little white boy. Frances Boyd Calhoun's *Miss Minerva and William Green Hill* tells the story of how a little boy's maiden aunt tries to turn him into a little gentleman by making him forget all the Negro lore he has learned while living on his late father's plantation. This, she discovers, is an impossible task. William Green Hill is a Negro in all but skin color. He and his colored playmate on the plantation, Wilkes Booth Lincoln, had lived so closely together since their birth that they considered themselves twins. Wilkes Booth Lincoln, Billy explains to his Aunt Minerva, is one of Aunt Blue-Gum Tempy's Peruny Pearline's many children. For his aunt's information Billy recites the names of all the children in this family.

"Admiral Farragut Moses the Prophet Esquire, he's the bigges'; an' Alice Ann Maria Dan Step-an'-Go-Fetch-It, she had to nuss all the res': she say fas' as she git th'oo nussin' one an' 'low she goin' to have a breathin' spell here come another one an' she got to nuss it. An' the nex' is Mount Sinai Tabernicle, he name fer the church where ol' Aunt Blue-Gum Tempy's Peruny Pearline takes her sackerment; an' the nex' is First Thessalonians; Second Thessalonians, he's dead an' gone to the Bad Place 'cause he skunt a cat,—I don't mean skin the cat on a actin' pole like me an' Wilkes Booth Lincoln does,—he skunt a sho' 'nough cat what was a ole witch, an' she come back an' ha'nt him an' he growed thinner an' thinner an' weasler an' weasler, tell finely he wan't nothin' 't all but a skel'ton, an' the Bad Man won't 'low nobody 't all to give his parch' tongue no water, an' he got to, ever after amen, be toast on a pitchfork. An' Oleander Magnolia Althea is the nex'," he continued, enumerating Peruny Pearline's offspring on his thin well-molded fingers; "she got the seven-year itch; an' Gettysburg, an' Biddle-& Brothers-Mercantile-Co; he name fer the sto' where ole Aunt Blue-Gum Tempy's Peruny Pearline gits credit so she can pay when she fetches in her cotton in the fall; an' Wilkes Booth Lincoln, him an' me's twins; we was borned the same day only I's borned to my mama an' he's borned to hisn an' Doctor Jenkins fetched me an' Doctor Shacklefoot fetched him. An' Decimus Ultimus,"—the little boy triumphantly put his right forefinger on his left little one, thus making the tenth,—"she's the baby an' she's got the colic an' cries loud 'nough to wake up Israel; Wilkes Booth Lincoln say he wish the little devil would die. Peruny Pearline firs' name her 'Doctor Shacklefoot' 'cause he fetches all her chillens, but the doctor he say that ain't no name fer a girl, so he name her Decimus Ultimus" (pp. 9-11).

This recitation by William Green Hill is defense enough for including the book in a chapter on Negro humor. The humor of the leading character derives directly and almost exclusively from the Negro. So popular were the creations of Mrs. Calhoun that after her death other writers wrote sequels to Miss Minerva. Among these is Emma Speed Sampson, *Miss Minerva on the Old Plantation.*

Until World War I the Negro was treated principally as a comic character, even in books and sketches not considered primarily humorous. Around the turn of the century, however, a movement began to present other facets of Negro character. Julia Peterkin and DuBose Heyward, both from South Carolina, were leaders in the attempt to eliminate the comic-animal tradition and to treat the Negro in recognizably human terms. An extreme reaction to this tradition is the Negro as tragic hero in the works of Negro writers like William M. Ashby, James Weldon Johnson, and W. E. B. DuBois. The Negro was rapidly becoming less a comic oddity and more an American whose skin was black. Late in the period, however, a Southern writer could still see enough individuality in the Negro to provide material for humor. "Let the pessimist who believes that the picturesque old-time Southern negro has been entirely denatured in the South's process of waking up take a first-hand look during the camp meeting season and he will admit that there is material for the dialect story in the freedman, even yet."[19] By the end of the period the Negro was no longer exclusively a Southern oddity. Northern migrations made him into a national type. In the Preface to *The Heart of Happy Hollow* Charles W. Chesnutt vouched for the change: "Happy Hollow; are you wondering where it is? Wherever Negroes colonize in the cities or villages, North or South, wherever the hod carrier, the porter, and the waiter are the society men of the town; wherever the picnic and the excursion are the chief summer diversion, and the revival the winter time of repentance, wherever the cheese cloth veil obtains at weddings, and the little white hearse goes by with black mourners in the one carriage behind, there—there—is Happy Hollow. Wherever laughter and tears rub elbows day by day, and the spirit of labour and laziness shake hands, there—there—is Happy Hollow" (pp. 320-21). To Chesnutt and to many later writers the Negro had not lost his unique identity in the national melting pot. The humor of the Negro would continue as long as he retained his racial identity.

Notes

1. "American Literary Comedians," 796.
2. "Negro in the Southern Short Story," 45.
3. In *Wit and Truth*, 25.
4. "American Letter," 258.
5. "Literature in the South," 755.
6. Boatright, *et al., Family Saga*, 49.
7. Heritage Club, *Sandglass*, VII, 23.
8. *Comic Tradition*, 320-21.
9. Howard, *This Is the South*, 178.
10. Holmes, *et al., Stories of Humor*, 64-65.
11. In Mason, *Humorous Masterpieces*, 268-79.
12. *Library of Southern Literature*, IV, 1443-44.
13. In Fulton, *Southern Life*, 412-13.
14. Quoted in Rankin, *Kate Chopin*, 156.
15. "Negro in the Southern Short Story," 60.
16. In Handford, *Elmo's Humorous Speaker*, 142-43.
17. In Mills, *Editorials, Sketches and Stories*, 838.
18. In Wilder, *Wit and Humor*, V, 121-23.
19. Mills, *Editorials, Sketches and Stories*, 838-39.

8. *The Poor White*

FROM WILLIAM BYRD TO ERSKINE CALDWELL the poor white man of the South has been a popular subject for humorists. Although ignored in large part by prewar Southern novelists, his uniqueness was exploited by the humorists of the Old Southwest. After the war, during the local-color era (1870-1900), he was again a popular subject for humorous sketches.

The later poor white, however, was typically not the Ham Rachel, or Ransy Sniffle, or Sut Lovingood of the earlier tradition.[1] Though there were notable exceptions, most Southern humorists after the war tried to picture an admirable and lovable South. Fiction dealing with the trashy poor Southerner would have done little toward convincing the rest of the country that the South was a refined, cultured section. Sometimes, in fact, not-too-poor whites were elevated by the writer. In *Southern Silhouettes* (94-104) Jeannette Walworth wrote of "Mrs. New and the Old Families." Mrs. New rose to respectability, though her father had been an overseer before the war. She won the admiration of the old families when she showed them how to meet the exigencies of the war by making coffee out of okra seed and roasted sweet potatoes, and candle molds out of cane roots. Her daughter would no longer have to bear the "poor white trash" label of derision.

The poor white was usually treated with a large element of pathos and emotion. The sketches by Joel Chandler Harris and Thomas Nelson Page are appealingly sentimental and lack much of the earlier clownishness. To Harris, Page, Cable, and most of the other leading Southern writers the poor white as a person was pitiable and likable. They treated him as a human being, not merely as a comic dirt-eater. As a man he was undeniably tragic, but to suit the taste of the time he was pictured in humor as pathetic. Perhaps nowhere else was the trend toward mixing humor and pathos more evident. B. O. Flower, editor of the *Arena*, published Will Allen Dromgoole's "Fiddling His Way to Fame," and then explained its attraction for him in his introduction to that author's collection, *The Heart of Old Hickory*. "I immediately accepted the sketch, as it was something I wanted to lighten the pages of my review, and because it possessed a certain charm which is rare among modern writers, being humorous and pathetic by turns, wonderfully true to life, and yet free from the repulsive elements so often present in realistic sketches." Because of "her artistic skill in bringing out the pathos and humor of the situations depicted," hers had been the most popular sketches appearing in the *Arena*. Her works reminded Flower of Charles Dickens. Obviously Miss Dromgoole was not alone in drawing inspiration from the English master of humor and pathos.

All areas of the little-known poor white's life were a field for humor: his fundamentalist religion, his ungrammatical and sometimes archaic English, his customs and superstitions, his attitude toward the Negro, his courting and marriage traditions, his frolics, his labors.

The popularity of the local-color story dealing with the Southern rural classes is attested to by the number of such sketches appearing in the national magazines. It is virtually impossible to thumb through any volume of such magazines as the *Century*, *Lippincott's*, or *Harper's* without coming across several stories set in the mountains of Kentucky, the wiregrass of Georgia or Alabama, the bayous of Louisiana, or the hills of North Carolina. In 1900 Benjamin Wells observed that the Negro was still the chief source of local color, but more and more the unfortunate white man was coming in for treatment by such writers as Ellen Glasgow, Robertson, and Edwards.[2]

Why in America after the Civil War was there so much interest in the almost isolated and largely illiterate Southerner? Why was he such a popular subject for humor? In *The American Mind* Bliss Perry noted that a type or a person becomes humorous through failure to adapt himself to the prevalent pattern. "Yankee, Southerner, Westerner, Californian, Texan, each type provokes certain connotations of humor when viewed by any of the other types. Each type in turn has its note of provinciality when compared with the norm of the typical American" (p. 195). Thus the provincial of the North, for whom most of the Southern sketches were written, looked upon the Southern provincial as a humorous type. The Yankee reader could feel superior to the unfortunates of the South and laugh at their clumsiness and their ignorance. To most readers North and South the Southern poor man was, like the Negro, comic per se. In 1884 Joel Chandler Harris lamented, "It is a fatal weakness of American literature that our novelists . . . can perceive only the comic side of what they are pleased to term 'provincial life.'"[3]

Dialect accentuated the difference between reader and literary character, and thus contributed to the humor and popularity of many local-color sketches. In his *Autobiography* Richard Malcolm Johnston justified his use of it in a good general defense of the method. "There are things in one's thoughts sometimes, particularly upon humorous themes, that cannot be put with near as much aptness and poignancy in entirely grammatical, rhetorical phrases. Even if this were possible, the characters that I have tried to illustrate spoke the language that I put into their mouths" (p. 85). Naturally there was some opposition. Perhaps the most valid criticism came from the living prototypes of the dialect characters. After reading a book by John Fox, Jr., a mountaineer is said to have commented: "Why, that feller don't know how to spell! That taleteller . . . is jest makin' fun of the mountain people by misspellin' our talk. You educated folks don't spell your own words the way you say them."[4]

Most writers and readers saw justification for dialect sketches. If the dialogue was not always accurate, it at least increased the humor. In 1875 the politician-humorist S. S. Cox described the situation. "Our dialect has not only swollen to a laughable bulk, but the wildest perversions of good words have resulted from it. . . . The metaphorical and other odd expressions belonging to the West and South . . . originate in some funny anecdote, which makes its way up through many mouths until it obtains the imprimatur of the *Congressional Record* and the currency of the metropolitan press. If the history of our lexicography were written, it would be a comic one. . . ."[5] Frequently, as Cox implied, the use of dialect got out of hand. An exaggerated example is a conjugation of the verb "to do," allegedly by an applicant for a teacher's certificate in Arkansas. "Imperfect—I have done it. Plural—Weuns done it, youns done it, theyuns done it. Perfect—I gone done it, you gone done it, he gone done it. Plural—Weuns gone done it, youns gone done it. Theyuns gone done it. Future—I guine done it, you guine done it, he guine done it. Plural—Weuns guine done it, youns guine done it, theyuns guine done it. Future perfect—I done guine done it, you done guine done it, he done guine done it. Plural—Weuns done guine done it, youns done guine done it, theyuns done guine done it."[6] Usually, however, dialect was used as a means to give reality and local color and not as the end.

After the war the Negro and the rural white man were often thrown into close contact. This relationship frequently bred jealousy and ill will, but there were a few white men who saw some good in the freedman. In *Old Si's Sayings* for example, Sam Small's "Only a Nigger Preacher" eulogizes in cracker dialect, a Holly Springs, Mississippi, colored preacher who, during a yellow fever epidemic, had ministered heroically to white and black. The cracker mouthpiece declares, "Thar'll be one nigger in heaven / I'll jine with ter praise an' ter sing."

Sarge Wier's comments on the freedman are mixed but generally favorable. The Georgia humorist wrote in *Old Times in Georgia* (pp. 42-45), "The nigger may steal a chicken now and then, but he's the best laborer for this country, and we like him, and he likes us, 'cepting when it comes to politics, and then he's gwine to vote with the yankee, and I don't blame him." He stated that at first he was skeptical about the Negro and the vote, but now he's changed his mind ("and it's all from what I've seed"). "When the negro went to voting, I thought it would collapse the world, but it didn't, and now I think it all right for the nigger to vote, and if I was running for office I'd get his vote if I could." Wier was afraid, however, that the new voters were being corrupted by the influence of white people. "The nigger is here and he's going to stay, and they are growing more and more like white folks every day. Whoever heard of a nigger having a headache before the war? . . . They complain of headache now, and grunt the same as white folks, and must have their coffee every morning—that is, when they are cooking for some white family." Not many poor whites were so kind to the Negro, who as a freedman was their competitor on the labor market.

The Arkansas Redneck

Most of the postwar humor dealing with the common white man centered around the mountaineer and the cracker; however, smaller groups were not ignored. The Arkansas rednecks, the Florida piney woods tacky, the Louisiana Cajun, and the Alabama wool hat were occasionally treated. The cowboy, largely outside the scope of this study, figures in much of the humor written in Texas. After the Civil War the cowboy's life continued many of the traits of the earlier Southern frontier: lawlessness, speculation, independence, and scorn for titles and protocol. His humor is characterized by exaggeration, the tall tale, the practical joke, and is often coarse, realistic, and sometimes cruel. While much of the humor in the states of the Old Southwest became refined and genteel after the Civil War, the Southwest of the cowboy continued in the frontier tradition. A recent anthology of cowboy humor is Stan Hoig, *The Humor of the American Cowboy.*

Unlikely though it may seem, Irwin Russell wrote some Irish sketches in verse. One of the poet's last published pieces was "Larry's on the Force," probably influenced by his brief stay in New York City. Russell's description of the Irish policeman shows his skill in handling non-Negro dialect.

He shtips that proud and shtately-loike, you'd think he owned the town,
And houlds his shtick convenient to be tappin' some wan down—
Aich blissed day, I watch to see him comin' up the shtrate,
For by the greatest bit of luck, our house is on his bate.[7]

The widely reprinted Hoffenstein sketches by Joe C. Aby of the New Orleans *Times-Democrat* reflect yet another white group in the South, the ubiquitous and nomadic Jewish peddler and storekeeper. The legendary Jewish dexterity in salesmanship was the usual target of Aby's wit. In the sketch called "Thermometer Pants" a Jewish merchant's sales spiel is shown to be ineffectual. He tries to sell a countryman a pair of cheap jean pants. When the farmer complains that they contain too much cotton and will shrink when washed, Hoffenstein puts his sales pitch into high gear. "Dey was de dermometer pants, und a plessing to every farmer vat wears a bair uf dem. Do you know, my frent, dose bants will dell you exactly vat de vedder will be. Ven it was going to be vet und cold, dose bants will begin to shrink up, und ven it was going to be dry und varm, dey comes right down, you know." The merchant follows these sales points with a testimonial from a man who bought a pair of the pants and became a successful farmer almost overnight. He ends with what he thinks is a sale clincher. "Dink of it, my frent; mit de thermometer bants, you can tell exactly ven to put in cabbage seed, und plant corn twice as better as mit an almanac, besides ven de vedder gets so cold und vet dot de bants goes up under your arms, you sew bottons on the front and vear him as a vest." When Hoffenstein finishes, the farmer abruptly turns and leaves the store. Angrily the merchant draws a cynical moral for his clerk. "Vell, it shust shows dot de more you dry to help beoble along, de more, py tam, you don't got any tanks for it."[8] In the Hoffenstein sketches the stereotyped traits of the Jewish tradesman were exaggerated and provoked laughter all over a South that was becoming increasingly commercial.

Another Jewish merchant treated satirically in humor was Mose Schaumburg, the subject of a series of sketches appearing in *Texas Siftings*. He was typically depicted as a conniving, money-mad anomaly. The following anecdote (July 10, 1886) reveals Alexander Sweet's attitude toward his creation.

Mose Schaumburg: "Isaac, mine son, ven I gives you a globe mit some gold fishes for a bresent, vat would you do mit 'em?"
Isaac: "I vould melt dose gold fishes down and put puy goots on credit mit dot gold vot I got from dose gold fishes."
Mose: "Vot a head for pishness! Come to my pusom, Isaac, my son."

The Arkansas and Louisiana redneck was another group exploited in local-color sketches by such writers as Alice French, Ruth McEnery Stuart, and Opie Read. He was a first cousin to the mountaineer and the cracker. In the sketches of Alice French he is frequently pictured as a creature of violence and immorality. Shields McIlwaine has pointed out that humor, sentiment, and naturalism, a relatively new element, blend in such sketches as "The Loaf of Peace," "Trusty, No. 49," and "Headlights." The latter contains a cottonpatch strumpet presaging those of Erskine Caldwell.[9]

Though Mrs. Ruth McEnery Stuart wrote of the poor Irish and Italians in New Orleans (see, for example, "Camelia Riccardo"), her best sketches deal with the country people of Arkansas. The author of "Bud Zundt's Mail" and "Christmas Geese"—stories of Arkansas—was called by Mildred Rutherford the "laureate of the lowly" whose "humor brightens everything it touches."[10] One of her best-known books is *Sonny,* which is a series of seven monologues about his son by Deuteronomy Jones, a backwoods Arkansas farmer. Though each chapter is separately complete, taken together they form the seven ages of Sonny. The first, "A Christmas Guest," is a tender and humorous account of his birth. "The Boy" shows Sonny at age two. "Sonny's Christenin' " is an amusing account of how the boy while perched atop a bean arbor is baptized by a minister who stands on the front porch. The next two monologues, 'Sonny's Schoolin' " and "Sonny's Diploma," are a humorous account of his education. The sixth, "Sonny's Keepin' Company," deals with his courtship; and the seventh, "Weddin' Presents," shows him on the way to marital bliss. The humor of situation in each of these sketches is reinforced by the humor of dialect and of provincial manners.

"The Deacon's Medicine" from *Moriah's Mourning* is a small masterpiece of humor by Mrs. Stuart. Each time Deacon Gregg has a spat with his wife, he goes outside and sits forlornly on his gatepost. One evening the doctor while riding by sees him sitting there and stops to find out the trouble. The deacon tells the doctor his wife has given him a pill to take because she got upset about a steer running into her clothesline and dirtying her wash. He has an intense aversion to pills and can get sick just thinking about them. The doctor suggests that he simply throw the pill away and tell his wife he has taken it. The deacon says he tried that once, but he knew his wife could sense that he had lied to her. "No, I won't never try to deceive her ag'in. It never has seemed to me thet she could have the same respect for me after ketchin' me at it, though she ain't never referred to it but once-t, an' that was the time I was elected deacon, an' even then she didn't do it outspoke." He is not sure why his wife gives him medicine when she is upset, but he has a theory. "I s'pose when she feels her temper a-risin' she's 'feerd thet she might be so took up with her troubles thet she'd neglect my health, an' so she wards off any attackt thet might be comin' on."

The doctor leaves the deacon still contemplating the awful task of swallowing the pill. Suddenly in a moment of strength he throws caution to the winds—and the pill also. He goes in to his wife and tries to appease her with his decision to sell the steer that ruined her wash, the very steer he has sworn never to sell. This generous act so touches his wife that she sets aside the gruel she intended for his supper and makes his favorite mush instead. Then she decides to add pudding. Her demeanor is too much for the guilty man, and he confesses that he "dropped" the pill outside and needs another. His confession melts his wife completely, and she places before him a plate of fried chicken. They are reconciled.

Opie Read's use of an Arkansas setting for his humor is largely mechanical; however, his sketches occasionally reveal an understanding of redneck personality and psychology born of many years of living among country people. The suspicion and distrust with which the native views the outsider, for example, are the core of the humor form most often associated with Read, the Arkansaw Traveler dialogue.

In *Opie Read in the Ozarks* a stranger attempts to identify himself when he asks for his mail at a rural postoffice. "Wall, if it's any information, I will remark that I am the man that made Jesse James run once." With this boast the colloquy is on.

"That's nuthin', so fur as personal 'complishment goes. These boys will tell you that I spit at a wild hog once and raised a three-cornered blister between his eyes."

"You don't begin to say so! And atter all it is a putty good personal 'complishment. It's strange, though, that you never hearn of me. I grabbed a panther once and tied a knot in his tail, and it took him three weeks of close attention to business to get it out."

"You don't say so! But after all that was doin' putty well fur a man that simply wanted to throw away his time. I uster idle away my time that a-way. I ricolleck once that I was out in the Rocky Mountains when who should come along but a grizzly bear that I wasn't acquainted with at all, but I spoke to him sorter polite like, and he ups with his paw and struck at me. I told him not to take such violent exercise just after dinner, but he frowned on my advice and struck at me agin. Then I got sorter riled, and I grabbed him, snatched out his tongue, split it, and tied the ends over the top of his head. Yes, I used to be a good deal of a idler" (pp. 10-12).

The clever, smart-alecky answer to a stranger's question is another characteristic of Read's dialogue structure. A conversation between an Eastern visitor and a native of Arkansas reveals absolutely no information.

"Hallo!" called the judge.
"Comin'!" the man replied, depositing a child in the doorway, and advancing.
"How's all the folks?"
"Children's hearty; wife's not well. Ain't what you might call bed-sick, but jest sorter stretchy."
"Got anything to eat in the house?"
"Ef I had it anywhere, I'd have it in the house."
"How many children have you?"
"Many as I want."
"How many did you want?"
"Wa'n't hankerin' arter a powerful chance, but I'm satisfied."
"How long have you been living here?"
"Too long."

"How many years?"

"Been here ever since my oldest boy was born."

"What year was he born?"

"The year I come here."

"How old is your boy?"

"Ef he had lived, he would have been the oldest until yit; but, as he died, Jim's the oldest."

"How old is Jim?"

"He ain't as old as the one what died."

"Well, how old was the one that died?"

"He was older than Jim."

"What do you do for a living?"

"Eat."

"How far is it to the next house?"

"It's called three miles, but the man what calls it that is a liar" (pp. 23-34).

The conversation continues in this frustrating manner for some time, with the stranger learning nothing from the Arkansan. This anecdote form became popular in Read's *Arkansaw Traveler,* and almost every issue of the paper contained an example. That this kind of humor was popular fifty years ago is proof that what to one age is amusing is to another age boring and absurd. Read's sketches of the poor white retain little interest for either the humorist or the sociologist.

The Mountaineer

Writing in 1897 A. G. Bradley said of the white people who had settled in the Virginia mountains: "There they have multiplied and stagnated, illiterate, squalid, poor, unambitious, despised by whites and by negroes alike, clinging together, inter-marrying and degenerating physically and morally." Despite their poverty, he added, mountain women were often very religious and humble. He described a typical woman of the mountains. "She will sit for hours before the fire in the broken rocking chair, crooning out disconnected lamentations, after some such wise as this—'The Lord is good! The Lord is mighty good! We're too sinful, too bad to live! Even this yer mountain's too good for such as us!' "[11] The complacency—or laziness—suggested by Bradley was concurred in by most humorists. They generally agreed with him too that the mountaineer was more likely to be shiftless and immoral than any other Southern type, including the Negro.[12]

Before Mary Noailles Murfree began writing, the mountaineer was little known in literature. With the discovery of the new type, there followed a flurry of sketches, short stories, anecdotes, and even poetry, in which the peculiarities of the mountaineer were the focus. Though he had many things in common with other Southerners, extreme fundamentalism—even cultism—in religion, feuds, moonshining, and sympathy for the Union during the Civil War were considered distinguishing traits. Humorists generally showed his life to

256

be more primitive, more passionate, and cruder than that of his kinsmen in the foothills and plains of the South. His earthy existence was, however, usually softened, sweetened, and romanticized. Charles H. Smith, for example, in a sketch he called "Tell and Kiss," wrote about one of the mountaineer's amusements. In East Tennessee the young men and women used to play a kissing game. A girl would say she was "a-pinin" for a certain boy, and the boy would get to kiss her. Then a boy would be taken with a sudden pining. He named the girl, she rushed outside, he chased her to claim his reward. The author attended a frolic where a newly married woman and her burly mountaineer husband were present; but the boys stayed clear of pining for the bride for fear of her husband. Presently, however, the young giant strode to the middle of the room. "My wife is as purty an nice an sweet as any gal here. You-uns has knowed her all her life. This game has been a-goin on half an hour, an nobody has pined for her once. If somebody don't pine for her purty soon, thar will be trouble!" Somebody did—very shortly.[13]

Although Miss Murfree's stories had wider publication and were more influential, Sherwood Bonner was a pioneer in exploiting (along with the Negro) the Tennessee mountain characters in dialect sketches. Three of the four stories in *Dialect Tales* that deal with the mountaineer are based on moonshining. "The Case of Eliza Bleylock" and "Lame Jerry" are humorous and pathetic stories of moonshiners and revenuers. "Jack and the Mountain Pink" is a comic sketch of a bored young man from Nashville who comes to the Cumberland Mountains for hiking. His guide is Sincerity Hicks. He soon finds out that she is not one of the lovely and willing "mountain pinks" of whom he has heard so much. He incidentally mentions that he has heard of a big raid on moonshiners being planned by the revenuers. Knowing of a nearby still, Sincerity rushes to warn the men. She is too late, and the revenue agents catch one of the distillers. That night, however, the agent and his prisoner stay at Sincerity's mother's house; and the girl aids the moonshiner to escape by slipping him a knife through a hole in the roof. The bored young man from Nashville comments on Sincerity: "A mountain pink! . . . Oh no, a bean stalk —a Cumberland bean stalk."

But the supreme artist-humorist of the mountaineer was Mary Noailles Murfree, better known by her pen name Charles Egbert Craddock. Though her field was primarily East Tennessee, her work equally applies to the Virginia, the Carolina, and the Kentucky mountain people. In her novels and sketches she delineated a panorama of types found in the Southern highlands of the late nineteenth century: moonshiners, murderers, farmers, millers, blacksmiths, storekeepers, revenuers, itinerant preachers, beautiful mountain girls. Unfortunately, like those of most local colorists, her characters tend to remain types.

F. L. Pattee placed her with the Georgia group of humorists, even though she wrote of Tennesseans.[14] Many of the early settlers in Tennessee, he pointed out, were from Georgia; therefore the mountaineers in her tales, set along the Georgia border, are sons and daughters of the characters in A. B.

Longstreet's "Gander Pulling" and cousins of Joel Chandler Harris' Teague and Puss Poteet. Her sketches, however, lack the masculinity of Longstreet's work. G. H. Baskette wrote that "Miss Murfree's stories are wholesome and pure, without a hint of the erotic, or of prurient suggestion, or any appeal to maudlin sentimentality."[15] Influenced significantly by Charles Dickens, her humor is seldom without its companion pathos.

In the Tennessee Mountains is her best-known book. It dealt with a picturesque region and people then almost unknown to the outside world. Typical of the sketches in the collection is "The 'Harnt' that Walks Chilhowee," which reveals the author's merits and her weaknesses. A young man walks up out of the deepening darkness one evening and tells a mountaineer's family of "a harnt that walks Chilhowee every night o' the worl'." It is the ghost, he says, of Reuben Crabb, born with one arm and shot by the sheriff four years ago. Later that night Clarsie, the mountaineer's daughter, steals from the house and suddenly finds herself face to face with the "ghost," who tells her to bring him food the next night "or it'll be the worse for ye." She delivers food scraps, even though she doesn't believe in stealing for a ghost. "A gal that goes a-robbin' fur a hongry harnt," was her moral reflection, "oughter be throwed bodaciously off'n the bluff." The ghost is discovered to be not a specter but the live Reuben Crabb, who had not been killed by the sheriff. Eventually he is given a fair trial for a crime he supposedly committed, and is found innocent. He is taken in by a kind man and made comfortable for the rest of his life. The humor in the sketch derives from the "oddity" of the mountain character: the credulity of a people to whom ghosts are as real as people, their childlike innocence, and their quaint dialect.

In *The Prophet of the Great Smoky Mountains* the title story shows the mixture of humor and pathos that is present in most of Miss Murfree's works. Seeing the "prophet" riding his mule and reading at the same time, a mountaineer decides to take his whole family to hear the preacher. "I 'low ez a man what kin ride a beastis an' read a book all ter wunst mus' be a powerful exhorter, an' mebbe ye'll lead us all ter grace." The parson stops by a house to "rest his bones," and an old woman, when she hears that he is going to preach the following Sunday, promises: "Then I'm a-comin'. It do me good ter hear you-uns fairly make the sinners spin. Sech a gift o' speech ye hev got! I fairly see hell when ye talk o' thar doom. I see wrath an' I smell brimstone. Lord be thanked, I hev fund peace! An' I'm jes' a-waitin' fur the good day ter come when the Lord'll rescue me from yearth!" Humor thus dominates the story until the parson is arrested in his pulpit the following Sunday. As he is delivering an impassioned recital of his fall from divine grace, the sheriff enters the church, strides to the altar, and lays his instrument of authority on the open Bible. "Ye can read, pa'son. Ye kin read the warrant fur your arrest." The prophet is accused of helping an outlaw escape from jail; and although he is acquitted, he later gives his life for the sheriff who arrested him. Pathos dominates the ending.

A sketch with less pathos and more humor is "A Blacksmith in Love." It deals with a comic episode in which a bashful, awkward blacksmith stops by his girl's house ostensibly to get a drink of water. Cynthia has just asserted to her mother, "I ain't studyin' 'bout marryin' nobody. . . . I hev laid off ter live single." The mother knows the two young people are courting, and teases the blacksmith. "Waal, waal, who would hev b'lieved ez Lost Creek would go dry nigh the shop, an' yit be a-scuttlin' along like that hyarbouts!" And she points toward the swift flow of the creek nearby.[16]

Miss Murfree's humor seldom provokes the belly laugh; like most of the work by the popular writers it calls forth the tender smile instead. Frequently because her humor is so subdued, it is underemphasized, sometimes entirely overlooked. German critic Alfred Reichert, for example, could find little "objective" humor in her works; in fact, he stated that humor played a small role in her stories. However, in *Charles Egbert Craddock und die Amerikanische Short-Story* he pointed out examples of situation humor, character humor, and "subjective" or incidental humor (pp. 108-9).

Another gifted portrayer of the mountaineer in humorous literature is John Fox, Jr. He concentrated on Kentuckians. In the short stories contained in *Bluegrass and Rhododendron, Hell Fer Sartain and Other Stories, Following the Sun Flag,* and *Christmas Eve on Lonesome* he chronicled Kentucky mountain life from birth to death. By treating humor and pathos as inseparable twins, he also showed that he was a man of his time.

The title story in *Hell Fer Sartain* was considered at least by John Patterson, a contemporary critic, to be the best short story ever written by an American.[17] This and most of the other sketches in the volume are comic monologues in dialect. The story is related by a mountaineer who recalls an exciting dancing party Christmas night on Hell fer Sartain. Although the situation is similar to that in Longstreet's "The Fight," the treatment is quite different. Two rivals are drawn into a fight by a Ransy Sniffles type named Abe Shivers. When they discover the trick, they turn upon him. The narrator states that at the next Christmas party one of the two will tote the "Widder Shivers" across the Cumberland River. Fox's treatment differs from Longstreet's mainly in his omission of realistic fight details. During the first fight, in fact, the participants are parted before they can draw blood.

"A Trick o' Trade" illustrates that most of the humor in Fox's sketches comes from the way they are told. The narrator begins, "Stranger, I'm a separate man, an' I don't inquizite into no man's business; but you ax me straight, an' I tell ye straight: You watch ole Tom!" The story he tells back up his admonition, which he repeats at the end.

Humor and religious pathos blend in "Preachin' on Kingdom-Come." This sketch concerns the controversy over calling a replacement for the dead preacher at the "meetin'-house." The narrator recalls one candidate for the job. "They'd heerd o' Henry endurin' the war, an' they knowed he was agin the rebs, an' they wanted Henry if they could jes git him to come." Soon

259

a feud breaks out between opposing factions in the church and continues until a preacher comes along and reconciles the enemies with his eloquent preaching.

Opie Read also traveled the mountain paths, but added little to the portrait of the mountaineer by Craddock and the others. In some of his books, however, he created an authentic atmosphere for his plots. William L. Visscher named as examples *My Young Master, A Kentucky Colonel,* and *The Jucklins.* "In those books you may taste the honey-dew; you can see a squirrel squat and hide in the forks of a tree; a 'possum, lonesome and listless, hangs by the prehensile end of his tail to the limb of a paw-paw bush; a drop of rain spatters in the living velvet of a rose; the scent of tobacco and the whitish hue of its smoke comes from the corn-cob pipe and the lips of a 'po white' woman; the plaintive, faraway call of a dove, deep in the woods, is heard; the melancholy pipe of a whippoorwill comes from a thicket, at night, and in the evening, the chatter of tree-frogs is heard; the rustle of a woman's starched skirt is near; the bay of hounds, on the trail of a fox, comes down a wooded hollow; the red tassel of the ironweed bends in the light wind that blows across blue-grass pastures; a meadow-lark sings his first spring-song, short, yet full of soulful melody."[18] Read's humor, like O. Henry's, became less and less Southern after he moved to Chicago. *Odd Folks,* published in 1897, includes sketches set in Northern Illinois. Of the Kentucky sketches in the volume few could not just as well have been written about Maine or Iowa. Pathos as well as humor pervades most of the pieces. The humor of the mountaineer was being diluted in a syrupy pool of sentiment. A later reaction against this trend led to realistic and naturalistic interpretations of mountaineer life. The main service of humor had been to uncover for the writer a rich vein of untapped ore in the Southern mountains.

The Cracker

The Georgia cracker—and his cousins in Alabama, Tennessee, the Carolinas, Mississippi, and the other Southern states—were tapped for extensive exploitation by the humorists. Continuing the tradition of A. B. Longstreet in writing of the humble life about them, such humorists as Harry Stillwell Edwards, William N. Harben, Charles H. Smith (Bill Arp), Joel Chandler Harris, and Frank L. Stanton used the cracker as the source of some of their best humor.

Like the Negro and the mountaineer, the cracker differed so much from the American norm in appearance and habit that he was often considered comic per se. His unkempt appearance, his slowness in manner and speech, his aversion to labor, his unprogressiveness, and his hostility to new gadgets and new ideas—these traits made him a fascinating discovery to the cosmopolitan reader, North and South. His dialect with its colorful and exaggerated imagery became a popular bit of anecdote machinery. On April 21, 1869, the Union Spring *Times* printed under the title "How I Did It" one such anecdote. "I hitched my chair close up to hern, shet my eyes and shudderingly said: 'Sally, I've been hankering arter you for a long time—that's so! I love you from the foot of your sole to the head of the crown, and I don't keer who nose it.' With that she fetched a screach, and arter a while she sez: 'Uriah!' 'Sally,' sez I. 'Yes,' sez she, hidin' her face. 'Glory, galory!' sez I. 'I can jump a ten rail fence. Hooray—hooray!' With that I sorter sloshed myself down by her side and clinched. O, my! O, broomstraws with lasses on 'em!" The humor in the sketch arises fully from the cracker speech.

Sidney Lanier used the dialect and character for several of his humorous poems, including "A Puzzled Ghost in Florida" (*Poems*). A traveler tells of a trip he took down the coast of Florida. At one stop he is approached by an "ancient mariner" type, a wild-looking man with a long beard. The old man relates an unusual experience. He says he once built "a c'lossal sanitarium" for a key nearby and loaded it on his steamboat ready to be taken to its destination. But the night after it was finished "a squall / Cum up from some'eres," and the next morning he saw "That boat laid right whar that hotel had stood, / An' it sailed out to sea!" Now, the bearded one says sadly, he is committed to a life of trying to figure out what happened.

> For here I walk for evermore,
>   A-tryin' to make it gee,
> How one same wind could blow my ship to shore,
>   And my hotel to sea!

The apotheosis of the cracker is Charles H. Smith's Bill Arp. In *Bill Arp's Scrap Book* Smith described the "original and real" Bill Arp, the Georgian from whom he took his pen name and on whom he based his fictional character. "He was an humble man and unlettered in books; never went to school but a month or two in his life, and could neither read nor write." Bill, however, had common sense or mother-wit, ingenuity, "plan and contrivance," and good humor. In his home community, Smith wrote, "He could out-run, out-jump, out-swim, out-rastle, out-shoot anybody . . . and was so far ahead that everybody else had give it up, and Bill reigned supreme" (pp. 8-10). Bill's prowess in fighting Smith demonstrated by telling of the time Bill had to fight Ben McGinnis, a rival from an adjoining community. The following excerpt will show how lacking in blood and pain the postwar fights were in contrast with those depicted in the earlier Southern humor. "As Ben straightened himself up, Bill let fly with his hard, bony fist right in his left eye, and followed it up with another. I don't know how it was, and never will know; but I do know this, that in less than a second, Bill had him down and was on him, and his fists and his elbows and his knees seemed all at work. He afterwards said that his knees worked on Ben's bread basket, which he knew was his weakest part. Ben hollered enough in due time, which was considered honorable to do, and all right, and Bill helped him up and brushed the dirt off his clothes, and said, 'Now, Ben is it all over betwixt us, is you and me all right?' And Ben said,

'It's all right 'twixt you and me, Bill; I give it up, and you are a gentleman.' Bill invited all hands up to the shelf, and they took a drink, and Bill paid for the treat as the generous victor, and he and Ben were friends" (p. 13). In prewar humor several ears and hunks of flesh gouged from cheeks and noses were usually left lying around after a fight; seldom did the contestants afterwards shake hands and make up. Again, writing of a wrestling match between Bill Arp and a braggart, Smith related that the braggart lost his balance and fell into the river below where they were tussling. Again the match ends with a reconciliation and a moral. "It cured Ike of braggin, and it cured Bob Moore of bettin, and that was a good thing" (pp. 14-15).

But if the popular humorists wrote more refined sketches of the poor white, the non-professional had no large audience to please and could speak his mind. Some of the sketches in Joseph Gault's *Reports*, for example, show the continuation of devices and approaches used by the humorists of the Old Southwest. "The Drunkard's Resurrection in His Morning Shroud" is a realistic comic sketch of a young man who goes on a spree and drinks too much. Here is Gault's description of the scene early the morning after. "He was a very red headed man, and had thrown up his late supper, stump water, and rat-tail, which made a pile as large as a quart bowl, and the jay birds, woodpeckers and old thrashers, were eating, fighting and frolicking over their early breakfast, derived from a late supper." When the drunk is aroused from his stupor, he lets loose a string of epithets. "Clear yourself from here you pigeon-toed, bowe legged, brissel nosed, tarapan-backed hypocrit, or I will shroud you with a convoy of buzzards."

Another of Gault's extremely realistic sketches is "Jealousy Accounted For." A cracker woman accuses her husband of adultery: "Yes you little spike legged son of a bitch, you have been spiking about until you have spiked old Sal Gunter; now you have got yourself in a hell of a fix." Her accusation is confirmed, she thinks, when one night she finds a basket at the door with a baby in it and a note addressed to her husband. The delighted, sadistic shrew calls in the neighbors to witness the unwrapping of the infant son of her unfaithful husband, "old spike legs." But the baby is actually an old tomcat, and the joke is on her. Her jealousy is exposed.

A sketch reminiscent of Simon Suggs' preaching experience is Gault's satirical "Faith, Hope, and Charity." The writer showed here a charlatan preacher well versed in the art of getting the congregation to fill his pockets with money. In "A Preacher Collecting Money" he described a fight between a Missionary Baptist preacher and a debtor. After the fight the parson treats the entire company to whiskey. Gault writes that the man of God had a Bible in one pocket and corn whiskey in the other.

But generally pathos had replaced realism as an almost necessary ingredient of humor. A poem by Sam Small in *Old Si's Humorous Sketches* illustrates the trend toward mixing humor and pathos. Perhaps influenced by Bret Harte's sympathetic portrayals of bad men, Small wrote in "A Bad Citizen" of

a gambler in Chattanooga who during a yellow fever epidemic had nursed a
family of orphans and had died himself. Pleading the gambler's case before a
"Jedge," the cracker narrator says that "he had er heart like a full grow'd
man / An' as warm as er woman's cheek." He had a good war record.
"He wuz brave uz old Caesar . . . / And allus in front of the line." Though
"a bad citizen" according to the letter of the law, he was not a bad man.

> *With the sick 'uns he stayed like er brother,*
> *An' he buried the dead like er priest;*
> *He took care jest ez fond ez er mother*
> *Of the orphins, from biggest ter least.*

The cracker concludes his argument on a note of religious sentiment.

> *This man lived a life that was hard, Jedge,*
> *An' chuck full of sin an' of shame,*
> *But don't yer forgit that the Lord, Jedge,*
> *Weighs the saint an' the gambler the same!*

Sam Small also wrote cracker sketches in prose, but their significance is negligible. "A Katterkism Lesson" is significant only for its revelation of an illiterate farmer's prejudice against dime novels. The farmer discovers his son at the
well-house reading a novel with a lurid picture on the cover. Since his father
cannot read, the boy tries to persuade him that he is reading a new catechism
and that the picture is of "the angel in the burnin' bush." Actually the novel
is about Indians burning a white woman at the stake; but although the father
doesn't know the subject, he does know the book is "a nasty, stinking dime
novel." Most of the cracker sketches by this newspaper humorist are like the
other features appearing in the Atlanta *Constitution* from day to day: written
for that time, they have little interest and meaning for later readers.

Another newspaper poet who wrote ephemeral cracker dialect verses was
Frank L. Stanton, also on the staff of the Atlanta *Constitution*. Though forgotten
today, he was one of the three writers of dialect poetry that Joel Chandler
Harris predicted would be remembered. (The other two were Robert Burns and
James Whitcomb Riley.) His poems contain humor and pathos in generous
amounts. Many of them are optimistic and pastoral. The cracker reciting "Down
on the Old Plantation" concludes.

> *In spite of politics an' sich*
> *A-worryin' of the nation,*
> *We're doin' well in Georgy lan'*
> *Down on the ol' plantation.*

This poem is typical of those appearing in *Up from Georgia,* the volume Stanton dedicated to Joel Chandler Harris. The cracker's fundamentalist and
emotional religion was as fascinating to Stanton as to other humorists. "In Camp-
meetin' Time" shows that the cracker's religion was not very different from the
Negro's.

The Smiling Phoenix

Some don't believe in shoutin', but to me it's cl'ar as day
Ef a feller has religion it'll sometimes act that way!

In this book, in *Songs of the Soil*, and in "Just from Georgia," the column Stanton conducted for the *Constitution*, are reflected his sunshiny humor, his wit and wisdom, and his skillful use of dialect. As a humorous poet he dealt mainly with the household joys of the common people. Some critics tagged him the James Whitcomb Riley of the South. "Me and Mary" from *Songs of the Soil* illustrates the kinship between the two poetasters. In this poem a hayseed relates how his milkmaid sweetheart dissuaded him from leaving the farm for the city. Now all is sweetness and light.

I'm mixed up with the meadows, an' I never want to roam,
Fer Mary does the milkin' an' I drive the cattle home!

In "The Lightning Age" the speaker expresses the cracker's skepticism of new inventions. He is amazed at man's ability to make ice and snow by machine—"rain in Texas without a word o' prayer"—and is afraid "the Lord ain't in it." But there is one bright spot.

But when I go—praise be to God!—it won't be in the night,
Fer my grave'll shine like glory in a bright electric light!

The volume *Comes One with a Song* contains one of Stanton's most popular poems, "The Billville Debate." Showing the fierce competition and antagonism among Protestant churches, the poem deals with a meeting of brethren to discuss the question "Is salvation really free?" Arguments on both sides are expounded emotionally; then a preacher settles the controversy by citing how poorly preachers are paid. He tells the church members,

You've been feedin' on the gospel till the souls of you are fat,
An' the preacher's coat is threadbare an' the wind howls through his hat!

Shamed by their parsimony, the parishioners take up a collection.

An' the last seen of the preachers—they wuz jottin' down their notes
An' havin' of their measures took fer bran new broadcloth coats!

The preacher, however, came in for a bit of satire in Stanton's "The Billville Spirit Meeting."[19] At a "sperrit meetin'" to call up the spirits of loved ones it is revealed that most of the congregation have things to hide from the departed ones and flee before the ghosts arrive. Even the minister cannot face the music.

The parson said he had a call 'bout ten miles off, to pray!
He didn't preach nex' Sunday, an' they tell it roun' a bit,
Accordin' to the best reports the parson's runnin' yit!

The satire in Stanton's verses is the gentle Horatian kind, not the cynical Juvenalian variety.

Popular though he was during his day, Stanton, like Sam Small, is unknown to later generations. His vogue, however, is a valuable index to public taste in the late nineteenth and early twentieth centuries. As a newspaper humorist he had to write what his public wanted to read.

On a somewhat higher literary level are the cracker sketches of Will Allen Dromgoole. One of the most effective is the farcical "Ole Logan's Courtship" in *The Heart of Old Hickory*. It is an account of the love adventure of a middle-aged bachelor. The narrator defends Ole Logan's foolish intention to court a young girl: "you see, bein' ez it had took Loge nigh about forty year to make up his mind to go court'n' it seemed sort o' big when he got it made up, naturly." Loge's mother, with whom he lives, still thinks of him "wearin knee pants an' caliker jackets" and is at first horrified at his courting plans, but she finally gives in. Loge is absentminded, she rationalizes—he often wears his socks for two weeks instead of the one week he is supposed to—and maybe a wife to look after him when she is gone wouldn't be a bad idea.

Ole Logan's first problem is to decide which girl to marry. Finally he narrows it down to one of Sid Fletcher's three girls, but he can't decide which one. He thinks he is obligated to all three; once at meeting he was asked to hand out the hymnals and gave Jinnie seven; he gave Mary the twenty-odd eggs he found in a hidden guinea nest; and he once opened a gate for Mandy. In this state of indecision he goes over to Fletcher's one Saturday evening to make up his mind and to bring back a wife. When he gets there, he is so shy all he can say is "I jes come over here . . . to git a goad o' water," not thinking how ridiculous it sounds to say he walked several miles for water.

It soon begins to rain, and he is invited to stay the night. Now the farce really begins. Taking off his clothes to go to bed, he puts his pants in the openings between the logs that have not been chinked in. The next morning they are gone. He looks everywhere for them—even up the chimney—but in vain. In desperation he goes back to bed, "an' give out that he wuz mighty sick, an' would some un please go fur his ma." His mother comes, returns home quickly, and comes back with a small bundle tied to the side of the saddle. Once dressed in the clothes his mother brought him, Ole Logan watches for a chance, and when no one is around sneaks off home through the woods. He makes up his mind to wait a little longer before marrying.

Harry S. Edwards' best work is the short humorous studies he made of the crackers of his native Georgia. A suitor more successful than Ole Logan is Ezekiel Obadiah Sykes in "An Idyl of 'Sinkin' Mount'in" (*Two Runaways*). While pining for the love of a girl who spurns him, Ezekiel Obadiah discovers his own true love in the orphan girl who has lived five years with his family. Most of the humor rises out of the young cracker's lament for his lost love—"O Sal; my heart ar' plum broke!"—and his flattery of his true love—"I declar' ter goodness, D'rindy . . . yuh han' 's sof' es er moss-patch, an' yuh es putty es th' sunset on the mount'in."

The title story from *His Defense* is about a farmer indicted for cursing his mother-in-law. After he admits his guilt to his lawyer and adds that the curse was not motivated by abuse or insult from her, the attorney recommends that he plead guilty. But the cracker wants a trial—actually he wants a sounding board for his many grievances. At the trial he presents his case: he and his young wife were living in bliss until the scolding, fault-finding mother-in-law moved in. Not able to stand this togetherness, the couple moved out, leaving their home to the intruder. A prolonged argument over the sewing machine left in the house finally caused the man to break down and curse his mother-in-law. The judge immediately dismisses the case. Even the woman is appalled at her own callousness and is reconciled with her son-in-law.

Two more sketches from *Two Runaways* are dominated by humor, but they show the characteristic decline into sentiment. "Elder Brown's Backslide" is the account of a churchman's misdoings in Macon while away from the domineering protection of his wife. He is thrown by his mule on the way to town, has trouble borrowing money on his unmade crop, and loses the shopping list his wife gave him. But all these episodes are minor compared to his complete undoing: for the first time in twenty years he succumbs to temptation, goes into a bar, and gets drunk. Before returning home, he decides to buy his wife a bonnet to appease her. He forgets to ride his mule home and when he is sent back to town to get the animal, he returns to the saloon; yet his wife, looking at the pink bonnet with the blue plume, forgives the old backslider.

"Sister Todhunter's Heart" is one of Edwards' most amusing stories. A new minister in a Georgia village discovers that one of his most interesting parishioners is Sister Todhunter, in the words of another lady member: "a disagreeable old thing who lives out on her farm about a mile from here." The parson's suspicion about a henpecked husband is confirmed when he visits the Todhunters. Colonel Todhunter tells the minister confidentially that he is leading a dog's life and needs help. He suggests that his wife be reported to the church for her actions toward him and publicly humiliated. Once, the timid little man reports, he came home somewhat tipsy and his wife almost killed him. "As I was preparing to lie down, being also ill, Mrs. Todhunter, with her superior strength and weight, forced me between the mattresses and sat down on me. And there she sat, Parson, three hundred pounds, and it a July day, and knitted all afternoon. 'I'll sweat that whiskey out er you,' she says; and she did. The perspiration that exuded from my pores soaked through the mattress and dripped on the floor. I do not know how I lived through it." The minister agrees that Sister Todhunter needs to be disciplined by the church; but sensing something in the air, the overbearing wife threatens "er bad day fur Moun' Zion" if she is brought up before the church.

The next Sunday is appointed for the hearing. The minister presents the case against her; then the little colonel gets up to give his testimonial. Before he can begin, his wife reaches out with her umbrella and jerks him over into her lap. Then she begins an exposé of prominent church members, from the minister's wife to the banker. "An' there's Tom Culpepper. *He's* er pretty nice one to be settin' hisself up fur er church-cleaner. I saw him pass my house so drunk last week he didn't know if he was goin' home er comin' back." When she becomes even more vituperative, the parson suggests that she be removed bodily from the church, and she is taken out kicking and screaming. On the way home she pushes Elder Hamlin into a creek. At home she slams a door on the colonel and holds his neck in it until they reach an understanding. Naturally she is voted out of the church.

But from here on pathos rules the sketch. When the parson's baby is deathly sick and given up for incurable, Sister Todhunter goes to stay at the parsonage and nurses the baby back to health with her love and mullein tea. The parson and the church are penitent. She pooh-poohs their apologies, but she offers the minister a bit of advice. "When yer go ter turn ernother woman out er church, don't yer go ter her husban', if he happens ter be a triflin' kind er man; but come straight to headquarters. Trouble and worry sometimes sorter crusts over er woman's heart, so that ev'ybody can't see hit, Parson, but hit's there all the same."

The Alabama cracker was not as prominent as his cousin in Georgia, but he was not ignored. Francis Bartow Lloyd, who used the pen name Rufus Sanders, revealed Alabama backwoods scenes in *Sketches of Country Life*. The cracker's interest in politics and in whiskey, his love of practical jokes, his indulgence in mule races and horse trades—these are the subjects of Rufus Sanders' sketches. "There Are Boys and Boys" uses the humorous dialogue that Opie Read and others had made a stock device. On a campaign trip in North Alabama in 1890, Rufus writes, he met a boy who was his match in verbal wit.

"Hello Buster! top of the mornin at you," says I.
"Howdy Mister," says he.
"How does your coperosity seem to egashuate?" says I.
"Tolerable fermently accordin to our doxology, how does yours seem to redoshiate?" says he.
"Are you travelin around today or jest goin somewheres?" says I.
"Goin summers," says he.
"What you got in that bucket?" says I.
"Butter," says he.
"What sort of butter is it?" says I.
"Cow's butter," says he.
"Is it fresh?" says I.
"No, sir, mammy salted it this mornin," says he.
"If you ever git down into the neck of woods where I live please pass in callin," says I.
"Same to you and all your family," says he.

The love of understatement is dramatically illustrated in "A Whole Lot the Matter." On a cold, drizzly day, riding in West Alabama, Rufus came upon a boy on his knees trying to start a fire beside a covered wagon. Touched by the pitiful picture of the forlorn, crying boy, Rufus asks what are his troubles. The boy bitterly replies that "taint no use," but he does recite his tribulations.

The Smiling Phoenix

"Old Buck has got the holler horn and got it bad, Daddy is laying out there in the wagin dead drunk, Sister Sal she loped off with a strange man last night, Mammy she took and run away wid a sewin machine peddler this mornin, our dog died last week, and the goldarned wood is wet, and dad-blame it I don't want to go to Texas nohow." Shaken by the boy's misfortunes, Rufus gives him his pocketknife, two bits in money, tells him to brace up like a man, and leaves. "That was all I could do."

Most of Lloyd's sketches are comic bagatelles of cracker life. "Handy Stribblin's Dog," for example, is about three brothers who pool their money and buy a dog. When they grow up and marry, they decide on a poetry contest to determine who will keep the dog. Each brother's entry, they decide, must "have something about possum in it." The two bright brothers have their verses ready and recite them. When the dull-witted Handy's turn comes, he is "trembling like a man with the buck ager," but he finally braces up and recites.

> *Possum up a simmon tree,*
> *Rabbit on the ground,*
> *Rabbit say you dad-blame*
> *slou-footed, box-ankled,*
> *bench-legged, long-tailed,*
> *gray-headed, blaze-faced,*
> *grass-bellied son-of-a-gun,*
> *Shake some simmons down!*

Handy wins the dog.

Another bagatelle is "Miss Garner and Her Soft Soap," wherein a country woman gets revenge on the railroad for running its trains too fast by her place and killing her chickens and ducks. She pours lye soap over two hundred yards of track at an incline near her farm, and the train is unable to climb it. Perhaps too often Lloyd used the cracker personality as a humor device; however, in the sketches he usually shows insight into the character.

Will Harben's North Georgia crackers are portrayed in the tradition of A. B. Longstreet, but with more emotion. In 1910 William Dean Howells praised Harben's local color sketches of contemporary North Georgia and the pioneer period still persistent there "with its wild passions, its fights and frolics, its intensely personalized religious experiences, its beliefs unshaken by modern question, its exaggerated sense of honor." Harben's characters are mainly poor-white farmers who were still in the backwoods stage of civilization. Howells said of them: "They express themselves, without straining for dialect, in the neighborly parlance which their experience and their observation have not transcended, and they express themselves with a fury of fun, of pathos and profanity which is native to their region."[20]

Although considered by his contemporaries as humorous pieces, *Northern Georgia Sketches* is generally a sober book. The titles of such stories as "The Tender Link" and "A Filial Impulse" suggest the triumph of sentiment. "A Rural

Visitor" does contain humor of the greenhorn-in-the-city type, but even it ends in romantic sentiment.

A better example of Harben's humor is found in *The Georgians*. The main character is Harben's best humorous creation, Abner Daniel. Abner is a cracker noted for his pranks and his wit. Harben begins by describing him: "Abner was a farmer, tall, lank, thin-faced, with a tuft of gray beard on his chin and a constant twinkle of merriment in his eyes." Although humor is not organic to the main plot—Abner saves the life of a man in jail for a murder he did not commit—its incidental use makes the novel much more readable.

James J. McDonald's sketches of life in remote isolated sections of Virginia deal with Old Dominion kinsmen of the crackers in the lower South (*Life in Old Virginia*). He wrote of peddlers traveling among the poor whites, of the farmer's custom of turning out hogs each winter, and of the popularity of camp meetings. At one meeting a woman suddenly bursts into tears after the song leader has begun to "raise" a hymn. The hymn raiser stops his singing, leans over to the woman, and asks if she is sick. "Brother Jeems, I couldn't help it. You know what bad luck I've had lately. I lost my poor dear husband just a month ago to-day, and my son went off last week, and yesterday my old mule 'Jennie' that I sot such store by, she up and died too. Poor thing! She used to come to the yard gate ev'ry morning and wake me up braying, and when I heard you raise that hymn, your voice was so much like the poor old critter I just couldn't help crying. God bless you brother Jeems" (p. 276).

Almost every humorist who treated the cracker wrote of horse-swapping, one of his favorite pastimes. McDonald was no exception.

"The swapping" was conducted usually in the tavern "horse lot," after some "sharp talk," and a few gallops of the animals, up the road and back again. A wily "swapper" from an adjoining county, would ride through the "Court House Bounds" on his "new, jaunty tail, frisky *hoss*," that betokened "go in him," and "hard to hold." Such a swapper was sure to attract the attention of the younger owners of horses. None but the poor animal, and its shrewd rider knew that a dried chestnut burr under the crupper was the main cause of its friskiness, and an inspection of his mouth, would disclose the fact that he had "cut his eye teeth" many moons antedating the birth of the new owner. The loser in a horse swap at one court was a winner at the next court, else he had made such a "bad swap" that it "broke him up." Every young horse owner, at some time or another, is desirous to make a swap. The earlier in life he makes the swap and "gets stuck good" the more he may profit in after years by this experience. The "Court House Bounds" on a court day, is a good place for the young swapper to begin, for there he is sure to meet with friends who will do for him that which his newly swapped horse may refuse to do—carry him home (pp. 191-92).

Thus was the cracker portrayed in humor from Virginia to Florida and Texas. His life was a hard one, but it offered many opportunities for the humorist and local colorist interested in exploring one of America's odd types. In his essay on Will Harben, Howells wrote: "His corner of that strange 'new South,' which is still for us such a *terra incognita* after our many inquiries and conjectures, is alive with what we feel to be genuine interests and real emotions."[20]

In the middle of the twentieth century Americans were still fascinated by the strange corners in the South. They continued reading humorous sketches of the cracker in Caldwell's *Tobacco Road* and Faulkner's *As I Lay Dying*.

Just Plain Folks

Not all humor about the common man in the South was about crackers, mountaineers, or rednecks. Some sketches concern people less easily identified than the cracker or the mountaineer. A large body of humor had to do with people who are not members of a group considered intrinsically humorous or odd. But among these ordinary people were many mavericks, who, by comparison with the norm, were funny. And many of them became involved in comical situations.

Calvin Stewart's Uncle Josh Weathersby is a country type but not a cracker. One chief difference between these types is the technical fact that the cracker appears in dialect stories and the country type does not. In the "Punkin Centre" stories Uncle Josh reported humorous incidents among the common people. (His monologues were once very popular on phonograph records.) In "Jim Lawson's Hoss Trade" he tells how a horse trader gets taken in by a gypsy, and how he in turn unloads the nag on Deacon Witherspoon. A peculiar feature of the horse is the fact that it would sit down when its sides were touched, and since the deacon is a big hunter Jim tells him that the horse is a setter. This talent he demonstrates on a hunt. On the way home, however, the deacon is riding his new "setter" across a creek and accidentally touches its side and the horse "squatted right down in the crick." The sly Jim Lawson maintains his reputation as the best horse trader in Punkin Centre with this explanation, "he's trained to set fer suckers same as fer rabbits."

In another sketch Uncle Josh relates his comic experiences in learning to play golf. He concludes that "all I know about playin' golf is, the feller what knocks the ball so durned far you can't find it or whar it does the most damage, wins the game."

Topical allusions are frequent in his sketches. In "Uncle Josh at a Camp Meeting" Stewart tells of a preacher (he was probably "ridin' on a free pass") who says that people shouldn't be too hard on the monopolists because "our forefathers wuz all monopolists." Adam and Eve had a monopoly on the Garden of Eden. Lot's wife had a corner on the salt market. "And while Pharoe's daughter was not in the milk business, yet we observe she took great profit out of the water." Before the baptism services in "A Baptizin' at the Hickory Corners Church" Deacon Witherspoon asks a Sunday School class "who slew the Philistines and whar at?" A little boy answered promptly. "Commodore Dewey, at Manila." The deacon corrects him with "Sampson," but another little boy says,

"No, Deacon, I think you've sort of got it mixed up; he wasn't there; Schley is the feller what done the job, at Santiague." The deacon is exasperated; the boys have "bin readin' too much about them war doin's in the papers." He asks an easy question: What is the First Commandment? "Remember the main" is the answer he gets.

One of the most popular books in America during the early twentieth century was Alice Hegan Rice's *Mrs. Wiggs of the Cabbage Patch*. George Madden Martin called the book "a piece of that rare product, pure comedy." She described *Mrs. Wiggs* and the sequel *Lovey Mary*. "Both stories deal charitably and affectionately with the lives of the plain people, a love of humanity pervading them, their creed being an optimistic and simple one. Their humor is natural and unforced, a mixture of comic appreciation and human sympathy."[21] Mrs. Wiggs, as characterized by Alice Hegan Rice, is a poor widow with four children, but she is cheerful and the "sum and substance of her philosophy lay in keeping the dust off her rose-colored spectacles." Her husband died by following "the alcohol route," but she buried his faults with him, "and for want of better virtues to extol she always laid stress on the fine hand he wrote." The family lives in the Cabbage Patch, not a real cabbage patch at all "but a queer neighborhood, where ramshackle cottages played hop-scotch over the railroad tracks." The Wiggs' house is the most impressive one in the neighborhood because it has two front doors (though one is nailed up) and the only tin roof in the Cabbage Patch. The book fitted perfectly the public demand for crying humor. It contained just enough humor and pathos to keep the reader smiling tenderly through his tears. The family's nursing of a dying horse back to health is an excellent example of this type of humor.

In *Southern Silhouettes* by Jeannette Walworth a sketch exploits the humor in pluralistic denominationalism among the common folk of the South. "A Bone of Contention" tells of the building of the Blue Lick community church. When completed, it has a spire which "terminates abruptly and looks not unlike a badly sharpened lead-pencil with a gall nut stuck in its point." The community was without a church until Miss Margery Banks, a spinster, became a "merciless woman with a mission." The church was inevitable, although there was some opposition. The Episcopalians, for example, are afraid that a neighborhood church will be too democratic. Most people are convinced of the need for a church, however, when they hear that the doctor's eight-year-old son has mistaken the picture of a church spire for a pigeon house. Miss Margery finally leads or coerces everyone in the neighborhood into supporting the church, and it is built. Then the denomination of the church has to be decided upon. The Presbyterians naturally assume that it will be Presbyterian; the Episcopalians naturally assume it will be Episcopal; and the Methodists naturally assume it will be Methodist. As a result of this disunion the congregation split into factions and the little church has a succession of ministers of different denominations. As no one minister is supported by the entire community, the church is finally closed. Mrs. Walworth makes her satirical intent explicit. "It is one of these snarls that time does little towards straightening out, and that is the reason why the grass grows over the walk in front of the little Brick Church, and the cows take their afternoon siestas on its shady side, and the bell does not ring in a harmonious flock of worshipers to sit at the feet of an established minister."

Several of Samuel Minturn Peck's *Alabama Sketches* deal with plain folk not identifiable as crackers or fallen aristocrats or any other recognizable type. "What Became of Mary Ellen" is the story of the escape of the world-famous anaconda "Mary Ellen" from the circus visiting a small Alabama town, Oakville. It is also the story of how the editor of the Oakville *Chronicle* exploited the anaconda's escape in sensational stories to increase his circulation enough to get married.

"Sister Taylor's Registered Letter" concerns the first such letter ever received at the Hickory Hollow post office. It is addressed to Widow Taylor, but she will not come down to sign for it because she is afraid it might contain bad news. The curious villagers try all sorts of ludicrous strategies to get the widow to claim the letter, but she remains adamant. Finally on the day it is to be returned, the widow's son dresses as his mother and claims it. Instead of bad news, he finds $200 and good tidings from the widow's brother.

One of the funniest of Peck's tales is "Mrs. McMurtrie's Rooster." A young bachelor lawyer is told by his friends that he should have an avocation. Considering this suggestion, he thinks of and discards many possibilities. "Art? He preferred the nearest window to any picture. Music? He could hardly whistle one tune. Bee-keeping? The little insects might swarm in the middle of court week: besides, he hated honey. Wood-carving? He could never whittle without cutting his fingers." While musing on the problem he happens to glance through the window and sees the local grocery store. Suddenly he decides that gardening will be his avocation. So he buys a house with a garden, and he tells Mrs. McMurtrie, "It is the dream of my life to raise fine radishes." In a very witty repartee the new neighbor tries unsuccessfully to discourage him. Later he discovers why: Mrs. McMurtrie raises chickens. Although he knows the two avocations will not go together, he is determined not to stop his hobbyhorse just to please her. He is completely unconcerned about what she thinks of him—until he meets her young niece. Then he decides he should stay on speaking and visiting terms with his neighbor. This he finds hard to do because the chickens frequently invade his garden, eating his seeds and scratching up his plants. When he complains, Mrs. McMurtrie explains that her chickens are not after his precious vegetables but after the bugs and worms that could harm them. For this service he should be grateful. When he replies that he doesn't want her chickens destroying his bugs and worms, "she said that if I was such a crank as to set up a nursery for bugs and worms, she'd be happy to tell the town, and I'd never get another case at the law."

Finally a friend comes up with a scheme to rid his garden of Mrs. McMurtrie's chickens, yet not insult her openly. He should make a rabbit trap to catch the "rabbits" that she insists have been eating his vegetables. This he does. As luck would have it, the day after he set the trap, Mrs. McMurtrie's favorite rooster disappears. Of course, she suspects the young lawyer and breaks off communication between him and her niece. Seeing the beautiful young niece secretly, he pleads, "I never robbed a hen-roost in my life," and suggests that a replacement ordered from Mobile might appease her wrath. But the niece says that her aunt would know the difference. The lawyer meditates on the crisis. "How absurd it was that his romance should be entangled with the fate of an old white rooster!" The situation remains at an impasse until the lawyer overhears several boys talking about a rooster they had stolen a few nights before and sold to a nearby chicken breeder. This leads to the recovery of Mrs. McMurtrie's rooster and the blossoming of a romance between her niece and the gardening lawyer.

Southern humor after the Civil War reflected the many colorful groups of white people in the South—people who with the end of slavery could begin to compete economically, socially, and politically with the aristocrat. These groups, and especially the cracker, formed the bulk of the emerging Southern middle class. The humor of the period shows the great vogue of white dialect stories set in the mountains, the bayous, and on back-country Southern farms. It shows how this vogue lessened with the decline of the local-color movement. "Mrs. McMurtrie's Rooster" and the other sketches in the last section of this chapter show the trend toward less emphasis on setting, time, and ethnic groups. Most of the humor of the Old Southwest could have been written only during the flush times of the frontier South. "Mrs. McMurtrie's Rooster" does not depend on any setting or time for its humor.

Notes

1. McIlwaine, *Southern Poor-White*, 106 ff.
2. "Southern Literature," 504.
3. Quoted in Julia Harris, *J. C. Harris*, 204.
4. Kephart, *Southern Highlanders*, 682.
5. "American Humor," 854.
6. Union Springs *Times*, Dec. 14, 1870.
7. In Clemens, *Famous Funny Fellows*, 92.
8. *Ibid.*, 186-88.
9. In *Otto the Knight;* see McIlwaine, *Southern Poor-White*, 153 ff.
10. *South in History*, 541.
11. *Sketches from Old Virginia*, 141.

12. Fox, "Southern Mountaineer."
13. In Aswell, *Native American Humor*, 296-97.
14. *American Literature Since 1870*, 308 ff.
15. *Library of Southern Literature*, VIII, 3726.
16. In Abbott, *Wit of Women*, 135-39.
17. *Library of Southern Literature*, IV, 1687.
18. *Ten Wise Men*, 126.
19. In Wilder, *Wit and Humor*, 224-25.
20. "Mr. Harben's Georgia Fiction," 363.
21. *Library of Southern Literature*, X, 4404.

9. Politics

IN A PERIOD FILLED with such issues as Reconstruction and civil rights, William Jennings Bryan and the gold question, the growth of big business and its corruption, and the Spanish-American War, much of the humor was bound to be political or to have political overtones. From the professional humorist like Joel Chandler Harris to the professional politician like "Private" John Allen of Mississippi humor was used to influence people politically. Newspapers and comic journals were filled with cartoons, satires, anecdotes, and funny stories by any about politicians. In 1901 W. P. Trent even included the political as one of the major divisions of American humor.[1] In the South political humor had been popular since colonial times.

In 1902 the Preface to *Wit and Humor of American Statesmen* explained this popularity. "Probably in no other country does politics enter so largely and so intimately into the daily life of the people as in the United States. . . ." Of American politicians the editors said, "Their clever sayings and pungent witticisms are chronicled and chuckled over from the Lakes to the Gulf, from the St. Lawrence to the Rio Grande." Certainly in a nation where universal suffrage is an ideal if not a reality, many people will be interested in one of the most fascinating categories of humor. And in a section of that nation where politics is often fiery and intensely personal this interest will be even greater. The Southern editor Henry Watterson wrote simply and succinctly, "Humor has played no small part in our politics."[2]

Southern political humor after 1865 was often quite partisan, but not usually as biting as that written immediately before and during the war. Samuel "Sunset" Cox showed the dominant attitude. "Studied invective implies malice aforethought, and no malicious man was ever great by either wit or humor. Malice corrodes the steel of the polished poniard. It unfits it for its work."[3] "Our Bob" by John T. Moore (in *Ole Mistis*), eulogizing Governor Bob Taylor of Tennessee, revealed the ingredients of Taylor's humor. They were typical.

> With humor as sweet as our Basin
> When the clover blooms gather the dew,
> And pathos as deep as our valley
> When the clouds shut the stars from our view,
> With wisdom as rich and as fertile
> As our plains when they first feel the plow. . . .

The general tendency to make humor sentimental and wise is thus evident in that dealing with politics.

The importance of humor in electoral campaigns was emphasized by Joel Chandler Harris. "First and last, humor has played a very large part in our political campaigns; in fact, it may be said that it has played almost as large a part as principles—which is the name that politicians give to their theories. It is a fact that . . . the happy allusion, the humorous anecdote . . . will change the whole prospects of a political struggle. . . ."[4] The Southern campaigner who could tell a folksy joke or a tall tale certainly had a better chance of being elected county commissioner—or governor—than his straight-talking opponent.

Anecdotes of the war were of course a favorite with politicians. In his memoirs Frank A. Montgomery illustrated how during Reconstruction a congressional candidate employed a war anecdote to win laughs and get votes. He used the story told by a Negro of how a certain white man narrowly avoided being drafted into the army. There was operative in the Confederacy a law known as the "twenty-negro law," which exempted from compulsory military service every man who owned as many as twenty slaves. The Negro said that his master owned hundreds of slaves, while a neighbor owned but a few. Shortly after the passage of the law the Negro was sent on an errand to the neighbor's and found him very depressed. The man's cook explained. "Master scared dey gwine to put him in the army 'cause he ain't got twenty niggers; he ain't got but nineteen." In desperation the poor white man tried to borrow a Negro to

275

round out his twenty, but failed. A month later the slave returned and found the master smiling and happy. Again the cook explained. "Sally had a baby last night and master's got twenty niggers now" (pp. 292-93).

Then as now religion was frequently an important issue in political campaigns. But then it was not so much a matter of Protestant versus Catholic as of Protestant versus Protestant. A story often told by Senator Zebulon Vance of North Carolina had to do with a campaign trip into the backwoods of the Tarheel state. At one crossroads community he was asked by an old man about his church affiliation. Although he did not belong to any church, he wanted the vote. He answered that his grandfather from Scotland was Presbyterian and his grandmother from England was Episcopalian, but that his father was born a Methodist in this country. His mention of these denominations failed to get the approval of the voter. He made one last effort. "But my mother was a Baptist, and it's my opinion that a man has got to go under water to get to heaven." The old man's face brightened, and he passed around a jug of mountain dew. Vance got all the votes in that Baptist community.[5]

Many candidates would do almost anything to get votes—from bribing voters with whiskey and money to letting their wives sleep with voters. In a sketch he called "Politics Makes Bedfellows" Henry R. Foote told of a circuit judge who stopped at an inn and upon inspecting his room for the night found the bed occupied by the innkeeper's wife and a stranger. Later in another room he came upon the wife in another bed with another man. The judge went to the innkeeper. The host explained. "You see, I am a candidate for constable here, and very hard up for votes. The election will come off tomorrow, after which I promise you there shall be no similar cause for complaint."[6]

Court days at the county seat were as popular with candidates for speechmaking as with farmers for horse-trading. McDonald in *Life in Old Virginia* described a speaker whose weight was a little too much for the platform on which he was speaking. "During one of the exciting elections, a candidate of heavy weight was making his speech from the head of a whisky barrel, across which was placed a narrow board for safety. In his ardor to impress a certain fact upon his hearers, which he emphasized by the statement: 'As sure as I stand upon this barrel----,' and with this statement unfinished, he leaped with both feet from the narrow plank upon the yielding barrel head, and disappeared 'up to his neck in spirits' which the anxious crowd had hoped to put into their own necks, and to test in a more convivial manner. Through this awkward incident of his canvass, he lost his election, but thereby acquired fame as 'Old Soak,' which name ever afterwards identified him" (p. 190). If some such campaign tales were fictional, many were surely based on fact.

Anecdotes were often circulated by one party at the expense of another. Said to have been told by E. R. Gunby, Republican candidate in 1896 for governor of Florida, the following joke ridicules William Jennings Bryan's money policy. A Negro one time bit a half dollar to see if it was made of silver or lead. While it was in his mouth it slipped into his throat and stuck halfway down. The doctor said he couldn't cut it out and recommended that the Negro immediately register "and vote for McKinley, because if Bryan is elected that half dollar will be a dollar, and then you'll choke to death, sure."[7]

In *The Heart of Old Hickory* Will Allen Dromgoole told how Bob Taylor ("Fiddling His Way to Fame") used humor in getting elected governor of the Volunteer state. "His strange, half-humorous, half-pathetic oratory was familiar in every county from the mountains to the Mississippi." The author allows the governor, whom she does not call by name, to tell in his own words the story of his political career. As a young man in East Tennessee, he recalled, his Republican family had disapproved violently of his becoming a Democrat. Once during a campaign for the legislature, he was whipped by his father for shouting "Hooray fur Dimocracy!" He received forty licks. "An' when the last un fell, I riz up an' tore off my hat, an' tossed it up ter the rafters, an' sez I, ez loud ez I could, 'Hooray fur Dimocracy! Forty lashes hev heat it ter red-hot heat.'" The Democrats carried the county and he won a seat in the legislature. Describing the way he campaigned with his fiddle, the governor recalled: "I teched the bow acrost the strings. 'Rabbit in the Pea-Patch,'—the boys began ter pat; soft at first, then a bit more peart. Then I played up—that old Rabbit went a-skippin' an' a-trippin', I kin tell ye. Far' well ter the peas in that patch." In this manner Taylor fiddled his way to the legislature, to Congress, into the governor's chair —and to fame.

The anecdotes and stories attributed to Taylor were read and told by people all over Tennessee and the South. A popular one, told by Taylor himself in *Life Pictures,* was the story of the old Dutchman who sought to foretell his son's occupation. To do so he placed a Bible, a silver dollar, and a bottle of whiskey on a table in the boy's room and hid to see which one would attract the boy. If the boy chose the Bible, the old Dutchman assumed, he would become a preacher; the dollar, a businessman; the whiskey, a drunkard. The boy put the dollar in his pocket, took a swig from the bottle, and began to read the Bible. The old man was horror-stricken. "Mein gracious! He iss going to be a politician!"

Although the peak of spread-eagle oratory came prior to the Civil War, Taylor frequently indulged in it. In later years (*Life Pictures*) he recalled the time he "stood on the stump in Tennessee as elector for Grover Cleveland, and thus I turned my eagle loose. . . ." One old fellow was so affected by the florid description of this "grandest country in the world" that he jumped up, threw his hat into the air, and shouted, "Let 'er stretch, durn 'er! Hurrah for the Dimocrat party!" (p. 26).

Like Governor Bob Taylor, John Allen of Mississippi used humor freely in running for office. It helped elect him congressman over Confederate General Tucker who had a brilliant war record. It is recorded that when the two candidates met on the stump, the general closed his speech like this. "Seventeen years ago last night, my fellow citizens, after a hard-fought battle on yonder hill, I bivouacked under yonder clump of trees. Those of you who remember as I do the times that tried men's souls will not, I hope, forget their humble servant when the primaries shall be held." This was a powerful appeal in the South, but Allen did him one better. "My fellow citizens, what General Tucker says to you about the engagement seventeen years ago on yonder hill is true. What General Tucker says to you about having bivouacked in yon clump of trees on that night is true. It is also true, my fellow citizens, that I was vedette picket and stood guard over him while he slept. Now then, fellow citizens, all of you who were generals and had privates to stand guard over you while you slept, vote for General Tucker; and all of you who were privates and stood guard over the generals while they slept, vote for Private John Allen!" This speech earned Private Allen a new title and a seat in Congress.[8]

Hasty and fickle response to the campaigns of the various parties in the presidential election of 1908 is satirized in Burtscher's "The Political Record of Squire Joines" (*Yellow Creek Humor*). When the Populists nominated Tom Watson of Georgia for President, the squire sold his pigs, bought Watson's books, and enthusiastically supported him. But when the Socialists nominated Eugene V. Debs, the squire sold eggs, subscribed to the *Appeal to Reason*, bought books on Socialism, and was converted to this nominee. After the Republicans selected William Howard Taft to head their ticket, the squire sold a calf, subscribed to a Republican paper, and became a Republican. Then the Democrats nominated William Jennings Bryan, and the squire sold a cow, read Bryan's *Commoner*, and was converted to free silver. Finally the Prohibitionist Party met and chose a candidate; the squire sold a horse, subscribed to the *Patriot Phalanx*, and became a Prohibitionist supporter. Such furious political activity should bespeak a conscientious voter; however, Burtscher concluded with a punch line. "But the strangest thing about it all was that when election day finally came Squire Joines did not vote at all."

The most widely printed political humor of the period was copied from the *Congressional Record*, which Henry Clay Lukens called "that universally acknowledged masterpiece of our national humor."[9] If the content of the *Record* is indicative, the Southern members kept their fellow politicians in stitches. Charles Heber Clark ("Max Adeler") suggested that it be made even more readable by putting the contents in verse.

> *Mr. Hill*
> *Introduced a bill*
> *To give John Smith a pension;*
> *Mr. Bayard*
> *Talked himself tired,*
> *But said nothing worthy of mention.*

Or a House session might be lyrically reported.

> *A very able speech was made by Cox, of Minnesota,*
> *Respecting the necessity of protecting the black voter,*
> *'Twas indignantly responded to by Smith, of Alabama,*
> *Whose abominable talk was silenced by the Speaker's hammer.*[10]

Champ Clark from Missouri, Speaker of the House, was an expert on congressional humor—probably because he had to listen to so much of it. In an essay he recorded the "Wit, Humor, and Anecdote" of many of his Southern colleagues.[11] He also defended the literary worth of humor against the detractors who said that the funny man lacked "the substantial qualities of mind." Clark would not stand for it. "The truth is that the man who is dowered with wit and humor is in first-class intellectual company—with Shakespeare and Bacon; Swift and Sheridan . . . and with our own Washington Irving, Tom Marshall . . . with Lowell and Holmes and Lincoln; with 'Sunset' Cox, Henry Watterson, and Proctor Knox; with Hoar, Ingersoll, and Thomas B. Reed . . . and with a bright and shining host of statesmen, orators, poets, and literati—not to mention all the professionals from 'John Phoenix' to 'Mark Twain.'" One of the stories Clark used to illustrate congressional wit and wisdom was told in the House by W. Jasper Talbert of South Carolina. Talbert, Clark commented, was a free trader; to show how a high protective tariff affected different parts of the country, the South Carolinian told an anecdote. "Down in my district a boy went to mill for the first time, and did not understand the modus operandi. So when the miller took out the toll, the boy thought he had stolen it; but as it was a small matter he said nothing about it. When the miller took up the sack, poured all the rest of the corn into the hopper, and threw the sack on the floor, the little chap thought he had stolen that too, and he thought furthermore that it was high time for him to take his departure. Consequently he grabbed the empty bag and started home as fast as his legs could carry him. The miller, deeming the boy crazy, pursued him. The boy beat him in the race home, and fell down in the yard out of breath. His father ran out and said: 'My son, what is the matter?' Whereupon the boy replied: 'That old fat rascal up at the mill stole all my corn and gave me an awful race for the sack!'" "Now," said Mr. Talbert, making the application, "that illustrates the working of the high protective tariff precisely. The tariff barons have been skinning the farmer for lo! these many years. They've gotten all our corn and now they are after the sack!" The expression of low-tariff sentiments in such humorous form was likely to win more support for the cause than a straight relating of facts.

George S. Hilton's anthology, *The Funny Side of Politics*, contains examples of humor by Talbert and others. The South Carolinian's concern for fiscal policies is reflected in several speeches he made in the House. Again telling his story of the boy and the miller, he applied it to the withdrawal by large corporations in 1893 of large sums of money from circulation. "So I tell you these corporations, these gold bugs, have withdrawn all the money from circulation, on the pretense that times are hard. . . . They have withdrawn the money from circulation, all except $5 per capita, and they are giving us a hell of a race for the $5 (laughter) and if we do not wake up they will get that" (pp. 122-23).

In 1893 in a speech on the bill to repeal the silver-purchasing clause of the Sherman Act of 1890, he admitted that he was confused by the debate on the issue. He told the story of the little boy whose mother, dressing him in his first pair of pantaloons, mistakenly put the front in the rear. "The little fellow started for school the next morning, and walked cheerfully along until he looked down and discovered the situation, when he burst out into a cry, and said, 'I don't know whether I am going to school or going back home.' (Laughter) I have listened to these arguments until I have been put almost in a similar position" (p. 132).

Speaking another time on the silver question, Talbert told of an old Negro preacher's sermon on the miracles of Christ. "My beloved friends and brethren, de greatest of all miracles was 'bout de loaves and de fishes. Dey was 5,000 loaves and 2,000 fishes, and de twelve 'postles had to eat 'em all. Now de miracle is dat dey didn't bust" (p. 133). Talbert's application: the people had lately been so stuffed with silver speeches that it was a miracle they hadn't "busted." In the same speech he commented on both sides of the silver controversy by recalling the Negro preacher who was preaching on the broad and the narrow ways open to a man. "My bredren, dere's but two roads for you to trabbel; one leads to eternal damnation, and de udder one to hell and destruction." Old brother Pompey, hearing this hopeless situation, grabbed his hat and made a break for the door. "Dat bein de case, dis darky takes to de bushes." This story, Talbert said, showed how each side of the silver question was picturing destruction if the other side prevailed.

Hilton's collection contains examples by major and minor statesmen. Some are shop quips like a remark by the Republican Leonidas C. Houk of Tennessee. "I never saw a Democrat in my life who did not understand the Constitution, whether he could read it or not" (pp. 18-19). Asher G. Caruth of Kentucky, speaking against a bill to increase the tariff on granite, said that he thought tax collecting stopped at the grave, but evidently he was wrong, for now "they pursue a man even beyond the tomb." Congressman Caruth continued: "Notwithstanding that they have taxed the shroud in which the corpse is clad, notwithstanding they have taxed the coffin in which he is placed, they now come along to tax the gravestone that is erected over him. . . . I trust that in the great hereafter, when we stand before the judgment seat of God, we shall at least find that 'salvation is free'" (p. 80).

Samuel W. Peel of Arkansas, in a House speech in 1886 against the suspension of the coinage of standard silver dollars under the Bland Act, said the act would be fine for banks and moneylenders but hard on the debtor and the working class generally. The situation reminded Peel of the retort of a boy to his father's description of the goodness of God in forming the crane. "See how good and wise the Lord is; He has given the crane a long, slim neck, a long, sharp bill, long legs, and a broad web foot. With his long legs he can wade the water, with his broad web foot he can hold down the fish until he reaches down with his long neck and a sharp bill and takes him in for food." The son replies, "Yes, father, that is mighty nice for the crane but it is hell on the fish."

The "War Governor of the South," Zebulon B. Vance of North Carolina, had encouraged the worn-out and discouraged Confederate soldiers during the war with his jokes and humor. In the Senate he continued his reputation as a humorist. Speaking on the protective tariff—the "plunder of the public" to protect "our 'infant' manufactures"—Vance used a metaphor. "The infant is, according to my researches, well on to a hundred years old and still it can't walk or even stand alone. (Laughter) It promises fair to become the deathless rival of the Wandering Jew, judging by its prolonged youth, only it can't wander, and therefore sticks fast by New England and Pennsylvania. . . . He may be properly called the Great American Infant. . . . Evidently, if not naturally, his infirmities and his appetite increase with age. His food don't seem to have the desired effect; but assuming an abnormal character, he has to all intents and purposes become a vast politico-economical tape-worm in the public anatomy, fit only to consume food provided by others. (Great Laughter.)" (pp. 54-55).

As a Congressman "Private" John Allen of Mississippi kept the House laughing —both Democrats and Republicans—from 1885 to 1901. From the beginning of his House tenure he had a reputation for humor. Champ Clark tells us that as a peroration to his maiden speech Allen said, "Now, Mr. Speaker, having fully answered all the arguments of my opponents, I will retire to the cloak-room for a few moments, to receive the congratulations of admiring friends." Like Vance and other Southern legislators, he was opposed to a high protective tariff. Hilton included a speech in which Allen replied to those who maintained that the high tariff was the making of New England by telling an anecdote with a moral. A boy took his father out with him to help train his dog to hunt bear. In the dry run the father took the part of the bear, and "the puppy got the old man by the nose and was giving him fits, when he shouted to the boy, 'Help, come take him off.' 'Oh,' said the boy, 'daddy, hold on, stand it, it is hard on you, but it is the making of the pup.'" The protective tariff might be the making of New England, but it was hard on the South.

Allen's humor occasionally carried barbs. In 1898 he spoke on the retirement of "Uncle Josiah" Patterson, a colleague, and commented on the man's farewell self-eulogy. It reminded Allen of the time he was running in Mississippi in 1884 and harangued a crowd with a list of his qualifications. A Negro carpenter was called upon to say a few words, and he told the crowd, "you's heerd Mr. Allen on hisself, and he has ricommended hisself so much higher than any of the rest of us kin ricommend him, it ain't wuth while for me to say nothin' about him." Now, Allen remarked, he would like to help retire Uncle Josiah, who had said that "he was thoroughly converted and ready to die in the faith." This confession reminded Allen of the Irishman and the Jew, in a boat, discussing Christianity. After a while the Irishman knocked the Jew over the head and threw him overboard because he said he didn't believe in the Lord Jesus Christ. To convert the Jew, the Christian held him under the water and pulled him up several times; but the Jew continued to disclaim any belief in Christ. Finally as the unbeliever was almost drowning, he confessed: "Yes, I believe." "Well," said the Irishman, "damn you, I'll drown you now while you are in the faith," and he sent the new convert to the bottom.

The Smiling Phoenix

Allen's humorous comments on American foreign policy were often realistic. Reviewing the excuses offered for the acquisition of the Philippines—manifest destiny, the leading of Divine Providence, the white man's burden—he drew a parallel between what the United States was claiming and what the old Negro meant when he said that his belief in special Providence depended on the wording of the "pra'r." He might pray all night for one of his neighbor's turkeys but it would never come, but if he prayed to be sent after it, it would surely be there the next morning.

The Mississippian's most famous House speech was "The Tupelo Fish Hatchery," delivered in 1901. He favored the hatchery proposed for the Mississippi town by informing the public, especially newspapermen and congressmen, of the merits of the location. "The main lines of American history converge in Tupelo or radiate from Tupelo." Columbus sailed from Spain in search of such a place. Ponce de León was actually searching for Tupelo. In the era of the great railroad expansion, there was a continual striving to get to Tupelo. Lincoln didn't want the South to secede because "this secession," the President had said, "takes from the Union Tupelo." Tupelo's fall during the Civil War had broken the Confederate spirit and caused the South to lose the war. The proud Allen invited everyone to visit Tupelo, "the only place in the South where we have the same beautiful moons we had before the war." He used monstrous logic. "Tupelo is very near, if not exactly in, the center of the world. The horizon seems about the same distance in every direction." He concluded with an explicit plea for a congressional appropriation of $20,000. "Why, sir, fish will travel over land for miles to get into the water we have at Tupelo. Thousands and millions of unborn fish are clamoring to this Congress for an opportunity to be hatched at Tupelo." The bill passed without a dissenting vote.

As Mississippi's most distinguished postwar statesman, John Sharp Williams was second only to Allen in representing his state as a humorist. Many of his political speeches were made funny by stories about "niggers" and poor-white farmers in Mississippi. In 1898, to illustrate the current Republican "prosperity," he told the story of the farmer who took two baskets to market—one filled with eggs and the other with affidavits showing that the eggs were fresh and sound. The eggs, however, didn't sell well because the affidavits aroused suspicion as to their soundness.

Responding to criticism of taking "tainted" money from robber barons like Rockefeller for humanitarian purposes, Williams told how the Methodist preacher in Mississippi explained his acceptance of twenty-five dollars from a gambler. "Well, here are twenty-five dollars badly and dirtily won that will be taken from a bad cause and made to serve the cause of God and humanity."

In a speech critical of continued Republican support for the Dingley tariff, which was not supplying sufficient revenue, he said: "It may be that the Republican Government can use Mr. Dingley and his bill for one more term of Congress as the fellow proposed to use the corpse of the man who was drowned and whose body was not discovered until some time afterwards, when it seems that it had formed food for the eels, a number being caught. After it was found and about to be buried in a decent and proper manner, one of the bystanders suggested: 'Boys, this fellow seems mighty near decomposed, but we can plant him once more, for one night. He is good bait for the eels.' "[12]

Kentucky was represented in congressional humor by Ben Hardin, Tom Corwin, and J. Proctor Knott. The latter was elected to the House in 1867, and Samuel S. Cox wrote in *Why We Laugh:* "Proctor Knott is now best known as a Congressional humorist. But his humor, like all genuine virtues, has little or no malice in its composition" (p. 207). At times, however, Knott could be satirical. In a burlesque of spread-eagle oratory he said that some people were urging the paving of Pennsylvania Avenue for the use of office seekers who thronged the city "in numbers almost equal to the hosts which were hurled by Lucifer from the battlements of heaven." Then he declaimed: "When I see one of that 'noble army of martyrs' bidding adieu to his home and all the sweets of private life, for which he is eminently fitted by nature, to immolate himself upon the altar of his country's service for four long years, Homer's touching picture of the last and sad scene between the noble Hector and his weeping family rises before my sympathetic imagination. (Great Laughter) When I see him plunging recklessly into an office of the duties of which he is profoundly and defiantly ignorant, I am reminded of the self-sacrificing heroism of Curtius when he leaped into the yawning gulf which opened in the Roman forum."[13]

Knott's most famous speech was delivered in 1870. Henry Watterson described the "Duluth Speech." "It made a great impression on the occasion of its production in the House, and has since stood the test of time, being still in greater demand than any other congressional document." Watterson added that it was "the most quaint and genial effusion ever delivered before a deliberative body" and noted that "it is replete with Southernisms. Its identity could nowhere be mistaken. It is essentially an offspring of the imagination and intellect, the humor of the South."[14] Samuel S. Cox declared that the mock-heroic speech "hits the American sense of extravagance, which . . . is the reservoir whence flows most of our fun. . . . His wit took down and off and out the most grandiose schemes and schemers, in the most superlative way." Cox added that "the special humor of this Duluth speech lies in its magnifying, with a roaring rush of absurdity, the exaggerations of a Western Eden (pp. 194, 221). The occasion was the consideration of a bill to construct a railroad from the St. Croix River to the west end of Lake Superior at Duluth. Knott began, with an air of mock seriousness, trying to locate Duluth. He finally found the town on a map furnished by the Minnesota legislature. Speculating on the delightful climate there, he quoted a Byron rhapsody; the poet must have had Duluth in mind when he wrote it. The great things in store for Duluth, however, might have unfortunate results because the natives might become educated. "How long would it be before they would take to studying the Declaration of Independence, and hatching out the damnable heresy of secession?" And then would follow the "painful process" of reconstruction and the amendments that would have to be added to the Constitution. In a delirium of praise for the town he said, "I think every gentleman on this floor is as well satisfied as I am that Duluth is destined to become the commercial metropolis of the universe, and that the road should be built at once." He proposed that every able-bodied female between eighteen and forty-five who believed in women's rights be drafted to work on the road. After such praise of the town, he surprised his colleagues by concluding that it was impossible for him to vote for the grant of land which would finance the railroad's construction. He explained that his constituents had no interest in the road and that actually the lands he was being asked to give away were not his to bestow. His peroration reaffirmed his loyalty to those whom he represented in Congress. "Rather perish Duluth! Perish the paragon of cities! Rather let the freezing cyclones of the bleak Northwest bury it forever beneath the eddying sands of the raging St. Croix!"[15]

Robert Love Taylor, governor of Tennessee and later United States senator, was one of the best specimens of the Southern politician-humorist. William L. Visscher in *Ten Wise Men* called him "the foremost humorist of his region and one of the merriest in history. . . . Senator Taylor is particularly gifted with the warm and flowery eloquence peculiar to Southern orators, but wit and jollity so pervade his nature that often in making a speech he will abruptly cut a well-rounded sentence with a flash of humor that explodes his audience." To illustrate this quality Visscher quoted Taylor's eulogy of his state in which he compared her to a beautiful woman. "There she rests, upon her verdant couch. At the west her dimpled feet bathed in the waters of the mighty Mississippi; at the east her glorious head pillowed upon the mountains—and there we have first-class mountains. Why, some of those mountains are so high that a tall man can stand on the tip top of a lofty peak and tickle the feet of the angels" (pp. 145-46).

Much of Taylor's humor was "state" humor, associated with Tennessee or other states. In *Echoes* he is found using tall tales on Texas Day at the Tennessee Centennial in 1897. "An old Texan once told me it was the quickest climate in the world. . . . He said that an old farmer was driving along one day; his team was composed of oxen, and it was so hot that one of the oxen fell dead from sunstroke, and while he was skinning him the other one froze to death." Traveling in Texas, the governor remarked, he came upon a typical sandbank "where the fleas are so thick that the engineer pulls his train up and has the flat cars loaded with sand, and when he gets to the place where the sand has to be unloaded, he gives his engine a toot or two and the whole thing hops off" (p. 22).

One of Taylor's most famous speeches, "The Paradise of Fools" (*Echoes*), contains with the humor much religious sentiment. But it probably was in his use of spread-eagle oratory that he was most appealing and amusing. He opened the lecture "Love, Laughter, and Song" (*Echoes*) with this elaborate description: "I saw the morning, with purple quiver and burnished bow, stand tip-toe on the horizon and shoot sunbeams at the vanishing darkness of night, and then reach up and gather the stars and hide them in her bosom, and then bend down and tickle the slumbering world with straws of light till it woke with laughter and song."

Governor Taylor himself was the subject of many poems and sketches by Southern humorists. "The Heart of Old Hickory" by Will Allen Dromgoole deals with the governor's kindheartedness while in office. It shows him in mental anguish pondering the fate of a woman scheduled to be executed for murder. Through the incidental visit of a crippled paperboy he is led to show mercy to the woman. To the present-day reader the sketch is completely submerged in pathos; it contains no obvious humor. However, an age fond of crying humor considered it a funny story, and in the Introduction to Miss Dromgoole's book B. O. Flower wrote that the story "is, in my judgment, one of the finest short stories of the present generation. It has proved unusually popular, and displays the wonderful power of its gifted author in blending humor and pathos, while investing with irresistible fascination a sketch which, in the hands of any other than an artist, would appear tame and insipid." Flower's evaluation has not been borne out by time, but it reveals much about an older taste in popular humor.

A common device of political humor North and South was the visit or letter to the President. Artemus Ward, Orpheus C. Kerr, and Petroleum V. Nasby entertained and edified their Northern readers with such sketches during and after the war. Southern attempts in this genre were not so well known, but they were motivated by similar circumstances. During the Civil War these sketches were usually caustic and satirical, but as time went on they became more sympathetic. As an impetuous young man, Joel Chandler Harris had written Lincoln a letter in cracker dialect, signed "Obadiah Skinflint," in which he got rough with the Union President and ended by threatening to "draw his blood with a lead pill the first time he sets his peepers on him." As a mature writer, Harris was a great admirer of Lincoln. In the person of Billy Sanders, Harris later paid a visit to President Theodore Roosevelt. "Well, I come away from the White House might'ly hope up, feelin' that Teddy is the President of the whole country, an' not of a party. I felt jest like I had been on a visit to some friend that I hadn't seed in years. An' I went back to the hotel an' snored as loud as ef I'd 'a' been on my own shuck mattress, an' dreamed that the men in Wall Street had promised to be reasonably honest atter the fust of Jinawary."[16]

Most postwar visits and letters to the President by Southern humorists were without serious intent; however, John A. Cockerill's "An Interview with the President," from *The Major in Washington City,* was written with a serious (or mock-serious) motive—to get President Cleveland to take some action on Confederate war claims. Before he goes for the interview, the major has a new calling card printed for the occasion. It reads: "Randolph Gore Hampton / Tuskegee, Ala., / 'The Juleps-by-the-Mint-Bed.'" The meeting begins pleasantly. The major is pleased to hear that the President had not fought against the South—he had hired a substitute to fight for him. But when the visitor mentions the Confederate war claims, and the President says the South must be patient, Hampton gets mad and rants. He even concludes that Cleveland is a moral coward.

"A Snapshot at the President," written by O. Henry in 1894 for the *Rolling Stone,* had no such serious intent. As a reporter waiting to interview President Cleveland, O. Henry is first mistaken for a dynamiter. Eventually, however, he gets in to see the President, who has to check the map to find out where Texas is located. O. Henry's first question is "What do you think of the political future of this country?" Cleveland's answer is politic. "I will state that political exigencies demand emergentistical promptitude, and while the United States is indissoluble in conception and invisible in intent, treason and internecine disagreement have ruptured the consanguinity of patriotism, and—" Not able to take any more of the President's gobbledegook, the reporter interrupts to ask: "Do you wear flannels? What is your favorite poet, brand of catsup, bird, flower, and what are you going to do when you are out of a job?" Unfortunately, the President refuses to answer these questions because "my private affairs do not concern the public."

Letters to the President were also written by Francis Bartow Lloyd and William Burtscher. Lloyd's Alabama cracker Black Jack Wiggins asked to be made revenue agent for Cyclone Streak. He wants to make some money, he says. Since his main job would be to break up illicit distilleries, he threatens in the postscript: "And in case you don't need me as general raider for Cyclone Streak, I do most fervently hope the boys will run 300 barrels before Christmas—and all unbeknowance to the general government" (pp. 263-69). Burtscher's Cal F. Head wrote a letter to "Mr. W. H. Taft, c/o Mrs. Roosevelt," asking that the general election in 1908 be moved up to July so he could vote; he was planning a trip in November (pp. 43-44).

Opie Read's *Arkansaw Traveler* also printed open letters to government executives, including Arkansas governors and the President. One to Grover Cleveland was ostensibly written by "an old fellow who lives near Buck Snort, Ark." on October 17, 1885. "I reckon you'll be sorter surprised to hear from me, 'specially as we have never had the pleasure o' meetin' each other. I voted for you an' thurfo' think that it is my duty as a ole citizen uv this place an' the owner uv a snatchin' team uv as good mules as you ever seed, to give you a little advice. I want you to turn them fetch-taked raskils out. They've had their fore feet in the troff long enough. It ain't often that I send advice away from home an' you oughter feel proud uv it. My father uster advise old Andy Jackson, he did. But givin' advice ain't all that causes me to write. I want a pardon fur makin' wild-cat whisky. I ain't made none yit, but I wish you would write me one an' send her down. Then ef I do make the whisky an' git kotch up with, I can haul out the dockyment an' make the deputy marshals open the'r eyes. I never like to be rash about anything. I always like to be prepar'd before I commence to cut an' slash."

The series known as "The Bill Snort Letters," published in *Texas Siftings* intermittently from 1889 to 1895, began as letters from a Texas newspaper editor to the newly elected Benjamin Harrison.[17] These satirical letters treat such topics as free trade, the protective tariff, civil service reform, soldiers' pensions, and the appointment of Negroes to office. Bill Snort ingratiates himself with the Republican President, becomes Harrison's confidential secretary, and is later made editor of the *Harrison Vindicator,* a Republican paper.

As the President's adviser, Snort counseled him on many topics, including how to "break up the solid Democratic South and change it into a Republican solid South." This was the opportunist's plan on April 6, 1889. "The South leans toward Protection and Republicanism. Nothing keeps it Democratic except the nigger. Just as soon as the next Presidential campaign opens, with your consent and approval, I'll kick your colored stenographer out of the White House and down Pennsylvania avenue. It will be telegraphed all over the country that President Harrison fully sustains the high-toned Southern gentleman, Col. Snort, in kicking the Senegambian out of the White House. The South will be solid, but it will be solid for Harrison and Snort, that is if a Southern man is put on the ticket." Snort offered a scheme for appeasing the North too. "I will put on my old Confed. uniform and you will put on your old Federal uniform, and we will pose as the blue and the gray. See? We will get up a yarn about me saving your life on the field of battle. We can enlist the sympathies of Gen. Sherman, Bob Ingersoll, Gen. Carl Schurz, Gen. Enthusiasm and all the rest. Mrs. Grant will write us a letter of sympathy and send us a check, and the North will be solid, too, for Harrison and Snort. With the North and the South solid, we will get the biggest majority ever received by a President."

Many of the choicest anecdotes in Southern humor deal with political figures. John Allen, Alexander H. Stephens, Zebulon B. Vance, Robert Toombs—such statesmen became a part of the South's stock of humor, written and oral. Some of the stories were based on fact. In 1885, for example, L. Q. C. Lamar of Mississippi was appointed Secretary of the Interior. He was promptly visited by John Youngblood, his former private secretary, who lived off him for some time, borrowing money frequently. After a while Lamar was said to have told an associate, "See here, Henry: Youngblood has got to get away from Washington. Find some place for him. Both of us can't live on $8,000 a year." The former secretary was promptly appointed superintendent of Arizona schools.[18]

Other stories cannot be so well substantiated. The anecdotes in circulation about "Private" John Allen have become a part of humorous folklore. This is one of them.

John Allen, the famous Mississippi wit, was traveling through his native state with a party of his northern friends, to whom he stated that the negroes of that section could talk and understand Indian. To dispel the doubt of the party he approached an old Negro standing on the platform at the next station and thus saluted him:

"Whah he?"

"Whah who?" replied the negro.[19]

The vice-president of the Confederacy was a popular anecdotal figure. Richard Malcolm Johnston told what is probably an apocryphal story of the time

Alexander H. Stephens was in Washington at a dinner, listening disgustedly to toasts to the various states. He was called upon to eulogize Georgia. "Gentlemen, dod-fetch it all! I can't make a speech; but that ain't goin' to hender me from drinkin' to the state o' Georgie. I'll do it, and I'll do it free. Here's to her! She come from nobody, she ain't beholden on nobody, and you better believe she don't care a continental cent *for* nobody!"[20] Under the caption "Some of Aleck Stephens' Jokes on Himself," the Union Springs *Times* on January 26, 1881, ran two stories about the Southern hero. This one was probably already a part of folklore. "Mr. Stephens was going to Cassville to speak. It was in the heyday of his fame and popularity as a stumper. He stayed all night with an old man up in Cass, now Bartow County. He didn't inquire the name of his host, nor did the host know who the guest was. The next morning as he told his kind entertainer good-bye, the old man told him that he would be up in Cassville after a while—that he was going to hear *Stephens* speak—and asked if his guest had ever seen Mr. Stephens. Mr. Stephens replied, 'Yes, I have seen him and heard him often, and expect to hear him today.' The good farmer was very much astonished when later in the day he saw the little man, but great commoner, take the stand, to sustain the fame of perhaps the first orator of the country."

Robert Toombs, of Georgia, was another popular subject for anecdotes. A story repeated defiantly by Southerners concerned the meeting in Augusta of Toombs and Thad Stevens, who asked the Georgian how he felt after being licked by the Yankees. Toombs answered that he felt like Lazarus, for he was "licked by the dogs, wasn't he?" Henry Watterson told in *Marse Henry* (I, 65) of Toombs' visit with President Grant. After spending several years in Europe after the war, the Georgian came back to the United States. Passing through Washington, he sent his card to the President, who invited him in for a visit. Toombs told him, "Mr. President, in my European migrations I have made it a rule when arriving in a city to call first and pay my respects to the Chief of Police." Another story was told at Toombs' expense. Jealous of General John B. Gordon's popularity, he once said that if Gordon's war-scar on his left cheek were on his neck instead he wouldn't be so popular. Gordon responded, "If Toombs had been where I was when I got that scar it would be on the back of his neck instead of on his face."[21] Thus went the anecdotes of Southern men of politics.

Much political humor was written by men who were not politicians, but to whom politics was a choice and easy target. A large part of what was written during Reconstruction was naturally biased and bitter. Later in the period, however, professional humorists turned to local politics or national issues and away from sectional partisanship.

Charles H. Smith (Bill Arp) was one of the most widely read commentators on partisan politics. Henry Watterson saw him as "a rough-and-tumble, random, local, current, and partisan dissertator upon the topics of the time." Smith was "a politician as well as humorist, and in much of his lucubration, produced just after the war, the feeling and sarcasm are in excess of humor."[22] Although Smith eventually moderated his bias, he continued to comment on political topics until his death. His "Bill Arp Letters," widely syndicated in the South, frequently dealt with politics.

Satire was a much-used device. The anonymous poem in heroic couplets, *Party Lights; or, The Monkey Congress,* published in 1869, satirically attacked the radical Congress that had been in power since the war. In the Introduction the anonymous author castigated the recent Congress for its huge giveaways to corporations and monopolies. "Then again, Congress, to keep itself in power, has degraded—nay, made the elective franchise a farce in ten of the Southern States. It conferred the right of citizenship on a barbarous, ignorant race, who no more understand its principles than do droves of chattering monkeys." The poem itself is a satire in the tradition of Pope and Byron, whom the author mentions in the Introduction. After a few lines, the poet announced his plan.

> I'll now to Congress, with my burnished pen,
> And show how monkeys ape the ways of men.

The author directed his satire at specific members of the radical Congress, including Sumner, Butler, and Thaddeus Stevens.

> All eyes are fixed on THAD, the mighty man,
> Who hawks, and talks, and spits where'er he can.

There is a summary.

> Alas, the shame! In Congress bigots prate,
> And blind fanatics rule the ruined State.

The South's hopes for a fair deal from the federal government lay with the Democratic party; so of course the Republicans were a perennial target of the Southerner's satire. The sentiments of Sarge Wier, the author of *Old Times in Georgia,* typify the increasing dissatisfaction of the South with its treatment at the hands of the radicals in both parties.

> We hain't axed nary question,
>   Since the nigger was set free,
> But went erlong up to the polls
>   To elect the nominee;
>
> But we're getting kinder jubus
>   And opening up one eye—
> For old Blaine has taught the lessen
>   That er 'yank' is mighty sly.

He concluded on a half-defiant note.

> The South's been fed upon the scraps,
>   Of the nation's chicken pie—
> We want a just division now,
>   They've learned us to be sly (p. 67).

289

Wier's political outlook was generally optimistic. Commenting on the election of President Harrison, he declared that though some folks were gloomy over the future, "I tell 'em that it's nothing like as bad as it was just after the war, and that it ain't er gwine to be" (p. 104).

Sam W. Small used his Negro mouthpiece in *Old Si's Sayings* to comment on political topics ranging from the rumor that Negroes would be re-enslaved by the Democrats to the controversy over the silver question. The outlook Old Si took was always that of a white man. To calm a scared ex-slave, he asked, "Is dat dar ralerode ingine gwine ter walk de tightrope? . . . Is a two-year ole boy gwine ter put dat depo' in his britches pocket an' run away wid hit? . . . Is de Demmycrats gwine ter put de niggers back inter slabery?" (pp. 58-59).

Old Si commented on a wide variety of political topics—even the President's veto of a bill to restrict Chinese immigration. He approved the action, saying, "Dere's so menny triflin' niggers an' po' white trash in dis country now dat I thinks er million er too ob Chinamens wouldn't hurt enneybody much 'ceptin' hit ar de washwomen" (pp. 65-66).

Once when questioned about why more Negroes did not exercise their right to vote, he cited the poll tax and the dog tax as obstacles. The Negro, Old Si asserted, will always pay his dog tax before his poll tax. "When de mussels ob a niggar's hart gits twined roun' a dog, he fines mor' comfort in dat proputy dan in all de votes dat yer could cram inter a fo' bushel ballot-box—an' dat's niggar 'sperience now" (p. 124). Old Si had little sympathy for the colored politician. The business of government should be left up to the white man. He even compared the Negro office seeker to the Georgia mule that "when he kant hab his own way no udder way, he jess ra'rs up befo' an' kicks up behine', an' 'fore yer kin tell which eend ob 'im is in de a'r dar aint nuffin lef' in sight but a cloud of dus' 'way down de big rode!" (p. 165).

The old Negro took the Republicans to task for failing in their promise to make the Negro rich and the white man poor. "Bress de Lord, de white fokes is jes' as rich as eber, an' it wus de niggar whar got busted, an' he been busted eber sence, an' is gwine ter stay busted! Dat's whar makes me mad an' ef de 'publicans eber git anodder chance at me, I'll go die wid de yaller jandise a chawin' ole yaller 'lecshun tickets!" (p. 40).

Uttering the sentiments of his Democratic creator, Old Si praised the new "dimmycrat" governor of Georgia, "Marse Colquitt." He reported to a group of Negroes after returning from the inauguration that the new governor would look after them. "I'me bettin' dis buck an' saw right now dat long ez he's Gubner he don't git lost so fer dat a blin' nigger can't fine him . . ." (p. 45). Thus a fictional Negro was used to help restore political control in the South to the white man.

One of the bitterest of postwar books of humor is John A. Cockerill's *The Major in Washington City*. Here are recorded the adventures and comments of an unreconstructed Rebel in the capital where he is attempting to get Confederate war claims paid and the Republican tariff lowered. A native of Tuskegee,

Alabama, and a former slaveowner, Major Hampton figures that the United States Government owes him $50,000—"30 head" at an average of $800 a head —for freeing his slaves and destroying his plantation.

Reporting to the folks back home by way of letters, he writes that his first successful item of business was to get their ex-slave postmaster replaced by a white man. Beginning with an attack, he soon goes into a genealogical digression. "I horsewhipped him on the road when he was a boy, and he never liked me. When Harrison appointed him P.M. I wanted to open an account with him for postage stamps, but he said it would be cash. I seen that he had his grudge and I laid it in for the wooly pated scoundrel. It took me just fifteen minutes to fix him yesterday. Mr. Maxwell, who is a perfect gentleman, apologized for overlooking the nigger for so long and appointed, on my recommendation, young Mirabeau Clay, son of Dabney Clay, of an old Virginia family, who was killed at Shiloh, and whose mother is directly related to the Rhetts of South Carolina. His grandfather owned the celebrated race horse Tallyhooter and raised the finest game chickens of any gentleman in our section. He cleaned out all the cocks in Mobile in 1845 and won over $3,000" (p. 8). Receiving news that the new white postmaster has taken office at Briar Root, he exults, "A gentleman can get his mail now without havin' to pass a half dozen greasy niggers sittin' around the postoffice door, spittin' tobacco juice and talkin' about 'coon huntin'!" (p. 14). In a postscript to another letter he writes that President Cleveland has insulted both the South and the Democratic party by appointing a Negro as postmaster at Wilberforce, Ohio. "In the South we despise a nigger because he is a nigger. The fact that he votes the Democratic ticket doesn't change the wool on his head, remove his smell or fit him for the society of gentlemen" (p. 70).

As a man with a burning mission—getting the federal government to pay the Confederate claims—he is often bitter about the lukewarm way he is received by fellow Southerners. Henry Watterson, he believes, is opposed to the claims. "I admire Watterson's genius and I believe he is a sincere Free Trader, but somehow he doesn't seem serious enough for a leader. . . . I haven't much use for funny men. I never knowed a man down our way who spent his time tellin' funny stories and entertainin' people with his jokes that ever amounted to a cuss" (p. 11). The major is unaware that as a caricature of the postwar Rebel he is a far more ludicrous figure than Watterson, whose humor was refined and subtle.

Southern congressmen, Hampton finds, are hesitant to support the claims. He warns Speaker Crisp of "Gaujah." "I'm no fool if I did git hit on the back of the head with a piece of Yankee shell at Sharpsburg, and if Mr. Crisp wants to go to the U.S. Senate from Georgia he'd better git a pair of my kind of spectacles" (pp. 22-23). The Southern Secretary of the Interior Hoke Smith suggests that the present recession be dealt with first. The major disagrees. "Poor South, to be represented here by timid jackrabbits and mannykins and dwarfed imitations of statesmen, how far away seems your day of deliverance and retribution!" (p. 40).

291

Somewhat sadistically the major has something to say about his enjoyment of the recession of 1893. "A man who has seen his niggers taken away from him, his mules stolen, his fences burned, his barns and his home pillaged can't help feeling some satisfaction when his enemies begin to know how it is themselves" (pp. 20-21).

Although he is not able to arouse much enthusiasm among Southern congressional delegations, he holds a successful rally attended by Southern sympathizers. Describing the vote of confidence they gave him, he says, "I hain't felt so popular since we Ku-Kluxed six nigger families out of our neighborhood at my suggestion in 1867" (p. 123).

The dominant mood of the book is defiance. In an argument with a Yankee he boasts that the Southern Negro is being rapidly disfranchised. "We own the nigger now just as much as we did and don't have to board and clothe and take care of him" (p. 61). Besides this, Washington has at last been taken over by the South, "and everybody seems to realize that the dear old South is not only in the saddle, but on the front seat and a-drivin'" (p. 15). Emboldened by this new Southern power in Washington, he tries unsuccessfully to have the earlier war on the South declared unconstitutional by the Supreme Court. Thwarted in this attempt, he decides that at least the war should not be referred to as the "late rebellion" or even the "war betwixt the States," but the "Second War for Independence" (p. 232).

Though the major often sounds like a Southern Petroleum V. Nasby, the popular creation of David Ross Locke whose propaganda humor effectively aided the North, his creator evidently meant for him to be taken as a caricature and not an an anti-Southern propagandist. The author gave a clue to his intention in the Introduction. "With all his faults, political and moral, the 'Major'—exaggeratedly typical as he is of the unreconstructed and unrepentant Southerner—has grown to be an entity from whom his creator would be reluctant to part. That he may continue to live to frankly express the true and undisguised, though fallacious, sentiments of his kind is the sincere wish of the author."

Joel Chandler Harris' political comments as a mature humorist seldom rang with a note of sectionalism. He was not a rabid partisan. He once said: "I am not a politician. I am a Democrat on election day, but that is as far as I go."[23] He did, however, comment freely on politics through the Billy Sanders articles in *Uncle Remus's Magazine*. He often espoused causes and issues that he considered worth while. He believed, for example, in free silver and thought it would be the salvation of the poor people. His editorials on the subject in the Atlanta *Constitution* called forth many attacks on him—some humorous—by opponents of the "Silveroons." The following squib from the Washington *Post* is an example. "Joel Chandler Harris, the financial editor of the 'Atlanta Constitution,' receives his salary of $450 per week in bright, silver dollars. Mr. Harris will touch no other kind of money, and if the 'Constitution' office doesn't happen to have silver on hand, Mr. Harris will allow his salary to accumulate until a supply is laid in. Last week, while attempting to carry home three weeks' salary,

Mr. Harris was so unfortunate as to seriously wrench his back. He has been confined to his home ever since, but the 'Post' sincerely hopes he will soon be able to be out and at his desk. The cause of free silver cannot well spare Mr. Harris."[24]

Much of the political humor by non-politicians was written by the editors of magazines and newspapers. Southern periodicals which printed it included the *Arkansaw Traveler,* the *Arkansaw Thomas Cat,* the *Nineteenth Century,* the *Sunny South,* the *Taylor-Trotwood Magazine* (especially in a section called "Editorial Etchings"), and *Texas Siftings.* Although the *Arkansaw Traveler* commented on national politics, its most representative political humor dealt with state matters. The governor and the state legislature came in for many jibes. Under a column headed "Legislative Humor" the paper on March 17, 1883, made the following comment: "The Arkansaw Senate is a very humorous body of law makers. Some times, during the discussion of an important question, a visitor would naturally suppose that he had stumbled upon a convention of 'paragraphers.' "

The Arkansaw Thomas Cat: A Journalistic Highball Run by a Heathen, published in Hot Springs, was principally a political newspaper. Jefferson Davis Orear, its editor, attacked his enemies in caustic terms. Writing on March 8, 1908, he said: "This grand and glorious country of ours, filled with boodle and graft, needs a few anarchists' funerals, more stringent immigration laws and a stricter surveillance over avowed anarchists from the South of Europe. . . . An anarchist is a mad animal, as cowardly as a mad cayote [*sic*], and as conscienceless as a wolf. Like the rattlesnake he strikes blindly and viciously. . . . The anarchist has no place under Old Glory. Anarchists should be strangled and anarchy stamped out. . . . The foreign anarchist, who comes to this country to set at defiance our laws, should be shown no more mercy than a mad dog. Mad dogs are slain."

As were virtually all the periodicals in the South, the *Nineteenth Century* was Democratic in sentiment. An anecdote printed in August, 1870, makes that point clear. "A certain physician, driving into town on election morning, was met by a friend, who hailed him with the question if he had voted. 'Not yet,' said the doctor, 'but I have been out all night after a voter. I got him, too.' 'When will he vote?' 'Oh, about twenty-one years from now.' 'Ah, I see. Not bad. Well, look after him, doctor, and see that he votes right.' 'No fear. He can't go wrong with the name he's got. His father is a Democrat, and when I told him he had got a boy, and asked him what he would name him, he said: "Thomas Jefferson, by thunder!" So he'll do.' "

Political overtones permeated much of the humor in Sweet and Knox's *Texas Siftings.* Two popular series in Negro dialect, "The Uncle Mose Letters" and "The Whangdoodle Letters," regularly used political subjects. Judgments on Texas politics, the tariff, the silver question, and the Populists appeared frequently. Short comments, like these of May 8, 1886, were often used as fillers. "President Cleveland's recommendation that a Commission of Labor be created, consisting of three members, who shall be regular officers of the Government, to whom shall be submitted for arbitration disputes between employers and employed, is received with general approval. We suggest that at least one of those officers should be a man who has been compelled to work for his living. He will then know how it is himself." "When Senator Sherman is in the chair Democratic members find it difficult to catch his eye. We are very much afraid that the Democratic members are not in the habit of inviting Sherman to step into the cloak room."

Most post-Reconstruction humor was good-natured. The Southerner's temper would occasionally flare when he felt his region was being discriminated against, but usually his fun was completely lacking in sectional bias or bitterness. Men like Frank L. Stanton and Francis Bartow Lloyd concerned themselves mainly with local—and often fictional—issues and politicians. Stanton's "A Sharp Politician" in *Songs of the Soil* tells of a man who was unsuccessful in his bid for a seat in Congress and later for a sheriff's badge. After finally winning an election and becoming mayor, he summoned all those who had beaten him in other elections.

> *An' he fined 'em each ten dollars—it was all jest like a dream—*
> *An' when they paid an' went away Jim Jones was rich as cream!*

The poem is a bagatelle. It has no serious message to preach.

Francis Bartow Lloyd in *Sketches of Country Life* about Panther Creek, in Alabama, dealt mainly with local politicians. One office seeker ran on this platform: "I fit plum through the war, and got my horse drowned in the Tennessee River" (p. 128). Aunt Nancy is something of a political philosopher. After much thought, she concludes that there should be but one voter per family, either the husband or the wife, according to whoever is the boss. Many women, she maintains, are qualified to vote. "Whensomever it comes to that pass where a woman has got to do the farmin and the cussin and the drinkin for the family it seems to me like she mought as well go on and do the votin" (p. 147). Politics sometimes became very fiery on Panther Creek, causing family and church feuds and grassy crops. Rufus Sanders, the author's cracker, reports such local matters and also comments on national questions, such as the real meaning of free silver. Some people think it means that silver will be given out free to everybody. Actually it is quite different, Rufus says, "free silver means that the government will take your old spoons, or your raw silver or silver bunyun, as some folks calls it, and make it up into money and not charge you anything for the work. It is like taking your corn to mill where they will grind it into meal and take out nothin for toll. But how in the thunderations is that goin to help me or you or old man Josh Ridley? My old lady ain't got no old silver spoons to fling in, and I know durn well his aint got none cause I eat at his house the other day, and their spoons are like ours—genuine pewter, and not the finest article of that" (p. 106).

By the time of Francis B. Lloyd the humor of politics had lost most of its "bloody shirt" aspect. The Civil War had ceased to dominate the outlook; it could even be treated lightly. A poem sometimes attributed to Henry Watterson dealt with the 1894 railroad labor riots.

> *Now, don't you do it, Mr. Debs—*
> *Don't tackle Uncle Sam;*
> *Ten thousand Johnny Rebs*
> *Can tell you that the projick, Debs,*
> *Ain't worth a "tinker's dam."* [25]

In 1865 such a facetious treatment of the war by a Southerner would have been unthinkable. In 1894 it was read and smiled over by many former Confederates. As tempers cooled, the humor changed.

Notes

1. "Retrospect of American Humor," 45 ff.
2. "*Marse Henry,*" II, 128.
3. *Why We Laugh,* 151.
4. *World's Wit and Humor: American,* I, xx.
5. *Wit and Humor of American Statesmen,* 151.
6. Aswell, *Native American Humor,* 105.
7. Hilton, *Funny Side of Politics,* 137-38.
8. *Library of Southern Literature,* XIV, 6235-36.
9. "American Literary Comedians," 791.
10. In Clemens, *Famous Funny Fellows,* 39-40.
11. *Library of Southern Literature,* XIV, 6225-37.
12. The speeches are in Hudson, *Humor of the Old Deep South,* 199-201, 202-3, 205, 208, 209, 211, where the *Congressional Rec-*

ord is cited.
13. In Hilton, *Funny Side of Politics,* 182.
14. *Oddities in Southern Life,* 265.
15. *Library of Southern Literature,* XIV, 6296-6308.
16. Quoted in Julia Harris, *J. C. Harris,* 46, 517.
17. See Linneman, "American Life," 12-15, and "Colonel Bill Snort."
18. *Wit and Humor of American Statesmen,* 58-59.
19. Piaggi, *Uncle Schnitz,* 61.
20. "Middle Georgia Rural Life," 738.
21. *Wit and Humor of American Statesmen,* 21.
22. *Oddities in Southern Life,* 285.
23. Julia Harris, *J. C. Harris,* 330.
24. *Ibid.,* 330-31.
25. Hilton, *Funny Side of Politics,* 305.

10. The Picaro

FROM THE BEGINNINGS of American humor, the traveler, or picaro, has been a popular figure in it. In eighteenth-century New England Sarah Kemble Knight's *Journal* recorded her serio-comic observations made on a trip from Boston to New York. In the colonial South William Byrd found humorous material on a surveying trip to Western Virginia and North Carolina. Of the many picaresque works by the humorists of the Old Southwest, W. T. Thompson's *Major Jones' Travels* (1848) and Johnson J. Hooper's *Some Adventures of Captain Simon Suggs* (1845) are noteworthy.

Following the war, the picaro continued popular, and the Negro was added to the list of characters. John T. Moore placed Old Wash in the tradition and had this to say in general of the black man's place in picaresque literature: "As he is pictured in fiction, the Southern Negro often bears a definite resemblance to the picaro in the picaresque novel of the eighteenth century. Wash is such a character, both clown and philosopher."[1] The dark picaro's adventures brought him into contact with most Southern classes, black and white. His comments on representatives of these classes often exposed their foibles and vices.

Although there are differences between the classical picaresque characters created by Cervantes, Le Sage, Defoe, and Fielding, and those treated in this chapter, there are enough resemblances to make it possible to call these latter-day creations picaresque. F. W. Chandler wrote that the tradition "has become since the advent of the nineteenth century most diffused, complex, and varied. . . . It adapts itself equally well to the purposes of the moralist and to those of the jester, to the propaganda of the humanitarian reformer, or to the inventions of the light hearted teller of tales."[2] Most of the postwar picaresque humor in the South can in fact be placed into three categories: the moralistic or satirical, the comical, and the rascally. The moral picaro exposes conditions for salutary effect. The comic picaro has no serious intent; he merely records his adventures. The rascal picaro takes as his motto Simon Suggs' slogan: "It is good to be shifty in a new country"; he is the confidence man of humor.

The Rascal

A popular embodiment of the rascal picaro was the Reconstruction carpetbagger who had come South to make his fortune. He was shifty, greedy, and often sadistic. Such a character is Bowman, the "nigger school" promoter and rogue in Will Harben's *The Georgians*. Traveling about over the Reconstruction South, Bowman swindled Negroes and whites. Abner Daniel, the cracker, checked into Bowman's past. "It certainly involves about the biggest rascal unhung—a feller that worked every pore, ignorant nigger in the State o' South Carolina, with a gigantic swindle in the way of a burial-outfit insurance company. Initiation fee ten dollars in advance, nigger buried O.K. ef he died on the spot. The skunk raked in some'n like five thousand before the scheme bu'sted an' he skipped." Whenever his chicanery was detected, he would move on and set up somewhere else. According to Abner, "He worked the nigger racket, in some form or other, wherever he went." After the Carolina burial swindle, he went to Texas where he sold a colored fluid "purportin' to take the kink out o' the original African wool." When his trickery was found out, he moved to Georgia, and there he tried and failed to swindle a rich philanthropist out of money intended for a Negro school. During his travels he married two women and left each with a baby. "But he's a good man all right; he was tryin' in South Carolina to bury all the dead niggers, an' here in Georgia he's tryin' to lift the live ones to a high plane" (pp. 239-40).

Opie Read's novel *The Carpetbagger* also deals with a picaro like Bowman, but Read had his rogue reform after serving a term as corrupt governor of Mississippi. Bowman and his colleagues had plenty of company in the scalawags who roamed like scavengers over their Southland. And an ingratiating

The Smiling Phoenix

Yankee peddler's tales of Southern adventures are the subject of "Hunting a Dragon" by Edward Spencer in the *Southern Magazine* (August, 1871).

Much of the picaresque literature was naturally based on the lives of criminals and outlaws. Farther west this was the age of Jesse James, and many tales were told and written about that well-known picaro. In 1874 J. R. S. Pitts published *The Life and Bloody Career of the Executed Criminal, James Copeland*. The adventures of this Southern land pirate ranged from stealing the knife a woman lent him to gather a sack of greens to the sacking and burning of Mobile in 1839. Copeland once seduced a young mulatto girl, persuaded her to run away with him, and then sold her into slavery. Pitts' racy narrative describes the many picaresque details of the outlaw's life: the organizing of a band of thieves, midnight murders by torchlight, bandits masquerading as preachers, and secret conclaves of thieves. Arthur Palmer Hudson called the outlaw "the Tamburlaine of Southern picaresque tales."[3] One episode reminiscent of Simon Suggs shows how a member of Copeland's gang disguised himself as a Methodist preacher and fooled the people attending a camp meeting. He explained the gun he was carrying by telling the gullible people that he was on his way to visit a sick relative two hundred miles away and had to carry the gun to fight off wild animals. This story so touched the good church people that they contributed money to buy him a new suit of clothes and a new saddle and saddlebags.

Many were the picaresque tales told and written about river gamblers and confidence men. The story of a daring Mississippi River boat gambler is told in the autobiographical *Forty Years a Gambler on the Mississippi* by George H. Devol. At eleven the author said he could steal cards and cheat in gambling. At fourteen he knew how to stack a deck. During the Mexican War he outgambled soldiers on the Rio Grande. Throughout his career, he reported, he won hundreds of thousands of dollars from paymasters, cotton buyers, defaulters, and thieves. He claimed that he fought more rough-and-tumble fights than any man in America and was the most daring gambler in the world.

Another scoundrel was Shocco Jones of North Carolina, whom Arthur Palmer Hudson named the "Prince of Humbuggers."[4] Jones' confidence games were motivated by a desire for money and fun. H. S. Fulkerson wrote of him in *Random Recollections of Early Days in Mississippi*: "The gullible trait in human character was the field of his operations, and he had unbounded confidence in its resources, in its capacity to yield him an abundant harvest of fun under his skillful cultivation."

The master portrayer of the rascal in American fiction was O. Henry. A picaro-type character himself, O. Henry delighted in writing about the man who deceived—or tried to deceive—gullible people. "Jeff Peters as a Personal Magnet" (in *The Gentle Grafter*) tells how Jeff and a friend get enough money to go into business. Peddling Resurrection Bitters in Fisher Hill, Arkansas, Jeff is threatened with jail unless he buys a town license. He goes to get one, but he is told the mayor is sick. The young man in the mayor's office asks him to use his widely known "psychic treatment" to cure his uncle. Jeff does so and collects the $250 promised him. The mayor throws off his sick disguise and announces that his nephew is really a detective who has fixed up the scheme to catch Jeff for practicing medicine without authority. But the mayor is the last one fooled, for the detective has one further disguise: he is actually Andy Tucker, Jeff Peters' confederate.

In "A Double-Eyed Deceiver" (*Roads of Destiny*) a young Texas rough kills a man in a card row and flees to South America. There he and an American consul plan a deception on a wealthy couple whose son had run away to the States twelve years before. The deception works and the Llano Kid is accepted as their long-lost son. After a few weeks as their son, the Texas renegade decides the life is too soft to leave, and double-crosses his partner in crime by refusing to carry out their plan to rob the old man.

The tables are turned on the rascal picaro in "The Ransom of Red Chief," one of the funniest of O. Henry's stories (*Whirligigs*). The narrator and his confederate, Bill Driscoll, decide to make some money by kidnaping and holding for ransom the son of Mr. Dorset, the leading citizen of Summit, Alabama. Their plan, however, backfires when they discover that both the boy and his father approve of the kidnaping. The boy, in fact, enjoys tormenting his captors with Indian games. In answer to their demand for $1,500, the father replies that he will take the boy back for $250. The two kidnapers survey the damage the captive has wrecked on them and agree to the latter terms. "Just at the moment when I should have been abstracting the fifteen hundred dollars from the box under the tree, according to the original proposition, Bill was counting out two hundred and fifty dollars into Dorset's hand." Thus O. Henry reduced another literary tradition to absurdity.

The Comic

The comic adventures of the picaro were generally written by little-known humorists and often had no other aim than that of entertainment. As a young writer before the Civil War, George W. Bagby wrote the picaresque adventures of a Virginia bumpkin on a trip to Washington. This was the beginning of the Mozis Addums sketches that were so popular after the war.

Although he was usually a moral picaro, the Negro occasionally figured in adventures that were comic. In *Old Si's Humorous Sketches* Sam Small sends his picaro to France. There, as valet to his boss, Old Si has much trouble with French money. He goes into an American bar where he also has trouble with the French language. "Dis 'sperience lets me out on dese bogus 'Merican bars whar dey kant talk ner drink 'Merican no mo' den I kin preech Latin to a bauky mule." He had been given a drink he had never heard of before—absinthe.

Most of the adventures and asides in *Mexican Mustang* by Sweet and Knox are comic and without serious satirical implications. In Galveston the travelers' landlord tells them a joke he played on an English visitor who had been bragging about the dogs and horses in England. "Says I to the Englishman, 'Major, talking about them dogs you mentioned this morning, do you have any rooter dogs in your country?'—'Any what?' says he. 'Rooter dogs,' says I: 'We use them for hunting tarantulas, and for harvesting goober peas. They're a cross between the wild Mexican hog and the bulldog. You see, the bite of a tarantula will kill a common dog in less'n a minute,' says I; 'whereas snakebites and such like don't fizzle on a hog. Well, the rooter being half hog, half dog,' says I, 'is just what we want. If it hadn't been for their introduction into the country, the tarantula trade would never have been developed; and as for gathering goober peas,—they grow under ground, you know,—the rooter dog is the greatest labor-saving animal known. You see, the hog part of him roots the goobers out, while the-sagacity-of-the-dog part enables him to be taught to pile the peas in little heaps all along the row'" (p. 45). The Englishman, the landlord boasts, was half-way skeptical until he was shown some dogs being nursed by a sow.

The Texan's alleged propensity for lying or exaggeration is the basis for much of the humor of *Mexican Mustang*. Even the visiting travelers seem to catch the disease. They write about Texas mosquitoes. "In Houston they showed me affidavits stating that in Galveston the mosquitoes were so large as to be included in the cow ordinance, while in Galveston I was told that the Houston mosquitoes wore forty-five-inch undershirts. There is probably a happy medium between the two. I do not know how happy the medium is; but, if he is not under a mosquito-bar, there is a limit to his bliss. The truth is, that the coast-town mosquito rarely exceeds in size the ordinary Texas mockingbird." A timely postscript is added. "When I left New York, I could not have told a lie to save my life; and here, after three-days' residence in Texas, this is what I have come to—and all the time I have been associating with the higher classes. They say in Houston that I caught the infection in passing through Galveston" (p. 53).

On their trip they meet up with a widely known Texas type: the liar. Texas has the biggest liars in the country, and they prove it. "The real-estate agent and the immigration agent have probably no superior in the art of decorative mendacity; but they have an equal,—the old Texas veteran. We met one of the old veterans at Eagle Lake while we were there. I cannot yet decide what form of capital punishment would be severe enough for his case" (p. 181).

Boasting is usually associated with Davy Crockett and the humor of the Old Southwest, but in *Mexican Mustang* Texans raise boasting to its highest power. A candidate for the rangers said: "I'm a scout from the Far West, whar the turkey-buzzard roosts on the fleshless ribs of the dead buffalo, and whar the *coyote* sleeps in the deserted wigwams of the skulpt Indian. Geehossifat! I'm the Long-range Roarer of the Sierra Mojada Mountains. I want to enlist in your company, and show you how to clean out the gory red-skins.

. . . I'm the Cavortin' Cataclysm of the Calaveras Canyon . . ." (pp. 246-47). Soon after the company's first encounter with Indians, the boaster was seen mixing drinks in a Waco saloon.

The trip through Texas had somewhat iconoclastic results for at least one of the authors. This shattering of youthful illusions started in Galveston, where he saw houses built on sturdy foundations of sand, "and showing no signs of crumbling to pieces" (p. 29). Another illusion had to do with the noble-savage concept of the Indian which he had formed from James Fenimore Cooper's novels. Before he met his first Indian he knew how "Nature's Nobleman" would look and talk—as Cooper depicted him, of course. The first Indian he meets he addresses in these Cooperesque words: "Does my red brother desire to replenish his depleted exchequer by the sale of the products of the chase,— the victims of his unerring aim?" The noble Indian responded: "Yes, six-bit one dam heap big turkey." The crestfallen traveler can only remark: "Here was another idol broken, another tradition shattered, a romance reduced to reality. The noble savage is a fraud, a fiction, a myth" (pp. 55-57).

The Texas picaros meet representatives of many classes and nationalities and occupations: Mexicans, Indians, Irish, Germans, Negroes, reporters, sewing-machine salesmen, farmers, preachers, inmates of a county poorhouse. Each group furnishes material for gentle satire. The Negro preacher's misinterpretation of Scripture is the subject of the sketch of a camp meeting "ob de African branch ob de Methodis' Church." At one service an old-time exhorter takes as his text "de fourth chapter ob de Secon' Book ob Kings: O man ob God! dar is death in de pot." Interpreting the text loosely, the parson says: "Dis yar tex' ob mine tells us dat dar's death in de pot. What pot? Brederin, de pot spoken ob hyar is a figger ob speech, an' means sin. It means de whiskey-bottle; it means stealin' an' lyin' an' sabbath-breakin' an' votin' de Dimerkratic ticket, an' de debbil's work ginrally" (p. 114).

Mildly satirizing the sewing-machine agent, they show how he sells with flattery. "He tells the daughter that he is unmarried, going to settle in the county, and hopes she will let him call on her when he is in the vicinity. He informs the old farmer that he—the old farmer—has more good agricultural sense than any man he has yet met in the State" (p. 472). Passing through the German settlement of Braunfels brings this comment: "All around we hear the guttural sounds of the German language, until I get a sore throat listening to it" (p. 393). A conversation in Spanish is carried on with a Mexican, and the American used sentences like these: "Have you my book, or the book of my neighbor? Has the merchant received the gold candlestick? Has the boy the cow of the carpenter, or the horse of the cook?" (pp. 456-57).

The Mexicans are a favorite target of the authors' humor. Someone once asked if the Mexicans are good-natured people. The answer was yes, because "they will take almost any kind of treatment without grumbling. They will even take the smallpox from each other without making any fuss about it." The authors describe the trial of a Mexican in San Antonio.

The accused was a Mexican who had been drunk and disorderly. His very appearance was suggestive of small-pox. As soon as the recorder took his seat, he riveted his eyes on the prisoner, and asked,—

"What is the name of that villainous-looking outcast on the mourner's bench?"

"His name," said the county attorney, "is Don Jose Maria de Valgeme Dios tres Palacios."

"I dismiss the case against him."

"But, your honor, the man is guilty."

"Maybe; but there are mitigating circumstances."

"What are those circumstances?"

Recorder (aside).—"I've not yet been vaccinated" (p. 319).

Much of the book's fun derives, naturally, from the places through which the travelers pass and from the Texas background. They tell the story of a man who was in a hurry to reach the pearly gates; he decided to get himself convicted of murder and have the state pay his way. But he has no luck, for each time he shoots or poisons a human being—his victims number four—a Texas jury finds him innocent. In disgust the impatient man moves to Pennsylvania, where he soon has his wishes fulfilled. He simply did not know how to go about getting himself hanged at home, the authors write. "It is very easy to get killed in Texas: steal a yearling, and you will be accommodated with a rope and a live-oak limb" (pp. 133-39).

Some Texas towns, they find out, have very unusual local prejudices. Take San Antonio, for example. "San Antonio is a land of liberty in all but one thing,—the people cannot bear the sight of a plug hat. They won't have 'em. A plug hat has the same effect on a San-Antonian that a red shawl has on a wild bull. You may go through the street barefooted, and nobody will notice you; you may cavort around, dressed like a Chinese, and they won't much more than throw a rock or two at you; you might even paint yourself, and go without clothes, and it wouldn't excite comment: but just walk into town with that hat on, and—The Lord help you!" (p. 404).

The state capitol in Austin comes in for humorous criticism. "The view from the Capitol Hill is beautiful, unless you allow your gaze to rest on the Capitol itself,—a miracle of architectural absurdity, that, at a distance, looks like a corn-crib with the half of a large watermelon on top it. When you come nearer, after making this comparison, you feel like apologizing to the corn-crib" (p. 641). Good-natured fun is thus poked at people and places all the way from Galveston to the Rio Grande. Only occasionally does the satire become serious or bitter.

The greenhorn has long been a popular subject of slapstick humor. Seldom do his adventures expose anyone's weaknesses except his own inability to adapt to a new environment. In the *Adventures of a Greenhorn in Gotham* by M. L. Byrn ("Phudge Phumble"), a Southern hayseed discovers the big city and decides it is no place for him. New York, he writes, is where a man can get a wife by putting a want ad in the paper. Its boarding houses are filled with types like Lawyer Fleece-um and Miss Moley Nose. Its papers are filled with notices like this: "Boy Wanted.—An orphant, who is not over 30, quick at figgers, understands the care of Hosses, and must live with his parents." Interspersed with the misadventures of the greenhorn are funny remedies—to cure yourself of corns, cut off your toes—and comic aphorisms—"Don't yu burn your phingers if you kan help it." All in all, the book is a hodgepodge of absurdities. Another comic picaresque novel of a Southerner in New York is "Col. Judson of Alabama," by F. Bean, which ran in the *Sunny South* (1887); and the experiences of a Yankee picaro in the South can be read in Hayden Carruth, *The Adventures of Jones*.

The adventures of Uncle Josh Weathersby in New York and Boston are related by Calvin E. Stewart in his Punkin Centre stories. Like most of the humor dealing with the Southerner out of his milieu, it shows his naïveté when he is confronted with the *beau monde*. Uncle Josh is perhaps ill fitted for northern big-city life, but his embarrassing experiences don't disillusion him. His optimism is indestructible. The author describes him in the Preface as "a character chuck full of sunshine and rural simplicity. Take him as you find him and in his experiences you will observe there is a bright side to everything."

Uncle Josh is unaware that he is a country bumpkin in town. He thinks that he has done a good job adapting to the big city. "Folks at home said I'd be buncoed or have my pockets picked fore I'd bin here mor'n half an hour; wall, I fooled 'em a little bit, I wuz here three days afore they buncoed me" (p. 15). "Uncle Josh in Society" is an account of his capers among the wealthy. His entree was provided by a wealthy man who had been a boyhood friend. At a dance a lady approaches him and asks if he dances the German, "but I told her I only danced in English." At dinner he is still the comic figure. He reports that "that durn fool with the knee britches on insulted me, he handed me a little wash bowl with a towl round it, and I told him he needn't cast no insinuations at me, cause I washed my hands afore I cum in."

His misadventures include visits to a Chinese laundry, where he meets "a critter with his head and tail on the same end"; Wall Street; a wax museum, where he talks to a wax figure; Coney Island; and the opera, where he sees on the program that five years elapse between the first and second acts, and he decides: "I knowed durned well I wouldn't have time to wait and see the second part, so I got up and went out" (p. 77).

One of his favorite pastimes is reading signs in store windows. A drug store announces, "Frog in your throat 10¢." He comments, "I wouldn't put one of them critters in my throat for ten dollars." In another shop he reads, "Boots blacked on the inside." Uncle Josh's reaction, "Now, any feller what gits his boots blacked on the inside ain't got much respect fer his socks" (pp. 54-55).

Another book written with the same lack of seriousness, but with a little more artistry, is Georgia Elizabeth Duncan's *Samanthy Billins of Hangin'-Dog*. The adventures are related in cracker dialect by a garrulous old spinster to a

"Mis' Sparks." Throughout the narrative runs a sex-craving that probably author and character alike were unaware of. It is seen in Samanthy's first monologue at Mrs. Sparks when she mentions the time she almost got a husband. Just before the wedding she had to leave to nurse a sick sister, and when she returned her man had married someone else. The moral: "Now, lemme tell you somp'n, my advice to a gal is if she has any notion of ketchin' a feller, she'd better set right down by him an' stay thar" (p. 11). Many of her digressions and asides have to do with how to catch a husband and frequently are wistful comments on marriage. Once she interrupts an account of her travels. "Hain't that Joe Kitchens a goin' 'long the road? I reckin he think he's done went an' burnt a river sence he's got married. Thar's been a lots of 'em a gittin' married here of late. I never heerd of the like" (p. 37). On one of her trips a friend and companion has an affair, and Samanthy is obviously envious of her and a little jealous. Reporting on a trip to Asheville, North Carolina, she says, "The main thing that Asheville is norated fer is, it's considered a good place fer new-married folks ter go an' spen' about two weeks a spoonin'" (p. 139). Indulging herself in sour-grapes philosophy, in her last monologue, she decides that being an old maid isn't so bad. To buttress her conclusion, she tells Mrs. Sparks of the man sent to jail for making whiskey. While he's in jail his wife dies and his children are parceled out to neighbors. "Yes, Mis' Sparks, I believe I'd ruther be jist whut the Lord made me—a woman, an' a ol' maid woman at that" (p. 199).

Samanthy's protest that married life is tragic is pathetically humorous. Most of the humor in the book, however, comes from her adventures on the road. Her first trip, to Washington, results from her failure in sparking. She saves her money and goes with two friends to the capital. Her reactions to the sights are what might be expected from a Georgia cracker. She comments on the equestrian statues that fill Washington. "I figgered it out that most of the big men that's passed over from Washin'ton wuz mighty fond of ridin' r'arin' horses. Why, nearly ever' one of 'em wuz a standin' on his hin' legs a pawin' of the air" (p. 27).

She frequently gives Mrs. Sparks the benefit of her broader knowledge of the world. For instance, in Washington she got sick on a pie. She warns her listener, "Don't you never eat a thing when you're away frum home that's got a kiver on it—'specially, if it don't cost no more'n a nickle" (p. 39).

She reports that in Washington she visited the White House, Mount Vernon, and Lee's home; she also went on a river excursion. On the size of the White House she says, "My land! I don't know whut on earth they kin do with so much house-room unless they calkerlate on takin' in boarders er orphans" (p. 44). She bought a souvenir at Mount Vernon. "This here hatchet is made frum a piece of the cherry-tree that George cut down when he wuz a youngster. I got it at a stan' outside the gate—jist fetched it over fer you ter see" (p. 46).

At other times she reports to Mrs. Sparks on her visits to Tennessee, to

Savannah, to the fair, to Asheville, to North Georgia, and to New York. Her Tennessee adventures centered principally around her attempts to catch a husband. In Savannah she goes to the beach and is shocked by the bathing suits the people are wearing, but she grits her teeth and puts one on too. She has a good time but adds, "I reckon I'll be a puzzlin' my brain ter know why it's decent fer women to cut off ther dresses at the bottom fer the seashore an' off at the top fer sociables" (p. 94). It's lucky, she tells Mrs. Sparks, that she and her friend Roxy went to New York together. "Law, if it hadn't a been fer Roxy I don't have no idee I'd a ever come back alive. It's the beatenest place that ever I wuz in. Why, it takes at leas' two with ther eyes peeled the whole endurin' time ter dodge the things that's a comin' an' a goin'—an' then that don't inshore yer life" (p. 162).

Samanthy Billins is one of the most accurately drawn cracker spinsters in American humor. Her dialect and her sentiments are authentic. She frequently stops her narratives to attend to various details in Mrs. Sparks' house—running the cat out or shooing a hen out of the sugar bucket. One time she remarks to her hostess, "If you'll skuse me, Mis' Sparks, I'll move my cheer over by the door so's I kin dip my snuff without bein' skeered I'll mess up yore floor. It'd be a pity ter git it all spattered up" (p. 42). A tone of religious sentiment permeates the accounts of her travels. Several times she leaves home to nurse sick relatives. As a gossipy woman, she rambles a great deal. Living close to Negroes, she often brings them naturally into her narratives. During one of her digressions she tells of a Negro woman's trance and vision of heaven and hell. When asked what the white folks were doing in hell, the woman replied, "Whut you 'spec' 'em ter be a doin'? Why, dey wuz a gittin' up a legislacher fer ter git de debbil ter make anudder fire fer de niggers ter set at. Said dey didn't like de idee ob settin' down on de grounds of 'quality'" (pp. 14-15). Samanthy reports that in New York she was startled to see a Negro singing in a church choir—and from a hymnal with a white woman. "Sich as that may suit some folks, but I've been brung up different!" (p. 166). There is, however, no bitterness in Duncan's humor. The book is merely an excellent picture of the female Georgia cracker on the road.

A series of anonymous travel sketches published in *Texas Siftings* from July 3 to October 16, 1886, entitled "Around the World on a Bicycle," is in the comic picaresque tradition. In these sketches a Mr. Theophilus Wobble takes a worldwide bicycle trip, visiting such countries as Canada, China, India, Turkey, Italy, Spain, France, and England.

The Moralist

In contrast to the comic, the moral picaro had a serious message to convey. Usually he had an object for bitter satire. Much of the picaresque humor written shortly after the war fits into this category. The device of having a character visit the North and report on the corruption and abuses there was used by Charles H. Smith in *Peace Papers* where "Bill Arp Visits Gotham." Bill wrote that when he was young "the biggest thing out was a trip to Augusty," but now it is a trip to New York. On the way he passes through Washington. "If there never had been a hell one would germinate spontaneously from the corruption that breeds within its walls, like maggots breeding in the karkases of the dead."

In New York his adventures are those of the country bumpkin in town with one thing added: excoriating satire on the North. The North, he reports, so eager to give the Negro equal rights in the South, denies them to him in New York. Seeing a crowd around the mayor's office, he asks the trouble, and an Irishman explains. "It's the domd nagur polees. . . . They talk about mixin up the black and the white togither and it cant be dun in this town. The first nagur that wears a shtar and a shillaly will hav his domd head smashed into a smithhreen—and that's all." Bill says the Irishman told him that the Civil Rights Bill was meant exclusively for the Rebel South.

Bill becomes infuriated when he attends a trial of Susan B. Anthony, arrested for her promotion of women's suffrage. He fumes, "They raise a hellybilloo over the old broken konstitution and mend it up so as to let the black babboons vote in the rebbel States, but if a white woman of sense and spunk dares to do it, it shocks their pewritan modesty." Although refusing to commit himself on the issue, he remarks, "I wont say she ort to vote if she don't want to, but I do say that no politishun could buy her vote with a drink." The Yankee, he suggests, places the Negro before his own wife and sister.

In 1886 several numbers of *Texas Siftings* carried satirical reports of a trip to Washington by Alexander Sweet. In one letter, after discussing the Texas delegation to the Forty-ninth Congress, he added, "In my next letter I shall drop the Congressmen and take up the other monstrosities and freaks which I inspected in the Smithsonian Institute."

William T. Thompson's *John's Alive* is organized in the manner of the picaresque story, but its purpose is moralistic. The justification used by the narrator of the title story is reminiscent of those used by Daniel Defoe's Moll Flanders and Henry Fielding's Joseph Andrews, "The sad experience and extraordinary vicissitudes through which I have passed were probably . . . necessary to teach me that degree of humility which should temper the disposition of every rational being. . . ."

The story is a hoax devised in Philadelphia by the narrator to chastise his fiancée, who he thinks is flirting with another man. John's jealousy leads to their estrangement and breakup. He becomes very gloomy and even thinks of suicide, but he is saved by a clever plan to win her back. He will swap clothes with a corpse and make Mary think he is dead. At the graveyard he startles a medical class exhuming a body for examination and dissection. The medics run off and leave him with the corpse, which he dresses in his clothes and takes down to the river. A watchman approaches. The scene is one of macabre humor. "I sat the corpse upon its feet, hastily threw my cloak about its shoulders and pulled my fur cap upon its head. It was cold and stiff, and stood erect with little assistance. As the honest old guardian of the night approached, I commenced an altercation, supplying my companion's part of the dialogue in a feigned voice. After a little muttering, I broke out in a louder tone, as I supported the corpse with one hand against the fire-plug, by which we were now standing, 'You're a liar!'—'You're another!'—'I'll break your mouth!'—'You'd better try it, you puppy!'—'Call me a puppy!' (here the footfalls of the watchman became more rapid) 'Take that, you infernal scoundrel!'" Leaving the body standing erect against a fireplug, John walks away just as the watchman comes up. As soon as the latter discovers the dead man's face, he also quickly leaves, thinking he has seen a ghost. Hiding nearby, John sees the old man's fright. "I could not refrain a hearty laugh, for the first time in a month, as the fast-receding sounds of the Dutchman's well-nailed boots died away in the distance." He then slips the body into the river. As he had hoped, everyone assumes that the body is his. He reads in his obituary that he probably committed suicide over an affair of the heart. He attends his own funeral in disguise and is delighted to see his sweetheart in deep grief.

Deciding to lie low for a while, he leaves Philadelphia for the South. He takes a ship at New York for New Orleans. There he becomes a book-keeper, but hard times set in. He spends time in jail, and even considers suicide. But again his life is saved when he joins a company of Louisiana volunteers and goes to Florida to fight the Seminoles. Life as a soldier is hard. After he is wounded, he is discharged from the service and heads back to Philadelphia. "I found it impossible to trace my misfortunes to any other source than to my own reckless, wayward, indomitable temper. My selfish jealousy had been the cause of my original despondency. . . ."

In Philadelphia he finds his old rival still suing for Mary's love, but by pretending to be a ghost he scares the suitor away. He and Mary finally marry and move to the South, where he is "the happiest John *alive!*"

Most of the remaining sketches in the volume deal with picaresque characters. "Going Ashore" tells of the lesson a New York dandy learned off Key West, Florida. Against the advice of the captain, Mr. J. Theophilus Hill decides to go ashore to see the natives; but as he steps into the little shore boat, he falls overboard. The sophisticated greenhorn presents a ludicrous picture. "Mr. Hill looked like a wilted poppy as he seated himself in the bottom of the boat, clinging convulsively to the sides. His blooming ruffles were gone, his exquisitely pointed shirt collar no longer maintained its erect position, and his shining beaver, which had set so gracefully upon the side of his head in the morning, was now the property of covetous old Neptune." This adventure teaches the New Yorker never to leave the city again.

A sketch recording an adventurer's army experiences fighting Indians is "Recollections of the Florida Campaign of 1836." In retrospect, army life seemed pleasant and funny to the narrator. He recalls that his company was filled with new recruits who were eager to kill Indians. "There was fighting enough done, but there were no Indians caught; there was powder enough burned, but there were more wounded pine trees discovered after the battle than wounded Seminoles; and I am strongly of opinion that there was more turpentine than Indian blood spilled on that occasion." He remembers a soldier found curled up on picket duty. "The truth of the matter was, Tom, not being disposed to stand two hours in a pelting storm, had, after having been placed upon his post, strayed up into the camp, where he found an empty flour-barrel, which he carried, as near as he could guess in the dark, back to his post, into which he crawled with his musket, and where he might have remained 'as snug as a bug in a rug' till morning, but for our intrusion."

Such characters as the Georgia Stag kept the troops entertained. "I am Ruga Dick, the big buck of the water, the Georgia Stag. Tie my leg to a swinging limb, and I'll whip all the Irish in Ireland." In these sketches and in the title sketch the narrator shows how either he or the central character has been educated by his adventures on the road of life. His picaresque experiences have been salutary for him, and they provide moral instruction for the reader.

Although most of the episodes in Sweet and Knox's *On a Mexican Mustang* are merely comic, occasionally satirical sketches and comments are directed against such groups as the braggart Texan, the early Catholic missionary, and the Indian.

The first sketch in the book is of a big blustering Texan drunk in a saloon. He reviews the disastrous effects of the war on him, "the loss of his plantation and negroes (he never owned a slave in his life, and the only connection he ever had with a plantation was through a hoehandle.)" He calls the Yankees liars and thieves. "I can make the biggest man of them eat dirt, *I* can. I'm hell on the Wabash, *I* am. The durned body-snatchers, they took all of my niggers; but I'll get even with 'em yet. There ain't one of them man enough to stand up with me in a fair fight. I just want one of them to contradict me, an' I'll bore holes in him till he can't hold water. I wish one of the cowardly *coyotes* would come along now, till I'd carve out the material for a funeral. I'm just pining away for a fight. I'm a raw-hide Texan, *I* am; but I can lick daylight out'n the biggest Yankee ever grew in New England." A man from Massachusetts hears the big words of the Texan, challenges him, pierces his ear lobe with a six-shooter, and knocks him unconscious with the butt of the weapon. Thus the braggart learned his lesson the hard way.

The ruthlessness of some early Catholic missionaries is the subject of the authors' bitterest satire. Of religious conversion devices they wrote, "Those old Spanish pioneers used to coax the Indians of Texas into the folds of Christianity under the soothing influences of the thumb-screw and other ancient Christian ordinances" (p. 79). Another popular converter was the "virgin," an iron overcoat into which a heathen Indian was placed. "Nine out of every ten of those operated on were converted after a certain number of turns of the screw: the other was usually spoiled in the process of conversion, and was useful only as an awful example" (p. 208).

Far from being the noble savage of romantic literature, the Indian of Sweet and Knox was likely to be a murderer and a thief—and dirty in addition. Even a good Indian was sometimes not to be trusted. "A friendly Indian is one who does not make a business of scalping the superior race; one who only kills his white benefactors at such odd times as he can safely and conveniently lay the blame on someone else. A friendly Indian will live five to ten years on the best of terms with his neighbors; that is, he will borrow all the corn-meal he needs, steal what pork he requires, and beg enough firewater to keep him mellow. Then, when he has sufficiently demonstrated his friendly disposition, he will select a favorable opportunity, and, assisted by his relatives, also amiable Indians, will murder and outrage all the whites in the settlement. Then he disappears, taking with him the settlers' horses, and becomes a bad Indian for a time, keeping away from the busy haunts of men until his gnawing conscience (which is situated in his stomach) forces him to go to the reservation and draw rations" (pp. 502-3). Getting more specific, the authors direct their satirical arrows at the Kickapoos and the Lipans, who are "absolutely unhampered with prejudice as to color, and have frequently shown a perfect willingness to scalp a Mexican on terms of social equality" (p. 506). The Kickapoo has one distinctive trait. "He is the dirtiest Indian on earth. His sanitary condition is such, that he would require to be dressed in a clean shirt, and be fired out of a cannon loaded with carbolic acid, before he would be fit to anchor at a quarantine station" (p. 518). The Comanches are not lily-white in character either. "The Fort-Stanton Comanches have been very regular in robbing the United-States mail on the El Paso route,—so much so, that on one occasion, when the stage came in unmolested, the local paper headed a column on the subject, 'Startling Innovation!—The San Antonio Stage Not Robbed!' " (p. 517). The federal government's policy of appeasement was responsible for much of the trouble. The authors have a design for better and more efficient relations with the redskins. "It is estimated that it costs the war department about half a million dollars for every Indian actually killed by the United States troops. Would it not be cheaper to have dead Indians furnished by contract, the same as the other supplies needed to keep up the army?" (p. 513). Much of this talk is, of course, comic bombast; however, underlying these comments are serious indictments.

The narrator of Isaac Whitely's *Rural Life in Texas* is a picaro who, for the edification of his readers, relates the vicissitudes of his life. This humorous autobiography shows the author living by his wits and learning from his mistakes. He first relates boyhood capers in Alabama: tying a tin bathtub to a horse's tail, scaring a new boy at school with a live lizard, tying two yearlings' tails together and having one pulled off, and insulting the preacher by reminding him that he has eaten all the biscuits. When he is sixteen the family moves to

Rome, Georgia, where he plays the greenhorn in town for some time. He goes to college for a while and has many ups and downs there. He travels to Baltimore, where he has many amusing and embarrassing experiences. He becomes an undertaker and then, "My health being bad I felt reckless and went to Texas."

He plans to play confidence games on the Texans, but soon changes his mind. "My idea was that Texas was a new country and filled up mostly with an ignorant class of people, in other words I was fishing for suckers, but I am candid to confess, I soon found out that I was the sucker, and that Texas was filled with the *sharpest, shrewdest* people on earth" (p. 30). He has to make a living, however, and tries many ways. He uses his embalming instruments and for a while practices veterinary surgery. He writes and peddles a book on the home treatment of horses and cows. He sells patent medicines. He becomes an assistant surgeon and operates to correct cross-eyes, harelips, and club feet. He is at various times a butcher, a grocery clerk, a grain merchant, and the owner of a ranch. He sells a preparation for lighting pipes and cigars and when one blows up, he pulls an old Simon Suggs trick, he says, and disappears.

As a picaro he is a master at improvisation. When his supply of pills gives out, for example, he uses what ingredients are available to him at the moment and makes some new ones. One time he makes pills out of Texas mud and spit from his chewing tobacco, rolling them in castor oil. Although he is a charlatan, he is not very harmful and fools his clients not merely for fun but for food and shelter. He does, however, take much delight in accumulating possessions; and his obvious joy in adding money to his treasury is reminiscent of a Defoe hero or heroine. At the conclusion of his memoirs he inserts a paragraph that reads like a passage from *Moll Flanders*. "I have enough of this world's goods now to keep me comfortable, even though I go down to old age. But, kind reader, I hope you may never be called on to pass through the many fiery trials through which I have passed." He adds words of advice to young people. Don't go roving. "Don't be changing around from one thing to another. Live an honest life and always tell the truth; live according to the directions of the Bible. If I had so done I would have been a much happier man" (pp. 75-77). Thus a nineteenth-century Southern picaro deprecates the life of the picaro. Texas, he adds, is a good place to live—if a man goes there with the right intention. "If a man goes to Texas, as Bill Arp says, 'spiling for a fight,' he will not remain long before he is accommodated, but if he goes there with the intention of being a good citizen, he will not be molested."

The author's last words again remind one of Defoe. "Since I have had so many ups and downs, I have concluded now, to settle down, and while my life has been of a checkered character, and my trials severe, don't think, kind reader, that I am the happy-go-lucky, unconcerned man that, perhaps, you have judged me to be during the perusal of this book" (pp. 81-82). His frequent disavowal of the picaresque life he has led leaves only the most superficial reader convinced that he would have preferred to live a more sedentary existence. The zest with which he relates his adventures proves the contrary.

The misadventures that befall a young hick from North Alabama make up *Sam Simple's First Trip to New Orleans,* by "A Georgian of the Good Old Times." The author has a definite moral purpose in relating how the naïve country boy is taken in by the unscrupulous ways of the sophisticated world and how in the end virtue triumphs.

Sam Simple thinks that Wolf's Bend, his birthplace in the mountains of North Alabama, is "one of the greatest places in the world"—until in school one day he hears about New Orleans. After he grows a little more, he sets out for the Crescent City to see the world. He arrives by stage in Montgomery and stays at the Exchange Hotel, which he describes "as big as all of dad's yard and horse-lot put together." He registers as "SAM SIMPLE FROM THE MOUNTAINS GWINE TO NEW ORLEANS." His adventures in Montgomery include a fight with the Negro porter who takes his suitcase at the hotel, and a misunderstanding over a restaurant menu.

Missing his boat to Mobile, Sam rushes to the banks of the Alabama River and tries to stop the boat by waving a pair of drawers. Down by the river he has a fight with a dock worker who "hitched that tarnal hook [used in moving cotton bales] into the seat er my britches, and, bless my old buttons, if he didn't turn me heels over head right into the river."

The young picaro finally gets aboard a boat headed for Mobile, but his troubles go on with him. He is accused of stealing money, and is about to be punished when the ship hits a snag in the river and begins to sink. In the confusion Sam jumps off and later hitches a ride on another boat to Mobile. On this he is given whiskey by a gambler and for the first time in his life gets drunk. "I'm the best man in Alabam'—out run, throw down, out jump, jump higher, jump fu'ther, jump longer, jump stronger, than enny man from Gen'ral Jackson to Billy Bowlegs."

Throughout the book Sam's colorful—but clean—exclamations enliven the narrative: "volcanoes and cotopaxi!"—"splugeration and wildcats!"—"earthquakes and alligators!"—"auger and gimlet holes!"—"Old Nick and Tar River!"—"pistols and cotton hooks!"—"blue blazes and lucifer matches!" In Mobile he is put in jail for fighting a man on board the ship.

He gets on a New Orleans boat at last, and his destination is not far away when a fire affords him the opportunity to be a hero by rescuing a beautiful young lady. In New Orleans he continues to be taken in by sharpsters. Once he buys sixty coats at an auction. "Now I had no money, but coats 'nough for a cross-roads store." Luckily he then receives a $200 gift from the lady whose life he had saved in the boat fire. A New Orleans strumpet attempts to swindle him by posing as a woman in distress, but Sam accidentally escapes her trap. Afterwards he correctly reasons, "I b'lieve the plot was all fixed 'forehan' to git me in er tite place, skeer me 'most ter death, and make me give up all my money." His innocence acts as a guardian angel.

The Smiling Phoenix

Leaving New Orleans, Sam Simple stops by the plantation on which lives the young lady he rescued on the boat. They fall in love and marry. The girl's old father turns over to Sam the administration of the plantation. His folks from Alabama move near them, and they all live happily ever after. The author's purpose is to show that virtue and innocence will win out eventually. This he does definitely, but not very skillfully or believably. His means and his objective he states succinctly in closing the narrative. "In what I've wrote I've not 'tempted to draw on the 'maginashun, in order to feed er morbid cravin' fur the romantic, but my desire has been to lay 'fore the public some true idee of the treach'ry and meanness oftentimes practiced on the unsuspectin', and to make prominent the power ov honesty and perseverance in attainin' the successes in life."

Humorous picaresque literature was a relatively minor but significant area of Southern humor. Restricting this category principally to extended treatments of travels has excluded many works—especially those dealing with the freedman—that could be properly classified as picaresque. Nevertheless, there is enough to show the continuing appeal of the narrative of discovery, satire, and humor.

Notes

1. Green, *J. T. Moore*, 38.
2. *Literature of Roguery*, II, 548.
3. See Hudson, *Humor*, 353-58.
4. *Ibid.*, 363.

11. The Philosopher

THE KEYNOTE OF AMERICAN HUMOR was struck at the signing of the Declaration of Independence when a signer said, "We must all hang together." Benjamin Franklin is reported to have replied with humor and wisdom, "Yes, we must all hang together, because if we do not it is certain that we shall all hang separately." James L. Ford later commented, "From that time to this, every humorous writer who has won distinct recognition from the American people has been a philosopher as well as a mere fun maker."[1] American humor, then, has been useful as well as entertaining. Americans have usually felt that the laughing philosophers are the wisest.

The South has had its share of the philosopher-humorists. Before the Civil War the Southerner living close to the land had evolved a philosophy usually expressed in humorous folk aphorisms. David Crockett was a backwoods thinker. Abraham Lincoln's proverbs—like "Don't swap horses when you are crossing a stream"—were directly indebted to the store of humorous wisdom common to every Kentuckian. After the war, proverbs continued to be a popular medium of humor. Since its first publication in 1890 the *Ladies Birthday Almanac*, a perennial favorite in the rural South, has devoted much space to such sayings as: "Plant your taturs when you will, they won't come up until April. The more thunder in May, the less in August and September. Be sure of hay 'til the end of May."[2] In the writings of most postwar Southern humorists philosophy played a significant role. Joel Chandler Harris, Charles H. Smith, Sam Small, Francis Bartow Lloyd, Anne Virginia Culbertson—these and many more undergirded their humor with philosophical messages. Sometimes the morals were expressly stated; sometimes they were implied. An English essayist, E. V. Lucas, had this to say of Irvin S. Cobb: "Beneath Mr. Cobb's fun is a mass of ripe experience and sagacity. However playful he may be on the surface, one is aware of an almost Johnsonian universality beneath. It would not be extravagant to call his humor the bloom on the fruit of the tree of knowledge."[3]

Attesting to the popularity of humorous wisdom were the "Wit and Wisdom" columns in Southern periodicals. The following epigrams appeared in the *Arkansaw Traveler* of February 17, 1883. "Money of all evils is called the root. / Give us the money, the devil give, to boot."—"Beauty by homely ones is often hated. / 'Tis thus that good looks are so poorly rated."—"Whiskey is a curse that all men damn, / Even he who cries out for a dram."

Proverbs were often used as fillers in *Texas Siftings,* as on May 15, 1886: "To make a name have an aim."—"Good laws are of little avail when bad men are depended upon to enforce them."

These gems of wisdom were gleaned from the pages of the *Sunny South* of August 17, 1901. "Bear with your neighbor's defects, that he in turn may put up with yours."—"A political economist says that 'the best wives are the cheapest.' Yet every man who has a good wife looks upon her as a little 'dear.'"

Throughout the nineteenth century and into the twentieth the newspaper was the most popular means of disseminating wisdom with fun. Almost every paper, no matter how small, had its paragrapher whose job it was to satisfy his readers' craving for humor and philosophy. Sometimes all he had to do was to clip funny stories and sayings from larger papers whose staff included full-time humorists; occasionally he wrote his own. They range from the popular Judd Mortimer Lewis who wrote the "Tampering with Trifles" column for the Houston *Post* to the anonymous paragrapher for the Union Springs *Times* in Alabama. The philosophical humor published in the newspapers was identical to that which appeared in the periodicals; indeed, there was much swapping of material. Much of this material consisted of aphorisms placed in columns variously headed by such rubrics as "Wit and Wisdom" and "Humor and Philosophy." Excerpts from the pages of the Union Springs *Times* of May 1, 1867, show the content and tone (some of it obviously derived from Benjamin Franklin). "If you wish to be well served serve yourself."—"Winter weather and women's thoughts often change."—"Hoops surround what ruin men—wine and women."

And on January 26, 1881, the paper satirized advertising proverbs. "What a monotonous sort of life it must have been in Eden, without those cheering aphorisms that now everywhere brighten up the landscape, making every rock, tree and fence to blazon out into such gratuitous advice as 'purify your blood!'— 'Chew Spherical Fine Cut!'—'Consumption can be cured!'" The same issue contained such pronouncements as the following: "An ounce of keep-your-mouth-shut is better than a pound of explanation after you have said it."— "Hymen is represented with a torch on account of the tortuous ways of matrimony."

The Countryman

From Hosea Biglow to Abe Martin wisdom uttered through a rustic mouthpiece has seemed to Americans to have a special authenticity. The man living close to the soil is supposed to be closer to the wisdom of the ages because, as William Faulkner has put it, "Only the earth endures."

The philosopher most widely read in the postwar South was Bill Arp (Charles H. Smith). His philosophical reflections on daily life and experience were published in the Atlanta *Constitution* and syndicated throughout the South. The collections of his writings became best sellers.

Almost all of his late sketches, like those in *The Farm and the Fireside,* are optimistic. In "The Ups and Downs of Farming" he wrote that farming is like fishing: you seldom get the results you expect. He added thankfully, "But we are not complainin' by no means, for we've got wheat enuf fer biskit every day and light-bread on Sunday, and a few bushels to spare for them angels that's to cum along unawares sum of these days." Because the lawmakers had been "protecting manufactures for seventy-five years and neglectin' agriculture," he made a utopian proposal. "I wonder if our law-makers who can save a State couldn't fix up an arrangement that would give everybody a good price for what they had to sell, and put everything down low that we had to buy, and then abolish taxes and work the roads with the chain gang, and let the bell-punch run the government."

In the Introduction to *Bill Arp's Scrap Book* a countrywoman is quoted on Smith's pleasant sketches. "Don't Bill Arp tell things the plainest? I have laughed till I cried over some of his letters; for the same things had happened in our own family, and it seemed that he must have been right here in the house when he wrote it." In the same place an anonymous critic comments. Smith's "writings are a delightful mixture of humor and philosophy. There is no cynicism in his nature, and he always pictures the brightest side of domestic life, and encourages his readers to live up to it and enjoy it. 'Carpe diem' is his motto. Old folks and children alike enjoy his genial writings. . . ." The writer's picture of himself in later life sets the scene and mood for his philosophical sketches. "It's a great comfort for me to set in my piazzer these pleasant evenings and look over the farm, and smoke the pipe of peace, and ruminate."

Much of Smith's later humor dealt, naturally, with farming and farm life, as in *The Farm and the Fireside*. The paternalism of the plantation owner is the subject of this comment on the original Bill Arp: "The genuine Bill Arp used to say he had rather belong to Col. Johnson than be free, for he had lived on the Colonel's land for twenty years, and his wife and children had never suffered, crop or no crops; for the Colonel's wife threw away enough to support them, and they were always nigh enough to pick it up." Farm work was hard, and Bill Arp had done enough to know it. "Diggin' taters" was a back-breaking and dirty chore, but it had to be done. "If I can't plow I can do something else, I can tote water for a rest." His father used to tell him: "William, when you get tired hoeing potatoes you may weed the onions for a rest." With his family he relaxed from work with such entertainments as coon hunts. He concluded in the *Scrap Book*: "And so we go, mixing in with our daily labor any fun that comes to hand."

The sketches in *The Farm* frequently included humorous advice. Sometimes this advice gently satirized cherished rural superstitions: "Now is the time to plant potatoes. Be shore to plant 'em in the dark of the moon and then plant some more just two weeks later, and they'll be 'allee samee.' I tried it last year" (p. 122). In the *Scrap Book* he gave advice on fence building. "A gate should be no higher than the fence. . . ." Bill confided confidentially, "I think I know a right smart about gates and about fencing, but I don't know how to drive steers, and I don't want to learn" (p. 71). Many of his rural observations are pragmatic and optimistic. "We have got a power of good things to be thankful for. A little boy was drownd in my nabor's mill-pond yesterday, but he wasent mine. The doctor passes my house most every day, but he don't stop. There was a barn full of corn and mules burnt up in the settlement last week, but it wasent mine. The poor house is just up the road a piece, but we don't board there" (p. 139).

When he viewed the so-called progress since the war, however, he saw less cause for optimism. In *The Farm* he blamed Yankee "progress" for substituting a furnace in the basement and a few iron pipes for "the 'old back log' and the blazing hearth-stone" (p. 150). The industrial age, he felt in the *Scrap Book*, meant a decline in morals and manners. "The old lines of social standing are broken down, and one man is as good as another, if he succeeds. Success is everything now, especially in making money. Statesmanship has gone down. Great learning is at a discount, money rules the roost, and everybody knows it, and everybody is pushing for it. Money makes presidents, and governors, and members of congress." Stoically, however, he added, "Nevertheless I am hopeful, and if I do sometimes take the shady side, I mean no harm by it. I am always reconciled to what I cannot help" (p. 143).

Politics, on the other hand, produced mildly pessimistic comments. After trying to explain to Mrs. Arp "the great general principles of the Democracy" and the opposite principles of the Republicans, he recorded her opinion. "I've been suspecting, for a long time, that those principles were to get in office and draw big salaries, and live high without work, and I reckon one party can do that about as well as another, don't you?" (p. 305).

The Negro question and especially Yankee interference in a Southern domestic problem generally irked him. "I've seen a good many pieces of late about the negro and the great Southern problem. The people up north begin to admit they can't see through it. . . . I would not give a farthing for any man's judgment about darkies who hadn't been born and raised with 'em and owned 'em. . . . The Yankee will never know what the negro is, for he never knew him in a state of slavery." He illustrated Southern paternalism. "I love these old darkies, not as my equals, but as I love my children. . . . The relation between the white and black race is by nature one of protection on the one side and dependence upon the other, and when it ceases to be that, I have no use for the nigger" (pp. 152-54). In another sketch he lamented the change in the labor market. "We can't hire cooks now-a-days, for these free niggers had rather beg or steal or starve than cook." As a solution he suggested that a fresh supply be brought over from Africa, where "those chiefs will sell 'em for beads and jewsharps" (pp. 166-67). This recommendation is, of course, humorous. The loving, paternalistic attitude evident in "The Negro" (*Scrap Book*) is representative of his real feelings toward the freedman. "I like the nigger. I like him better than I did ten years ago. I can look back and remember what he was soon after the war, and I am satisfied he is improving." The Negro, he revealed, has certain weaknesses, but most white people are indulgent. "When our cook hides away a little flour Mrs. A. shuts her eyes and says nothing, for it hurts their feelings so bad to be accused when they are guilty." The childlike Negro, he said, needs a guardian. "I like the darkeys, I do, but I haven't got much hope of 'em being anything but the same old careless, contented, thoughtless creatures they always was. If we don't own 'em as we used to we have got to act like we do, for there is no other way to get along with 'em."

Most of Dr. George W. Bagby's philosophical humor was presented as the lucubrations of Mozis Addums. The essay "Uv Wimmin" is typical of the Virginian's meditative productions. Female suffrage, he wrote, has made women a popular topic. "As wimmin is a gointer voat sune, every dog uv a man that kin hole a pin is a takin uv a chants at 'em in the gnuspapers." He also is qualified to pass judgment on the gender. "I has known and luved 'em these menny a year, but I has my ubjekshun to wimmin. It ar this—everything about 'em is too long." Then he specifically listed all those things about women that are too long: "thar cotetail," "thar shoo-strings," "thar ixtremmytis"—ability to kick from a long distance—"thar waste," "thar necks," and "tungs," "nose," "heds," "har," "memmyris." He ended with, "In cunclewshun, they livs too long, givin uv a man (preechurs is diffrunt) no chants to marry but one in a lifetiem. . . ."⁴ Thus Mozis gave his readers the benefit of his many years of experience and thought about women.

The title and subtitle of Francis Bartow Lloyd's collected sketches epitomize the humor of the bucolic sages: *Sketches of Country Life: Humor, Wisdom and Pathos from the "Sage of Rocky Creek." The homely life of the Alabama Back Country has its sunny side: rough but wise and kindly talk.* All the ingredients are there: humor, wisdom, pathos, optimism, homeliness, and kindliness. The introductory essay emphasizes these traits. "The literary productions of Mr. Lloyd had three leading characteristics—humor, sense, pathos; the gentle humor of a heart in love with all about it; the sense that finds no description half so apt as to call it 'homely wisdom'; the pathos always trembling on the lip that laughs whole-heartedly at the foibles of mankind."

As a newspaper humorist, Lloyd assumed the personality of the rustic Rufus Sanders, whose name the same critic called "a synonym for household philosophy in many thousand American homes." The philosophy of Rufus Sanders is found chiefly in his aphorisms, in his stories and sketches with moral reflections, and in his philosophical essays. "A Visit to the Old Home" is a nostalgic account of a visit to the scenes of his youth, where everything has changed. His concluding wisdom after seeing again "the old trompin ground" is that "the sun goes swingin on to the Western hills, and after the gold of evenin will come the dusk of night." "The Saddest Case in Rocky Creek" is the story of an old man who, like King Lear, was "crowded to death." He gave away most of his land and goods to his children, and then they cast him out. "The Farmer and the Broncho" warns of the swap shark. Too many farmers, Rufus believed, are taken in by this kind of fellow. "He's a clever sort of fellow; he can tell a funny story or a wild and thrilling romance about Indians and cowboys, drink by note and ride like Gilpin, sing a song or dance the cancan, kiss the babies, smile at the ladies, while he swaps your very socks off."

The moral of "Rev. Zeb Newton's Career" is that preachers should stick to preaching and not mix in politics. After the Reverend Zeb Newton was elected justice of the peace, he quit preaching and started drinking, cursing, and fighting. He was once a good man, "But when a preacher kicks out of the traces and runs to politics you never can tell right exactly where he will make a landin." The story "Rufus Goes to College" teaches that a man doesn't have to be educated to become a success. At college Rufus was told by the president that it would take a surgical operation to put a college education into his head. Rufus then quit college and became a successful farmer.

With another story the Alabama philosopher agrees that a man should not leave the influence of his wife. "The sorriest white man that ever made a track or flung a card in the settlement" meets a woman who decides to reform him. "So they pitched in and got married and went to hangin their clothes on the same peg." At first he listens to his wife and works hard; but when the sun begins to bear down in June, he starts wasting his time again fiddling and telling smutty stories. Finally his wife can take no more. She tells him, "Pack your wallet now, and take your old fiddle and hit the grit." After he leaves home he steadily goes downhill. While his wife is prospering on the farm she works with a hired hand, his decline continues, until "The last time I heard from him he had jined the chain gang for ridin off on a horse that belongs to some other man, and if he has ever unjined himself, *its* more than I know." All this because the man had cut the apron strings that should have bound him to his wife—according to Rufus Sanders.

Some of the genial old countryman's aphorisms are based on superstitions. Such sayings as the following were common to most Alabama farmers: "It is bad luck to kill a frog, cause it makes the cows go dry. It is bad luck to cuss in the spring of the year, cause the fish won't bite." Others were more original. Under the head "Rocky Creek Philosophy," Rufus Sanders placed a group of local proverbs.

A sheepskin ain't always big enough to hide the wolf's teeth, but it takes some men a long time to git the lesson.

My religion is short and sweet and simple. Put your trust in the good Lord, and keep your liver movin.

A man may ride a poor horse, and borrow his neighbor's paper, and let his wife tote the wood and water, and still have religion, but I have got some mighty serious doubts about it.

Briars and berries grow together, and if you git the berries you will have to go through the briars.

The "tumble bug politician" is a man that looks one way and pushes the other at the same time.

Next to the man that will promise anything to git elected, the blamdest, biggest fool in this country is the man that would give a cent a thousand for the promise.

Rufus Sanders' sunny and wise humor was popular because he wrote it down in the language of the people who read his columns, and he used farm and home imagery and incidents with which they were all familiar.

Joel Chandler Harris' rural philosopher Billy Sanders appeared first in "The Kidnapping of President Lincoln" (1900); and until his creator's death the sage of Shady Dale, Georgia, spoke the mind of Harris on many things. He appears, for example, in *Gabriel Tolliver,* in *The Bishop and the Boogerman,* and in *Uncle Remus's Magazine* and other periodicals. The old Georgia cracker's optimistic philosophy is much in evidence throughout *Gabriel Tolliver.* One character quotes Sanders as saying "that it is the most comfortable world he has ever found . . ." (p. 388). Philosophizing on a Reconstruction project that had taken him months to accomplish and that had later proved useless, he says that the work had helped him over the rough spots of Reconstruction by giving him something to do. He illustrates by telling a short story. "Why, I knowed a gal, an' a mighty fine one she war, who knit socks for a feller she had took a fancy to. The feller died, but she went right ahead wi' her knittin' just the same. Now, that didn't do the feller a mite of good, but it holp the gal up might'ly" (p. 431). Southern humorists like Billy Sanders, Rufus Sanders, and Bill Arp helped Southern readers to get over many rough spots in their Spartan existence.

Will Harben's Abner Daniel in *The Georgians* is a type of humorous philosopher who is related in many ways to Harris' Billy Sanders. He frequently uttered maxims that are both funny and wise. He also helped people out of trouble by giving them advice and showing them how to take it. To an unorthodox, free-thinking Sunday School class he said: "Them ancient fellers that got up that Garden o' Eden tale was jest tryin' to inculcate some livin' truth, I reckon. All my life I've wondered what they meant by Adam an' Eve bein' told they must n' eat o' the tree of the Knowledge o' Good an' Evil, an' I've come to the conclusion that them old writers found the'rselves right whar I am to-day, and whar you-uns are. We've ate o' the forbidden fruit, an' are turned out o' house an' home. The rest o' this community are in the Garden o' Eden" (pp. 69-70).

To the promoter of a Negro school who said that some people will have to be made over to fit the new era, Abner remonstrated: "I *do* believe, ef any makin' over *has* to be done, that it will be a sight easier to make over a few colored people that never are troublesome, until some person gits to devilin' 'em an' incitin' 'em to disorder, than to make over a race that never has been made over by nobody nur never will. Niggers kin be made over *some*, ur they never would 'a' been fetched agin the'r will so fur from home; but the puore white blood never was led about an' dictated to, nur it never will be" (p. 108). Abner often spoke in aphorisms like "Man was meant to work, an' he was meant to enjoy it" (p. 299). His role throughout *The Georgians* is frequently that of adviser to people and commentator on people and events.

Major Tom Noodle of Pulaski was the *Tennessee Ignoramus*, created by W. Thomas Carden, and the major was another country philosopher type. As a philosopher, his purpose was to help young people live a more rewarding, less painful life. He stated the purpose of the book in these words: "While it is desired to grow two smiles where only one grew before, the motif is to instill into young (ignorant) hearts correct views of many phases of life by portrayal of real scenes, that they may be warned of the dangers incident to humanity and to teach them so as for them to avoid many of the mistakes of the encyclopedia of life" (pp. 7-8). Major Noodle's memoirs abound with philosophical treatises: on love, on ambition, on trouble. In the essay on love he observes: "The hoss and woman . . . air the two most useful animules ter man in all creation. They pervide the greater part of his pleesures and sustenance. . . . Nothin' on earth will attract a man more, er ruin him quicker, than a butiful hoss and a purty woman" (p. 142). The theme of trouble leads him to discuss in a mock-serious vein such topics as love, debt, and the seven-year itch. He concludes hopefully, "There is a way out of the bad things of life. If you have to scratch, scratch. I glory in your spunk if you scratch" (p. 114). He ends his observations on life with a stoical acceptance of the inevitable. "Death is a blessing—a relief from a bitter struggle; a release from a burden, a weight; rest from labors; peace after a weary battle, and freedom from pain and care" (p. 195).

Burtscher's *Yellow Creek Humor* reserves a chapter for "Yellow Creek Philosophy." Most of his wisdom appears in the form of aphorisms and resolutions, and there is an occasional anecdote showing the evils of whiskey. He loved to offer pithy kernels of advice. "Beginning on a small scale is a good weigh."— "There is no blue Monday to the man who makes his Sunday white."—"When a man preaches the doctrine of sunshine he must practice the doctrine of sweat."—"Two-faced people are never double-brained."—"Following the advice he gives to others leads a man to perfection." Burtscher's philosophical humor was obviously moral and practical. The additional element of optimism comes up in the "Resolutions." "That I will read a chapter in the Bible before breakfast and live one afterwards."—"That I will be an optimist every hour in the day."—"That I will smile more and frown less, think more and talk less, praise more and scold less."

The prevailing mood of the stories told by Eliza Caroline Obenchain's Aunt Jane is philosophical repose. In both *The Land of Long Ago* and *Aunt Jane of Kentucky* the homely philosophy of Aunt Jane permeates her stories of the past. Though she may tell of worthless drunkards, she is always tolerant and willing to overlook such minor vices, provided the men are good-hearted.

The framework for Aunt Jane's "ricollections" was a popular one: an elderly person recalling the past for the entertainment and edification of a young listener. Her humorous stories are told for a young lady who listens avidly. Aunt Jane fills them with philosophical comments. "There's a heap o' women to be pitied, child . . . but, of all things, deliver me from livin' with a man that has to have hot bread three times a day."

Most of Aunt Jane's wisdom is integrated into the stories she tells and the attitudes she takes toward the people and events. Her contemporaries definitely considered her a wise storyteller. An advertisement for *Aunt Jane of Kentucky* read in part: "Aunt Jane is a philosopher in homespun, and in her 'ricollections' we see the beauty, the romance, and the pathos that lie in humble lives."[5]

The Kentucky widow is tolerant of new ideas and ways. She is not like the unprogressive Uncle Billy in *Land of Long Ago*. He says, "They've got their gas and their 'lectricity, so's it don't make a bit o' difference whether the sun or the moon or the stars shines or not. And they've got their 'lectric fans, which makes 'em independent of the wind blowin', and now they're fixin' the roads so's they won't have to pray for rain, oiling them to keep down dust. . . . It looks like they're tryin' to git rid of all sense o' dependence on the Almighty; but as for me . . . I've got my pegs sot, and I ain't goin' to have my brains all tore up follerin' after new ways" (pp. 12-13). Aunt Jane philosophically sets Uncle Billy right. "There's no use stickin' to old ways unless they're better than the new ways."

The Smiling Phoenix

Verse was a favorite form for country humor, and much of this verse was reflective. A selection from "Solomon Nokes' Views" by Will T. Hale of Tennessee is typical.

> "Hate the bad in your natur'," is the way he would warn,
> "An' encourage the good, is the lesson to l'arn:
> *The weeds need no hoein', but you hatter to work corn,"*
> Said Solomon Nokes.
>
> "Don't blame people quickly until you have seen
> All p'ints of a question, from startin' to een':
> *Ripe fruit's ever better than that pulled green,"*
> Held Solomon Nokes.
>
> "The thoughts you're ashamed fer the good folks to know
> Ain't elevatin' guest's better hint 'em to go:
> *With ants at the roots, roses have a pore show,"*
> Claimed Solomon Nokes.[6]

Madison Cawein also used verse form for his "Corncob Jones: An Oldham-County Weather Philosopher." Corncob Jones, the "beateningest man and the talkingest," believes that if one notices and keeps a record of the weather, he'll be able to predict the future weather:

> *Hit's not whut the weather is,*
> *But whut hit wuz oncet, long back*
> *In the times whut's gone.—Gee whiz!*
> *No man needs an almanack*
> *If he only notices.*

Cawein's poems were typically optimistic.

> *Take heart again, Joy may be lost awhile.*
> *It is not always Spring.*
> *And even now from some far Summer Isle*
> *Hither the birds may wing.*[7]

The newspaper humorist Frank L. Stanton also wrote optimistic verses which stressed that behind every cloud was a silver lining—or as he expressed it in "This World":

> *This old world we're livin' in*
> *Is mighty hard to beat;*
> *You get a thorn with every rose,*
> *But ain't the roses sweet!*[8]

Although almost all of Stanton's poetry is superficial, his optimistic philosophy won him great popularity and an appointment as Georgia's first poet laureate. He preached a message—humorous, sentimental, optimistic—that his readers delighted to believe. Like most country philosophers, he wrote for an immediate audience—and his job was to please them. Like Bill Arp, Rufus Sanders, and Billy Sanders, he did what he set out to do.

The Negro

Many Southern humorists used a Negro as a medium for their speculations on life, death, taxes, and the Republican party. An anecdote attributed to Henry Watterson, "Abram Jasper's Parable," teaches a "truth" about the Republican party. Speaking at a barbecue for Negroes near Louisville, Abram begins: "I has seed de Republicans up. I has seed de Democrats up. But I is *yit* to see de nigger up." He says he dreamed he died and went to heaven, but at the pearly gates he was denied admittance by Saint Peter because he was not mounted. On the way down the hill from the Celestial City he met Charles Sumner and Horace Greeley. They were walking and he warned them they couldn't get inside the gates unless they were mounted. At Greeley's suggestion Abram got down on all fours and rode the two Republicans up to the gates. This way, they figured, all three could get in; but at the gate Peter called out to them: "All right . . . jes' hitch yo hoss outside, gentlemen, an come right in."[9]

Three writers for the Atlanta *Constitution*—Frank L. Stanton, Sam Small, and Joel Chandler Harris—frequently used the Negro personality for their comments. Stanton often interspersed bits of prose philosophy with his poetry, crediting the expressions to such pseudonymous persons as "Brer Williams," "Brother Dickey," and the "Old Deacon." Epigrams were the forms in which he revealed their wisdom.

Satan wuz a' angel in heaven, but lak de res' of us, he couldn't stan' prosperity.

It wouldn't be such a cold world if we'd make bonfires of the old stumbling blocks, and warm up to happiness.

You can't 'scape Trouble, but you kin whistle a jig tune an' make him fergit what he come fer.

De sayin' is, you can't take your money to de hereafter, but it'll give you easy ridin' on a paved road till you git dar.

De wise man said dar's nothin' new under de sun, but de worl' looks so new ever' mornin' dat you has to ax yestiddy whar you is today.[10]

Some folks spen' mo time in grievin' over spilt milk dan dey does to drinkin' whut's on hand.

Dey's so much light in de worl' dat I hez come to de conclusion dat hit's a crime fer anybody ter stumble.

Heaven is so clost ter you, dat if you des had faith enough you could tiptoe en reach it.[11]

Sam Small's Old Si served as oracle for comments on subjects ranging from the parvenu Negro to round dancing. He was asked in the *Sayings* what he thought of the Murphy Movement, a temperance campaign. "Well, er man cums out ez a temprence man an' talks like a sojer, but he goes in wid der boys an' drinks like er fish" (p. 33). He was as realistic in commenting on high prices. "Darfo' de only tings dat de wah made cheap is de niggers, an' whar dat is de state ob de case de country is 'bleeged to be po'!" (p. 91).

In the *Humorous Sketches* Si defended the robber barons like Jay Gould who had publicly sent aid to the yellow fever sufferers in Memphis. "I allus tho't dat Mister Goule 'ud some day riz up an' sho' dat de good Lord made him, too, an' hed er use fur him" (p. 6). He objected to the critics of dancing, and asked them probing questions. "Ar' it onhealthy when er ole 'oman waltzes 'round at er camp-meetin' wid fo' presidin' elders exercizin' dar mussel tryin' ter hold her on de groun'? . . . An' I wants ter kno' ef hit's sinful fer de parson ter put his arm 'round de gals an' go in washin' wid 'em at dese big creek baptisin's?" (p. 28).

Most of Old Si's advice and comments were reserved for members of his own race. After an insurrection in Macon, he was ready (in *Sayings*) with a recommendation. "I tink de niggers better rouse up and freeze to de white fokes, 'kase sence I know'd freedom de niggers is had a cussed sight too much polyticks an' too little bread . . ." (p. 97). Like Sam Small himself, Old Si could find little to praise about educating the Negro. He contended that "dere's no use ob book larnin' fer er nigger dat don't 'splane ter him how ter make er libbin in der good ole way. Dar's too many eddycated niggers playin' lottery er finishin' dar larnin' in the penitenchery now, yer heah dat!" (p. 129). And in the *Sketches* he believed that the effect of new inventions was not always beneficial to the race. "I's mighty jubious on nigger progriss in sech times ez dese. Ennybody whar kno's er nigger kno's dat he warn't cut out ter lib in er country full er yankee noshins an' double-back-ackshun convenshuns ter beat 'em outen de odd jobs dey wuz fotched up ter do" (pp. 20-21).

During a freak snowstorm in Decatur, Georgia, Old Si asked a white man if it was like Yankee snow. He was told it was, "An' dat's de country dat you white folks wants to sen' we darkies to jes for ter gib de yankees a taste of the niggah, am it?" Then he warns, "Well, now, Boss, when dey gits this niggah up dar, he's gwine ter know all about hit, he is! He's got to be too dead to skin an' ropped up in a wooden obercoat, ter boot, yer hear me—dat's white man's talk" (pp. 63-64). In the *Sayings* he explained why he was so critical of his own race. "Dat's 'kase I'se 'quainted wid 'em. I ain't bin ten yeahs 'round de court house widout larnin' dat hits nip an' tuck twixt er nigger theef an' er suck-egg dog ez ter w'ich kin hole out de longes'!" (p. 35).

A regular feature of the *Arkansaw Traveler* was a "Plantation Philosophy" column, which contained the sage sayings of a darky.

A man can't afford ter go at a piece ob work wid too much rashness. A dog sometimes runs over the rabbit.

De fame ob a man is only show'd by comparison. De lower yer turns de lamp in de room, de brighter de fire seems to burn.

A man what can go inter a spring house an' keep from drinkin' de milk outen de crock jar is as much ob a fool as he is honest.

A man what's got a mortgage on a nigger's farm is a wus marster den de one he had 'fore de wah.

When I sees a couple ob nigger women meet each udder an' try ter ack like white women what has all dar lives been practicin' deceit ob s'ciety, I gits sick right dar.[12]

Two supposed racial characteristics—complacency and flightiness—are censured in Eloise Sherman's *Plantation Poems*. "Disappointed" pictures Brer Raccoon who sits under a persimmon tree waiting for fruit to fall. He says to himself, "I've hyeard dat all things come / To him who des will wait." He falls asleep and Brer Possum comes along, climbs the tree, and eats all the persimmons. Awaking and seeing the tree barren of fruit, Brer Raccoon catches on. "Things come to dem whut waits / 'Less some one gits 'em fus'."

"Stick to Yo' Blackbe'y Vine" is a shrewd commentary on people who hop around from one thing to another. The wise people, however, are in another category.

> *De ones dat gits de mos' is dem*
> *Dat des makes up dey mine*
> *To choose dey place an' a'ter dat*
> *Stick to dey blackbe'y vine.*

These are representative examples of wisdom in Negro dialect verse among Southern humorists.

Uncle Remus is, of course, Joel Chandler Harris' Negro philosopher, and he is the best of the lot. He looks into and sees the truth of the human heart. Usually he clothes his observations in homely metaphor. "Put a boy within smellin' distance uv a piece er tater custard, an' it seem like de custard will fly up an' hit him in de mouf, no matter how much he try ter dodge." Uncle Remus' philosophy was a genial one, filled with moral truths and kind-hearted observations. The old storyteller speaks many truisms based on his animal tales. After relating the story of how Brer Possum is falsely accused of stealing butter and then burned to death, Uncle Remus explains it to his little friend. "In dis worril lot er folks is gotter suffer for udder folks' sins. . . . Tribbalashun seems like she's awaitin' roun' de cornder fer ter kotch one en on us, honey."[13]

Throughout the Georgian's work there are bits of philosophical commentary, but the "Sayings" of Uncle Remus and "Plantation Proverbs" are oracular pronouncements. Like Old Si, Uncle Remus spends much of his energy advising, instructing, and chastising the freedman. In *Uncle Remus: His Songs and His Sayings* he satirizes the bickering and pettiness in churches, lazy men, those who move from Georgia to Mississippi and Arkansas, the temperance movement, and the educated Negro. In "Race Improvement" he indicts the freedman, but indicates hope for his improvement. "Dere's a kind er limberness 'bout niggers dese days dat's mighty cu'us." He takes to task "dese yer young bucks w'at goes a gallopin' 'roun' huntin' up devilment." He notes sarcastically, however, that there is hope for them. "Dey er gittin' so dey b'leeve dat dey ain't no better dan de w'ite fokes. W'en freedom come out de

325

niggers sorter got dere humps up, an' dey staid dat way, twel bimeby dey begun fer ter git hongry." Now, with a chance for improvement, he suggests, "You slap de law onter a nigger a time er two, an' larn 'im dat he's got fer to look attern his own rashuns an' keep out'n udder fokes' chick'n-coops, an' sorter coax 'im inter de idee dat he's got to feed 'is own chilluns, an' I be blessed ef you ain't got 'im on risin' groun'."

In "The Emigrants" he warns one would-be emigrant, "I done seed deze yer Arkinsaw emmygrants come lopein' back, an' some un 'em didn't have rags nuff on 'em fer ter hide dere nakidness." He advises him to "pull out fer de place whar you come fum."

Uncle Remus was another who opposed education for the Negro. As he said, "W'at a nigger gwineter l'arn outen books? I kin take a bar'l stave an' fling mo' sense inter a nigger in one minnit dan all de school-houses betwixt dis en de State er Midgigin." Education, he maintains, is "de ruinashun er dis country. Look at my gal. De ole 'oman sont 'er ter school las' year, an' now we dassent hardly ax 'er fer ter kyar de washin' home. . . . I ain't larnt nuthin' in books, en yit I kin count all de money I gits. No use talkin', boss. Put a spelling-book in a nigger's han's, en right den en dar' you loozes a plow-hand."

Uncle Remus' "Plantation Proverbs" are capsule wisdom. Using plantation imagery Harris preserved in permanent form the folk wisdom of the observant Negro.

> Dem w'at eats kin say grace.
> Ole man Know-All died las' year.
> Tattlin' 'oman can't make de bread rise.
> Rails split 'fo' bre'fus' 'll season de dinner.
> Dogs don't bite at de front gate.
> Pullet can't roost too high for de owl.
> Empty smoke-house makes de pullet holler.
> Nigger dat gets hurt wukkin oughter show de skyars.
> Nigger wid a pocket-han'kcher better be looked atter.
> Hongry rooster don't cackle w'en he fine a wum.
> Hit's a mighty deaf nigger dat don't year de dinner-ho'n.
> Sleepin' in de fence-cornder don't fetch Chrismus in de kitchen.

Good advice has always been more acceptable when enclosed in a framework of humor. This sugar-coating certainly accounted for the popularity of most of the didactic literature written in the South between 1865 and 1914. During this period Southern wisdom most frequently appeared as the random observations of an old country philosopher or an old-time darky. Their philosophy was typically optimistic, retrospective—even nostalgic—conservative, and domestic.

Notes

1. "Century of American Humor," 482.

2. Quoted in Clark, *Pills, Petticoats and Plows,* 254.

3. *Library of Southern Literature,* XVII, 159.

4. *Selections,* II, 352-59.

5. In Obenchain, *Sally Ann's Experience.*

6. *Library of Southern Literature,* V, 2040-41.

7. *The Republic,* 68, 97.

8. *Frank Libby Stanton,* 14.

9. Aswell, *Native American Humor,* 380-81.

10. *Frank Libby Stanton,* 29-31.

11. *Sunny South,* Nov. 30, 1901.

12. Dec. 10, 1882; Jan. 6, 1883.

13. Quoted in Toulmin, *Social Historians,* 140.

12. Shapes

SOUTHERN HUMORISTS usually disregarded form in itself. That is, they did not permit form to determine content any more than the novel form today determines its material. However, in addition to the general classifications of the sketch, the novel, and verse, it is possible to classify the humor further into such genres as the essay, the tall tale, parody, allegory, light verse, the epistle, the hoax, and the burlesque. A study of postwar Southern humor, therefore, would not be complete without at least a cursory glance at these shapes of humor.

Southern humor has always been influenced in part by location and climate. The rural South, for example, is peculiarly suited to the development of the yarn. Robert West Howard has recently pictured the result. "The Yankee is inherently a go-getter; the Southerner is inherently a porch-sitter. The one scarcely pauses to make a wisecrack; the other takes half an hour to weave one simple joke."[1] The slower moving life of the South, then, had its effect on the form of humor. Perhaps Joel Chandler Harris' delineation in *Gabriel Tolliver* of Billy Sanders' method could be applied more broadly to the indigenous humor of the entire South. "One peculiarity of Mr. Sanders' humour was that it could not be imitated with any degree of success. His raciest anecdote lost a large part of its flavour when repeated by some one else. It was the way he told it, a cut of the eye, a lift of the eyebrow, a movement of the hand, a sudden air of solemnity—these were the accessories that gave point and charm to the humour" (p. 113). Manner or form, therefore, was important to much of the oral humor; it necessarily suffered when it was transmitted to the printed page.

The Essay

Frequently the juvenilia of a humorist consisted of a goodly number of essays, and he occasionally returned to the form throughout his life. Usually a ridiculous subject was chosen: the human ear, flirts, the onion, the mule. One of George W. Bagby's essays was called "My Notion About the Human Ear," published in *Putnam's* of February, 1870. Before the war he had written several such essays, including "My Wife and My Theory About Wives" and "The Virginia Editor," both published in *Harper's Magazine* (November, 1855; December, 1856).

Sidney Lanier wrote several mock-serious essays. An article dated "San Francisco, December 9, 1872" is actually a short essay containing many puns. He described, for example, his companions in the stagecoach as "a Michigoose, or female Michigander, with her daughter, a very sprightly little gosling indeed, going to San Antonio to set up in the millinery line." Touching on his affliction with consumption, he pictured himself as "traveling as valet to his right lung—a service in which he had been engaged for some years."[2]

"Peace," which Lanier wrote in 1870, has been called "a burlesque essay, full of the facetiousness of his early prose, with the humor derived from the mock-serious tone."[3] Here Lanier showed himself volunteering to keep his son and his nephew while their mothers went out. Choosing toys with careful attention to child psychology, he hopes to keep the boys pacified while he writes an essay on peace. But there is no peace for him because the children begin to hurt themselves with the toys he so carefully selected for them. They quarrel and fight and eventually overturn Lanier's desk. In reality he is ignorant of child psychology, and he invites the reader to laugh with him over the trouble resulting from his pretended knowledge. Warfare not peace, he concludes, is the natural state of man.

The first published work of Mary Noailles Murfree (who wrote as Charles Egbert Craddock) was a humorous essay. "Flirts and Their Ways" classifies its subject in seven categories: the dashing, demure, musical, literary, pious, sympathetic, and the sentimental flirt. The author refused to single out any one type for praise. "I shake my head and sagely opine all are good and none are best. Yet something of moment I can impart. Not long since I heard a retired flirt of great brilliance say that she had during a long and successful career adopted each role in turn, and if she could recall the years of misdirected zeal and energy, she would reduce her former elaborate *modus operandi* to the following simple regime: Buy a hogshead of prayer-books and do the pious flirt."[4]

A mock-serious essay by Alexander E. Sweet treats the excellent climate of Texas. The climate there is so good, he remarks, that many invalids from other states threatened with a serious throat disease migrate to the state. "So sudden and dangerous is this disease that the slightest delay in moving to a new and milder climate is apt to be fatal, the sufferer dying of dislocation of the spinal vertebra at the end of a few minutes and a rope."[5]

Among the writings of the Georgian Lucian L. Knight, collected in *Memorials of Dixie-Land,* are many funny essays. "Justice to the Onion" is a defense of a vegetable too long "the butt of the world's ridicule." In "Our Friend, the Mule"—reminiscent of Josh Billings' more famous essay on the same topic—the writer praised the beast of burden and concluded with a question. "Is it not time for Nebuchadnezzar to be getting something besides fodder?" Another light effort, "Fido—the Real Hero of the Polar Conquest," eulogized the polar dog.

The Lie and the Tall Tale

Absurd exaggeration found sympathetic soil in the South, especially during the "flush times" of the Old Southwest. The genre continued after the Civil War, but was still primarily associated with the frontier. In the popular imagination "liar" became almost synonymous with "Texan."

The stock victim of the Texas liar was the Eastern greenhorn. In *The Adventures of Big-Foot Wallace* by John C. Duval the title character describes a Texas "varmint" to credulous tenderfoots. The creature is called the "Santa Fe" and is worse than the tarantula, with "a hundred legs and a sting on every one of them, besides two large stings in its forked tail, and fangs as big as a rattlesnake's." Attacked by the Sante Fe, a person is stone dead in five minutes. Big-Foot brags that his boots are made of alligator skin and that his hunting shirt is made of tanned rattlesnake hide. The only way for a Texan to protect himself against Santa Fes, scorpions, and other such varmints is to chew tobacco and drink whiskey, "and that is the reason the Temperance Society never flourished much in Texas."[6]

But other Southerners sometimes gave the Texan liar a run for his money. In "A Dog Fall with a Texas Liar," one of the best of the *Sketches of Country Life* by Francis Bartow Lloyd, the champion liar of Rocky Creek, Alabama, is challenged by a native whom he meets on a trip to the Lone Star State. The Texan opens the contest by claiming that everything is "pore out there in Alabamy—pore lands, pore stock, pore folks and pore ways." The Alabaman wins the first fall with a stretcher which runs its teller's a close second to Ovid Bolus' lying artistry. "Well, sir . . . you are about half right and about half wrong. We don't have no graveyards in Alabama—they have gone clean and clear out of fashion. The land is powerful pore in spots—too pore to sprout cow peas or grow bull nettles, but if crops are extra short and times uncommon hard we can chaw rosum and eat fried light wood knots and drink branch water and keep out of the porehouse. And we have got a monstrous healthy country over there. People used to die in that country sometimes, but they don't do that way now. They just live on and on and on till they turn to something good to eat or dry up and blow away. Now and then and here and there you will run across a man that put most too much salt in his dirt when he was a boy and has turned into what they call a petrified rock. But they don't get sick and lay down and die like they use to, and whensoever a fellow citizen gits old and wrinkled and broke down and tired out and weary with life and takes up a fool notion to commit suicide, all he has got to do is to pack up and move his washin out of Alabama. Generally speakin, in three days after he crosses the state line and strikes a country where they sell coffins and build graveyards he will keel over and go dead. We may be pore folks and we may have pore ways, stranger, but you can bet your chin whiskers that we have got a monstrous healthy country where I come from."

Talk of the relative speed of Texas and Alabama trains brings on a boast from the Alabaman. "Very frequently I have been on the cars when they got over the ground at such a brisk rate till the telegraph poles looked exactly like the teeth of a fine comb." The Texan does him one better, however, telling of "a cannon ball train" in West Texas. After visiting his sweetheart one time, he boarded the train and started to kiss her goodby when "the train shot out at such a rate till before I knowed it I had kissed a cow in the mouth two miles up the road."

The Texan relates the feat of a dog tied to the rear of a train going up to a hundred miles an hour. The conductor was startled to find "that durn dog runnin alongside the train on three legs lickin the grease of a hot box." The Texan brags a little. "Yes, siree, it takes a power of speed to keep up with things out here on the plains of the great and glorious west." And there is his experience with a "mule yeared" rabbit. "I shot at one out there onct upon a time and a stray birdshot struck him in the burr of the ear. It didn't kill him, but it kinder addled his mind so till he lost what sense he started with and went off in a ziz-zag run like a streak of lightnin. When the New Orleans papers come out the next day they told about a mule-yeared rabbit from Texas that was killed in the streets of that town the night before, and went on to say it had a fresh birdshot wound in the burr of the ear. It was my rabbit to a dead moral certainty, but I couldn't lay claims to him at that long distance."

Eventually each man agreed that the other was no apprentice in the art of storytelling. The Alabaman concludes: "By this time my feet and legs had gone to sleep and I was powerful durn dizzy about the head. So we called it a dog fall as to the first round and quit."

Parody

A prerequisite to the writing of parody is, of course, a knowledge of literature and style by the writer. Evidently Southern writers had this knowledge, for parody was a popular form with them. Most of the professional humorists regarded what they produced in the genre as bagatelles, and dashed them off without much revision or polishing.

Probably the most popular subject was the poetry of Edgar Allan Poe. Of the many parodies of Poe that were embalmed in print, one of the most unusual was "The Medical Raven," first published anonymously in the *Atlanta Medical and Surgical Journal*.

> *Once upon a midnight dreary,*
> *The doctor slumbered weak and weary,*
> *And all the town could*
>   *Hear him snore.*
>
> *While he lay there sweetly napping,*
> *Suddenly there came a tapping*
> *Like a ramgoat madly rapping*
> *His hard head*
>   *Upon the door.*
>
> *"Get thee up," a voice said loudly,*
> *"Come in haste," it added proudly,*
> *Like a man who owned a million*
>   *Or much more.*
>
> *But the Doctor never heeded:*
> *Back to dreamland fast he speeded,*
> *For such men as that he needed*
> *In his practice*
>   *Nevermore.*
>
> *For long months that man had owed him,*
> *Not a cent he ever paid him,*
> *And the doctor now will dose him*
>   *Nevermore.*[7]

John Trotwood Moore wrote many parodies, taking special delight in lampooning James Whitcomb Riley. One stanza from "When the Colts are in the Ring" (*Ole Mistis*) will show the humorous imitation of the Hoosier's style.

> *O the fair time, the rare time, I can feel it in the air,*
> *As we take our brimming baskets and go out to see the fair;*

The lasses decked with ribbons red, the colts with ribbons blue—
What a trial for the gallant lads to choose between the two!
No season of old mother earth can half such blessings bring
When the bloom is on the maiden and the colts are in the ring.

Moore also produced "When de Fat Am on de Possum," a poem in Negro dialect. Each stanza ends in a Rileyesque couplet similar to this one: "O I don' want no better times den dese my life to fill, / When de fat am on de possum an' de taters in de hill!"

Moore turned his attention to the impressionistic school of poets, and the result was published in the *Horse Review* on July 16, 1895.

> *The sun has donned his nightcap,*
> *Upon his head of red,*
> *The clouds have ceased to play about,*
> *They're in their trundle bed;*
> *But mother moon is on her wheel*
> *And riding out with Mars,*
> *She's put her biggest bloomers on*
> *And buttoned them with stars.*[8]

Two better known writers—O. Henry and George Washington Cable—also wrote parodies. O. Henry's "The Bridge of Ryes" was a take-off on Thomas Hood's "The Bridge of Sighs," and a poem which parodied Longfellow's "The Bridge" were among those appearing in the writer's paper, *The Rolling Stone.* Cable called his often reprinted parody of Thomas Campbell "The New Arrival."

> *There came to port last Sunday night*
> *   The queerest little craft,*
> *Without an inch of rigging on;*
> *   I looked and looked—and laughed!*
> *It seemed so curious that she*
> *   Should cross the Unknown water,*
> *And moor herself within my room—*
> *   My daughter! Oh, my daughter!*
>
> *Yet by these presents witness all*
> *   She's welcome fifty times,*
> *And comes consigned in hope and love—*
> *   And common-metre rhymes.*
> *She has no manifest but this,*
> *   No flag floats o'er the water;*
> *She's too new for the British Lloyds—*
> *   My daughter! Oh, my daughter!*
>
> *Ring out, wild bells—and tame ones too,*
> *   Ring out the lover's moon;*

The Smiling Phoenix

Ring in the little worsted socks,
Ring in the bib and spoon.
Ring out the muse, ring in the nurse,
Ring in the milk and water;
Away with paper, pen, and ink—
My daughter! Oh, my daughter![9]

The genre was even called into the service of prohibition. William Burtscher's verses on the evils of liquor are reminiscent of Longfellow.

Lives of drunk men all remind us
We should oust the traffic quick.
And, departing, leave behind us
Footprints everywhere we kick.[10]

Parodies of obituary poetry reached a high-water mark in the poem by Emmeline Grangerford in *Huckleberry Finn*, but the gloomy form was also spoofed by other humorists. A widow's lament was put by O. Henry into his *Rolling Stone* (October 13, 1894).

I will miss you, Jabez, miss you
When the stars begin to shine,
In fact it will be hard to get along without you
But I will have to be resign [sic].

You will wait for me in heaven
Just within the pearly gates
He died just a quarter past seven
But Providence rules our fates.

But true hearts death cannot sever
There never was a kinder man,
I never expect to do better ever;
But I'll try and do the best I can.

Allegory

The best examples of allegory are, of course, the animal tales of Uncle Remus, already discussed. Another example, also already mentioned, Lanier's "Hard Times in Elfland," can be read as an allegory of Reconstruction. Although frequently a device for serious satire, allegories were also light and comic. One of the most amusing in Southern literature is John T. Moore's "How the Bishop Broke the Record" (in *Ole Mistis*). Invited to attend services in an Episcopal Church (he sits in the colored gallery), Old Wash later writes his account of the occasion, using horse-racing imagery throughout. He assumes first of all that the church is a track, "an' jes' off to de lef' dey had de nices' leetle jedges' stan' all painted in silver an' trimmed wid gold, while

334

de timers' box on de right wid leetle peep holes in it an' pictures of flyin' things wid wings jes' erbove—hosses dat had broken de recurds, I spec." Little angel boys bring in "programs fur de races." He speculates that with all these facilities the track will be fast; and he is right, for when the Bishop is put on exhibition Old Wash is transported and cries "lak er baby." Then comes the aftermath. "I heurd de white folks all pass quietly out; I heurd de notes ob de organ die erway, but I sot in de cornder, way off by mysef, an' thanked God dat I'd seed de light an' heurd de recurd ob salvation busted."

A satirical allegory is Charles E. Nash's "Bicycle Road to Hell" in *Donkey, Horse and Bicycle.* Nash uses the bicycle fad to symbolize the descent of man into the Devil's lair through Progress. A female cyclist states the book's anti-scientific theme when she says: "Mr. Devil, what God has made occult, let no man make apparent." The sketch is built around conversations between the Devil and Mr. and Mrs. Cyclist.

Although Mr. Cyclist doesn't believe in heaven or hell—he has read Tom Paine, Voltaire, Thomas Henry Huxley, and Darwin—he suddenly finds himself going down the bicycle road to the center of the earth where dwells the Devil. There, Mr. Cyclist is shown around by Satan, who says that Paine and the other skeptics are his agents and that his worst enemies are the old-time Methodist and Presbyterian camp meetings. Much of the satire, however, is directed at religious groups. Mr. Cyclist attacks the Jews as skeptics, infidels, liars, swindlers. "They think they have no need of a Savior, for they don't want to be saved from their sins—it would interfere greatly with their trade." Other targets of Nash's satire include the Christian Scientists, saloons, Sunday bicycling, birth control, homeopaths, specialists, pure scientists, and the X-ray.

But Progress is the real enemy. Bragging about the achievements of the nineteenth century, Mr. Cyclist says, "If the earth were to move five thousand miles an hour, it would take ten years to catch up with us, and this wheel has set her an example of speed. . . . Don't you suppose she will get ashamed of herself and increase her motion?" In reply to the question "Who should ride the bicycle?" the Devil answers: "If anyone, an old bachelor, who is too stingy and mean to marry; and an old maid, who is too ugly and cross to get a husband. These two it can make no worse." Continuing to speak out of character—but revealing the mind of his creator—the Devil attacks material progress: "Too much machinery makes idlers, too many idlers make paupers, too many paupers make tramps, too many tramps make penitentiaries and gallows. I agree with Dr. Petrie that the average mind has been weakened by our higher education, for where memory is weakened there can be no advance."

The Smiling Phoenix

Light Verse

Sidney Lanier wrote several trifles about turkeys.

> *Observe yon plum'd biped fine!*
> *To effect his captivation*
> *Deposit particles saline*
> *Upon his termination.*

A popular proverb is the theme of another Lanier stanza.

> *While self-inspection it neglects,*
> *Nor its own foul condition sees,*
> *The kettle to the pot objects*
> *Its sordid superficies.*

A proverb also becomes a couplet.

> *The earliest winged songster soonest sees,*
> *And first appropriates, the annelides.*

For a lady who had sent him some grapes Lanier returned "To Mrs. S. C. Bird (With an Empty Basket)."

> *Elijah (so in Holy Writ 'tis said)*
> *Was in the wilderness by raven fed;*
> *But my lone wastes a fairer wing supplies,*
> *I'm pampered by a Bird-of-Paradise!*[11]

Written in rimed regular verse, "When Mrs. Hays Laughed," by Lucian Knight, tells of the time the Daughters of the American Revolution met in Macon and Mrs. Hays became amused about something ("I've forgotten now" what) and "almost split the conference." "Just Send for the Parson" is a comic love poem. A swain is in love with a certain lady and pleads: "Don't send for the fireman! Water won't do. / But send, doublequick, for the parson!" Only this can put out the blaze that she has ignited in him. Even lighter is "The Parson's Compliment."

> *Said Parson Bland to Deacon Bluff*
> *Seated before the fire:*
> *"Deacon, I like you well enough,*
> *But you're an awful liar."*[12]

Samuel M. Peck wrote perhaps the best society verse of any Southerner. Almost all his poems of this type dealt with love themes. In "Rose" a bashful lover attempted to express his passion by plagiarizing Byron, Scott, and Thomas Moore; but he failed. Suddenly, however, "from my tongue the fetters fell" and the muse came to him.

> *Then came a flood of poetry;*
> *I spouted yards of rhyme;*
> *And she is going to marry me*
> *In apple-blossom time.*

In another verse Little Bopeep falls asleep and is found by Little Boy Blue. He is so bewitched by her that "he dropped his horn / And thought no more of the cows in the corn." Then he kissed her.

> *At the smack the woolies stood all in a row,*
> *And whispered to each other, "We're clearly de trop;*
> *Such conduct is perfectly shocking—let's go!"*[13]

Letters

Letter form was used for a variety of humorous situations. It was employed by John A. Cockerill (Randolph Gore Hampton) for *The Major in Washington City* and by George W. Bagby for "Mozis Addums to Billy Ivvins" in reporting the adventures of a humorous character in a strange place. "The Letters of Cal F. Head" by William Burtscher is centered around an attempt by a hayseed to order a book on poultry—he planned to read it to his chickens. Brander Matthews parodied the English lord's letters of advice to his son in "Chesterfield's Postal-Cards to His Son." In addition to this fictional use of letters, humor is found in the personal letters of such writers as Sidney Lanier and Joel Chandler Harris.

A series of letters from "Jesse Holmes, the Fool Killer," written by Charles Napoleon Bonaparte Evans, editor of the Milton (North Carolina) *Chronicle* from 1841 to 1883, gained some popularity and created a character that eventually entered folklore. As Daniel Patterson has noted, the original Fool Killer letters have been virtually forgotten because of their numerous topical allusions and weak structure. The series consisted principally of loosely connected anecdotes and character sketches allegedly written by Jesse Holmes while traveling through North Carolina and Virginia. The letters expose various follies, ranging from pre-Civil-War white patrols who harass innocent slaves to a Tarheel belle who jilts her lover. Although the letters are generally artistic failures, they provide the modern reader with intimate glimpses of Southern life in the middle of the nineteenth century by way of the amusing peripatetic adventures of the Fool Killer. The type has since been used by O. Henry ("The Fool Killer"), George Ade ("The Fable of How the Fool-Killer Backed out of a Contract"), Stephen Vincent Benet ("Johnny Pye and the Fool Killer"), Helen Eustis (*The Fool Killer*), Carl Sandburg ("Ossawatomie"), and Helen Bevington ("The Fool Killer").[14]

The editor of the *Saturday Evening Post,* the Kentuckian George Horace Lorimer, wrote prudential letters to his son on how to become a success. *Letters of a Self-Made Merchant to His Son* was ostensibly written by a successful businessman while his son was in college and continued until the son went into business and got married. Almost any sentence taken at random from the letters is an aphorism. This passage, for example, comes from the first letter. "You'll find that education's about the only thing lying around loose in this world, and that it's about the only thing a fellow can have as much of as he's willing to haul away. Everything else is screwed down tight and the screw-driver lost."

Lorimer comments on the need for a person to be sound at the core. "You can cure a ham in dry salt and you can cure it in sweet pickle, and when you're through you've got pretty good eating either way, provided you started in with a sound ham." With this metaphor he reminds his son that a man can turn out good or bad regardless of whether he goes to college. Another aphoristic comment is in his "Education's a good deal like eating—a fellow can't always tell which particular thing did him good, but he can usually tell which one did him harm."

Responding to his son's desire to take the Grand Tour before starting to work in the family packing plant, the father wrote, "Procrastination is the longest word in the language, but there's only one letter between its ends when they occupy their proper place in the alphabet." About traveling, "Seeing the world is like charity—it covers a multitude of sins, and, like charity, it ought to begin at home."

Much of Lorimer's wisdom centers about commerce and business.

A business man's conversations should be regulated by fewer and simpler rules than any other function of the human animal. They are:

Have something to say.

Say it.

Stop talking.

The Caricature

Caricature has always been a valuable method of the humorist. More often than not, characters in humorous literature are exaggerated and distorted. In Southern humor the Negro, for example, was generally caricatured. Certain sketches, however, were acknowledged to be caricatures. George W. Bagby maintained that his "The Virginia Editor"[15] was a caricature, but when it first appeared many Virginia editors took personal offense. One even challenged him to a duel. This reaction could be understood if some of Bagby's statements were taken straight.

The Virginia Editor is a young, unmarried, intemperate, pugnacious, gambling gentleman. Between drink and dueling-pistols he is generally escorted to a premature grave.

His abhorrence of the vice of solitary drinking has a good deal to do with this popularity. . . . Rather than drink alone he will drink with a negro, provided the negro is at all genteel, and has a gentleman for his master.

He loves to talk, and his great theme, after politics, is himself.

Finally, half an ounce of lead is "honorably and satisfactorily adjusted" in his heart or brain, and the Virginia Editor dies, to the great joy of himself and to the intense grief of his party,—the faro-dealers, the bar-keepers, and of everybody who is entitled to an unexpected fifty cents simply because he is a negro and can run an errand.

The Hoax

In newspapers, magazines, and short stories the hoax was frequently used as a humor form. Henry Clay Lukens once observed, "There is one feature of American humor entirely distinct from any characteristics of which I have hitherto written. Hoaxing of the too credulous reading public has been nowhere so successfully practised as in this country."[16] In the South from Poe ("The Balloon Hoax") to Faulkner (*The Hamlet*) the hoax has been an important structure for humor.

Sherwood Bonner's "The Gentlemen of Sarsar," in *Dialect Tales,* is an example of the hoax in short-story form. Told by his father that he can have a $1,000 bad debt if he will go to the backwoods community of Sarsar to collect it, the narrator arrives at the village and seeks out the debtor, one Mr. Andy Rucker. The friendly Mr. Rucker invites the greenhorn to go on a chase for some Negroes who have broken out of jail. The gentlemen of Sarsar in company with the narrator set out on the chase. Accidentally the visitor shoots and fatally wounds one of the men they are after. The men take the dying fugitive to his mother, who wails that her son has been murdered. To appease her the stranger gives her $25. Then the girl friend quiets down only after also being given money. The pastor arrives, and the murderer gives him money for building a new church. The narrator is about to take Andy Rucker's advice and get out of town, but a woman stops him and asks for money to raise the dead man's illegitimate children. Even a doctor duns the greenhorn for money the Negro had owed him. The narrator, however, manages to get safely back to the city. On Christmas Day his luggage is brought to him by the Negro he had supposedly killed, who explains that it had all been one of Mr. Rucker's practical jokes.

The Burlesque

Joel Chandler Harris, Charles H. Smith, George W. Bagby, and George W. Hooper are but a few of the Southern humorists who tried their hand at burlesques. Harris' "The Late Mr. Watkins of Georgia" is a take-off on folklorists. He draws a humorous parallel between a supposedly Oriental folktale and a legend of Middle Georgia. James Wood Davidson said of Smith soon after the Civil War, "Of the many humorous writers in the broad-burlesque vein who have obtained at various times popularity in the South, none, I venture—not even Thompson, Hooper, or Longstreet—has ever struck a deeper and more universal current of popular sympathy than 'Bill Arp—So Called.'" The same critic said of Mrs. Fanny Murdaugh Downing's "Pluto: The Origin of Mint Julep" (1867): "It is a playful effusion, marked by unmistakable ability, and full of fine hints, sly humour, and playful fancy, with no want of genuine fire. It is a species of *mélange* humour, in which the burlesque and mock-heroic prevail. . . ."[17] According to Walter Blair, such burlesques, in company with the work of Mark Twain and others, ridiculed extreme romanticism and thus promoted the growth of realism in American literature.[18]

The Jud Brownin burlesques by George W. Bagby were among the most popular in the South. Jud's description of an opera in "Fray Devilo" is hilarious. "Well, a operer is nothin' mo' nor less than a play set to music; somethin' like a sermon preached out of a hand organ, only at a operer they all go in full dress. . . . But thar is the big chandalier, the pit, boxes, galleries, and just like a reglar theatre, only thar is mo' fiddlers in the fiddler's pen, with a man to beat time for 'em, and another man jobbed in a hole on the stage with his head hid under a greengig top to beat time for the sings, and I tell you between them time beaters old time has a hard old time uv it." Jud's retelling of the absurd plot is comic. He innocently recalls that he had intervened once when a woman on the stage was undressing.[19]

A burlesque account of how to conduct an affair of honor is given in George W. Hooper's *Down the River; or, Practical Lessons Under the Code Duello.* In the opening paragraph the author mock-seriously sets forth as his objective "to inform the public as to the mode of conducting an affair of honor in the most enlightened and modern style." The remainder of the book details the protocol of dueling in all of its absurd minutiae. Reminiscent of Mark Twain's account of a French duel in *A Tramp Abroad* (1880), the burlesque is a devastating attack on the dueling tradition.

Set variously in Alabama, Georgia, and Florida, the book purports to tell of an affair of honor over an implied insult in an Atlanta newspaper. Actually no offense was ever intended, and the offended party merely imagined the insult. The first step is to have the challenge delivered. The procedure is long and involved, but Hercules D. Lofty, M.D., a cowardly vestige of the Middle Ages, is an expert on duels and takes care of that step for the challenger. An extreme devotee of the code of honor, Lofty is impaled on a lance of satire. His dress, his speech, and especially his affected courtly bow are described in detail by the narrator, who feigns to be impressed by it all.

Dr. Lofty insists that all the amenities of the code of honor be observed with extreme caution. He is offended when a slight infringement occurs, as when a bow is not returned in the prescribed manner. The narrator, obviously with tongue in cheek, states that "it had never been my fortune to associate with a gentleman so courteous and so accomplished in bowing as Doctor Lofty."

The preliminaries to the duel take months and require the full-time service of several people. Once the preliminaries are over, the challenge delivered and accepted, the duel is called off—the affair having been settled off the field of honor. But the author's evident purpose of exposing a nineteenth-century dandy, phony, alcoholic, and coward has been served. From Lofty's home in Mobile, an acquaintance writes his brother of the dandy: "I have known him for about four or five years, and know him to be a most consummate dead-beat, and a coward. You cannot have any correspondence or intercourse with him other than to use a horse-whip on him should he insult you." Although ostensibly the hero of the book, Dr. Lofty, in some ways an earlier Miniver Cheevy, is actually the anti-hero. He is the principal character in one of the most elaborate burlesques in Southern humor.

Satire

In a period of rapid change, such as the postwar South was going through, it was inevitable that much of the humor would be satire or have satirical overtones. Objects ranged from the radical Republicans and the bicycle to Darwin and the Baptist church. Immediately after the war—before tempers had a chance to cool—the satire was bitter, but later it became good-natured. For example, J. Fairfax McLaughlin's *The American Cyclops* (1868), a satire on "Beast" Butler, is venomous; but Bagby's *What I Did with My Fifty Millions* (1874) is a gentle dreamlike joshing of the foibles of his fellow Virginians.

Darwin's recently publicized theory of evolution became the butt of much of the good-natured fun. There was published anonymously in New Orleans in 1873 a poem in heroic couplets, *Ye Mistick Crewe of Comus: The Missing Links to Darwin's Origin of Species;* it made fine sport of the idea. The opening is an invocation to the famous biologist, "Who thread'st the line of life to Nature's germs, / To find God's image in ancestral worms." The poet carefully traces "those pre-historic sires / Whose loves and lives a wondering race admires." The zoöphyte appears in the waters, and soon there are shrimp, lobster, and whale; the tadpole and salamander climb out on land; the land mammal develops there and through many gradations produces the noble line. An individual of each species named by the poet—there are many—is pictured, in a drawing, with a brutish half-human face. So far, so good.

> As countless rills, from fountains far and wide,
> United to form the river's rushing tide,
> So all these types, in Darwin's matchless plan,
> Converged, assert the lineage of Man.

The ineluctable process goes on. Monkeys, baboons, chimpanzees evolve, and then,

> Oh! rosy hues of Time's dim twilight morn!
> In such an hour the "Missing Link" was born;
> The great Gorilla, flinging wide the gate,
> Of Darwin's Eden, and our high estate.

> Our father Ape, by all with pride confessed,
> But she, whose love his ardent passion blessed;
> Like Pleiad lost, is hid behind Time's veil,
> We only know,—her offspring dropped the tail.

341

The Smiling Phoenix

The problem vast new Darwins shall engage
To swell the knowledge of a future age,
Until the secret countless cycles sealed
Bursts into life, and Man stands forth revealed.

Katherine MacDowell went to Boston from Mississippi in the early 1870's, served as Longfellow's amanuensis, and as Sherwood Bonner wrote local-color sketches of her native South. In Boston she also produced "The Radical Club," a satirical poem in imitation of Poe's "The Raven," and the members were shocked when the author read the poem as a guest of that elite group. Katharine Abbott, who wrote as Kate Sanborn, said that "Sherwood Bonner's hit on the Radical Club of Boston was almost inexcusable. She was admitted as a guest, and her subsequent ridicule was in violation of all good breeding. But like so many wicked things it is captivating, and while you are shocked, you laugh." The first stanza of the poem sets the tone.

Dear friends, I crave attention to some facts that I shall mention
About a Club called "Radical," you haven't heard before;
Got up to teach the nation was this new light federation,
To teach the nation how to think, to live, and to adore;
To teach it of the heights and depths that all men should explore;
Only this and nothing more.

Miss Bonner proceeded to lampoon various well-known members of the club, and concluded with this stanza:

But, dear friends, I now must close, of these Radicals dispose,
For I am sad and weary as I view their folly o'er;
In their wild Utopian dreaming, and impracticable scheming
For a sinful world's redeeming, common sense flies out the door,
And the long-drawn dissertations come to—words and nothing more;
Only words, and nothing more.[20]

One of the most unusual works of humor was George W. Bagby's *What I Did with My Fifty Millions*, praised by John Esten Cooke for its "bizarre and original humor which is richer and rarer, in our opinion, at least, than that of any other American. . . ."[21] The novel shows how Mozis Addums, as a wealthy Southerner, would dispose of his vast fortune. As a loyal Virginian, he would not spend any money outside the state. Actually Mozis' fortune is a delusion, for he earns a meager living as a cutter of hoops in a barrel factory.

While under the delusion, Mozis spends money to make his beloved state a better one and to perpetuate his name. But fifty million is hardly enough, he decides. "I want to give Virginia a perfect system of country roads, so that one may get off at a station and go to the nearest country house without breaking his neck, and it would take five hundred millions to do that" (p. 245).[22] He also spends money on parks, churches, streets, the poor, and other public projects. But to make sure that he would be remembered, he builds what came to be known as "Adams' Folly." "It is an octagonal mass of rough-hewn siennite, that rises some one thousand one hundred . . . feet in air. Upon its top there is a bell, compared to which the big bell at Moscow is but an infant's thimble. This bell rings of itself on stormy nights, and its mournful sound is heard in Philadephia" (p. 281). It takes five hundred thousand men ten years to complete the monument.

After years of such ridiculous schemes, Mozis fails to find happiness. Eventually he loses all his money and dies a pauper. This was the only notice of his death to appear in any paper: "Moses Adams, a pauper, died at the poor-house yesterday soon after dinner. He was very old—said to be upwards of one hundred—and labored under the delusion that he had been enormously rich. His knowledge of grammar was defective" (p. 318). Bagby's satire exposes the poor but proud Virginian who builds castles in the air that nobody can see or enjoy but himself. His contemporaries were said to be able to identify real Virginians in the satire.

Although Bagby's novel is unusual, it cannot be given the prize as the strangest satire of the period. This dubious honor goes to *Historical and Humorous Sketches of the Donkey, Horse, and Bicycle* by Charles E. Nash, a Little Rock physician. In the Preface the author stated that his purpose was "to give my own views on the leading questions of religion, science, morals, and manners. . . . The motive for writing this book is to try to improve the morals and manners of those who stand in the way of good manners and right living. . . ."

To Nash the most serious threat to morals and the economy was the bicycle. Throughout his satire he tried to show "that the bicycle produces nothing but ill health and poverty to the masses." He even took local doctors to task for being "willing to discount their bills at one hundred per cent and take bicycles at cost for their pay" (p. 42). He specified the results. "What do bicycles give to the public? The old homesteads are going to wreck, lands are washing away, and the young girls and the old maids and the boys of the farms are hastening to the towns and cities to catch this insane fad that they may be noticed for their expert riding" (p. 46). The infernal wheel was bad for the anatomy and usually brought bankruptcy to its owner. Nash sputtered: "Don't cry 'Hard times!' when you can throw away millions on a fad which has a tendency to destroy the morals, deplete the pocket and cripple the body" (p. 51). Nash saw in the bicycle fad a symbol of all the newfangled notions that were turning the heads of Southerners and corrupting the youth.

Although not a native Southerner (he was born in Illinois), W. C. Brann made his reputation in Waco, Texas, where as editor of *The Iconoclast* he won international renown and notoriety for his satire. Biographer J. D. Shaw said of him: "Mr. Brann has been classed as a humorist. This he was, and of a type peculiar to himself, but he was not content with merely having amused or entertained the people, he aspired to arouse public sentiment in the interest of certain reforms. He was a hater of shams and defied every form of fraud, hypocrisy and deceit. He made of his humor a whip with which to scourge from the temple of social purity every intruder there."[23]

In Texas he found many handy targets for his satire: the Baptist church, Baylor University, prohibition, revivalism, white supremacy, and other locally cherished idols. Taking the position of a freethinker and skeptic, Brann exposed weaknesses and fallacies wherever he found them. He did not restrict himself to Texas idols and institutions; he called James Whitcomb Riley "the poetical ass with the three-story name."[24] He was such a controversial figure that he split Waco into gun-toting factions. His life was ended on the streets of Waco in 1898 by an assassin who could take no more of the inconoclast's satire.

The Mock-Heroic Poem

The genre for which the eighteenth century was so much noted, the mock-heroic poem, was used by such "literary" comedians as Sidney Lanier, Samuel M. Peck, and Bakus W. Huntington. Having fun with an unheroic subject treated heroically was especially popular with writers who were suspicious of the literary value of other humor forms.

Perhaps no subject could be more appropriate for a medium which treats the insignificant as significant than a flea; and *The Flea* is the title and subject of a poem written by an anonymous author and dedicated "To the Hon. George S. Hawkins, Distinguished as a Jurist and Humorist, of Marianna, Fla." Written in heroic couplets, it opens with a defense of its subject.

> In little things true greatness oft is found,
> While oft in bulks naught but the bulks abound.

The poet went on to define his scope. "The flea, his travels and exploits I sing." Although many of the couplets are forced and wrenched, there are many as clever as this one.

> "*Let there be fleas!*" the Great Creator said,
> And fingers ope'd to see—the flea had fled!

Another trivial subject is treated seriously by Samuel M. Peck. This poet defended a dying custom.

> *The pride of the forest was slaughtered to make*
> *My grandmother's turkey-tail fan.*

The fan, he continued, was never meant for common occasions but for such spectacular events as camp meetings, where "It beckoned backsliders to re-seek the right, / And exhorted the sinners to pray." The era of the turkey-tail fan, Peck lamented, was past. "A fig for the fans that are made nowadays, / Suited only to frivolous mirth!"[25]

344

A favorite Southern dish is the subject of William R. Smith's "Bacon and Greens," published in *Reminiscences of a Long Life* under the pseudonym Bakus W. Huntington. In one stanza the poet showed the efficacy of the dish in helping a forlorn lover forget a lost love.

> *Ah! well I remember when sad and forsaken,*
> *Heart-wrung by the scorn of a miss in her teens,*
> *How I rushed from her sight to my loved greens and bacon,*
> *And forgot my despair over bacon and greens.*

In another stanza he pushed his adoration for the food to the ultimate extreme.

> *If some fairy a grant of three wishes would make one*
> *So worthless as I, and so laden with sins,*
> *I'd wish all the greens in the world—then the bacon—*
> *And then wish a little more bacon and greens.*

One of the most successful attempts to write a mock-heroic poem in the manner of the eighteenth century was "To Our Mocking-Bird Died of a Cat, May, 1878," in *Poems of Sidney Lanier*. Using an elevated tone and diction, Lanier wrote of the life and death of his family's favorite pet. He described the songs of the bird in elaborate figures of speech.

> *Tissues of moonlight shot with songs of fire;—*
> *Bright drops of tune, from oceans infinite*
> *Of melody. . . .*

This is Lanier's account of the death of the songster.

> *thus of late*
> *Thou camest, Death, thou Cat! and leapst my gate,*
> *And, long ere Love could follow, thou hadst passed*
> *Within and snatched away, how fast, how fast,*
> *My bird—wit, songs, and all. . . .*
> *Thy yellow claws unsheathed and stretched, and cast*
> *Sharp hold on Keats, and dragged him slow away.*

The lamentation follows the death.

> *'Twas wrong! 'twas wrong! I care not, wrong's the word—*
> *To munch our Keats and crunch our mockingbird.*

But the poet takes consolation in the probability that the Lord wanted the bird to "set all Heaven's woods in rhyme." He speculates that Beethoven and Keats would have their conversations arrested by the beauty of the bird's music and call out "Brother, O thou heavenly Bird!" Although Lanier probably intended the bird as a symbol of the poet, the poem still reads well as a mock-heroic.

345

The Smiling Phoenix

The Lecture and Confederate Rhetoric

After the Civil War the indigent Southern humorist frequently turned to the lecture platform as a means of keeping body and wit together. Almost every humorist at one time or another went on a lecture tour. Next to Mark Twain and Joel Chandler Harris, probably the most popular Southern lecturer was George W. Bagby.

Before the war Bagby had written several lectures, including the popular "An Apology for Fools" which he continued to use in his tours after the war. A typical evening's entertainment might include one of his lectures and readings from his Mozis Addums sketches.

His most popular subjects included "The Old Virginia Gentleman," "Women Folks," "The Disease Called Love," "The Virginia Negro, Slave and Free"; the best-known lecture in Southern humor was his "Bacon and Greens." This masterpiece was a favorite with audiences not only in Bagby's native Virginia but throughout the United States.[26] The lecture purports to tell of "that strange variety of mankind which is compounded of bacon on the one hand, and cabbage or greens on the other hand." The true Virginian, Bagby maintains, can be identified by his preference for the dish. He also eats other delicacies of the state: pot-liquor, fried chicken, stewed chicken, broiled chicken, chicken pie, barbecued shoat, roas'n'ears, buttermilk, hoecake, sweet milk, cracklin' bread, hominy, gooba-peas, persimmon beer, mushmelons, hickory nuts, snappin'-turtle eggs, catfish, cornfield peas; but bacon and greens he cannot do without.

One who would be a Virginian must also "butt heads with little negroes," "wear white yarn socks with green toes and yarn gallowses," get the cow-itch, meddle with Negro men at hog-killing time, upset beehives, bring big wasp nests into the house, try to tame a catbird, call doodlebugs out of their holes—"and keep on eating bacon and greens." He must, as a boy, fish for minnows with a pin-hook, carry his worms in a cymling, tie June bugs to strings, stump his toe and have it tied in a rag, go possum hunting at night, and "keep steadily eating bacon and greens."

After the Virginian is dismissed from school, the lecture continues, "he consoles himself with bacon and greens." He keeps a country store for a while; then he leaves for a sojourn in the Deep South. He returns home, "eats bacon and greens, and determines to be a better man." He gets religion at a camp meeting but loses it at a fish fry. He studies law, runs for the legislature, gets beaten, gets drunk, reforms, and "eats plenty of bacon and greens." He then marries "much to the satisfaction of his own, and greatly to the horror of his wife's family—and thus becomes a thorough-going Virginian." Thus through all the stages which one must pass who wishes to be a true Virginian. The only carry-over is the indispensable bacon and greens.

A section of William Burtscher's *Yellow Creek Humor* (pp. 13-18) pictures the local Chautauqua, whose lecture platform features such personalities as

346

Funshine Hawks and Opie Read. Most of the humor in the sketch derives from the reaction and interruptions of the audience. When Opie Read begins to tell a story, for example, he is stopped by a voice from the audience that suggests that he not tell that story because the people will not think it funny. After other suggested deletions, Read winds up with a much-abbreviated lecture.

The golden era of spread-eagle oratory came before the war, but inflated rhetoric continued to be a popular device for Southern speakers and writers throughout the century. Governor Bob Taylor of Tennessee was perhaps the best practitioner in the florid speech tradition. Although he was a humorist, much of the fun that the present-day reader finds in his orations was not intended by him. A speech he delivered at St. Louis on January 8, 1898, printed in *Echoes* (pp. 103-4), will show his artistry with the tradition. "I sometimes think that when the Lord God had banished the first guilty pair from Paradise, and when the gleaming sword of his angel had mounted guard over the barred portal, loath to destroy its glories and its beauties, he transferred them all to Tennessee. And when civilization first peeped over the Alleghanies and looked down upon the gorgeous landscape below, I think she shouted back to the advancing hosts, Lo, this is Paradise regained! Is it any wonder, then, that this beauty-spot on the face of the earth long ago became the shrine of heroes and statesmen? Is it any wonder that the star of destiny guided the peerless Jackson here to live and die?"

The Georgia historian Lucian L. Knight used allusion-studded spread-eagle devices in many of the speeches in *Memorials of Dixie-Land*. In one delivered in 1909 at Greenville, South Carolina, entitled "South Carolina and Georgia," he remarked that the faces before him looked familiar. "The explanation may be found in a kinship which takes us back to the other side of cradledom—which traces our habits of thought and our lineaments of expression to the same ancestral molds—which points us, it may be, to the potrait of some gentle mother of the Elizabethan age—perchance to the knee buckles of some pampered sire who feasted with Louis or who fought with Charles—and, which, leading us to the bastions of the old manor, unites us in the hearthstone ties of some common fireside beyond the seas." Although obviously not intended to be humorous, most of Knight's orations are made funny to us today by the same devices that seriously appealed to his audiences: his use of elaborate rhetorical devices and his appeal to state and sectional chauvinism by pointing up a Cavalier past. Even his funeral pieces can hardly be read today with a straight face. Read a section from his memorial to Joel Chandler Harris, with whom he had worked on the Atlanta *Constitution*. "Strong and gentle, he was oak and violet. In the chaplet of his clustering virtues, modesty was the queen-regent of all the flowers. No thorn of malice lay concealed beneath his laurels. No bitterness rankled within his bosom. He was the apostle of sunshine; and like Ben Adhem he loved his fellowman."

By the twentieth century the day of the great orator was almost over. In

The Smiling Phoenix

July, 1908, the *Taylor-Trotwood Magazine* carried Philip Lindsley's lament over the passing of the old-time Tennessee orator. But he did see reason for hope. "Nevertheless, oratory, in this country, will never become a lost art. So long as eloquence thrills the blood, or wit awakens mirth, or invective storms abuses, so long will the great orator meet with a welcome. . . ."

Paragraphs

Before the Civil War certain newspapers developed a form of humor that by the 1880's had become characteristic throughout the United States. Every paper of any size had its own paragrapher. As a critic of newspaper humor, Will M. Clemens defined the type. "A paragrapher is a writer of paragraphs, and paragraphs, in an American newspaper, are commonly understood to be short, concise, spicy and readable gems of wit and humor."[27]

A pioneer in the field was George D. Prentice, whose paragraphs for the Louisville *Journal* continued popular after the war and spawned many imitations. S. S. Cox explained that "there is a little silvery vein which runs through our newspapers, and which Prentice, of Louisville, first worked successfully. It consists in adroitly garbling a brief extract from an opponent's article, and diverting the meaning into a dash at some frailty of the opponent. The manner in which this is done is humorous, though the matter generally has the pungency of sarcasm and wit."[28]

Henry Watterson praised the collected *Prenticeana*. "I can recall no book of wit and humor . . . in which the salt is fresher or more savory; and the student of that brevity which is the soul of wit can hardly find a better model of all that is neat, racy, and concise."[29] Published in 1860, *Prenticeana* became, indeed, a model for postwar paragraphers. Most of the paragraphs consist of from three to six lines, and the book is not restricted in subject matter. The following randomly selected examples will show its tone.

A quizzical editor in Arkansas, who rejoices in the rather quizzical name of Harry Hurry, says that "truth is generally slow in its progress." Probably it is never in such a Hurry as he (p. 6).

A man recently got married in Kentucky one day and hung himself the next. No doubt he wanted to try all the varieties of nooses to see which he liked best (p. 7).

An Illinois editor asks how to kill humbugs. Let him swallow a little prussic acid, and he will dispatch one (p. 91).

We don't think Whiggery is worth anything except to be laughed at.—*Democrat*. It has lost much of its value in that respect since you left it (p. 123).

Some things are much better eschewed than chewed; tobacco is one of them (p. 298).

O. Henry wrote a column of humor for the Houston *Post* in 1895-96. Typical of such columns is an anecdote taken from the issue of October 21, 1895.

"Speaking of the $140,000,000 paid out yearly by the government in pensions," said a prominent member of Hood's Brigade to the Post's representative, "I am told that a man in Indiana applied for a pension last month on account of a surgical operation he had performed on him during the war. And what do you suppose that surgical operation was?"

"Haven't the least idea."

"He had his retreat cut off at the battle of Gettysburg."[30]

C. Alphonso Smith wrote of O. Henry's reputation at the time he quit the *Post*: "Had he died at this time those who had followed his career closely would have seen in him a mixture of Bill Nye and Artemus Ward with an undeveloped vein of Eugene Field" (p. 134).

O. Henry's witty paragraphs derived from the work of Alexander Sweet in *Texas Siftings,* who is generally credited with adding movement to the wit of the paragraph. Sweet's paragraphs actually were miniature comedies.

Mrs. McCoble, an Austin lady, rebuked her colored cook, Matilda Snowball, in the following words:—

"When I hired you, you said you didn't have any male friends, and now I find a man in the kitchen half the time."

"Lor bress your soul, he ain't no male friend of mine."

"Who is he, then?"

"He am only my husband."[31]

During the period from 1865 to 1914 humorous paragraphs were the most appealing part of small weekly papers. The following are representative samples taken from newspapers published in Union Springs, Alabama, between 1867 and 1889.

We once saw a young man gazing at the *ry heavens, with a † in 1 ☞ & ⌒ of pistols in the other. We Ndeavored to attract his at10tion by pointing to a ¶ in a paper we held in our hand, rel8ting to a young man in that § of the country, who had left home in a st8 of mental derangement. He dropped the † & pistols from his ☞ ☞ with the !: "It is I of whom U read. I left home B4 my friends knew of my design. I had s0 the ☞ of a girl who refused to lis10 to me; but smiled B9ly on another. I ——ed madly from the house, uttering a wild ! to the God of love, and without replying to the ? ? of my friends, came here with this † and ⌒ of pistols to put a . to my Xis10ce."

This story has no ‖ in ancient history. (*Times,* Dec. 7, 1867.)

What proof have we that Noah navigated an American river? Because he was on the Ark and saw (Arkansaw). (*Times,* Dec. 7, 1867.)

An Essay

An S A now, I mean 2 write,
2 U, sweet K T J,
The girl without a ‖
The bell of U T K.

Ten verses follow, with the final one reading:

> Now, fare U well dear K T J
> I trust that U R true;
> When this U C, then U can say
> An S A I O U (*Times,* May 4, 1870.)

Why is a man beaten in the street like a pickled donkey? Because he's ass-salted (assaulted). (*Times,* August 3, 1870.)

I know not which of the twain lifts man the higher—genius or gentleness.—Henry Ward Beecher. No more do we; but we'll back a mule against either. (*Herald and Times,* January 26, 1881.)

Throughout 1884 the *Herald and Times* printed a page-one column called "Humorous." The following are examples of the humor in the column: "A rising business—Making yeast." "A clean steal—Taking a bath." "Dead beats—The stopped clock."

In 1889 the humor column of the Bullock County *Reporter* had been absorbed by one called "Quaint and Curious," which contained such miscellaneous bits of information as the following: "The Emperor of China runs 426 servants." "It costs about $6 per head more to carry cattle from Boston to Liverpool than it does to buy a steerage ticket for an adult person."

From a peak of popularity in the late nineteenth century, Southern newspaper humor has declined to its present relatively insignificant status. Aside from the comic strips carried in daily papers, very little humor appears today in Southern papers. The decline is especially evident in the small weekly. A check in June and July, 1961, of the Union Springs *Herald,* successor to the *Times,* revealed that its only humor consists of syndicated cartoons.

Notes

1. *This Is the South,* 177.
2. Quoted in Starke, *Sidney Lanier,* 161.
3. *Ibid.,* 156; *Southern Magazine,* VIII (Oct., 1874), 406-10.
4. Parks, *C. E. Craddock,* 62; *Lippincott's,* May, 1874.
5. In Aswell, *Native American Humor,* 375-76.
6. In Tidwell, *American Folk Humor,* 603-4.
7. Lillard, *Medical Muse,* 37-38.
8. In Green, *J. T. Moore,* 50.
9. In Wells, *Parody Anthology,* 72.
10. *Yellow Creek Humor,* 67.
11. *Poems and Poem Outlines,* I, 203.
12. *Memorials of Dixie-Land,* 512-13, 527, 585.
13. *Rings and Love-Knots,* 64-66, 141-42.
14. Patterson, "Letters from the Fool Killer."
15. *Selections,* I, 109-21.
16. "American Literary Comedians," 795.
17. *Living Writers,* 157, 530-31.
18. "Burlesques."
19. *Selections,* II, 222-23.
20. In Abbott, *Wit of Women,* 96-100.
21. Quoted in J. King, *Bagby,* 156.
22. Page citations are to *Selections,* II.
23. In Brann, *the Iconoclast,* 5.
24. Quoted in Carver, *Brann and The Iconoclast,* 56.
25. In Wilder, *Wit and Humor,* II, 224-25.
26. In Rosenberger, *Virginia Reader,* 435-38.
27. *Famous Funny Fellows,* 7-8.
28. "American Humor," 847.
29. *Library of Southern Literature,* IX, 4192-93.
30. In C. A. Smith, *O. Henry Biography,* 130-31.
31. In Watterson, *Oddities in Southern Life,* 458.

13. Southern Humor: A Consensus

AS I HAVE SUGGESTED in the Preface, the humor written in the South between the Civil War and World War I may be read today not only for its literary significance (which is sometimes rather dubious) but also for its historical and sociological implications. A close examination of this humor reveals that it actually provides us with a mirror of the age. In the mirror is reflected the mind of the South during one of its most critical periods. The image which the humor projects is admittedly a sometimes distorted one, even at times appearing chaotic and inconsistent. Many of the stock characters are caricatures—the valiant Confederate soldier of Thomas Nelson Page, the faithful slave of Harry Stillwell Edwards, the benevolent slaveholder of Eloise Sherman, the unscrupulous carpetbagger of Opie Read, the mellowing philosopher of Charles H. Smith, the unreconstructed Rebel of John A. Cockerill, the "white man's Negro" of Sam Small. In addition, it must be admitted that Southern writers from Joel Chandler Harris to Mrs. LaSalle Pickett tended to drape the veil of romance over much of the harshness of the ante-bellum and post-bellum South. In their defense, however, we might remind ourselves that Southerners were, for much of the period, living in a "conquered province," which alone provided enough of stark reality. Lest we forget the contribution of humor to the rise of a realistic literature, however, we might reread the war memoirs and sketches of backwoods life which often included coarse— even crude—scenes and characters. Sam Watkins' description of the Chickamauga battlefield is naturalistic in its realism, and Bill Arp's gander pulling is anything but a refined sport.

But Southern humorists had a far greater task than recording reality. They recognized that in order for the Southerner to survive the ignominy of defeat and oppression, he had to regain and hold his self-respect. And humor provided a ready vehicle for the restoration of a good image for the Southerner himself and for the Southerner to hold up to the rest of the nation. Through the writings of men like Joel Chandler Harris, James Lane Allen, John Trotwood Moore, Dr. George W. Bagby, and Sidney Lanier, the South began the process of rehabilitation in her own and in the national mind. This process involved the formulation and presentation of a favorable image.

The image which the South wished to convey through humor had three main parts. First, the slaveholder who had been condemned by Harriet Beecher Stowe, John Greenleaf Whittier, and other Abolitionists had to be made over into a lovable, paternalistic manor lord who would not knowingly harm a fly—and certainly not a dependent slave. Jeannette Walworth is typical of the writers who took the position that the slaveowner had actually done the Negro a favor by owning and caring for him. William Lightfoot Visscher's "Chrismus in de Ole Time," with its picture of the generous master and mistress dispensing gifts on Christmas morning to their adoring slaves gathered around the steps of the Big House, is emblematic of this part of the image. Will Harben and Mary Ross Banks are but two additional writers who wrote from the point of view that the white Southerner had unselfishly agreed to shoulder the "white man's burden" for a time—until the Negro could emerge from the childhood of his racial development. The Negro needed someone to look out for him, and the white Southerner graciously assumed the responsibility. The resulting slavocracy was, the humorists posited, the best society the world had known since the days of ancient Greece—or outside the pages of a Sir Walter Scott novel. This part of the image was so impressively portrayed that it even convinced the Northern Negroes Paul Laurence Dunbar and Charles Chesnutt, whose writings are filled with freedmen nostalgic for "slavery times." Though no one—not even Thomas Nelson Page—seriously anticipated a return to those halcyon days of yesteryear, the Southerner could be pleased with the success of this rehabilitation of the slave system. It was a vindication of the "Southern Way of Life."

But this idyllic agrarian society had been irrevocably destroyed by Sherman's cannons, and the Southerner was ironically faced with the necessity of competing with an industrial civilization which as an aristocrat he had thoroughly condemned. Again humor aided in the preparation of an appropriate image to meet the demands of the new day. The reversal of attitude toward commerce and industry demanded by the new image was achieved smoothly and with a minimum of embarrassment with the help of writers who pleaded for a "new South." Dave Sloan's pride in the rebuilt Atlanta was duplicated in thousands of Southern hearts—in Petersburg, in Selma, in Natchez, in Charleston, in Nashville. Henry Grady's "Picken's County Funeral" was but one of the humorous productions by progressive realists bent on turning the South into an industrial paradise. The North Carolina clergyman's cry of "Next to the Grace of God, what Salisbury needs is a cotton mill" was echoed from the Potomac to the Rio Grande to the Ohio, where Henry Watterson sat in the editor's chair of the Louisville *Courier-Journal* writing editorials and speeches urging the South to recognize the Industrial Revolution. The second part of the image was thus helping the South to compete with the North on her own ground.

The South was waking up to the facts of life in an industrial-commercial age, but this did not mean a wholesale acceptance of all the concomitant social ideas. The former aristocrats who were now industrial realists were still convinced of the necessity to protect the purity of their race and the elegance of their society. It was, therefore, mandatory that the "inferior" Negro be kept in his place. The third part of the image which humor helped to create consequently concerns the attempt of the white Southerner to convince himself, the non-Southerner, and the Negro that the races are not equal, and that therefore they should never be allowed to meet on equal terms—socially, politically, or economically. Segregation was thereby deemed requisite and mandatory. (To a lesser extent this same idea is reflected in the humor dealing with the relationship between the Southern ruling classes and the poor whites. From A. B. Longstreet's Ransy Sniffle through the crackers and mountaineers of Will Allen Dromgoole, Mary Noailles Murfree, and Samuel Minturn Peck down to William Faulkner's Flem Snopes, the Southern aristocrat has been typically depicted as condescending in his relationship with his white inferiors.) The Negro mouthpieces created by Joel Chandler Harris, Sam Small, Irwin Russell, and Anne Virginia Culbertson are all "white folks' Negroes" who never presume to equality with their erstwhile owners. They know their place and because they do they are accorded a genuine affection by their white overlords. Like Ruth McEnery Stuart's Aunt Amity and Joel Chandler Harris' Aunt Minervy Ann, they know they can depend upon their white friends to continue to look after them. The humor showed the former slaveowner willing to take up the burden from which Lincoln's Proclamation of January 1, 1863, had seemed to relieve him. The white man would allow the Negro to return to his cabin and become a sharecropper or a paid servant. The story of the freedman who becomes disillusioned with the demands of freedom and desires to return to the security of his former life is perhaps no better illustrated than in Harry Stillwell Edwards' *Eneas Africanus*. The prewar friendly relations between white and black could thus be preserved, but only on the white man's terms. Truly as Charles H. Smith's Bill Arp put it, the South had been "conquered but not convinced."

This three-faceted image which the mirror of humor reflects appears clearly and uniformly in all Southern humor and is an underlying factor in today's racial troubles. The image governs the human Uncle Remus and the synthetic Uncle Si; Billy Sanders was just as much a part of it as was Rufus Sanders. From Mrs. Pickett and Dr. Bagby through all the professional and amateur humorists the image grew and grew until doubtless it was as real in the minds of Henry Grady and Booker T. Washington as it was unreal in the society they thought they were describing. By the 1890's the South had been so successful in promulgating this image that relatively little opposition was heard when Southern lawmakers accelerated their disfranchisement of the Negro. The effectiveness and permeating influence of the image is attested to by the Supreme Court's separate-but-equal decision of 1896. By 1914 Southern society was virtually back on the same racial road from which Lincoln's troops had earlier routed it. Readers of Martha Young, Howard Weeden, Thomas Nelson Page, and Joel Chandler Harris sometimes wondered if the Civil War had not been a mistake. One can only speculate as to whether the Little Rock, Jackson, and Birmingham incidents would have occurred had Southern writers not been quite so successful in their propagandizing of the "Southern Way of Life." Nevertheless, the South had proved that she could be reborn from ashes like the Phoenix. Sam Watkins once told an allegory of a rooster named Southern Confederacy killed in an Atlanta cock fight. The owner says a serio-comic farewell to the slain bird, plucks its feathers, fries it, and dips his biscuit in its gravy. Though Watkins ended his story here, his work and the work of other humorists helped to make possible a sequel in which the dead barnyard fowl arises as a beautiful bird of mythology. Indeed, the Southern Phoenix arising from the ashes of Richmond and Atlanta was more glorious than the one sacrificed on the battle field at Gettysburg. Southern humorists had helped transform the humble feathers of the rooster into the splendid plumage of the Phoenix.

An Afterword

In the Foreword to *Sherwood Anderson and Other Famous Creoles* (1926) William Faulkner wrote: "We have one priceless universal trait, we Americans. That trait is our humor. What a pity it is that it is not more prevalent in our art." In *As I Lay Dying,* "Spotted Horses," *Mosquitoes,* and in many other pieces, Faulkner used this "one priceless universal trait" freely. And he was not alone. Drawing on a tradition that goes back to the humorists of the Old Southwest and beyond, Southern writers have continued to find rich materials for humor in their native region.

Faulkner's humor is "Southern." So is much of the humor in the writings of Erskine Caldwell, Flannery O'Connor, J. P. Alley, Vinnie Williams, Tennessee Williams, and Harper Lee. However, to some extent the exodus north by Southerners that started after the Civil War has affected the regional nature of the humor they have written. F. Hopkinson Smith of Maryland went to New York after the war; his Colonel Carter sketches are his best-known humor, but he also wrote much humor not related to the South. Most of O. Henry's humor has little or no organic connection with his native South. George Horace Lorimer and Brander Matthews are two other Southerners who migrated to Northern cities and wrote non-Southern humor. Since World War I this trend toward de-Southernizing Southern humor has increased; and the humor of Irvin Cobb and Thomas Wolfe reveals little that can be called distinctly Southern. A gloomy future for "Southern" literature was predicted by Robert Penn Warren and Albert Erskine in the Introduction to *A New Southern Harvest* (1957). "Perhaps twenty years forward from now there will be no place for a collection of Southern writers; the category may by then have outlived its usefulness. Just as regional differences generally in this country are being broken down by the growing influence of mass communications techniques (movies, radio, television), by the increasing ease and speed of travel and by deliberate educational policies, so probably will differences among American writers become less and less regional in nature." Warren and Erskine probably overstated the case, but their point is well taken because the melting pot that has been the United States in theory since our founding is rapidly becoming one in fact. American literature of the future—whether written by a Minnesotan or a Mississippian—should increasingly reflect this uniformity of American life. In "The Rose of Dixie" O. Henry pricked the bubble of "Southern literature." The bubble has continued slowly to deflate.

But although the trend has been toward a national literature and a national humor, I believe that even down to the present Southern character and life have retained enough individuality to justify the labeling of a significant portion of contemporary American humor "Southern." Southern writers apparently agree with this observation because they continue to exploit their region for humor. Consequently, I have undertaken a further investigation of Southern humor to bring the present study up-to-date. Faulkner's comic masterpiece, *The Reivers* (1962), is alone proof of the continuing vitality of the Southern tradition in American humor.

Bibliography

Periodicals

Arkansaw Thomas Cat. Hot Springs, 1890-1948.
Arkansaw Traveler. Little Rock, 1882-87; Chicago, 1887-1916?
Bob Taylor Magazine. Nashville, 1905-7.
Fetter's Southern Magazine. Louisville, 1892. Name changed to *Southern Magazine* in 1893. Merged with *Scribner's Magazine,* 1895.
McClure's Magazine. New York, 1893-1929.
The Rolling Stone. Austin, 1894-95.
Scott's Monthly Magazine. Atlanta, 1865-69.
Southern Bivouac. Louisville, 1882-87.
The Spirit of the Times. New York, 1831-58.
The Sunny South. Atlanta, 1875-1907.
Taylor-Trotwood Magazine. Nashville, 1907-10.
Texas Siftings. Austin, 1881-85; New York, 1885-97.
Uncle Remus's Magazine. Atlanta, 1907-8. Name changed to *Uncle Remus's Home Magazine* in 1908; published at least until 1912.
Union Springs (Ala.) *Times.* (Succeeded by the Bullock County *Breeze* and the Union Springs *Herald.*) 1866-1914.

Dissertations

Brinson, Lessie Brannen. "An Abstract of a Study of the Life and Works of Richard Malcolm Johnston." Vanderbilt University, 1937.
Linneman, William Richard. "American Life as Reflected in Illustrated Humor Magazines: 1877-1900." University of Illinois, 1960.
Smith, Rebecca Washington. "The Civil War and Its Aftermath in American Fiction: 1861-1899." University of Chicago, 1937.

Articles and Stories

Baker, Ray Stannard. "Joel Chandler Harris," *Outlook,* LXXVIII (Nov. 5, 1904), 595-603.
Baskervill, William M. "Southern Literature," *PMLA,* VII (1892), 89-100.
Bean, F. "Col. Judson of Alabama; or A Southerner's Experiences in New York City." Serialized in *The Sunny South* beginning in the Feb. 5, 1887 issue.
Blair, Walter. "Burlesques in 19th Century American Humor," *American Literature,* II (Nov., 1930), 236-47.
_____. "The Popularity of 19th Century American Humorists," *American Literature,* III (April, 1931), 175-94.
"Bred en Bawn in a Brier-Patch," The Heritage Club *Sandglass,* VII, 23.
Chase, Richard. "Cable and His Grandissimes," *Kenyon Review,* XVIII (Summer, 1956), 373-83.
Cox, S. S. "American Humor," *Harper's New Monthly Magazine,* L (May, 1875), 847-59.
Current-Garcia, Eugene. "Newspaper Humor in the Old South: 1835-1855," *Alabama Review,* II (April, 1949), 102-21.
Edwards, Harry Stillwell. "A Battle in Crackerdom," *Century Magazine,* XXI (Jan., 1892), 457-67.
Eggleston, George Cary. "Southern Literature," in *Extempore Speaking,* Edwin D. Shurter, ed., (Boston, 1908), 139-140. Originally a speech delivered at a banquet of the New York Southern Society, Feb. 22, 1887.
Elam, W. C. "On Scalawags," *The Southern Magazine,* VIII (April, 1871), 456-59.

357

Ford, James L. "A Century of American Humor," *Munsey's Magazine*, XXV (April, 1901, 482-90.

Fox, John, Jr. "The Southern Mountaineer," *Scribner's Magazine*, XXIX (April, May, 1901), 387-99, 556-70.

Hale, Will T. "Solomon Nokes' Views," in Alderman and Harris, *Library of Southern Literature*, V, 2040-41.

Harris, Joel Chandler. "The Comedy of War," *McClure's Magazine*, I (June, 1893), 69-82.

Henneman, John Bell. "The National Element in Southern Literature," *Sewanee Review*, XI (July, 1903), 345-66.

Howells, William Dean. "American Letter: The Southern States in Recent American Literature," *Literature*, No. 47 (London, Sept. 10, 1898), 231-32; No. 48 (Sept. 17, 1898), 257-58; No. 49 (Sept. 24, 1898), 280-81.

———. "Mr. Harben's Georgia Fiction," *North American Review*, CXCI (March, 1910), 356-63.

Johnston, Richard Malcolm. "Middle Georgia Rural Life," *Century Magazine*, XLIII (March, 1892), 737-42.

———. "Review of James Whitcomb Riley's Rhymes of Childhood," *Lippincott's Magazine*, XLVIII (Oct., 1891), 511-12.

Leach, Anna. "Literary Workers of the South," *Munsey's Magazine*, XIII (April, 1895), 57-65.

Link, Samuel A. "Southern Humorists," in *Pioneers of Southern Literature*, Nashville, 1900, II, 465-548.

Linneman, William R. "Colonel Bill Snort: A Texas Jack Downing," *Southwestern Historical Quarterly*, LXIV (Oct., 1960), 185-99.

———. "Opie Read and *The Arkansaw Traveler*: The Trials of a Regional Humor Magazine," *Midwest Folklore Magazine*, X (Spring, 1960), 5-10.

Lukens, Henry Clay. "American Literary Comedians," *Harper's New Monthly Magazine*, LXXX (April, 1890), 783-97.

Mabie, H. W. "Literature in the South," *Outlook*, LXIII (Dec. 2, 1899), 768-70.

Newsom, D. W. "Bill Arp," in An Annual Publication of Historical Papers by the Historical Society of Trinity College, Durham, N. C., Series V (1905), 57-66.

Ormond, John Raper. "Some Recent Products of the New School of Southern Fiction," *South Atlantic Quarterly*, III (July, 1904), 285-89.

Page, Thomas Nelson. "Literature in the South Since the War," *Lippincott's Magazine*, XLVIII (Dec., 1891), 740-56.

Partin, Robert. "Alabama Newspaper Humor: A Post-Bellum Case," *Alabama Review*, IX (April, 1956), 83-99.

Patterson, Daniel W. "A Letter from the Fool Killer," *North Carolina Folklore*, VIII (Dec., 1960), 22-25.

Rollins, Hyder E. "The Negro in the Southern Short Story," *Sewanee Review*, XXIV (Jan., 1916), 42-60.

Simms, William Gilmore. "How Sharp Snaffles Got His Capital and Wife," *Harper's New Monthly Magazine*, XLI (Oct., 1870), 667-87.

Smith, C. Alphonso. "The Possibilities of the South in Literature," *Sewanee Review*, VI (July, 1898), 298-305.

Spencer, Edward. "Hunting a Dragon," *Southern Magazine*, August, 1871.

Stuart, Ruth McEnery. "The Gentleman of the Plush Rocker," *Century Magazine*, LXIII (Jan., 1902), 409-30.

Trent, W. P. "A Retrospect of American Humor," *Century Magazine*, LXIII (Nov., 1901), 45-64.

Wells, Benjamin W. "Southern Literature of the Year," *Forum*, XXIX (June, 1900), 501-12.

Books and Pamphlets

Abbott, Katharine (Kate Sanborn). *The Wit of Women*. New York, 1886. (3rd ed.)

Abe Lincoln's Jokes, ed. Max Stein. Chicago, 1943.

Adeler, Max. *See* Clark, Charles Heber.

Alderman, Edwin Anderson, and Joel Chandler Harris, eds. *Library of Southern Literature.* 17 vols. New Orleans, 1907-1909.

Allen, James Lane. *Flute and Violin and Other Kentucky Tales.* New York, 1891.

Alley, J. P. *Hambone's Meditations,* ed. Sara Beaumont Kennedy. Memphis, n.d. (1919 dates on several cartoons).

Arnold, Robert. *Uncle Alek and His Mule; or The Author's Recollections of the Dismal Swamp and Lake Drummond. Early Recollections: Vivid Portrayal of Amusing Scenes.* Norfolk, 1888.

Arp, Bill. *See* Smith, Charles H.

Aswell, James R., ed. *Native American Humor.* New York, 1947.

Avary, Myrta Lockett. *Dixie After the War: An Exposition of Social Conditions Existing in the South, during the Twelve Years Succeeding the Fall of Richmond.* New York, 1906.

Bagby, George W. *The Old Virginia Gentleman and Other Sketches,* ed. Thomas Nelson Page. New York, 1911.

————. *Original Letters of Mozis Addums to Billy Ivvins* (rev. ed.). Richmond, 1878.

————. *Selections from the Miscellaneous Writings of Dr. George W. Bagby.* 2 vols. Richmond, Va., 1884.

————. *What I Did with My Fifty Millions.* Edited from the Posthumous MS by Caesar Maurice, Esq., of the Richmond (Va.) Whig. Philadelphia, 1874.

Baldwin, Joseph Glover. *The Flush Times of Alabama and Mississippi.* New York, 1853.

Banks, Mary Ross. *Bright Days in the Old Plantation Time.* Boston, 1882.

Barr, James, ed. *The Humour of America.* London, 1893.

Bikle, Lucy Cable. *George Washington Cable: His Life and Letters.* New York, 1928.

Bill Arp. *See* Smith, Charles H.

Blackford, W. W. *War Years with Jeb Stuart.* New York, 1945.

Blair, Walter. *Horse Sense in American Humor: From Benjamin Franklin to Ogden Nash.* Chicago, 1942.

————. *Native American Humor: 1800-1900.* New York, 1937.

Boatright, Mody C. *Folk Laughter of the American Frontier.* New York, 1949.

Boatright, Mody C., John T. Flanagan, and Robert B. Downs. *The Family Saga and Other Phases of American Folklore.* Urbana, 1958.

Boner, John Henry. *Boner's Lyrics.* New York, 1903.

Bonner, Sherwood. *See* MacDowell, Katherine.

A Book of American Humorous Verse, by the Best Known American Writers. Chicago, 1904.

Botkin, B. A., ed. *A Treasury of Southern Folklore.* New York, 1949.

Bradford, Roark. *Ol' Man Adam an' His Chillun.* New York, 1928.

Bradley, A. G. *Sketches from Old Virginia.* London, 1897.

Brann, W. C. *Brann, the Iconoclast: A Collection of the Writings of W. C. Brann,* ed. J. D. Shaw, 2 vols. Waco, Texas, 1959.

Brashear, Minnie M., and Robert M. Rodney, eds. *The Art, Humor, and Humanity of Mark Twain.* Norman, Okla., 1959.

Bruere, Martha Bensley, and Mary Ritter Beard, eds. *Laughing Their Way: Women's Humor in America.* New York, 1934.

Burke, T. A., ed. *Polly Peablossom's Wedding and Other Tales.* Philadelphia, 1851.

Burtscher, William J. *Yellow Creek Humor: A Book of Burtscher Drolleries.* Baltimore, 1909.

Byrd, William. *History of the Dividing Line Run in the Year 1728;* published in 1841 in *The Westover Manuscripts,* ed. by E. Ruffin. A recent edition is *William Byrd's Histories of the Dividing Line betwixt Virginia and North Carolina,* with introduction and notes by William K. Boyd. Raleigh, 1929.

Byrn, M. L. (Phudge Phumble). *Adventures of a Greenhorn in Gotham.* New York, 1885.

Cable, George Washington. *Bonaventure.* New York, 1888.

————. *The Cavalier.* New York, 1901.

————. *Dr. Sevier.* New York, 1885.

————. *The Grandissimes.* New York, 1880.

————. *John March, Southerner.* New York, 1894.

Cable, George Washington. *Madame Delphine*. New York, 1881.
————. *Old Creole Days*. New York, 1879.
Calhoun, Frances Boyd. *Miss Minerva and William Green Hill*. Chicago, 1909.
Carden, W. Thomas (Major Tom Noodle). *A Tennessee Ignoramus: Impressions and Confessions*. Lebanon, Tenn., 1907.
Carruth, Hayden. *The Adventures of Jones*. New York, 1895.
Carver, Charles. *Brann and the Iconoclast*. Austin, Texas, 1957.
Cash, Wilbur J. *The Mind of the South*. New York, 1941.
Caskey, T. W. *See* Srygley, Fletcher Douglas.
Cawein, Madison. *The Republic: A Little Book of Homespun Verse*. Cincinnati, 1913.
Chandler, Frank W. *The Literature of Roguery*. Boston, 1907.
Chase, Richard. *The American Novel and Its Tradition*. New York, 1957.
Chesnutt, Charles W. *The Conjure Woman*. Boston, 1899.
Chopin, Kate. *Bayou Folk*. Boston, 1894.
————. *A Night in Acadie*. Boston, 1897.
Churchill, Allen, ed. *All in Fun: An Omnibus of Humor*. New York, 1940.
Churchill, Winston, *et al. Anecdotes of the Hour*. London, 1912.
Clark, Charles Heber (Max Adeler). *Out of the Hurly-Burly; or, Life in an Odd Corner*. Philadelphia, 1874.
Clark, Richard H. *Memoirs of Judge Richard H. Clark*, ed. Lollie Belle Wylie. Atlanta, 1898.
Clark, Thomas D. *Pills, Petticoats and Plows: The Southern Country Store*. Indianapolis, 1944.
Clemens, Will M. *Famous Funny Fellows: Brief Biographical Sketches of American Humorists*. Cleveland, 1882.
Cockerill, John A. (Randolph Gore Hampton). *The Major in Washington City: A Series of Timely Letters from a Strict Southern Standpoint*. New York, 1893.
Cooper, Frederic Taber. *Some American Story Tellers*. London, 1912.
Cox, Samuel S. *Why We Laugh*. New York, 1877.
Craddock, Charles Egbert. *See* Murfree, Mary Noailles.
Cross, Jane Tandy. *Six Months Under a Cloud*.
Culbertson, Anne Virginia. *At the Big House Where Aunt Nancy and Aunt 'Phrony Held Forth on the Animal Folks*. Indianapolis, 1904.
————. *Banjo Talks*. Indianapolis, 1905.

Dabney, Virginius. *The Story of Don Miff*. 1886.
Daniel, F. E. *Recollections of a Rebel Surgeon and Other Sketches; or, In the Doctor's Sappy Days*. Chicago, 1901.
Davidson, James Wood. *The Living Writers of the South*. New York, 1869.
Davis, Molly Moore. *An Elephant's Track and Other Stories*. New York, 1896.
Davis, Robert H., and Arthur B. Maurice. *The Caliph of Bagdad, Being Arabian Nights Flashes of the Life, Letters, and Work of O. Henry*. New York, 1931.
DeForest, John W. *The Bloody Chasm*. New York, 1881.
DeLeon, Thomas C. *Belles, Beaux and Brains of the 60's*. New York, 1907.
De Vere, Tom. *Pointed Pickings from the Arkansaw Traveler*. Chicago, 1913.
Devol, George H. *Forty Years a Gambler on the Mississippi*. Cincinnati, 1887. Excerpt in Hudson, *Humor of the Old Deep South*, pp. 358-62.
De Voto, Bernard. *Mark Twain's America*. Boston, 1932.
Dowdey, Clifford. *Experiment in Rebellion*. New York, 1946.
Downing, Fanny Murdaugh. *Pluto: Being the Sad Story and Lamentable Fate of the Fair Minthe*. Raleigh, N. C., 1867.
Doyle, Jefferson E. (Major Jep Joslynn). *Tar-Heel Tales in Vernacular Verse*. New York, 1873.
Dromgoole, Will Allen. *Cinch and Other Stories of Tennessee*. Boston, 1898.
————. *The Heart of Old Hickory and Other Stories of Tennessee*, ed. B. O. Flower. Boston, 1895.
Dunbar, Paul Laurence. *The Best Stories of Paul Laurence Dunbar*, ed. Benjamin Brawley. New York, 1938.
————. *Complete Poems of Paul Laurence Dunbar*. New York, 1913.

Dunbar, Paul Laurence. *Folks from Dixie.* New York, 1898.
————. *The Heart of Happy Hollow.* New York, 1904.
————. *Howdy, Honey, Howdy.* New York, 1896.
————. *In Old Plantation Days.* New York, 1903.
————. *Lyrics of the Hearthside.* New York, 1899.
————. *Lyrics of Love and Laughter.* New York, 1903.
————. *Poems of Cabin and Field.* New York, 1896.
————. *The Strength of Gideon.* New York, 1900.
Duncan, Georgia Elizabeth. *Samanthy Billins of Hangin'-Dog.* Atlanta, 1905.
Duval, John C. *The Adventures of Big-Foot Wallace.* 1870. Excerpt in James N. Tidwell, *A Treasury of American Folk Humor,* pp. 603-4.

Edwards, Harry Stillwell. *Eneas Africanus.* Macon, Ga., 1920.
————. *His Defense and Other Stories.* New York, 1892.
————. *Two Runaways and Other Stories.* New York, 1889.
Eggleston, George Cary. *A Rebel's Recollections.* New York, 1905. (First published in 1874.)
Evans, Leo C. "The Color Line" in *Wit and Truth: Humorous Sketches Selected by the New York Enamel Paint Company.* New York, n.d.

Falk, Robert P., ed. *The Antic Muse: American Writers in Parody.* New York, 1955.
Faulkner, William. *Light in August.* New York, 1932.
————. *Salmagundi.* Milwaukee, 1932.
Fiske, Horace Spencer. *Provincial Types in American Fiction.* Chautauqua, N. Y., 1903.
The Flea, "By You." New York, 1869.
Fleming, Walter Lynwood. *The Sequel of Appomattox.* New Haven, 1919.
Fletcher, William A. *Rebel Private Front and Rear.* Austin, Texas, 1954. Preface by Bell Irwin Wiley. (First published in Beaumont, Texas, 1908.)
Fortier, Alcée. *Louisiana Studies.* New Orleans, 1894.
Fox, John, Jr. *Bluegrass and Rhododendron.* New York, 1901.
————. *Christmas Eve on Lonesome.* New York, 1904.
————. *Following the Sun Flag.* New York, 1905.
————. *Hell Fer Sartain and Other Stories.* New York, 1897.
French, Alice (Octave Thanet). *Otto the Knight and Other Trans-Mississippi Stories.* Boston, 1900.
French, Joseph Lewis, ed. *Sixty Years of American Humor.* Boston, 1924.
Fulkerson, H. S. *Random Recollections of Early Days in Mississippi.* Vicksburg, 1885. Excerpt in Hudson, *Humor of the Old Deep South,* p. 363.
Fulton, Maurice Garland. *Southern Life in Southern Literature.* Boston, 1917.

Gaines, Francis Pendleton. *The Southern Plantation: A Study in the Development and the Accuracy of a Tradition.* New York, 1925.
Gault, Joseph. *Fifth Edition of His Reports Entitled A Coat of Many Colors.* Americus, Ga., 1902.
Gielow, Martha S. *Old Plantation Days.* New York, 1902.
A Gift for Young and Old. Baltimore, 1879. (Sponsored by St. Jacob's Oil.)
Gloster, Hugh M. *Negro Voices in American Fiction.* Chapel Hill, N. C., 1948.
Goldsborough, Edmund K. *Ole Mars an' Ole Miss.* Washington, 1900.
Gonzales, Ambrose E. *The Black Border: Gullah Stories of the Carolina Coast.* Columbia, S. C., 1922.
Grady, Henry W. *Life of Henry W. Grady Including His Writings and Speeches,* ed. Joel Chandler Harris. New York, 1890.
————, Joel Chandler Harris, and Frank L. Stanton. *A Message from Atlanta's Immortals.* Atlanta, 1921.
Green, Claud B. *John Trotwood Moore: Tennessee Man of Letters.* Athens, Ga., 1957.

Hall, Eliza Calvert. *See* Obenchain, Eliza Caroline.
Hampton, Randolph Gore. *See* Cockerill, John A.
Handford, Thomas W., ed. *Elmo's Humorous Speaker.* Chicago, 1890.

Harben, Will N. *The Georgians.* New York, 1904.

————. *Northern Georgia Sketches.* Chicago, 1900.

Harris, George Washington. *Sut Lovingood Travels with Old Abe Lincoln,* ed. Edd Winfield Parks. Chicago, 1937.

————. *Sut Lovingood: Yarns Spun by a "Nat'ral Born Durn'd Fool." Warped and Wove for Public Wear.* New York, 1867.

Harris, Joel Chandler. *The Bishop and the Boogerman.* New York, 1901.

————. *The Chronicles of Aunt Minervy Ann.* New York, 1899.

————. *Free Joe and Other Georgian Sketches.* New York, 1887.

————. *Gabriel Tolliver: A Story of Reconstruction.* New York, 1902.

————. *Little Mr. Thimblefinger and His Queer Country, and What the Children Saw and Heard There.* New York, 1894.

————. *A Little Union Scout.* New York, 1904.

————. *On the Plantation: A Story of a Georgia Boy's Adventures During the War.* New York, 1892.

————. *The Shadow Between His Shoulder-Blades.* Boston, 1907.

————. *Tales of the Home Folks in Peace and War.* Boston, 1898.

————. *Uncle Remus: His Songs and His Sayings,* ed. Marc Connelly. New York, 1957. (First published in 1880.)

Harris, Julia Collier. *The Life and Letters of Joel Chandler Harris.* Boston, 1918.

Hearn, Lafcadio. *"Gombo Zhébes": Little Dictionary of Creole Proverbs.* New York, 1885.

Henry, O. *See* Porter, William Sydney.

Herzberg, Max J., and Leon Mones. *Humor of America.* New York, 1945.

Hibbard, Addison, ed. *Stories of the South.* Chapel Hill, N. C., 1931.

Higginson, Thomas Wentworth. *Army Life in a Black Regiment.* Boston, 1870.

Hilton, George S. *The Funny Side of Politics.* New York, 1899.

Hogue, Albert R. *Peculiar Laws and Lawsuits in Tennessee, 1796-1926.* Jamestown, Tenn., n.d.

Hoig, Stan. *The Humor of the American Cowboy.* New York, 1960.

Holliday, Carl. *A History of Southern Literature.* New York, 1906.

Holmes, Oliver Wendell, Bill Nye, Mark Twain, *et al. Stories of Humor.* New York, 1908.

Hooper, George W. (An Amateur). *Down the River; or, Practical Lessons Under the Code Duello.* New York, 1874.

Hooper, Johnson J. *Some Adventures of Simon Suggs, late of the Tallapoosa Volunteers; together with "Taking the Census," and Other Alabama Sketches.* By a country editor. Philadelphia, 1846.

————. *The Widow Rugby's Husband, A Night at the Ugly Man's, and Other Tales of Alabama.* Philadelphia, 1851.

Howard, Robert West, ed. *This Is the South.* Chicago, 1959.

Howells, William Dean, and Henry Mills Alden, eds. *The Heart of Childhood.* New York, 1906.

————. *Southern Lights and Shadows.* New York, 1894.

Hubbell, Jay B. *Southern Life in Literature.* Athens, Ga., 1960.

Hudson, Arthur Palmer, ed. *Humor of the Old Deep South.* New York, 1936.

Humorous Masterpieces from American Literature. Vol. I. New York, 1886.

Insurance at Piney Woods. Louisville, 1896.

Johnson, Burges. *More Necessary Nonsense.* New York, 1931.

Johnston, Richard Malcolm. *Autobiography.* Washington, 1900.

————. *Dukesborough Tales.* Baltimore, 1871.

————. *Georgia Sketches.* Augusta, Ga., 1864.

————. *Old Mark Langston, A Tale of Duke's Creek.* New York, 1883.

The Jolly Bear: A Story for the Amusement of Young and Old. Baltimore, n.d. (Sponsored by St. Jacob's Oil.)

Jones, Charles Colcock. *Negro Myths from the Georgia Coast Told in the Vernacular.* Boston, 1888.

Jones, Katharine M., ed. *New Confederate Short Stories.* Columbia, S. C., 1954.

Jones, Major. *See* Thompson, William Tappan.

Joslynn, Major Jep. *See* Doyle, Jefferson E.

"Junius, E.," ed. *Critical Dialogue Between Aboo and Caboo on a New Book; or, A Grandissime Ascension.* Mingo City [New Orleans], 1880.

Kendrick, Benjamin Burks, and Alex Mathews Arnett. *The South Looks at Its Past.* Chapel Hill, N. C., 1935.

Kephart, Horace. *Our Southern Highlanders.* New York, 1913.

Kern, John Dwight. *Constance Fenimore Woolson: Literary Pioneer.* Philadelphia, 1934.

King, Grace. *Balcony Stories.* New York, 1925.

————. *Monsieur Motte.* New York, 1888.

————. *Tales of a Time and Place: A Collection of Short Stories.* New York, 1888.

King, Joseph Leonard, Jr. *Dr. George William Bagby: A Study of Virginian Literature, 1850-1880.* New York, 1927.

King, W. C., and W. P. Derby, eds. *Camp-Fire Sketches and Battlefield Echoes of the Rebellion.* Springfield, Mass., 1887.

Knight, Grant C. *James Lane Allen and the Genteel Tradition.* Chapel Hill, N. C., 1935.

Knight, Lucian Lamar. *Memorials of Dixie-Land.* Atlanta, Ga., 1919.

Lang, Andrew. *Lost Leaders.* London, 1889.

Langford, Gerald. *Alias O. Henry: A Biography of William Sydney Porter.* New York, 1957.

Lanier, Sidney. *Bob: The Story of Our Mocking-Bird.* New York, 1899.

————. *Poems and Poem Outlines,* ed. Charles R. Anderson. 10 vols. Baltimore, 1945.

————. *Poems of Sidney Lanier,* edited by His Wife, with a Memorial by William Hayes Ward. New York, 1884.

————. *Tiger-Lilies.* New York, 1867.

Laugh and Let Laugh Way Down in Dixie: Three Hundred Funny Negro Stories, By Grandma. Talladega, Ala., n.d.

Lawson, Albert, ed. *War Anecdotes and Incidents of Army Life: Reminiscences from Both Sides of the Conflict Between the North and South.* Cincinnati, 1888.

Leacock, Stephen. *The Greatest Pages of American Humor: A Study of the Rise and Development of Humorous Writings with Selections from the Most Notable of the Humorists.* Garden City, N. Y., 1936.

Lee, James W. *Henry W. Grady.* St. Louis, 1896.

Lewis, Henry Clay (Madison Tensas). *Odd Leaves from the Life of a Louisiana "Swamp Doctor,"* n.d. Reprinted as a part of *The Swamp Doctor's Adventures in the South-West,* by Madison Tensas and "Solitaire." Philadelphia, 1858.

Lewis, Henry Taliaferro. *Harp of a Thousand Strings, with Waifs of Wit and Pathos,* 1907.

Lillard, John F. B., ed. *The Medical Muse: Grave and Gay.* New York, 1895.

Lloyd, Francis Bartow (Rufus Sanders). *Sketches of Country Life: Humor, Wisdom and Pathos from the "Sage of Rocky Creek." The homely life of the Alabama Back Country has its sunny side: rough but wise and kindly talk.* Birmingham, Ala., 1898.

Loggins, Vernon. *The Negro Author: His Development in America.* New York, 1931.

Long, E. Hudson. *O. Henry: The Man and His Work.* Philadelphia, 1949.

Longstreet, A. B. *Georgia Scenes.* 1835.

————. *Stories with a Moral: Humorous and Descriptive of Southern Life a Century Ago,* ed. Fitz R. Longstreet. Philadelphia, 1912.

Looney, Louise Preston. *Tennessee Sketches.* Chicago, 1901.

Lorimer, George H. *Letters from a Self-Made Merchant to His Son.* Boston, 1902.

Lydston, G. Frank. *Over the Hookah: The Tales of a Talkative Doctor.* Chicago, 1896.

Lynn, Kenneth S., ed. *The Comic Tradition in America: An Anthology.* New York, 1958.

————. *Mark Twain and Southwestern Humor.* Boston, 1959.

McCarthy, Carlton. *Detailed Minutiae of Soldier Life in the Army of Northern Virginia, 1861-1865.* Richmond, Va., 1882.

McDonald, James J. *Life in Old Virginia: A Description of Virginia . . . together with Many Humorous Stories.* Norfolk, Va., 1907.

MacDowell, Katherine (Sherwood Bonner). *Dialect Tales.* New York, 1883.

————. *Like Unto Like.* New York, 1878.

MacDowell, Katherine. *Suwanee River Tales*. Boston, 1876.
McIlwaine, Shields. *The Southern Poor-White: From Lubberland to Tobacco Road*. Norman, Okla., 1939.
McLaughlin, J. Fairfax (Pasquino). *The American Cyclops*. Baltimore, 1868.
McWilliams, Carey. *The New Regionalism in American Literature*. University of Washington Chapbooks, No. 46. Seattle, 1930.
Manly, Louise. *Southern Literature: From 1579-1895*. Richmond, Va., 1907.
Martin, George Madden (Mrs.). *Emmy Lou, Her Book and Heart*. New York, 1902.
Mason, Edward T., ed. *Humorous Masterpieces from American Literature*, 3 vols. New York, 1886.
Meine, Franklin J., ed. *Tall Tales of the Southwest: An Anthology of Southern and Southwestern Humor, 1830-1860*. New York, 1930.
Mills, Quincy Sharpe. *Editorials, Sketches and Stories*. New York, 1930.
Miner, Ward L. *The World of William Faulkner*. New York, n.d. (Originally published in Durham, N. C., 1952.)
Montgomery, Frank A. *Reminiscences of a Mississippian in Peace and War*. Cincinnati, 1901.
Moore, Frank, ed. *Anecdotes, Poetry and Incidents of the War: North and South*. New York, 1866.
Moore, John Trotwood. *The Bishop of Cottontown*. 1906.
———. *Ole Mistis and Other Songs and Stories from Tennessee*. Nashville, 1897.
———. *Songs and Stories from Tennessee*. Chicago, 1897.
———. *Uncle Wash: His Stories*. Philadelphia, 1910.
Mott, Frank Luther. *A History of American Magazines: 1865-1885*. Cambridge, Mass., 1938.
———. *A History of American Magazines: 1885-1905*. Cambridge, Mass., 1957.
Murfree, Mary Noailles (Charles Egbert Craddock). *The Bushwhackers and Other Stories*. Chicago, 1899.
———. *In the Tennessee Mountains*. Boston, 1885.
———. *The Prophet of the Great Smoky Mountains*. Boston, 1885.
———. *Where the Battle Was Fought*. Boston, 1900.
———. *The Young Mountaineers*. Boston, 1897.

Nash, Charles Edward. *Historical and Humorous Sketches of the Donkey, Horse and Bicycle*. . . . Little Rock, 1896.
Noodle, Major Tom. *See* Carden, W. Thomas.
Nye, Bill, Max Adeler, *et al*. *Snap Shots*. New York, n.d.

Obenchain, Eliza Caroline (Eliza Calvert Hall). *Aunt Jane of Kentucky*. Boston, 1907.
———. *The Land of Long Ago*. Boston, 1909.
———. *Sally Ann's Experience*. Boston, 1910.
Odum, Howard W. *Southern Pioneers in Social Interpretation*. Chapel Hill, N. C., 1925.
O. Henry. *See* Porter, William Sydney.
Old Times in West Tennessee: Reminiscences—Semi-Historic—of Pioneer Life and the Early Emigrant Settlers in the Big Hatchie Country, by A Descendant of one of the First Settlers. Memphis, 1873.
Overton, Grant. *The Women Who Make Our Novels*. New York, 1928.

Page, Thomas Nelson. *Bred in the Bone*. New York, 1904.
———. *The Burial of the Guns*. New York, 1894.
———. *In Ole Virginia*. New York, 1887.
———. *Pastime Stories*. New York, 1894.
———. *Two Little Confederates*. New York, 1888.
———, and A. C. Gordon. *Befo' de War*. New York, 1895.
Page, Walter Hines (Nicholas Worth). *The Southerner: A Novel; Being the Autobiography of Nicholas Worth*. New York, 1909.
Palmer, Henrietta Raymer, ed. *In Dixie Land: Stories of the Reconstruction Era by Southern Writers*. New York, 1926.
Parks, Edd Winfield. *Charles Egbert Craddock*. Chapel Hill, N. C., 1941.

Parks, Edd Winfield. *Segments of Southern Thought.* Athens, Ga., 1938.
Parrington, Vernon Louis. *Main Currents in American Thought,* 3 vols. New York, 1927.
Party Lights; or, The Monkey Congress. Hudson City, N. J., 1869.
Pattee, Fred Lewis. *A History of American Literature Since 1870.* New York, 1915.
_____. *Side-Lights on American Literature.* New York, 1922.
Payne, Leonidas Warren. *A Survey of Texas Literature.* New York, 1928.
Peck, George W. *How Private George W. Peck Put Down the Rebellion; or, The Funny Experiences of a Raw Recruit.* Chicago, 1887.
Peck, Samuel Minturn. *Alabama Sketches.* Chicago, 1902.
_____. *Rings and Love-Knots.* New York, 1892.
Perley, Mrs. T. E. (An Early Settler). *From Timber to Town: Down in Egypt.* Chicago, 1891.
Perry, Bliss. *The American Mind.* Boston, 1912.
_____. *The American Spirit in Literature.* New Haven, 1918.
Piaggi, Henry Rego, ed. *Uncle Schnitz: Being a Collection of Dutch, Irish, Coon, Rube, Dago Stories and Conundrums.* Chicago, 1912.
The Picket Line and Camp Fire Stories, by a Member of the G. A. R., n. d.
Pickett, LaSalle Corbell. *Pickett and His Men.* Washington, 1899.
_____. *What Happened to Me.* New York, 1917.
_____. *Yule Log.* Washington, 1900.
Pitts, J. R. S. *The Life and Bloody Career of the Executed Criminal, James Copeland.* Jackson, Miss., 1874. Excerpt in Hudson, *Humor of the Old Deep South,* pp. 353-58.
A Pocket Book of the Early American Humorists: Selections from Ben Franklin, Joseph C. Neal [et al.] Boston, 1907.
Porter, William Sydney (O. Henry). *The Gentle Grafter.* New York, 1904.
_____. *Heart of the West.* Garden City, N. Y., 1916.
_____. *Roads of Destiny.* New York, 1914.
_____. *Rolling Stones.* Garden City, N. Y., 1912.
_____. *Strictly Business: More Stories of the Four Million.* New York, 1910.
_____. *Whirligigs.* New York, 1910.
Porter, William T., ed. *The Big Bear of Arkansas and Other Sketches, Illustrative of Characters and Incidents in the South and South-west.* New York, 1845.
_____. *A Quarter Race in Kentucky.* Philadelphia, 1846. Reprinted as *Colonel Thorpe's Scenes in Arkansas.* Philadelphia, n.d.
Prentice, George D. *Prenticeana; or, Wit and Humor in Paragraphs.* New York, 1860.
Pryor, Sara Agnes. *Reminiscences of Peace and War.* 1904.
Pyrnelle, Louisa Clarke. *Diddy, Dumps and Tot.* New York, 1882.

Rankin, Daniel S. *Kate Chopin and Her Creole Stories.* Philadelphia, 1932.
Raymond, Walter Marion. *Rebels of the New South.* Chicago, 1905.
Read, Opie. *I Remember.* New York, 1930.
_____. *The Jucklins.* Chicago, 1896.
_____. *A Kentucky Colonel.* Chicago, 1890.
_____. *My Young Master.* Chicago, 1896.
_____. *Odd Folks.* New York, 1897.
_____. *Opie Read in the Ozarks, Including Many of the Rich, Rare, Quaint, Eccentric, Ignorant and Superstitious Sayings of the Natives of Missouri and Arkansaw.* Chicago, 1905.
_____, and Frank Pixley. *The Carpetbagger.* Chicago. 1899.
Reddall, Henry Frederick, ed. *Wit and Humor of American Politics.* Philadelphia, 1903.
Reichert, Alfred. *Charles Egbert Craddock und die Amerikanische Short-Story.* Leipzig, 1912.
Rhodes, R. S., ed. *Wit.* Chicago, 1903.
Rice, Alice Hegan. *Mrs. Wiggs of the Cabbage Patch.* New York, 1901.
Rosenberger, Francis Coleman, ed. *Virginia Reader: A Treasury of Writings from the First Voyages to the Present.* New York, 1948.
Rourke, Constance. *American Humor: A Study of the National Character.* Garden City, N. Y., 1931.
Russell, Irwin. *Christmas Night in the Quarters.* Kansas City, 1913.
_____. *Poems.* Introduction by Joel Chandler Harris. New York, 1888.
Rutherford, Mildred. *American Authors: A Hand-Book of American Literature.* Atlanta, 1894.

Rutherford, Mildred. *The South in History and Literature: A Handbook of Southern Authors.* Atlanta, 1907.

Sampson, Emma Speed. *Miss Minerva on the Plantation.* Chicago, 1923.
Sam Simple's First Trip to New Orleans, by "A Georgian of the Good Old Times." Macon, Ga., 1901. (Originally published in 1896.)
Sanborn, Kate. *See* Abbott, Katharine.
Sanders, Rufus. *See* Lloyd, Francis Bartow.
Scott, Mrs. C. C. *Sis and Bud: Plantation Sketches of the Ante-Bellum South.* c. 1891.
Sheppard, Eli. *See* Young, Martha.
Sherman, Eloise Lee. *Plantation Poems.* New York, 1910.
Shoemaker, Charles C. *Choice Humor for Reading and Recitation.* Philadelphia, 1894.
Shurter, Edwin D., ed. *Extempore Speaking.* Boston, 1908.
Simpson, Claude M., ed. *The Local Colorists: American Short Stories, 1857-1900.* New York, 1960.
Sloan, Dave U. *Fogy Days, and Now; or, The World Has Changed.* Atlanta, 1891.
Small, Sam W. *Old Si's Humorous Sketches.* No. 126 in the Surprise Series. New York, 1890.
————. *Old Si's Sayings.* Chicago, 1886.
Smith, C. Alphonso. *O. Henry Biography.* Garden City, N. Y., 1916.
Smith, Charles H. (Bill Arp). *Bill Arp: From the Uncivil War to Date, 1861-1903.* Atlanta, 1903.
————. *Bill Arp's Scrap Book: Humor and Philosophy.* Atlanta, 1884.
————. *Bill Arp, So Called: A Side Show of the Southern Side of the War.* New York, 1866.
————. *Bill Arp's Peace Papers.* New York, 1873.
————. *The Farm and the Fireside: Sketches of Domestic Life in War and Peace Written and Published for the Entertainment of the Good People at Home, and Dedicated Especially to Mothers and Children.* Atlanta, 1892.
Smith, F. Hopkinson. *Colonel Carter and Other Tales of the South.* Vol. III of the *Novels, Stories and Sketches of F. Hopkinson Smith.* New York, 1908.
————. *Colonel Carter of Cartersville.* Boston, 1891.
————. *The Other Fellow.* Boston, 1899.
Smith, William R. *Reminiscences of a Long Life.* Washington, c. 1889. Excerpt in Hudson, *Humor of the Old Deep South,* pp. 547-48.
Srygley, Fletcher Douglas. *Seventy Years in Dixie: Recollections and Sayings of T. W. Caskey and Others.* Nashville, 1893.
Stanton, Frank L. *Comes One with a Song.* Indianapolis, 1898.
————. *Songs from Dixie Land.* Indianapolis, 1900.
————. *Songs of the Soil.* New York, 1913.
————. *Up from Georgia.* New York, 1902.
————. *Frank Lebby Stanton: Georgia's First Poet Laureate,* ed. Wightman F. Melton. Atlanta, Ga., 1938.
Starke, Aubrey Harrison. *Sidney Lanier: A Biographical and Critical Study.* Chapel Hill, N. C., 1933.
Stewart, Calvin E. *Uncle Josh Weathersby's "Punkin Centre" Stories.* Chicago, 1903.
Stewart, William H. *The Spirit of the South.* New York, 1908.
Stories of the South: Stories from Scribner's. New York, 1894.
Story of Esquire Brown and His Mule. Baltimore, n.d.
Stroyer, Jacob. *My Life in the South.* Salem, 1885. Excerpt in Botkin, *A Treasury of Southern Folklore,* pp. 107-35.
Stuart, Ruth McEnery. *Aunt Amity's Silver Wedding and Other Stories.* New York, 1909.
————. *Moriah's Mourning,* New York, 1898.
————. *Napoleon Jackson: The Gentleman of the Plush Rocker.* New York, 1902.
————. *Sonny: A Christmas Guest.* New York, 1894.
Sullivan, Timothy Paul. *Plantation and Up-to-Date Humorous Negro Stories.* Chicago, 1905.
Sweet, Alexander E., and J. Armory Knox. *On a Mexican Mustang through Texas, from the Gulf to the Rio Grande.* Hartford, Conn., 1883.
————. *Sketches from Texas Siftings.* New York, 1882.

Taliaferro, H. E. (Skitt). *Fisher's River (North Carolina) Scenes and Characters.* New York, 1859.

Tandy, Jeannette. *Crackerbox Philosophers in American Humor and Satire.* New York, 1925.

Taylor, Robert L. *Echoes: Centennial and Other Notable Speeches, Lectures and Stories.* Nashville, 1899.

————. *Life Pictures.* Nashville, 1907.

Tensas, Madison. *See* Lewis, Henry Clay.

Thanet, Octave. *See* French, Alice.

Thompson, William Tappan (Major Jones). *John's Alive; or, The Bride of a Ghost, and Other Sketches.* Philadelphia, 1883.

————. *Major Jones's Sketches of Travels, Comprising the Scenes, Incidents, and Adventures in His Tour from Georgia to Canada.* Philadelphia, 1848.

Tidwell, James N. *A Treasury of American Folk Humor.* New York, 1956.

Toulmin, Harry Aubrey, Jr. *Social Historians.* Boston, 1911.

Trent, William P. *A History of American Literature, 1607-1865.* New York, 1903.

Turner, Arlin. *George Washington Cable: A Biography.* Durham, N. C., 1956.

Vedder, Henry C. *American Writers of To-Day.* New York, 1894.

Visscher, William Lightfoot. *Black Mammy: A Southern Romance.* Chicago, 1897.

————. *Harp of the South and Other Poems.* Chicago, 1894.

————. *Ten Wise Men and Some More.* Chicago, 1909.

Von Koch, Siegfried. *Farmertypen nach dem Amerikanischen Roman.* Hamburg, 1933.

Wade, John Donald. *Augustus Baldwin Longstreet: A Study of the Development of Culture in the South.* New York, 1924.

Walworth, Jeannette H. *The Other Fellow.* Boston, 1899.

————. *Southern Silhouettes.* New York, 1887.

————. *Uncle Scipio: A Story of Uncertain Days in the South.* New York, 1896.

Warren, Robert Penn, and Albert Erskine, eds. *A New Southern Harvest: An Anthology.* New York, 1957.

Watkins, Samuel R. *"Co. Aytch," Maury Grays, First Tennessee Regiment; or, A Side Show of the Big Show.* Nashville, 1882. Reprinted in Jackson, Tenn., 1952, with an Introduction by Bell Irwin Wiley.

Watterson, Henry. *"Marse Henry," An Autobiography.* 2 vols. New York, 1919.

————. *Oddities in Southern Life and Character.* Boston, 1882.

Wauchope, George Armstrong. *The Writers of South Carolina.* Columbia, 1910.

Weeden, Howard (Miss). *Bandanna Ballads.* New York, 1899.

————. *Old Voices.* New York, 1904.

————. *Shadows on the Wall.* New York, 1898.

————. *Songs of the Old South.* New York, 1901.

Wells, Carolyn, ed. *A Parody Anthology.* New York, 1904.

White, E. B., and Katharine S. White, eds. *A Subtreasury of American Humor.* New York, 1955.

Whitely, Isaac H. *Rural Life in Texas.* Atlanta, 1891.

Wier, A. M. (Sarge). *Old Times in Georgia: Good Times and Bad Times.* Atlanta, 1889.

Wiggins, Lida Keck. *The Life and Works of Paul Laurence Dunbar.* Memphis, 1896.

Wiggins, Robert Lemuel. *The Life of Joel Chandler Harris: From Obscurity in Boyhood to Fame in Early Manhood with Short Stories and Other Early Work Not Heretofore Published in Book Form.* Nashville, 1918.

Wilder, Marshall P., ed. *The Wit and Humor of America.* 10 vols. New York, 1907.

[Williams, Henry L.] *Hawthorne's Comic Reciter.* New York, 1881.

Williams, Vinnie. *Walk Egypt.* New York, 1960.

Wilson, Edmund. *Patriotic Gore: Studies in the Literature of the American Civil War.* New York, 1962.

Wilt, Napier. *Some American Humorists.* New York, 1929.

Wit and Humor of American Statesmen: A Collection from Various Sources Classified Under Appropriate Subject Headings. Philadelphia, 1902.

Wit and Humor of the Age, by Mark Twain, *et al.* Chicago, 1883.

Wit and Truth: Humorous Sketches Selected by the New York Enamel Paint Company, by the Detroit Press Man, *et al.* New York, n.d.

Wood, William N. *Reminiscences of Big I.* Jackson, Tenn., 1956.

Woodberry, George E. *America in Literature.* New York 1903.

Woolson, Constance Fenimore. *Rodman the Keeper: Southern Sketches.* New York, 1880.

The World's Wit and Humor. Introduction by Joel Chandler Harris. 15 vols. New York, 1906.

Worth, Nicholas. *See* Page, Walter Hines.

Wright, Henrietta C. *Children's Stories in American Literature, 1861-1896.* New York, 1914.

Ye Mistick Krewe of Comus: The Missing Links to Darwin's Origin of Species. New Orleans, 1873.

Young, Martha (Eli Sheppard). *Plantation Songs for My Lady's Banjo and Other Negro Lyrics & Monologues.* New York, 1901.

Index

Index